Arms Control Agreements

sipri

Stockholm International Peace Research Institute

Sipri is an independent institute for research into problems of peace and conflict, especially those of arms control and disarmament. It was established in 1966 to commemorate Sweden's 150 years of unbroken peace.

The Institute is financed by the Swedish Parliament. The Staff, the Governing Board and the Scientific Council are international.

sipri

Stockholm International Peace Research Institute

Bergshamra, S-171 73 Solna, Sweden
Cable: Peaceresearch, Stockholm
Telephone: 08-55 97 00

Arms Control Agreements

A Handbook

Jozef Goldblat

sipri

Stockholm International Peace Research Institute

PRAEGER

PRAEGER SPECIAL STUDIES • PRAEGER SCIENTIFIC

Library of Congress Cataloging in Publication Data

Goldblat, Jozef.
    Agreements for arms control.

    "SIPRI, Stockholm International Peace Research
Institute."
    Bibliography: p.
    1. Arms control. I. Stockholm International Peace
Research Institute. II. Title.
JX1974.G518 1983   341.7'33   83-2167
ISBN 0-03-063709-0

Published in 1983 by Praeger Publishers
CBS Educational and Professional Publishing
a Division of CBS Inc.
521 Fifth Avenue, New York, NY 10175 USA
First published in 1982 by Taylor & Francis Ltd.

456789 052 98765432

Preface

The United Nations declaration proclaiming the 1980s as the Second Disarmament Decade stressed the need to mobilize world public opinion on behalf of peace and disarmament. Such a mobilization can be achieved by spreading objective information about the arms race and about the efforts made to stop it. This book serves the latter purpose by providing an analysis and assessment of the arms control agreements and of current negotiations, free from the usual bias of official government reports. It is a revised and abridged version of the book which was originally prepared at the Stockholm International Peace Research Institute (SIPRI) on the occasion of the 1982 UN General Assembly Special Session devoted to disarmament. This edition is intended as a handbook for students of arms control and disarmament as well as for politicians and other concerned citizens.

Acknowledgements: Acknowledgement is given to Ragnhild Ferm for compiling the documentary and statistical material in the book, and to Connie Wall for editing the manuscript.

Jozef Goldblat

Contents

Introduction

Measures for the limitation of armaments can take various forms. They can be taken by states on a voluntary basis, without reciprocity. They can be part of agreed armistice arrangements following armed conflicts. They can also be imposed upon defeated countries, as in the case of Germany after both World Wars. This book, however, is concerned only with agreements freely arrived at in time of peace among sovereign states, through a process of formal intergovernmental negotiation, and providing for mutual rights and obligations.

A multitude of proposals for regulation of armaments, including proposals for the complete elimination of armed forces and weapons, have been made in various forums, but so far only so-called arms control measures have been agreed upon, imposing certain restrictions on the armament policies of states. Originally, the term 'arms control', coined in the USA, was meant to denote internationally agreed rules limiting the arms competition rather than reversing it; it had a connotation distinct from the reduction of armaments or disarmament. Subsequently, however, diverse measures intended to freeze, limit or abolish specific categories of weapons; to prevent certain military activities; to regulate the deployment of forces; to proscribe transfers of militarily important items; to reduce the risk of an accidental war; to constrain or prohibit the use of certain arms in war; or to build up confidence among states through greater openness in the military field, and thereby produce an international climate conducive to disarmament, have come to be included under the rubric of arms control. It is in this broad sense that the term 'arms control' will be used here, often interchangeably with 'arms limitation' or 'disarmament'.

This publication deals primarily with the bilateral and multilateral arms control agreements reached since World War II. In the latter category of agreements, several are of a regional nature in the sense that they are valid only for a given geographical zone or continent. The forms of the agreements discussed in this book vary from treaties, conventions or protocols, to memoranda, declarations or common understandings, to statutes, charters and special binding decisions of international bodies or final acts of international conferences, to joint or simultaneous statements by governments, to exchanges of letters among the states concerned.

Chapter 1 is a brief historical survey of the pre-World War II efforts towards disarmament, beginning with the Hague Peace Conferences, held at the turn of this century, through the naval conferences convened in the inter-war period, to the League of Nations' attempts to bring about a universal reduction in armaments.

Chapter 2 covers the activities of the United Nations in the field of arms regulation during the first years following World War II. Special attention is devoted to problems relating to nuclear weapons, proposals for the reduction of armaments, and plans for general and complete disarmament.

Chapter 3 reviews the scope of the obligations undertaken by the parties to the post-war arms control agreements and attempts to assess whether, and to what extent, each agreement has affected the arms race, reduced the likelihood of war or otherwise contributed to the overall goal of disarmament. The agreements have been divided into seven categories, according to the nature and type of the undertakings.

Chapter 4 deals with the verification of compliance and discusses, in particular, the shortcomings of the existing arrangements.

Chapter 5 contains the official texts of the relevant documents, preceded by a note on the so-called final clauses of the agreements. Certain pre-World War II agreements related to the topics considered in Chapter 3 are also included.

Chapter 6 contains a tabular presentation of the status of the implementation of the most important multilateral agreements.

Chapter 7 describes the existing arms control negotiating machinery, while Chapter 8 summarizes the arms control experience gained up until the time of writing, spring 1982.

Arms Control Agreements

1. Pre-World War II efforts towards multilateral control of arms

The practice of negotiating arms control in an international forum with a view to making the measures adopted applicable to several or all nations is relatively recent. Some outstanding examples of the first efforts in this field which are of remarkable relevance to topics now under discussion are briefly described and evaluated in this chapter.

I. The humanitarian rules of war

Among the earliest international efforts were the two International Peace Conferences convened before World War I. They were held in 1899 and 1907 at The Hague and contributed to codifying the laws of war by prohibiting or restricting the use of certain specific weapons. This was an international recognition of the need for collective action to control the effects of 'modern warfare'. (The relevant agreements are reviewed in chapter 3, section VII.) Moreover, conventions regarding the rights and duties of neutral states were signed.

The two conferences also brought advances in establishing institutions and procedures for settling international disputes. The Permanent Court of Arbitration set up at the Hague was the predecessor of the present International Court of Justice.

The reduction of 'excessive armaments' originally intended by the initiators of the Peace Conferences was not achieved, but a resolution was adopted declaring that a restriction of military expenditure was extremely desirable, and a wish was expressed that governments examine the possibility of an agreement regarding the limitation of armed forces and war budgets. Plans for a third peace conference had to be abandoned in view of the intensified inter-state antagonisms that preceded World War I.

II. The peace treaties

In the years immediately following World War I, considerable efforts were spent in the search for devices to preserve world peace.

The 1919 Treaty of Versailles imposed important restrictions on Germany: the strength of its army was to be reduced to a fixed ceiling, compulsory military service abolished, armaments limited, the general staff dissolved and fortifications on the Rhine dismantled. Restrictions were also introduced on German naval forces, and tanks, submarines, and military or naval aircraft were prohibited. Moreover, the manufacture and importation of asphyxiating, poisonous or other gases and all analogous liquids, materials or devices in Germany were strictly forbidden.

The Covenant of the League of Nations, which forms one of the Parts of the Treaty of Versailles and of the other post-World War I peace treaties as well, required the reduction of armaments of all nations "to the lowest point consistent with national safety and the enforcement by common action of international obligations". The Council of the League was to formulate plans for such reduction for the consideration and action of governments.

III. The naval treaties

Of the proposals aimed at stabilizing world conditions, the one that appeared to hold the greatest promise of success concerned the limitation of naval armaments. The initial step in this direction was made in 1921–22, when representatives of the USA, Great Britain, Japan, France and Italy met in Washington, D.C. and concluded a treaty limiting the sizes of their navies.

The 1922 Washington Treaty

The 1922 Washington Treaty established limits for the size of individual capital ships (the term used at that time to denote the largest warships) and aircraft carriers, and set a definite ratio of tonnages of such types of ships among the signatory countries. Other essential obligations included:

(a) scrapping an agreed number of warships by sinking or breaking them up, or converting them to target use;

(b) prohibiting the construction and acquisition of warships, other than capital ships or aircraft carriers, exceeding 10 000 tons standard displacement, and limiting the calibre of guns carried by all warships; and

(c) undertaking not to establish new fortifications or naval bases in the territories and possessions of the USA, Great Britain and Japan, as specified in the Treaty, and not to take any measures to increase the existing naval facilities for the repair and maintenance of naval forces and not to make any increases in the coastal defences of the mentioned territories and possessions.

The Treaty, which was to remain in force until 1936 (subject to the withdrawal of any signatory on two years' notice), was generally considered a success in spite of the fact that no agreement could be reached on the total tonnage of cruisers, destroyers and submarines. But as a consequence of this omission, the signatories began extensive programmes of warship construction in the categories which were not restricted.

It is worth noting that in the early 1920s there was a strong trend of opinion, especially in Great Britain, favouring the complete abolition of

2

submarines, considered a means of warfare inconsistent with the laws of war. However, the opponents of such a disarmament measure, mainly France, considered the submarine a legitimate defensive weapon. They argued, in particular, that it was the only means of defence a small naval power possessed against a nation with an overwhelming superiority in capital ships.

The 1930 London Treaty

At the second naval conference, held in London in 1930, attempts were made to extend the provisions of the 1922 Washington Treaty to include additional naval craft. However, France refused to follow the Washington Treaty ratio of tonnages rule and rejected Italy's right to parity with France in cruisers, destroyers and submarines, while Italy would accept nothing less than parity. As a result, the most important part of the London Treaty (Part III)—that establishing limits on these types of warships—applied only to the USA, Great Britain and Japan. Nevertheless, the pact was significant in that for the first time in history the three major sea powers accepted, by international arrangement, quantitative and qualitative limitations on all categories of warships.

Other parts of the 1930 London Naval Treaty reaffirmed the general provision of the Washington Treaty governing capital ships and aircraft carriers, and included an agreement reached by the same five nations not to exercise their rights to lay down capital ship replacement tonnage (as provided for in the Washington Treaty) during the period 1931-36. In addition, the number of capital ships of the USA, Great Britain and Japan was to be reduced.

In 1934 Japan, considering the capital ship ratio to be unjust, abrogated the 1922 Washington Treaty. At a conference subsequently called in London, it soon became apparent that Japan's proposal for a common upper limit and its claim to parity would be denied. Japan then decided to withdraw from the conference.

The 1936 London Treaty

As distinct from the 1922 and 1930 treaties, the 1936 London Naval Treaty provided neither for quantitative limitations nor for reductions in the existing fleets. It did, however, regulate certain aspects of naval competition through qualitative restrictions which were to govern ship construction until 1942, namely, restrictions on ship displacement and gun calibres by class of ship. The Treaty also introduced an interesting innovation: the parties were required regularly to exchange detailed information regarding construction and acquisition of all vessels.

The main drawback of the Treaty was that it did not bind such important powers as Japan, the Soviet Union, Italy or Germany. Any of these countries could bring about a collapse of the Treaty by constructing vessels which did not conform to its provisions, because this would release the signatories from the limitations on displacement and armaments. Denmark, Finland, Norway and Sweden acceded to the Treaty in 1938. Separate agreements incorporating the principal features of the 1936 London Naval Treaty were signed by Great Britain with Germany and the Soviet Union in 1937, and with Italy in 1938. However, the outbreak of World War II in 1939 put an end to all these agreements.

IV. Attempts to regulate arms trade and production

The 1890 Brussels Act

An early attempt to regulate the international trade in arms was made in the General Act for the repression of African slave trade, the so-called Brussels Act, signed in 1890. The Act prohibited the introduction into Africa between latitudes 20° North and 22° South of fire-arms and ammunition other than flint-lock guns and gunpowder, except under effective guarantees.

The 1906 Act of Algeciras

The General Act of Algeciras, which introduced reforms in Morocco to ensure "order, peace and prosperity", contained the following provision concerning the repression of the contraband of arms: throughout the Shereefian Empire (Morocco) the importation and sale of arms of war, parts of guns, ammunition of any nature, powder, saltpeter, gun cotton or nitroglycerine were forbidden. Explosives necessary for industry and public works were not covered by this prohibition, but their importation was to be subject to strict regulation. The arms, parts of guns and ammunition intended for the Shereefian troops were to be admitted after the fulfilment of the formal requirements specified in the Act. Confiscation, punishment and fines were provided for illegal introduction and sale of the prohibited items.

The 1919 St Germain Convention

A legal basis for subsequent actions to control the arms trade as well as the manufacture of arms was provided by the 1919 Covenant of the League of Nations. In particular, the League was to be entrusted with general supervision of the trade in arms and ammunition with the countries in which the control of this traffic was "necessary in the common interest", while the Council of the League was to advise how the "evil effects" attendant upon the manufacture by private enterprise of munitions and implements of war could be prevented. States also undertook to exchange information regarding their armaments, military programmes and war industries.

Under the 1919 St Germain Convention for the control of the trade in arms and ammunition, worked out in compliance with the relevant provisions of the League of Nations Covenant, there was to be no arms export, save for exceptions to be permitted by means of export licences granted by governments. A comprehensive list of armaments was drawn up, to which different regulations were applicable, and full publicity for the arms trade was required. However, the Convention never came into force, mainly because of the refusal of the USA to ratify it.

The League of Nations *Armaments Year-book*

The Secretariat of the League of Nations began in 1924 to publish the *Armaments Year-book* on the strength and equipment of states' armed forces, based on public sources. Certain editions of the yearbook included data on the production and exchange of goods related to national defence, as well as information on paramilitary formations and police forces. Some indication of the size and trends of military spending was also provided. Yet another publication, the *Statistical Year-book* of the League of Nations, was issued in 1924. It contained particulars of the international trade in arms and ammunition and showed the values of imports and exports according to official national statistics. The figures were approximate, incomplete and generally non-comparable, while the trade in certain important categories of arms was not covered at all. Nevertheless, both yearbooks provided a background for the conference which was convened in Geneva in 1925 to consider the "supervision of the international trade in arms and ammunition and in implements of war".

The 1925 Geneva Convention on the arms trade

The Convention produced by the 1925 Geneva conference distinguished five categories of arms: (*a*) arms exclusively designed and intended for land, sea and air warfare; (*b*) arms capable of use both for military and other purposes; (*c*) war vessels and their normal armament; (*d*) aircraft (assembled or dismantled) and aircraft engines; and (*e*) gunpowder, explosives and arms not covered by the first two categories.

An export licence or declaration was required for export of any item in the first category; authorization by the government of the importing country was also necessary for the export of these items to private persons. Equally, items in the second category could be exported solely under cover of an export document, but prior authorization of the government of the importing country was not necessary. In the case of items covered by the third category, detailed information was to be published regarding vessels transferred and those constructed on behalf of the government of another state, including armaments installed on board. As regards the fourth category, a return giving quantities of aircraft and aircraft engines exported and the country of destination was to be made public. Trade in commodities belonging to the fifth category was not to be subject to any restrictions, unless the commodities were destined for certain territorial and maritime zones in Africa or the Middle East, referred to as 'special zones' and specified in the Convention.

The purpose of the Geneva Convention was not to reduce the international arms trade, which was considered a legitimate activity, but to prevent illicit traffic. This was to be accomplished through 'supervision', meaning universal export licensing by governments, and publicity in the form of statistical returns of the foreign trade in arms. However, no supervision of arms production was provided for. This inequity was the main reason why many countries, especially non-producing, arms-importing countries, refused to ratify the Convention, which consequently failed to enter into force.

Of the documents signed simultaneously with the Convention for the supervision of the international arms trade, only the Geneva Protocol for the prohibition of the use in war of asphyxiating, poisonous or other gases, and of bacteriological methods of warfare became effective; it is now adhered to by over 100 states. (For a detailed discussion of the Geneva Protocol, see chapter 3.)

The 1929 proposal for supervision of arms production

After the 1925 Geneva conference, a special committee was set up by the Council of the League of Nations to deal with the problem of arms production. In 1929, the committee submitted a draft convention regarding the "supervision of the private manufacture and publicity of the manufacture of arms and ammunition and of implements of war". The draft proposed that no private manufacture of arms included in any of the first four categories established by the 1925 Geneva Convention should be permitted, unless licensed by governments. Moreover, data were to be published showing the value, number and weight of arms in the first, second and fourth categories and manufactured in private enterprises (under licence) or in establishments owned by the state.

Reservations expressed with regard to different provisions of the above draft, namely, opposition to restrictions upon private manufacture and objections against publicizing data relating to state arms industry, as well as a requirement to abolish private manufacture of arms and insistence on internationalizing all arms manufacture, made it impossible to reach any agreement whatsoever.

V. Limitation of armaments in Central America

In 1922, following an outbreak of armed clashes among states in Central America, the US government called a conference of these states in order to bring them closer together and avert a large conflict. The conference took place in Washington, D.C. and in 1923 adopted a General Treaty of peace and amity establishing a code of inter-state behaviour as well as a series of conventions, including one on the limitation of armaments. Under the latter document, Guatemala, El Salvador, Honduras, Nicaragua and Costa Rica agreed not to maintain standing armies or national guards in excess of the numbers which were fixed in the Convention and which were based on such considerations as the population, area or extent of frontiers. Export of arms or munitions from one Central American country to another was prohibited. None of the parties had the right to possess more than 10 war aircraft, and the acquisition of war vessels, except for armed coast guard boats, was not allowed. However, these limitations were not to be binding in case of civil war or threatened attack by a foreign state.

Moreover, the signatories obligated themselves not to use in war asphyxiating gases, poisons or similar substances, as well as analogous liquids, materials or devices.

Reports on measures taken in the implementation of the Convention were to be submitted semi-annually by the parties themselves. No other means of control was envisaged.

VI. The First World Disarmament Conference

The most remarkable agreement reached in the inter-war period to abolish the use of violence in relations among nations was the General Treaty for the renunciation of war, the so-called Briand-Kellogg Pact, signed at Paris in 1928. The parties to this Pact condemned recourse to war for the solution of international controversies and declared that they renounced it as an instrument of national policy in their relations with one another. They also agreed that the settlement or solution of all disputes or conflicts which might arise among them would always be sought by pacific means.

The Pact of Paris provided impetus for the 1932 Disarmament Conference, the only conference held prior to World War II to discuss a universal reduction and limitation of all types of armaments. Convened under the auspices of the League of Nations, it was attended by representatives of more than 60 states, making it the largest international gathering up till that date. Without prejudging the decisions of the Conference, the governments were asked to refrain, for a period of one year, from any measure involving an increase in their armaments. This so-called armaments truce was later extended for a few months.

The following questions were examined in detail by specialized commissions, sub-commissions and committees of the Disarmament Conference: (a) establishment of a system of collective security; (b) limitation of the strength of the armed forces; (c) limitation of land, naval and air armaments; (d) limitation of national defence expenditures; (e) prohibition of chemical, incendiary and bacteriological warfare; (f) control of arms manufacture and trade; (g) supervision and guarantees of the implementation of the obligations by the parties; and (h) "moral disarmament" intended to create an atmosphere favourable to the peaceful solution of international problems.

7

A draft convention, drawn up by the Preparatory Commission which had been in session since 1926, was first submitted to the Conference for consideration. Subsequently, a British draft was accepted as the basis of the future convention, and a provisional text prepared in light of the modifications to this draft was published in September 1933, along with amendments proposed and statements made by different delegations. Summaries of the points of agreement and disagreement revealed at the Conference follow.

Renunciation of war

The participating states were willing to enter into immediate consultations in the event of a breach, or threat of breach, of the 1928 Pact of Paris. A draft agreement not to resort to force, to be signed by all European states, was also adopted, and the President of the USA, in a message to the Conference, proposed that all nations should conclude a pact of non-aggression. The positions were less clear as regards the definition of an aggressor, the procedure for the establishment of facts constituting aggression, and the problem of mutual assistance.

Armed forces, armaments and defence expenditures

An agreement existed in principle that a strict numerical limitation and substantial reduction of armed forces should be brought about. However, no common decision could be reached regarding the assignment to individual states of definite figures of effectives or regarding the method of their computation.

Among the proposals for the limitation of land armaments, the most remarkable was that submitted by the USA requiring that tanks and heavy mobile land guns should be abolished. However, the draft convention went no further than to suggest a maximum limit for the calibre of land mobile guns as well as for the weight of a tank, and the abolition of all guns and tanks exceeding the fixed limits. Various suggestions were made concerning the maxima to be prescribed and the time limits for the destruction of excess material, while the French delegation moved that weapons exceeding the prescribed limits should be internationalized.

The discussions of naval armaments were determined to a large extent by the fact that the 1922 and 1930 Naval Treaties were subject to revision at an international conference planned for 1935. Pending this conference, Great Britain proposed that the stipulations of both treaties should be retained, while France and Italy were to be brought within the framework of the 1930 London Naval Treaty. States not bound by the Naval Treaties were to maintain the *status quo*, meaning that any new warship construction undertaken before 1935 would only be to replace 'over age' tonnage. These proposals met with protests on the part of the delegates who considered that incorporation in a general disarmament convention of provisions contained in treaties between only certain naval powers was an inadequate solution of the problem of naval disarmament.

The agreed text relating to air armaments recognized that abolition of military and naval aircraft must depend on the effective supervision of civil aviation. (The French delegation pleaded for internationalization of civil aviation.) Alternatively, should it prove impossible to ensure such supervision, it was proposed to determine the number of machines required by each party, consistent with its national safety and obligations, and considering the particular circumstances of each country. Adoption of concrete measures was left to the next disarmament conference. Nevertheless, the draft convention already provided for limits on numbers of aeroplanes capable of use in war. There was also agreement in principle that bombardment from the air should be prohibited.

According to the text prepared by a technical committee of the Conference, the parties would undertake, on a basis of reciprocity, periodically to give full publicity to their national defence expenditures, irrespective of the nature and origin of the resources from which the expenditure was met. The committee also specified the instruments necessary for the application of the system of publicity.

Chemical, incendiary and bacteriological warfare

The draft convention prohibited the use of chemical weapons, including lachrymatory, irritant or vesicant substances, as well as incendiary or bacteriological weapons, against any state and in any war, whatever its character. (It thus constituted an advance as compared to the 1925 Geneva Protocol, which covered only chemical and bacteriological means of warfare.) Preparations for such use, including instruction or training, would also be prohibited in time of peace as in time of war. A procedure of enquiry, on-the-spot investigation and prompt reporting for establishing an instance of the use of a prohibited weapon was provided for. The right of reprisals, however, was recognized, as was the right to material and installations intended exclusively to ensure individual or collective protection against the effects of chemical, incendiary or bacteriological weapons, or to training with a view to such protection.

Arms trade and manufacture

Many delegations to the Conference expressed the desire to introduce a system of arms regulation which would be more complete than that proposed in the 1925 Geneva Convention on the arms trade or the 1929 draft convention on arms manufacture. Others were unwilling to accept more radical measures. The fundamental questions to be resolved concerned the principle of state responsibility for, and the kind of publicity to be given to, the manufacture of and trade in arms, as well as the principle of qualitative and quantitative limitations on manufacture. The report published in 1935 by a special committee of the Conference included texts reflecting the unanimous view that an effective system for the control and regulation of the trade in and the manufacture of arms was essential. However, considerable differences of opinion remained on the character and extent of the measures of control and publicity considered necessary. The Committee appreciated the need to ensure equality between producing and non-producing countries, but opinions differed as regards the manner in which such equality could be achieved. Certain delegations made their position on arms trade and manufacture conditional upon the nature and extent of the obligations which the governments would undertake under a general disarmament convention.

Verification and sanctions

The need for effective international control was strongly emphasized throughout the debates of the Conference. There was an agreement to set up at the seat of the League of Nations a Permanent Disarmament Commission composed of representatives of the parties, and it was felt that the Commission should be ready to assume its duties as soon as the convention came into force. These duties were to include investigations of alleged infractions of the convention on the territory of any party. Moreover, there were to be regular inspections of the armaments of each state at least once a year on the basis of equality between the contracting powers.

As regards guarantees of implementation, it was assumed that in the case of an established violation of the provisions of the convention, the Council of the League would exercise its rights under the Covenant. However, the French delegation insisted on defining more precisely the action to be taken in the event of a violation. It proposed that the Permanent Disarmament Commission should demand that the party at fault observe its undertakings within a fixed period, and appoint a committee of inspection to satisfy itself that the demand was heeded. If the violation continued, the parties were to employ, in common, the necessary means of pressure against the defaulting party to ensure the implementation of the convention; and, if war ensued, the defaulting party was to be subject to sanctions in accordance with the appropriate provisions of the Covenant.

Moral disarmament

Under the heading of moral disarmament the Conference discussed questions relating to education, co-operation among intellectuals, the press, broadcasting, theatre and cinema. The committee which dealt with moral disarmament adopted a text according to which the parties would undertake to ensure that education at every stage, including teacher training, should be so conceived as to inspire mutual respect between peoples and to emphasize their interdependence. The parties would further undertake to ensure that persons entrusted with education and preparing textbooks were inspired by these principles, to encourage the use of the cinema and broadcasting for increasing the spirit of goodwill among nations, and to use their influence to

10

avoid the showing of films, the broadcasting of programmes or the organization of performances obviously calculated to insult the legitimate sentiments of other countries.

A proposal to adapt the municipal laws of various countries to the requirements of international relations was also submitted. It provided for legislation to be introduced by the parties which would enable them to inflict punishment for certain acts detrimental to good international relations. These acts would include the preparation and execution in the territory of a state of measures directed against the security of a foreign power, efforts to induce a state to commit a violation of its international obligations, the aiding or abetting of armed bands formed in the territory of a state and invading the territory of another state, the dissemination of false information likely to disturb international relations, and the false attribution to a foreign state of actions likely to bring it into public contempt or hatred. It was also suggested that the parties should pledge themselves, when reviewing their state constitutions, to consider the introduction of articles prohibiting resort to force as an instrument of national policy, thus embodying the principles of the 1928 Pact of Paris.

The withdrawal of Germany from the League of Nations, and German rearmament in violation of the Treaty of Versailles, brought about the breakdown of attempts to achieve a general limitation of armaments. At the beginning of 1936, the Council of the League of Nations decided to suspend the Disarmament Conference.

The Conference never reconvened, but much can be learned from the record of its deliberations, which includes the most thorough examination of the technical, economic, legal and moral aspects of general disarmament ever made. Many ideas put forward at the League of Nations have been revived in recent years, and a number of points made then remain topical now.

2. Early United Nations arms control activities

International efforts to regulate armaments on a world-wide scale resumed after World War II within the framework of the United Nations Organization, which was created "to save succeeding generations from the scourge of war".

I. The UN Charter

Unlike the Covenant of the League of Nations, which had attached considerable importance to disarmament and had clearly defined the obligations of the League and of its members with regard to the reduction and limitation of armaments, the Charter of the United Nations made only passing reference to disarmament. Principles "governing disarmament and the regulation of armaments" were included among the general principles of co-operation in the maintenance of international peace and security to be considered by the UN General Assembly, while the UN Security Council was to formulate plans for the establishment of a "system for the regulation of armaments". One reason for this difference in emphasis lies in the fact that when the League Covenant was written many believed that World War I was caused by the arms race prior to that war, whereas a few decades later the prevalent feeling was that World War II could have been avoided if the great powers had maintained an adequate military potential as well as a readiness to use it. Moreover, unlike the League Covenant, the UN Charter was drafted when the war was still in full progress, and when planning a system of disarmament might have seemed ill-timed.

The system of peacekeeping and enforcement measures envisaged by the Charter is predicated on the continued existence of national armed forces, which are to be made available to the Security Council to maintain or restore international peace and security, and which may be used for self-defence in the case of armed attack against a UN member until the Security Council takes the necessary measures.

Nevertheless, the United Nations very early became involved in the matter of disarmament. This had been prompted chiefly by the use of atomic bombs shortly after the signing of the UN Charter and by the fear that this new weapon of unprecedented destructiveness might be used again. Indeed, the very first UN General Assembly resolution, of January 1946, established a commission to deal with the problems raised by the discovery of atomic energy and to make specific proposals for elimination from national armaments of atomic weapons and of all other major weapons of mass destruction. In December of the same year, the United Nations formally recognized that the problem of security was closely connected with that of disarmament and recommended a general, progressive and balanced reduction of national armed forces. Since then, disarmament has been regarded as the most important item on the international agenda.

II. Nuclear disarmament

The Baruch Plan

At the first meeting of the Atomic Energy Commission, set up by the UN General Assembly, the USA put forward what came to be known as the Baruch Plan under which an international atomic development authority would be created. This authority would be entrusted with managerial control or ownership of all atomic energy activities potentially dangerous to world security; with the power to control, inspect and license all other atomic activities; as well as with the duty to foster the beneficial uses of atomic energy. In particular, the authority was to conduct continuous surveys of supplies of uranium and thorium and bring these materials under its control, and to possess the exclusive right both to conduct research in the field of atomic explosives and to produce and own fissionable material. All nations were to grant the freedom of inspection deemed necessary by the authority. The United States stressed the importance of immediate punishment for infringements of the rights of the authority, maintaining that there must be no veto to protect those who violated their agreements not to develop or use atomic energy for destructive purposes.

In memoranda submitted later, the USA explained that it had in mind the ownership and exclusive operation by the international authority of all facilities for the production of uranium-235 as well as plutonium, and that the authority was to be non-political, although its decisions were to have a considerable degree of finality. Once a system of control and sanctions was effectively operating, further production of atomic weapons would cease, existing stocks would be destroyed, and all technological information would be communicated to the authority. In other words, control would have to come first; atomic disarmament would follow.

The Soviet response

The Soviet Union rejected this plan on the premises that it would interfere with national sovereignty and internal affairs of states, and that the provision denying the right of veto was contrary to the UN Charter. For its part, it submitted a draft convention which reversed the priorities put forward by the United States: the production and use of atomic weapons were to be prohibited and all atomic weapons were to be destroyed within three months, whereupon an international system to supervise the implementation of these commitments would be established. Violations were to be considered a serious crime against humanity and severe penalties were to be provided by domestic legislation. The convention would be of indefinite duration and would come into force after approval by the UN Security Council and ratification by the Council's permanent members. The composition, rights and obligations of the envisaged international commission for the control of atomic energy (to be established within the framework of the UN Security Council) would be determined by a special international convention. The commission would periodically inspect facilities for the mining of atomic raw material and for the production of atomic materials and atomic energy, as well as carry out special investigations of suspected violations. It would also have the right to submit recommendations to the Security Council on measures to be taken against violators of the convention on the prohibition of atomic weapons and of the convention on the control of atomic energy.

US–Soviet differences

The basic differences between the two positions were, *first*, the stage at which atomic weapons were to be prohibited, that is, whether a convention outlawing these weapons and providing for their destruction should precede or follow the establishment of a control system; and, *second*, the role of the Security Council in dealing with the possible violations, or whether the rule of veto would be applicable. The deadlock proved impossible to break, mainly because the Soviet Union was then considerably less advanced than the United States in the atomic field and would not accept the Baruch Plan, which could have led to a US monopoly of atomic weapons. Equally, the Soviet proposal for the abolition of atomic weapons before establishing an effective international control to ensure compliance with the ban was unacceptable to the United States.

In 1948, at US insistence, the UN General Assembly approved the Baruch Plan by an overwhelming majority. Nevertheless, despite the adoption of what was then called the 'United Nations Plan' for the control of atomic energy, hopes for taking effective measures in this field and for averting a nuclear arms race were dissipated.

'Atoms for Peace'

In 1953 US President Eisenhower proposed the so-called 'Atoms for Peace' plan. The idea, as stated by the sponsor of the plan, was to promote disarmament by an indirect approach, that of building up the peaceful uses of atomic energy. The atomic powers were to contribute fissionable material for such uses to an agency, which would be set up under the aegis of the United Nations and which would help countries to obtain the benefits of atomic energy. This proposal led to the establishment in 1956 of the International Atomic Energy Agency (IAEA) having the following main functions: to assist research, development and practical application of atomic energy for peaceful purposes; to make provision for relevant materials, services, equipment and facilities, with due consideration for the needs of the underdeveloped areas of the world; to foster the exchange of scientific and technical information and to encourage the exchange and training of experts in the field of peaceful uses of atomic energy; to administer safeguards designed to ensure that relevant materials, equipment and information were not used in such a way as to further any military purpose; and to establish standards of safety for the protection of health and the minimization of danger to life and property.

Since 1970 the IAEA has had a key role in safeguarding compliance with the Treaty on the non-proliferation of nuclear weapons (the NPT).

III. Limitation of armed forces and armaments

Parallel to the consideration of atomic weapons, efforts continued in a separate UN commission to reach an agreement on the limitation of conventional weapons. But no negotiations comparable in thoroughness to those in the League of Nations have ever been conducted in the United Nations.

Soviet and Western approaches

In 1948 the Soviet Union proposed, as a first step, that the permanent members of the Security Council (China, France, the UK, the USA and the USSR) should immediately reduce by one-third all land, naval and air forces; that atomic weapons be prohibited; and that an international control body be established within the framework of the Security Council for the supervision and control of the implementation of these measures. At that time, the Soviet Union insisted that atomic weapons and conventional weapons must be dealt with together in any plan for disarmament, while the United States and its allies argued that a start could be made on conventional disarmament.

In 1949 the Western powers presented a plan for a census and verification of information on armed forces and conventional armaments, and envisaged a central control authority to be directly under the Security Council. The Soviet Union opposed this plan because it considered it as an unacceptable preliminary condition for the reduction of armaments and armed forces, and also because collecting information on atomic weapons was not provided for. The Western plan was approved by the UN General Assembly but was never implemented.

The UN commissions for atomic energy and for conventional armaments merged in 1952 into the Disarmament Commission. The argument continued there as to whether disarmament must begin with atomic or conventional weapons and as to whether the disclosure of information on armed forces and armaments and verification of the accuracy of this information should be carried out before or after the adoption of a programme of disarmament. Neither side was prepared to compromise on priorities; each side accused the other of wishing to retain the weapons in which it was strongest. In any event, the political climate of the early 1950s was hardly propitious for arms control talks, as the main protagonists deeply distrusted each other. The war in Korea threatened to degenerate into a world-wide conflagration, and recourse to nuclear weapons was being seriously considered. An additional irritant was the charge put forward in the United Nations by the USSR that the USA had used bacteriological and chemical weapons in Korea and China. The accusations specified the localities affected, the number of casualties and the damage caused. But the evidence produced by the investigating commissions appointed by organizations which sided with the accusers was considered unconvincing by the majority of UN members, while US proposals for impartial investigation were rejected by the accusing side.

Only in 1953, with the end of the Korean War and the changes in the governments of the Soviet Union (following the death of Stalin) and of the United States (following the election of Eisenhower as President), did the international atmosphere improve sufficiently to allow reconsideration of the problem of disarmament. Moreover, the new relationship of forces between the two great powers seemed to favour arms control talks. The United States, which before the Korean War had been greatly inferior in conventional arms as compared to the Soviet Union, rearmed considerably in the early 1950s, while the USSR achieved an important atomic capability. A new body, a five-power (Canada, France, the United Kingdom, the Soviet Union and the United States) sub-committee of the UN Disarmament Commission, was established to seek, in private, agreement on a "comprehensive and co-ordinated" disarmament programme with adequate safeguards. There was an explicit understanding that efforts to reach such an agreement were to be made concurrently with progress in the settlement of international disputes.

Soviet and Western disarmament programmes in 1954–55

In 1954 France and the United Kingdom jointly put forward a programme based on the following principles: (a) the measures of reduction, of prohibition, and of disclosure and verification, regarding military manpower, military expenditure, conventional armaments and nuclear weapons[1] had to be linked together in order to increase the security of all parties at all stages; (b) the transition from one stage of the programme to another should be automatic, subject to the competence of the control organ to verify the next stage; and (c) the measures prohibiting weapons of mass destruction should be sub-divided among use, manufacture and possession, and should take effect at different stages. At the outset, the nuclear powers would regard

---

[1] After the invention of the thermonuclear fusion weapon (also referred to as the hydrogen weapon) the term 'nuclear weapons' came to be used to include both this and the atomic fission weapon.

themselves as prohibited from using nuclear weapons except "in defence against aggression".

A few months later the Soviet Union submitted a draft international convention based on the French–British proposal, but with amendments. In particular, the Soviet plan set specific time-limits for reductions, and required a total and unconditional ban on the use of nuclear weapons. The main concession to the West consisted in accepting that half of the agreed reductions in armed forces and conventional armaments might take place before any action to prohibit nuclear weapons.

In 1955 Canada and the United States joined France and the United Kingdom in submitting a memorandum which repeated in general terms the French–British programme of 1954. France and the United Kingdom further suggested that the ceilings for the armed forces of the Soviet Union, the United States and China should be between 1 and 1.5 million men each, and that those of the United Kingdom and France should be 650 000 men each. For other countries, the permitted levels were to be considerably lower. France and the UK also proposed that the total prohibition of nuclear weapons should be effected when 75 per cent of the reduction of conventional armaments and armed forces had been completed (not at the end of the disarmament programme, as proposed earlier). An effective system of control was to operate throughout the whole disarmament programme.

The Soviet Union at first opposed the Western plan, but subsequently, on 10 May 1955, put forward its own plan in which it accepted the specific ceilings proposed by France and the United Kingdom as well as the postponement of the prohibition of nuclear weapons until after 75 per cent of the agreed reduction in armed forces and conventional armaments had been carried out.

The Soviet plan was to be completed in two stages of one year each.

In the first stage, the five great powers — China, France, the UK, the USA and the USSR — would reduce their armed forces and armaments by 50 per cent of the difference between the levels at the end of 1954 and the ceilings of 1–1.5 million men and 650 000 men, respectively. A world conference would establish ceilings for the other countries. Simultaneously with carrying out the agreed reduction of armed forces, states possessing nuclear weapons would undertake to discontinue tests of these weapons and would commit themselves not to use them except for purposes of defence against aggression when a decision to that effect was taken by the Security Council. Finally, some of the military bases in the territories of other states would be eliminated.

During the second stage, the second half of the reductions would be carried out. When 75 per cent of the total reduction had been completed, a complete prohibition of the use of nuclear weapons would come into force. These weapons would be destroyed simultaneously with the last 25 per cent of the reduction of armed forces.

A separate section of the Soviet plan, dealing with international control, stated that there was no way of assuring that all stocks of nuclear weapons had been eliminated, and that there were therefore possibilities whereby some nuclear weapons could be hidden. Hence the Soviet Union proposed setting up an early-warning system to monitor large troop movements, arguing that a surprise nuclear attack was likely to be preceded by a considerable build-up and movement of conventional forces. A control agency would install in the territories of all states concerned, on a basis of reciprocity, control posts at major ports, at railway junctions, on main highways and at airfields, so that the observers could alert the world to possible dangers. The control agency would have the right to request from states the necessary information on the implementation of measures of reduction of armaments and armed forces, as well as the right of unhindered access to documents pertaining to budgetary appropriations for military purposes. It would also have the power to exercise control, including inspection, on a permanent basis and on a scale necessary to ensure the implementation of the disarmament programme.

The Soviet proposal was the most comprehensive and detailed programme of general disarmament submitted at the United Nations up to that time. And the timing for its presentation seemed opportune as the international situation began to look hopeful. The year 1955 saw the conclusion of the State Treaty re-establishing an independent Austria and prohibiting the possession, construction or testing by Austria of weapons of mass destruction, and of certain other types of weapons; a formal undertaking by the Federal Republic of Germany not to manufacture on its territory atomic, chemical or biological weapons; the convening of the first international conference on the peaceful uses of atomic energy; and the meeting of the heads of government of France, the UK, the USA and the USSR, which created a relaxed international atmosphere known as the 'Geneva spirit'.

The 1955 Geneva Summit

The Geneva Summit Conference discussed the Soviet programme for the reduction of armaments and the prohibition of nuclear weapons, a British memorandum on joint inspection of forces confronting each other in Europe, a French proposal for reductions in military budgets and using the savings to assist underdeveloped countries and the US plan for 'open skies' to ensure against a large-scale surprise attack.

Under the US plan, the United States and the Soviet Union were to exchange military 'blueprints', that is, information about the strength, command structure and disposition of personnel, units and equipment of all major land, sea and air forces, as well as a complete list of military plants, facilities and installations. Verification of information was to be accompanied by ground observation and by mutual, unrestricted aerial reconnaissance. The Soviet Union considered this to be "control without disarmament", which would increase international mistrust and tension. The United States emphasized that an effective method of inspection and control was the first requirement of an agreement.

Shortly thereafter in 1955 the USA placed a reservation on all of its "pre-Geneva substantive positions" pending the outcome of the study of inspection methods. This in fact amounted not only to the withdrawal of the Western disarmament proposal after a very large and essential portion of it had been accepted by the Soviet Union, but also to the formal abandonment of the Baruch Plan, which had been approved by the majority of UN members. Thus, the efforts to achieve agreement on a programme of disarmament involving all armaments in a co-ordinated manner were brought to a standstill by the Geneva Summit and its decision to pursue consideration of the plans of the four heads of government.

Subsequently, attention shifted to partial arms control approaches, such as: discontinuance of nuclear weapon tests; restriction of the production of fissionable materials to non-weapon purposes only; establishment of a European zone of arms limitation; reduction of force levels; reduction of military budgets; prohibiting the use of nuclear weapons; ensuring that the launching of objects through outer space would be exclusively for peaceful purposes; safeguarding against the possibility of surprise attack; and eliminating foreign military bases. There were also sharp disagreements in each of these fields. The sub-committee, which for more than three years had been negotiating measures of arms control, ended its work on a note of acrimony in 1957.

IV. Arms control conferences in 1958

Several conferences dealing with arms control issues took place in 1958 outside the aegis of the United Nations. The first of these, a conference of experts on the detection of nuclear tests, was convened to meet an international concern which had been growing ever since Indian Prime Minister Nehru appealed, in 1954, for a 'standstill agreement' on nuclear explosions. The conference presented a unanimous report outlining a rather extensive system of control and led to the conference on the discontinuance of nuclear weapon tests—a diplomatic negotiation of the three nuclear weapon powers (the UK, the USA and the USSR) that continued until 1962.

Another conference of experts was to study measures for the prevention of surprise attack. But the delegations could not even agree on the terms of reference: the Western countries insisted on working out a technical, military analysis of the problem and evaluating the effect of various systems of inspection and observation, without considering possible disarmament measures, while the Eastern countries proposed to discuss proposals for a system of inspection and disarmament in Europe as a means of preventing surprise attack. The conference broke down.

With the exception of the 1959 Treaty for the demilitarization of the Antarctic, which was also negotiated outside of the United Nations, no agreement could be reached on any single arms control measure during the first 18 years following World War II.

V. General and complete disarmament

On 17 September 1959 the United Kingdom submitted to the UN General Assembly a plan for 'comprehensive' disarmament, based on the principle of balanced stages towards the abolition of all nuclear weapons and the reduction of all other weapons to levels which would rule out the possibility of aggressive war. The next day, the Soviet Union proposed a disarmament programme aimed at eliminating all armed forces and armaments[2] within four years. A revised detailed version of this programme, in the form of a "draft treaty on general and complete disarmament under strict international control", became a basis for discussion in the Committee on Disarmament in Geneva, along with the US proposed "outline of basic provisions of a treaty on general and complete disarmament in a peaceful world".

The parties had before them a set of principles, as agreed between the USSR and the USA in a joint statement of 1961 (the so-called McCloy–Zorin agreement), which were to guide them in finding solutions to the complex problem of general and complete disarmament. The main agreed principles were those regarding a balanced, staged and verified elimination of all armed forces and armaments. However, the parties could not agree on how to apply these principles. The plans were amended by each side in the course of the following years, but the differences remained unresolved. The main divergencies can be summarized as follows.

The principle of balance

The Soviet Union placed the main emphasis on the completion of the disarmament process within a short, fixed period of time: the more quickly nuclear delivery vehicles were eliminated, the sooner would equality, and hence balance, be achieved. The United States proposed to keep the relative military positions and the pattern of armaments within each military establishment similar to those at the beginning of the disarmament process. To this end, disarmament, beginning with a freeze, was to be gradual; as confidence developed, the military establishment would, by progressive reductions, shrink to zero.

Duration and stages

Both sides envisaged three stages of the disarmament process and made the transition from one stage to the next dependent on the completion of previous disarmament measures. The Soviet Union proposed a four-year

---

[2] It is worth noting that already in 1928, at the Preparatory Commission for the World Disarmament Conference, the USSR proposed, in a draft convention for "immediate, complete and general disarmament", that all armed forces should be disbanded, existing armaments destroyed, military training stopped, war ministries and general staffs abolished, military expenditure discontinued, and military propaganda prohibited.

programme, with 15 months for each of the first two stages, and was later prepared to extend the period for implementing the whole programme to five years and the first stage to two years. The US plan provided for two stages of three years each, to be followed by a third stage, the duration of which would be fixed at the time the treaty on general and complete disarmament was signed.

Reduction of armed forces and conventional armaments

The United States provided for a reduction of the armed forces of both the USSR and the USA to 2.1 million and 1.05 million in the first and second stages, respectively, with a 30 per cent reduction of all major armaments by categories and types of weapon in the first stage and a 35 per cent reduction in each of the second and third stages. Subsequently, the USA amended its proposal to prohibit the production of certain major armaments in the first stage except for replacement purposes, in order to ensure that the 30 per cent reduction would in fact reduce both the quantity and quality of all armaments covered by the reduction. A reduction of agreed military bases, without distinction between foreign and domestic bases, would take place in the second stage. The Soviet Union originally provided for the reduction of Soviet and US armed forces to the level of 1.7 million and 1 million men in the first and second stages, respectively, but later proposed a compromise first-stage level of 1.9 million men. The revised draft envisaged reductions of 30 per cent, 35 per cent and 35 per cent of conventional armaments in each successive stage, and a reduction in the production of conventional armaments, parallel to the reductions of armed forces, through the elimination of factories engaged in such production. The total elimination of all foreign military bases would take place in the first stage, starting with the liquidation of such bases located in Europe.

Nuclear disarmament

Both plans contained first-stage obligations for the nuclear powers not to transfer control of nuclear weapons or information on their production to non-nuclear states. In all other respects they differed. The original Soviet draft provided for the complete elimination of nuclear weapon delivery vehicles and the cessation of the production of such vehicles in the first stage, but it was subsequently amended to permit the USSR and the USA to retain on their own territories a so-called nuclear umbrella, that is, a limited number of intercontinental missiles, anti-missile missiles and anti-aircraft missiles of the ground-to-air variety, until the end of the third stage. The total elimination of nuclear weapons and fissionable material for weapon purposes and the discontinuance of their production would take place during the second stage. The US plan provided in the first stage for ending the production of fissionable material for weapon purposes and for transferring, for peaceful uses, agreed quantities of such material already produced and stockpiled. The number of nuclear weapon delivery vehicles would be reduced by 30 per cent in the second stage, while stocks of nuclear weapons would be reduced by an agreed percentage, and the production of nuclear weapons would be subject to agreed limitations. The total elimination of such weapons would take place in the third stage.

Verification

Both sides agreed on the need to verify what was being reduced, destroyed or converted to peaceful uses, as well as to control the cessation of production of armaments. In addition, the United States stressed the need to verify remaining quantities of armaments and forces and to ensure that undisclosed, clandestine forces, weapons or production facilities did not exist. The Soviet Union was opposed to the inspection of remaining stocks but was willing to consider budgetary controls.

Peace-keeping

The United States proposed that in the first stage a United Nations peace observation corps should be established. At the start of the second stage, a UN peace force would be created; during the remainder of that stage the jurisdiction of the International Court of Justice would become compulsory for legal disputes, and measures would be adopted against indirect aggression and subversion. The question of whether the peace force, which was to be fully developed in the third stage, should be equipped with nuclear weapons was to be left open for future decision. The Soviet draft provided that in the course of and following the disarmament process, force contingents with non-nuclear weapons would be made available to the Security Council under Article 43 of the Charter. The USSR opposed the creation of supra-national institutions and objected to any possibility of providing the UN peace force with nuclear weapons.

The talks on general and complete disarmament failed. They were doomed to fail, among other reasons, because no one could provide a satisfactory answer to such a fundamental question as what would be the political order governing international relations in a completely disarmed world. The same applies to mechanisms and procedures for settling interstate disputes and maintaining peace. But the more immediate obstacle was that the parties were unable even to agree on how much disarmament should be undertaken in the first stage of a disarmament process. The Soviet Union claimed that only a very substantial reduction in military power during the first stage could eliminate the danger of nuclear war, while the Western powers maintained that they could not accept radical first-stage measures or give up the nuclear deterrent until confidence was established between East and West and until an international peace force was formed to replace national forces.

The realization of the insuperable difficulties in agreeing on a programme for general and complete disarmament had the effect of turning attention once again to, and stimulating interest in, specific partial measures of disarmament. In fact, a few first-stage measures proposed in the Soviet and US plans, such as a ban on nuclear weapon testing and prevention of nuclear weapon proliferation, became the subject of separate negotiations. General and complete disarmament has for the United Nations remained an ultimate goal worth striving for rather than a practical policy objective.

Since 1963 a number of arms control agreements have been negotiated, both bilaterally (mainly between the USA and the USSR) and multilaterally. The obligations assumed by the parties to these agreements are reviewed in chapter 3.

3. A review of the obligations in the arms control agreements

The main undertakings which have been assumed by states in the arms control agreements concluded up until 31 December 1981, or which are to be assumed in agreements under negotiation, include: (*a*) restrictions on nuclear weapon testing; (*b*) strategic arms limitation; (*c*) the non-proliferation of nuclear weapons; (*d*) the prohibition of non-nuclear weapons of mass destruction; (*e*) the demilitarization, denuclearization and other measures of restraint in certain environments or geographic areas; (*f*) the prevention of war; and (*g*) the humanitarian laws of war. In the sections below, each arms control agreement is discussed under one of these seven subject-headings, and the specific arms control obligations are analysed.

I. Restrictions on nuclear weapon testing

The question of stopping all nuclear weapon tests has been on the agenda of multilateral, bilateral (US–Soviet) and trilateral (UK–US–Soviet) negotiations since the early 1950s, but no comprehensive ban has been reached by 1982. The three partial agreements signed so far have only circumscribed the environment for nuclear testing and reduced the size of the explosions.

Partial Test Ban Treaty

The 1963 multilateral Partial Test Ban Treaty (PTBT) prohibited any nuclear explosions (that is, including those which may be intended for non-military purposes) in the atmosphere, outer space or under water, or in any other environment if the explosion would cause radioactive debris to be present outside the territorial limits of the country conducting it. In agreeing to this limitation, the original parties—the UK, the USA and the USSR—stated that they were seeking to put an end to the contamination by radioactive substances of man's environment, to slow down the nuclear arms race, to check the spread of nuclear weapons to other nations and to facilitate progress towards disarmament.

The PTBT has certainly helped to curb the radioactive pollution caused by nuclear explosions, but it could not stop it altogether: the non-party nuclear powers, France and China, continued testing in the atmosphere (France stopped atmospheric tests only in 1975). Moreover, underground explosions, permitted under the Treaty, often also release radioactive products into the air.

The PTBT was hailed as the first international agreement of world-wide scope reached in the field of arms control. But by the time it was concluded, the two main testing states, the USA and the USSR, had already carried out extensive series of nuclear explosions in the atmosphere and knew that this activity could be continued underground, thus providing most of the information required for further weapon development. In fact, since 1963 they have carried out considerably more nuclear explosions than during the period preceding the signing of the PTBT. This has enabled them to develop new generations of nuclear warheads and of related delivery vehicles. The nuclear arms race has been allowed to continue unhampered. (For the nuclear explosions conducted since 1945, see table 3.1.)

Table 3.1. Nuclear explosions, 1945–81

A certain, relatively small number of explosions were carried out outside the known nuclear weapon testing sites and may therefore be presumed to form part of a programme for peaceful uses of nuclear energy.

I. 16 July 1945 (the first nuclear explosion) to 5 August 1963 (the signing of the PTBT)

USA	USSR	UK	France			Total
293	164	23	8			488

II. 6 August 1963 to 31 March 1976 (the cut-off date for explosions above the yield limit set by the TTBT)

USA	USSR	UK	France	China	India	Total
315	175	3	52	18	1	564

III. 1 April 1976 to 31 December 1981

USA	USSR	UK	France	China		Total
75	130	8	48	8		269

IV. 6 August 1963 to 31 December 1981

USA	USSR	UK	France	China	India	Total
390	305	11	100	26	1	833

V. 16 July 1945 to 31 December 1981: totals

USA	USSR	UK	France	China	India	Total
683	469	34	108	26	1	1 321

Sources: US Geological Survey, US Department of Energy, Hagfors Observatory of the Research Institute of the Swedish National Defence, and press reports.

The PTBT may have paved the way for the Treaty on the non-proliferation of nuclear weapons, but it did not prevent China, a non-party, from joining the 'nuclear club' in 1964, and there is no indication that, by itself, it has played a role in inhibiting the spread of nuclear weapons among the states which have subscribed to it. While it may be less convenient for an incipient nuclear weapon state to conduct tests underground than in the atmosphere, a country determined to acquire a nuclear weapon capability would not be deterred by such technical difficulties. Thus, India, a party to the PTBT, managed to explode a nuclear device underground.[1]

It is, however, generally recognized that the ban on atmospheric tests helped to improve US–Soviet relations, which were strained by the 1962 Cuban missile crisis, and contributed to the promotion of arms control. Indeed, it led to unilateral reductions in the production of highly enriched uranium and plutonium for nuclear weapons, simultaneously announced by the USA and the USSR in 1964. (These announcements were followed by a UK statement to the effect that military plutonium production in the United Kingdom was being gradually terminated.)

As envisaged by the PTBT, talks on a comprehensive test ban (CTB) were resumed after the entry into force of the Treaty, but the consideration of technical matters replaced, rather than contributed to, the negotiation of the provisions of a new agreement. For years, appeals for transitional measures of restraint that would suspend nuclear weapon testing, or limit or reduce the size and number of nuclear weapon tests, pending the entry into force of a comprehensive ban, had been ignored by the main testing powers. Both the USA and the USSR had insisted on the solution of the testing problem as a whole. However, in 1974, they agreed on a limitation of underground nuclear weapon tests.

Threshold Test Ban Treaty

Under the 1974 US–Soviet Threshold Test Ban Treaty (TTBT), the parties have undertaken to prohibit, to prevent, and not to carry out any underground nuclear weapon test having a yield which exceeds 150 kilotons (the equivalent of 150 000 metric tons of TNT) at any place under their jurisdiction or control, from 31 March 1976. The official reason for setting such a distant date for the entry into force of the yield limitation was that considerable time was needed to make all the necessary verification arrangements. However, the fact is that certain nuclear warheads then under development were planned to have a yield exceeding the agreed limit, and their testing had to take place before the restrictions became effective. Indeed, tests with yields exceeding the threshold were conducted by the USA and the USSR in the period between the signing of the TTBT and 31 March 1976.

In addition to the limit placed on the size of underground nuclear weapon tests, each party to the TTBT committed itself to restrict the number of tests to a minimum. This commitment has had little or no effect on the testing activities of the major powers in subsequent years.

The TTBT may complicate the development of new high-yield warheads by both sides and make it difficult for them to carry out stockpile sampling, because the large thermonuclear weapons could not be tested at their full yield. The cessation of explosions in the megaton range may also have a

---

[1] A complaint by Pakistan about the radioactive contamination of its territory from the Indian nuclear underground explosion, in violation of the PTBT, was rejected by India and the matter was not pursued.

favourable environmental effect in reducing the risks of radioactive venting. However, the 150-kt yield threshold is so high (more than 10 times higher than the yield of the Hiroshima bomb) that the parties cannot be experiencing onerous restraint in continuing their nuclear weapon programmes. In any event, the multiplication of warheads and the increased accuracy of missiles which carry them make up for the lowering of the nuclear explosive yield. The USA and the USSR have even agreed, in a separate understanding, that one or two "slight, unintended" breaches per year would not be considered a violation of the Treaty, because of the technical uncertainties associated with predicting the precise yield of nuclear weapon tests. Neither does the threshold reflect the existing capabilities to verify compliance with test limitations; it is generally admitted that detection and identification of nuclear explosions of much lower size are possible.

Peaceful Nuclear Explosions Treaty

The 1976 US-Soviet Peaceful Nuclear Explosions Treaty (PNET) regulates the explosions which may be conducted outside the nuclear weapon test sites and which may, therefore, be considered to serve peaceful purposes. Possible peaceful applications of nuclear explosions include digging canals or harbours, building roads through mountains, creating underground storage cavities or water reservoirs, stimulation of natural gas and petroleum resources, or extinguishing gas-well fires. To ensure that such explosions should not provide weapon-related information that is not obtainable from limited weapon testing, the parties established the same yield threshold for peaceful applications as had been imposed on weapon tests under the TTBT, namely 150 kt. The restriction applies to individual explosions, while a "group explosion" may exceed the 150-kt limit and reach an aggregate yield as high as 1 500 kt, or one and one-half megatons.

There is considerable scepticism as to the technical feasibility and economic viability of nuclear explosions for peaceful purposes.[2] A question has also arisen about the implications of peaceful explosions for existing arms control agreements, such as the PTBT or the Non-Proliferation Treaty (NPT), and about the compatibility of such explosions with a future agreement banning all nuclear weapon test explosions. Consequently, the PNET must be seen only as an indispensable complement to the TTBT. The latter treaty would be deprived of meaning if peaceful application explosions were allowed without restrictions, for it is impossible to develop nuclear explosive devices which could not be used as weapons. But the PNET has not increased the very limited arms control value of the TTBT. By 1 January 1982, neither treaty had formally entered into force. The parties stated that they would observe the agreed limitations during the pre-ratification period.

---

[2] The USA stopped conducting its peaceful nuclear explosion programme several years ago.

Comprehensive test ban

In 1977, the UK, the USA, and the USSR engaged in trilateral talks for the achievement of a Comprehensive Test Ban Treaty (CTBT), but in 1980, with the change of the US Administration, the talks were adjourned *sine die*. The main points of agreement reached among the negotiators up to that time can be summarized as follows. (*a*) The treaty should prohibit any nuclear weapon test explosion in any environment and be accompanied by a protocol on nuclear explosions for peaceful purposes, which would establish a moratorium on such explosions. (*b*) Any amendments to the treaty would require the approval of a majority of parties, which majority should include all parties that are permanent members of the UN Security Council, and a conference would be held at an appropriate time to review the operation of the treaty. (*c*) The parties would use national technical means of verification at their disposal to verify compliance, and would undertake not to interfere with such means of verification; an international exchange of seismic data would be established. (*d*) The treaty would provide for consultations to resolve questions that may arise concerning compliance, and any party would have the right to request an on-site inspection for the purpose of ascertaining whether or not an event on the territory of another party was a nuclear explosion.

While verification no longer seems to be a major obstacle, a series of complex technical problems related to verification remains to be solved. Among other problems there is the status of laboratory tests which could, for example, consist of extremely low-yield nuclear experiments or the so-called inertial confinement fusion. Extremely low-yield nuclear experiments could involve an explosion of a device which may have characteristics of a nuclear explosive device but uses fissile material of an amount or kind that produces only a fraction of the yield of the chemical explosion that sets off the release of the nuclear energy. The question is whether such a test, which could be conducted in a laboratory, should be considered a nuclear weapon test explosion. The inertial confinement concept is to use lasers or other high-power sources to heat and compress small pellets containing fusionable fuel (deuterium and tritium). If a properly shaped pulse of sufficient energy can be delivered to the pellet, the density and temperature may become high enough for fusion. This would be a laboratory nuclear explosion of tiny proportions.

It may be argued that in order to be effective, a comprehensive test ban should cover all explosions without exception, including laboratory tests. On the other hand, it can be contended that a comprehensive test ban could not cover laboratory tests because they are contained and not verifiable, and also because some of them may be useful for various peaceful purposes, including the development of new sources of energy.

It is important to note that the test ban negotiated trilaterally was planned to have a duration of no more than three years. The USA did not want to make a provision for a possible extension of the ban, while the USSR preferred to stipulate that the ban would continue unless the other nuclear weapon powers, not party to the treaty, continued testing. A ban of fixed duration would not fulfil the pledge included in the PTBT to achieve the discontinuance of all test explosions of nuclear weapons for all time. Moreover, a treaty of short duration would create a problem with respect to the adherence of non-nuclear weapon states, particularly parties to the NPT, which have renounced the possession of nuclear explosive devices for a much longer period. And, finally, the resumption of tests upon the expiration of a short-lived comprehensive test ban treaty would probably hurt the cause of arms limitation and disarmament more than if the treaty had never been entered into.

The discontinuation of nuclear weapon test explosions could not stop all improvements in nuclear warheads; certain improvements do not require tests involving nuclear reactions. There also exists authoritative evidence that the continued operability of stockpiled nuclear weapons can be ensured by non-nuclear testing. Moreover, considerable increases in nuclear capabilities can result mainly from the modernization of the delivery vehicles. Nevertheless, a CTBT would have an arms limitation impact in that it would make it difficult, if not impossible, for the nuclear weapon parties to develop new designs of nuclear warheads, and would also place constraints on the modification of existing weapon designs. It would narrow, thereby, one channel of arms competition among the major powers. The arms control benefits could be further enhanced if the CTBT were followed by a ban on the production of fissionable material for weapon purposes. Such a 'cut-off' would decelerate the rate of manufacture of nuclear weapons and could perhaps even be a step toward eventually stopping this manufacture.

A CTB would also reinforce the NPT by demonstrating the major powers' awareness of their legal obligation under this treaty to bring the nuclear arms race to a halt. On the other hand, it is not certain that it would actually hinder the further proliferation of nuclear weapons, since a test explosion may not be absolutely essential for constructing at least a simple fission device. Neither is it certain that a CTBT would provide sufficient incentives for the present non-NPT states to join the NPT, especially if these states have kept their nuclear weapon option open irrespective of the behaviour of the great powers, or if they consider that the mere cessation of tests by the nuclear weapon states is not a sufficient *quid pro quo* for their renunciation of nuclear weapons.

II. Strategic arms limitation

In 1969, the USA and the USSR initiated bilateral negotiations on possible restrictions regarding their strategic nuclear arsenals. The first phase of these Strategic Arms Limitation Talks (SALT) ended in 1972 with the conclusion of a treaty limiting anti-ballistic missile (ABM) systems and an interim agreement on the limitation of strategic offensive arms. The second phase led to the signing in 1979 of a strategic offensive arms limitation treaty and of a series of related documents.

ABM Treaty

The 1972 US–Soviet ABM Treaty prohibits the deployment of ABM systems for the defence of the whole territory of the USA and the USSR or of an individual region, except when expressly permitted. Permitted deployments are limited to two sites in each country—one for the protection of the national capital, and the other for the protection of an intercontinental ballistic missile (ICBM) complex. The centres of the two ABM deployment areas for each party must be at least 1 300 km apart. No more than 100 ABM launchers and 100 ABM interceptor missiles may be deployed in each ABM deployment area. ABM radars should not exceed specified numbers and are subject to qualitative restrictions. The parties may not transfer to other states, and not deploy outside their national territories, the ABM systems or components thereof which are limited by the Treaty. The Treaty is accompanied by agreed and unilateral statements as well as common understandings.

In 1974, in a Protocol to the ABM Treaty, the USA and the USSR introduced further restrictions on ballistic missile defence. They agreed to limit themselves to a single area for deployment of ABM systems instead of two areas allowed by the Treaty. Each party may dismantle or destroy its ABM system and the components thereof in the area where they were deployed at the time of the signing of the Protocol and deploy an ABM system or its components in the alternative area permitted by the ABM Treaty, provided that proper advance notification is given. This right may be exercised only once. The deployment of an ABM system within the area selected shall remain limited by the levels and other requirements established by the ABM Treaty.

It will be noted that the agreed limitations concerned anti-missile systems in the form in which they existed at the time the ABM Treaty and its Protocol were signed. These systems were deemed unreliable as well as costly and vulnerable to countermeasures and, therefore, patently inadequate for preventing nuclear warheads from reaching the target. But their modernization was allowed. Moreover, the development of ABM systems based on other physical principles than the systems limited by the ABM Treaty and including components capable of substituting for ABM interceptor missiles, ABM launchers or ABM radars, has not been prohibited. In a statement attached to the Treaty the parties merely agreed that in the event of such new means of anti-ballistic missile protection being created in the future, their specific limitations would be subject to discussion and agreement.

Considerable progress has already been made in developing new concepts of ballistic missile defence, namely, in target-detection, -recognition, -tracking, and -interception. It is now believed that in the near future the technology of laser beams powerful enough to destroy incoming missiles will be developed. All this, combined with pressure, especially in the USA, to protect fixed missile silos which are deemed to become increasingly vulnerable, constitutes a latent danger to the ABM Treaty. At the time of signing the Treaty, the USA formally stated that if an agreement providing for more complete strategic offensive arms limitations were not achieved within five years, US supreme interests could be jeopardized, and that, should that occur, it would constitute a basis for withdrawal from the Treaty. Although of unlimited duration, the Treaty is subject to review at five-year intervals (the first review took place in 1977) and may be denounced on six months' notice. Only a complete and unconditional renunciation of any type of ballistic missile defence, whatever its components, could be significant from the point of view of arms control, as it would signify the acceptance of a state of mutual vulnerability to ballistic missiles, and of a no-damage-limitation posture, the important requirements of strategic stability ostensibly sought by the two sides.

SALT I Interim Agreement

The first limitation of strategic offensive arms was introduced by the 1972 US–Soviet Interim Agreement, which provides for a freeze for a period of five years on the aggregate number of fixed land-based ICBM launchers and ballistic missile launchers on modern submarines. The parties are free to choose the mix, except that conversion of land-based launchers for light ICBMs, or for ICBMs of older types, into land-based launchers for modern heavy ICBMs is prohibited. Strategic bombers are not covered by the limitations.

A Protocol, which is an integral part of the Interim Agreement, specifies that the USA may have not more than 710 ballistic missile launchers on submarines and 44 modern ballistic missile submarines, while the USSR may have not more than 950 ballistic missile launchers on submarines and 62 modern ballistic missile submarines. Up to those levels, additional ballistic missile launchers in the USA over 656 launchers on nuclear-powered submarines and in the USSR over 740 launchers on nuclear-powered submarines, operational and under construction, may become operational as replacements for equal numbers of ballistic missile launchers of older types deployed before 1964, or of ballistic missile launchers on older submarines. Like the ABM Treaty, the Interim Agreement is accompanied by agreed and unilateral statements, as well as common understandings.

In September 1977, the USA and the USSR made formal statements that, although the Interim Agreement was to expire on 3 October 1977, they intended to refrain from any actions incompatible with its provisions, or with the goals of the current talks on a new agreement.

The land-based launchers specified in the Agreement are those capable of firing ballistic missiles at a range in excess of 5 500 km, so as to reach the territory of the other power. Soviet intermediate-range rockets aimed at US European allies, or at other countries, but unable to reach the USA, are not covered. On the other hand, US forward-based aircraft in Europe and bombers aboard US aircraft carriers, which can deliver nuclear strikes on the USSR or its allies, are not covered either. While the number of ballistic missile launchers in the possession of the two sides may not increase beyond a fixed limit, there are no restrictions in the Interim Agreement on the improvement of the quality of these weapons (with the exception of the freeze on the size of the ICBM launchers)—on their survivability, accuracy or range. The agreed replacement procedures have made it possible for the parties to substitute modern models for obsolete types of weapons, and the number of nuclear warheads each missile can carry has not been circumscribed at all. The absence of qualitative limitations on offensive missiles considerably reduced the value of the quantitative limitations on launchers, and the competition in arms continued to be fuelled by technological advances.

In the Agreement on basic principles of negotiations on the further limitation of strategic offensive arms, signed in 1973, the USA and the USSR undertook to work out a *permanent* arrangement on more complete measures for the limitation of these arms, as well as their subsequent reduction. They stated that they would be guided by the recognition of each other's equal security interests as well as by the recognition that efforts to obtain unilateral advantage, directly or indirectly, would be inconsistent with the strengthening of peaceful relations between them. These guidelines were drawn from the 1972 Agreement on basic principles of relations between the USA and the USSR signed at the same time as the first SALT agreements. According to other agreed principles, limitations on strategic offensive weapons should apply to both their quantitative aspects and their qualitative improvement. But it was not clear what was meant by limitations on "qualitative improvement" since modernization and replacement of arms were to be permitted.

Vladivostok accord

More essential elements of a new SALT treaty were agreed upon in 1974. In a Joint Statement made at the summit meeting at Vladivostok, the USA and the USSR established the principle of equal ceilings on strategic nuclear delivery vehicles. It was later revealed that the agreed aggregate limit for each side was 2 400 intercontinental ballistic missile (ICBM) launchers, submarine-launched ballistic missile (SLBM) launchers and heavy bombers. Of these 2 400 delivery vehicles, only 1 320 launchers of ICBMs and SLBMs equipped with multiple independently targetable re-entry vehicles (MIRVs) would be allowed. Under these ceilings, each side would be free to compose its forces as it wished. Further progress in negotiations was delayed, among other reasons, by a disagreement on whether or how the so-called Backfire aircraft and cruise missiles should be limited. 'Backfire' is the NATO designation for a modern swing-wing, twin-engine Soviet bomber—the Tu-22M—which is deployed for theatre and anti-ship roles but which on certain flight profiles (high altitude, low speed) or with in-flight refuelling could have an intercontinental capability. Cruise missiles are pilotless vehicles, which can fly at very low altitudes and can be air-, ground- or sea-launched.

In March 1977, the US government tried to go beyond the Vladivostok formula and offered the USSR a so-called comprehensive proposal which would have significantly reduced the nuclear arsenals, and imposed strict limits on the deployment of new systems and on the modernization of existing ones. In particular, the overall ceiling on strategic nuclear delivery vehicles would have been lowered from the Vladivostok level of 2 400 to between 1 800 and 2 000; the ceiling on MIRVed strategic ballistic missiles would have been fixed between 1 100 and 1 200, as compared to 1 320 agreed at Vladivostok; and limitations on the permitted number of MIRVed ICBMs and 'heavy' ICBMs would have been set at, respectively, 550 and 150. In concentrating on ICBMs, which constitute the most important component of the Soviet nuclear forces, the comprehensive approach would have had a greater limiting impact on Soviet strategic nuclear weapon programmes than on US programmes. It was, therefore, immediately rejected by the USSR. Another US proposal, which incorporated the Vladivostok terms while deferring consideration of the Backfire bomber and cruise missile issue, was also rejected. Subsequently, in the negotiations which resumed in Geneva in May 1977, the parties adopted a new framework that permitted a long-term agreement on limits below the overall Vladivostok ceiling, a short-term arrangement for the most contentious issues, and a statement of more far-reaching goals to be achieved in the next phase of SALT. This 'three-tier' arrangement became the structure of the SALT agreements reached two years later.

SALT II agreements

The 1979 US–Soviet Treaty on the limitation of strategic offensive arms, the so-called SALT II Treaty (not in force by 1982), sets for both parties an initial ceiling of 2 400 on ICBM launchers, SLBM launchers, heavy bombers, and air-to-surface ballistic missiles (ASBMs) capable of a range in excess of 600 km. This ceiling was to be lowered to 2 250 and the reduction was to begin on 1 January 1981, while the dismantling or destruction of systems which exceeded that number was to be completed by 31 December 1981. A sublimit of 1 320 is imposed upon each party for the combined number of launchers of ICBMs and SLBMs equipped with MIRVs, ASBMs equipped with MIRVs, and aeroplanes equipped for long-range (over 600 km) cruise missiles. Moreover, each party is limited to a total of 1 200 launchers of MIRVed ICBMs, SLBMs and ASBMs, and of this number no more than 820 may be launchers of MIRVed ICBMs. (For the aggregate limits, see figure 3.1.)

A freeze is introduced on the number of re-entry vehicles on current types of ICBMs, with a limit of 10 re-entry vehicles on the one new type of ICBM allowed each side, a limit of 14 re-entry vehicles on SLBMs and a limit of 10 re-entry vehicles on ASBMs. An average of 28 long-range air-launched cruise missiles (ALCMs) per heavy bomber is allowed, while current heavy bombers may carry no more than 20 ALCMs each. Ceilings are established

Figure 3.1. The SALT II aggregate limits

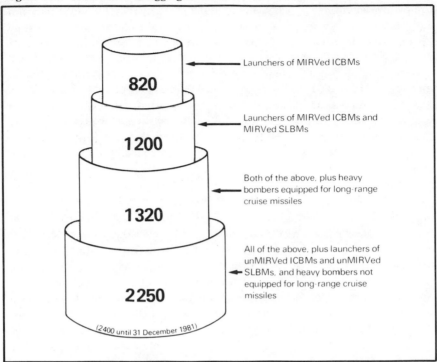

Launchers of MIRVed ICBMs

Launchers of MIRVed ICBMs and MIRVed SLBMs

Both of the above, plus heavy bombers equipped for long-range cruise missiles

All of the above, plus launchers of unMIRVed ICBMs and unMIRVed SLBMs, and heavy bombers not equipped for long-range cruise missiles

820

1200

1320

2250

(2400 until 31 December 1981)

Note: Neither side was known to have plans for deploying long-range ASBMs before the expiration of the Treaty.

on the launch-weight and throw-weight[3] of light and heavy ICBMs. There are the following bans: on the testing and deployment of new types of ICBMs, with one exception for each side; on building additional fixed ICBM launchers; on converting fixed, light ICBM launchers into heavy ICBM launchers; on heavy mobile ICBMs, heavy SLBMs, and heavy ASBMs; on surface–ship ballistic missile launchers; on systems to launch missiles from the sea-bed or the beds of internal waters; as well as on systems for the delivery of nuclear weapons from Earth orbit, including fractional orbital missiles. The Treaty was to remain in force until 31 December 1985.

The parties also signed a series of agreed statements and common understandings clarifying their obligations under particular articles of the Treaty. Before signing these documents, the USSR officially informed the USA that the Soviet Backfire aircraft was a medium-range bomber, that the Soviet Union did not intend to give this bomber an intercontinental capability and that it would not increase its radius of action to enable it to strike targets on US territory. It also pledged to limit the production of the Backfire aircraft to the 1979 rate, that is, not to exceed 30 per year.

---

[3] Launch-weight is the weight of the fully loaded missile at the time of launch, while throw-weight is the useful weight which is placed on a trajectory toward the target.

The Protocol to the SALT II Treaty banned, until 31 December 1981, the deployment of mobile ICBM launchers or the flight-testing of ICBMs from such launchers; the deployment (but not the flight-testing) of long-range cruise missiles on sea-based or land-based launchers; the flight-testing of long-range cruise missiles with multiple warheads from sea-based or land-based launchers; and the flight-testing or deployment of ASBMs.

At the same time, a Memorandum of Understanding between the USA and the USSR established a data-base on the numbers of strategic offensive arms. The parties agreed, for the purposes of the SALT II Treaty, on the numbers of strategic offensive arms in each of the 10 categories limited by the Treaty, as of 1 November 1978. In separate statements of data, each party declared that it possessed the stated number of strategic offensive arms subject to the Treaty limitations as of the date of signature of the Treaty (18 June 1979).

Finally, in a Joint Statement of principles and basic guidelines for subsequent negotiations on the limitation of strategic arms, the parties undertook to pursue the objectives of significant and substantial reductions in the numbers of strategic offensive arms, qualitative limitations on these arms, and resolution of the issues included in the Protocol to the SALT II Treaty.

Due to differences in geography, technology, strategy and defence arrangements with their allies, the USA and the USSR have placed different emphasis on various components of their forces. The Soviet Union has more land-based ballistic missiles with larger megatonnage, and better air defences, while the USA has more warheads and greater missile accuracy, as well as other advantages in submarine and bomber forces. Nevertheless the establishment by the SALT II Treaty of a quantitative parity may help in reaching agreement on significant reductions of force levels by creating an equal basis for such reductions. It is, therefore, a step forward as compared to the 1972 SALT I Interim Agreement, which did not provide for quantitative parity. Already the SALT II Treaty requires the dismantling, without replacement, of a certain number of nuclear weapon delivery vehicles: the USSR would have to dismantle some 250 operational missile launchers or bombers, while the USA would have to dismantle 33 strategic nuclear delivery vehicles to comply with the Treaty's overall aggregate limit.

Moreover, the provision of information on the numbers of strategic offensive arms was an important advance in the US–Soviet negotiating technique. In addition to its role as a confidence-building measure, the exchange of data facilitates the uniform interpretation of the Treaty provisions and can facilitate the verification of compliance with the obligations.

However, the SALT II agreements also have serious shortcomings. The numerical limits on strategic nuclear forces have been set very high. There is a remarkable compatibility between the Treaty limitations and the projected strategic nuclear weapon programmes of both sides. It is disturbing that such destabilizing elements of the strategic nuclear forces as MIRVed ICBMs have been allowed to increase in numbers: the Treaty permits the number of US and Soviet MIRVed ICBMs, taken together, to increase by more than 40 per cent from the time of signing the Treaty to the end of 1985.

Figure 3.2. The strategic nuclear warhead inventories of the USA and the USSR, 1972–85

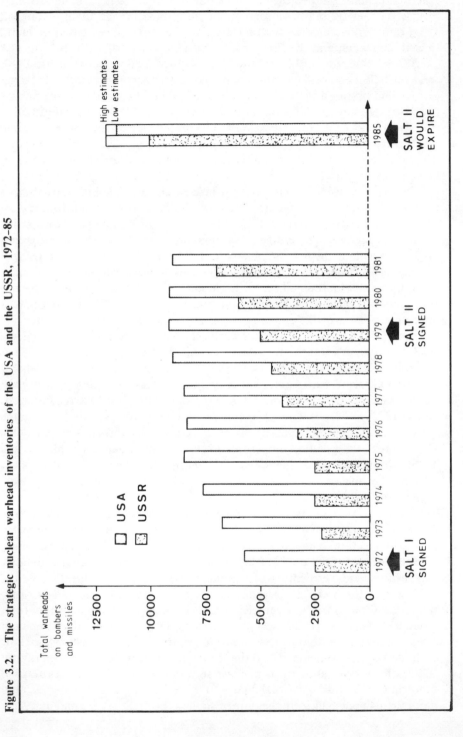

It is even more disturbing that with the high number of warheads permitted on ballistic missiles and with the high number of cruise missiles permitted per bomber, the total figure for US and Soviet missile re-entry vehicles and bomber weapons—an important measure of strategic power—may rise in the period from the signing to the expiration of the Treaty by roughly 50–70 per cent. (For the US and Soviet strategic nuclear warhead inventories, see figure 3.2.) A rationale for such formidable increases in warhead inventories can be found in the strategic doctrines requiring constant enlargement of the range of nuclear targets in the pursuit of nuclear war-fighting capabilities. Thus, notwithstanding the SALT II limitations, the strategic nuclear fire-power of both sides would grow, and the strategic stability might be affected because the parties are allowed to increase their counterforce (mostly anti-silo) potential not only by increasing the yield and accuracy of warheads on current ICBMs, but also by introducing a new type of ICBM. Indeed, the provision permitting each side to deploy a new type of ICBM seems to be incongruous with the arms limitation purpose of SALT. Should this new missile turn out to be mobile, new stimuli would be provided for the nuclear arms competition. Furthermore, as distinct from ICBMs, there are no restrictions at all on new types of SLBMs. The lack of such restrictions may, in time, add to the counterforce capabilities of both sides. Neither are there any restrictions on anti-submarine weapons, equipment or operations which could eventually endanger the survivability of missile-launching submarines.

Equally dangerous from the arms control perspective would be the deployment of ground- and sea-launched long-range cruise missiles. It is true that the Protocol prohibited the deployment of these weapons, as well as mobile ICBM launchers, but the prohibition was pointless because the Protocol was scheduled to expire at the end of 1981, that is, before the time when either party would be ready to deploy the weapons in question. Even the restrictions contained in the SALT Treaty itself had a lower value because of their limited duration (through 1985); the development and deployment plans were already aiming at a period after the expiration of the Treaty. By replacing one SALT interim agreement, that of 1972, by another, the parties have failed to fulfil their commitment to work out a "permanent" arrangement, as stipulated in the 1973 Agreement on basic principles of negotiations on the further limitation of strategic offensive arms.

The nuclear arms competition would continue under the SALT II regime, but it would be more predictable, and there would be certain limits on how fast it might proceed. Since unilateral military constraints of any importance by the USA or the USSR are inconceivable in the present international atmosphere of mistrust, mutually regulated arms competition, which diminishes the stimulus for 'worst-case' military planning, is safer than unregulated arms competition. However, the significance of the 1979 SALT agreements lies mainly in the promise of more meaningful nuclear arms limitation measures. Therefore, entry into force of the signed agreements, or at least observance by both parties of the essential limitations provided for in these agreements until a new, mutually acceptable accord has been reached, is necessary to maintain the continuity of the SALT process and to facilitate related arms control talks.

Apart from the linkage made with the global policies of the USSR, including Soviet armed intervention in Afghanistan and military presence in Cuba, US opponents of the SALT Treaty have argued that the deal is militarily inequitable, mainly because it leaves unaffected the heavy ICBMs, deployed by the USSR but not possessed by the USA, and also because it does not include in its numerical ceilings the Soviet Backfire bomber, considered to have some intercontinental strategic capabilities.

As regards ICBMs, it may be noted that already in the late 1950s the USA made a conscious decision, based on technological and military factors, to switch from large to smaller missiles. Present Soviet advantage in throw-weight is commonly considered to be compensated by the greater accuracy of US missiles, and the limitation of the number of re-entry vehicles on ICBMs reduces the value of extra payload capability.

As to the Soviet Backfire bombers, it is true that under certain conditions these aircraft, not covered by the SALT limits, may reach US territory. But this is equally true for US aircraft stationed in Europe or on aircraft carriers, and even for certain aircraft based on the territory of the USA—all capable of striking targets in the USSR—which are exempt from the SALT limitations. Whatever the asymmetries, there undoubtedly exists an overall, rough equivalence in the strategic military power of the USA and the USSR.

A resumption of strategic arms negotiations was expected in 1982. The United States announced that it would seek "truly substantial" reductions in nuclear arms, which would result in levels that are equal and verifiable. To symbolize the change in direction, the USA has proposed to call these negotiations START—Strategic Arms Reduction Talks.

Real progress would require not only substantial reductions in the number of MIRVed missiles and warheads, but also tight constraints, if not a total prohibition, on the modernization of strategic nuclear delivery systems. This will depend on whether the negotiating parties will actually give up aspirations for military superiority, as was postulated in the joint US–Soviet Communiqué issued at the end of the Vienna summit meeting on 18 June 1979. For such aspirations, considering the present size of the forces on both sides, have less to do with strategic deterrence than with the desire to acquire a nuclear first-strike capability.

III. Non-proliferation of nuclear weapons

The need to halt the spread of nuclear weapons was evident from the early days of the nuclear age. Nevertheless, the USA, which was the first state to apply nuclear energy for military purposes, was soon followed by the USSR and the UK and, some 15–20 years later, by France and China. Moreover, the spread of peaceful nuclear programmes to many parts of the world has been providing the wherewithal for nuclear weapon programmes.

The realization that the possession of nuclear weapons by many countries would increase the threat to world security led to the unanimous adoption, in 1961, of a UN General Assembly resolution calling on all states to conclude an international agreement to refrain from the transfer or acquisition of these weapons. This resolution formed a basis for the Non-Proliferation Treaty signed in 1968.

Non-Proliferation Treaty

The NPT prohibits the transfer by nuclear weapon states to any recipient whatsoever of nuclear weapons or other nuclear explosive devices or of control over them. The Treaty also prohibits the receipt by non-nuclear weapon states from any transferor whatsoever, as well as the manufacture or other acquisition by those states, of nuclear weapons. Non-nuclear weapon states undertook to conclude safeguards agreements with the International Atomic Energy Agency (IAEA) with a view to preventing the diversion of nuclear materials from peaceful uses to nuclear weapons or other nuclear explosive devices. (Unlike the Treaty of Tlatelolco, described in section V of this chapter, the NPT has not defined 'nuclear weapon' or 'nuclear explosive device'.) In addition, the nuclear weapon states are not allowed to assist, encourage or induce any non-nuclear weapon state to manufacture or acquire the devices in question. There is no express prohibition for non-nuclear weapon states party to the NPT to provide such assistance, encouragement or inducement to other non-nuclear weapon states which are not party to the NPT. But the USA and the USSR, the powers that were responsible for the formulation of the relevant provisions, have made it clear that such a case would be regarded as a violation of the Treaty.

The concept of a treaty prohibiting the acquisition of weapons by an overwhelming majority of states, while tolerating the retention of the same weapons by a few, has given rise to controversies relating to the balance of rights and obligations of parties under international agreements. Indeed, in renouncing the nuclear weapon option under the NPT, the non-nuclear weapon states have assumed the main burden of obligation. The nuclear weapon states, in undertaking not to disseminate the weapons, have sacrificed little if anything: it would be against their interests to encourage or permit the spread of nuclear weapons. In addition to retaining their nuclear arsenals, the nuclear weapon powers are free to assist each other in developing nuclear warheads and testing them, to receive from any state the material necessary to pursue their nuclear weapon programmes and to deploy nuclear weapons on the territories of other states; and, unlike the non-nuclear weapon countries, they are not obligated to subject their peaceful nuclear activities to international safeguards.

To attenuate the asymmetries inherent in the NPT, the nuclear weapon powers have undertaken to facilitate the exchange of equipment, materials and scientific and technological information for the peaceful uses of nuclear energy, with due consideration for the needs of the developing areas of the world; to make available their services, at low cost, for peaceful applications of nuclear explosions; to pursue negotiations on measures relating to the cessation of the nuclear arms race and to nuclear disarmament, and on a treaty on general and complete disarmament; and, under a separate arrangement, to provide security guarantees to non-nuclear weapon states.

Peaceful uses of nuclear energy

Assistance in the development of nuclear energy for peaceful purposes could have been a powerful inducement to join the NPT if it had been reserved only for the parties. But nuclear transactions continued to be conducted according to the rules and customs of commercial competition and in keeping with the political interests of the supplier states, rather than in conformity with the international non-proliferation strategy. Non-parties have not been excluded from participation in international co-operation in the nuclear field. In a few instances they have even managed to secure more material supplies and technical aid than have the parties. Moreover, and paradoxically enough, non-parties have been subject to less stringent control over their nuclear activities than have the parties; some of them could, thereby, reach the nuclear weapon threshold.

In refusing to join the NPT the non-nuclear weapon countries with civilian nuclear activities, especially those operating unsafeguarded nuclear facilities which are important from the point of view of production of weapons-usable material (for example, India, Israel, Pakistan or South Africa), have preserved the option to acquire nuclear weapons. Nuclear supplies to these countries can facilitate the exercise of such an option and pose, therefore, a direct threat to the survival of the NPT. The countries in question are the most likely candidates for membership in the 'nuclear club', and if further proliferation takes place, withdrawal from the Treaty by certain present parties may prove unavoidable.

In view of the different safeguards conditions for parties and non-parties to the Treaty, and because India, a non-party, had taken advantage of the more lenient safeguards applied to its nuclear activities to explode a nuclear device termed 'peaceful', the major nuclear suppliers started meeting in London in 1975 to work out a common approach to their nuclear exports. In 1977, this supplier group, the so-called London Club, which eventually comprised .15 countries (Belgium, Canada, Czechoslovakia, France, the German Democratic Republic, the Federal Republic of Germany, Italy, Japan, the Netherlands, Poland, Sweden, Switzerland, the UK, the USA and the USSR), finalized the Guidelines for Nuclear Transfers which were intended to tighten the terms of such transfers and reduce the advantages that non-parties may derive from remaining outside the NPT. A catalogue was drawn up of materials, equipment and technology which, when provided to any non-nuclear weapon state, would 'trigger' IAEA safeguards. This catalogue extended the list, agreed upon in the so-called Zangger Committee of suppliers (which did not include France) and communicated to the IAEA in 1974, specifying those items which require safeguards under the NPT when exported to non-parties (the parties being already covered by safeguards on all their nuclear activities).

Under the London Guidelines, the recipients of the trigger-list items must pledge not to use them for the manufacture of nuclear explosives and to provide effective physical protection of the imported materials. The safeguards requirements are to be applied not only to facilities utilizing technology directly transferred by the supplier or derived from transferred facilities, but even to any facility of the same type as that imported which was constructed indigenously during an agreed period. Retransfers of trigger-list items are to be subject to the same conditions as those applying to the original transfer.

Since there was also increasing concern over the ease with which materials from a peaceful nuclear programme could be diverted to military purposes with the help of uranium enrichment or plutonium reprocessing plants capable of producing fissile materials directly usable for weapons, the London Club suppliers recommended restraint in the transfer of these sensitive facilities. France and FR Germany announced that, until further notice, new deals for exports of reprocessing equipment and technology would not be allowed, while Canada and Australia forbade all nuclear exports to countries that did not accept safeguards on their entire nuclear programmes. They also required prior consent for retransfer of their nuclear material supplies and for reprocessing or enrichment (over 20 per cent) of these supplies.

In 1978 the USA also set strict unilateral restrictions by adopting the Nuclear Non-Proliferation Act. In addition to confirming the US embargo on enrichment and reprocessing plants, the Act stated that new commitments to export significant amounts of separated plutonium and highly enriched uranium were to be avoided. Other conditions included the requirement of prior US consent for retransfer of any US-supplied materials or any fissionable material produced through the use of US equipment; prior US approval for reprocessing, enrichment (over 20 per cent) or alteration of nuclear materials supplied by the USA or derived from these supplies; and a guarantee of physical security for any special nuclear material transferred. The Act also required international safeguards on all the nuclear activities of the importing states, as a condition for receiving US nuclear supplies. Because its provisions were made retroactive, the Act entailed renegotiation of existing US nuclear co-operation agreements. The main purpose of these measures was to ensure control over plutonium-producing technology. At the same time, the USA launched the International Nuclear Fuel Cycle Evaluation (INFCE) to devise means to minimize the danger of the proliferation of nuclear weapons without jeopardizing energy supplies or the development of nuclear energy for peaceful purposes. The hope was that some alternative to a plutonium-producing cycle would be found.

INFCE concluded its work in February 1980, having achieved a wide measure of agreement on complex technical problems. It was therefore generally regarded as a useful exercise, and its report gained support from nuclear suppliers and recipients. However, the main conclusion was that, although certain measures could make misuse of the nuclear fuel cycle more

Figure 3.3. The nuclear fuel cycle

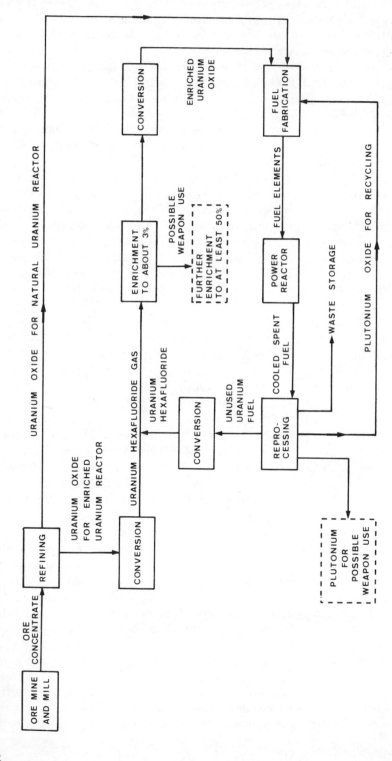

difficult, there is no technical way to produce nuclear energy without at the same time producing fissile material usable for weapons. Plutonium derived from the spent fuel of nuclear power reactors, so-called reactor-grade plutonium, has a higher content of plutonium isotopes undesirable for nuclear weapons than weapon-grade plutonium produced in special facilities committed to military use, but it can nevertheless be used to manufacture nuclear explosive devices.[4] (See figure 3.3 for an illustration of the nuclear fuel cycle.)

The restrictive export policies recommended in the Guidelines for Nuclear Transfers, as well as those imposed by individual suppliers in the name of non-proliferation, provoked dissatisfaction, especially among the Third World countries fearing that their acquisition of civilian nuclear technology might be frustrated. It will be noted, in this connection, that under the NPT both the obligation to provide and the right to obtain equipment, materials and scientific and technological information for the peaceful uses of nuclear energy are not without limits: any such supplies are subordinated to non-proliferation goals, which means that they must not in any way facilitate the acquisition of nuclear weapons. In case of a collision between these arms control goals and the economic interests of the suppliers or recipients, the arms control aspect must prevail. For example, there can hardly be justification for shipments of large quantities of weapon-grade nuclear material to countries having no immediate need for such material, even if they are subject to full-scope international controls. Neither can one argue that refusal to supply plutonium reprocessing facilities to a country with a nuclear industry still in an embryonic state is contrary to the NPT. Equally, an unrestricted right to retransfer of nuclear material, especially to non-parties, safeguards notwithstanding, would run counter to the objectives of non-proliferation.

Since 1980, the USA has been gradually modifying its non-proliferation policy, as determined in the 1978 Nuclear Non-Proliferation Act, by lowering the requirements to be met by the recipients of its nuclear supplies.

Physical protection of nuclear material

An important step towards reducing the risks of the diversion of nuclear material to non-peaceful purposes was made with the conclusion in 1980 of the Convention on the physical protection of nuclear material. The provisions of the Convention oblige the parties to ensure that, during international transport across their territory or on ships or planes under their jurisdiction, nuclear material for peaceful purposes as categorized in a special annex (plutonium, uranium-235, uranium-233 and irradiated fuel) is protected at the agreed level. Furthermore, the parties undertake not to export or import nuclear material or allow its transit through their territory unless they have received assurances that this material will be protected

---

[4] Reactor-grade plutonium can be purified isotopically, but the existing methods are very slow. New techniques which are still in the research and development stage are likely to be too sophisticated and costly for most of the non-nuclear weapon countries.

during international transport in accordance with the levels of protection determined by the Convention, and to apply these levels of protection also to material which, during transit from one part of their territory to another, will pass through international waters or airspace. The parties to the Convention agree to share information on missing nuclear material to facilitate recovery operations. Robbery, embezzlement or extortion in relation to nuclear material, and acts without lawful authority involving nuclear material which cause or are likely to cause "death or serious injury to any person or substantial damage to property", are to be treated as punishable offences.

Uniform application of measures of physical protection of nuclear material for peaceful purposes in international transport is essential. It seems, however, equally vital that internationally agreed levels of physical protection should be applied to nuclear material in domestic use, storage and transport. As regards nuclear weapons themselves, responsibility for their physical protection against misuse must rest entirely with the nuclear weapon states. Accidents or negligence, especially with regard to nuclear weapons stationed in foreign territories, may create proliferation risks more serious than those created by the diversion of nuclear material.

Peaceful nuclear explosions

The NPT article dealing with services in the field of peaceful applications of nuclear explosions was included in the Treaty in exchange for the surrender by non-nuclear weapon states of the right to conduct any nuclear explosions, because 'peaceful' devices could also be used as weapons. It should be noted, however, that in referring to benefits derived from peaceful explosions, the Treaty employs the term "potential", which implies that the advantages remain to be demonstrated.

The hopes held by certain states that peaceful uses of nuclear explosions would help to resolve some of their economic problems have not materialized. The prevailing opinion now seems to be that such explosions might entail greater risks than the benefits they would bring. By tacit agreement, the implementation of the relevant Treaty provision has been kept in abeyance.

Vertical proliferation

The provision dealing with disarmament embodies the basic bargain of the NPT. It was included at the insistence of the non-nuclear weapon states, with a view to matching the cessation of 'horizontal' proliferation with the cessation of 'vertical' proliferation. The idea was that the NPT should become a transitional stage in a process of nuclear disarmament. But it soon became clear that the nuclear weapon powers considered the NPT to be an end in itself. In fact, the obligation undertaken was not to disarm, but to negotiate disarmament. Moreover, the term "cessation", as applied to the nuclear arms race, does not convey the same meaning for all states. For example, the US–Soviet SALT agreements, which allow for the multiplication of nuclear warheads and place no restrictions on the improvement of weapons, are considered by some as a measure meeting the requirements of the NPT; others regard "cessation" as meaning an end to quantitative increases and qualitative refinements of weapons.

Without a process of actual disarmament, which would reduce the role and utility of nuclear weaponry in world diplomacy and military strategy, the future of the NPT may be at risk. The arms race undermines the credibility of the Treaty in the eyes of its non-nuclear weapon parties and provides an excuse to non-parties for not joining the Treaty. Under these conditions, it may be difficult to contain the nuclear weapon ambitions of certain non-nuclear weapon states.

The interest of the major nuclear powers in preserving and strengthening the non-proliferation regime[5] has been expressed in a number of international documents, in particular in the US–Soviet Communiqué issued in connection with the signing of the 1979 SALT agreements, and in the 1975 British–Soviet and the 1977 French–Soviet Declarations on the non-proliferation of nuclear weapons. However, it would not be correct to maintain that the NPT serves the interests only of the great powers. The non-nuclear weapon states benefit at least to the same degree as the great powers from the renunciation of nuclear weapons by the parties to the NPT. Indeed, although it was unable to adopt a consensus declaration, the Second NPT Review Conference, held in 1980, confirmed the view that the NPT plays a vital role in the efforts to prevent the further proliferation of nuclear weapons, as well as the general interest of the parties in ensuring the universality of the Treaty. But the non-nuclear weapon states have been insistent that the nuclear weapon powers must live up to their disarmament obligations under the NPT. Moreover, in surrendering their nuclear option, the non-nuclear weapon states feel that they are entitled to effective security assurances.

Security assurances

According to the 1968 UN Security Council Resolution No. 255, the states forgoing the acquisition of nuclear weapons under the NPT received a pledge of immediate assistance, in conformity with the UN Charter, in the event they became "a victim of an act or an object of a threat of aggression in which nuclear weapons are used". But the value of these so-called positive assurances is questionable. France and four non-nuclear weapon members of the Security Council abstained on the vote. Moreover, the resolution and the associated declarations by the UK, the USA and the USSR did not add to but merely reaffirmed the existing UN Charter obligation to provide assistance to a country attacked, irrespective of the type of weapon employed. Since all the nuclear weapon powers are now also permanent members of the Security Council, a decision concerning military or non-military measures against a delinquent state could not be taken if

---

[5] The non-proliferation regime is a notion larger than the NPT; it encompasses all rules, norms and institutions which discourage nuclear weapon proliferation.

any one of them cast a negative vote, inasmuch as it is inconceivable that a nation which had used or threatened to use nuclear weapons would consent to a collective action being taken against itself. Furthermore, immediate active intervention, as envisaged by the resolution, is deemed unacceptable by some non-aligned and neutral states, unless assistance has been specifically requested by them. The most serious deficiency of the resolution resides in the fact that it provides for action only when a threat of nuclear attack has been made or an attack has already occurred.

In recent years, there has been a growing demand for 'negative assurances', that is, formal guarantees by the nuclear weapon states that they would not use or threaten to use nuclear weapons against non-nuclear weapon states. Steps in this direction were taken at the 1978 UN General Assembly Special Session on Disarmament when the USA, the UK and the USSR each made an official policy statement giving such assurances. The USSR declared that it would never use nuclear weapons against those states which "renounce the production and acquisition of such weapons and do not have them on their territories". In addition, it expressed readiness to conclude appropriate bilateral security agreements with non-nuclear weapon countries. The USA announced that it would not use nuclear weapons against any non-nuclear weapon state which is party to the NPT or "any comparable internationally binding agreement not to acquire nuclear explosive devices", except in the case of an attack on the USA or its allies by a non-nuclear weapon state "allied to" or "associated with" a nuclear weapon state in carrying out or sustaining the attack. A similar statement was issued by the UK.[6] This constituted an advance, but the assurances offered showed significant disparities and contained qualifications which were so phrased as to suit the military doctrines of the nuclear weapon states and could be subject to divergent interpretations. Doubts have also been expressed as to the binding force of unilateral statements. Most countries see a need to develop a uniform formula for security assurances and to incorporate it in an international legal instrument. In 1982, at the Second UN General Assembly Special Session on Disarmament, the Soviet Union formally pledged itself "not to be the first to use nuclear weapons." If it were undertaken by all the nuclear weapon powers (which is unlikely in the immediate future), a no-first-use commitment would make the elaboration of negative security assurances exclusively for non-nuclear weapon countries superfluous.

---

[6]France and China, which are not parties to the NPT, also made statements on this subject at the UN General Assembly Special Session on Disarmament in 1978. The position of France was that it would give assurances of the non-use of nuclear weapons, in accordance with arrangements to be negotiated, only to those states which have "constituted among themselves non-nuclear zones". China reiterated its commitment made long ago not to be the first to use nuclear weapons at any time and under any circumstances. At the Second UN General Assembly Special Session on Disarmament in 1982, France developed its position by stating that it would not use nuclear arms against a state that "does not have these weapons and has pledged not to seek them." France made it clear that its no-use guarantee would not apply in the case of an act of aggression carried out "in association or in alliance with" a nuclear weapon state against France or against a state with which France has a security commitment.

It is clear that formal assurances, in whatever form, cannot guarantee the security of non-nuclear weapon states. Only nuclear disarmament can remove the risk that nuclear weapons will be used. Nuclear war is unlikely to respect the borders between states that benefit from negative security guarantees and those that do not. Nonetheless, security assurances must be considered as a legitimate minimum *quid pro quo* for renouncing nuclear weapons, even though no specific clause to this effect was included in the NPT.

IV. Prohibition of non-nuclear weapons of mass destruction

In 1948 the UN Commission for Conventional Armaments, wishing to distinguish its terms of reference from those of the UN Atomic Energy Commission, defined weapons of mass destruction as "atomic explosive weapons, radioactive material weapons, lethal chemical and biological weapons, and any weapons developed in the future which have characteristics comparable in destructive effect to those of the atomic bomb or other weapons mentioned above". One category of these weapons was abolished in 1972.

BW Convention

The 1972 Biological Weapons (BW) Convention prohibits the development, production, stockpiling or acquisition by other means, or retention of biological agents or toxins, as well as weapons, equipment or means of delivery designed to use such agents or toxins for hostile purposes or in armed conflict.

In its 1969 report on the health aspects of chemical and biological weapons, the World Health Organization defined "biological agents" as those that depend for their effects on multiplication within the target organism, and are intended for use in war to cause disease or death in man, animals or plants. But neither this, nor any other definition, has been incorporated in the Convention.

The definition of "toxins" is more difficult. These poisonous substances are products of organisms; however, they are inanimate and incapable of reproducing themselves. But some toxins may also be produced by chemical synthesis. The language of the Convention is meant to avoid ambiguity and to ensure that the concept of toxins is understood broadly: both biological and synthetically produced or modified compounds that can be used as warfare agents are covered by the prohibition, "whatever their origin or method of production".

It should be noted that the prohibition on developing, producing, stockpiling or otherwise acquiring or retaining is not absolute under the BW Convention: it applies only to types and to quantities of biological agents and toxins that have no justification for prophylactic, protective or other peaceful purposes.

While the term "prophylactic" encompasses medical activities, such as diagnosis, therapy and immunization, the term "protective" covers the development of protective masks and clothing, air and water filtration systems, detection and warning devices, and decontamination equipment. (In no case, as it was made clear in the course of the negotiations on the Convention, should the word "protective" be interpreted as permitting possession of biological agents or toxins for 'defensive' warfare, retaliation or deterrence.) Thus, research on and production of certain quantities of biological agents and toxins, over and above those needed to prevent diseases, will continue, as they will be necessary to develop the protective equipment and devices. There is also bound to be some testing in the laboratories and possibly even in the field, as well as appropriate military training.

The very maintenance of defensive preparations, which at certain stages are indistinguishable from offensive preparations, may generate suspicion, and the continued production of warfare agents contains a risk of infringement or of allegations of infringement of the provisions of the Convention.

The qualification that there should be "justification" for the development, production, stockpiling or retention does not carry much weight. There are no agreed standards or criteria for the quantities of agents and toxins that may be required for different purposes, especially for military protective purposes. In other words, it is not at all clear how much of a substance possessed would constitute a violation. The risk inherent in the retention of some warfare agents could be considerably reduced if defensive work were internationalized to the greatest possible extent, and also if secrecy surrounding biological research were removed. This has not been provided for in the Convention.

Because of their uncontrollability and unpredictability, biological weapons have always been considered of little utility. But, in prohibiting the further development of biological weapons, the BW Convention has aimed at eliminating the possibility that scientific advances modifying the conditions of production, stockpiling and use of these weapons could make them militarily more attractive. The Convention is also meant to prevent the spread of biological and toxin weapons to countries which do not possess them. However, its most remarkable feature is the requirement to destroy the agents and toxins, as well as related weapons, equipment and means of delivery which are in the possession of the parties, or to divert them to peaceful purposes. This is the first international agreement since World War II which involves some measure of military 'sacrifice'. After the entry into force of the Convention, the USA stated that its entire stockpile of biological and toxin agents and weapons had been destroyed and that its former biological warfare facilities had been converted to peaceful uses. As a matter of fact, the decision to dispose of existing stocks of weapons in question was taken unilaterally by the US government long before the signing of the BW Convention: in 1969, with regard to biological weapons, and in 1970, with regard to toxin weapons. The USSR formally announced that it did not possess any bacteriological (biological) agents or toxins, weapons, equipment or means of delivery, as prohibited in the Convention. The UK stated that it had no stocks of biological weapons.

France and China refused to sign the BW Convention. The main arguments put forward by France were that the Convention did not include any satisfactory provision for international control, and that the biological weapons prohibition should not have been separated from a chemical weapons prohibition. Nevertheless, in 1972 France adopted a law whose main provisions are almost identical to those of the BW Convention. Similarly, China criticized the Convention for not including the prohibition of chemical weapons and for not banning the use of biological weapons.

Indeed, the BW Convention does not explicitly prohibit the *use* of biological and toxin weapons, the general understanding being that the non-use obligation has already been included in the 1925 Geneva Protocol. The dilemma is that in ratifying the Geneva Protocol many countries reserved the right to use the banned weapons against non-parties or in retaliation. These reservations are incompatible with the BW Convention, which excludes the possibility of biological agents being used as weapons under any circumstances. The reservations regarding biological weapons should, therefore, be withdrawn, and a few states have already done so. On the other hand, a number of parties to the BW Convention have not yet adhered to the 1925 Geneva Protocol, in spite of the UN resolutions urging them to do so.

The BW Convention provides for a review of its operation, in particular with respect to relevant scientific and technological developments. Such developments were examined in connection with the Review Conference of the parties to the BW Convention, held in 1980. The conclusion reached in a report prepared by experts of the depositary governments (of the UK, the USA and the USSR) was that microbial or other biological agents or toxins with enhanced military utility could be developed, but these agents are unlikely to improve upon known agents to the extent of providing compelling advantages for illegal production or military use in the foreseeable future. Moreover, the Review Conference reaffirmed the comprehensive nature of the prohibitions under the BW Convention by stating that the language of the Convention fully covered all agents which could result from the application of such new techniques as the 'recombinant DNA techniques' for manipulation of the deoxyribonucleic acid molecules, which form the genetic material of organisms.

Biological weapons have been considered together with chemical weapons from the early 1920s, and have continued to be associated with them in the public mind. It is therefore regrettable that both categories were not prohibited at the same time. Chemical weapons may be militarily more useful than biological weapons: they are more predictable and can produce immediate effects, which are important qualities in combat. They are maintained in the arsenals of certain states and have already been used on a large scale in war with disastrous consequences for those attacked. For these reasons, the parties to the BW Convention recognized that the Convention was only a step towards an agreement effectively prohibiting chemical weapons as well and providing for their destruction. Without a formal commitment which was included in the BW Convention, that such an agreement should be reached at an "early" date, many countries would probably have refrained from joining the Convention.

Chemical weapons

The prohibition of chemical means of warfare has been the subject of discussions held in the United Nations and the Geneva Committee on Disarmament, as well as of negotiations conducted between the USA and the USSR. The most important points of agreement hitherto reached in the bilateral negotiations are as follows.

(a) The parties should assume the obligation not to develop, produce, otherwise acquire, stockpile or retain super-toxic lethal, other lethal or other harmful chemicals, or precursors of such chemicals, or munitions or devices specifically designed to cause death or other harm through the toxic properties of chemicals released as a result of the employment of these munitions or devices, or equipment specifically designed for use directly in connection with the employment of such munitions or devices. The obligation should not extend to those substances in the above-mentioned categories which are intended for non-hostile purposes[7] or military purposes not involving the use of chemical weapons (as in the case of missile or torpedo fuels), provided their types and quantities are consistent with such purposes. The convention would include definitions of the basic terms used in its provisions.

(b) In addition to the general purpose criterion, toxicity criteria would be used to define the prohibited chemicals.

(c) The parties should undertake not to transfer to anyone, directly or indirectly, any chemical weapons, and not to assist, encourage or induce any person, organization, state or group of states to engage in activities they themselves would be obligated to refrain from under the convention.

(d) States should make declarations—within 30 days after they become parties to the convention—regarding both their stocks of chemical weapons and their means of production of such weapons. Plans for the destruction or, where appropriate, diversion for permitted purposes of declared stocks of chemical weapons should also be declared. Plans for the destruction or dismantling of relevant means of production should be declared not later than one year prior to the beginning of the destruction or dismantling.

(e) Destruction or diversion of declared stocks should be completed not later than 10 years after a state becomes party to the convention.

(f) Destruction or dismantling of the declared means of production should be initiated not later than eight years, and completed not later than 10 years after the state possessing them becomes a party to the convention.

(g) The aggregate quantity of super-toxic lethal chemicals for non-hostile military purposes, produced, diverted from stocks, and otherwise acquired

---

[7] By non-hostile purposes the negotiators mean industrial, agricultural, research, medical or other peaceful purposes, law-enforcement purposes, or purposes directly related to protection against chemical weapons.

annually or possessed at any given time, should be minimal. In any event, that amount should not exceed one metric ton for any party, and a party producing super-toxic lethal chemicals for non-hostile military purposes should carry out such production at a single specialized facility, the location of which should be declared and the capacity of which should not exceed a fixed limit.

(*h*) The fulfilment of the obligations must be subject to adequate verification.

(*i*) The parties should have the right to turn to the UN Security Council with a complaint, which would include appropriate evidence.

(*j*) The convention would contain a withdrawal clause similar to the relevant provision in other arms control agreements.

The important questions which by 1982 had remained unresolved are as follows: (*a*) To what extent should toxins, herbicides, irritants and precursors be covered by the convention? (*b*) What should be the time-limit for declaring plans for the destruction or diversion of chemical weapon stocks, and when should such destruction or diversion begin? What should be the specific content of the declarations pertaining to stocks of weapons and means of production? (*c*) What would be the scope of the international measures of verification? (*d*) What kind of confidence-building measures could be brought into effect in connection with the prohibition of chemical weapons?

The bilateral US–Soviet negotiations have revealed a convergence of views between the two most powerful chemical weapon states on a series of key issues. The solution of the outstanding questions requires an input also by other nations concerned with chemical disarmament, especially those that are known to possess militarily significant supplies of chemical weapons (that is, also by France), or are in a position to manufacture them. In any event, since a CW convention is meant to be a generally applicable agreement, it is important that it should be negotiated and agreed upon multilaterally. Indeed, in 1980–81, the Committee on Disarmament carried out a detailed examination of the issues related to a multilateral chemical weapons convention and considered the draft elements of such a convention.

As stated by the 1978 UN Special Session on Disarmament, the complete and effective prohibition of all chemical warfare agents and weapons and their destruction represent one of the most urgent measures of disarmament. The envisaged mass production of binary chemical weapons[8] adds urgency to this measure because binaries are safer to store and handle, which means that their supplies can be carried by combat units, while 'conventional' poison gas may be made available only through special channels from distant depots.

---

[8] A binary chemical weapon is a device filled with two chemicals of low toxicity which mix and react while the device is being delivered to the target, the reaction product being a supertoxic warfare agent, such as nerve gas.

ENMOD Convention

Other means of warfare capable of inflicting mass destruction were banned under the Environmental Modification (ENMOD) Convention, signed in 1977. The Convention prohibits military or any other hostile use of "environmental modification techniques", which are defined as techniques for changing—through the deliberate manipulation of natural processes—the dynamics, composition or structure of the Earth, including its biota, lithosphere, hydrosphere and atmosphere, or of outer space.

The negotiations on the ENMOD Convention were motivated *inter alia* by concern that environmental forces could be used to produce serious consequences for human welfare. (For a list of possible environmental modification techniques, see table 3.2.) But the resulting agreement has not

Table 3.2. Environmental modification

This list, based on the documents presented to the Geneva Committee on Disarmament, is tentative, but it includes most of the environmental modification techniques referred to in the scientific literature.

Type of modification	Technique employed
Atmospheric modification (incl. the high atmosphere and ionosphere)	Fog and cloud dispersion
	Fog and cloud generation
	Hailstone production
	Release of materials which might alter the electrical properties of the atmosphere
	Introduction of electromagnetic fields into the atmosphere
	Generating and directing destructive storms
	Rain and snow making
	Control of lightning
	Climate modifications
	Disruption of the ionized or ozone layers
Modification of the oceans	Change of the physical, chemical and electrical parameters of the seas and oceans
	Addition of radioactive material into the oceans and seas
	Destruction of oil wells on the sea-bed
	Generation of large tidal waves (tsunamis)
Modification of land masses and associated water systems	Stimulation of earthquakes
	Stimulation of volcanoes
	Generation of avalanches and landslides
	Surface modification in permafrost areas
	Large-scale burning or other destruction of vegetation
	River diversion
	Destruction of dams on rivers
	Destruction of nuclear industry

entirely allayed this concern since it has not banned all environmental modification techniques for hostile purposes. Only the use of those techniques which have widespread, long-lasting or severe effects as the means of destruction, damage or injury to states party to the Convention has been prohibited.

According to the understandings reached during the negotiations (but not written into the Convention), the term "widespread" means encompassing an area on the scale of several hundred square kilometres; "long-lasting" refers to a period of months, or approximately a season; while "severe" is to be interpreted as involving serious or significant disruption or harm to human life, natural and economic resources or other assets. Exempted from the prohibition are non-hostile uses of environmental modification techniques, even if they produce destructive effects above the threshold described above. Equally permissible are hostile uses which produce destructive effects below the threshold.

According to the same understandings, the hostile use of techniques which produce earthquakes, tsunamis, an upset in the ecological balance of a region, or changes in weather patterns (clouds, precipitation, cyclones of various types and tornadic storms), changes in climate patterns, in ocean currents, in the state of the ozone layer, and in the state of the ionosphere, is unconditionally prohibited. However, none of these phenomena seems likely to be caused through deliberate action for rational warlike purposes, that is, in such a way that the effects would be felt only, or primarily, by the enemy. Techniques that can produce more limited effects—such as precipitation modification (short of changing the weather patterns), fire storms, or formation or dissipation of fog—and are likely to be used to influence the environment with hostile intent in a selected area, especially in tactical military operations (facilitating the effectiveness of other weapons), have escaped proscription. And it is precisely such techniques that may enter the sphere of military competition.

In an agreement which bans the use of a specific method of warfare and thereby establishes a new humanitarian law of war, the notion of a threshold of damage or injury below which the parties would retain freedom of action seems incongruous. In the case of the ENMOD Convention, there is not even a commitment to remove the established threshold in a follow-up agreement. Nor have restrictions been imposed on the development of environmental modification techniques for warlike purposes. The significance of the ENMOD Convention is therefore very limited.

Radiological weapons

The development of nuclear energy has made highly radioactive material available in great amounts to many countries. To prevent the misuse of this material, the USA and the USSR referred to the UN definition of weapons of mass destruction, which includes "radioactive material weapons", and proposed in 1979 the conclusion of a treaty prohibiting the development, production, stockpiling, acquisition by other means or possession, and use of radiological weapons. The two powers defined a radiological weapon as any device, including any weapon or equipment, other than a nuclear explosive device, specifically designed to employ radioactive material by disseminating it to cause destruction, damage or injury by means of the radiation produced by the decay of such material, as well as any radioactive material, other than that produced by a nuclear explosive device, specifically designed for such use. Thus, a clear distinction was drawn between a weapon relying for its destructive effect on radiation emitted by radioactive material contained in it, and a weapon relying for its destructive effect both on heat, blast and radiation caused by the nuclear process occurring at the time of the explosion. The former would be prohibited, the latter would not. A definition of radiological weapons which contained a clause excluding nuclear explosives was objected to by several nations, as it would, in their opinion, legitimize the use of nuclear weapons.

A radiological weapon killing *exclusively* by radiation should not be confused with the enhanced radiation/reduced blast weapon, commonly referred to as a 'neutron' weapon, which is a nuclear explosive device killing *mainly* by radiation. The prohibition of the production, stockpiling, deployment and use of neutron weapons was proposed in 1978 by the Soviet Union as a separate measure. The USSR then argued that the introduction of neutron weapons would lower the so-called nuclear threshold and would thereby increase the possibility of an armed conflict escalating to the level of an all-out nuclear war. However, the Soviet proposal, reiterated in 1981 when the USA decided to start the production of neutron weapons (intended to repel possible massed tank attacks in Europe by incapacitating the crews manning the tanks), was rejected by the Western powers chiefly on the ground that there was no reason to single out this particular nuclear weapon, which was less destructive than others, for special arms control treatment.

As far as is known, no nation has manufactured a radiological weapon. In view of the enormous practical difficulties connected with the use of such a weapon in war, it is even doubtful whether any serious thought is being given to developing one. A very high radiation dose would be required to kill or injure people on the battlefield. One would need radioactive isotopes having a very short half-life, but these cannot be stored (they would decay before being used); or alternatively, one would need such large amounts of isotopes with long half-lives that the whole proposition would be impractical. In general, transport of radioactive material to the battlefield would be a very cumbersome task, mainly because of the heavy protective shielding which would be needed. Delivery of this material to intercontinental targets, for so-called strategic purposes, is hard to conceive. On the other hand, it is technically possible to use material of lower activity for causing long-term effects, harmful to life or health after months or years, or even to future generations. For this purpose one might use materials having a relatively long half-life, for instance strontium-90, which has a half-life of about 28 years. These materials can be obtained from the radioactive waste of reactors. But there would be little military rationale for producing long-term harmful effects.

To make the envisaged ban more meaningful, a suggestion has been made to prohibit deliberate damage to nuclear reactors or other nuclear fuel facilities, which could cause release of radioactive material and contamination of the environment. In fact, such acts would seem to be at present the only conceivable way of waging radiological warfare. It will be noted that, according to the 1977 Protocol relating to the protection of victims of international armed conflicts, "nuclear electrical generating stations" shall not be made the object of attack, if such attack may cause the release of dangerous forces and consequent severe losses among the civilian population. However, the protection will cease if the station provides electric power "in regular, significant and direct support of military operations and if such attack is the only feasible way to terminate such support". This reservation is vague enough to bring to naught the ban to which it is attached.[9] Moreover, the Protocol prohibition does not cover facilities committed to military use, while in the field of civilian use it leaves aside installations with large quantities of radioactivity, such as research reactors; cooling ponds, which contain fuel elements removed from the reactor before they are shipped to reprocessing plants; reprocessing plants, where the spent fuel elements are chemically treated to separate uranium and plutonium from the waste products; or storage tanks, containing high-level radioactive wastes. Therefore, a more adequate and a much stricter international legal norm is needed. But there is no immediate or serious threat that a specific, militarily useful radiological weapon will be developed.

New weapons of mass destruction

The widely shared recognition that weapons might be developed on the basis of scientific or technological principles other than those used in the weapons listed in the 1948 definition of weapons of mass destruction led to an international discussion of the possibility to prohibit new types of weapons and new systems of weapons of mass destruction. Such a prohibition may be difficult to achieve in a single treaty. For an agreement encompassing all imaginable new types of weapons could not be sufficiently clear as regards its object or sufficiently precise as regards its scope to produce real arms control effects. Also verification of an omnibus treaty would encounter enormous difficulties, as it would involve monitoring a wide gamut of scientific activities, the military implications of which are often not obvious. It would seem more practical to tackle each specific and clearly identified new weapon of mass destruction separately, with due account being taken of its peculiarities. On the other hand, it is generally considered easier to ban arms which are at the research and experimentation

---

[9] It is noteworthy that the Israeli Air Force attack of 7 June 1981 on the Iraqi nuclear centre was motivated by considerations of "self-defence".

stage than to eliminate those already developed, manufactured and stock-piled. To detect signs of a new weapon being developed, pertinent scientific discoveries would have to be internationally reviewed on a current basis, and their possible military impact examined.

V.   Measures of restraint in certain environments or geographical areas

Because of conflicting national interests which make it difficult to devise measures applicable on a global scale, the attention of the arms control negotiators has turned to those environments which are generally considered to be *res nullius* or *res communis omnium*, that is, belonging to no one or belonging to all. Two such environments, outer space and the sea-bed, have been subject to some denuclearization measures.

Certain environments

Outer space

The 1967 Outer Space Treaty laid down the principles governing peaceful activities of states in outer space. However, only one clause of this Treaty (Article IV) is directly related to arms control: elaborating on a UN General Assembly resolution unanimously adopted in 1963, it prohibits the placing in orbit around the Earth of any objects carrying nuclear weapons or any other kinds of weapons of mass destruction, the installation of such weapons on celestial bodies, or the stationing of them in outer space in any other manner. (Although "weapons of mass destruction" have not been defined in the Treaty, the general understanding of the negotiators was that, in addition to nuclear, they included at least chemical and biological weapons as well.) The establishment of military bases, installations and fortifications, the testing of any type of weapons and the conduct of military manoeuvres on celestial bodies have been also forbidden.

From the technological point of view, weapons of mass destruction, if placed in orbit around the Earth, would have serious drawbacks. Hitting a predetermined target on the Earth's surface, which lies on the path defined by the orbit, would be feasible only at certain hours or on certain days. A malfunction of the orbiting weapon could cause unintentional large-scale damage on the territory of the enemy, of a third state, or even of the launching state itself. There would also be problems of maintenance and command and control. The weapon could be relatively easily intercepted or rendered inoperative. Putting the weapons in question on manned orbiting stations would remove only some of these operational inconveniences. On balance, the disadvantages of placing nuclear or other weapons of mass destruction in outer space outweigh their military usefulness. Therefore, in agreeing to ban them, the USA and the USSR have not sacrificed much. Both powers continue to rely on ground-based and sea-based nuclear weapons which can be both better maintained and controlled, and launched with greater accuracy.

Other arms control measures regarding outer space include the prohibition on testing nuclear weapons in this environment (under the 1963 Partial Test Ban Treaty); the ban on the development, testing or deployment of specified space-based anti-ballistic missile systems or their components (under the 1972 ABM Treaty); an undertaking not to engage in military or any other hostile use of environmental modification techniques, defined as techniques for changing the dynamics, composition or structure of the Earth or of outer space (under the 1977 ENMOD Convention); and the proscription of fractional orbital bombardment systems (FOBS) capable of launching nuclear weapons into an orbital trajectory and bringing them back to Earth before the weapons complete one full revolution (under the 1979 SALT II Treaty). In addition, the Agreement governing the activities of states on the Moon and other celestial bodies, which was worked out in 1979, has amplified the relevant provisions of the Outer Space Treaty by prohibiting any threat or use of force or any other hostile act or threat of hostile act on the Moon, as well as the use of the Moon in order to commit any such act or to engage in any such threat in relation to the Earth, the Moon, spacecraft, the personnel of spacecraft or man-made space objects.

The 1968 Agreement on the rescue of astronauts, the return of astronauts and the return of objects launched into outer space, the 1972 Convention on international liability for damage caused by space objects, and the 1975 Convention on registration of objects launched into outer space all address themselves to technical and legal aspects of international co-operation in the exploration and use of outer space for peaceful purposes.

However, the outer space environment has not been fully denuclearized. In particular, the flight through outer space of ballistic missiles carrying nuclear weapons from one point to another on the Earth's surface has not been forbidden. Nor has the deployment in outer space of weapons not capable of mass destruction been subject to any restriction. The USA and the USSR are engaged in developing devices capable of intercepting or disabling satellites in orbit, adding a new dimension to the arms race.

Since the danger of a war conducted from another planet against a state on Earth is an unrealistic prospect, the arms control effect of the undertaking to use celestial bodies exclusively for peaceful purposes is even scantier than that of banning orbiting weapons of mass destruction.

The complete demilitarization of outer space is unattainable as long as ballistic missiles exist in weapon arsenals. Nevertheless, certain further measures to prevent an arms race and reduce the risk of military confrontation in outer space are conceivable, and the 1978 UN Special Session devoted to disarmament called for appropriate negotiations to be held in conformity with the spirit of the Outer Space Treaty.

In 1979 Italy suggested that an additional protocol to the Outer Space Treaty be signed to establish that outer space, including the Moon and other celestial bodies, shall be used for peaceful purposes "only", and, to this end, to extend the prohibition contained in Article IV of the Treaty. In particular, the parties to the protocol would undertake to refrain from engaging in, encouraging, or authorizing or participating in "any measures of a military or other hostile nature" in outer space, such as the establishment of military bases, installations and fortifications, the stationing of devices having the same effect, the launching into Earth orbit or beyond of objects carrying weapons of mass destruction or any other types of device designed for offensive purposes, the conduct of military manoeuvres, as well as the testing of any type of weapon. The main objective pursued by Italy was to prohibit the development and use of Earth-based and space-based systems designed to damage, destroy or interfere with the operations of other states' satellites.

In 1981 the Soviet Union proposed a treaty of unlimited duration, which would prohibit the stationing of weapons of any kind in outer space, including stationing on "reusable" manned space vehicles (a clear reference to the US space shuttle programme). Moreover, the parties to the treaty would undertake not to destroy, damage, or disturb the normal functioning or change the flight trajectory of space objects of other states, if such objects were placed in orbit in "strict accordance" with the above-mentioned provision. Compliance with the treaty would be assured with the national technical means of verification at the disposal of the parties and, when necessary, the parties would consult each other, make inquiries and provide relevant information.

The Soviet proposal does not specify whether the development and testing of anti-satellite systems would be prohibited, and whether states would be obliged to dismantle those systems which they have already developed and tested. As a matter of fact, the draft treaty does not seem to prohibit anti-satellite weapons as such; only their deployment in space and use would be banned. One clause implies that these weapons may even be resorted to in case of violation of the agreement. In this context, it is not at all clear who would make the judgement as to whether or not objects were placed in orbit in accordance with the provisions of the treaty and, consequently, under what circumstances parties would be relieved from their undertaking not to interfere with the space objects of other states. Notwithstanding the apparent deficiencies of the Soviet text, the envisaged ban would be of significant importance as an arms control measure, were it to cover not only weapons placed in orbit but also weapons that could strike space objects from the ground and from the atmosphere.

A few rounds of talks on the possibility to control anti-satellite systems were held in 1978–79 between the USA and the USSR with the declared aim of preserving strategic stability and ensuring that treaties verified from space by satellites are being complied with. But, given the states' growing dependence on space technology for communications or meteorology, for example, it is the international community as a whole that has the right and the responsibility to negotiate the appropriate measures. The Soviet proposal constitutes an important step towards the multilateralization of such negotiations. An eventual agreement would have to be open for adherence by all states.

The prevailing opinion is that an anti-satellite weapons treaty should be a point of departure of the process of averting the risk of war in outer space. But a formidable obstacle to reaching such an arms control agreement is the fact that most satellites are used for military purposes. And, since satellites will remain highly vulnerable to attack for a long time to come, they will continue to be tempting military targets. On the other hand, unbridled great-power competition in the field of anti-satellite weaponry could be unbearably costly for both sides, as it would inevitably involve both offensive and defensive measures. Such competition would, moreover, generate pressure for pre-emptive action and would thereby decrease rather than increase the sense of security of the powers in question, bringing no advantage to either side.

Sea-bed

The 1971 Sea-Bed Treaty prohibits emplanting or emplacing on the sea-bed and the ocean floor and in the subsoil thereof beyond the outer limit of a sea-bed zone (coterminous with the 12-mile outer limit of the zone referred to in the 1958 Geneva Convention on the Territorial Sea and the Contiguous Zone) any nuclear weapons or any other types of weapons of mass destruction as well as structures, launching installations or any other facilities specifically designed for storing, testing or using such weapons.

Arms control with respect to the sea-bed first began to receive attention in the 1960s. At that time, advances in the technology of oceanography were feared to lead to the use of the sea-bed for warlike purposes. The original idea was to reserve the sea-bed beyond the limits of national jurisdiction for peaceful undertakings alone, which for many nations was tantamount to a prohibition on all military activities. But the Sea-Bed Treaty has failed to bring about the demilitarization of the area in question.

Even the denuclearization undertaking was only partial: the portion of the sea-bed which is adjacent to the coast of nuclear weapon states was excluded from the prohibition. Nor does the Treaty prevent the nuclear weapon powers from installing nuclear weapons beneath the territorial waters of other states, if those states authorize such installation and if the operation is carried out within the 12-mile sea-bed zone. The USA, which together with the USSR sponsored the Treaty, also explained that submersible vehicles carrying nuclear weapons on board, and able to navigate in the water above the sea-bed, would be viewed as any other ship and not as violating the Treaty when they are anchored to, or resting on, the ocean bottom.

The 1979 SALT II Treaty extended, for the USA and the USSR, the ban on military activities in the sea-bed environment. It prohibited the development, testing or deployment of fixed ballistic or cruise missile launchers for emplacement on the ocean floor, on the sea-bed, or on the beds of internal waters and inland waters, or in the subsoil thereof, or mobile launchers of such missiles, which move only in contact with the ocean floor, the sea-bed, or the beds of internal waters and inland waters, or missiles for such launchers. Thus, only fixed nuclear installations or bottom-crawling vehicles, specifically designed to use nuclear weapons, would be banned.

Such devices, being very vulnerable, appear not to be militarily attractive. But the Sea-Bed Treaty permits the use of the sea-bed for facilities which service free-swimming nuclear weapon systems. In joining the Treaty some states have reserved the right to remove any weapon, installation, facility or device emplaced by other countries on their continental shelves beyond the outer limit of the sea-bed zone referred to in the Treaty.

The Treaty was presented to the international community as a step towards excluding the sea-bed area from the domain of the arms race. The parties undertook to conduct negotiations in good faith concerning measures in the field of disarmament which would lead to this goal, but no such negotiations have yet been held. The review conference of the parties, convened five years after the entry into force of the Sea-Bed Treaty, was to examine the effects of developments in both underwater and weapon technologies on the military uses of the sea-bed and the implications of such developments for efforts aimed at the demilitarization of the sea-bed. But such examination proved impossible because relevant information was not made available to the conference by the great powers, which are the only ones to possess both sophisticated underwater technology as well as military resources.

Geographical areas

Arms control arrangements regarding certain geographical areas in one country or in neighbouring countries, or covering certain islands or straits, were made many times in the past. As early as in 1817, the US–British so-called Rush–Bagot Agreement reduced, limited and equalized the two sides' naval forces on the Great Lakes. The more recent examples include the 1905 Convention between Sweden and Norway for the establishment of a neutral zone and for dismantling fortifications, or the 1921 Convention relating to the non-fortification and neutralization of the Aaland Islands, forming part of the Finnish Archipelago.

However, the application of an arms control regime to a whole continent is a new development. Three continents, Antarctica, Latin America and Europe, are already subject, or are planned to be subject, to certain restrictive measures in the military field.

Antarctica

The 1959 Antarctic Treaty declared that the area south of 60° South latitude, including all ice shelves, shall be used exclusively for peaceful purposes. The Treaty prohibits any measures of a military nature, such as the establishment of military bases or fortifications, the carrying out of military manoeuvres or the testing of any type of weapon. There is also a ban on nuclear explosions in the Antarctic, whatever their nature, as well as on the disposal of radioactive waste material, subject to possible future international agreements on these subjects.

The Antarctic Treaty is an important preventive measure, the first of its kind to be concluded after World War II. Its denuclearization clause, which has helped to prevent the use of the empty expanses of the Antarctic as a nuclear testing ground or a nuclear weapon base, is particularly significant. An outstanding example of a similar pre-World War II agreement is the 1920 Treaty regulating the status of Spitsbergen, which prohibits the establishment of any naval base or the construction of any fortification in Spitsbergen (Svalbard), a group of islands lying north of Scandinavia and with no indigenous population.

The arms control purpose of the Antarctic Treaty was derived from its other three main objectives: to establish a foundation for international co-operation in scientific investigation in Antarctica, successfully initiated during the 1957/58 International Geophysical Year; to protect the unique Antarctic environment; and to avert discord over territorial claims.

Co-operative exploration of the Antarctic continent has been ensured by the undertaking of the parties to exchange scientific personnel and

Figure 3.4. Territorial claims in the Antarctic

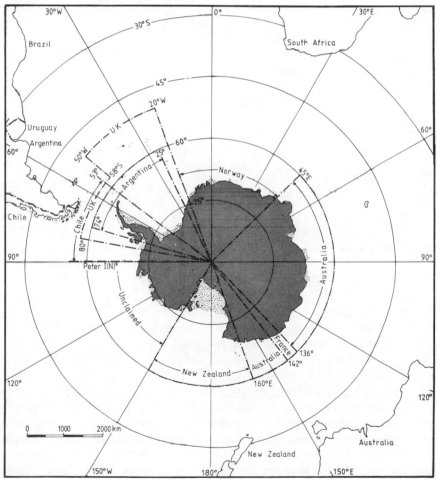

information. Preservation and conservation of living resources in Antarctica have been included in the list of the topics regularly to be reviewed by consultative meetings, and have figured prominently on the agenda of these meetings. As regards the politically sensitive question of territorial claims, the Treaty introduced a moratorium, implying neither renunciation nor recognition of "previously asserted rights of or claims to" territorial sovereignty in Antarctica, and prohibiting the making of new claims or the extension of existing ones. By the 1950s, seven states—Argentina, Australia, Chile, France, New Zealand, Norway and the UK—had claimed sovereignty over areas of Antarctica on the basis of discovery, exploration, geographic proximity or territorial continuity; in the case of Argentina, Chile and the UK, the claims overlap. (For a map of the territorial claims in the Antarctic, see figure 3.4.) Only some 15 per cent of the Antarctica land mass remains unclaimed. The moratorium established by the Antarctic Treaty can be terminated 30 years from the date of entry into force of the Treaty, that is, after 1991, at which time any party may request the convening of a conference to review its operation.

Although the Antarctic Treaty is an international agreement of universal interest, the number of parties to it is rather small but includes all of the nuclear weapon states except China. One reason why states have felt no particular urge to participate may be the very structure of the Treaty, which is marked with exclusiveness. There are two categories of parties. The 12 signatories, former participants in the scientific investigation in the Antarctic during the International Geophysical Year, enjoy full rights under the Treaty. They are entitled to participate in consultative meetings; they have the right to carry out inspections; they may modify or amend the Treaty at any time through an agreement among themselves; they are empowered to decide whether or not non-UN members should be allowed to accede; and only they may call a conference to review the operation of the Treaty. The parties which accede to the Treaty do not have those rights, unless they conduct "substantial scientific research activity" in the Antarctic, such as the establishment of a scientific station or the despatch of a scientific expedition, while the original parties to the Antarctic Treaty would maintain their privileged position even if they ceased to be actively engaged in the Antarctic research.

The scarcity of food and mineral and hydrocarbon resources has increased mankind's interest in the potential of areas as yet untapped; it has been known for some time that there are deposits of precious minerals on the Antarctic continent and that the waters in that part of the world are rich in living resources. The special interest of the past few years in Antarctica is related to indications that its continental shelf may contain oil and gas, although estimates of these resources are speculative.

Economic activity in Antarctica has been neither expressly permitted nor prohibited by the Antarctic Treaty, but it is not considered contrary to its principles or its purposes. In fact, exploitation of the living marine resources of the area has already begun. In 1980 the parties signed a Convention on the conservation (including rational use) of these resources (complementing the provisions of the Convention for the regulation of whaling and the Convention for the conservation of Antarctic seals), which requires that both the population levels of the exploited species and the balance of the ecosystem (that is, the complex of relationships of living marine resources with each other and with their physical environment) be conserved. However, if and when exploitation of the Antarctic mineral resources becomes a practical proposition, a struggle might erupt for national rights to territorial possessions containing these non-renewable resources. This could be a struggle among the original claimants, especially where claims overlap, or between them and non-claimants active in Antarctica or also with new claimants demanding a share, whether party or non-party to the Antarctic Treaty. (It should be noted that the USA and the USSR have neither made nor recognized territorial claims, but have established their *de facto* presence all over the continent through scientific stations and resource-oriented geological and other research programmes.) It is conceivable that a nation may resort to the use of force to assert its declared rights over other contenders, or to guard against infringements on its economic activities. Such action would bring about a collapse of the legal order currently prevailing under the Treaty: Antarctica would cease to be a non-militarized zone and would become a danger zone instead.

The Antarctic Treaty consultative meetings held in recent years recommended the timely adoption of an agreed regime concerning Antarctic mineral resources. But, to forestall developments dangerous to the environment and ecology, to preserve Antarctica as an area of unprecedented international scientific co-operation and to secure peace, it would be best to impose a total ban on hydrocarbon and other mineral exploitation. Failing such a ban, Antarctica, which has never been effectively occupied or under the control of any state, should be formally recognized as a common heritage of mankind rather than an exclusive preserve of a limited group of states, and its resources should be exploited in the interest of all nations, just as the sea-bed beyond the limits of national jurisdiction is planned to be used. These areas, as well as outer space, which has already been declared the province of all mankind, have, from the legal point of view, similar characteristics. Internationalization would be a fair solution from the economic point of view. It would also remove the sources of inter-state friction and conflict, and would reinforce the demilitarized status of the Antarctic.

Latin America

The 1967 Treaty of Tlatelolco prohibits the testing, use, manufacture, production or acquisition by any means, as well as the receipt, storage, installation, deployment and any form of possession of nuclear weapons in Latin America. The extra-continental or continental states which are internationally responsible for territories lying within the limits of the geographical zone established by the Treaty (that is, France, the Netherlands, the UK and the USA) undertake to apply the statute of military denuclearization to these territories by adhering to Additional Protocol I annexed to the Treaty. Under Additional Protocol II, the nuclear weapon states undertake to respect the statute of military denuclearization of Latin America, and not to contribute to acts involving a violation of the Treaty, nor to use or threaten to use nuclear weapons against the parties to the Treaty.

The importance of the nuclear weapon-free zone established by the Treaty of Tlatelolco is undeniable. Nevertheless, the Treaty contains a few ambiguous points which may weaken its arms control impact. One of them is related to so-called peaceful nuclear explosions.

Explosions of nuclear devices for peaceful purposes are allowed under the Treaty and procedures for carrying them out are specified. A proviso is made that such activities must be in accordance with the article which prohibits the testing, use, manufacture, production or acquisition of nuclear weapons, as well as with the article which defines a nuclear weapon as "any device which is capable of releasing nuclear energy in an uncontrolled manner, and which has a group of characteristics that are appropriate for use for warlike purposes". Some countries interpret these provisions as prohibiting the manufacture of nuclear explosive devices for peaceful purposes unless or until nuclear devices are developed which cannot be used as weapons. Other countries consider that the Treaty has sanctioned peaceful explosions involving devices used in nuclear weapons. Thus, the important problem of compatibility of an indigenous development of nuclear explosive devices for peaceful purposes with participation in this nuclear weapon-free zone agreement has remained unresolved.

Another controversial point is the geographical extent of the Latin American nuclear weapon-free area. The zone of application of the Treaty embraces the territory, territorial sea, airspace and any other space over which the zonal state exercises sovereignty in accordance with "its own legislation". But such legislation varies from state to state. In signing Additional Protocol II of the Treaty of Tlatelolco, France, the UK, the USA and the USSR stated that they would not recognize any legislation which did not, in their view, comply with the relevant rules of international law, that is, the law of the sea. There may be more problems when large areas of the high seas in the Atlantic and Pacific Oceans, hundreds of kilometres off the coasts of signatory states and over which no state has claimed jurisdiction, are included in the nuclear weapon-free zone.[10] This will happen upon fulfilment of the following requirements specified in the Treaty of Tlatelolco: adherence to the Treaty by all states in the region which were in existence when the Treaty was opened for signature; adherence to Additional Protocols I and II of the Treaty by all states to which they are open for signature; and the conclusion of safeguards agreements with the IAEA. (For the zone of application of the Treaty of Tlatelolco, see figure 3.5.)

Furthermore, since neither transport nor transit of nuclear weapons has

---

[10]One argument put forward against the proposals to establish a 'zone of peace' in the Indian Ocean, or a nuclear weapon-free zone in the Pacific, was that such zones would restrict the freedom of navigation in the high seas.

Figure 3.5.   The Treaty of Tlatelolco

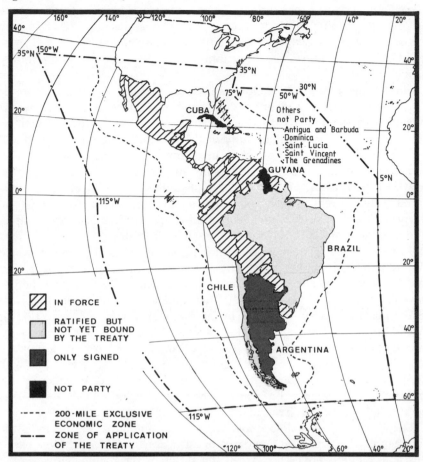

include the term ''transport'' in the article dealing with the obligations of the parties. If the carrier state were one of the zonal states, transport would be covered by the prohibition on any form of possession of nuclear weapons, ''directly or indirectly, by the Parties themselves, by anyone on their behalf or in any other way''. If the carrier were a state not party to the Treaty, transport would be considered identical with ''transit''. In this case, as the Preparatory Commission argued, the principles and rules of international law must apply, according to which it is the prerogative of the territorial state, in the exercise of its sovereignty, to grant or deny permission for transit. In joining the Additional Protocols of the Treaty, the USA and France made a declaration of understanding to the same effect, while the USSR reaffirmed its position that authorizing the transit of nuclear weapons in any form would be contrary to the objectives of the Treaty. China considers that the passage of means of transportation or delivery carrying nuclear weapons through Latin American territory, territorial sea or airspace is prohibited. Indeed, once nuclear weapons are allowed to be in transit in Latin America, even if such transit is limited to port visits or over-

China considers that the passage of means of transportation or delivery carrying nuclear weapons through Latin American territory, territorial sea or airspace is prohibited. Indeed, once nuclear weapons are allowed to be in transit in Latin America, even if such transit is limited to port visits or over-flights, it will be difficult to maintain that the zone has been totally denuclearized.

Finally, the Treaty of Tlatelolco stipulates that the rise of a new power "possessing nuclear weapons" shall have the effect of suspending the execution of the Treaty for those countries which have ratified it without waiving the requirement that Additional Protocol II should be signed and ratified by all the countries concerned, and which request such suspension and that the Treaty shall remain suspended until the new power ratifies the Protocol. However, the applicability of these provisions to a country like India, which exploded a nuclear device for "peaceful purposes", is disputable. India denies that it has acquired a nuclear weapon and does not consider itself a possible party to Protocol II.

The Treaty of Tlatelolco is significant as the first agreement which embodies a legally binding restriction on the use of nuclear weapons. But not all the assurances of non-use are unconditional. The USA and the UK have reserved the right to reconsider their obligations with regard to a state in the nuclear weapon-free zone in the event of any act of aggression or armed attack by that state which is carried out with the support or assistance of a nuclear weapon power. The USSR made a similar reservation with regard to a party to the Treaty committing an act of aggression with the support of, or together with, a nuclear weapon state. Whether or not such hedged guarantees conform to the spirit of Additional Protocol II is open to question. The Treaty itself does not allow reservations.

The Treaty of Tlatelolco was specifically intended to preclude the emergence of nuclear weapon powers in Latin America. The achievement of this goal requires adherence by all the states of the region. However, in 1982, 15 years after the signing of the Treaty, several countries of Latin America were still not bound by its provisions.

Cuba, which in 1962 allowed Soviet nuclear weapons to be stationed on its territory, has refused to join the Treaty, motivated mainly by the state of US–Cuban relations. Argentina has so far only signed the Treaty.

Brazil and Chile have signed and ratified it but, unlike other parties, have not waived the requirements that are to be met (but have not yet been met) before the Treaty enters into force for any given country. However, according to the generally accepted principles of international law, Argentina, Brazil and Chile, as signatories of the Treaty of Tlatelolco, are obligated to refrain from acts which would defeat the object and purpose of the Treaty. These countries have substantial nuclear activities and are not parties to the NPT. Additional Protocols to the Treaty of Tlatelolco have been ratified by the powers concerned with the exception of France, which by the end of 1981 had signed but not ratified Protocol I.

It is the attitudes of Argentina and Brazil, the two largest countries in Latin America and practically the only ones in the area with any present nuclear weapon potential or aspiration, that will mainly determine whether Latin America remains free of nuclear weapons. Each of these countries has stated that, according to its interpretation, the Treaty gives the parties the right to carry out, by their own means or in association with third parties, nuclear explosions for peaceful purposes, including explosions which involve devices similar to those used in nuclear weapons.[11] However, 'peaceful' nuclear explosive devices could also be used as weapons: they are transportable and the amount of energy they are able to release could cause mass destruction. Any of these countries exploding such a device would *de facto* become a nuclear power, defeating the purpose of the Treaty of Tlatelolco.

Proposals for having nuclear weapon-free zones set up in *other* regions, as put forward over the years in the United Nations and elsewhere, include Europe, in particular the central and northern parts, Africa, the Middle East, South Asia and the South Pacific. There also exist proposals for 'zones of peace' to be set up in the Indian Ocean, South-East Asia, the Mediterranean or the Balkans, which imply at least some measure of denuclearization.

It is clear that the withdrawal of nuclear weapons deployed outside the territories of the nuclear weapon states would have a considerable arms control impact. But the likelihood of areas already nuclearized becoming denuclearized, especially where the two main military alliances confront each other, is slight unless at the same time the levels of armed forces and conventional armaments accumulated there are very substantially reduced. On the other hand, nuclear weapon-free zones could play an important role in preventing nuclearization. To the extent that the incentive to acquire nuclear weapons may emerge from regional considerations, the establishment of such zones in various regions of the world would be an asset for the cause of the non-proliferation of nuclear weapons. However, the areas where a denuclearized regime is most needed are conflict areas, in which hostility and mistrust prevail, while the conclusion of regional agreements presupposes at least a modicum of good-neighbourly relations.

It is of interest to note that there have also been attempts to limit conventional armaments in Latin America. In the 1974 Declaration of Ayacucho, the six members of the so-called Andean Group (Bolivia, Chile, Colombia, Ecuador, Peru and Venezuela)[12] plus two non-members (Argentina and Panama) undertook to create conditions permitting an effective limitation of armaments and putting an end to their acquisition for offensive purposes. The stated aim of these measures was to devote all possible resources to the economic and social development of the countries in Latin America. Several consultative meetings of the Andean countries took place

---

[11] Nicaragua, a party to the Treaty of Tlatelolco, has also reserved the right to use nuclear energy for such peaceful purposes as the removal of earth for the construction of canals or irrigation works.

[12] The Andean Group was created in 1969 for the purpose of subregional economic integration.

after the signing of the Declaration of Ayacucho with a view to translating its provisions into an internationally binding instrument.

In 1978 a conference was convened, the first of this kind in the history of Latin America, to deal exclusively with the problem of conventional arms control in the region. This conference, held in Mexico City, was attended by representatives of Argentina, Bolivia, Colombia, Costa Rica, Cuba, the Dominican Republic, Ecuador, El Salvador, Guatemala, Haiti, Honduras, Jamaica, Mexico, Nicaragua, Panama, Peru, Suriname, Trinidad and Tobago, Uruguay and Venezuela. The participants recommended, *inter alia*, initiation of studies and talks concerning possible limitations on transfer of certain types of conventional armaments to Latin America, and among the countries in the area, as well as limitations or prohibitions on conventional weapons considered to be excessively injurious or indiscriminate in their effects.

An agreement on conventional weapon restraints in Latin America could have positive effects for peace and security in the area, especially if adhered to by all militarily significant countries of the region. Since the relations between Latin American states are in many cases characterized by rivalry or open conflict, confidence building aimed at reducing inter-state tension might create prerequisites for such an agreement. This approach is being tried out in Europe.

Europe

The 1975 Final Act of the Conference on Security and Co-operation in Europe contains a Document on confidence-building measures and certain aspects of security and disarmament. The rationale for adopting the Document was formulated as follows: "to contribute to reducing the dangers of armed conflict and of misunderstanding or miscalculation of military activities which could give rise to apprehension, particularly in a situation when the participating states lack clear and timely information about the nature of such activities". However, most provisions of the Document are vague or non-committal, or simply confirm a practice already existing among nations maintaining normal relations.

The only provision stated in concrete terms concerns the notification of major military manoeuvres in Europe, to be given at least 21 days in advance or, in the case of a manoeuvre arranged at shorter notice, at the earliest possible opportunity before its starting date. The term "major" means that at least 25 000 troops are involved. Manoeuvres with fewer troops can also be considered as major if they involve "significant numbers" of either amphibious or airborne troops, or both. Manoeuvres of naval and air forces, conducted independently or jointly, are not covered by the notification requirement. The following information is to be provided for each major manoeuvre: its designation (code-name), if any; its general purpose; the states involved; the types and numerical strength of the forces engaged; and the area and estimated time-frame of its conduct. States may give additional information, particularly that related to the components of the forces engaged and the period of involvement of the troops, and may invite observers to attend the manoeuvres.

The preamble of the Document states that the notification of manoeuvres "rests upon a voluntary basis"; it is, therefore, not a legally binding commitment. Nonetheless, it is a declaration of intent solemnly adopted by the representatives of the participating states at the highest possible level. The parties expressed their conviction of the political importance of prior notification of major military manoeuvres for "the promotion of mutual understanding and the strengthening of confidence, stability and security", and accepted the "responsibility of each of them" to implement this measure. The record of the implementation of the relevant provisions of the Document has proved satisfactory in that "major" manoeuvres have apparently been notified. However, the information required by the Document has not in all cases been included in the notification.

The concept of advance notification of manoeuvres was introduced into the international debate at the beginning of the 1960s as part of a programme to reduce the risk of war by accident, miscalculation, failure of communications or surprise attack. It was then discussed along with the proposed establishment of observation posts, mobile observation teams and exchange of military missions, or in conjunction with a proposed prohibition on certain types of military exercise. Isolated from the above-mentioned measures, notification can hardly fulfil the original role allotted to it, namely, that of a warning signal for the two major military blocs, especially at a time when the means of satellite surveillance are considered sufficiently reliable to monitor significant military activities in any part of the world. Notification may contribute to minimizing the danger that the detection of such activities might give rise to misunderstandings and provoke a rapid, possibly disproportionate military response, initiating unpremeditated hostilities. But the notification would then have to apply even to military manoeuvres of fewer than 25 000 troops, and preferably be given more in advance of the start of the manoeuvres. It would also have to cover, on an obligatory basis, military movements other than manoeuvres, since transfers of combat-ready army, naval and air force units outside their permanent garrison or base areas, especially over long distances and close to the borders of other states, may cause even greater concern than manoeuvres. Furthermore, the role of invited foreign observers would have to be clearly defined. Hitherto, it has been left entirely to the host country to determine whether the attendance of observers at the manoeuvres was to be a meaningful or simply a ceremonial act.

Consequently, at the follow-up meeting of the Conference on Security and Co-operation in Europe in 1980–81, a group of non-aligned and neutral countries proposed that: (a) notification should be given of major military manoeuvres and movements exceeding a total of 18 000 troops 30 days or more in advance; and (b) observers invited to attend manoeuvres should be given ample information about the purpose and progress of the exercises, as well as the opportunity to follow the activities of command staffs and field units and to have personal contacts with troops. Prior notification of major naval exercises in European waters, especially exercises involving amphibious forces, was also suggested.

The undertaking to notify military activities signifies a step towards openness, but it does not imply restrictions. The Soviet Union, which is in favour of extending the scope of confidence-building measures in Europe, suggested in 1979 that an upper limit should be fixed on the size of military manoeuvres, while the Western countries have been advocating a "coherent system" of militarily significant, binding and appropriately verified confidence-building measures applicable from the Atlantic to the Urals.

Actual limitations on the military potential of European states are being dealt with at the negotiations on "mutual reduction of forces and armaments and associated measures in Central Europe", held in Vienna since 1973. Eleven states, with indigenous or stationed forces in Central Europe, are full participants in the Vienna talks—the USA, Canada, the UK, the Federal Republic of Germany, Belgium, the Netherlands and Luxembourg, on the NATO side; and the USSR, the German Democratic Republic, Czechoslovakia and Poland, on the Warsaw Treaty Organization (WTO) side. Eight more countries have a special observer status—Denmark, Greece, Italy, Norway, Turkey, Bulgaria, Romania and Hungary. The envisaged reductions are to take place on the territories of Belgium, FR Germany, Luxembourg and the Netherlands, as well as Czechoslovakia, the GDR and Poland, and are also to cover foreign troops.

Over the years, each side has presented proposals that have been rejected by the other side. The WTO countries seek such reductions that would not affect the existing correlation of forces in Europe, while NATO insists that measures should be taken to remove the present superiority of the WTO in the numbers of ground forces and tanks in the agreed area of reductions, and to compensate for the differences in reinforcements capabilities caused by the disparity in geographic situations which favours the Soviet Union. The proposals of the two sides converge on a few points: both envisage reductions by stages, deal with US and Soviet troop strengths separately from those of the remaining nine states, and include tanks and nuclear warheads, as well as aircraft and other nuclear weapon delivery vehicles, in the categories of weapons to be reduced. But since different national perspectives have generated conflicting perceptions of what is an acceptable military balance, the controversy with regard to the scope of the reductions and the manner in which they have to be carried out—symmetrically, according to the East, or asymmetrically, according to the West—remains unresolved.

Given the dissimilarity of motivations of the main parties, it would be unrealistic to expect, at least in the first phase, much more than some thinning-out of the troops due to force restructuring and improvements in mobility, in particular airlifting capabilities, or replacement of certain obsolete arms by less numerous but more effective modernized weapons. Moreover, the sector of Europe at which the negotiations are aimed cannot be isolated from an area which, from the geographic and strategic points of view, constitutes an entity, and be subject to an entirely different regime, without affecting the military balance on the European continent as a whole. In particular, the exclusion of Hungary and Italy from the designated zone of possible reductions, as if these countries were unconcerned with the disposition of forces in the central part of the continent, and the absence of France from the negotiating table illustrate the artificiality of the exercise. Hence the need to convene an all-European conference to negotiate substantial arms control measures in a broader context, including means to prevent a major surprise attack against any state in the region.

The spotlight has recently fallen on the so-called long-range European theatre nuclear weapons, that is, nuclear weapons located in or targeted on Europe and having a range longer than that of the existing short-range tactical nuclear weapons, but shorter than that of the intercontinental strategic nuclear weapons often referred to as "central systems". The current debate is focused on the newest generation of these weapons. They are, on the Soviet side, mobile land-based SS-20 missiles, which can carry three independently targetable nuclear warheads to ranges of about 5 000 km, thereby covering the whole of Europe. They may replace the obsolescent fixed land-based SS-4 and SS-5 missiles carrying a single warhead. On the US side, the theatre nuclear weapons would include ground-launched cruise missiles and Pershing II ballistic missiles, both possessing exceptional accuracy and capable of penetrating a significant distance into the Soviet Union from Western Europe where they are to be deployed largely as a response to the SS-20 deployment. (For the ranges of the European theatre nuclear weapons, see figure 3.6.) Control of these weapons must be negotiated by those who possess them, that is, the USA and the USSR. But, since nuclear weapons deployed in Europe or targeted on Europe create the risk of a nuclear war on this continent, and since there is widespread suspicion that the USA and the USSR envisage the possibility of a limited nuclear exchange in Europe, the views of the European nations directly concerned, both aligned and non-aligned, must be taken into account.

On 30 November 1981, the United States and the Soviet Union started in Geneva "intermediate nuclear force negotiations", as they were called by the USA, or "talks on the reduction of nuclear arms in Europe", as they were called by the USSR. The two labels for the talks reflected the different starting negotiating positions of the two powers.

The United States advocated the so-called zero option, meaning that the deployment of US Pershing II and ground-launched cruise missiles in Europe would be cancelled if the Soviet SS-20, SS-4 and SS-5 missiles were dismantled. The Soviet Union proposed a moratorium on the deployment in Europe of all 'medium'-range nuclear missiles, to be in force until a permanent treaty was concluded to limit or reduce such weapons. Should both sides agree to a moratorium, the Soviet Union was prepared to effect significant reductions of its medium-range nuclear weapons, its declared aim being to free Europe from both medium-range and tactical nuclear weapons. Subsequently, the USSR made it clear that it had in mind mutual reductions of weapons, in Europe and in the waters adjacent to Europe,

Figure 3.6. European theatre nuclear weapons

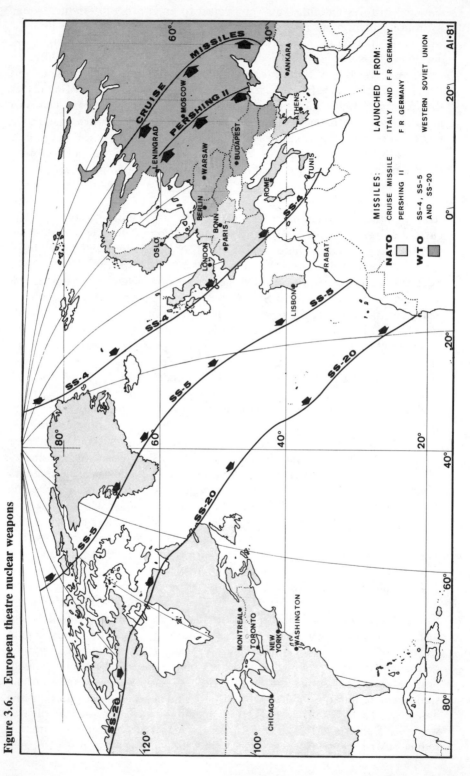

with a range exceeding 1 000 km. Reductions by one-third would have to be carried out before 1985, and by two-thirds before 1990.

These positions were widely publicized, and it is significant that the two powers felt the need to appeal to public opinion in Western Europe with far-reaching proposals even before they engaged in formal negotiations.

In view of the nature and complexity of the issue—in particular of the difficulty in differentiating between strategic and non-strategic missions of weapons—it is highly uncertain whether a satisfactory measure to limit the European theatre nuclear forces can be found independently of limitations on US and Soviet strategic nuclear arms, and without taking into consideration the state of conventional armaments in Europe.

VI. Prevention of war

The Cuban missile crisis of 1962 demonstrated the need for quick and reliable communications between heads of government to reduce the danger that a war might break out due to a technical failure, misunderstanding or miscalculation. The first agreement setting up such a communication was concluded between the USA and the USSR in 1963 for use in time of emergency, when normal consultative procedures between the states involved appear insufficient or impossible.

'Hot lines'

The US–Soviet Memorandum of Understanding regarding the establishment of a direct communications link, the so-called Hot Line Agreement, provides that each government should be responsible for arrangements for the communications link on its own territory, including continuous functioning of the link and prompt delivery of communications to its head of government. An annex attached to the Memorandum specified that the link would comprise: (a) two terminal points with teletype equipment; (b) a full-time duplex wire telegraph circuit routed Washington–London–Copenhagen–Stockholm–Helsinki–Moscow; and (c) a full-time duplex radiotelegraph circuit routed Washington–Tangier–Moscow. If the wire circuit should be interrupted, messages would be transmitted by the radio circuit.

Advances in satellite communications technology offered a possibility to increase the reliability of the 'hot line'. Thus, the Agreement on measures to improve the US–Soviet direct communications link, signed in 1971, supplemented and modified the 1963 Memorandum of Understanding by providing for the establishment of two satellite communications circuits between the USA and the USSR, with a system of multiple terminals in each country. Under this Hot Line Modernization Agreement, the USA was to provide one circuit via the Intelsat system, and the USSR a circuit via its Molniya system. The original circuits were to be maintained. When the two satellite communications circuits became operational in 1978, the radio circuit provided for in the 1963 Memorandum was terminated, but the wire telegraph circuit has been retained as a back-up.

The hot line has turned out to be a useful measure. It has been used many times in communications between Moscow and Washington, mainly during military crises, such as the 1967 and 1973 Arab–Israeli wars. In 1966, France signed an accord establishing a direct communications link between the Elysée Palace and the Kremlin, while a direct communications line between the Kremlin and 10 Downing Street was set up following the 1967 British–Soviet agreement.

Whatever the precautions taken to ensure the safety of arms, and whatever the sophistication of command-and-control procedures, accidental or unauthorized use of nuclear weapons cannot be ruled out. According to official US reports, there have been many false alarms of possible missile attack, caused mainly by misleading or ambiguous information from sensors aboard satellites or from early-warning radars, but also by computer malfunctions or failures in communications equipment; in several cases intercontinental bombers and missiles were ordered to a higher state of alert which lasted long enough to use up a good portion of the time allotted for a decision. Thousands of lesser alarms are caused primarily by atmospheric disruptions. In addition, dozens of accidents have occurred directly involving nuclear weapons. (For a list of serious accidents involving nuclear weapons, see table 3.3.) All this creates the risk of an unintended nuclear war breaking out, especially at a time of high international tension: US and Soviet land-based missiles can reach the other side's territory in about 30 minutes, while sea-borne missiles may take only half that time or less, depending on the location of the submarine. The danger is increasing due to the continued advocacy by certain military strategists of the 'launch-on-warning' policy, which implies automatic firing of missiles in response to warning signals.

Prevention of nuclear accidents

The first attempt to deal with the dilemma was made in 1971, when the USA and the USSR signed an agreement on measures to reduce the risk of outbreak of nuclear war.

Under the so-called Nuclear Accidents Agreement, the parties undertake to notify each other immediately in the event of an accidental, unauthorized or any other unexplained incident involving a possible detonation of a nuclear weapon which could create a risk of the outbreak of nuclear war. In the event of such an incident, the party whose nuclear weapon is involved will immediately make every effort to take necessary measures to render harmless or destroy such weapon without its causing damage.

The parties shall also notify each other immediately in the event of detection by missile warning systems of unidentified objects, or in the event of signs of interference with these systems or with related communications facilities. Advance notification is to be given of any planned missile launches if such launches extend beyond the national territory of one party in the direction of the other party.

In other situations involving unexplained nuclear incidents, each party shall act in such a manner as to reduce the possibility of its actions being misinterpreted by the other party; primary use will be made of the hot line to transmit urgent information.

It will be noted that the 1979 SALT Treaty would extend the obligations of the parties with regard to advance notification of missile launches. In addition to planned extra-territorial launches of missiles, all planned multiple launches would have to be notified according to the SALT Treaty, even if the planned trajectories were to be entirely within the side's national territory. (A multiple launch has been defined as one which would result in two or more ICBMs being in flight at the same time.)

The French–Soviet and British–Soviet Nuclear Accidents Agreements, concluded in 1976 and 1977, respectively, are patterned after the US–Soviet agreement.

Prevention of nuclear war

In 1973, as a follow-up to the 1971 accord, the USA and the USSR signed an Agreement on the prevention of nuclear war. The parties pledged themselves to act in such a manner as to prevent the development of situations capable of causing a dangerous exacerbation of their relations, as to avoid military confrontations, and as to exclude the outbreak of nuclear war.

It is obviously in the interest of both great powers to shun any nuclear confrontation, with or without a legal commitment to this effect, which might jeopardize the viability of each of them as a nation. The 1973 Agreement is, therefore, more significant in its multilateral implications. It aims at preventing a nuclear war also "between either of the Parties and other countries". Furthermore, the parties agreed to proceed from the premise that each will refrain from the threat or use of force "against the allies of the other Party and against other countries".

The non-use of force against the territorial integrity or political independence of any state is the most fundamental undertaking of UN members and, under the UN Charter, this undertaking is unconditional. But in the US–Soviet Agreement on the prevention of nuclear war it applies only "in circumstances which may endanger international peace and security", and no indication is given as to who will judge whether such circumstances have arisen or not.

The Agreement also provides for action to be taken if the risk of nuclear conflict appears. The two parties would then enter immediately into urgent consultations and make every effort to avert the risk. Although the UN Security Council bears the main responsibility for international peace and security, it would not be involved in handling such situations. However, each party would be "free" to inform the Council, as well as the UN Secretary-General and the governments of allied or other countries, of the progress and outcome of the said consultations.

It is noteworthy that, according to the Agreement, the two-power exclusive consultation procedure should also apply to relations of the USA and the USSR with other countries. It is even applicable whenever relations between countries "not parties" to the Agreement appear to involve the risk

Table 3.3. Serious accidents involving US nuclear weapons, 1950–80

An 'accident involving nuclear weapons' is defined by the US Department of Defense as an unexpected event involving nuclear weapons or nuclear weapon components that results in any of the following: accidental or unauthorized launching, firing or use, by US forces or supported allied forces, of a nuclear-capable weapon system which could create the risk of an outbreak of war; nuclear detonation; non-nuclear detonation or burning of a nuclear weapon or radioactive weapon component, including a fully assembled nuclear weapon, an unassembled nuclear weapon or a radioactive nuclear weapon component; radioactive contamination; seizure, theft or loss of a nuclear weapon or radioactive nuclear weapon component, including jettisoning; and public hazard, actual or implied.

This table is based on official US reports. Similar information regarding the USSR is not available.

Date	Weapon system involved	Location	Comments
1950			
13 Feb	B-36	Pacific Ocean, off coast of British Columbia	Aircraft dropped weapon from 2 400 m. Weapon's high-explosive material detonated.
11 Apr	B-29	Manzano Base, New Mexico	Aircraft crashed into a mountain. Bomb case was demolished and high-explosive material burned in gasoline fire. Both weapon and capsule of nuclear material were on board aircraft, but capsule was for safety reasons not inserted.
13 Jul	B-50	Lebanon, Ohio	Aircraft flew into ground. High-explosive portion of weapon on board detonated on impact. No nuclear capsule on board.
5 Aug	B-29	Fairfield-Suisun Air Force Base, California	Aircraft, carrying a weapon but no capsule, crashed and burned. Weapon's high-explosive material detonated.
10 Nov	B-50	Over water, outside USA	A weapon, containing no capsule of nuclear material, was jettisoned. A high-explosive detonation was observed.
1956			
10 Mar	B-47	Mediterranean Sea	Search failed to locate traces of missing aircraft or crew. Two capsules of nuclear weapon material were on board in carrying cases.
27 Jul	B-47	Overseas base (north-east of Cambridge, England)	Aircraft went out of control and slid off runway, crashing into storage igloo containing several nuclear weapons. Bombs did not burn or detonate.

Date	Aircraft	Location	Description
1957			
22 May	B-36	Kirtland Air Force Base, New Mexico	Both weapon and capsule were on board aircraft, but for safety reasons capsule was not inserted. Weapon dropped from bomb bay taking bomb bay doors with it. High-explosive material detonated, completely destroying weapon. Radiological survey of area disclosed no radioactivity beyond lip of crater.
28 Jul	C-124	Atlantic Ocean	Two weapons were jettisoned off east coast of USA. Nuclear components were not installed in weapons. No detonation occurred.
11 Oct	B-47	Homestead Air Force Base, Florida	Aircraft, carrying one weapon in bomb bay and one nuclear capsule in a carrying case in crew compartment, crashed. Weapon was enveloped in flames. Two high-explosive detonations occurred during burning. Nuclear capsule and its carrying case were recovered intact.
1958			
31 Jan	B-47	Overseas base (probably northern Africa)	Aircraft with one weapon caught fire and burned. High explosive did not detonate, but there was some contamination in the immediate area of crash.
5 Feb	B-47	Savannah River, Georgia	Aircraft had a mid-air collision. Nuclear capsule was not on board. No detonation occurred. Weapon was jettisoned into water.
11 Mar	B-47	Florence, South Carolina	Aircraft accidentally jettisoned an unarmed nuclear weapon. Bomb's high-explosive material exploded on impact. No capsule of nuclear materials was on board or installed in weapon.
4 Nov	B-47	Dyess Air Force Base, Texas	Aircraft caught fire. One nuclear weapon was on board when aircraft crashed. Resultant detonation of high explosive made a crater. Nuclear materials were recovered.
26 Nov	B-47	Chennault Air Force Base, Louisiana	Aircraft caught fire on ground. Nuclear weapon on board was destroyed. Contamination found in immediate vicinity.
1959			
18 Jan	F-100	Pacific Base	External load of aircraft consisted of a nuclear weapon and three fuel tanks. An explosion and fire occurred on ground when fuel tanks inadvertently jettisoned. Nuclear capsule was not in vicinity of aircraft nor involved in accident.

Date	Weapon system involved	Location	Comments
6 Jul	C-124	Barksdale Air Force Base, Louisiana	Aircraft was destroyed by fire which also destroyed one weapon. No nuclear or high-explosive detonation occurred.
25 Sep	P-5M	Off Whidbey Island, Washington	Aircraft ditched. It was carrying an unarmed nuclear anti-submarine weapon containing no nuclear material.
15 Oct	B-52, KC-135	Hardinsberg, Kentucky	The two aircraft collided. B-52's two unarmed nuclear weapons were recovered. One had been partially burned.
1960 7 Jun	BOMARC	McGuire Air Force Base, New Jersey	Air defence missile in ready storage condition was destroyed by explosion and fire after a high-pressure helium tank exploded and ruptured missile's fuel tanks. Warhead was also destroyed by fire although high explosive did not detonate.
1961 24 Jan	B-52	Goldsboro, North Carolina	Structural failure of right wing resulted in two weapons separating from aircraft during aircraft breakup. One bomb parachute deployed, and weapon received little impact damage. Other bomb fell free and broke apart upon impact. No explosion occurred.
14 Mar	B-52	Yuba City, California	Two nuclear weapons on board were torn from aircraft on ground impact. High explosive did not detonate.
1963 13 Nov	Atomic Energy Commission Storage Igloo	Medina Base, Texas	An explosion involving 55 350 kg of high-explosive components of nuclear weapons caused injuries to three employees. Components were from obsolete weapons being disassembled.
1964 13 Jan	B-52	Cumberland, Maryland	Aircraft was carrying two weapons. Both weapons remained in aircraft until it crashed and were relatively intact in approximate centre of wreckage area.

Date	Weapon	Location	Description
5 Dec	LGM 30B (Minuteman ICBM)	Ellsworth Air Force Base, South Dakota	Missile was on strategic alert at launch facility. In midst of checkout, one retro-rocket below re-entry vehicle (RV) fired, causing RV to fall about 22.5 m to floor of silo. When RV struck bottom of silo, subsystem containing batteries was torn loose, thus removing all sources of power from RV. RV structure received considerable damage. There was no detonation or radioactive contamination.
8 Dec	B-58	Bunker Hill Air Force Base, Indiana	Aircraft caught on fire. Portions of the five nuclear weapons on board burned. Contamination found in immediate area.
1965 11 Oct	C-124	Wright-Patterson Air Force Base, Ohio	Fuselage of aircraft, containing components of nuclear weapons, was destroyed by fire.
5 Dec	A-4	At sea, Pacific Ocean	Aircraft loaded with one nuclear weapon rolled off elevator of US aircraft carrier and fell into sea.
1966 17 Jan	B-52, KC-135	Palomares, Spain	Aircraft collided and crashed. B-52 carried four nuclear weapons. High-explosive materials of two weapons exploded on impact with ground, releasing radioactive materials. Contaminated soil and vegetation were removed to USA for storage.
1968 21 Jan	B-52	Thule, Greenland	Aircraft crashed while approaching base to land. Bomber carried four nuclear weapons all destroyed by fire. Radioactive contamination occurred. Contaminated ice, snow and water, with crash debris, were removed to a storage site in USA.
Spring 1968	Classified	At sea, Atlantic Ocean	Accident probably refers to nuclear-powered US attack submarine. It sank 640–720 km south-west of the Azores. Nuclear weapons aboard may have been an anti-submarine missile and a nuclear torpedo.
1980 19 Sep	Titan II ICBM	Damascus, Arkansas	During routine maintenance in a silo, a heavy wrench socket struck missile, causing a leak from a pressurized fuel tank. Fuel vapours within silo ignited and exploded. Missile's re-entry vehicle, which contained a nuclear warhead, was recovered intact.

of nuclear war between the USA and the USSR or between either of them and other countries. These provisions may have been motivated by a desire to prevent the possible degeneration of a local conflict into a major great-power confrontation. Nevertheless, they gave rise to suspicions that the two powers accord absolute priority to their bilateral relations over their multilateral alliance commitments, and that they arrogate to themselves the role of referee in matters relating to the security of others.

The 1973 US–Soviet Agreement was politically significant in the sense that for the first time the two powers formally, and in a bilateral document, expressed the intention not only to avoid the accidental use of nuclear weapons, but also to minimize the probability of a nuclear war started by design. In practical terms, however, the importance of the Agreement is questionable. The new code of nuclear behaviour has not reduced the danger of nuclear war between the two big powers or between either of them and another nuclear power. Moreover, in the context of the main provisions of the Agreement, the clause which reiterates the right of self-defence implies that the parties continue to consider themselves free to employ nuclear weapons against an adversary that uses only conventional weapons, that is, against a non-nuclear weapon state as well. As a matter of fact, the existing doctrines of nuclear deterrence are predicated upon the willingness to use nuclear weapons.

Prevention of incidents at sea

Special undertakings of a preventive nature concerning bilateral US–Soviet naval relations were agreed upon in 1972. The Agreement on the prevention of incidents on and over the high seas provides for measures to assure the safety of navigation of the ships of the armed forces of the USA and the USSR on the high seas and flight of their military aircraft over the high seas, including rules of conduct for ships engaged in the surveillance of other ships as well as ships engaged in launching or landing aircraft. The parties also pledged themselves to give notification of actions on the high seas which represent a danger to navigation or to aircraft in flight, and to exchange information concerning instances of collisions, instances which result in damage, or other incidents at sea between their ships and aircraft.

In a Protocol signed in 1973, the two sides recognized that the objective of this Agreement could be furthered by understandings concerning actions with respect to the non-military ships of each side. In particular, the parties pledged themselves that their ships and aircraft would not make simulated attacks by aiming guns, missile launchers, torpedo tubes and other weapons at non-military ships of the other party, nor launch nor drop any objects near non-military ships of the other party in such a manner as to be hazardous to these ships or to constitute a hazard to navigation.

The Agreement on incidents at sea is a useful instrument for reducing peacetime naval tension between the USA and the USSR. The navies continue to shadow each other in the pursuit of electronic and photographic intelligence, but incidents have decreased in number, and the risks of escalation have declined.

VII.   Humanitarian laws of war

Efforts to reduce brutality in war, motivated by humanitarian and religious as well as practical considerations, have a very long history. Thus, a body of restrictions and limitations upon what states might do when at war has developed as customary law.

Declaration of St Petersburg

During the second half of the 19th century, conventional law in the form of multilateral agreements began to supplement customary law. The Declaration of St Petersburg of 1868 was of special significance. It proclaimed that the only legitimate objective which states should endeavour to accomplish during war is to weaken the military forces of the enemy, and that the employment of arms which uselessly aggravate the suffering of disabled men, or render their death inevitable, would be contrary to the laws of humanity. From this principle, the Declaration went on to forbid the use of a specific weapon, namely, a projectile of a weight below 400 grams which is explosive or charged with "fulminating or inflammable substances". For, due to the physiological effects of shock, loss of body fluid and infection, the severe wounds created by such a projectile may inevitably result in death.

Hague Declarations and Conventions

Following the spirit of the St Petersburg Declaration, Declaration IV,3 of the Hague Conference, held in 1899, prohibited the use of so-called dumdum bullets, which expanded or flattened easily in the human body and caused more serious wounds than other bullets.

The Second Hague Conference, held in 1907, adopted a convention on laws and customs of land warfare, Convention IV, which confirmed the principles of the St Petersburg Declaration. It stated that the right of belligerents to adopt means of injuring the enemy is not unlimited, and it prohibited the employment of arms, projectiles or material calculated to cause unnecessary suffering. In particular, the Convention prohibited the use of poison, or poisonous weapons, the treacherous killing or wounding of individuals belonging to the hostile nation or army, or the killing or wounding of an enemy who had either laid down his arms or surrendered. The same conference restricted and regulated, in Convention VIII, the use of submarine mines: it forbade the laying of unanchored automatic contact mines, except when they are so constructed as to become harmless one hour at most after the person who laid them ceases to control them; the laying of such anchored mines which do not become harmless as soon as they have broken loose from their moorings; the use of torpedoes which do not become harmless when they have missed their target; and the laying of automatic contact mines off the coasts and ports of the enemy with the sole object of intercepting commercial shipping. Convention IX prohibited the bombardment by naval forces of ports, cities, villages, habitations or buildings which were not defended, while Declaration XIV proclaimed a prohibition on the discharge of projectiles and explosives from balloons or by other methods of a similar nature.

Regulations on submarines and noxious gases

The five victorious powers of World War I signed a Treaty in Washington in 1922 related to the use of submarines and noxious gases in warfare. The aim was to make more effective the rules for the protection of the lives of neutrals and non-combatants at sea, as well as to reaffirm in a treaty the customary law prohibiting the use of gases in war. Strict restrictions were to be imposed on the employment of submarines in naval warfare, and their use as "commerce destroyers" was to be entirely prohibited. However, France did not ratify the Treaty, which consequently did not come into effect.

The problem of submarines was raised again at the 1930 Naval Conference in London. In Part IV, Article 22 of the 1930 Naval Treaty signed at that Conference, the participants agreed that, in their action with regard to merchant ships, submarines must conform to the rules of international law to which surface vessels are subject. When the treaty expired in 1936, its Article 22 was recast as a separate protocol and signed by many other nations.

1925 Geneva Protocol

The problem of gases was settled in the 1925 Geneva Protocol, which prohibited the use of asphyxiating, poisonous or other gases, and of all analogous liquids, materials or devices, as well as the use of bacteriological methods of warfare. In the part dealing with gases, the Protocol actually ratified a prohibition previously declared in international documents. These included the 1899 Hague Declaration IV,2, under which the contracting powers had agreed to abstain from the use of projectiles for the diffusion of asphyxiating or deleterious gases, as well as the 1907 Hague Convention IV, mentioned above. The need to restate the prohibition of acts already held in abhorrence and condemned by world opinion was prompted by the experience of World War I, during which the extensive use of poisonous gas resulted in many casualties. Of the direct antecedents of the Geneva Protocol, as far as the prohibition of chemical weapons is concerned, the 1919 Treaty of Versailles and the other peace treaties of 1919–20 were applicable only to the vanquished countries (Germany, Austria, Bulgaria and Hungary), while the 1923 Convention on the limitation of armaments in Central America was binding only on Guatemala, El Salvador,

Honduras, Nicaragua and Costa Rica.

The interpretation of the scope of the Geneva Protocol has for many years been a matter of dispute. In 1969 a majority UN resolution expressed the view that the Protocol embodied the generally recognized rules of international law prohibiting the use in international armed conflicts of *all* biological and chemical methods of warfare, regardless of any technical developments, and declared as contrary to those rules the use in international armed conflicts of: (*a*) any chemical agents of warfare—chemical substances, whether gaseous, liquid or solid—which might be employed because of their direct toxic effects on man, animals or plants; and (*b*) any biological agents of warfare—living organisms, whatever their nature, or infective material derived from them—which are intended to cause disease or death in man, animals or plants, and which depend for their effects on their ability to multiply in the person, animal or plant attacked.

The United States has been in the forefront of the states which gave the Geneva Protocol a narrow interpretation and which contended, in particular, that the use of irritants, such as tear gas, and anti-plant chemicals was not covered by the Protocol. In 1975 the USA decided to renounce, as a matter of national policy, both the first use of herbicides in war, except for control of vegetation within US bases and installations or around their immediate defensive perimeters, and the first use of riot control agents in war, except in defensive military methods of saving lives, such as: (*a*) to control rioting prisoners of war in areas under US military control; (*b*) to reduce or avoid civilian casualties when civilians are used to mask or screen attacks; (*c*) to recover downed aircrews and passengers, and escaping prisoners, in rescue missions in remotely isolated areas; or (*d*) to protect convoys outside the combat zone from civil disturbances, terrorists and paramilitary organizations. This interpretation is more liberal than the one previously advocated: some of the permitted uses relate to non-combatant situations or are similar to domestic police uses. Nevertheless, the US interpretation fell short of the understanding of the scope of the Geneva Protocol, as formulated in the above-mentioned UN resolution. Since then, the US government has accepted, on a permanent basis, formal international treaty constraints that outlaw the use of some forms of herbicidal warfare. This happened in 1980 when the USA deposited the instruments of ratification of the 1977 ENMOD Convention. Although the Convention does not explicitly include antiplant chemical warfare among the military or any other hostile uses of environmental modification techniques, a US government spokesman stated during the ratification hearings before the US Senate Committee on Foreign Relations that the Convention does prohibit the use of herbicides for destruction, damage or injury, and if the effects are "widespread, long-lasting or severe" (the terms used in the Convention to qualify the ban on environmental modification).

As a legal constraint, the Geneva Protocol has been weakened by reservations made by a number of states, which limit its applicability to nations party to it and to first use only, thereby preserving the right to retaliate with the weapons in question (see section IV).

1949 Geneva Conventions

When World War II broke out, the following agreements for the protection of war victims were in force: the Convention for the amelioration of the condition of the wounded and sick in armies in the field (which replaced the Red Cross Geneva Conventions of 22 August 1864 and 6 July 1906) and the Convention relative to the treatment of prisoners of war, both of which were signed on 27 July 1929. Hague Convention X, of 1907, for the adaptation to maritime warfare of the principles of the 1906 Geneva Convention was also in force. But neither these nor other international instruments then in existence proved sufficient to provide humanitarian safeguards during World War II. Indeed, the shock of the discovery of mass crimes committed during that war led to the 1948 Convention on the prevention and punishment of the crime of genocide, known as the Genocide Convention. This Convention declares genocide (defined as the commission of acts intended to destroy, in whole or in part, a national, ethnical, racial or religious group, as such) to be a punishable crime.

Further rules were worked out at a conference held in Geneva in 1949, and were included in the following four conventions: Convention I for the amelioration of the condition of the wounded and sick in armed forces in the field; Convention II for the amelioration of the condition of the wounded, sick and shipwrecked members of armed forces at sea; Convention III relative to the treatment of prisoners of war; and Convention IV relative to the protection of civilian persons in time of war.

The 1949 Geneva Conventions for the protection of war victims, almost universally adhered to, were conceived primarily as a code of behaviour in wars of the traditional type, conducted between states and between regular armed forces. (Convention IV primarily concerned the protection of the civilian population under the control of an enemy power.) However, since World War II, most armed conflicts have been civil wars, or have started as such. Guerrilla warfare has been the prevalent type of armed conflict and has complicated the application of the principle that a distinction must be observed between the civilian and the military. As a result, the protection of civilians has weakened considerably. Furthermore, the laws of war which relate directly to the methods and means of warfare, as distinct from rules designed to accord protection to certain persons, places or objects in armed conflicts, had not developed since the 1907 Hague Conventions, with the sole exception of the 1925 Geneva Protocol. In particular, air warfare had remained to a great extent uncodified; area bombardment, which caused the destruction of many cities in World War II, was not expressly forbidden; and weapons which had come into existence during the past decades and which were of an especially cruel nature had not been specifically prohibited.

Protocols

To deal with all these matters, a Diplomatic Conference on the reaffirmation and development of international law applicable in armed conflicts was convened in Geneva in 1974. In 1977, at the end of the fourth session of the Conference, two protocols were adopted: Protocol I, relating to the protection of victims of international armed conflicts; and Protocol II, relating to the protection of victims of non-international armed conflicts.

Protocol 1 reiterates the basic 'Hague rules': namely, that the right of the parties to an armed conflict to choose methods or means of warfare is not unlimited, and that it is prohibited to use weapons, projectiles and material and methods of warfare of a nature that causes superfluous injury or unnecessary suffering. In addition, the parties are under an obligation to determine in their study, development, acquisition or adoption of a new weapon, means or methods of warfare, whether its employment would in some or all circumstances be prohibited by the Protocol or other rules of international law. But there seems to be a tacit understanding among states belonging to the two major military alliances that the new rules of warfare established by the Protocol do not regulate the use of nuclear weapons.

The Protocol also reiterates and expands the traditional rules regarding the protection of the civilian population. The prohibition against indiscriminate attacks now covers attacks by bombardment via any methods or means which treat as a single military objective a number of distinct objectives located in a city, town, village or other area containing a similar concentration of civilians or civilian objects. It also covers attacks expected to cause incidental losses or injuries to civilians, which would be excessive in relation to the direct military advantage anticipated. Reprisals against the civilian population are forbidden.

Furthermore, it is prohibited to destroy foodstuffs, agricultural areas for the production of foodstuffs, crops, livestock, drinking water installations and supplies and irrigation works, for the specific purpose of denying the civilian population those objects which are indispensable for its survival. However, in recognition of the vital requirements of any party to the conflict in the defence of its national territory against invasion, derogation of these prohibitions may be made by a party within such territory under its own control where required by "imperative military necessity". Dams, dykes and nuclear electric power generating stations have been placed under special protection and shall not be attacked if an attack on them may cause severe losses among civilians. This protection will cease if the installations in question are used in significant and direct support of military operations and if an attack on them is the only feasible way to terminate such support.

Detailed precautionary measures are prescribed to spare the civilian population and civilian objects in the conduct of military operations. There is a prohibition to attack, by any means, non-defended localities, declared as such by the appropriate authorities of a party, or to extend military operations to zones on which the parties have conferred by agreement the status of demilitarized zone. Members of civil defence organizations and journalists engaged in dangerous professional missions in areas of armed conflict shall also be protected.

Several articles dealing with relief actions in favour of the civilian population have strengthened the corresponding clauses of the 1949 Geneva

Convention IV. The duties of the occupying power include the provision, to the fullest extent of the means available, of supplies essential to the survival of the civilian population of the occupied territory.

A special provision is devoted to the protection of the natural environment against widespread, long-term and severe damage.[13] It includes a prohibition on the use of methods and means of warfare that are intended or may be expected to cause such damage to the natural environment and thereby to prejudice the health or survival of the population.

Protocol I is applicable not only to inter-state armed conflicts, but also to conflicts in which peoples are fighting against colonial domination and alien occupation and against racist regimes in the exercise of their right to self-determination. In this way, guerrilla fighters have been covered by international protection. In particular, they have been given the right to prisoner-of-war status if they belong to organized units subject to an internal disciplinary system and under a command responsible to the party concerned. They also have to carry their arms openly during each military engagement, and during such time as they are visible to the adversary before launching an attack. On the other hand, mercenaries, as defined in the Protocol, have not been granted the combatant or prisoner-of-war status.

Protocol II develops and supplements Article 3, which appears in all four Geneva Conventions of 1949, and which deals with armed conflicts not of an international character. It prescribes humane treatment of all the persons involved in such conflicts, care for the wounded, sick and shipwrecked, as well as protection of civilians against the dangers arising from military operations. It does not apply to internal disturbances, such as riots, sporadic acts of violence and similar acts.

Convention on 'inhumane' weapons

Protocols I and II of 1977 constitute an important step forward in the development of the humanitarian laws of war, even though some of the provisions lack clarity or have been weakened by exemptions, and certain definitions are imprecise. From the point of view of arms control, their main shortcoming is that they have not restricted or forbidden the use of any specific weapon. To fill this gap, a special UN conference was convened in 1979. It discussed the problem of so-called inhumane weapons. While no weapon can be considered humane, there are substantial differences in the effects weapons produce on individual combatants or civilians, in particular as regards the magnitude and severity of the wounds and the duration of the injury caused, as well as in the extent of the area covered and the degree of control that can be exercised by their user.

In 1980, at the conclusion of its second session, the UN conference adopted the text of the Convention on prohibitions or restrictions on the use

---

[13] This formulation is more restricted than that included in the 1977 Environmental Modification Convention, because it requires the presence of all the three effects—widespread, long-term and severe—for the method and means of warfare to be prohibited.

of certain conventional weapons which may be deemed to be excessively injurious or to have indiscriminate effects.

Signed in 1981, the Convention applies to international conflicts in the same way as Protocol I of the 1949 Geneva Conventions. It has the format of an 'umbrella treaty', under which specific agreements can be subsumed in the form of protocols. Three protocols were agreed in the first instance.

Protocol I prohibits the use of any weapon whose "primary" effect is to injure by fragments which in the human body escape detection by X-rays. Prohibiting a weapon whose design makes medical treatment very difficult has a clear humanitarian appeal, but in this particular case it is of little consequence, as the weapon prohibited does not exist, and no one seems to have any serious military interest in developing it. The use of other fragmentation weapons that exist has not been banned.

On the other hand, Protocol II, which prohibits or restricts the use of mines, booby-traps and similar devices, deals with a real problem, as it aims at preventing or at least reducing civilian casualties caused by these devices during and after the hostilities. Mines are defined as any munitions placed under, on, or near the ground or other surface area and designed to be detonated or exploded by the presence, proximity or contact of a person or vehicle. Booby-traps are defined as any devices or materials designed, constructed or adapted to kill or injure, and which function unexpectedly when a person disturbs or approaches an apparently harmless object or performs an apparently safe act. "Other devices" covered by Protocol II are defined as manually emplaced munitions and devices designed to kill, injure or damage which are actuated by remote control or automatically after a lapse of time.

The use of mines, booby-traps and other devices against the civilian population as such, or against individual civilians, is prohibited in all circumstances, whether in offence or defence or by way of reprisal. Also prohibited is the indiscriminate use of all these devices against military objectives in conditions which may be expected to cause incidental loss of civilian life, injury to civilians or damage to civilian objects, excessive in relation to the concrete and direct military advantage anticipated. Booby-traps designed to cause superfluous injury or unnecessary suffering are prohibited in all circumstances.

The Protocol bans the use of remotely delivered mines, that is, those delivered by artillery, rocket, mortar or similar means, or dropped from an aircraft, unless such mines are only used within an area which is itself a military objective or which contains military objectives, and unless the location of mines can be accurately recorded, or a neutralizing mechanism is used to render a mine harmless or cause it to destroy itself when it no longer serves the military purpose for which it was placed in position. Guidelines on recording the location of minefields, mines and booby-traps are contained in an annex to the Protocol. International co-operation in the removal of the devices in question after the cessation of hostilities is provided for in a separate article.

The Protocol does not apply to the use of anti-ship mines at sea or in inland waterways. In this respect, the rules which were adopted at the beginning of the century, and which deal with automatic submarine contact mines, are still valid.

Protocol III refers to the use of incendiary weapons. Incendiary weapons are defined as those weapons or munitions which are primarily designed to set fire to objects or to cause burn injury to persons through the action of flame, heat, or a combination thereof, produced by a chemical reaction of a substance delivered on the target, as for example: flame throwers, fougasses, shells, rockets, grenades, mines, bombs and other containers of incendiary substances. Munitions which may have only incidental incendiary effects, such as illuminants, tracers, smoke or signalling systems, are excluded from the scope of the Protocol. The same applies to munitions designed to combine penetration, blast or fragmentation effects with an additional incendiary effect. Such munitions are armour-piercing projectiles, fragmentation shells, explosive bombs and similar combined-effects munitions in which the incendiary effect is not specifically designed to cause burn injury to persons, but to be used against such military objectives as armoured vehicles, aircraft and installations or facilities.

The prohibitions and restrictions introduced by Protocol III aim only at the protection of civilians. Thus, it is prohibited in all circumstances to make the civilian population as such, individual civilians or civilian objects the object of attack by incendiary weapons. It is also prohibited to make a military objective situated within a concentration of civilians the object of attack by air-delivered incendiary weapons. (This prohibition would protect some military personnel as well.)

But even the protection of civilians is qualified: military objectives which are located within populated areas but which are clearly separated from a concentration of civilians are excluded from the restriction in respect of ground-delivered incendiary weapons. The Protocol stipulates that all feasible precautions should be taken in order to limit the incendiary effects to the military objective and to avoid or minimize incidental loss of civilian life, injury to civilians and damage to civilian objects. The meaning of "feasible precautions" is explained in the Protocol but may be subject to divergent interpretations.

The Protocol also prohibits attacks with incendiary weapons on forests or other kinds of plant cover, except when these are used to cover, conceal or camouflage combatants or other military objectives, or are themselves military objectives. A general prohibition of the use of incendiary weapons in war, as advocated by a group of non-aligned and neutral nations, could not be reached.

The most serious deficiency of Protocol III is that it does not protect combatants. Evidently, incendiary weapons are still considered by certain countries as too militarily useful to be outlawed. Thus, the scope of the ban on the use of incendiary weapons is considerably narrower than the one concerning chemical weapons.

In spite of the described shortcomings, the 1981 Convention must be regarded as an achievement, because in regulating the use of certain weapons in certain circumstances it has given precedence to humanitarian imperatives over military considerations. An appropriate legal framework has been created within which further advances in the field of humanitarian rules of law can be made. The next step could be, for example, the introduction of restrictions on small-calibre weapon systems. In 1979, at the first session of the Conference which drafted the Convention, a resolution was adopted appealing to all governments to exercise the utmost care in the development of these systems, so as to avoid an unnecessary escalation of their injurious effects. In this context, reference was made to the 1899 Hague Declaration, under which states agreed to abstain from the use of dum dum bullets. In any event, in the preamble of the Convention, the parties expressed their determination that in cases not covered by international agreements, the civilian population and the combatants shall at all times remain under the protection and authority of the principles of international law "derived from established custom, from the principles of humanity and from the dictates of public conscience".[14]

It should be noted that nuclear and other weapons of mass destruction were not considered at the Conference which adopted the Convention on inhumane weapons, even though weapons of mass destruction obviously fall under the category of arms which are excessively injurious or have indiscriminate effects. Possible bans or restrictions on the use of these weapons are being dealt with in other international bodies, both multilateral and regional, often in conjunction with prohibitions on their development, production, stockpiling or proliferation. Nevertheless, even in the absence of specific legal norms, the legality of the use of weapons of mass destruction is open to question in the light of the principles of international law, as enshrined in the conventions already in force.

Laws of war and disarmament

All laws of war suffer from one common weakness: the rules of conduct established for belligerents in time of peace may not resist the pressure of military expedience generated in the course of hostilities, and the attempts to 'humanize' war may sometimes prove futile. The danger that the weapons prohibited may, under certain circumstances, be resorted to—as has occurred on several occasions—will not disappear as long as these weapons remain in the arsenals of states. Hence the intrinsic link between the development of the humanitarian laws of war and progress in the field of disarmament.

---

[14] This is a paraphrase of the so-called Martens clause which appears in the Hague Conventions.

4. Verification and enforcement of arms control obligations

The problems associated with breaches of obligation have been an important issue in all arms control negotiations because states are generally reluctant to depend solely on good faith when such vital matters as national security are involved.

I. Role and functions of verification

There is, of course, no way of preventing sovereign governments from openly or secretly violating international commitments if they choose to disregard the potential consequences of their actions. They may, however, be deterred from committing violations if they fear losing the advantages they have originally gained from the treaty, if they dread an expected or unpredictable response from the injured states, or if they are sufficiently sensitive to public disapproval to wish to avoid an unfavourable reaction in their own or in other countries. Deterrence of secret violations presupposes the ability to detect them, and timely detection is important, particularly in cases constituting an immediate military threat, because it might enable the injured party to redress the situation. The deterrence function is the main purpose of verification clauses in arms control treaties. In addition, through possible 'negative' results, that is, by confirming that activities prohibited by agreements are *not* taking place and that the parties are fulfilling their obligations, verification may help to generate a climate of international confidence which is indispensable for progress in arms control.

Insistence on verification measures which are obviously unacceptable to another party, or refusal to accept verification measures which are obviously indispensable, have often been used as convenient excuses for blocking an arms control agreement when the real reason was inconvenient to admit. Normally, verification provisions should cover procedures for acquiring information about the parties' performance with respect to their undertakings, for instituting an inquiry in cases requiring clarification, and for dealing with complaints of violations. Not all these requirements have been met in each of the arms control agreements concluded hitherto.

II. Acquisition of information under bilateral agreements

Strategic arms limitations

Under the US–Soviet strategic arms limitation agreements, information necessary to ascertain compliance is to be collected by use of the "national technical means of verification''. These means include satellites[1] for reconnaissance (photographic and electronic) and early warning, as well as radar and other intelligence-gathering systems. (Satellites launched from 1972 to 1981 are listed in table 4.1.) The use of satellites for legitimate supervision purposes gave international recognition to the principle of 'open skies', which the United States had advocated since the 1950s. There is also a ban on interference with the permissible means of verification which covers the use (but not the development or testing) of anti-satellite systems against another state's satellites serving verification purposes.

Table 4.1. Satellites for reconnaissance and early warning, launched during 1972[a]–81

Note: On the whole, Soviet satellites have a considerably shorter life-time than US satellites; this may explain the higher figures for the USSR.

Year	Photographic reconnaissance satellites			Electronic reconnaissance satellites		Early-warning satellites	
	USA	USSR	China	USA	USSR	USA	USSR
1972	8	30	–	3	7	2	1
1973	5	35	–	2	12	2	1
1974	5	28	–	3	10	–	1
1975	4	34	1	2	8	2	2
1976	4	34	1	1	11	1	1
1977	3	33	–	–	8	2	3
1978	2	35	1	1	6	2	2
1979	2	35	–	1	5	2	2
1980	2	35	–	1	6	–	5
1981	2	37	–	–	4	2	5
Total by country	37	336	3	14	77	15	23
Total by mission	**376**			**91**		**38**	

[a] The year 1972 was chosen since it is the year when the SALT I agreements, verified mainly by satellites, were signed.

Deliberate concealment measures which impede verification by national technical means (e.g., placing shelters over silos for intercontinental ballistic missile (ICBM) launchers or over submarine pens) are also banned. The 1979 SALT II Treaty specifies that even testing activities must not be concealed. Thus, measures to conceal the association between ICBMs and their launchers during testing are prohibited, and the deliberate denial of telemetric information (radio signals normally sent from a missile to ground monitors during a flight test), for example by encryption, is not allowed whenever such denial impedes verification.

---

[1] In the debate on the Outer Space Treaty, it was assumed that satellite reconnaissance, like any other form of observation of a state from outside its territorial limits, violates no provision of international law.

The USA and the USSR agreed on appropriate notification to aid verification. There is a requirement for prior notification of certain ICBM flight tests, of the inclusion in nuclear inventories of new types of heavy bombers and of additional types of MIRVed ballistic missiles (i.e., those equipped with multiple independently targetable re-entry vehicles), as well as of the location of any new ICBM test range. Rules for counting many of the systems limited by the SALT agreements, as well as criteria for distinguishing between different systems, have also been established.

A series of allegations were made of non-compliance with the 1972 ABM (Anti-Ballistic Missile) Treaty and the 1972 Interim Agreement for the limitation of strategic offensive arms. (By spring 1982, the 1979 SALT II agreements were not yet ratified.) In particular, the USSR was formally accused of constructing additional ICBM silos, testing an air defence system radar in an ABM mode, increasing the number of heavy missiles above the permitted level, concealing relevant activities from detection by US national technical means of verification, not following the agreed procedures in dismantling excess launchers at an ABM test range, establishing a new ABM test range, and failing to dismantle older ICBM launchers being replaced with launchers on ballistic missile submarines.

Only in one case did the USSR admit that it had not fulfilled its commitments, namely that it had not met the stipulated time-limits for dismantling the ICBM launchers being replaced by SLBMs. It undertook to complete the operation within a few months.

The Soviet Union has also put forward accusations. It challenged the construction of a new US phased-array radar as inconsistent with the provisions of the ABM Treaty, the dismantling of ABM facilities not in full accord with the agreed procedures, and the placement of shelters over ICBM silos. The USA denied the charges.

On the whole, considering the complexity and the ambiguous language of the SALT I agreements, the record of the implementation of the formal clauses of the accords does not seem to be unsatisfactory. With the exception of the admitted failure to dismantle ICBM launchers, allegations have arisen from misunderstandings or excessive reliance on statements made during the negotiations by one side (and subsequently included in a separate document initialed by the heads of the delegations) but not accepted by the other side. This was, for example, the case of the US definition of "heavy missile" or the US interpretation of the term "tested in an ABM mode". Complaints about non-compliance with the spirit, as opposed to the letter, of the accords were based on different perceptions of the goals pursued by each side in the arms limitation exercise. At the same time, the debate about violations has disclosed some information about the degree of accuracy of national means of verification, which is rated rather high.

Intelligence-gathering systems operate irrespective of arms control obligations, but while intelligence is meant to determine the characteristics or activities of the adversary's weapons and forces, verification must assess whether these characteristics or activities exceed the limitations imposed by treaties. The verification requirements under the SALT agreements facilitate the performance of the latter tasks.

Nuclear test limitations

National means are also stipulated for assuring compliance with the 1974 US–Soviet Threshold Test Ban Treaty (TTBT). In this case, seismic monitoring is the most useful method for determining whether a seismic event has a strength exceeding the agreed limit (threshold) and, if so, whether it is an explosion or a natural earthquake. Existing seismic methods can identify nuclear explosions by the shock wave pattern or 'signature' of the event, but yield determination also requires knowledge about the environment in which the test has been carried out and about the explosions previously performed at the same site. Accordingly, the USA and the USSR have agreed to exchange the information needed to establish a correlation between yields of explosions at specific sites and the seismic signals produced. An undertaking under the TTBT not to interfere with the national technical means of verification of the other party can be understood as an undertaking not to use evasion techniques. Most important is the commitment of the parties to conduct all nuclear weapon tests solely within specified testing areas. At the time of signing the TTBT, the USA stated that it had a substantial degree of confidence, within a factor that is fully tolerable for military purposes, that it would recognize violations of the ban as long as the testing took place at known sites.

In recent years the USA has complained that several Soviet explosions have exceeded the agreed yield limit. Conclusive proof of such a breach would have to be based on world-wide seismic recordings, but these recordings were not concordant. The exchange of information, envisaged by the TTBT and necessary to improve each side's assessments of the yields of explosions based on the measurements derived from its own seismic instruments, has not taken place, pending ratification of the Treaty.

The provisions of the TTBT did not extend to underground nuclear explosions which may have peaceful applications. Since such explosions cannot be distinguished from tests serving military ends, a possibility was left open to circumvent the threshold limitation. Moreover, the information to be provided under the TTBT was not meant for monitoring the size of explosions conducted in areas where peaceful applications would take place, namely, outside the designated weapon test sites. For these reasons, the Peaceful Nuclear Explosions Treaty (PNET), concluded in 1976, established the same yield threshold for peaceful application as had been imposed on weapon tests under the TTBT, namely 150 kt. A group explosion for peaceful purposes may exceed the limit if it is carried out in such a way that individual explosions in the group can be identified and their yields determined to be no more than 150 kt. To facilitate verification, the parties undertook to supply each other with information on the purpose, location, depth of the emplacement of the explosive, date and yield of the explosion, as well as the geological and geophysical characteristics of the site which could influence the determination of yield.

Since it is difficult, with distant seismic measuring instruments alone, to determine the yield of individual explosions if they occur within a few seconds of each other, observers of the verifying party are to be given access to the site of a group explosion. They could check that the local circumstances were consistent with the stated peaceful purposes, examine the validity of the geological and geophysical information provided, observe the emplacement of each explosive, and observe the explosions. Their main function, however, would be to measure the yield of each individual explosion in the group with the use of special equipment. If the verifying side wanted to use its own equipment instead of that provided by the party carrying out the explosion, an elaborate procedure would be followed to assure that there was no abuse and that the observers did not acquire unwarranted information. Thus, two identical sets of instruments would be made available by the verifying side; the side conducting the explosion would choose one set for actual use by the verifying side, while the other set could be taken apart and examined. Acquisition of photographs would be permitted only under specified conditions and only with cameras having a built-in, rapid film-developing capability, so that the pictures could be immediately inspected.

For any group explosion with a planned aggregate yield exceeding 500 kt, the observers would, in addition, have the right to install and operate a local seismic network to help ascertain that no undeclared explosions were taking place along with the announced explosions.

On-site observation is envisaged also for some explosions with a planned aggregate yield of between 100 and 150 kt, but the need for such observation would have to be mutually agreed between the parties; it is not mandatory, as with explosions exceeding 150 kt. The scope of the observer functions in this case would be narrower than in the case of explosions with higher yields.

The protocol to the PNET contains detailed provisions regulating the number of observers, the geographical extent of their access, and their equipment, records and immunities. The observers are expressly forbidden to have or to seek access by physical, visual or technical means to the interior of the canister containing an explosive, to documentary or other information descriptive of the design of an explosive, or to equipment for the control and firing of explosives.

Occasions for inviting representatives of the other side to observe peaceful nuclear explosions would probably arise only rarely, if ever, because apparently neither nuclear power has, as yet, established practical applications for such explosions. But the very acceptance of on-site observation is noteworthy as a breakthrough in the great powers' approach, notably in the Soviet Union's approach, to the problem of verification. It could become a precedent for future arms control measures.

III. Acquisition of information under multilateral agreements

Antarctic Treaty

The best developed system for the acquisition of information for verification purposes is found in the 1959 Antarctic Treaty, which declared that Antarctica shall be used exclusively for peaceful purposes. Each party to this Treaty is obliged to inform the other parties of all expeditions to and within Antarctica, of all stations occupied there by its nationals, and of any military personnel or equipment intended to be introduced into Antarctica for scientific research or other peaceful purposes. The Treaty provides for complete freedom of access by the parties, at any time, to any area of Antarctica. All areas, including stations, installations and equipment within these areas, and all ships and aircraft at points of discharging or embarking cargoes or personnel are to be open at all times to inspection. Aerial observation is allowed. In addition, scientific personnel may be exchanged between expeditions and stations. However, only the original parties are entitled to designate observers to carry out inspections or aerial observation. Acceding states may participate in these activities if they conduct "substantial" scientific research in Antarctica.

Outer Space Treaty

The verification principles embodied in the Antarctic Treaty have been applied to a certain extent in the 1967 Outer Space Treaty, which prohibits the stationing in outer space of weapons of mass destruction. The parties have agreed to inform the UN Secretary-General as well as the public and the international scientific community, "to the greatest extent feasible and practicable", of the nature, conduct, locations and results of their activities in outer space. It is in fulfilment of this provision that the 1975 Convention on registration of objects launched into outer space was concluded. Moreover, under the 1979 Agreement concerning the Moon and other celestial bodies, which has developed the relevant provisions of the Outer Space Treaty, all space vehicles, equipment, facilities, stations and installations on the Moon are to be open to other parties. However, there is no provision for verifying the ban on placing weapons of mass destruction in orbit around the Earth (earlier proposals for inspecting space vehicles on their launch pads were abandoned), nor has the requirement of international verification been included in the draft treaty prohibiting the stationing of weapons of any kind in outer space, as proposed by the Soviet Union in 1981. Compliance with this treaty would have to be assured with the national technical means of verification at the disposal of the parties.

Treaty of Tlatelolco

Under the 1967 Treaty prohibiting nuclear weapons in Latin America, each

95

party must apply the International Atomic Energy Agency (IAEA) safeguards to its nuclear activities. It must also submit periodic reports stating that no activity prohibited under the Treaty has occurred on its territory. Supplementary information regarding any event or circumstance connected with compliance with the Treaty may be requested by the General Secretary of the Agency for the Prohibition of Nuclear Weapons in Latin America. Special inspections, in addition to those routinely conducted by the IAEA, can be carried out either in accordance with the agreements concluded with the IAEA, or when a party suspects that some activity prohibited by the Treaty has been carried out or is about to be carried out on the territory of another party, or following a request by a party suspected of or charged with having violated the Treaty. Those carrying out special inspections must be granted full and free access to all places and to all information which may be necessary for the performance of their duties and which are directly connected with the suspicion of violation of the Treaty. There are no provisions for verifying the obligation undertaken by the nuclear weapon states under Additional Protocol II—to respect the status of the Latin American nuclear weapon-free zone.

Non-Proliferation Treaty

Under the terms of the 1968 NPT, non-nuclear weapon parties must accept IAEA safeguards for the purpose of verification of the fulfilment of their obligation not to acquire nuclear weapons or other nuclear explosive devices. The safeguards are to be applied to all source or special fissionable material in all peaceful nuclear activities within the territories of such states, under their jurisdiction, or carried out under their control anywhere. The structure and content of agreements between the Agency and states required in connection with the NPT (as distinct from safeguards agreements which had been in existence prior to the NPT, and which applied only to specific materials and to individual plants exported under bilateral nuclear co-operation agreements) were agreed to in 1971 and incorporated in an IAEA document. The NPT provides that these agreements must be concluded either by individual states or by groups of states (the latter provision was included to meet the request by EURATOM, the European Atomic Energy Community, which has its own system of control) within the prescribed time-limits of 24 months for the original parties and 18 months for states acceding later. Pursuant to a safeguards agreement, the IAEA also concludes subsidiary arrangements which contain technical and operational details.

NPT safeguards consist of three main elements: material accountancy, containment and surveillance. These should enable timely detection of the diversion of significant quantities of nuclear material from peaceful activities to the manufacture of nuclear explosive devices, as well as the deterrence of diversion by creating the risk of early detection. A Standing Advisory Group on safeguards implementation, established in 1975, provides the IAEA with recommendations on the formulation of such basic criteria as "timely" detection and "significant" quantities, in order to make it possible to measure the effectiveness of safeguards activities. As an additional precautionary measure against diversion, the 1980 Convention on the physical protection of nuclear material requires that storage of such material, incidental to international transport, must be within an area under constant surveillance by guards or electronic devices and surrounded by a physical barrier with a limited number of points of entry. According to IAEA annual reports, nuclear material under Agency safeguards has so far remained in peaceful nuclear activities or has been otherwise adequately accounted for.

It should be noted, however, that fully effective safeguards for the most sensitive parts of the fuel cycle—enrichment and reprocessing—remain to be elaborated. Although optimistic statements have been made about the accuracy of material accountancy in enrichment plants, there has not been much experience with international safeguarding of these plants. Similarly, the only IAEA experience to date in safeguarding reprocessing facilities has been with small or pilot plants. The large quantities of plutonium involved in commercial reprocessing will considerably complicate material account-ancy; a margin of error in the accountancy may facilitate the diversion of plutonium in quantities which are significant from the point of view of nuclear weapon proliferation.

There is no provision in the NPT for controlling compliance with the obligation not to transfer nuclear weapons or other nuclear explosive devices.

Sea-Bed Treaty

Parties to the 1971 Sea-Bed Treaty, which prohibits the emplacement of nuclear and other weapons of mass destruction beyond the limits of a defined sea-bed zone, have the right to verify, by observation, the activities of other states on the sea-bed and the ocean floor and in the subsoil thereof outside the zone, provided that observation does not interfere with such activities. The possibility of "appropriate" inspection of objects, structures, installations or other facilities, which may reasonably be expected to be of a kind prohibited in the Treaty, is also envisaged.

Partial Test Ban Treaty

The 1963 multilateral Partial Test Ban Treaty, prohibiting nuclear weapon tests in the atmosphere, outer space or under water, contains no provision for checking whether the parties are complying with their commitments. The parties are presumed to monitor the terms of the Treaty unilaterally, using their own means of verification. These means, which may include both physical methods and conventional intelligence gathering, were deemed to be sufficient. Actually, the ban is not likely to be violated by the nuclear weapon parties to the Treaty, as long as they are permitted to test underground. The prospective gains from secret atmospheric explosions are relatively small when compared to the cost of concealment and the risk of detection.

However, a clandestine atmospheric test by a nascent nuclear weapon state, carried out outside its territory to conceal the identity of the tester, cannot be ruled out. The mysterious event which was detected on 22 September 1979 by a US satellite in the southern hemisphere, in a region which includes parts of the Indian and South Atlantic Oceans as well as Southern Africa and Antarctica and which may have been a low-yield nuclear explosion in the atmosphere, has not been cleared up. South Africa, which was accused by many members of the United Nations of being the testing nation, denied having any knowledge of a nuclear explosion occurring in its vicinity.

The clause of the PTBT that prohibits any nuclear explosion causing the debris to be present outside the territorial limits of the state conducting the explosion is difficult to enforce. There have been complaints of radioactive leakages spreading outside the territory of the testing states party to the PTBT, but all such occurrences were treated as 'technical' rather than deliberate violations. Indeed, radioactive material venting from an underground test to the surface cannot always be entirely contained within national boundaries.

Comprehensive test ban

In a comprehensive test ban the problem of verification would be more complex. It is believed that covert testing can provide an advantage to the cheating party, either in the field of weapon development or in maintaining confidence in the reliability of weapons already stockpiled. It is also impossible to obtain, through national means alone, the same degree of assurance that the prohibition is being observed as in the partial ban. Verification provisions must, therefore, be included in a treaty banning underground nuclear tests.

Whatever additional methods might be used by individual nations, seismological means of verification will certainly constitute the principal component of an international control system for an underground test ban. With this in mind, the Geneva-based Committee on Disarmament established an *ad hoc* group of scientific experts to consider international co-operative measures to detect and identify seismic events. The group has suggested that these measures should include a systematic improvement of procedures at seismological observatories around the globe, an international exchange of seismic data and the processing of the data at special international data centres.

The experts consider that a seismological verification system should comprise about 50 globally distributed teleseismic stations selected in accordance with seismological requirements and that there should be routine reporting by these stations of basic parameters of detected seismic signals, as well as transmission of data in response to requests for additional information regarding events of particular interest. (The desirable global network of seismograph stations to detect, locate and identify seismic events is shown in figure 4.1.) International centres would receive the data mentioned above, apply agreed analysis procedures to these data in order to estimate the location, magnitude and depth of seismic events, associate identification parameters with these events, distribute compilations of the complete results of these analyses and act as a data bank.

Figure 4.1.   Desirable global network of seismograph stations

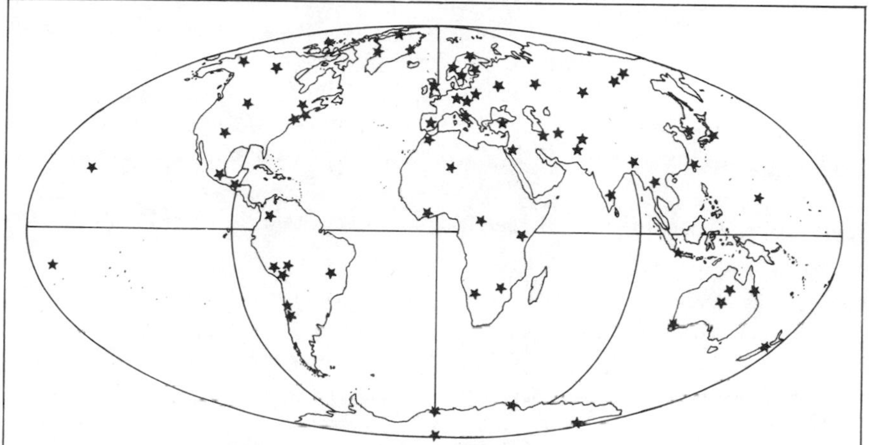

Although the global seismic network can provide a high degree of confidence that a comprehensive test ban is not being violated, there may still be events of uncertain origin. One way to reduce this uncertainty, which in most cases will be related to earthquake areas, could be for the state in question to provide seismic data for the suspected event from local stations not belonging to the global network.

The UK, the USA and the USSR, partners in the tripartite test ban negotiations, agreed to develop measures of reciprocal verification, independent of the envisaged international co-operative measures, in order to obtain supplemental seismic data from high-quality, tamper-proof national seismic stations (NSSs) of agreed characteristics. Ten NSSs would be installed on the territories of the USA and of the USSR, but no agreement could be reached regarding the number of such stations in the UK. Questions regarding specific locations of the NSSs, their emplacement and maintenance as well as the transmission of data produced by them have not been settled.

Assuming that the above problems may eventually be satisfactorily solved, the clarification of possible remaining doubts as to the nature of a seismic event would still require on-site inspection. The three negotiating powers agreed on the possibility of having such inspections, but the procedure for setting in motion the inspection process (including the nature of the evidence needed to justify a request for on-site inspection), the modalities of the inspection itself (including the equipment to be used), as well as the number, rights and functions of the inspectors, remain to be specified.

Other unresolved questions pertaining to the verification of a comprehensive test ban are whether the data from British, US and Soviet NSSs would be generally available, and whether on-site inspections on the territories of the three powers would be conducted with the participation of other states as well.

Prohibitions on biological and chemical weapons

In the 1972 BW Convention, no verification measures were envisaged *vis-à-vis* the obligations not to develop or produce biological or toxin weapons. The parties are not even formally obliged to prove that they have complied with the commitment to destroy the stocks of these weapons or to divert them to peaceful purposes. Nevertheless, statements were made by a

Table 4.2. Alleged instances of chemical and biological warfare, 1975[a]–81

Alleged user and occasion	Period	Weapons allegedly used
Laotian and Vietnamese forces in Laos	1975–81	Mustard gas, irritants, nerve gas and mycotoxins spread by aircraft
Both sides during Shaba rebellion in Zaire	May 1977	Poison arrows
South African forces during air attack on Kassinga, Angola	May 1978	"Paralyzing gas"
Vietnamese forces in Kampuchea	1978–81	Irritants, cyanide, tabun and mycotoxins spread by aircraft or artillery; poisoning of water
US covert action (CIA) in Cuba	1978–81	Causing sugar-cane rust, blue mould of tobacco, African swine fever and, in people, dengue fever and haemorrhagic conjunctivitis
Vietnamese forces against Chinese	February 1979	"Poison gas"
Chinese forces in Viet Nam	February 1979	"Toxic gas" and "poisoning of drinking water sources"
Soviet forces in Afghanistan	1979–81	Nerve gas, irritants, incapacitants and mycotoxins spread by aircraft and ground weapons; toxic bullets
Insurgent forces in Afghanistan	1980–81	"Lethal chemical grenades" allegedly supplied by the USA
Ethiopian forces against Eritrean secessionists and in conflict with Somalia	Summer 1980	"Chemical warfare" (allegations coincide with reports of nerve-gas supplies)
	April 1981	"Chemical spraying"
Iraqi forces in occupied territory of Iran	November 1980	"Chemical bombs"
Salvadorean Army and National Guard in El Salvador against guerrilla forces	1981	"Toxic gas", "chemical bombs" and "acid spray"

[a] The year 1975 was chosen since it is the year when the BW Convention entered into force.

number of countries that no prohibited weapons or equipment were present on their territories.

In recent years, serious accusations have been put forward regarding the actual use of biological and toxin weapons. The governments implicated in the reports of use of these weapons as well as of chemical means of warfare include those of China, El Salvador, Ethiopia, Iraq, Laos, South Africa, the USA, the USSR and Viet Nam. (For a summary of alleged instances of chemical and biological warfare during 1975–81, see table 4.2.)

Particularly wide international press coverage was given to US reports on the employment by Soviet and Vietnamese forces in military operations in Afghanistan, Laos and Kampuchea of mycotoxins, known as T2 toxins (in the form of a "yellow powder"), that cause blisters, vomiting, haemorrhaging of mucous membranes, diarrhoea and death. The accusations followed those repeatedly made by the USA since 1978 about the use of some undefined chemical warfare agents against the guerrilla or civilian populations in south-east Asia.

The BW Convention does not contain a provision explicitly prohibiting the use of biological agents or toxins, but it proclaims the determination of the parties to "exclude completely" the possibility of these agents or toxins being used as weapons. Indeed, since both production and retention are explicitly banned, so must also be the use, because use presupposes possession. Moreover, the Convention has recognized the important significance of the 1925 Geneva Protocol, which prohibits the use of both chemical and biological weapons. It reaffirms the principles and objectives of that Protocol and calls upon all states to comply strictly with them. It will be noted in this connection that the prohibition on the use of CB weapons has become part of customary international law, and all states must therefore be regarded as being bound to refrain from such use, whether or not they are parties to the Protocol. Nevertheless, there exists no mechanism for checking allegations concerning the employment of the prohibited weapons, nor a mechanism to protect parties against ill-considered allegations of violation.

To remedy this serious deficiency, the UN General Assembly decided in 1980 to carry out an impartial investigation to ascertain the facts pertaining to reports of the alleged use of such weapons and to assess the extent of the damage caused.[2] A group of experts was set up to seek relevant information and to "collect and examine evidence, including on-site with the consent of the countries concerned". The first report of the group, submitted in 1981, was inconclusive. Indeed, since it was impossible to ensure timely access to the areas where the prohibited warfare agents had allegedly been used, no definitive conclusions could be reached.

There have also been allegations of illegal production or retention of biological warfare agents.

In 1980 the USA said that the outbreak a year before in Sverdlovsk,

---

[2] The reports submitted by the USA regarding south-east Asia were based on information provided by the refugees and on medical records, including public health data.

USSR, of a disease caused by anthrax, a bacterium generally considered to be a candidate for biological warfare activities, had raised questions concerning compliance by the USSR with the BW Convention. The Western press reported that an accident had taken place in a plant producing biological warfare agents. The Soviet Union denied that it had acted contrary to the provisions of the Convention, and explained that the anthrax epidemic had been caused by infected meat. The USA proposed holding consultations, but no more information about the event was provided by the USSR and no investigation of the allegation was carried out.

After the Sverdlovsk allegations, the Soviet press suggested that the USA continues to store biological weapons, among other places, at a US military base in Spain.

All these suspicions of breaches, none of which has been either proved or disproved, have negatively affected the international climate. In addition, they may have weakened confidence in the relevant treaties and cast a shadow on arms control efforts.

A convention prohibiting the production and stockpiling of chemical weapons and requiring their destruction is inconceivable without provisions for checking compliance with the commitments undertaken. In fact, consensus already exists that verification of a CW convention should be based on national and international measures which complement each other.

National measures would comprise the use of national technical means and the parties would be obliged not to impede, including through deliberate concealment, the use of such means by other parties. International measures would include the establishment of a consultative committee to solve problems relating to the application of the convention. In addition, any party would have the right to request on-site investigations. While the negotiators agreed that such an optional inspection, "by challenge", would be enough in certain cases, they differed as regards the need for mandatory inspection in other cases (in particular, during stockpile destruction operations), and as regards procedures to be applied to on-site investigation. The functions of the proposed consultative committee also remain to be specified. Moreover, many states recognize the need for a permanent international machinery within the framework of a CW convention or as a supplement to the 1925 Geneva Protocol, which could be set in motion at short notice to investigate charges of use of the banned weapons.

WEU arms limitations

The Agency for the control of armaments of the Western European Union (WEU) has for many years been engaged in verifying compliance by the WEU member states (Belgium, France, FR Germany, Italy, Luxembourg, the Netherlands and the United Kingdom) with the limitations to which they agreed in 1954 under the Protocols to the 1948 Brussels Treaty for collaboration and collective self-defence. The tasks of the Agency are to satisfy itself that the undertakings not to manufacture certain types of weapon (mainly atomic, biological and chemical) are being observed, and to control the level of stocks of other specified armaments, including production and imports. For this purpose, the Agency is to scrutinize statistical and budgetary information supplied by members of the WEU and by NATO authorities, and to undertake on the mainland of Europe test checks, visits and inspections at production plants, depots and forces.

Participation in the verification process

The verification procedures, as embodied in most existing multilateral arms control agreements, suffer from lack of consistency. Checking compliance with arms control obligations often requires the use of sophisticated equipment. The few nations possessing such resources can, to a great extent, rely on their own national means of verification. But for nations lacking the means, the mere right to verify is nearly meaningless. In other words, treaty obligations are placed on all parties, but verification is in the hands of a few.

Some improvement in this respect has been made in the 1971 Sea-Bed Treaty, under which verification may be undertaken by any party with the full or partial assistance of any other party, or through international procedures. (A similar clause can be found in the 1979 Agreement concerning the Moon and other celestial bodies.) However, many states may be reluctant to resort to the aid of the technologically advanced states and to rely for their security on such uncertain factors as the goodwill of the great powers. Non-aligned or neutral states seeking direct assistance from one or another power would run the risk of compromising their status. On the other hand, the possibility of using international procedures to verify suspected Sea-Bed Treaty violations has not been specified.

It is noteworthy that none of the multilateral agreements presently in force provides for access to the territories of the great powers for verification of arms control obligations. Only in connection with the NPT have the United Kingdom and the United States voluntarily submitted certain civilian nuclear installations to IAEA safeguards, including inspection. (France has done the same, although it is not party to the Treaty.) However, the right of these powers to use their nuclear material for military purposes has remained unaffected. More openness on the part of the nuclear weapon states may alleviate the sense of 'discrimination' of the non-nuclear weapon states and satisfy the commercial interests of the nuclear industry, but, from the point of view of non-proliferation, safeguarding peaceful activities in selected facilities in countries unrestricted in their military nuclear programmes has no arms control significance. It amounts to verifying non-existing obligations.

Most arms control agreements provide for consultations between the states directly concerned to clarify problems which may arise in relation to the objective of, or in the application of the provisions of, these agreements. Such consultations are of importance to states capable of monitoring compliance. For those deprived of knowledge about the behaviour of others, there may be no opportunity for consultation. Moreover, direct contacts among countries may not always be feasible. As regards indirect, international consultation, most treaties use vague language to cover such an eventuality: the procedure must be "appropriate" and take place within the framework of the United Nations in accordance with its Charter. To the extent that this implies the right to approach the United Nations through the usual channels, the clause may prove to be redundant. Thus, since the means of verifying compliance are a virtual monopoly of the great powers, the main dilemma is how the other parties to multilateral arms control agreements could acquire information to justify requests for consultation and investigation. There is always a danger that, for political or other reasons (for example, unwillingness to disclose the nature or the source of the evidence), the great powers may deliberately overlook transgressions committed by some states to the detriment of others.

The first UN Special Session on Disarmament, held in 1978, emphasized the requirement for all parties to participate in the verification process. It is in this context that a proposal was made by France to establish an international satellite monitoring agency (ISMA).

Multilateral verification by satellites

In 1981, a group of UN experts who had studied the French proposal concluded that the technical facilities for an ISMA could be acquired in stages, beginning with an image processing and interpretation centre, to stations receiving appropriate data from observation satellites of various states, and ending with the ISMA having its own space segment (in addition to the ground segment), comprising a number of satellites. The presumption is that by the time an ISMA becomes operational, several countries might be able to offer their services in launching the satellites.

It should be noted that an ISMA could provide supporting information rather than replace the existing means of verification. Certain intrusive methods, such as on-site inspection, would probably remain irreplaceable in a number of cases. Nevertheless, monitoring by satellites could make a valuable contribution to the verification of compliance with arms control obligations and also to the prevention and settlement of certain international crises.

In the short run, the success or failure of the ISMA proposition will depend on the attitudes of the United States and the Soviet Union, which are the main countries possessing reconnaissance satellites. So far, these attitudes have been negative; neither country participated in the work of the group of experts which prepared the ISMA report. The USA sees overwhelming political, organizational, technical and financial difficulties associated with an international institution charged with collecting and assessing satellite information. In particular, it considers that the establishment of satisfactory decision-making procedures in such an institution would pose exceedingly difficult and probably insoluble problems. In the opinion of the USSR, the creation of a monitoring organ not connected with the implementation of concrete disarmament measures would merely give the appearance of progress in the field of disarmament, and might even lead to a heightening of mutual suspicion among states.

In the long run, since the US–Soviet monopoly on military reconnaissance by satellites cannot continue for ever, the situation may change when other countries acquire such a capability.

IV. Non-compliance with treaty obligations

Breaches

Under the Treaty of Tlatelolco, the General Conference of the Agency for the Prohibition of Nuclear Weapons in Latin America is to take note of cases in which a party is not complying with its obligations and make such recommendations as it deems appropriate. In the event that non-compliance constitutes a violation which might endanger peace and security, the General Conference must report simultaneously to the UN Security Council and the General Assembly, and to the Council of the Organization of American States (OAS); it should report to the IAEA for such purposes as are relevant in accordance with its Statute.

Cases of non-compliance with the nuclear safeguards are to be reported by the IAEA Director General to the Board of Governors, which in turn reports these cases to the IAEA member states as well as to the UN Security Council and General Assembly.

Normally, complaints of breaches of the multilateral arms control agreements can be lodged with the UN Security Council, but they must contain evidence "confirming" or "supporting" their validity. A state lacking sufficiently reliable information and therefore not possessing such evidence may have its request for consideration rejected by the Council. And even if the Council agrees to discuss a charge which does not entirely satisfy the above requirement, there is always a danger that the case will not be given proper examination and will remain unsolved. The Council "may" initiate an investigation, but it is not obliged to do so. The great power veto has been used to block not only substantive decisions, but even proposals for investigation or observation, when the interests of the permanent members of the Council, or their allies, were involved. Should an investigation be initiated, it is not at all clear to what extent the parties are committed to co-operate in carrying it out and, in particular, whether they are under an obligation to allow inspection on their territory. Moreover, it may be awkward for a complainant if Council members not party to a given treaty are called upon to judge the conduct of a party.

Sanctions

In view of the above uncertainties, countries may hesitate to embark on a procedure which extends the inequality of states under the UN Charter to relations regulated by arms control agreements. The legitimate option left open is to withdraw if there is an appropriate clause in the treaty (the most important arms control treaties, both bilateral and multilateral, do contain such a clause), or to suspend the operation of the treaty with the defaulting state, according to the general principles of international law. Actually, even if an offender has been condemned by the Security Council, an injured country could not expect from the United Nations more than an internationally recognized justification for the abrogation of the treaty. In prevailing political circumstances, a collective military punitive action against a transgressor of an arms control treaty is unthinkable, and the coercive value of economic sanctions is very limited, except in hypothetical cases of total economic dependence on the states imposing sanctions or universal economic ostracism. Since international opprobrium, as expressed in governmental declarations, diplomatic notes, resolutions of international organizations or critical editorials in the world press, is a sanction of dubious efficacy, the threat of abrogation is the primary means of enforcing a treaty.

Other sanctions, if found politically feasible, do not necessarily need the approval of the UN Security Council to become effective. For example, according to the Statute of the IAEA, its Board of Governors may, in the event of non-compliance with the safeguards agreements, direct curtailment or suspension of assistance being provided by the IAEA or a member state and call for the return of materials and equipment made available to the recipient member or group of members. In 1981, following an Israeli attack on the Iraqi Nuclear Research Centre, the IAEA General Conference decided to suspend the provision to Israel of any assistance under the Agency's technical assistance programme. In taking this decision, the IAEA stated that it considered the Israeli act against the safeguarded nuclear installations as an attack against the Agency and its safeguards regime, which is the foundation of the Non-Proliferation Treaty. The IAEA may also, upon the recommendation of its Board of Governors, suspend any non-complying member from the exercise of the privileges and rights of membership.[3]

The nuclear supplier states which are members of the London Club have agreed on measures to be taken in case of non-compliance. In the event that one or more of them believe that there has been a violation of

---

[3] Somewhat more elaborate measures are provided for against violators of the control provisions under the Treaty which established EURATOM. The sanctions to be imposed by the Commission of EURATOM depend on the gravity of the offence, and range from a warning to the withdrawal of financial or technical assistance, to the placing of the respective enterprise under the administration of an appointed person or board for a period not exceeding four months, to the partial or total withdrawal of source or special fissionable materials.

supplier/recipient understandings resulting from the 1977 Guidelines for Nuclear Transfers, particularly in the case of an explosion of a nuclear device or illegal termination or violation of IAEA safeguards by a recipient, suppliers should promptly consult through diplomatic channels in order to determine and assess the reality and extent of the alleged violation. Upon the findings of such consultations and bearing in mind the relevant provisions of the IAEA Statute, the suppliers should agree on an appropriate response and possible action, which could include the termination of nuclear transfers to that recipient.

The 1972 BW Convention and the 1977 ENMOD Convention contain an undertaking to provide support or assistance to any party, in accordance with the UN Charter, if the Security Council decides that such party has been harmed or exposed to danger as a result of violation of these conventions. While it would probably be for the requesting party to determine the form of assistance it wishes to receive, it is not clear how strong the commitment is to assist. It would seem that, since assistance is to be given in accordance with the UN Charter, the relevant provision of Chapter VII of the Charter should apply, under which UN members "shall join in affording mutual assistance in carrying out the measures decided upon by the Security Council". But in the understanding of the UK and the USA recorded during the negotiations for the BW Convention, each party would decide whether it could or was prepared to supply the aid requested. In other words, assistance would be optional, not obligatory: it could be refused without incurring the charge of non-compliance. If this is so, one can hardly see the purpose of including a clause on the subject in an arms control agreement.

International fact-finding

The withdrawal or denunciation clauses in arms control agreements are not keyed specifically to violations, but to events related to the subject-matter of the treaty which have jeopardized the "supreme interests" of the party in question. Under certain agreements, notice of withdrawal must be given both to other parties and to the UN Security Council, with a statement of the events which the withdrawing party regards as having jeopardized its interests. Although this requirement has narrowed the margin for possible arbitrary action, the ultimate judge of such extraordinary events remains the government of the country considering abrogation. The most plausible reason for a country's decision to withdraw from, to denounce or to suspend the operation of a treaty, especially a multilateral treaty, would be non-compliance by others with the treaty provisions. However, in the absence of a formal verdict that a violation has been committed, such a decision could be politically costly and hazardous, both domestically and internationally. To be on the safe side, a state planning abrogation but unwilling to depend on the uncertain outcome of the UN Security Council procedures would need to be in possession of convincing evidence of misdemeanour. To impress world opinion, the proof would have to be authoritatively confirmed by an impartial expert inquiry.

First steps towards separating international fact-finding from UN political judgement have been made in the Convention prohibiting the use of environmental modification techniques for hostile purposes. The ENMOD Convention stipulates that consultations to clarify problems relating to its objectives and application may include the services of a consultative committee of experts, to be convened upon request. The role of the committee is to establish facts and to provide expert views on issues raised by the party requesting its services. Voting on matters of substance is not allowed, but the right to decide, by majority vote, procedural questions relative to the organization of its work may enable the committee to order an inquiry. Since a summary of the findings, which incorporates all views and information presented to the committee during its proceedings, is to be distributed to the parties, the prevailing range of opinions on matters of substance can be made discernible without recourse to voting. The essential point here is that experts will be given an opportunity to examine the particulars of each case and make their views widely known, irrespective of whether the case will eventually be considered by the Security Council. It would be left to the complaining country to draw its own conclusions from the information received and to decide upon further action. (Since the problem of response to violations is principally political and calls for discretion, denunciation or withdrawal may not always be resorted to, even if the other party's guilt is manifest.)

The procedure described above was a precedent-setting improvement on previous practice. Subsequently, at the initiative of the neutral and non-aligned countries the 1980 Review Conference of the parties to the BW Convention declared that the "international procedures" referred to in the Convention in connection with the provision on consultation must be understood as including the right of any party to request that a consultative meeting, open to all parties, should be convened at expert level. The United Kingdom recorded its view that if such a request were made, all the parties should co-operate in holding the meeting in order to make appropriate findings of fact and to provide expert views. The UK expressed its readiness to assume its responsibilities in this respect as one of the depositaries of the BW Convention. As regards the convener of a possible consultative meeting, Sweden stated the opinion, not contested by the participants at the BW Review Conference, that any party had the right to request that the meeting should be convened by the UN Secretary-General.

The existing proposals for a CW convention envisage even wider terms of reference for the consultative committee. In addition to the functions specified above, such a committee would be entrusted with monitoring the destruction, or diversion for permitted purposes, of stocks of chemical weapons, as well as of means of their production; monitoring the production of super-toxic lethal chemicals for non-hostile military purposes; developing an international standardization of methods to be applied by national and international verification bodies; and undertaking on-site inspections. An annual report of the consultative committee's activities would have to be presented to states parties to the convention.

The 1977 Protocol additional to the 1949 Geneva Conventions and relating to the protection of victims of international armed conflicts (Protocol I) also provides for the establishment of an international fact-finding commission to enquire into any "facts alleged to be a grave breach", and to facilitate, through its good offices, the restoration of an attitude of respect for the Conventions and the Protocol. Regretfully, the 1981 Convention prohibiting or restricting the use of certain conventional weapons has failed to include provisions for the verification of alleged violations of the undertakings subscribed to. However, some signatories have reserved the right to submit proposals for filling this gap within the framework of the amendments procedure.

Limits to verification

It is usually postulated that verification should be "adequate", "effective", "strict" or "thorough", but fool-proof verification is impossible; the degree of tolerable uncertainty is a judgement based on a possible violation's impact on the national security of the parties. Because of the relatively small disarmament value of the treaties concluded hitherto, their violation would probably have no significant impact on the security of states. If disclosed, the effect would be political rather than military, and the disadvantage would be primarily for the violator rather than for the injured party. However, for more substantial treaties which may be reached in the future, tighter procedures would have to be devised guaranteeing equal rights for all parties to ensure that the agreements function properly and that the obligations are being complied with by all.

V. Verification institutions

Institutions dealing with the verification of arms control agreements may either serve the purpose of clarifying ambiguous situations that might generate suspicions regarding compliance, as in the case of the Standing Consultative Commission (SCC) set up in accordance with the SALT agreements, or be directly engaged in the verification operations, as in the case of the IAEA checking the observance of the NPT.

US–Soviet Standing Consultative Commission

Within the framework of the SCC, the USA and the USSR are to provide information considered necessary to assure confidence in the fulfilment of the obligations assumed by them, and to discuss questions involving interference with national technical means of verification or impeding verification by such means. In addition, the parties agreed to consider possible changes in the strategic situation which have a bearing on the provisions of the SALT agreements; to set procedures for replacement, conversion and dismantling or destruction of arms, as provided for in the agreements, and to notify each other periodically of actions completed and those in process; to examine possible proposals for further increasing the viability of the agreements, including proposals for amendments; and to maintain the agreed data base of each side's arms subject to limitations.

The SCC is a bilateral US–Soviet arrangement. Each government is represented by a commissioner and a deputy commissioner, assisted by such staff as is deemed necessary. So far, the SCC has been successful in getting questionable activity either explained or stopped before it became a serious problem.

Multilateral institutions

There is no institution for multilateral arms control treaties comparable to the SCC. The consultative committees of experts which are provided for in the existing agreements may be convened only upon request, and their authority is strictly circumscribed. The establishment of standing multilateral bodies, possibly with terms of reference similar to those of the SCC, would certainly be useful in assuring the implementation of the multilateral arms control undertakings. It would even be worthwhile attempting to set up a centre to co-ordinate the consultative activities, preferably within the framework of the United Nations.

On the other hand, there does not seem to be much use in centralizing actual verification operations. The choice of control methods depends on the type of activity prohibited and on the technical means available. The ways in which information about compliance is acquired and the expertise needed to analyse and interpret such information differ from one treaty to another. An ISMA could become an institution specializing in checking compliance with specific obligations verifiable by satellites, while a special consultative committee could, according to current proposals, carry out monitoring functions under a CW convention. Use can also be made of UN–affiliated or other authoritative international institutions dealing with related peaceful activities.

The only verification institution in existence which deals with a wide variety of arms control measures is the WEU Agency, but the Agency can hardly serve as a model since it operates within the boundaries of a single military alliance. Moreover, its verification duties are different with regard to different parties. This asymmetry is based on the fact that the 1954 Protocol to the 1948 Brussels Treaty, which set up the Agency, pursued two rather uncommon goals for arms control agreements—to strengthen a military alliance (NATO) with the participation of a new member state (FR Germany) and, at the same time, to allay the misgivings of the allies about that new member's rearmament.

Comprehensive and general disarmament may require a comprehensive treatment of verification, on a global scale, to guard against all risks to the security interests of states. This was recognized as early as 1961 in the Joint

US–Soviet Statement of agreed principles for disarmament negotiations (the so-called McCloy–Zorin statement), approved by the UN General Assembly. One of the agreed principles stipulated that during and after the implementation of general and complete disarmament, the most thorough control should be exercised and that, to implement control over and inspection of disarmament, an International Disarmament Organization should be created within the framework of the United Nations. Accordingly, the Soviet draft treaty on general and complete disarmament provided that an organization of the parties to the Treaty would begin operating as soon as disarmament measures were initiated. The organization would receive information from the parties about their armed forces, armaments, military production and military appropriations. It would have its own internationally recruited staff to exercise control, on a temporary or permanent basis, depending on the nature of the measure being carried out. In its proposal, the USA envisaged the establishment of an international organization to ensure that all obligations were honoured and observed during and after disarmament, and requested that inspectors from the organization should have unrestricted access to all places necessary for the purpose of effective verification. However, as long as arms control agreements deal only with partial measures, the establishment of one world-wide organization to deal with both consultative activities and verification operations would be premature.

5. Arms control agreements: the texts and parties

I. Introductory note

Certified texts of all the important arms control agreements—either full texts or excerpts—are reproduced in sections II and III of this chapter. Each agreement is prefaced by the dates of signature and entry into force and the designation of the depositary, and is followed by a list of parties. The documents in section II are those pre-World War II agreements selected for their relevance to topics on the present international arms control agenda. Section III covers comprehensively the post-war agreements. All texts are presented in chronological order, by the date on which they were opened for signature. The status of the agreements is as of 1 October 1981, with additional new information that reached SIPRI by the time this book went to press.

A number of problems arise with the so-called final clauses of the agreements. The most important of these are explained below in this introductory note.

Succession

The agreements reproduced in this chapter cover the period from 1868 to 1981. Over these more than 100 years, certain signatories have ceased to exist as independent states. This is, for example, the case of Estonia, Latvia and Lithuania, incorporated in the Soviet Union during World War II. Such states are not listed as parties to agreements.

In the case of states signatories which have united in a federation, the newly established state is listed as party if it has made a declaration confirming the continuity of obligations undertaken by one or more of the predecessor states. The same principle has been followed with regard to successors of dissolved political unions of states.

The case of Germany is special in that this state was split after World War II into two independent German entities. The Federal Republic of Germany considers itself bound by the agreements to which the German Reich had been party, in so far as they are not incompatible with the constitution of FR Germany and in so far as their validity has been formally confirmed by a competent authority of the Republic. The German Democratic Republic does not consider itself bound by the treaties of the Reich unless it has formally declared and notified the depositary about the renewed applicability of a pre-war treaty.

The People's Republic of China has declared that, as regards multilateral treaties to which China was party before the establishment of the People's

Republic (1 October 1949), the government will decide in light of the circumstances whether it should recognize them; on this basis it issued a statement recognizing as binding upon it the accession of China to the 1925 Geneva Protocol prohibiting chemical and bacteriological warfare. As to treaties concluded by the Republic of China (Taiwan) after 1 October 1949, the People's Republic stated that it considers them 'null and void'. China has stated that it may nevertheless decide to accede to such treaties.

Viet Nam underwent a reverse process. The Republic of Viet Nam (South) signed a few arms control agreements, acceded to the 1949 Geneva Conventions for the protection of war victims, ratified the Non-Proliferation Treaty, and concluded safeguards agreements with the IAEA. The Democratic Republic of Viet Nam (North) joined only the 1949 Conventions. But in 1975, the Republic of Viet Nam (South) ceased to exist as a separate political entity, and as from July 1976 North and South Viet Nam constitute a single state—the Socialist Republic of Viet Nam. The government of this single state has now acceded to certain arms control treaties on behalf of Viet Nam.

The procedure of succession to arms control agreements by former non-self-governing territories has not been uniform. Some newly independent states have officially informed the depositaries of arms control agreements that they consider themselves bound by these agreements by virtue of ratification by the power formerly responsible for their international relations. Other such states have acceded to arms control treaties without referring to the obligations undertaken on their behalf by the predecessor state. Some confusion arose with respect to states which, upon attaining independence, have made general statements of continuity to all treaties concluded by the predecessor state but which have not notified the depositaries of the arms control agreements that their statements specifically applied to these agreements. According to international law, a *general* unilateral declaration of continuity, made by a successor state, is not sufficient to constitute that state as party to *specific* treaties.[1] On the other hand, a newly independent state is not bound to maintain in force, or to become a party to, any treaty by reason only of the fact that at the date of the succession the treaty was in force in respect of the territory to which the succession relates. This rule recognizes that newly independent states may not be entirely familiar with the obligations which have been contracted on their behalf; irrespective of a general statement of continuity, they usually engage in examination of the individual treaties in order to determine whether they should formally succeed to them.

Potential parties

Most multilateral arms control agreements in force (with the exception of regional agreements) are open for signature by all states, without quali-

---

[1] Article 9 of the 1978 Vienna Convention on succession of states in respect of treaties.

fication. This is a recognition of the principle that, by their very nature, arms control treaties ought to have universal application.

In this context the question has arisen as to whether, by subscribing to a treaty, an entity or a regime can gain recognition as a state or a government by other parties which do not formally recognize it. To guard against such implications, certain countries have found it expedient to issue special declarations. Most of these declarations relate to the German Democratic Republic, Israel or Taiwan. It is generally understood that neither signature nor the deposit of any instrument in relation to a general multilateral treaty brings about recognition between parties to the treaty that do not recognize each other. As a matter of fact, states could even have dealings with a non-recognized regime within the framework of multilateral treaties open for general adherence without thereby recognizing it. Nevertheless, neither Taiwan, which is considered as part of China and is thus excluded from all United Nations bodies, nor South Africa, which has been barred from participating in certain UN organs and activities, has been invited to attend the conferences reviewing the treaties signed and ratified by these states.

Depositaries

The principle that recognition cannot be gained automatically and is primarily a matter of the intent of each recognizing state also applies to relations between a government acting as a depositary of a multilateral treaty and other governments wishing to take action in respect of the treaty. Normally it is possible to make arrangements for such actions to be taken even if there are no diplomatic relations between these governments. However, if the depositary government denies the very existence of another entity or the legitimacy of its government, then such arrangements may not be feasible. The solution which is increasingly frequently resorted to—to have some intergovernmental organ act as depositary—may not be possible either, if the membership of the organization concerned is too divided on the acceptability of a particular entity or government. It was for such political reasons, related to the cold war controversies rather than to the contents of the treaties, that in the early 1960s a novel device was developed. Instead of specifying a single depositary, the Partial Test Ban Treaty, the Outer Space Treaty, the Non-Proliferation Treaty, the Sea-Bed Treaty and the Biological Weapons Convention designate three depositaries: the governments of the UK, the USA and the USSR. This device has helped to relieve the depositaries from the international obligation to act impartially in the performance of their functions under all circumstances.

The duties of treaty depositaries include accepting signatures; receiving instruments of ratification and accession; informing signatory and acceding states of the date of each signature, the date of deposit of each instrument of ratification or of accession, and the date of entry into force of the treaty; as well as receiving and circulating other notices, which may include notifications of succession to the treaty and proposals for amendment. The wording of the relevant paragraphs of arms control agreements is not entirely clear on several points: whether, to be valid, the signature and the instrument of ratification or accession had to be deposited with more than one depositary; what was the official date of entry into force of the treaty for a party which had deposited its instrument of ratification or accession with the depositary governments at different dates; whether each depositary government had the duty to inform each signatory and acceding state of each signature and deposit of instrument of ratification or accession; and whether the depositary governments were under obligation to accept any such notifications. In practice, it has proved to be sufficient for a state to sign a treaty or to deposit its instrument of ratification or accession in one of the three capitals—London, Moscow or Washington—to become formally committed. This has facilitated wider adherence to agreements without embarrassing any depositary or potential party. In case a given state takes the same action in different capitals on different dates, a frequent occurrence, the earliest date is considered the effective one.

The depositaries do not feel obliged to accept a signature or a communication from an authority they do not recognize. For example, prior to 1973 the USA failed to take account of the notification of signature and deposit of ratification in Moscow by the government of the German Democratic Republic, and considered itself exempt from the duty of transmitting to that government the information required by the treaties, without denying that the GDR was bound by the arms control agreements ratified by it. The USA also regards the signatures and ratifications by Byelorussia and Ukraine, which have joined all the major multilateral arms control agreements except the NPT,[2] as included under the signature and ratification of the USSR. On the other hand, the USSR considers the deposit of instruments of ratification by Taiwan in Washington as illegal because it recognizes only the government of the People's Republic of China. Consequently, the official records of signatories and parties kept by the several depositary governments differ. So far, this has not caused serious inconveniences, due to the fact that the number of countries which are not universally recognized is rather small.

Be that as it may, with the GDR and the PRC recognized by practically all states, the cumbersome practice of dealing with three depositaries has hardly any *raison d'être* and has been abandoned in subsequent agreements. The 1977 Convention prohibiting environmental modification for hostile

---

[2] The adherence of Byelorussia and Ukraine to the NPT would have posed inextricable problems. The two Soviet republics could not sign as nuclear weapon states, because it was generally agreed that there were only five such states in existence at the time the treaty was concluded: the USA, the USSR, the UK, France and China. Should they have adhered to the NPT as non-nuclear weapon states, they would have had to undertake not to receive the transfer of nuclear weapons, directly or indirectly, and not to manufacture or otherwise acquire these weapons. However, such undertakings on the part of Byelorussia and Ukraine are inconceivable, since according to the Constitution of the USSR (Article 73, paragraph 8) the all-Union government has competence in matters of defence, while the constituent republics have not.

purposes, and the 1981 Convention prohibiting or restricting the use of certain conventional weapons, assign the task of depositary to the UN Secretary-General, while the 1980 Convention on the physical protection of nuclear material has been deposited with the IAEA Director General.

Entry into force

Certain agreements may enter into force simultaneously with the signing. Agreements requiring ratification enter into force after the deposit of instruments of ratification. In multilateral agreements the required minimum number of instruments of ratification is specified. When the treaty as such has entered into force, it does so only for the states that have already ratified it. A state which does not sign a multilateral agreement before its entry into force may accede to it. For those states whose instruments of ratification or accession are deposited after the entry into force of the agreement, the agreement enters into force either immediately or after a specified period of time following the deposit of these instruments. On the other hand, a notification of succession by a newly independent state is considered to be made on the date on which it is received by the depositary. Until that date, the operation of the treaty is suspended as between that state and the other parties. A newly independent state which makes a notification of succession is considered a party to the treaty from the date of the succession or from the date of entry into force of the treaty, whichever is the later date.

Having signed but not ratified a treaty subject to ratification, a state is generally considered obligated to refrain from acts which would defeat the object and purpose of the treaty, until such a time as it has made its intention clear not to become party to it.[3] Thus, even though the Threshold Test Ban Treaty had not entered into force by 31 March 1976, the agreed cut-off date for nuclear explosions above the established threshold, the USA and the USSR stated that they would observe the limitation during the pre-ratification period.

The number of ratifications necessary for a multilateral arms control treaty to enter into force is related to the nature of the prohibition or the limitation it contains. Thus, the Antarctic Treaty, which was negotiated among and signed by 12 countries, all active in Antarctica, required the deposit of instruments of ratification by all these countries. The Partial Test Ban Treaty became effective upon its ratification by the original parties—the UK, the USA and the USSR—three of the four powers which were at that time engaged in nuclear weapon testing. (France, then the only other nuclear weapon state, refused to participate in the treaty or to abide by its terms.) For the Outer Space Treaty, ratification by five governments was needed. These had to include the governments of the USA, the USSR and the UK, even though only the first two powers were conducting

---

[3] Article 18 of the 1969 Vienna Convention on the Law of Treaties.

116

significant activities in outer space at the time the Treaty was opened for signature.

Under the Treaty prohibiting nuclear weapons in Latin America (Treaty of Tlatelolco), several requirements must be met for the Treaty's entry into force even for the states that have ratified it—among others, the requirement that all the Latin American states which were in existence on the date the Treaty was opened for signature should deposit their instruments of ratification. But any state has the right wholly or in part to waive these requirements by means of a declaration annexed to the instrument of ratification or made subsequently. For those states which exercise this right, the Treaty enters into force upon deposit of the declaration, or as soon as the requirements which have not been expressly waived have been met. As a consequence of this provision, the Treaty entered into force as soon as two countries ratified it, waiving wholly the specified requirements. By 1981, 22 countries had made use of the waiver, and only two ratifying countries had refused to do so, thus remaining not bound by the Treaty.

The Non-Proliferation Treaty, which imposed obligations mainly on non-nuclear weapon states, required ratification by 40 such states in addition to the three nuclear weapon powers that are depositaries of the Treaty.

The Sea-Bed Treaty and the Biological Weapons Convention entered into force after the deposit of the instruments of ratification by 22 governments, which number again had to include the UK, the USA and the USSR. The Environmental Modification Convention, signed in 1977, became effective upon ratification by 20 governments, but it did not require that this number should include any particular state. The 1981 Convention prohibiting or restricting the use of certain conventional weapons contains a similar provision. But conventions of a humanitarian nature did not follow the same pattern. The 1925 Geneva Protocol prohibiting the use of chemical and bacteriological methods of warfare entered into force upon the deposit of two instruments of ratification. This was also the case with the 1949 Geneva Conventions for the protection of war victims, and a similar procedure applied to the 1977 Protocol I and II to these Conventions.

Amendments

Arms control agreements may be modified by a number of different procedures. Under bilateral agreements, each party may propose amendments; agreed amendments enter into force in accordance with the procedures governing the entry into force of the agreement. In multilateral agreements the amendment clauses are more complex.

The Antarctic Treaty may be amended at any time by unanimous agreement of the parties, except those which have acceded to the Treaty but do not conduct substantial scientific research in Antarctica. The Partial Test Ban Treaty provides for a two-stage amending process. At the first stage, the amendment must be approved by a majority, including all the original parties, that is, the UK, the USA and the USSR.[4] At the second stage, when the instruments of ratification of the amendment have been deposited by a majority, including the original parties, the amendment enters into force for all parties, that is, even for those who oppose it. Thus, each of the three nuclear powers has the right to veto any change, at either stage, while an amendment adopted by a majority can be automatically imposed upon a dissenting minority, if the latter does not include an original party.

Such patently inequitable amendment clauses have not appeared in subsequent arms control agreements. The NPT, concluded five years after the Partial Test Ban Treaty, has weakened the prerogatives of the great powers by requiring that a majority approving an amendment must include not only the votes of nuclear weapon states party to the Treaty, but also those of all other parties which are at the time members of the Board of Governors of the International Atomic Energy Agency. One could question the wisdom of extending the power to veto amendments to those nations that happen to be members of the IAEA Board of Governors at the time the amendment is to be approved (a power they do not enjoy in the IAEA itself); nevertheless, the curtailment of the exclusive rights of the nuclear powers has been a progressive step. Furthermore under the NPT, an amendment enters into force upon ratification by a majority, including the above-mentioned states, but cannot be imposed on non-ratifying states. For each party it becomes effective only upon the deposit of its instrument of ratification of the amendment—an important provision for an agreement dealing with national security matters. As a result of pressure exercised by smaller nations, the nuclear weapon powers' special prerogatives concerning possible modifications of treaty provisions have been abolished altogether in subsequent multilateral arms control agreements, for example, in the Sea-Bed Treaty, the Biological Weapons Convention and the Environmental Modification Convention.

Review conferences

Many arms control agreements provide for periodic review conferences in order to assure that the purposes and provisions of the agreements are being realized. Five such conferences have already been held: the US–Soviet ABM Treaty was reviewed in 1977, the Sea-Bed Treaty also in 1977, the Non-Proliferation Treaty in 1975 and 1980, and the Biological Weapons Convention in 1980. Review conferences offer an opportunity for the parties to urge improvements in the operation of the agreements and the fulfilment of non-implemented provisions. They also stimulate, to some extent, wider ad-

---

[4] In this respect, the rights of the great powers exceed even those provided for in the amendment process of the UN Charter (Article 108). The permanent members of the Security Council do not have a veto in the first stage of this process, when any Charter amendment has to be adopted by a vote of two-thirds of the members of the General Assembly. Each can, however, prevent the entry into force of an amendment at the ratification stage, by refraining from ratifying.

herence to the treaties in question. However, all attempts made at these conferences to initiate amendments to multilateral treaties, or complement them with additional protocols, have so far failed. A number of countries are reluctant to embark upon an amendment procedure which may lead to a weakening of the treaty in case the amendment is not accepted by all the parties.

Duration and denunciation

Nearly all the arms control treaties hitherto concluded are to remain in force indefinitely. The exceptions include the SALT agreements, valid for 5 or 6 years; the Threshold Test Ban Treaty and the Peaceful Nuclear Explosions Treaty, which are to be effective for 5 years, unless replaced by another agreement, or extended for successive five-year periods; the Antarctic Treaty, which has a duration of at least 30 years; and the NPT, which 25 years after its entry into force may be extended for an indefinite period or for an additional fixed period.

The major arms control agreements contain a withdrawal clause. But even in the absence of such a clause, parties have the right to denounce an agreement in accordance with the general principles of international law. Notice of withdrawal or denunciation must be given a few months in advance. This clause is somewhat stricter in certain humanitarian conventions. Thus, denunciation of the 1949 Conventions for the protection of war victims and of the Protocols to these Conventions would take effect one year after receipt of the instrument of denunciation instead of a few months. Moreover, if on the expiry of that year the denouncing party were engaged in an armed conflict the denunciation would not take effect until the end of the conflict.

On the other hand, parties may decide to extend the validity of an agreement after its formal termination. For example, in the case of the SALT I Interim Agreement the USA and the USSR stated their intention to refrain from any actions incompatible with the provisions of this Agreement, even though it had already expired, or with the goals of the ongoing talks on a new agreement.

Reservations

A state may, when signing, ratifying or acceding to a multilateral treaty or when making a notification of succession,[5] formulate a reservation whereby it excludes or modifies the legal effect of certain provisions of the treaty, unless the reservation is prohibited by the treaty or is incompatible with the object and purpose of the treaty. Many states have made reservations with regard to the 1925 Geneva Protocol, the 1948 Genocide Convention, and the 1949 Geneva Conventions. Some of these reservations have been

---

[5] A reservation expressed by the predecessor state is deemed to be maintained by the successor state if the latter remains silent on that point.

objected to.[6] Fewer reservations have been made with respect to multilateral arms control agreements concluded in recent years. But in statements of understanding attached to signatures or ratifications, some states have reserved their positions on a number of important issues. This was the case under the Treaty of Tlatelolco which has explicitly ruled out reservations. In the US–Soviet SALT I agreements, the parties put on record unilateral interpretations of certain provisions.

---

[6] In 1951, the International Court of Justice was asked by the UN General Assembly for an advisory opinion on the legal effect of reservations to the Genocide Convention. The opinion issued was that a state which has made and maintained a reservation which has been objected to by one or more of the parties to the Convention, but not by others, can be regarded as being a party to the Convention if the reservation is compatible with the object and purpose of the Convention. The Court further stated that if a party to the Convention objects to a reservation which it considers to be incompatible with the object and purpose of the Convention, it can in fact consider that the reserving state is not a party to the Convention. This question is now largely regulated by Articles 20–22 of the 1969 Vienna Convention on the Law of Treaties.

II. Selected pre-World War II agreements

DECLARATION (IV,2) CONCERNING ASPHYXIATING GASES

Signed at The Hague on 29 July 1899
Entered into force on 4 September 1900
Depositary: Netherlands government

The undersigned, plenipotentiaries of the Powers represented at the International Peace Conference at The Hague, duly authorized to that effect by their Governments, inspired by the sentiments which found expression in the Declaration of St. Petersburg of the 29th November (11th December), 1868,
Declare as follows:
The contracting Powers agree to abstain from the use of projectiles the sole object of which is the diffusion of asphyxiating or deleterious gases.
The present Declaration is only binding on the contracting Powers in the case of a war between two or more of them.
It shall cease to be binding from the time when in a war between the contracting Powers, one of the belligerents shall be joined by a non-contracting Power.
The present Declaration shall be ratified as soon as possible.
The ratifications shall be deposited at The Hague.
A *procès-verbal* shall be drawn up on the receipt of each ratification, a copy of which, duly certified, shall be sent through the diplomatic channel to all the contracting Powers.
The non-signatory Powers can adhere to the present Declaration. For this purpose they must make their adhesion known to the contracting Powers by means of a written notification addressed to the Netherland Government, and by it communicated to all the other contracting Powers.
In the event of one of the high contracting Parties denouncing the present Declaration, such denunciation shall not take effect until a year after the notification made in writing to the Government of the Netherlands, and forthwith communicated by it to all the other contracting Powers.
The denunciation shall only affect the notifying Power.

Source: Scott, J. B. (ed.), *The Hague Conventions and Declarations of 1899 and 1907*, 2nd ed. (Oxford University Press, New York, 1915)

Parties: Austria, Belgium, Bulgaria, Byelorussia, China, Denmark, Ethiopia, France, Fiji, Germany†, Greece, Iran, Italy, Japan, Luxembourg, Mexico, Netherlands, Nicaragua, Norway, Portugal, Romania, South Africa, Spain, Sweden, Switzerland, Thailand, Turkey, UK, USSR, Yugoslavia

† The Federal Republic of Germany considers itself bound by the pre-war treaties which were binding on the German Reich in so far as they are not incompatible with the Constitution of FR Germany and in so far as their validity has been formally confirmed by a competent authority of the Republic.
The German Democratic Republic notifies the depositary about the renewed applicability of a pre-war treaty each time it wishes the treaty to be binding on the GDR.

CONVENTION (IV) RESPECTING THE LAWS AND CUSTOMS OF WAR ON LAND

Signed at The Hague on 18 October 1907
Entered into force on 26 January 1910
Depositary: Netherlands government

His Majesty the German Emperor, King of Prussia; [etc.]:

Seeing that, while seeking means to preserve peace and prevent armed conflicts between nations, it is likewise necessary to bear in mind the case where the appeal to arms has been brought about by events which their care was unable to avert;

Animated by the desire to serve, even in this extreme case, the interests of humanity and the ever progressive needs of civilization;

Thinking it important, with this object, to revise the general laws and customs of war, either with a view to defining them with greater precision or to confining them within such limits as would mitigate their severity as far as possible;

Have deemed it necessary to complete and explain in certain particulars the work of the First Peace Conference, which, following on the Brussels Conference of 1874, and inspired by the ideas dictated by a wise and generous forethought, adopted provisions intended to define and govern the usages of war on land.

According to the views of the high contracting Parties, these provisions, the wording of which has been inspired by the desire to diminish the evils of war, as far as military requirements permit, are intended to serve as a general rule of conduct for the belligerents in their mutual relations and in their relations with the inhabitants.

It has not, however, been found possible at present to concert regulations covering all the circumstances which arise in practice;

On the other hand, the high contracting Parties clearly do not intend that unforeseen cases should, in the absence of a written undertaking, be left to the arbitrary judgment of military commanders.

Until a more complete code of the laws of war has been issued, the high contracting Parties deem it expedient to declare that, in cases not included in the Regulations adopted by them, the inhabitants and the belligerents remain under the protection and the rule of the principles of the law of nations, as they result from the usages established among civilized peoples, from the laws of humanity, and the dictates of the public conscience.

They declare that it is in this sense especially that Articles 1 and 2 of the Regulations adopted must be understood.

The high contracting parties, wishing to conclude a fresh Convention to this effect, have appointed the following as their plenipotentiaries:

[Here follow the names of plenipotentiaries.]

Who, after having deposited their full powers, found in good and due form, have agreed upon the following:

Article 1

The contracting Powers shall issue instructions to their armed land forces which shall be in conformity with the Regulations respecting the laws and customs of war on land, annexed to the present Convention.

Article 2

The provisions contained in the Regulations referred to in Article 1, as well as in the present Convention, do not apply except between contracting Powers, and then only if all the belligerents are parties to the Convention.

Article 3

A belligerent party which violates the provisions of the said Regulations shall, if the case demands, be liable to pay compensation. It shall be responsible for all acts committed by persons forming part of its armed forces.

Article 4

The present Convention, duly ratified, shall as between the contracting Powers, be substituted for the Convention of the 29th July 1899, respecting the laws and customs of war on land.

The Convention of 1899 remains in force as between the Powers which signed it, and which do not also ratify the present Convention.

Article 5

The present Convention shall be ratified as soon as possible.

The ratifications shall be deposited at The Hague.

The first deposit of ratifications shall be recorded in a *procès-verbal* signed by the Representatives of the Powers which take part therein and by the Netherland Minister for Foreign Affairs.

The subsequent deposits of ratifications shall be made by means of a written notification, addressed to the Netherland Government and accompanied by the instrument of ratification.

A duly certified copy of the *procès-verbal* relative to the first deposit of ratifications, of the notifications mentioned in the preceding paragraph, as well as of the instruments of ratification, shall be immediately sent by the Netherland Government, through the diplomatic channel, to the Powers invited to the Second Peace Conference, as well as to the other Powers which have adhered to the Convention. In the cases contemplated in the preceding paragraph the said Government shall at the same time inform them of the date on which it received the notification.

Article 6

Non-signatory Powers may adhere to the present Convention.

The Power which desires to adhere notifies in writing its intention to the Netherland Government, forwarding to it the act of adhesion, which shall be deposited in the archives of the said Government.

This Government shall at once transmit to all the other Powers a duly certified copy of the notification as well as of the act of adhesion, mentioning the date on which it received the notification.

Article 7

The present Convention shall come into force, in the case of the Powers which were a party to the first deposit of ratifications, sixty days after the date of the *procès-verbal* of this deposit, and, in the case of the Powers which ratify subsequently or which adhere, sixty days after the notification of their ratification or of their adhesion has been received by the Netherland Government.

Article 8

In the event of one of the contracting Powers wishing to denounce the present Convention, the denunciation shall be notified in writing to the Netherland Government, which shall at once communicate a duly certified copy of the notification to all the other Powers, informing them of the date on which it was received.

The denunciation shall only have effect in regard to the notifying Power, and one year after the notification has reached the Netherland Government.

Article 9

A register kept by the Netherland Ministry of Foreign Affairs shall give the date of the deposit of ratifications made in virtue of Article 5, paragraphs 3 and 4, as well as the date on which the notifications of adhesion (Article 6, paragraph 2), or of denunciation (Article 8, paragraph 1) were received.

Each contracting Power is entitled to have access to this register and to be supplied with duly certified extracts.

ANNEX TO THE CONVENTION

Regulations respecting the laws and customs of war on land

EXCERPT:

...

SECTION II. HOSTILITIES

Chapter I. Means of injuring the enemy, sieges, and bombardments

Article 22

The right of belligerents to adopt means of injuring the enemy is not unlimited.

Article 23

In addition to the prohibitions provided by special Conventions, it is especially forbidden—

(*a*) To employ poison or poisoned weapons;

(*b*) To kill or wound treacherously individuals belonging to the hostile nation or army;

(*c*) To kill or wound an enemy who, having laid down his arms, or having no longer means of defence, has surrendered at discretion;

(*d*) To declare that no quarter will be given;

(*e*) To employ arms, projectiles, or material calculated to cause unnecessary suffering;

(*f*) To make improper use of a flag of truce, of the national flag or of the military insignia and uniform of the enemy, as well as the distinctive badges of the Geneva Convention;*

(*g*) To destroy or seize the enemy's property, unless such destruction or seizure be imperatively demanded by the necessities of war;

(*h*) To declare abolished, suspended, or inadmissible in a court of law the rights and actions of the nationals of the hostile party.

A belligerent is likewise forbidden to compel the nationals of the hostile party to take part in the operations of war directed against their own country, even if they were in the belligerent's service before the commencement of the war.

Article 24

Ruses of war and the employment of measures necessary for obtaining information about the enemy and the country are considered permissible.

Article 25

The attack or bombardment, by whatever means, of towns, villages, dwellings, or buildings which are undefended is prohibited.

Article 26

The officer in command of an attacking force must, before commencing a bombardment, except in cases of assault, do all in his power to warn the authorities.

Article 27

In sieges and bombardments all necessary steps must be taken to spare, as far as possible, buildings dedicated to religion, art, science, or charitable purposes, historic monuments, hospitals, and places where the sick and wounded are collected, provided they are not being used at the time for military purposes.

It is the duty of the besieged to indicate the presence of such buildings or places by distinctive and visible signs, which shall be notified to the enemy beforehand.

Article 28

The pillage of a town or place, even when taken by assault, is prohibited.

...

---

* The Red Cross Convention of 22 August 1864 for the amelioration of the condition of the wounded in armies in the field.

Source: Scott, J. B. (ed.), *The Hague Conventions and Declarations of 1899 and 1907*, 2nd ed. (Oxford University Press, New York, 1915)

Parties: Austria, Belgium, Bolivia, Brazil, Byelorussia, China, Cuba, Denmark, Dominican Republic, El Salvador, Ethiopia, Fiji, Finland, France, Germany† (German Democratic Republic by virtue of 1959 notification of renewed applicability), Guatemala, Haiti, Japan, Liberia, Luxembourg, Mexico, Netherlands, Nicaragua, Norway, Panama, Poland, Portugal, Romania, South Africa, Sweden, Switzerland, Thailand, UK, USA, USSR

Many provisions of this Convention are identical to the provisions included in Convention (II) with respect to the laws and customs of war on land, signed at The Hague on 29 July 1899. The 1899 Convention was ratified or acceded to by: Argentina, Austria-Hungary, Belgium, Bolivia, Brazil, Bulgaria, Chile, China, Colombia, Cuba, Denmark, Dominican Republic, Ecuador, El Salvador, France, Germany, Great Britain, Greece, Guatemala, Haiti, Honduras, Italy, Japan, Korea, Luxembourg, Mexico, Montenegro, Netherlands, Nicaragua, Norway, Panama, Paraguay, Persia, Peru, Portugal, Romania, Russia, Serbia, Siam, Spain, Sweden, Switzerland, Turkey, United States, Uruguay and Venezuela.

States which ratified the 1899 Convention, but did not ratify the 1907 Convention, remain formally bound by the former in their relations with the other parties thereto. As between the parties to the 1907 Convention, this Convention has replaced the 1899 Convention.

† See note on page 120

COVENANT OF THE LEAGUE OF NATIONS

Signed at Versailles on 28 June 1919
Entered into force on 10 January 1920

EXCERPT:

...

Article 8

1. The Members of the League recognise that the maintenance of peace requires the reduction of national armaments to the lowest point consistent with national safety and the enforcement by common action of international obligations.

2. The Council, taking account of the geographical situation and circumstances of each State, shall formulate plans for such reduction for the consideration and action of the several Governments.

3. Such plans shall be subject to reconsideration and revision at least every ten years.

4. After these plans have been adopted by the several Governments, the limits of armaments therein fixed shall not be exceeded without the concurrence of the Council.

5. The Members of the League agree that the manufacture by private enterprise of munitions and implements of war is open to grave objections. The Council shall advise how the evil effects attendant upon such manufacture can be prevented, due regard being had to the necessities of those Members of the League which are not able to manufacture the munitions and implements of war necessary for their safety.

6. The Members of the League undertake to interchange full and frank information as to the scale of their armaments, their military, naval and air programmes and the condition of such of their industries as are adaptable to warlike purposes.

Article 9

A permanent Commission shall be constituted to advise the Council on the execution of the provisions of Articles 1 and 8 and on military, naval and air questions generally.

...

Article 23

Subject to and in accordance with the provisions of international conventions existing or hereafter to be agreed upon, the Members of the League:

...

(*d*) will entrust the League with the general supervision of the trade in arms and ammunition with the countries in which the control of this traffic is necessary in the common interest;

...

Source: *Essential Facts about the League of Nations*, 9th ed., revised (Geneva, 1938)

Members of the League of Nations as of 31 December 1937: Afghanistan, Albania, Argentina, Australia, Austria, Belgium, Bolivia, Bulgaria, Canada, Chile, China, Colombia, Cuba, Czechoslovakia, Denmark, Dominican Republic, Ecuador, Egypt, El Salvador, Estonia, Ethiopia, Finland, France, Greece, Guatemala, Haiti, Honduras, Hungary, India, Iran, Iraq, Ireland, Italy, Latvia, Liberia, Lithuania, Luxembourg, Mexico, Netherlands, New Zealand, Nicaragua, Norway, Panama, Peru, Poland, Portugal, Romania, Siam, Spain, Sweden, Switzerland, Turkey, South Africa, UK, Uruguay, USSR, Venezuela, Yugoslavia

PROTOCOL FOR THE PROHIBITION OF THE USE IN WAR OF ASPHYXIATING, POISONOUS OR OTHER GASES, AND OF BACTERIOLOGICAL METHODS OF WARFARE

Signed at Geneva on 17 June 1925
Entered into force on 8 February 1928
Depositary: French government

The Undersigned plenipotentiaries, in the name of the respective Governments:

Whereas the use in war of asphyxiating, poisonous or other gases, and of all analogous liquids materials or devices, has been justly condemned by the general opinion of the civilised world; and

Whereas the prohibition of such use has been declared in Treaties to which the majority of Powers of the world are Parties; and

To the end that this prohibition shall be universally accepted as a part of International Law, binding alike the conscience and the practice of nations;

Declare:

That the High Contracting Parties, so far as they are not already Parties to Treaties prohibiting such use, accept this prohibition, agree to extend this prohibition to the use of bacteriological methods of warfare and agree to be bound as between themselves according to the terms of this declaration.

The High Contracting Parties will exert every effort to induce other States to accede to the present Protocol. Such accession will be notified to the Government of the French Republic, and by the latter to all signatory and acceding Powers, and will take effect on the date of the notification by the Government of the French Republic.

The present Protocol, of which the French and English texts are both authentic, shall be ratified as soon as possible. It shall bear today's date.

The ratifications of the present Protocol shall be addressed to the Government of the French Republic, which will at once notify the deposit of such ratification to each of the signatory and acceding Powers.

The instruments of ratification of and accession to the present Protocol will remain deposited in the archives of the Government of the French Republic.

The present Protocol will come into force for each signatory Power as from the date of deposit of its ratification, and, from that moment, each Power will be bound as regards other Powers which have already deposited their ratifications.

Source: *League of Nations Treaty Series*, Vol. 94 (1929)

Parties: Argentina, Australia, Austria, Barbados, Belgium, Bhutan, Brazil, Bulgaria, Byelorussia, Canada, Central African Republic, Chile, China, Cuba, Cyprus, Czechoslovakia, Denmark, Dominican Republic, Ecuador, Egypt, Ethiopia, Fiji, Finland, France, Gambia, Germany† (German Democratic Republic by virtue of 1959 notification of renewed applicability), Ghana, Greece, Holy See, Hungary, Iceland, India, Indonesia, Iran, Iraq, Ireland, Israel, Italy, Ivory Coast, Jamaica, Japan, Jordan, Kenya, Kuwait, Lebanon, Lesotho, Liberia, Libya, Luxembourg, Madagascar, Malawi, Malaysia, Maldives, Malta, Mauritius, Mexico, Monaco, Mongolia, Morocco, Nepal, Netherlands, New Zealand, Niger, Nigeria, Norway, Pakistan, Panama, Papua New Guinea, Paraguay, Philippines, Poland, Portugal, Qatar, Romania, Rwanda, Saudi Arabia, Senegal, Sierra Leone, South Africa, Spain, Sri Lanka, Sudan, Sweden, Switzerland, Syria, Thailand, Togo, Tonga, Trinidad and Tobago, Tunisia, Turkey, Uganda, UK, United Republic of Tanzania, Upper Volta, Uruguay, USA, USSR, Venezuela, Viet Nam, Yemen Arab Republic, Yugoslavia

† See note on page 120

PACT OF PARIS (BRIAND-KELLOGG PACT)

Signed at Paris on 27 August 1928
Entered into force on 24 July 1929
Depositary: US government

EXCERPT:

The President of the German Reich, [etc.]:
. . .

Deeply sensible of their solemn duty to promote the welfare of mankind;

Persuaded that the time has come when a frank renunciation of war as an instrument of national policy should be made to the end that the peaceful and friendly relations now existing between their peoples may be perpetuated;

Convinced that all changes in their relations with one another should be sought only by pacific means and be the result of a peaceful and orderly process, and that any signatory Power which shall hereafter seek to promote its national interests by resort to war should be denied the benefits furnished by this Treaty;

Hopeful that, encouraged by their example, all the other nations of the world will join in this humane endeavor and by adhering to the present Treaty as soon as it comes into force bring their peoples within the scope of its beneficent provisions, thus uniting the civilized nations of the world in a common renunciation of war as an instrument of their national policy;

Have decided to conclude a Treaty and for that purpose have appointed as their respective Plenipotentiaries:
. . .

who, having communicated to one another their full powers found in good and due form have agreed upon the following articles:

Article I

The High Contracting Parties solemnly declare in the names of their respective peoples that they condemn recourse to war for the solution of international controversies, and renounce it as an instrument of national policy in their relations with one another.

Article II

The High Contracting Parties agree that the settlement or solution of all disputes or conflicts of whatever nature or of whatever origin they may be, which may arise among them, shall never be sought except by pacific means.

Article III

The present Treaty shall be ratified by the High Contracting Parties named in the Preamble in accordance with their respective constitutional requirements, and shall take effect as between them as soon as all their several instruments of ratification shall have been deposited at Washington.

This Treaty shall, when it has come into effect as prescribed in the preceding paragraph, remain open as long as may be necessary for adherence by all the other Powers of the world. Every instrument evidencing the adherence of a Power shall be deposited at Washington and the Treaty shall immediately upon such deposit become effective as between the Power thus adhering and the other Powers parties hereto.

. . .

Source: *Treaties and Other International Agreements of the United States of America 1776-1949,* Vol 2, Department of State Publication 8441 (Washington, D.C., 1969)

Parties: Afghanistan, Albania, Australia, Austria, Barbados, Belgium, Brazil, Bulgaria, Canada, Chile, Colombia, Costa Rica, Cuba, Czechoslovakia, Denmark, Dominican Republic, Ecuador, Egypt, Ethiopia, Fiji, Finland, France, Germany†, Greece, Guatemala, Haiti, Honduras, Hungary, Iceland, India, Iraq, Ireland, Italy, Japan, Liberia, Luxembourg, Mexico, Netherlands, New Zealand, Nicaragua, Norway, Panama, Paraguay, Peru, Poland, Portugal, Romania, Saudi Arabia, South Africa, Spain, Sweden, Switzerland, Taiwan, Thailand, Turkey, UK, USA, USSR, Venezuela, Yugoslavia

† See note on page 120

III. The post-World War II agreements

CHARTER OF THE UNITED NATIONS

*Signed at San Francisco on 26 June 1945
Entered into force on 24 October 1945*

EXCERPT:

. . .

Article 11

1. The General Assembly may consider the general principles of cooperation in the maintenance of international peace and security, including the principles governing disarmament and the regulation of armaments, and may make recommendations with regard to such principles to the Members or to the Security Council or to both.

. . .

Article 26

In order to promote the establishment and maintenance of international peace and security with the least diversion for armaments of the world's human and economic resources, the Security Council shall be responsible for formulating, with the assistance of the Military Staff Committee referred to in Article 47, plans to be submitted to the Members of the United Nations for the establishment of a system for the regulation of armaments.

. . .

Article 47

1. There shall be established a Military Staff Committee to advise and assist the Security Council on all questions relating to the Security Council's military requirements for the maintenance of international peace and security, the employment and command of forces placed at its disposal, the regulation of armaments, and possible disarmament.

. . .

Source: *Charter of the United Nations, Statute and Rules of Court and other Documents* (International Court of Justice, The Hague, 1978)

Members of the United Nations: Afghanistan, Albania, Algeria, Angola, Antigua and Barbuda, Argentina, Australia, Austria, Bahamas, Bahrain, Bangladesh, Barbados, Belgium, Belize, Benin, Bhutan, Bolivia, Botswana, Brazil, Bulgaria, Burma, Burundi, Byelorussia, Cameroon, Canada, Cape Verde, Central African Republic, Chad, Chile, China, Colombia, Comoros, Congo, Costa Rica, Cuba, Cyprus, Czechoslovakia, Denmark, Djibouti, Dominica, Dominican Republic, Ecuador, Egypt, El Salvador, Equatorial Guinea, Ethiopia, Fiji, Finland, France, Gabon, Gambia, German Democratic Republic, FR Germany, Ghana, Greece, Grenada, Guatemala, Guinea, Guinea-Bissau, Guyana, Haiti, Honduras, Hungary, Iceland, India, Indonesia, Iran, Iraq, Ireland, Israel, Italy, Ivory Coast, Jamaica, Japan, Jordan, Kampuchea, Kenya, Kuwait, Lao People's Democratic Republic, Lebanon, Lesotho, Liberia, Libya, Luxembourg, Madagascar, Malawi, Malaysia, Maldives, Mali, Malta, Mauritania, Mauritius, Mexico, Mongolia, Morocco, Mozambique, Nepal, Netherlands, New Zealand, Nicaragua, Niger, Nigeria, Norway, Oman, Pakistan, Panama, Papua New Guinea, Paraguay, Peru, Philippines, Poland, Portugal, Qatar, Romania, Rwanda, Saint Lucia, Saint Vincent and the Grenadines, Samoa, Sao Tome and Principe, Saudi Arabia, Senegal, Seychelles, Sierra Leone, Singapore, Solomon Islands, Somalia, South Africa, Spain, Sri Lanka, Sudan, Suriname, Swaziland, Sweden, Syria, Tanzania, Thailand, Togo, Trinidad and Tobago, Tunisia, Turkey, Uganda, UK, Ukraine, United Arab Emirates, Upper Volta, Uruguay, USA, USSR, Vanuatu, Venezuela, Viet Nam, Yemen Arab Republic, People's Democratic Republic of Yemen, Yugoslavia, Zaire, Zambia, Zimbabwe

BRUSSELS TREATY OF COLLABORATION AND COLLECTIVE SELF-DEFENCE AMONG WESTERN EUROPEAN STATES

Signed at Brussels on 17 March 1948
Entered into force on 25 August 1948
Depositary: Belgian government

EXCERPT:

His Royal Highness the Prince Regent of Belgium, the President of the French Republic, President of the French Union, Her Royal Highness the Grand Duchess of Luxembourg, Her Majesty the Queen of the Netherlands and His Majesty the King of Great Britain, Ireland and the British Dominions beyond the Seas,
Resolved
. . .
To afford assistance to each other, in accordance with the Charter of the United Nations, in maintaining international peace and security and in resisting any policy of aggression;
To take such steps as may be held to be necessary in the event of a renewal by Germany of a policy of aggression;
To associate progressively in the pursuance of these aims other States inspired by the same ideals and animated by the like determination;
Desiring for these purposes to conclude a treaty for collaboration in economic, social and cultural matters and for collective self-defence;
. . .
have agreed as follows:
. . .

Article IV

If any of the High Contracting Parties should be the object of an armed attack in Europe, the other High Contracting Parties will, in accordance with the provisions of Article 51 of the Charter of the United Nations, afford the Party so attacked all the military and other aid and assistance in their power.

Article V

All measures taken as a result of the preceding Article shall be immediately reported to the Security Council. They shall be terminated as soon as the Security Council has taken the measures necessary to maintain or restore international peace and security.

The present Treaty does not prejudice in any way the obligations of the High Contracting Parties under the provisions of the Charter of the United Nations. It shall not be interpreted as affecting in any way the authority and responsibility of the Security Council under the Charter to take at any time such action as it deems necessary in order to maintain or restore international peace and security.

Article VI

The High Contracting Parties declare, each so far as he is concerned, that none of the international engagements now in force between him and any other of the High Contracting Parties or any third State is in conflict with the provisions of the present Treaty.

None of the High Contracting Parties will conclude any alliance or participate in any coalition directed against any other of the High Contracting Parties.
. . .

Article IX

The High Contracting Parties may, by agreement, invite any other State to accede to the present Treaty on condition to be agreed between them and the State so invited.
. . .

Article X

The present Treaty shall be ratified and the instruments of ratification shall be deposited as soon as possible with the Belgian Government.

It shall enter into force on the date of the deposit of the last instrument of ratification and shall thereafter remain in force for fifty years.
. . .

Source: *Treaty Series*, Vol. 19 (United Nations, New York)

Parties: Belgium, France, Luxembourg, Netherlands, UK

See also Protocols of 1954.

GENEVA CONVENTION (IV) RELATIVE TO THE PROTECTION OF CIVILIAN PERSONS IN TIME OF WAR

Signed at Geneva on 12 August 1949
Entered into force on 21 October 1950
Depositary: Swiss Federal Council

EXCERPT:

PART I. GENERAL PROVISIONS

Article 1

The High Contracting Parties undertake to respect and to ensure respect for the present Convention in all circumstances.

Article 2

In addition to the provisions which shall be implemented in peacetime, the present Convention shall apply to all cases of declared war or of any other armed conflict which may arise between two or more of the High Contracting Parties, even if the state of war is not recognized by one of them.

The Convention shall also apply to all cases of partial or total occupation of the territory of a High Contracting Party, even if the said occupation meets with no armed resistance.

Although one of the Powers in conflict may not be a party to the present Convention, the Powers who are parties thereto shall remain bound by it in their mutual relations. They shall furthermore be bound by the Convention in relation to the said Power, if the latter accepts and applies the provisions thereof.

Article 3

In the case of armed conflict not of an international character occurring in the territory of one of the High Contracting Parties, each Party to the conflict shall be bound to apply, as a minimum, the following provisions:

1. Persons taking no active part in the hostilities, including members of armed forces who have laid down their arms and those placed *hors de combat* by sickness, wounds, detention, or any other cause, shall in all circumstances be treated humanely, without any adverse distinction founded on race, colour, religion or faith, sex, birth or wealth, or any other similar criteria.

To this end, the following acts are and shall remain prohibited at any time and in any place whatsoever with respect to the above-mentioned persons:

(*a*) violence to life and person, in particular murder of all kinds, mutilation, cruel treatment and torture;

(*b*) taking of hostages;

(*c*) outrages upon personal dignity, in particular humiliating and degrading treatment;

(*d*) the passing of sentences and the carrying out of executions without previous judgment pronounced by a regularly constituted court, affording all the judicial guarantees which are recognized as indispensable by civilized peoples.

2. The wounded and sick shall be collected and cared for.

An impartial humanitarian body, such as the International Commitee of the Red Cross, may offer its services to the Parties to the conflict.

The Parties to the conflict should further endeavour to bring into force, by means of special agreements, all or part of the other provisions of the present Convention.

The application of the preceding provisions shall not affect the legal status of the Parties to the conflict.

Article 4

Persons protected by the Convention are those who, at a given moment and in any manner whatsoever, find themselves, in case of a conflict or occupation, in the hands of a Party to the conflict or Occupying Power of which they are not nationals.

Nationals of a State which is not bound by the Convention are not protected by it. Nationals of a neutral State who find themselves in the territory of a belligerent State, and nationals of a co-belligerent State, shall not be regarded as protected persons while the State of which they are nationals has normal diplomatic representation in the State in whose hands they are.

The provisions of Part II are, however, wider in application, as defined in Article 13.

Persons protected by the Geneva Convention for the Amelioration of the Condition of the Wounded and Sick in Armed Forces in the Field of August 12, 1949, or by the Geneva Convention for the Amelioration of the Condition of Wounded, Sick and Shipwrecked Members of Armed Forces at Sea of August 12, 1949, or by the Geneva Convention relative to the Treatment of Prisoners of War of August 12, 1949, shall not be considered as protected persons within the meaning of the present Convention.

. . .

PART II. GENERAL PROTECTION OF POPULATIONS AGAINST CERTAIN CONSEQUENCES OF WAR

Article 13

The provisions of Part II cover the whole of the populations of the countries in conflict, without any adverse distinction based, in particular, on race, nationality, religion or political opinion, and are intended to alleviate the sufferings caused by war.

Article 14

In time of peace, the High Contracting Parties and, after the outbreak of hostilities, the Parties thereto, may establish in their own territory and, if the need arises, in occupied areas, hospital and safety zones and localities so organized as to protect from the effects of war, wounded, sick and aged persons, children under fifteen, expectant mothers and mothers of children under seven.

Upon the outbreak and during the course of hostilities, the Parties concerned may conclude agreements on mutual recognition of the zones and localities they have created. They may for this purpose implement the provisions of the Draft Agreement annexed to the present Convention, with such amendments as they may consider necessary.

The Protecting Powers and the International Committee of the Red Cross are invited to lend their good offices in order to facilitate the institution and recognition of these hospital and safety zones and localities.

Article 15

Any Party to the conflict may, either direct or through a neutral State or some humanitarian organization, propose to the adverse Party to establish, in the regions where fighting is taking place, neutralized zones intended to shelter from the effects of war the following persons, without distinction:

(a) wounded and sick combatants or non-combatants;

(b) civilian persons who take no part in hostilities, and who, while they reside in the zones, perform no work of a military character.

When the Parties concerned have agreed upon the geographical position, administration, food supply and supervision of the proposed neutralized zone, a written agreement shall be concluded and signed by the representatives of the Parties to the conflict. The agreement shall fix the beginning and the duration of the neutralization of the zone.

Article 16

The wounded and sick, as well as the infirm, and expectant mothers, shall be the object of particular protection and respect.

As far as military considerations allow, each Party to the conflict shall facilitate the steps taken to search for the killed and wounded, to assist the shipwrecked and other persons exposed to grave danger, and to protect them against pillage and ill-treatment.

Article 17

The Parties to the conflict shall endeavour to conclude local agreements for the removal from besieged or encircled areas, of wounded, sick, infirm, and aged persons, children and maternity cases, and for the passage of ministers of all religions, medical personnel and medical equipment on their way to such areas.

Article 18

Civilian hospitals organized to give care to the wounded and sick, the infirm and maternity cases, may in no circumstances be the object of attack, but shall at all times be respected and protected by the Parties to the conflict.

States which are Parties to a conflict shall provide all civilian hospitals with certificates showing that they are civilian hospitals and that the buildings which they occupy are not used for any purpose which would deprive these hospitals of protection in accordance with Article 19.

Civilian hospitals shall be marked by means of the emblem provided for in Article 38 of the Geneva Convention for the Amelioration of the Condition of the Wounded and Sick in Armed Forces in the Field of August 12, 1949, but only if so authorized by the State.

The Parties to the conflict shall, in so far as military considerations permit, take the necessary steps to make the distinctive emblems indicating civilian hospitals clearly visible to the enemy land, air and naval forces in order to obviate the possibility of any hostile action.

In view of the dangers to which hospitals may be exposed by being close to military objectives, it is recommended that such hospitals be situated as far as possible from such objectives.

Article 19

The protection to which civilian hospitals are entitled shall not cease unless they are used to commit, outside their humanitarian duties, acts harmful to the enemy. Protection may, however, cease only after due warning has been given, naming, in all appropriate cases, a reasonable time limit, and after such warning has remained unheeded.

The fact that sick or wounded members of the armed forces are nursed in these hospitals, or the presence of small arms and ammunition taken from such combatants and not yet handed to the proper service, shall not be considered to be acts harmful to the enemy.

Article 20

Persons regularly and solely engaged in the operation and administration of civilian hospitals, including the personnel engaged in the search for, removal and transporting of and caring for wounded and sick civilians, the infirm and maternity cases, shall be respected and protected.

In occupied territory and in zones of military operations, the above personnel shall be recognizable by means of an identity card certifying their status, bearing the photograph of the holder and embossed with the stamp of the responsible authority, and also by means of a stamped, water-resistant armlet which they shall wear on the left arm while carrying out their duties. This armlet shall be issued by the State and shall bear the emblem provided for in Article 38 of the Geneva Convention for the Amelioration of the Condition of the Wounded and Sick in Armed Forces in the Field of August 12, 1949.

Other personnel who are engaged in the operation and administration of civilian hospitals shall be entitled to respect and protection and to wear the armlet, as provided in and under the conditions prescribed in this Article, while they are employed on such duties. The identity card shall state the duties on which they are employed.

The management of each hospital shall at all times hold at the disposal of the competent national or occupying authorities an up-to-date list of such personnel.

Article 21

Convoys of vehicles or hospital trains on land or specially provided vessels on sea, conveying wounded and sick civilians, the infirm and maternity cases, shall be respected and protected in the same manner as the hospitals provided for in Article 18, and shall be marked, with the consent of the State, by the display of the distinctive emblem provided for in Article 38 of the Geneva Convention for the Amelioration of the Condition of the Wounded and Sick in Armed Forces in the Field of August 12, 1949.

Article 22

Aircraft exclusively employed for the removal of wounded and sick civilians, the infirm and maternity cases, or for the transport of medical personnel and equipment, shall not be attacked, but shall be respected while flying at heights, times and on routes specifically agreed upon between all the Parties to the conflict concerned.

They may be marked with the distinctive emblem provided for in Article 38 of the Geneva Convention for the Amelioration of the Condition of the Wounded and Sick in Armed Forces in the Field of August 12, 1949.

Unless agreed otherwise, flights over enemy or enemy-occupied territory are prohibited.

Such aircraft shall obey every summons to land. In the event of a landing thus imposed, the aircraft with its occupants may continue its flight after examination, if any.

. . .

PART IV. EXECUTION OF THE CONVENTION

. . .

Article 146

The High Contracting Parties undertake to enact any legislation necessary to provide effective penal sanctions for persons committing, or ordering to be committed, any of the grave breaches of the present Convention defined in the following Article.

Each High Contracting Party shall be under the obligation to search for persons alleged to have committed, or to have ordered to be committed, such grave breaches, and shall bring such persons, regardless of their nationality, before its own courts. It may also, if it prefers, and in accordance with the provisions of its own legislation, hand such persons over for trial to another High Contracting Party concerned, provided such High Contracting Party has made out a *prima facie* case.

Each High Contracting Party shall take measures necessary for the suppression of all acts contrary to the provisions of the present Convention other than the grave breaches defined in the following Article.

In all circumstances, the accused persons shall benefit by safeguards of proper trial and defence, which shall not be less favourable than those provided by Article 105 and those following of the Geneva Convention relative to the Treatment of Prisoners of War of August 12, 1949.

Article 147

Grave breaches to which the preceding Article relates shall be those involving any of the following acts, if committed against persons or property protected by the present Convention: wilful killing, torture or inhuman treatment, including biological experiments, wilfully causing great suffering or serious injury to body or health, unlawful deportation or transfer or unlawful confinement of a protected person, compelling a protected person to serve in the forces of a hostile Power, or wilfully depriving a protected person of the rights of fair and regular trial prescribed in the present Convention, taking of hostages and extensive destruction and appropriation of property, not justified by military necessity and carried out unlawfully and wantonly.

Article 148

No High Contracting Party shall be allowed to absolve itself or any other High Contracting Party of any liability incurred by itself or by another High Contracting Party in respect of breaches referred to in the preceding Article.

Article 149

At the request of a Party to the conflict, an enquiry shall be instituted, in a manner to be decided between the interested Parties, concerning any alleged violation of the Convention.

If agreement has not been reached concerning the procedure for the enquiry, the Parties should agree on the choice of an umpire who will decide upon the procedure to be followed.

Once the violation has been established, the Parties to the conflict shall put an end to it and shall repress it with the least possible delay.

. . .

Article 151

The present Convention, which bears the date of this day, is open to signature until February 12, 1950, in the name of the Powers represented at the Conference which opened at Geneva on April 21, 1949.

Article 152

The present Convention shall be ratified as soon as possible and the ratifications shall be deposited at Berne.

A record shall be drawn up of the deposit of each instrument of ratification and certified copies of this record shall be transmitted by the Swiss Federal Council to all the Powers in whose name the Convention has been signed, or whose accession has been notified.

Article 153

The present Convention shall come into force six months after not less than two instruments of ratification have been deposited.

Thereafter, it shall come into force for each High Contracting Party six months after the deposit of the instrument of ratification.

Article 154

In the relations between the Powers who are bound by The Hague Conventions respecting the Laws and Customs of War on Land, whether that of July 29, 1899, or that of October 18, 1907, and who are parties to the present Convention, this last Convention shall be supplementary to Sections II and III of the Regulations annexed to the above mentioned Conventions of The Hague.

Article 155

From the date of its coming into force, it shall be open to any Power in whose name the present Convention has not been signed, to accede to this Convention.

Article 156

Accessions shall be notified in writing to the Swiss Federal Council, and shall take effect six months after the date on which they are received.

The Swiss Federal Council shall communicate the accessions to all the Powers in whose name the Convention has been signed, or whose accession has been notified.

Article 157

The situations provided for in Articles 2 and 3 shall give immediate effect to ratifications deposited and accessions notified by the Parties to the conflict before or after the beginning of hostilities or occupation. The Swiss Federal Council shall communicate by the quickest method any ratifications or accessions received from Parties to the conflict.

Article 158

Each of the High Contracting Parties shall be at liberty to denounce the present Convention.

The denunciation shall be notified in writing to the Swiss Federal Council, which shall transmit it to the Governments of all the High Contracting Parties.

The denunciation shall take effect one year after the notification thereof has been made to the Swiss Federal Council. However, a denunciation of which notification has been made at a time when the denouncing Power is involved in a conflict shall not take effect until peace has been concluded, and until after operations connected with the release, repatriation and re-establishment of the persons protected by the present Convention have been terminated.

The denunciation shall have effect only in respect of the denouncing Power. It shall in no way impair the obligations which the Parties to the conflict shall remain bound to fulfil by virtue of the principles of the law of nations, as they result from the usages established among civilized peoples, from the laws of humanity and the dictates of the public conscience.

...

Source: *Treaty Series*, Vol. 75 (United Nations, New York)

Parties: Afghanistan, Albania, Algeria, Argentina, Australia, Austria, Bahamas, Bahrain, Bangladesh, Barbados, Belgium, Benin, Bolivia, Botswana, Brazil, Bulgaria, Burundi, Byelorussia, Cameroon, Canada, Central African Republic, Chad, Chile, China, Colombia, Congo, Costa Rica, Cuba, Cyprus, Czechoslovakia, Denmark, Djibouti, Dominica, Dominican Republic, Ecuador, Egypt, El Salvador, Ethiopia, Fiji, Finland, France, Gabon, Gambia, German Democratic Republic, FR Germany, Ghana, Greece, Grenada, Guatemala, Guinea-Bissau, Guyana, Haiti, Holy See, Honduras, Hungary, Iceland, India, Indonesia, Iran, Iraq, Ireland, Israel, Italy, Ivory Coast, Jamaica, Japan, Jordan, Kampuchea, Kenya, Democratic People's Republic of Korea, Republic of Korea, Kuwait, Lao People's Democratic Republic, Lebanon, Lesotho, Liberia, Libya, Liechtenstein, Luxembourg, Madagascar, Malawi, Malaysia, Mali, Malta, Mauritania, Mauritius, Mexico, Monaco, Mongolia, Morocco, Nepal, Netherlands, New Zealand, Nicaragua, Niger, Nigeria, Norway, Oman, Pakistan, Panama, Papua New Guinea, Paraguay, Peru, Philippines, Poland, Portugal, Qatar, Romania, Rwanda, Saint Lucia, Saint Vincent and the Grenadines, San Marino, Sao Tomé and Principe, Saudi Arabia, Senegal, Sierra Leone, Singapore, Solomon Islands, Somalia, South Africa, Spain, Sri Lanka, Sudan, Suriname, Swaziland, Sweden, Switzerland, Syria, Tanzania, Thailand, Togo, Tonga, Trinidad and Tobago, Tunisia, Turkey, Tuvalu, Uganda, UK, Ukraine, United Arab Emirates, Upper Volta, Uruguay, USA, USSR, Venezuela, Viet Nam, Yemen Arab Republic, People's Democratic Republic of Yemen, Yugoslavia, Zaire, Zambia

Geneva Convention IV was worked out at the Diplomatic Conference held from 21 April to 12 August 1949. Other conventions adopted at the same time:

Convention (I) for the amelioration of the condition of the wounded and sick in armed forces in the field.

Convention (II) for the amelioration of the condition of the wounded, sick and shipwrecked members of armed forces at sea.

Convention (III) relative to the treatment of prisoners of war.

See also Protocols of 1977.

PROTOCOLS TO THE 1948 BRUSSELS TREATY OF COLLABORATION AND COLLECTIVE SELF-DEFENCE AMONG WESTERN EUROPEAN STATES

Signed at Paris on 23 October 1954
Entered into force on 6 May 1955
Depositary: Belgian government

EXCERPT:

Protocol No. I Modifying and completing the above-mentioned Treaty

His Majesty the King of the Belgians, the President of the French Republic, President of the French Union, Her Royal Highness the Grand Duchess of Luxembourg, Her Majesty the Queen of the Netherlands and Her Majesty the Queen of the United Kingdom of Great Britain and Northern Ireland and of Her other Realms and Territories, Head of the Commonwealth, Parties to the Treaty of Economic, Social and Cultural Collaboration and Collective Self-Defence, signed at Brussels on March the 17th, 1948, hereinafter referred to as the Treaty, on the one hand,

and the President of the Federal Republic of Germany and the President of the Italian Republic on the other hand,
. . .

Have agreed as follows:

Article 1

The Federal Republic of Germany and the Italian Republic hereby accede to the Treaty as modified and completed by the present Protocol.

The High Contracting Parties to the present Protocol consider the Protocol on Forces of Western European Union (hereinafter referred to as Protocol No. II), the Protocol on the Control of Armaments and its Annexes (hereinafter referred to as Protocol No. III), and the Protocol on the Agency of Western European Union for the Control of Armaments (hereinafter referred to as Protocol No. IV) to be an integral part of the present Protocol.

Article 2

The sub-paragraph of the Preamble to the Treaty: «to take such steps as may be held necessary in the event of renewal by Germany of a policy of aggression» shall be modified to read: «to promote the unity and to encourage the progressive integration of Europe».
. . .

Article 3

The following new Article shall be inserted in the Treaty as Article IV: «In the execution of the Treaty the High Contracting Parties and any organs established by Them under the Treaty shall work in close co-operation

with the North Atlantic Treaty Organization».
. . .

Article 6

The present Protocol and the other Protocols listed in Article I above shall be ratified and the instruments of ratification shall be deposited as soon as possible with the Belgian Government.

They shall enter into force when all instruments of ratification of the present Protocol have been deposited with the Belgian Government and the instrument of accession of the Federal Republic of Germany to the North Atlantic Treaty has been deposited with the Government of the United States of America.
. . .

Protocol No. II on forces of Western European Union
. . .

Article 1

1. The land and air forces which each of the High Contracting Parties to the present Protocol shall place under the Supreme Allied Commander Europe in peacetime on the mainland of Europe shall not exceed in total strength and number of formations:

(*a*) for Belgium, France, the Federal Republic of Germany, Italy and the Netherlands, the maxima laid down for peacetime in the Special Agreement annexed to the Treaty on the Establishment of a European Defence Community signed at Paris, on 27th May, 1952;* and

(*b*) for the United Kingdom, four divisions and the Second Tactical Air Force;

(*c*) for Luxembourg, one regimental combat team.

2. The number of formations mentioned in paragraph 1 may be brought up to date and adapted as necessary to make them suitable for the North Atlantic Treaty Organization, provided that the equivalent fighting capacity and total strengths are not exceeded.

3. The statement of these maxima does not commit any of the High Contracting Parties to build up or maintain forces at these levels, but maintains their right to do so if required.

Article 2

As regards naval forces, the contribution to NATO Commands of each of the High Contracting Parties to the present Protocol shall be determined each year in the course of the Annual Review (which takes into account the recommendations of the NATO military authorities). The naval forces of the Federal Republic of Germany shall consist of the vessels and formations necessary for the defensive missions assigned to it by the North Atlantic Treaty Organization within the limits

---

* This Treaty, signed by Belgium, France, FR Germany, Italy, Luxembourg and the Netherlands, did not enter into force.

laid down in the Special Agreement mentioned in Article 1, or equivalent fighting capacity.

...

Article 5

The strength and armaments of the internal defence and police forces on the mainland of Europe of the High Contracting Parties to the present Protocol shall be fixed by agreements within the Organization of Western European Union, having regard to their proper functions and needs and to their existing levels.

...

Protocol No. III (with Annexes) on the Control of Armaments

Part I. *Armaments not to be manufactured*

Article 1

The High Contracting Parties, members of Western European Union, take note of and record their agreement with the Declaration of the Chancellor of the Federal Republic of Germany (made in London on 3rd October, 1954, and annexed hereto as Annex I) in which the Federal Republic of Germany undertook not to manufacture in its territory atomic, biological and chemical weapons. The types of armaments referred to in this Article are defined in Annex II. These armaments shall be more closely defined and the definitions brought up to date by the Council of Western European Union.

Article 2

The High Contracting Parties, members of Western European Union, also take note of and record their agreement with the undertaking given by the Chancellor of the Federal Republic of Germany in the same Declaration that certain further types of armaments will not be manufactured in the territory of the Federal Republic of Germany, except that if in accordance with the needs of the armed forces a recommendation for an amendment to, or cancellation of, the content of the list of these armaments is made by the competent Supreme Commander of the North Atlantic Treaty Organization, and if the Government of the Federal Republic of Germany submits a request accordingly, such an amendment or cancellation may be made by a resolution of the Council of Western European Union passed by a two-thirds majority. The types of armaments referred to in this Article are listed in Annex III.

Part II. *Armaments to be controlled*

Article 3

When the development of atomic, biological and chemical weapons in the territory on the mainland of Europe of the High Contracting Parties who have not given up the right to produce them has passed the experimental stage and effective production of

them has started there, the level of stocks that the High Contracting Parties concerned will be allowed to hold on the mainland of Europe shall be decided by a majority vote of the Council of Western European Union.

Article 4

Without prejudice to the foregoing Articles, the types of armaments listed in Annex IV will be controlled to the extent and in the manner laid down in Protocol No. IV.

Article 5

The Council of Western European Union may vary the list in Annex IV by unanimous decision.

...

ANNEX I

The Federal Chancellor declares:

that the Federal Republic undertakes not to manufacture in its territory any atomic weapons, chemical weapons or biological weapons, as detailed in paragraphs I, II and III of the attached list,

that it undertakes further not to manufacture in its territory such weapons as those detailed in paragraphs IV, V and VI of the attached list. Any amendment to or cancellation of the substance of paragraphs IV, V and VI can, on the request of the Federal Republic, be carried out by a resolution of the Brussels Council of Ministers by a two-thirds majority, if in accordance with the needs of the armed forces a request is made by the competent Supreme Commander of the North Atlantic Treaty Organization;

that the Federal Republic agrees to supervision by the competent authority of the Brussels Treaty Organization to ensure that these undertakings are observed.

ANNEX II

This list comprises the weapons defined in paragraphs I to III and the factories earmarked solely for their production. All apparatus, parts, equipment, installations, substances and organisms, which are used for civilian purposes or for scientific, medical and industrial research in the fields of pure and applied science shall be excluded from this definition.

I. *Atomic Weapons*

(*a*) An atomic weapon is defined as any weapon which contains, or is designed to contain or utilise, nuclear fuel or radioactive isotopes and which, by explosion or other uncontrolled nuclear transformation of the nuclear fuel, or by radioactivity of the nuclear fuel or radioactive isotopes, is capable of mass destruction, mass injury or mass poisoning.

(*b*) Furthermore, any part, device, assembly or material especially designed for, or primarily useful in, any weapon as set forth under paragraph (*a*), shall be deemed to be an atomic weapon.

(*c*) Nuclear fuel as used in the preceding

definition includes plutonium, Uranium 223, Uranium 235 (including Uranium 235 contained in Uranium enriched to over 2.1 per cent by weight of Uranium 235) and any other material capable of releasing substantial quantities of atomic energy through nuclear fission or fusion or other nuclear reaction of the material. The foregoing materials shall be considered to be nuclear fuel regardless of the chemical or physical form in which they exist.

II. Chemical Weapons

(a) A chemical weapon is defined as any equipment or apparatus expressly designed to use, for military purposes, the asphyxiating, toxic, irritant, paralysant, growth-regulating, anti-lubricating or catalysing properties of any chemical substance.

(b) Subject to the provisions of paragraph (c), chemical substances, having such properties and capable of being used in the equipment of apparatus referred to in paragraph (a), shall be deemed to be included in this definition.

(c) Such apparatus and such quantities of the chemical substances as are referred to in paragraphs (a) and (b) which do not exceed peaceful civilian requirements shall be deemed to be excluded from this definition.

III. Biological Weapons

(a) A biological weapon is defined as any equipment or apparatus expressly designed to use, for military purposes, harmful insects or other living or dead organisms, or their toxic products.

(b) Subject to the provisions of paragraph (c), insects, organisms and their toxic products of such nature and in such amounts as to make them capable of being used in the equipment or apparatus referred to in (a) shall be deemed to be included in this definition.

(c) Such equipment or apparatus and such quantities of the insects, organisms and their toxic products as are referred to in paragraphs (a) and (b) which do not exceed peaceful civilian requirements shall be deemed to be excluded from the definition of biological weapons.

ANNEX III

This list comprises the weapons defined in paragraphs IV to VI and the factories earmarked solely for their production. All apparatus, parts, equipment, installations, substances and organisms, which are used for civilian purposes or for scientific, medical and industrial research in the fields of pure and applied science shall be excluded from this definition.

IV. Long-range Missiles, Guided Missiles and Influence Mines

(a) Subject to the provisions of paragraph (d), long-range missiles and guided missiles are defined as missiles such that the speed or direction of motion can be influenced after the instant of launching by a device or mechanism inside or outside the missile, including V-type weapons developed in the recent war and subsequent modifications thereof. Combustion is considered as a mechanism which may influence the speed.

(b) Subject to the provisions of paragraph (d), influence mines are defined as naval mines which can be exploded automatically by influences which emanate solely from external sources, including influence mines developed in the recent war and subsequent modifications thereof.

(c) Parts, devices or assemblies specially designed for use in or with the weapons referred to in paragraphs (a) and (b) shall be deemed to be included in this definition.

(d) Proximity fuses, and short-range guided missiles for anti-aircraft defence with the following maximum characteristics are regarded as excluded from this definition:
Length, 2 metres;
Diameter, 30 centimetres;
Speed, 660 metres per second;
Ground range, 32 kilometres;
Weight of war-head, 22.5 kilogrammes.

V. Warships, with the exception of smaller ships for defence purposes

«Warships, with the exception of smaller ships for defences purposes are:

(a) Warships of more than 3,000 tons displacement;

(b) Submarines of more than 350 tons displacement;

(c) All warships which are driven by means other than steam, Diesel or petrol engines or by gas turbines or by jet engines.»

VI. Bomber aircraft for strategic purposes

ANNEX IV

List of Types of Armaments to be Controlled

1. (a) Atomic
   (b) biological, and
   (c) chemical weapons.
In accordance with definitions to be approved by the Council of Western European Union is indicated in Article I of the present Protocol.

2. All guns, howitzers and mortars of any types and of any rôles of more than 90 mm. calibre including the following component for these weapons, viz., the elevating mass.

3. All guided missiles.

Definition: Guided missiles are such that the speed or direction or motion can be influenced after the instant of launching by a device or mechanism inside or outside the missile; these include V-type weapons developed in the recent war and modifications thereto. Combustion is considered as a mechanism which may influence the speed.

4. Other self-propelled missiles of a weight exceeding 15 kilogrammes in working order.

5. Mines of all types except anti-tank and anti-personnel mines.

6. Tanks, including the following

component parts for these tanks, viz:

(*a*) the elevating mass;

(*b*) turret castings and/or plate assembly.

7. Other armoured fighting vehicles of an overall weight of more than 10 metric tons.

8. (*a*) Warships over 1,500 tons displacement;

(*b*) submarines;

(*c*) all warships powered by means other than steam, diesel or petrol engines or gas turbines;

(*d*) small craft capable of a speed of over 30 knots, equipped with offensive armament.

9. Aircraft bombs of more than 1,000 kilogrammes.

10. Ammunition for the weapons described in paragraph 2 above.

11. (*a*) Complete military aircraft other than:

(i) all training aircraft except operational types used for training purposes;

(ii) military transport and communication aircraft;

(iii) helicopters;

(*b*) air frames, specifically and exclusively designed for military aircraft except those at (i), (ii) and (iii) above;

(*c*) jet engines, turbo-propeller engines and rocket motors, when these are the principal motive power.

Protocol No. IV on the Agency of Western European Union for the Control of Armaments

Part I. *Constitution*

Article 1

The Agency for the Control of Armaments (hereinafter referred to as «the Agency») shall be responsible to the Council of Western European Union (hereinafter referred to as «the Council»). It shall consist of a Director assisted by a Deputy Director, and supported by a staff drawn equitably from nationals of the High Contracting Parties, Members of Western European Union.

. . .

Part II. *Functions*

Article 7

1. The tasks of the Agency shall be:

(*a*) to satisfy itself that the undertakings set out in Protocol No. III not to manufacture certain types of armaments mentioned in Annexes II and III to that Protocol are being observed;

(*b*) to control, in accordance with Part III of the present Protocol, the level of stocks of armaments of the types mentioned in Annex IV to Protocol No. III held by each member of Western European Union on the mainland of Europe. This control shall extend to production and imports to the extent required to make the control of stocks effective.

2. For the purposes mentioned in paragraph 1 of this Article, the Agency shall:

(*a*) scrutinise statistical and budgetary

information supplied by members of Western European Union and by the NATO authorities;

(*b*) undertake on the mainland of Europe test checks, visits and inspections at production plants, depots and forces (other than depots or forces under NATO authority);

(*c*) report to the Council.

. . .

Part III. *Levels of stocks of armaments*

Article 13

1. Each member of Western European Union shall, in respect of its forces under NATO authority stationed on the mainland of Europe, furnish annually to the Agency statements of:

(*a*) the total quantities of armaments of the types mentioned in Annex IV to Protocol No. III required in relation to its forces;

(*b*) the quantities of such armaments currently held at the beginning of the control years;

(*c*) the programmes for attaining the total quantities mentioned in (*a*) by:

(i) manufacture in its own territory;

(ii) purchase from another country;

(iii) end-item aid from another country.

2. Such statements shall also be furnished by each member of Western European Union in respect of its internal defence and police forces and its other forces under national control stationed on the mainland of Europe including a statement of stocks held there for its forces stationed overseas.

3. The statements shall be correlated with the relevant submissions to the North Atlantic Treaty Organization.

. . .

Source: *Treaty Series*, Vol. 211 (United Nations, New York)

Parties: Belgium, France, FR Germany, Italy, Luxembourg, Netherlands, UK

STATUTE OF THE INTERNATIONAL ATOMIC ENERGY AGENCY

Opened for signature on 26 October 1956
Entered into force on 29 July 1957

EXCERPT:
. . .

Article III. *Functions*

A. The Agency is authorized:

. . .

5. To establish and administer safeguards designed to ensure that special fissionable and other materials, services, equipment,

facilities, and information made available by the Agency or at its request or under its supervision or control are not used in such a way as to further any military purpose; and to apply safeguards, at the request of the parties, to any bilateral or multilateral arrangement, or at the request of a State, to any of that State's activities in the field of atomic energy.

...

Article XII. *Agency safeguards*

A. With respect to any Agency project, or other arrangement where the Agency is requested by the parties concerned to apply safeguards, the Agency shall have the following rights and responsibilities to the extent relevant to the project or arrangement:

1. To examine the design of specialized equipment and facilities, including nuclear reactors, and to approve it only from the view-point of assuring that it will not further any military purpose, that it complies with applicable health and safety standards, and that it will permit effective application of the safeguards provided for in this article;

2. To require the observance of any health and safety measures prescribed by the Agency;

3. To require the maintenance and production of operating records to assist in ensuring accountability for source and special fissionable materials used or produced in the project or arrangement;

4. To call for and receive progress reports;

5. To approve the means to be used for the chemical processing of irradiated materials solely to ensure that this chemical processing will not lend itself to diversion of materials for military purposes and will comply with applicable health and safety standards; to require that special fissionable materials recovered or produced as a by-product be used for peaceful purposes under continuing Agency safeguards for research or in reactors, existing or under construction, specified by the member or members concerned; and to require deposit with the Agency of any excess of any special fissionable materials recovered or produced as a by-product over what is needed for the above-stated uses in order to prevent stock-piling of these materials, provided that thereafter at the request of the member or members concerned special fissionable materials so deposited with the Agency shall be returned promptly to the member or members concerned for use under the same provisions as stated above;

6. To send into the territory of the recipient State or States inspectors, designated by the Agency after consultation with the State or States concerned, who shall have access at all times to all places and data and to any person who by reason of his occupation deals with materials, equipment, or facilities which are required by this Statute to be safeguarded, as necessary to account for source and special fissionable materials supplied and fissionable products and to determine whether there is compliance with the undertaking against use in furtherance of any military purpose referred to in sub-paragraph F-4 of article XI, with the health and safety measures referred to in sub-paragraph A-2 of this article, and with any other conditions prescribed in the agreement between the Agency and the State or States concerned. Inspectors designated by the Agency shall be accompanied by representatives of the authorities of the State concerned, if that State so requests, provided that the inspectors shall not thereby be delayed or otherwise impeded in the exercise of their functions;

7. In the event of non-compliance and failure by the recipient State or States to take requested corrective steps within a reasonable time, to suspend or terminate assistance and withdraw any materials and equipment made available by the Agency or a member in furtherance of the project.

B. The Agency shall, as necessary, establish a staff of inspectors. The staff of inspectors shall have the responsibility of examining all operations conducted by the Agency itself to determine whether the Agency is complying with the health and safety measures prescribed by it for application to projects subject to its approval, supervision or control, and whether the Agency is taking adequate measures to prevent the source and special fissionable materials in its custody or used or produced in its own operations from being used in furtherance of any military purpose. The Agency shall take remedial action forthwith to correct any non-compliance or failure to take adequate measures.

C. ... The inspectors shall report any non-compliance to the Director General who shall thereupon transmit the report to the Board of Governors. The Board shall call upon the recipient State or States to remedy forthwith any non-compliance which it finds to have occurred. The Board shall report the non-compliance to all members and to the Security Council and General Assembly of the United Nations. In the event of failure of the recipient State or States to take fully corrective action within a reasonable time, the Board may take one or both of the following measures: direct curtailment or suspension of assistance being provided by the Agency or by a member, and call for the return of materials and equipment made available to the recipient member or group of members. The Agency may also, in accordance with article XIX, suspend any non-complying member from the exercise of the privileges and rights of membership.

...

Article XX. *Definitions*

As used in this Statute:

1. The term "special fissionable material" means plutonium-239; uranium-233; uranium enriched in the isotopes 235 or 233; any material containing one or more of the foregoing; and such other fissionable material as the Board of Governors shall from time to

time determine; but the term "special fissionable material" does not include source material.

2. The term "uranium enriched in the isotopes 235 or 233" means uranium containing the isotopes 235 or 233 or both in an amount such that the abundance ratio of the sum of these isotopes to the isotope 238 is greater than the ratio of the isotope 235 to the isotope 238 occurring in nature.

3. The term "source material" means uranium containing the mixture of isotopes occurring in nature; uranium depleted in the isotope 235; thorium; any of the foregoing in the form of metal, alloy, chemical compound, or concentrate; any other material containing one or more of the foregoing in such concentration as the Board of Governors shall from time to time determine; and such other material as the Board of Governors shall from time to time determine.
. . .

Source: *Statute* as amended up to 1 June 1973 (IAEA, Vienna, 1980)

Members of the IAEA: Afghanistan, Albania, Algeria, Argentina, Australia, Austria, Bangladesh, Belgium, Bolivia, Brazil, Bulgaria, Burma, Byelorussia, Cameroon, Canada, Chile, Colombia, Costa Rica, Cuba, Cyprus, Czechoslovakia, Denmark, Dominican Republic, Ecuador, Egypt, El Salvador, Ethiopia, Finland, France, Gabon, German Democratic Republic, FR Germany, Ghana, Greece, Guatemala, Haiti, Holy See, Hungary, Iceland, India, Indonesia, Iran, Iraq, Ireland, Israel, Italy, Ivory Coast, Jamaica, Japan, Jordan, Kampuchea, Kenya, Democratic People's Republic of Korea, Republic of Korea, Kuwait, Lebanon, Liberia, Libya, Liechtenstein, Luxembourg, Madagascar, Malaysia, Mali, Mauritius, Mexico, Monaco, Mongolia, Morocco, Netherlands, New Zealand, Nicaragua, Niger, Nigeria, Norway, Pakistan, Panama, Paraguay, Peru, Philippines, Poland, Portugal, Qatar, Romania, Saudi Arabia, Senegal, Sierra Leone, Singapore, South Africa, Spain, Sri Lanka, Sudan, Sweden, Switzerland, Syria, Tanzania, Thailand, Tunisia, Turkey, Uganda, UK, Ukraine, United Arab Emirates, Uruguay, USA, USSR, Venezuela, Viet Nam, Yugoslavia, Zaire, Zambia, Zimbabwe

ANTARCTIC TREATY

Signed at Washington on 1 December 1959
Entered into force on 23 June 1961
Depositary: US government

The Governments of Argentina, Australia, Belgium, Chile, the French Republic, Japan, New Zealand, Norway, the Union of South Africa, the Union of Soviet Socialist Republics, the United Kingdom of Great Britain and Northern Ireland, and the United States of America,

Recognizing that it is in the interest of all mankind that Antarctica shall continue for-ever to be used exclusively for peaceful purposes and shall not become the scene or object of international discord;

Acknowledging the substantial contributions to scientific knowledge resulting from international cooperation in scientific investigation in Antarctica;

Convinced that the establishment of a firm foundation for the continuation and development of such cooperation on the basis of freedom of scientific investigation in Antarctica as applied during the International Geophysical Year accords with the interests of science and the progress of all mankind;

Convinced also that a treaty ensuring the use of Antarctica for peaceful purposes only and the continuance of international harmony in Antarctica will further the purposes and principles embodied in the Charter of the United Nations;

Have agreed as follows:

Article I

1. Antarctica shall be used for peaceful purposes only. There shall be prohibited, *inter alia*, any measures of a military nature, such as the establishment of military bases and fortifications, the carrying out of military maneuvers, as well as the testing of any type of weapons.

2. The present Treaty shall not prevent the use of military personnel of equipment for scientific research or for any other peaceful purpose.

Article II

Freedom of scientific investigation in Antarctica and cooperation toward that end, as applied during the International Geophysical Year, shall continue, subject to the provisions of the present Treaty.

Article III

1. In order to promote international cooperation in scientific investigation in Antarctica, as provided for in Article II of the present Treaty, the Contracting Parties agree that, to the greatest extent feasible and practicable:

(*a*) Information regarding plans for scientific programs in Antarctica shall be exchanged to permit maximum economy and efficiency of operations;

(*b*) scientific personnel shall be exchanged in Antarctica between expeditions and stations;

(*c*) scientific observations and results from Antarctica shall be exchanged and made freely available.

2. In implementing this Article, every encouragement shall be given to the establishment of cooperative working relations with those Specialized Agencies of the United Nations and other international organizations having a scientific or technical interest in Antarctica.

Article IV

1. Nothing contained in the present Treaty

shall be interpreted as:

(*a*) a renunciation by any Contracting Party of previously asserted rights of or claims to territorial sovereignty in Antarctica;

(*b*) a renunciation or diminution by any Contracting Party of any basis of claim to territorial sovereignty in Antarctica which it may have whether as a result of its activities or those of its nationals in Antarctica, or otherwise;

(*c*) prejudicing the position of any Contracting Party as regards its recognition or non-recognition of any other State's right of or claim or basis of claim to territorial sovereignty in Antarctica.

2. No acts or activities taking place while the present Treaty is in force shall constitute a basis for asserting, supporting or denying a claim to territorial sovereignty in Antarctica or create any rights of sovereignty in Antarctica. No new claim, or enlargement of an existing claim, to territorial sovereignty in Antarctica shall be asserted while the present Treaty is in force.

Article V

1. Any nuclear explosions in Antarctica and the disposal there of radioactive waste material shall be prohibited.

2. In the event of the conclusion of international agreements concerning the use of nuclear energy, including nuclear explosions and the disposal of radioactive waste material, to which all of the Contracting Parties whose representatives are entitled to participate in the meetings provided for under Article IX are parties, the rules established under such agreements shall apply in Antarctica.

Article VI

The provisions of the present Treaty shall apply to the area south of 60° South Latitude, including all ice shelves, but nothing in the present Treaty shall prejudice or in any way affect the rights, or the exercise of the rights, of any State under international law with regard to the high seas within that area.

Article VII

1. In order to promote the objectives and ensure the observance of the provisions of the present Treaty, each Contracting Party whose representatives are entitled to participate in the meetings referred to in Article IX of the Treaty shall have the right to designate observers to carry out any inspection provided for by the present Article. Observers shall be nationals of the Contracting Parties which designate them. The names of observers shall be communicated to every other Contracting Party having the right to designate observers, and like notice shall be given of the termination of their appointment.

2. Each observer designated in accordance with the provisions of paragraph 1 of this Article shall have complete freedom of access at any time to any or all areas of Antarctica.

3. All areas of Antarctica, including all stations, installations and equipment within those areas, and all ships and aircraft at points of discharging or embarking cargoes or personnel in Antarctica, shall be open at all times to inspection by any observers designated in accordance with paragraph 1 of this Article.

4. Aerial observation may be carried out at any time over any or all areas of Antarctica by any of the Contracting Parties having the right to designate observers.

5. Each Contracting Party shall, at the time when the present Treaty enters into force for it, inform the other Contracting Parties, and thereafter shall give them notice in advance, of

(*a*) all expeditions to and within Antarctica, on the part of its ships or nationals, and all expeditions to Antarctica organized in or proceeding from its territory;

(*b*) all stations in Antarctica occupied by its nationals; and

(*c*) any military personnel or equipment intended to be introduced by it into Antarctica subject to the conditions prescribed in paragraph 2 of Article I of the present Treaty.

Article VIII

1. In order to facilitate the exercise of their functions under the present Treaty, and without prejudice to the respective positions of the Contracting Parties relating to jurisdiction over all other persons in Antarctica, observers designated under paragraph 1 of Article VII and scientific personnel exchanged under subparagraph 1 (*b*) of Article III of the Treaty, and members of the staffs accompanying any such persons, shall be subject only to the jurisdiction of the Contracting Party of which they are nationals in respect of all acts or omissions occurring while they are in Antarctica for the purpose of exercising their functions.

2. Without prejudice to the provisions of paragraph 1 of this Article, and pending the adoption of measures in pursuance of subparagraph 1 (*e*) of Article IX, the Contracting Parties concerned in any case of dispute with regard to the exercise of jurisdiction in Antarctica shall immediately consult together with a view to reaching a mutually acceptable solution.

Article IX

1. Representatives of the Contracting Parties named in the preamble to the present Treaty shall meet at the City of Canberra within two months after the date of entry into force of the Treaty, and thereafter at suitable intervals and places, for the purpose of exchanging information, consulting together on matters of common interest pertaining to Antarctica, and formulating and considering, and recommending to their Governments, measures in furtherance of the principles and objectives of the Treaty, including measures regarding:

(*a*) use of Antarctica for peaceful purposes only;

(*b*) facilitation of scientific research in Antarctica;

(*c*) facilitation of international scientific cooperation in Antarctica;

(*d*) facilitation of the exercise of the rights of inspection provided for in Article VII of the Treaty;

(*e*) questions relating to the exercise of jurisdiction in Antarctica;

(*f*) preservation and conservation of living resources in Antarctica.

2. Each Contracting Party which has become a party to the present Treaty by accession under Article XIII shall be entitled to appoint representatives to participate in the meetings referred to in paragraph 1 of the present Article, during such time as that Contracting Party demonstrates its interest in Antarctica by conducting substantial scientific research activity there, such as the establishment of a scientific station or the despatch of a scientific expedition.

3. Reports from the observers referred to in Article VII of the present Treaty shall be transmitted to the representatives of the Contracting Parties participating in the meetings referred to in paragraph 1 of the present Article.

4. The measures referred to in paragraph 1 of this Article shall become effective when approved by all the Contracting Parties whose representatives were entitled to participate in the meetings held to consider those measures.

5. Any or all of the rights established in the present Treaty may be exercised as from the date of entry into force of the Treaty whether or not any measures facilitating the exercise of such rights have been proposed, considered or approved as provided in this Article.

Article X

Each of the Contracting Parties undertakes to exert appropriate efforts, consistent with the Charter of the United Nations, to the end that no one engages in any activity in Antarctica contrary to the principles or purposes of the present Treaty.

Article XI

1. If any dispute arises between two or more of the Contracting Parties concerning the interpretation or application of the present Treaty, those Contracting Parties shall consult among themselves with a view to having the dispute resolved by negotiation, inquiry, mediation, conciliation, arbitration, judicial settlement or other peaceful means of their own choice.

2. Any dispute of this character not so resolved shall, with the consent, in each case, of all parties to the dispute, be referred to the International Court of Justice for settlement; but failure to reach agreement on reference to the International Court shall not absolve parties to the dispute from the responsibility of continuing to seek to resolve it by any of the various peaceful means referred to in paragraph 1 of this Article.

Article XII

1. (*a*) The present Treaty may be modified or amended at any time by unanimous agreement of the Contracting Parties whose representatives are entitled to participate in the meetings provided for under Article IX. Any such modification or amendment shall enter into force when the depositary Government has received notice from all such Contracting Parties that they have ratified it.

(*b*) Such modification or amendment shall thereafter enter into force as to any other Contracting Party when notice of ratification by it has been received by the depositary Government. Any such Contracting Party from which no notice of ratification is received within a period of two years from the date of entry into force of the modification or amendment in accordance with the provisions of subparagraph 1 (*a*) of this Article shall be deemed to have withdrawn from the present Treaty on the date of expiration of such period.

2. (*a*) If after the expiration of thirty years from the date of entry into force of the present Treaty, any of the Contracting Parties whose representatives are entitled to participate in the meetings provided for under Article IX so requests by a communication addressed to the depositary Government, a Conference of all the Contracting Parties shall be held as soon as practicable to review the operation of the Treaty.

(*b*) Any modification or amendment to the present Treaty which is approved at such a Conference by a majority of the Contracting Parties there represented, including a majority of those whose representatives are entitled to participate in the meetings provided for under Article IX, shall be communicated by the depositary Government to all the Contracting Parties immediately after the termination of the Conference and shall enter into force in accordance with the provisions of paragraph 1 of the present Article.

(*c*) If any such modification or amendment has not entered into force in accordance with the provisions of subparagraph 1 (*a*) of this Article within a period of two years after the date of its communication to all the Contracting Parties, any Contracting Party may at any time after the expiration of that period give notice to the depositary Government of its withdrawal from the present Treaty; and such withdrawal shall take effect two years after the receipt of the notice by the depositary Government.

Article XIII

1. The present Treaty shall be subject to ratification by the signatory States. It shall be open for accession by any State which is a Member of the United Nations, or by any other State which may be invited to accede to the Treaty with the consent of all the Contracting Parties whose representatives are entitled to participate in the meetings provided for under Article IX of the Treaty.

2. Ratification of or accession to the present Treaty shall be effected by each State

in accordance with its constitutional processes.

3. Instruments of ratification and instruments of accession shall be deposited with the Government of the United States of America, hereby designated as the depositary Government.

4. The depositary Government shall inform all signatory and acceding States of the date of each deposit of an instrument of ratification or accession, and the date of entry into force of the Treaty and of any modification or amendment thereto.

5. Upon the deposit of instruments of ratification by all the signatory States, the present Treaty shall enter into force for those States and for States which have deposited instruments of accession. Thereafter the Treaty shall enter into force for any acceding State upon the deposit of its instrument of accession.

6. The present Treaty shall be registered by the depositary Government pursuant to Article 102 of the Charter of the United Nations.

Article XIV

The present Treaty, done in the English, French, Russian and Spanish languages, each version being equally authentic, shall be deposited in the archives of the Government of the United States of America, which shall transmit duly certified copies thereof to the Governments of the signatory and acceding States.

Source: *Treaty Series*, Vol. 402 (United Nations, New York)

For the list of states which have signed, ratified or acceded to the Antarctic Treaty, see Chapter 6.

JOINT STATEMENT BY THE USA AND THE USSR OF AGREED PRINCIPLES FOR DISARMAMENT NEGOTIATIONS

Made at New York on 20 September 1961

Having conducted an extensive exchange of views on disarmament pursuant to their agreement announced in the General Assembly on 30 March 1961,

Noting with concern that the continuing arms race is a heavy burden for humanity and is fraught with dangers for the cause of world peace,

Reaffirming their adherence to all the provisions of the General Assembly resolution 1378 (XIV) of 20 November 1959,

Affirming that to facilitate the attainment of general and complete disarmament in a peaceful world it is important that all States abide by existing international agreements, refrain from any actions which might aggravate international tensions, and that they seek settlement of all disputes by peaceful means,

The United States and the USSR have agreed to recommend the following principles as the basis for future multilateral negotiations on disarmament and to call upon other States to co-operate in reaching early agreement on general and complete disarmament in a peaceful world in accordance with these principles.

1. The goal of negotiations is to achieve agreement on a programme which will ensure that (*a*) disarmament is general and complete and war is no longer an instrument for settling international problems, and (*b*) such disarmament is accompanied by the establishment of reliable procedures for the peaceful settlement of disputes and effective arrangements for the maintenance of peace in accordance with the principles of the United Nations Charter.

2. The programme for general and complete disarmament shall ensure that States will have at their disposal only those non-nuclear armaments, forces, facilities, and establishments as are agreed to be necessary to maintain internal order and protect the personal security of citizens; and that States shall support and provide agreed manpower for a United Nations peace force.

3. To this end, the programme for general and complete disarmament shall contain the necessary provisions, with respect to the military establishment of every nation, for:

(*a*) Disbanding of armed forces, dismantling of military establishments, including bases, cessation of the production of armaments as well as their liquidation or conversion to peaceful uses;

(*b*) Elimination of all stockpiles of nuclear, chemical, bacteriological, and other weapons of mass destruction and cessation of the production of such weapons;

(*c*) Elimination of all means of delivery of weapons of mass destruction;

(*d*) Abolishment of the organization and institutions designed to organize the military effort of States, cessation of military training, and closing of all military training institutions;

(*e*) Discontinuance of military expenditures.

4. The disarmament programme should be implemented in an agreed sequence, by stages until it is completed, with each measure and stage carried out within specified time-limits. Transition to a subsequent stage in the process of disarmament should take place upon a review of the implementation of measures included in the preceding stage and upon a decision that all such measures have been implemented and verified and that any additional verification arrangements required for measures in the next stage are, when appropriate, ready to operate.

5. All measures of general and complete disarmament should be balanced so that at no stage of the implementation of the treaty

could any State or group of States gain military advantage and that security is ensured equally for all.

6. All disarmament measures should be implemented from beginning to end under such strict and effective international control as would provide firm assurance that all parties are honouring their obligations. During and after the implementation of general and complete disarmament, the most thorough control should be exercised, the nature and extent of such control depending on the requirements for verification of the disarmament measures being carried out in each stage. To implement control over and inspection of disarmament, an International Disarmament Organization including all parties to the agreement should be created within the framework of the United Nations. This International Disarmament Organization and its inspectors should be assured unrestricted access without veto to all places as necessary for the purpose of effective verification.

7. Progress in disarmament should be accompanied by measures to strengthen institutions for maintaining peace and the settlement of international disputes by peaceful means. During and after the implementation of the programme of general and complete disarmament, there should be taken, in accordance with the principles of the United Nations Charter, the necessary measures to maintain international peace and security, including the obligation of States to place at the disposal of the United Nations agreed manpower necessary for an international peace force to be equipped with agreed types of armaments. Arrangements for the use of this force should ensure that the United Nations can effectively deter or suppress any threat or use of arms in violation of the purposes and principles of the United Nations.

8. States participating in the negotiations should seek to achieve and implement the widest possible agreement at the earliest possible date. Efforts should continue without interruption until agreement upon the total programme has been achieved, and efforts to ensure early agreement on and implementation of measures of disarmament should be undertaken without prejudicing progress on agreement on the total programme and in such a way that these measures would facilitate and form part of that programme.

Source: Official Records of the General Assembly, Fifteenth Session, A/4879, 20 September 1961

In resolution A/RES/1722 (XVI) of 20 December 1961, approved unanimously, the UN General Assembly welcomed the above joint statement of the governments of the USA and the USSR (the McCloy-Zorin Statement) and recommended that negotiations on general and complete disarmament should be based upon the agreed principles.

EXCHANGE OF LETTERS BETWEEN THE USA AND THE USSR:

Letter from Presidential Adviser McCloy to Deputy Foreign Minister Zorin: verification of retained forces and armaments, 20 September 1961

Dear Mr. Zorin:

At the 18 September 1961 session of our bilateral discussions on disarmament you indicated that the draft of a joint statement of agreed principles which I submitted to you on behalf of the United States Government on 14 September 1961 would be acceptable to the Government of the Soviet Union provided the following clause were omitted from paragraph 6:

"Such verification should ensure that not only agreed limitations or reductions take place but also that retained armed forces and armaments do not exceed agreed levels at any stage."

This sentence expresses a key element in the United States position which we believe is implicit in the entire joint statement of agreed principles that whenever an agreement stipulates that at a certain point certain levels of forces and armaments may be retained, the verification machinery must have all the rights and powers necessary to ensure that those levels are not exceeded.

It appears from your statements that the Soviet Union will be unwilling to agree to a joint statement of agreed principles unless the above-mentioned clause is omitted therefrom. My Government has authorized me to inform you that, in the interest of progress toward resuming disarmament negotiations, it is willing to remove the above-mentioned sentence from paragraph 6 of the joint statement of agreed principles since it is an item to which the Soviet Union has not agreed.

This is done upon the express understanding that the substantive position of the United States Government as outlined in the above-quoted sentence and in our memorandum of 14 September 1961 remains unchanged, and is in no sense prejudiced by the exclusion of this sentence from the joint statement of agreed principles.

The United States continues to adhere to and will continue to advance the principle contained in the omitted sentence as a necessary element in any comprehensive disarmament negotiations or agreement.

Very truly yours,

John J. McCloy

Source: UN document A/4880, 20 September 1961

Letter from Deputy Foreign Minister Zorin to Presidential Adviser McCloy, 20 September 1961

Dear Mr. McCloy,

I have received your letter of 20 September 1961, in which you express a reservation with regard to the position which the United States of America intends to adopt in subsequent negotiations on disarmament.

According to the agreement which we reached in the course of a bilateral exchange of views, the United States agreed not to include, in the joint statement by the Governments of the USSR and the United States on the principles for disarmament negotiations, the proposal with which you are conversant and the adoption of which would imply acceptance of the concept of the establishment of control over armaments instead of control over disarmament. In your letter you say that this proposal "expresses a key element in the United States position".

In this connexion I must state that, as you know, the position of the USSR on the question of control over general and complete disarmament has been thoroughly and clearly explained in the statements of the Soviet Government and its leader N. S. Khrushchev. The Soviet Union favours the most thorough and strict international control over the measures of general and complete disarmament. While strongly advocating effective control over disarmament and wishing to facilitate as much as possible the achievement of agreement on this control, the Soviet Union is at the same time resolutely opposed to the establishment of control over armaments.

It appears from your letter that the United States is trying to establish control over the armed forces and armaments retained by States at any given stage of disarmament. However, such control, which in fact means control over armaments, would turn into an international system of legalized espionage, which would naturally be unacceptable to any State concerned for its security and the interests of preserving peace throughout the world. The position of the United States on this question, if it insists on the proposal described above, will inevitably complicate agreement on a programme of general and complete disarmament, on the general principles of which we have agreed.

The Soviet Union will continue to make every effort towards the earliest preparation of a treaty on general and complete disarmament under effective international control.

I have the honour to be, etc.

V. Zorin
Permanent Representative of the USSR to the United Nations

Source: UN document A/4887, 25 September 1961

MEMORANDUM OF UNDERSTANDING BETWEEN THE USA AND THE USSR REGARDING THE ESTABLISHMENT OF A DIRECT COMMUNICATIONS LINK

Signed at Geneva on 20 June 1963
Entered into force on 20 June 1963

For use in time of emergency the Government of the United States of America and the Government of the Union of Soviet Socialist Republics have agreed to establish as soon as technically feasible a direct communications link between the two Governments.

Each Government shall be responsible for the arrangements for the link on its own territory. Each Government shall take the necessary steps to ensure continuous functioning of the link and prompt delivery to its head of government of any communications received by means of the link from the head of government of the other party.

Arrangements for establishing and operating the link are set forth in the Annex which is attached hereto and forms an integral part hereof.

ANNEX

The direct communications link between Washington and Moscow established in accordance with the Memorandum, and the operation of such link, shall be governed by the following provisions:

1. The direct communications link shall consist of:

(*a*) Two terminal points with telegraph-teleprinter equipment between which communications shall be directly exchanged;

(*b*) One full-time duplex wire telegraph circuit, routed Washington-London-Copenhagen-Stockholm-Helsinki-Moscow, which shall be used for the transmission of messages;

(*c*) One full-time duplex radio telegraph circuit, routed Washington-Tangier-Moscow, which shall be used for service communications and for coordination of operations between the two terminal points.

If experience in operating the direct communications link should demonstrate that the establishment of an additional wire telegraph circuit is advisable, such circuit may be established by mutual agreement between authorized representatives of both Governments.

2. In case of interruption of the wire circuit, transmission of messages shall be effected via the radio circuit, and for this purpose provision shall be made at the terminal points for the capability of prompt switching of all necessary equipment from one circuit to another.

3. The terminal points of the link shall be so equipped as to provide for the transmission and reception of messages from Moscow to Washington in the Russian language and from Washington to Moscow in the English language. In this connection, the

USSR shall furnish the United States four sets of telegraph terminal equipment, including page printers, transmitters, and reperforators, with one year's supply of spare parts and all necessary special tools, test equipment, operating instructions, and other technical literature, to provide for transmission and reception of messages in the Russian language.

The United States shall furnish the Soviet Union four sets of telegraph terminal equipment, including page printers, transmitters, and reperforators, with one year's supply of spare parts and all necessary special tools, test equipment, operating instructions and other technical literature, to provide for transmission and reception of messages in the English language.

The equipment described in this paragraph shall be exchanged directly between the parties without any payment being required therefor.

4. The terminal points of the direct communication link shall be provided with encoding equipment. For the terminal point in the USSR, four sets of such equipment (each capable of simplex operation), with one year's supply of spare parts, with all necessary special tools, test equipment, operating instructions and other technical literature, and with all necessary blank tape, shall be furnished by the United States to the USSR against payment of the cost thereof by the USSR.

The USSR shall provide for preparation and delivery of keying tapes to the terminal point of the link in the United States for reception of messages from the USSR. The United States shall provide for the preparation and delivery of keying tapes to the terminal point of the link in the USSR for reception of messages from the United States. Delivery of prepared keying tapes to the terminal points of the link shall be effected through the Embassy of the USSR in Washington (for the terminal of the link in the USSR) and through the Embassy of the United States in Moscow (for the terminal of the link in the United States).

5. The United States and the USSR shall designate the agencies responsible for the arrangements regarding the direct communications link, for its technical maintenance, continuity and reliability, and for the timely transmission of messages.

Such agencies may, by mutual agreement, decide matters and develop instructions relating to the technical maintenance and operation of the direct communications link and effect arrangements to improve the operation of the link.

6. The technical parameters of the telegraph circuits of the link and of the terminal equipment, as well as the maintenance of such circuits and equipment, shall be in accordance with CCITT [1] and CCIR [2] recommendations.

Transmission and reception of messages over the direct communications link shall be effected in accordance with applicable recommendations of international telegraph and radio communications regulations, as well as with mutually agreed instructions.

7. The costs of the direct communications link shall be borne as follows:

(a) The USSR shall pay the full cost of leasing the portion of the telegraph circuit from Moscow to Helsinki and 50% of the cost of leasing the portion of the telegraph circuit from Helsinki to London. The United States shall pay the full cost of leasing the portion of the telegraph circuit from Washington to London and 50% of the cost of leasing the portion of the telegraph circuit from London to Helsinki.

(b) Payment of the cost of leasing the radio telegraph circuit between Washington and Moscow shall be effected without any transfer of payments between the parties. The USSR shall bear the expenses relating to the transmission of messages from Moscow to Washington. The United States shall bear the expenses relating to the transmission of messages from Washington to Moscow.

[1] International Telegraph and Telephone Consultative Committee.
[2] International Radio Consultative Committee.

Source: *Treaties and Other International Acts, Series 5362* (US Department of State, Washington, D.C., 1963)

See also Agreement on measures to improve the direct communications link (1971) and Agreement amending the 1971 Agreement (1975).

TREATY BANNING NUCLEAR WEAPON TESTS IN THE ATMOSPHERE, IN OUTER SPACE AND UNDER WATER

Signed at Moscow on 5 August 1963
Entered into force on 10 October 1963
Depositaries: UK, US and Soviet governments

The Governments of the United States of America, the United Kingdom of Great Britain and Northern Ireland, and the Union of Soviet Socialist Republics, hereinafter referred to as the "Original Parties",

Proclaiming as their principal aim the speediest possible achievement of an agreement on general and complete disarmament under strict international control in accordance with the objectives of the United Nations which would put an end to the armaments race and eliminate the incentive to the production and testing of all kinds of weapons, including nuclear weapons,

Seeking to achieve the discontinuance of all test explosions of nuclear weapons for all time, determined to continue negotiations to this end, and desiring to put an end to the contamination of man's environment by radioactive substances,

Have agreed as follows:

Article I

1. Each of the Parties to this Treaty undertakes to prohibit, to prevent, and not to carry out any nuclear weapon test explosion, or any other nuclear explosion, at any place under its jurisdiction or control:

(a) in the atmosphere; beyond its limits, including outer space; or under water, including territorial waters or high seas; or

(b) in any other environment if such explosion causes radioactive debris to be present outside the territorial limits of the State under whose jurisdiction or control such explosion is conducted. It is understood in this connection that the provisions of this subparagraph are without prejudice to the conclusion of a treaty resulting in the permanent banning of all nuclear test explosions, including all such explosions underground, the conclusion of which, as the Parties have stated in the Preamble to this Treaty, they seek to achieve.

2. Each of the Parties to this Treaty undertakes furthermore to refrain from causing, encouraging, or in any way participating in, the carrying out of any nuclear weapon test explosion, or any other nuclear explosion, anywhere which would take place in any of the environments described, or have the effect referred to, in paragraph 1 of this Article.

Article II

1. Any Party may propose amendments to this Treaty. The text of any proposed amendment shall be submitted to the Depositary Governments which shall circulate it to all Parties to this Treaty. Thereafter, if requested to do so by one-third or more of the Parties, the Depositary Governments shall convene a conference, to which they shall invite all the Parties, to consider such amendment.

2. Any amendment to this Treaty must be approved by a majority of the votes of all the Parties to this Treaty, including the votes of all of the Original Parties. The amendment shall enter into force for all Parties upon the deposit of instruments of ratification by a majority of all the Parties, including the instruments of ratification of all of the Original Parties.

Article III

1. This Treaty shall be open to all States for signature. Any State which does not sign this Treaty before its entry into force in accordance with paragraph 3 of this Article may accede to it at any time.

2. This Treaty shall be subject to ratification by signatory States. Instruments of ratification and instruments of accession shall be deposited with the Governments of the Origi-

nal Parties—the United States of America, the United Kingdom of Great Britain and Northern Ireland, and the Union of Soviet Socialist Republics—which are hereby designated the Depositary Governments.

3. This Treaty shall enter into force after its ratification by all the Original Parties and the deposit of their instruments of ratification.

4. For States whose instruments of ratification or accession are deposited subsequent to the entry into force of this Treaty, it shall enter into force on the date of the deposit of their instruments of ratification or accession.

5. The Depositary Governments shall promptly inform all signatory and acceding States of the date of each signature, the date of deposit of each instrument of ratification of and accession to this Treaty, the date of its entry into force, and the date of receipt of any requests for conferences or other notices.

6. This Treaty shall be registered by the Depositary Governments pursuant to Article 102 of the Charter of the United Nations.

Article IV

This Treaty shall be of unlimited duration.

Each Party shall in exercising its national sovereignty have the right to withdraw from the Treaty if it decides that extraordinary events, related to the subject matter of this Treaty, have jeopardized the supreme interests of its country. It shall give notice of such withdrawal to all other Parties to the Treaty three months in advance.

Article V

This Treaty, of which the English and Russian texts are equally authentic, shall be deposited in the archives of the Depositary Governments. Duly certified copies of this Treaty shall be transmitted by the Depositary Governments to the Governments of the signatory and acceding States.

Source: *Treaty Series*, Vol. 480 (United Nations, New York)

For the list of states which have signed, ratified, acceded or succeeded to the Partial Test Ban Treaty, see Chapter 6.

UNILATERAL STATEMENTS BY THE USA, THE USSR AND THE UK REGARDING REDUCTION OF FISSIONABLE MATERIALS PRODUCTION

ADDRESS BY PRESIDENT JOHNSON

Made on 20 April 1964

EXCERPT:

...

I am taking two actions today which reflect both our desire to reduce tensions and our unwillingness to risk weakness. I have ordered a further substantial reduction in our production of enriched uranium, to be carried out over a 4-year period. When added to previous reductions, this will mean an overall decrease in the production of plutonium by 20 per cent, and of enriched uranium by 40 per cent. By bringing production in line with need—and the chart shows now that our production is here, and our need is here, and our reduction today will bring it here—we think we will reduce tension while we maintain all the necessary power.

We must not operate a WPA nuclear project, just to provide employment, when our needs have been met. And in reaching these decisions, I have been in close consultation with Prime Minister Douglas-Home. Simultaneously with my announcement now, Chairman Khrushchev is releasing a statement in Moscow, at 2 o'clock our time, in which he makes definite commitments to steps toward a more peaceful world. He agrees to discontinue the construction of two big new atomic reactors for the production of plutonium over the next several years, to reduce substantially the production of U-235 for nuclear weapons, and to allocate more fissionable material for peaceful uses.

...

Source: *Documents on Disarmament 1964* (United States Arms Control and Disarmament Agency, Washington, D.C., 1965)

STATEMENT BY PREMIER KHRUSHCHEV

Made on 20 April 1964

EXCERPT:

...

Now the time has come when an opportunity has emerged to take steps to reduce the production of fissionable materials for military purposes. The Soviet Government has considered the question of to what extent in the present correlation of nuclear power in the world arena our country can go in this direction without in any way weakening the defence capacity of the Soviet Union and the solidity of the nuclear missile shield which reliably safeguards the security of all the countries of the socialist community.

Having carefully weighed up all the data relating to the nuclear potentials of the Soviet Union, on the one hand, and of the nuclear Powers-members of NATO, on the other, and having analysed all the circumstances of the matter, the Soviet Government has taken the following decision:

1. To stop straightaway the construction of two new large atomic reactors for the pro-duction of plutonium.

2. During the next few years to reduce substantially the production of uranium-235 for nuclear weapons.

3. To allocate accordingly more fissionable materials for peaceful uses in atomic power stations, in industry, agriculture, medicine and in the implementation of major scientific-technical projects, including the distillation of sea water.

The President of the United States of America, Mr. L. Johnson, and the Prime Minister of the United Kingdom, Sir Alexander Douglas-Home, have informed me that they will make announcements on the practical measures in regard to reducing the production of fissionable materials for military purposes, which will be taken accordingly by the United States of America and the United Kingdom.

...

Source: *Documents on Disarmament 1964* (United States Arms Control and Disarmament Agency, Washington, D.C., 1965)

STATEMENT BY PRIME MINISTER DOUGLAS-HOME

Made on 21 April 1964

EXCERPT:

...

Production of fissile material in the United Kingdom has, of course, always been on a very much smaller scale than in the United States of America or the Union of Soviet Socialist Republics. For their part, as was explained in the recently published White Paper on Defence, Her Majesty's Government have already adjusted their supplies of fissile material to the minimum necessary to maintain our independent nuclear deterrent and to meet all our defence requirements for the foreseeable future.

Military plutonium production is being gradually terminated. The civil reactors which have been, and are being, brought into service in this country are part of the United Kingdom programme for electric power generation or for research and development of new techniques in the use of atomic energy for peaceful purposes. By the nature of their operations these reactors produce plutonium. Part of this will be used for civil purposes in the United Kingdom and part will be sent to the United States under an agreement of which Parliament was informed on 19th November, 1962, whereby U-235 is supplied in exchange by the United States Government.

Our plans do not envisage the use of any of the plutonium produced by our civil reactors in the United Kingdom weapons programme and I am informed by the United States Government that they have no intention of using the plutonium received from us for weapons purposes.

Source: *Documents on Disarmament 1964* (United States Arms Control and Disarmament Agency, Washington, D.C., 1965)

TREATY ON PRINCIPLES GOVERNING THE ACTIVITIES OF STATES IN THE EXPLORATION AND USE OF OUTER SPACE, INCLUDING THE MOON AND OTHER CELESTIAL BODIES

Signed at London, Moscow and Washington on 27 January 1967
Entered into force on 10 October 1967
Depositaries: UK, US and Soviet governments

The States Parties to this Treaty,

Inspired by the great prospects opening up before mankind as a result of man's entry into outer space,

Recognizing the common interest of all mankind in the progress of the exploration and use of outer space for peaceful purposes,

Believing that the exploration and use of outer space should be carried on for the benefit of all peoples irrespective of the degree of their economic or scientific development,

Desiring to contribute to broad international co-operation in the scientific as well as the legal aspects of the exploration and use of outer space for peaceful purposes,

Believing that such co-operation will contribute to the development of mutual understanding and to the strengthening of friendly relations between States and peoples,

Recalling resolution 1962 (XVIII), entitled "Declaration of Legal Principles Governing the Activities of States in the Exploration and Use of Outer Space", which was adopted unanimously by the United Nations General Assembly on 13 December 1963,

Recalling resolution 1884 (XVIII), calling upon States to refrain from placing in orbit around the earth any objects carrying nuclear weapons or any other kinds of weapons of mass destruction or from installing such weapons on celestial bodies, which was adopted unanimously by the United Nations General Assembly on 17 October 1963,

Taking account of United Nations General Assembly resolution 110 (II) of 3 November 1947, which condemned propaganda designed or likely to provoke or encourage any threat to the peace, breach of the peace or act of aggression, and considering that the aforementioned resolution is applicable to outer space,

Convinced that a Treaty on Principles Governing the Activities of States in the Exploration and Use of Outer Space, including the Moon and Other Celestial Bodies, will further the Purposes and Principles of the Charter of the United Nations,

Have agreed on the following:

Article I

The exploration and use of outer space, including the moon and other celestial bodies, shall be carried out for the benefit and in the interests of all countries, irrespective of their degree of economic or scientific development, and shall be the province of all mankind.

Outer space, including the moon and other celestial bodies, shall be free for exploration and use by all States without discrimination of any kind, on a basis of equality and in accordance with international law, and there shall be free access to all areas of celestial bodies.

There shall be freedom of scientific investigation in outer space, including the moon and other celestial bodies, and States shall facilitate and encourage international co-operation in such investigation.

Article II

Outer space, including the moon and other celestial bodies, is not subject to national appropriation by claim of sovereignty, by means of use of occupation, or by any other means.

Article III

States Parties to the Treaty shall carry on activities in the exploration and use of outer space, including the moon and other celestial bodies, in accordance with international law, including the Charter of the United Nations, in the interest of maintaining international peace and security and promoting international co-operation and understanding.

Article IV

States Parties to the Treaty undertake not to place in orbit around the earth any objects carrying nuclear weapons or any other kinds of weapons of mass destruction, install such weapons on celestial bodies, or station such weapons in outer space in any other manner.

The moon and other celestial bodies shall be used by all States Parties to the Treaty exclusively for peaceful purposes. The establishment of military bases, installations and fortifications, the testing of any type of weapons and the conduct of military manoeuvres on celestial bodies shall be forbidden. The use of military personnel for scientific research or for any other peaceful purposes shall not be prohibited. The use of any equipment or facility necessary for peaceful exploration of the moon and other celestial bodies shall also not be prohibited.

Article V

States Parties to the Treaty shall regard astronauts as envoys of mankind in outer space and shall render to them all possible assistance in the event of accident, distress, or emergency landing on the territory of another State Party or on the high seas. When astronauts make such landing, they shall be safely and promptly returned to the State of registry of their space vehicle.

In carrying on activities in outer space and on celestial bodies, the astronauts of one State Party shall render all possible assistance to the astronauts of other States Parties.

States Parties to the Treaty shall immediately inform the other States Parties to the Treaty or the Secretary-General of the United Nations of any phenomena they discover in outer space, including the moon and other celestial bodies, which could constitute a danger to the life or health of astronauts.

Article VI

States Parties to the Treaty shall bear international responsibility for national activities in outer space, including the moon and other celestial bodies, whether such activities are carried on by governmental agencies or by non-governmental entities, and for assuring that national activities are carried out in conformity with the provisions set forth in the present Treaty. The activities of non-governmental entities in outer space, including the moon and other celestial bodies, shall require authorization and continuing supervision by the appropriate State party to the Treaty. When activities are carried on in outer space, including the moon and other celestial bodies, by an international organization, responsibility for compliance with this Treaty shall be borne both by the international organization and by the States Parties to the Treaty participating in such organization.

Article VII

Each State Party to the Treaty that launches or procures the launching of an object into outer space, including the moon and other celestial bodies, and each State Party from whose territory or facility an object is launched, is internationally liable for damage to another State Party to the Treaty or to its natural or juridical persons by such object or its component parts on the Earth, in the air space or in outer space, including the moon and other celestial bodies.

Article VIII

A State Party to the Treaty on whose registry an object launched into outer space is carried shall retain jurisdiction and control over such object, and over any personnel thereof, while in outer space or on a celestial body. Ownership of objects launched into outer space, including objects landed or constructed on a celestial body, and of their component parts, is not affected by their presence in outer space or on a celestial body or by their return to the Earth. Such objects or component parts found beyond the limits of the State Party to the Treaty on whose registry they are carried shall be returned to that State Party, which shall, upon request, furnish identifying data prior to their return.

Article IX

In the exploration and use of outer space, including the moon and other celestial bodies, States Parties to the Treaty shall be guided by the principle of co-operation and mutual assistance and shall conduct all their activities in outer space, including the moon and other celestial bodies, with due regard to the corresponding interests of all other States Parties to the Treaty. States Parties to the Treaty shall pursue studies of outer space, including the moon and other celestial bodies, and conduct exploration of them so as to avoid their harmful contamination and also adverse changes in the environment of the Earth resulting from the introduction of extraterrestrial matter and, where necessary, shall adopt appropriate measures for this purpose. If a State Party to the Treaty has reason to believe that an activity or experiment planned by it or its nationals in outer space, including the moon and other celestial bodies, would cause potentially harmful interference with activities of other States Parties in the peaceful exploration and use of outer space, including the moon and other celestial bodies, it shall undertake appropriate international consultations before proceeding with any such activity or experiment. A State Party to the Treaty which has reason to believe that an activity or experiment planned by another State Party in outer space, including the moon and other celestial bodies, would cause potentially harmful interference with activities in the peaceful exploration and use of outer space, including the moon and other celestial bodies, may request consultation concerning the activity or experiment.

Article X

In order to promote international co-operation in the exploration and use of outer space, including the moon and other celestial bodies, in conformity with the purposes of this Treaty, the States Parties to the Treaty shall consider on a basis of equality any requests by other States Parties to the Treaty to be afforded an opportunity to observe the flight of space objects launched by these States.

The nature of such an opportunity for observation and the conditions under which it could be afforded shall be determined by agreement between the States concerned.

Article XI

In order to promote international co-operation in the peaceful exploration and use of outer space, States Parties to the Treaty conducting activities in outer space, including the moon and other celestial bodies, agree to inform the Secretary-General of the United Nations as well as the public and the international scientific community, to the greatest extent feasible and practicable, of the nature, conduct, locations and results of such activities. On receiving the said information, the Secretary-General of the United Nations should be prepared to disseminate it immediately and effectively.

Article XII

All stations, installations, equipment and space vehicles on the moon and other celestial bodies shall be open to representatives of other States Parties to the Treaty on a basis of reciprocity. Such representatives shall give reasonable advance notice of a projected visit, in order that appropriate consultations may be held and that maximum precautions may be taken to assure safety and to avoid interference with normal operations in the facility to be visited.

Article XIII

The provisions of this Treaty shall apply to the activities of States Parties to the Treaty in the exploration and use of outer space, including the moon and other celestial bodies, whether such activities are carried on by a single State Party to the Treaty or jointly with other States, including cases where they are carried on within the framework of international inter-governmental organizations.

Any practical questions arising in connexion with activities carried on by international inter-governmental organizations in the exploration and use of outer space, including the moon and other celestial bodies, shall be resolved by the States Parties to the Treaty either with the appropriate international organization or with one or more States members of that international organization, which are Parties to this Treaty.

Article XIV

1. This Treaty shall be open to all States for signature. Any State which does not sign this Treaty before its entry into force in accordance with paragraph 3 of this Article may accede to it at any time.

2. This Treaty shall be subject to ratification by signatory States. Instruments of ratification and instruments of accession shall be deposited with the Governments of the United Kingdom of Great Britain and Northern Ireland, the Union of Soviet Socialist Republics and the United States of America, which are hereby designated the Depositary Governments.

3. This Treaty shall enter into force upon the deposit of instruments of ratification by five Governments including the Governments designated as Depositary Governments under this Treaty.

4. For States whose instruments of ratification or accession are deposited subsequent to the entry into force of this Treaty, it shall enter into force on the date of the deposit of their instruments of ratification or accession.

5. The Depositary Governments shall promptly inform all signatory and acceding States of the date of each signature, the date of deposit of each instrument of ratification of and accession to this Treaty, the date of its entry into force and other notices.

6. This Treaty shall be registered by the Depositary Governments pursuant to Article 102 of the Charter of the United Nations.

Article XV

Any State Party to the Treaty may propose amendments to this Treaty. Amendments shall enter into force for each State Party to the Treaty accepting the amendments upon their acceptance by a majority of the States Parties to the Treaty and thereafter for each remaining State Party to the Treaty on the date of acceptance by it.

Article XVI

Any State Party to the Treaty may give notice of its withdrawal from the Treaty one year after its entry into force by written notification to the Depositary Governments. Such withdrawal shall take effect one year from the date of receipt of this notification.

Article XVII

This Treaty, of which the English, Russian, French, Spanish and Chinese texts are equally authentic, shall be deposited in the archives of the Depositary Governments. Duly certified copies of this Treaty shall be transmitted by the Depositary Governments to the Governments of the signatory and acceding States.

...

Source: *Treaty Series*, Vol. 610 (United Nations, New York)

For the list of states which have signed, ratified, acceded or succeeded to the Outer Space Treaty, see Chapter 6.

TREATY FOR THE PROHIBITION OF NUCLEAR WEAPONS IN LATIN AMERICA (TREATY OF TLATELOLCO)

Signed at Mexico, Distrito Federal on 14 February 1967
Entered into force on 22 April 1968
Depositary: Mexican government

Preamble
In the name of their peoples and faithfully interpreting their desires and aspirations, the Governments of the States which sign the Treaty for the Prohibition of Nuclear

Weapons in Latin America,

Desiring to contribute, so far as lies in their power, towards ending the armaments race, especially in the field of nuclear weapons, and towards strengthening a world at peace, based on the sovereign equality of States, mutual respect and good neighbourliness,

Recalling that the United Nations General Assembly, in its Resolution 808 (IX), adopted unanimously as one of the three points of a coordinated programme of disarmament "the total prohibition of the use and manufacture of nuclear weapons and weapons of mass destruction of every type",

Recalling that militarily denuclearized zones are not an end in themselves but rather a means for achieving general and complete disarmament at a later stage,

Recalling United Nations General Assembly Resolution 1911 (XVIII), which established that the measures that should be agreed upon for the denuclearization of Latin America should be taken "in the light of the principles of the Charter of the United Nations and of regional agreements",

Recalling United Nations General Assembly Resolution 2028 (XX), which established the principle of an acceptable balance of mutual responsibilities and duties for the nuclear and non-nuclear powers, and

Recalling that the Charter of the Organization of American States proclaims that it is an essential purpose of the Organization to strengthen the peace and security of the hemisphere,

Convinced:

That the incalculable destructive power of nuclear weapons has made it imperative that the legal prohibition of war should be strictly observed in practice if the survival of civilization and of mankind itself is to be assured,

That nuclear weapons, whose terrible effects are suffered, indiscriminately and inexorably, by military forces and civilian population alike, constitute, through the persistence of the radioactivity they release, an attack on the integrity of the human species and ultimately may even render the whole earth uninhabitable,

That general and complete disarmament under effective international control is a vital matter which all the peoples of the world equally demand,

That the proliferation of nuclear weapons, which seems inevitable unless States, in the exercise of their sovereign rights, impose restrictions on themselves in order to prevent it, would make any agreement on disarmament enormously difficult and would increase the danger of the outbreak of a nuclear conflagration,

That the establishment of militarily denuclearized zones is closely linked with the maintenance of peace and security in the respective regions,

That the military denuclearization of vast geographical zones, adopted by the sovereign decision of the States comprised therein, will exercise a beneficial influence on other regions where similar conditions exist,

That the privileged situation of the signatory States, whose territories are wholly free from nuclear weapons, imposes upon them the inescapable duty of preserving that situation both in their own interests and for the good of mankind,

That the existence of nuclear weapons in any country of Latin America would make it a target for possible nuclear attacks and would inevitably set off, throughout the region, a ruinous race in nuclear weapons which would involve the unjustifiable diversion, for warlike purposes, of the limited resources required for economic and social development,

That the foregoing reasons, together with the traditional peace-loving outlook of Latin America, give rise to an inescapable necessity that nuclear energy should be used in that region exclusively for peaceful purposes, and that the Latin American countries should use their right to the greatest and most equitable possible access to this new source of energy in order to expedite the economic and social development of their peoples,

Convinced finally:

That the military denuclearization of Latin America—being understood to mean the undertaking entered into internationally in this Treaty to keep their territories forever free from nuclear weapons—will constitute a measure which will spare their peoples from the squandering of their limited resources on nuclear armaments and will protect them against possible nuclear attacks on their territories, and will also constitute a significant contribution towards preventing the proliferation of nuclear weapons and a powerful factor for general and complete disarmament, and

That Latin America, faithful to its tradition of universality, must not only endeavour to banish from its homelands the scourge of a nuclear war, but must also strive to promote the well-being and advancement of its peoples, at the same time co-operating in the fulfilment of the ideals of mankind, that is to say, in the consolidation of a permanent peace based on equal rights, economic fairness and social justice for all, in accordance with the principles and purposes set forth in the Charter of the United Nations and in the Charter of the Organization of American States,

Have agreed as follows:

Article 1. *Obligations*

1. The Contracting Parties hereby undertake to use exclusively for peaceful purposes the nuclear material and facilities which are under their jurisdiction, and to prohibit and prevent in their respective territories:

(*a*) The testing, use, manufacture, production or acquisition by any means whatsoever of any nuclear weapons, by the

Parties themselves, directly or indirectly, on behalf of anyone else or in any other way, and

(b) The receipt, storage, installation, deployment and any form of possession of any nuclear weapons, directly or indirectly, by the Parties themselves, by anyone on their behalf or in any other way.

2. The Contracting Parties also undertake to refrain from engaging in, encouraging or authorizing, directly or indirectly, or in any way participating in the testing, use, manufacture, production, possession or control of any nuclear weapon.

Article 2. *Definition of the Contracting Parties*

For the purposes of this Treaty, the Contracting Parties are those for whom the Treaty is in force.

Article 3. *Definition of territory*

For the purposes of this Treaty, the term "territory" shall include the territorial sea, air space and any other space over which the State exercises sovereignty in accordance with its own legislation.

Article 4. *Zone of application*

1. The zone of application of this Treaty is the whole of the territories for which the Treaty is in force.

2. Upon fulfilment of the requirements of article 28, paragraph 1, the zone of application of this Treaty shall also be that which is situated in the western hemisphere within the following limits (except the continental part of the territory of the United States of America and its territorial waters): starting at a point located at 35° north latitude, 75° west longitude; from this point directly southward to a point at 30° north latitude, 75° west longitude; from there, directly eastward to a point at 30° north latitude, 50° west longitude; from there, along a loxodromic line to a point at 5° north latitude, 20° west longitude; from there, directly southward to a point at 60° south latitude, 20° west longitude; from there, directly westward to a point at 60° south latitude, 115° west longitude; from there, directly northward to a point at 0 latitude, 115° west longitude; from there, along a loxodromic line to a point at 35° north latitude, 150° west longitude; from there, directly eastward to a point at 35° north latitude, 75° west longitude.

Article 5. *Definition of nuclear weapons*

For the purposes of this Treaty, a nuclear weapon is any device which is capable of releasing nuclear energy in an uncontrolled manner and which has a group of characteristics that are appropriate for use for warlike purposes. An instrument that may be used for the transport or propulsion of the device is not included in this definition if it is separable from the device and not an indivisible part thereof.

Article 6. *Meeting of signatories*

At the request of any of the signatory States or if the Agency established by article 7 should so decide, a meeting of all the signatories may be convoked to consider in common questions which may affect the very essence of this instrument, including possible amendments to it. In either case, the meeting will be convoked by the General Secretary.

Article 7. *Organization*

1. In order to ensure compliance with the obligations of this Treaty, the Contracting Parties hereby establish an international organization to be known as the Agency for the Prohibition of Nuclear Weapons in Latin America, hereinafter referred to as "the Agency". Only the Contracting Parties shall be affected by its decisions.

2. The Agency shall be responsible for the holding of periodic or extraordinary consultations among Member States on matters relating to the purposes, measures and procedures set forth in this Treaty and to the supervision of compliance with the obligations arising therefrom.

3. The Contracting Parties agree to extend to the Agency full and prompt co-operation in accordance with the provisions of this Treaty, of any agreements they may conclude with the Agency and of any agreements the Agency may conclude with any other international organization or body.

4. The headquarters of the Agency shall be in Mexico City.

Article 8. *Organs*

1. There are hereby established as principal organs of the Agency a General Conference, a Council and a Secretariat.

2. Such subsidiary organs as are considered necessary by the General Conference may be established within the purview of this Treaty.

Article 9. *The General Conference*

1. The General Conference, the supreme organ of the Agency, shall be composed of all the Contracting Parties; it shall hold regular sessions every two years, and may also hold special sessions whenever this Treaty so provides or, in the opinion of the Council, the circumstances so require.

2. The General Conference:

(a) May consider and decide on any matters or questions covered by this Treaty, within the limits thereof, including those referring to powers and functions of any organ provided for in this Treaty;

(b) Shall establish procedures for the control system to ensure observance of this Treaty in accordance with its provisions;

(c) Shall elect the Members of the Council and the General Secretary;

(d) May remove the General Secretary from office if the proper functioning of the Agency so requires;

(e) Shall receive and consider the biennial

and special reports submitted by the Council and the General Secretary.

(f) Shall initiate and consider studies designed to facilitate the optimum fulfilment of the aims of this Treaty, without prejudice to the power of the General Secretary independently to carry out similar studies for submission to and consideration by the Conference.

(g) Shall be the organ competent to authorize the conclusion of agreements with Governments and other international organizations and bodies.

3. The General Conference shall adopt the Agency's budget and fix the scale of financial contributions to be paid by Member States, taking into account the systems and criteria used for the same purpose by the United Nations.

4. The General Conference shall elect its officers for each session and may establish such subsidiary organs as it deems necessary for the performance of its functions.

5. Each Member of the Agency shall have one vote. The decisions of the General Conference shall be taken by a two-thirds majority of the Members present and voting in the case of matters relating to the control system and measures referred to in article 20, the admission of new Members, the election or removal of the General Secretary, adoption of the budget and matters related thereto. Decisions on other matters, as well as procedural questions and also determination of which questions must be decided by a two-thirds majority, shall be taken by a simple majority of the Members present and voting.

6. The General Conference shall adopt its own rules of procedure.

Article 10. *The Council*

1. The Council shall be composed of five Members of the Agency elected by the General Conference from among the Contracting Parties, due account being taken of equitable geographic distribution.

2. The Members of the Council shall be elected for a term of four years. However, in the first election three will be elected for two years. Outgoing Members may not be re-elected for the following period unless the limited number of States for which the Treaty is in force so requires.

3. Each Member of the Council shall have one representative.

4. The Council shall be so organized as to be able to function continuously.

5. In addition to the functions conferred upon it by this Treaty and to those which may be assigned to it by the General Conference, the Council shall, through the General Secretary, ensure the proper operation of the control system in accordance with the provisions of this Treaty and with the decisions adopted by the General Conference.

6. The Council shall submit an annual report on its work to the General Conference as well as such special reports as it deems necessary or which the General Conference requests of it.

7. The Council shall elect its officers for each session.

8. The decisions of the Council shall be taken by a simple majority of its Members present and voting.

9. The Council shall adopt its own rules of procedure.

Article 11. *The Secretariat*

1. The Secretariat shall consist of a General Secretary, who shall be the chief administrative officer of the Agency, and of such staff as the Agency may require. The term of office of the General Secretary shall be four years and he may be re-elected for a single additional term. The General Secretary may not be a national of the country in which the Agency has its headquarters. In case the office of the General Secretary becomes vacant, a new election shall be held to fill the office for the remainder of the term.

2. The staff of the Secretariat shall be appointed by the General Secretary, in accordance with rules laid down by the General Conference.

3. In addition to the functions conferred upon him by this Treaty and to those which may be assigned to him by the General Conference,—the General Secretary shall ensure, as provided by article 10, paragraph 5, the proper operation of the control system established by this Treaty, in accordance with the provision of the Treaty and the decisions taken by the General Conference.

4. The General Secretary shall act in that capacity in all meetings of the General Conference and of the Council and shall make an annual report to both bodies on the work of the Agency and any special reports requested by the General Conference or the Council or which the General Secretary may deem desirable.

5. The General Secretary shall establish the procedures for distributing to all Contracting Parties information received by the Agency from governmental sources and such information from non-governmental sources as may be of interest to the Agency.

6. In the performance of their duties the General Secretary and the staff shall not seek or receive instructions from any Government or from any other authority external to the Agency and shall refrain from any action which might reflect on their position as international officials responsible only to the Agency; subject to their responsibility to the Agency, they shall not disclose any industrial secrets or other confidential information coming to their knowledge by reason of their official duties in the Agency.

7. Each of the Contracting Parties undertakes to respect the exclusively international character of the responsibilities of the General Secretary and the staff and not to seek to influence them in the discharge of their responsibilities.

Article 12. *Control system*

1. For the purpose of verifying compliance with the obligations entered into by the Contracting Parties in accordance with article 1, a control system shall be· established which shall be put into effect in accordance with the provisions of articles 13-18 of this Treaty.

2. The control system shall be used in particular for the purpose of verifying:

(*a*) That devices, services and facilities intended for peaceful uses of nuclear energy are not used in the testing or manufacture of nuclear weapons;

(*b*) That none of the activities prohibited in article 1 of this Treaty are carried out in the territory of the Contracting Parties with nuclear materials or weapons introduced from abroad, and

(*c*) That explosions for peaceful purposes are compatible with article 18 of this Treaty.

Article 13. *IAEA safeguards*

Each Contracting Party shall negotiate multilateral or bilateral agreements with the International Atomic Energy Agency for the application of its safeguards to its nuclear activities. Each Contracting Party shall initiate negotiations within a period of 180 days after the date of the deposit of its instrument of ratification of this Treaty. These agreements shall enter into force, for each Party, not later than eighteen months after the date of the initiation of such negotiations except in case of unforeseen circumstances or *force majeure*.

Article 14. *Reports of the Parties*

1. The Contracting Parties shall submit to the Agency and to the International Atomic Energy Agency, for their information, semi-annual reports stating that no activity prohibited under this Treaty has occurred in their respective territories.

2. The Contracting Parties shall simultaneously transmit to the Agency a copy of any report they may submit to the International Atomic Energy Agency which relates to matters that are the subject of this Treaty and to the application of safeguards.

3. The Contracting Parties shall also transmit to the Organization of American States, for its information, any reports that may be of interest to it, in accordance with the obligations established by the Inter-American System.

Article 15. *Special reports requested by the General Secretary*

1. With the authorization of the Council, the General Secretary may request any of the Contracting Parties to provide the Agency with complementary or supplementary information regarding any event or circumstance connected with compliance with this Treaty, explaining his reasons. The Contracting Parties undertake to co-operate promptly and fully with the General Secretary.

2. The General Secretary shall inform the Council and the Contracting Parties forthwith of such requests and of the respective replies.

Article 16. *Special inspections*

1. The International Atomic Energy Agency and the Council established by this Treaty have the power of carrying out special inspections in the following cases:

(*a*) In the case of the International Atomic Energy Agency, in accordance with the agreements referred to in article 13 of this Treaty;

(*b*) In the case of the Council:

(i) When so requested, the reasons for the request being stated, by any Party which suspects that some activity prohibited by the Treaty has been carried out or is about to be carried out, either in the territory of any other Party or in any other place on such latter Party's behalf, the Council shall immediately arrange for such an inspection in accordance with article 10, paragraph 5.

(ii) When requested by any Party which has been suspected of or charged with having violated this Treaty, the Council shall immediately arrange for the special inspection requested in accordance with article 10, paragraph 5.

The above requests will be made to the Council through the General Secretary.

2. The costs and expenses of any special inspection carried out under paragraph 1, sub-paragraph (*b*), sections (i) or (ii) of this article shall be borne by the requesting Party or Parties, except where the Council concludes on the basis of the report on the special inspection that, in view of the circumstances existing in the case, such costs and expenses should be borne by the Agency.

3. The General Conference shall formulate the procedures for the organization and execution of the special inspections carried out in accordance with paragraph 1, sub-paragraph (*b*), sections (i) and (ii) of this article.

4. The Contracting Parties undertake to grant the inspectors carrying out such special inspections full and free access to all places and all information which may be necessary for the performance of their duties and which are directly and intimately connected with the suspicion of violation of this Treaty. If so requested by the authorities of the Contracting Party in whose territory the inspection is carried out, the inspectors designated by the General Conference shall be accompanied by representatives of said authorities, provided that this does not in any way delay or hinder the work of the inspectors.

5. The Council shall immediately transmit to all the Parties, through the General Secretary, a copy of any report resulting from special inspections.

6. Similarly, the Council shall send through the General Secretary to the Secretary-General of the United Nations, for transmission to the United Nations Security

Council and General Assembly, and to the Council of the Organization of American States, for its information, a copy of any report resulting from any special inspection carried out in accordance with paragraph 1, sub-paragraph (*b*), sections (i) and (ii) of this article.

7. The Council may decide, or any Contracting Party may request, the convening of a special session of the General Conference for the purpose of considering the reports resulting from any special inspection. In such a case, the General Secretary shall take immediate steps to convene the special session requested.

8. The General Conference, convened in special session under this article, may make recommendations to the Contracting Parties and submit reports to the Secretary-General of the United Nations to be transmitted to the United Nations Security Council and the General Assembly.

Article 17. *Use of nuclear energy for peaceful purposes*

Nothing in the provisions of this Treaty shall prejudice the rights of the Contracting Parties, in conformity with the Treaty, to use nuclear energy for peaceful purposes, in particular for their economic development and social progress.

Article 18. *Explosions for peaceful purposes*

1. The Contracting Parties may carry out explosions of nuclear devices for peaceful purposes—including explosions which involve devices similar to those used in nuclear weapons—or collaborate with third parties for the same purpose, provided that they do so in accordance with the provisions of this article and the other articles of the Treaty, particularly articles 1 and 5.

2. Contracting Parties intending to carry out, or to co-operate in carrying out, such an explosion shall notify the Agency and the International Atomic Energy Agency, as far in advance as the circumstances require, of the date of the explosion and shall at the same time provide the following information:

(*a*) The nature of the nuclear device and the source from which it was obtained;

(*b*) The place and purpose of the planned explosion;

(*c*) The procedures which will be followed in order to comply with paragraph 3 of this article;

(*d*) The expected force of the device, and

(*e*) The fullest possible information on any possible radioactive fall-out that may result from the explosion or explosions, and measures which will be taken to avoid danger to the population, flora, fauna and territories of any other Party or Parties.

3. The General Secretary and the technical personnel designated by the Council and the International Atomic Energy Agency may observe all the preparations, including the explosion of the device, and shall have unrestricted access to any area in the vicinity

of the site of the explosion in order to ascertain whether the device and the procedures followed during the explosion are in conformity with the information supplied under paragraph 2 of this article and the other provisions of this Treaty.

4. The Contracting Parties may accept the collaboration of third parties for the purpose set forth in paragraph 1 of the present article, in accordance with paragraphs 2 and 3 thereof.

Article 19. *Relations with other international organizations*

1. The Agency may conclude such agreements with the International Atomic Energy Agency as are authorized by the General Conference and as it considers likely to facilitate the efficient operation of the control system established by this Treaty.

2. The Agency may also enter into relations with any international organization or body, especially any which may be established in the future to supervise disarmament or measures for the control of armaments in any part of the world.

3. The Contracting Parties may, if they see fit, request the advice of the Inter-American Nuclear Energy Commission on all technical matters connected with the application of this Treaty with which the Commission is competent to deal under its Statute.

Article 20. *Measures in the event of violation of the Treaty*

1. The General Conference shall take note of all cases in which, in its opinion, any Contracting Party is not complying fully with its obligations under this Treaty and shall draw the matter to the attention of the Party concerned, making such recommendations as it deems appropriate.

2. If, in its opinion, such non-compliance constitutes a violation of this Treaty which might endanger peace and security, the General Conference shall report thereon simultaneously to the United Nations Security Council and the General Assembly through the Secretary-General of the United Nations, and to the Council of the Organization of American States. The General Conference shall likewise report to the International Atomic Energy Agency for such purposes as are relevant in accordance with its Statute.

Article 21. *United Nations and Organization of American States*

None of the provisions of this Treaty shall be construed as impairing the rights and obligations of the Parties under the Charter of the United Nations or, in the case of States Members of the Organization of American States, under existing regional treaties.

Article 22. *Privileges and immunities*

1. The Agency shall enjoy in the territory of each of the Contracting Parties such legal

capacity and such privileges and immunities as may be necessary for the exercise of its functions and the fulfilment of its purposes.

2. Representatives of the Contracting Parties accredited to the Agency and officials of the Agency shall similarly enjoy such privileges and immunities as are necessary for the performance of their functions.

3. The Agency may conclude agreements with the Contracting Parties with a view to determining the details of the application of paragraphs 1 and 2 of this article.

Article 23. *Notification of other agreements*

Once this Treaty has entered into force, the Secretariat shall be notified immediately of any international agreement concluded by any of the Contracting Parties on matters with which this Treaty is concerned; the Secretariat shall register it and notify the other Contracting Parties.

Article 24. *Settlement of disputes*

Unless the Parties concerned agree on another mode of peaceful settlement, any question or dispute concerning the interpretation or application of this Treaty which is not settled shall be referred to the International Court of Justice with the prior consent of the Parties to the controversy.

Article 25. *Signature*

1. This Treaty shall be open indefinitely for signature by:

(*a*) All the Latin American Republics, and

(*b*) All other sovereign States situated in their entirety south of latitude 35° north in the western hemisphere; and, except as provided in paragraph 2 of this article, all such States which become sovereign, when they have been admitted by the General Conference.

2. The General Conference shall not take any decision regarding the admission of a political entity part or all of whose territory is the subject, prior to the date when this Treaty is opened for signature, of a dispute or claim between an extra-continental country and one or more Latin American States, so long as the dispute has not been settled by peaceful means.

Article 26. *Ratification and deposit*

1. This Treaty shall be subject to ratification by signatory States in accordance with their respective constitutional procedures.

2. This Treaty and the instruments of ratification shall be deposited with the Government of the Mexican United States, which is hereby designated the Depositary Government.

3. The Depositary Government shall send certified copies of this Treaty to the Governments of signatory States and shall notify them of the deposit of each instrument of ratification.

Article 27. *Reservations*

This Treaty shall not be subject to reservations.

Article 28. *Entry into force*

1. Subject to the provisions of paragraph 2 of this article, this Treaty shall enter into force among the States that have ratified it as soon as the following requirements have been met:

(*a*) Deposit of the instruments of ratification of this Treaty with the Depositary Government by the Governments of the States mentioned in article 25 which are in existence on the date when this Treaty is opened for signature and which are not affected by the provisions of article 25, paragraph 2;

(*b*) Signature and ratification of Additional Protocol I annexed to this Treaty by all extra-continental or continental States having *de jure* or *de facto* international responsibility for territories situated in the zone of application of the Treaty;

(*c*) Signature and ratification of the Additional Protocol II annexed to this Treaty by all powers possessing nuclear weapons;

(*d*) Conclusion of bilateral or multilateral agreements on the application of the Safeguards System of the International Atomic Energy Agency in accordance with article 13 of this Treaty.

2. All signatory States shall have the imprescriptible right to waive, wholly or in part, the requirements laid down in the preceding paragraph. They may do so by means of a declaration which shall be annexed to their respective instrument of ratification and which may be formulated at the time of deposit of the instrument or subsequently. For those States which exercise this right, this Treaty shall enter into force upon deposit of the declaration, or as soon as those requirements have been met which have not been expressly waived.

3. As soon as this Treaty has entered into force in accordance with the provisions of paragraph 2 for eleven States, the Depositary Government shall convene a preliminary meeting of those States in order that the Agency may be set up and commence its work.

4. After the entry into force of this Treaty for all countries of the zone, the rise of a new power possessing nuclear weapons shall have the effect of suspending the execution of this Treaty for those countries which have ratified it without waiving requirements of paragraph 1, sub-paragraph (*c*) of this article, and which request such suspension; the Treaty shall remain suspended until the new power, on its own initiative or upon request by the General Conference, ratifies the annexed Additional Protocol II.

Article 29. *Amendments*

1. Any Contracting Party may propose amendments to this Treaty and shall submit its proposals to the Council through the

General Secretary, who shall transmit them to all the other Contracting Parties and, in addition, to all other signatories in accordance with article 6. The Council, through the General Secretary, shall immediately following the meeting of signatories convene a special session of the General Conference to examine the proposals made, for the adoption of which a two-thirds majority of the Contracting Parties present and voting shall be required.

2. Amendments adopted shall enter into force as soon as the requirements set forth in article 28 of this Treaty have been complied with.

Article 30. *Duration and denunciation*

1. This Treaty shall be of a permanent nature and shall remain in force indefinitely, but any Party may denounce it by notifying the General Secretary of the Agency if, in the opinion of the denouncing State, there have arisen or may arise circumstances connected with the content of this Treaty or of the annexed Additonal Protocol I and II which affect its supreme interests or the peace and security of one or more Contracting Parties.

2. The denunciation shall take effect three months after the delivery to the General Secretary of the Agency of the notification by the Government of the signatory State concerned. The General Secretary shall immediately communicate such notification to the other Contracting Parties and to the Secretary-General of the United Nations for the information of the United Nations Security Council and the General Assembly. He shall also communicate it to the Secretary-General of the Organization of American States.

Article 31. *Authentic texts and registration*

This Treaty, of which the Spanish, Chinese, English, French, Portuguese and Russian texts are equally authentic, shall be registered by the Depositary Government in accordance with article 102 of the United Nations Charter. The Depositary Government shall notify the Secretary-General of the United Nations of the signatures, ratifications and amendments relating to this Treaty and shall communicate them to the Secretary-General of the Organization of American States for its information.

Transitional Article

Denunciation of the declaration referred to in article 28, paragraph 2, shall be subject to the same procedures as the denunciation of this Treaty, except that it will take effect on the date of delivery of the respective notification.

ADDITIONAL PROTOCOL I

The undersigned Plenipotentiaries, furnished with full powers by their respective Governments,
Convinced that the Treaty for the Prohibition of Nuclear Weapons in Latin America, negotiated and signed in accordance with the recommendations of the General Assembly of the United Nations in Resolution 1911 (XVIII) of 27 November 1963, represents an important step towards ensuring the non-proliferation of nuclear weapons,
Aware that the non-proliferation of nuclear weapons is not an end in itself but, rather, a means of achieving general and complete disarmament at a later stage, and
Desiring to contribute, so far as lies in their power, towards ending the armaments race, especially in the field of nuclear weapons, and towards strengthening a world at peace, based on mutual respect and sovereign equality of States,

Have agreed as follows:

Article 1

To undertake to apply the statute of denuclearization in respect of warlike purposes as defined in articles 1, 3, 5 and 13 of the Treaty for the Prohibition of Nuclear Weapons in Latin America in territories for which, *de jure* or *de facto*, they are internationally responsible and which lie within the limits of the geographical zone established in that Treaty.

Article 2

The duration of this Protocol shall be the same as that of the Treaty for the Prohibition of Nuclear Weapons in Latin America of which this Protocol is an annex, and the provisions regarding ratification and denunciation contained in the Treaty shall be applicable to it.

Article 3

This Protocol shall enter into force, for the States which have ratified it, on the date of the deposit of their respective instruments of ratification.

ADDITIONAL PROTOCOL II

The undersigned Plenipotentiaries, furnished with full powers by their respective Governments,
Convinced that the Treaty for the Prohibition of Nuclear Weapons in Latin America, negotiated and signed in accordance with the recommendations of the General Assembly of the United Nations in Resolution 1911 (XVIII) of 27 November 1963, represents an important step towards ensuring the non-proliferation of nuclear weapons,
Aware that the non-proliferation of nuclear weapons is not an end in itself but, rather, a means of achieving general and complete disarmament at a later stage, and
Desiring to contribute, so far as lies in their power, towards ending the armaments race, especially in the field of nuclear weapons, and towards promoting and strengthening a

world at peace, based on mutual respect and sovereign equality of States,

Have agreed as follows:

Article 1

The statute of denuclearization of Latin America in respect of warlike purposes, as defined, delimited and set forth in the Treaty for the Prohibition of Nuclear Weapons in Latin America of which this instrument is an annex, shall be fully respected by the parties to this Protocol in all its express aims and provisions.

Article 2

The Governments represented by the undersigned Plenipotentiaries undertake, therefore, not to contribute in any way to the performance of acts involving a violation of the obligations of article 1 of the Treaty in the territories to which the Treaty applies in accordance with article 4 thereof.

Article 3

The Governments represented by the undersigned Plenipotentiaries also undertake not to use or threaten to use nuclear weapons against the Contracting Parties of the Treaty for the Prohibition of Nuclear Weapons in Latin America.

Article 4

The duration of this Protocol shall be the same as that of the Treaty for the Prohibition of Nuclear Weapons in Latin America of which this Protocol is an annex, and the definitions of territory and nuclear weapons set forth in articles 3 and 5 of the Treaty shall be applicable to this Protocol, as well as the provisions regarding ratification, reservations, denunciation, authentic texts and registration contained in articles 26, 27, 30 and 31 of the Treaty.

Article 5

This Protocol shall enter into force, for the States which have ratified it, on the date of the deposit of their respective instruments of ratification.

Source: *Treaty Series*, Vol. 634 (United Nations, New York)

For the list of states which have signed and ratified the Treaty of Tlatelolco, and of those which have signed and ratified Additional Protocols I and II, see Chapter 6.

SECURITY COUNCIL RESOLUTION ON SECURITY ASSURANCES TO NON-NUCLEAR WEAPON STATES

Adopted at New York on 19 June 1968

The Security Council,

Noting with appreciation the desire of a large number of States to subscribe to the treaty on the Non-Proliferation of Nuclear Weapons, and thereby to undertake not to receive the transfer from any transferor whatsoever of nuclear weapons or other nuclear explosive devices or of control over such weapons or explosive devices directly or indirectly, not to manufacture or otherwise acquire nuclear weapons or other nuclear explosive devices, and not to seek or receive any assistance in the manufacture of nuclear weapons or other nuclear explosive devices,

Taking into consideration the concern of certain of these States that, in conjunction with their adherence to the Treaty on the Non-Proliferation of Nuclear Weapons, appropriate measures be undertaken to safeguard their security,

Bearing in mind that any aggression accompanied by the use of nuclear weapons would endanger the peace and security of all States,

1. *Recognizes* that aggression with nuclear weapons or the threat of such aggression against a non-nuclear-weapon State would create a situation in which the Security Council, and above all its nuclear-weapon State permanent members, would have to act immediately in accordance with their obligations under the United Nations Charter;

2. *Welcomes* the intention expressed by certain States that they will provide or support immediate assistance, in accordance with the Charter, to any non-nuclear-weapon State Party to the Treaty on the Non-Proliferation of Nuclear Weapons that is a victim of an act or an object of a threat of aggression in which nuclear weapons are used;

3. *Reaffirms* in particular the inherent right, recognized under Article 51 of the Charter, of individual and collective self-defense if an armed attack occurs against a Member of the United Nations, until the Security Council has taken measures necessary to maintain international peace and security.

Source: UN document S/RES/255 (1968) in *Resolutions and Decisions of the Security Council 1968,* Security Council Official Records: Twenty-third year (United Nations, New York, 1970)

The Security Council approved this resolution by a vote of 10 to 0, with 5 abstentions. It was supported by Canada, Republic of China (Taiwan), Denmark, Ethiopia, Hungary, Paraguay, Senegal, UK, USA and USSR. The following countries abstained: Algeria, Brazil, France, India and Pakistan.

TREATY ON THE NON-PROLIFERATION OF NUCLEAR WEAPONS

*Signed at London, Moscow and
  Washington on 1 July 1968
Entered into force on 5 March 1970
Depositaries: UK, US and Soviet
  governments*

The States concluding this Treaty, hereinafter referred to as the "Parties to the Treaty",

Considering the devastation that would be visited upon all mankind by a nuclear war and the consequent need to make every effort to avert the danger of such a war and to take measures to safeguard the security of peoples,

Believing that the proliferation of nuclear weapons would seriously enhance the danger of nuclear war,

In conformity with resolutions of the United Nations General Assembly calling for the conclusion of an agreement on the prevention of wider dissemination of nuclear weapons,

Undertaking to co-operate in facilitating the application of International Atomic Energy Agency safeguards on peaceful nuclear activities,

Expressing their support for research, development and other efforts to further the application, within the framework of the International Atomic Energy Agency safeguards system, of the principle of safeguarding effectively the flow of source and special fissionable materials by use of instruments and other techniques at certain strategic points,

Affirming the principle that the benefits of peaceful applications of nuclear technology, including any technological by-products which may be derived by nuclear-weapon States from the development of nuclear explosive devices, should be available for peaceful purposes to all Parties to the Treaty, whether nuclear-weapon or non-nuclear-weapon States,

Convinced that, in furtherance of this principle, all Parties to the Treaty are entitled to participate in the fullest possible exchange of scientific information for, and to contribute alone or in co-operation with other States to, the further development of the applications of atomic energy for peaceful purposes,

Declaring their intention to achieve at the earliest possible date the cessation of the nuclear arms race and to undertake effective measures in the direction of nuclear disarmament,

Urging the co-operation of all States in the attainment of this objective,

Recalling the determination expressed by the Parties to the 1963 Treaty banning nuclear weapon tests in the atmosphere, in outer space and under water in its Preamble to seek to achieve the discontinuance of all test explosions of nuclear weapons for all time and to continue negotiations to this end,

Desiring to further the easing of international tension and the strengthening of trust between States in order to facilitate the cessation of the manufacture of nuclear weapons, the liquidation of all their existing stockpiles, and the elimination from national arsenals of nuclear weapons and the means of their delivery pursuant to a Treaty on general and complete disarmament under strict and effective international control,

Recalling that, in accordance with the Charter of the United Nations, States must refrain in their international relations from the threat or use of force against the territorial integrity or political independence of any State, or in any other manner inconsistent with the Purposes of the United Nations, and that the establishment and maintenance of international peace and security are to be promoted with the least diversion for armaments of the world's human and economic resources,

Have agreed as follows:

Article I

Each nuclear-weapon State Party to the Treaty undertakes not to transfer to any recipient whatsoever nuclear weapons or other nuclear explosive devices or control over such weapons or explosive devices directly, or indirectly; and not in any way to assist, encourage, or induce any non-nuclear-weapon State to manufacture or otherwise acquire nuclear weapons or other nuclear explosive devices, or control over such weapons or explosive devices.

Article II

Each non-nuclear-weapon State Party to the Treaty undertakes not to receive the transfer from any transferor whatsoever of nuclear weapons or other nuclear explosive devices or of control over such weapons or explosive devices directly, or indirectly; not to manufacture or otherwise acquire nuclear weapons or other nuclear explosive devices; and not to seek or receive any assistance in the manufacture of nuclear weapons or other nuclear explosive devices.

Article III

1. Each non-nuclear-weapon State Party to the Treaty undertakes to accept safeguards, as set forth in an agreement to be negotiated and concluded with the International Atomic Energy Agency in accordance with the Statute of the International Atomic Energy Agency and the Agency's safeguards system, for the exclusive purpose of verification of the fulfilment of its obligations assumed under this Treaty with a view to preventing diversion of nuclear energy from peaceful uses to nuclear weapons or other nuclear explosive devices. Procedures for the safeguards required by this Article shall be followed with respect to source or special fissionable material whether

it is being produced, processed or used in any principal nuclear facility or is outside any such facility. The safeguards required by this Article shall be applied on all source or special fissionable material in all peaceful nuclear activities within the territory of such State, under its jurisdiction, or carried out under its control anywhere.

2. Each State Party to the Treaty undertakes not to provide: (*a*) source or special fissionable material, or (*b*) equipment or material especially designed or prepared for the processing, use or production of special fissionable material, to any non-nuclear-weapon State for peaceful purposes, unless the source or special fissionable material shall be subject to the safeguards required by this Article.

3. The safeguards required by this Article shall be implemented in a manner designed to comply with Article IV of this Treaty, and to avoid hampering the economic or technological development of the Parties or international co-operation in the field of peaceful nuclear activities, including the international exchange of nuclear material and equipment for the processing, use or production of nuclear material for peaceful purposes in accordance with the provisions of this Article and the principle of safeguarding set forth in the Preamble of the Treaty.

4. Non-nuclear-weapon States Party to the Treaty shall conclude agreements with the International Atomic Energy Agency to meet the requirements of this Article either individually or together with other States in accordance with the Statute of the International Atomic Energy Agency. Negotiation of such agreements shall commence within 180 days from the original entry into force of this Treaty. For States depositing their instruments of ratification or accession after the 180-day period, negotiation of such agreements shall commence not later than the date of such deposit. Such agreements shall enter into force not later than eighteen months after the date of initiation of negotiations.

Article IV

1. Nothing in this Treaty shall be interpreted as affecting the inalienable right of all the Parties to the Treaty to develop research, production and use of nuclear energy for peaceful purposes without discrimination and in conformity with Articles I and II of this Treaty.

2. All the Parties to the Treaty undertake to facilitate, and have the right to participate in, the fullest possible exchange of equipment, materials and scientific and technological information for the peaceful uses of nuclear energy. Parties to the Treaty in a position to do so shall also co-operate in contributing alone or together with other States or international organizations to the further development of the applications of nuclear energy for peaceful purposes, especially in the territories of non-nuclear-weapon States

Party to the Treaty, with due consideration for the needs of the developing areas of the world.

Article V

Each Party to the Treaty undertakes to take appropriate measures to ensure that, in accordance with this Treaty, under appropriate international observation and through appropriate international procedures, potential benefits from any peaceful applications of nuclear explosions will be made available to non-nuclear-weapon States Party to the Treaty on a non-discriminatory basis and that the charge to such Parties for the explosive devices used will be as low as possible and exclude any charge for research and development. Non-nuclear-weapon States Party to the Treaty shall be able to obtain such benefits, pursuant to a special international agreement or agreements, through an appropriate international body with adequate representation of non-nuclear-weapon States. Negotiations on this subject shall commence as soon as possible after the Treaty enters into force. Non-nuclear-weapon States Party to the Treaty so desiring may also obtain such benefits pursuant to bilateral agreements.

Article VI

Each of the Parties to the Treaty undertakes to pursue negotiations in good faith on effective measures relating to cessation of the nuclear arms race at an early date and to nuclear disarmament, and on a treaty on general and complete disarmament under strict and effective international control.

Article VII

Nothing in this Treaty affects the right of any group of States to conclude regional treaties in order to assure the total absence of nuclear weapons in their respective territories.

Article VIII

1. Any Party to the Treaty may propose amendments to this Treaty. The text of any proposed amendment shall be submitted to the Depositary Governments which shall circulate it to all Parties to the Treaty. Thereupon, if requested to do so by one-third or more of the Parties to the Treaty, the Depositary Governments shall convene a conference, to which they shall invite all the Parties to the Treaty, to consider such an amendment.

2. Any amendment to this Treaty must be approved by a majority of the votes of all the Parties to the Treaty, including the votes of all nuclear-weapon States Party to the Treaty and all other Parties which, on the date the amendment is circulated, are members of the Board of Governors of the International Atomic Energy Agency. The amendment shall enter into force for each Party that deposits its instrument of ratification of the

amendment upon the deposit of such instruments of ratification by a majority of all the Parties, including the instruments of ratification of all nuclear-weapon States Party to the Treaty and all other Parties which, on the date the amendment is circulated, are members of the Board of Governors of the International Atomic Energy Agency. Thereafter, it shall enter into force for any other Party upon the deposit of its instrument of ratification of the amendment.

3. Five years after the entry into force of this Treaty, a conference of Parties to the Treaty shall be held in Geneva, Switzerland, in order to review the operation of this Treaty with a view to assuring that the purposes of the Preamble and the provisions of the Treaty are being realised. At intervals of five years thereafter, a majority of the Parties to the Treaty may obtain, by submitting a proposal to this effect to the Depositary Governments, the convening of further conferences with the same objective of reviewing the operation of the Treaty.

Article IX

1. This Treaty shall be open to all States for signature. Any State which does not sign the Treaty before its entry into force in accordance with paragraph 3 of this Article may accede to it at any time.

2. This Treaty shall be subject to ratification by signatory States. Instruments of ratification and instruments of accession shall be deposited with the Governments of the United Kingdom of Great Britain and Northern Ireland, the Union of Soviet Socialist Republics and the United States of America, which are hereby designated the Depositary Governments.

3. This Treaty shall enter into force after its ratification by the States, the Governments of which are designated Depositaries of the Treaty, and forty other States signatory to this Treaty and the deposit of their instruments of ratification. For the purposes of this Treaty, a nuclear-weapon State is one which has manufactured and exploded a nuclear weapon or other nuclear explosive device prior to 1 January, 1967.

4. For States whose instruments of ratification or accession are deposited subsequent to the entry into force of this Treaty, it shall enter into force on the date of the deposit of their instruments of ratification or accession.

5. The Depositary Governments shall promptly inform all signatory and acceding States of the date of each signature, the date of deposit of each instrument of ratification or of accession, the date of the entry into force of this Treaty, and the date of receipt of any requests for convening a conference or other notices.

6. This Treaty shall be registered by the Depositary Governments pursuant to Article 102 of the Charter of the United Nations.

Article X

1. Each Party shall in exercising its national sovereignty have the right to withdraw from the Treaty if it decides that extraordinary events, related to the subject matter of this Treaty, have jeopardized the supreme interests of its country. It shall give notice of such withdrawal to all other Parties to the Treaty and to the United Nations Security Council three months in advance. Such notice shall include a statement of the extraordinary events it regards as having jeopardized its supreme interests.

2. Twenty-five years after the entry into force of the Treaty, a conference shall be convened to decide whether the Treaty shall continue in force indefinitely, or shall be extended for an additional fixed period or periods. This decision shall be taken by a majority of the Parties to the Treaty.

Article XI

This Treaty, the English, Russian, French, Spanish and Chinese texts of which are equally authentic, shall be deposited in the archives of the Depositary Governments. Duly certified copies of this Treaty shall be transmitted by the Depositary Governments to the Governments of the signatory and acceding States.

Source: *Treaty Series*, Vol. 729 (United Nations, New York)

For the list of states which have signed, ratified, acceded or succeeded to the Non-Proliferation Treaty, see Chapter 6.

TREATY ON THE PROHIBITION OF THE EMPLACEMENT OF NUCLEAR WEAPONS AND OTHER WEAPONS OF MASS DESTRUCTION ON THE SEABED AND THE OCEAN FLOOR AND IN THE SUBSOIL THEREOF

Signed at London, Moscow and Washington on 11 February 1971
Entered into force on 18 May 1972
Depositaries: UK, US and Soviet governments

The States Parties to this Treaty,

Recognizing the common interest of mankind in the progress of the exploration and use of the seabed and the ocean floor for peaceful purposes,

Considering that the prevention of a nuclear arms race on the seabed and the ocean floor serves the interests of maintaining world peace, reduces international tensions and strengthens friendly relations among States,

Convinced that this Treaty constitutes a step towards the exclusion of the seabed, the ocean floor and the sub-soil thereof from the arms race,

Convinced that this Treaty consitutes a step towards a treaty on general and complete disarmament under strict and effective international control, and determined to continue negotiations to this end,

Convinced that this Treaty will further the purposes and principles of the Charter of the United Nations, in a manner consistent with the principles of international law and without infringing the freedoms of the high seas,

Have agreed as follows:

Article I

1. The States Parties to this Treaty undertake not to emplant or emplace on the seabed and the ocean floor and in the subsoil thereof beyond the outer limit of a seabed zone, as defined in article II, any nuclear weapons or any other types of weapons of mass destruction as well as structures, launching installations or any other facilities specifically designed for storing, testing or using such weapons.

2. The undertakings of paragraph 1 of this article shall also apply to the seabed zone referred to in the same paragraph, except that within such seabed zone, they shall not apply either to the coastal State or to the seabed beneath its territorial waters.

3. The States Parties to this Treaty undertake not to assist, encourage or induce any State to carry out activities referred to in paragraph 1 of this article and not to participate in any other way in such actions.

Article II

For the purpose of this Treaty, the outer limit of the seabed zone referred to in article I shall be coterminous with the twelve-mile outer limit of the zone referred to in part II of the Convention on the Territorial Sea and the Contiguous Zone, signed at Geneva on April 29, 1958, and shall be measured in accordance with the provisions of part I, section II, of that Convention and in accordance with international law.

Article III

1. In order to promote the objectives of and insure compliance with the provisions of this Treaty, each State Party to the Treaty shall have the right to verify through observation the activities of other States Parties to the Treaty on the seabed and the ocean floor and in the sub-soil thereof beyond the zone referred to in article I, provided that observation does not interfere with such activities.

2. If after such observation reasonable doubts remain concerning the fulfilment of the obligations assumed under the Treaty, the State Party having such doubts and the State Party that is responsible for the activities giving rise to the doubts shall consult with a view to removing the doubts. If the doubts persist, the State Party having such doubts shall notify the other States Parties, and the Parties concerned shall cooperate on such further procedures for verification as may be agreed, including appropriate inspection of objects, structures, installations or other facilities that reasonably may be expected to be of a kind described in article I. The Parties in the region of the activities, including any coastal State, and any other Party so requesting, shall be entitled to participate in such consultation and cooperation. After completion of the further procedures for verification, an appropriate report shall be circulated to other Parties by the Party that initiated such procedures.

3. If the State responsible for the activities giving rise to the reasonable doubts is not identifiable by observation of the object, structure, installation or other facility, the State Party having such doubts shall notify and make appropriate inquiries of States Parties in the region of the activities and of any other State Party. If it is ascertained through these inquiries that a particular State Party is responsible for the activities, that the State Party shall consult and cooperate with other Parties as provided in paragraph 2 of this article. If the identity of the State responsible for the activities cannot be ascertained through these inquiries, then further verification procedures, including inspection, may be undertaken by the inquiring State Party, which shall invite the participation of the Parties in the region of the activities, including any coastal State, and of any other Party desiring to cooperate.

4. If consultation and cooperation pursuant to paragraphs 2 and 3 of this article have not removed the doubts concerning the activities and there remains a serious question concerning fulfilment of the obligations assumed under this Treaty, a State Party may, in accordance with the provisions of the Charter of the United Nations, refer the matter to the Security Council, which may take action in accordance with the Charter.

5. Verification pursuant to this article may be undertaken by any State Party using its own means, or with the full or partial assistance of any other State Party, or through appropriate international procedures within the framework of the United Nations and in accordance with its Charter.

6. Verification activities pursuant to this Treaty shall not interfere with activities of other States Parties and shall be conducted with due regard for rights recognized under international law, including the freedoms of the high seas and the rights of coastal States with respect to the exploration and exploitation of their continental shelves.

Article IV

Nothing in this Treaty shall be interpreted as supporting or prejudicing the position of any State Party with respect to existing international conventions, including the 1958

Convention on the Territorial Sea and the Contiguous Zone, or with respect to rights or claims which such State Party may assert, or with respect to recognition or non-recognition of rights or claims asserted by any other State, related to waters off its coasts, including, *inter alia*, territorial seas and contiguous zones, or to the seabed and the ocean floor, including continental shelves.

Article V

The Parties to this Treaty undertake to continue negotiations in good faith concerning further measures in the field of disarmament for the prevention of an arms race on the seabed, the ocean floor and the subsoil thereof.

Article VI

Any State Party may propose amendments to this Treaty. Amendments shall enter into force for each State Party accepting the amendments upon their acceptance by a majority of the States Parties to the Treaty and, thereafter, for each remaining State party on the date of acceptance by it.

Article VII

Five years after the entry into force of this Treaty, a conference of Parties to the Treaty shall be held at Geneva, Switzerland, in order to review the operation of this Treaty with a view to assuring that the purposes of the preamble and the provisions of the Treaty are being realized. Such review shall take into account any relevant technological developments. The review conference shall determine, in accordance with the views of a majority of those Parties attending, whether and when an additional review conference shall be convened.

Article VIII

Each State Party to this Treaty shall in exercising its national sovereignty have the right to withdraw from this Treaty if it decides that extraordinary events related to the subject matter of this Treaty have jeopardized the supreme interests of its country. It shall give notice of such withdrawal to all other States Parties to the Treaty and to the United Nations Security Council three months in advance. Such notice shall include a statement of the extraordinary events it considers to have jeopardized its supreme interests.

Article IX

The provisions of this Treaty shall in no way affect the obligations assumed by States Parties to the Treaty under international instruments establishing zones free from nuclear weapons.

Article X

1. This Treaty shall be open for signature to all States. Any State which does not sign the Treaty before its entry into force in accordance with paragraph 3 of this article may accede to it at any time.

2. This Treaty shall be subject to ratification by signatory States. Instruments of ratification and of accession shall be deposited with the Governments of the United States of America, the United Kingdom of Great Britain and Northern Ireland, and the Union of Soviet Socialist Republics, which are hereby designated the Depositary Governments.

3. This Treaty shall enter into force after the deposit of instruments of ratification by twenty-two Governments, including the Governments designated as Depositary Governments of this Treaty.

4. For States whose instruments of ratification or accession are deposited after the entry into force of this Treaty, it shall enter into force on the date of the deposit of their instruments of ratification or accession.

5. The Depositary Governments shall promptly inform the Governments of all signatory and acceding States of the date of each signature, of the date of deposit of each instrument of ratification or of accession, of the date of the entry into force of this Treaty, and of the receipt of other notices.

6. This Treaty shall be registered by the Depositary Governments pursuant to Article 102 of the Charter of the United Nations.

Article XI

This Treaty, the English, Russian, French, Spanish and Chinese texts of which are equally authentic, shall be deposited in the archives of the Depositary Governments. Duly certified copies of this Treaty shall be transmitted by the Depositary Governments to the Governments of the States signatory and acceding thereto.

Source: *Treaties and Other International Acts, Series 7337* (US Department of State, Washington, D.C., 1972)

For the list of states which have signed, ratified or acceded to the Sea-Bed Treaty, see Chapter 6.

AGREEMENT BETWEEN THE USA AND THE USSR ON MEASURES TO IMPROVE THE DIRECT COMMUNICATIONS LINK

Signed at Washington, D.C. on 30 September 1971
Entered into force on 30 September 1971

The United States of America and the Union of Soviet Socialist Republics, hereinafter referred to as the Parties,

Noting the positive experience gained in the process of operating the existing Direct

Communications Link between the United States of America and the Union of Soviet Socialist Republics, which was established for use in time of emergency pursuant to the Memorandum of Understanding Regarding the Establishment of a Direct Communications Link, signed on June 20, 1963,

Having examined, in a spirit of mutual understanding, matters relating to the improvement and modernization of the Direct Communications Link,

Have agreed as follows:

Article 1

1. For the purpose of increasing the reliability of the Direct Communications Link, there shall be established and put into operation the following:

(*a*) two additional circuits between the United States of America and the Union of Soviet Socialist Republics each using a satellite communications system, with each Party selecting a satellite communications system of its own choice,

(*b*) a system of terminals (more than one) in the territory of each Party for the Direct Communications Link, with the locations and number of terminals in the United States of America to be determined by the United States side, and the locations and number of terminals in the Union of Soviet Socialist Republics to be determined by the Soviet side.

2. Matters relating to the implementation of the aforementioned improvements of the Direct Communications Link are set forth in the Annex which is attached hereto and forms an integral part hereof.

Article 2

Each Party confirms its intention to take all possible measures to assure the continuous and reliable operation of the communications circuits and the system of terminals of the Direct Communications Link for which it is responsible in accordance with this Agreement and the Annex hereto, as well as to communicate to the head of its Government any messages received via the Direct Communications Link from the head of Government of the other Party.

Article 3

The Memorandum of Understanding Between the United States of America and the Union of Soviet Socialist Republics Regarding the Establishment of a Direct Communications Link, signed on June 20, 1963, with the Annex thereto, shall remain in force, except to the extent that its provisions are modified by this Agreement and Annex hereto.

Article 4

The undertakings of the Parties hereunder shall be carried out in accordance with their respective Constitutional processes.

Article 5

This Agreement, including the Annex hereto, shall enter into force upon signature.

ANNEX

Improvements to the USA–USSR Direct Communications Link shall be implemented in accordance with the provisions set forth in this Annex.

I. Circuits

(*a*) Each of the original circuits established pursuant to paragraph 1 of the Annex to the Memorandum of Understanding, dated June 20, 1963, shall continue to be maintained and operated as part of the Direct Communications Link until such time, after the satellite communications circuits provided for herein become operational, as the agencies designated pursuant to paragraph III (hereinafter referred to as the "designated agencies") mutually agree that such original circuit is no longer necessary. The provisions of paragraph 7 of the Annex to the Memorandum of Understanding, dated June 20, 1963, shall continue to govern the allocation of the costs of maintaining and operating such original circuits.

(*b*) Two additional circuits shall be established using two satellite communications systems. Taking into account paragraph I (*e*) below, the United States side shall provide one circuit via the Intelsat system and the Soviet side shall provide one circuit via the Molniya II system. The two circuits shall be duplex telephone band-width circuits conforming to CCITT[1] standards, equipped for secondary telegraphic multiplexing. Transmission and reception of messages over the Direct Communications Link shall be effected in accordance with applicable recommendations of international communications regulations, as well as with mutually agreed instructions.

(*c*) When the reliability of both additional circuits has been established to the mutual satisfaction of the designated agencies, they shall be used as the primary circuits of the Direct Communications Link for transmission and reception of teleprinter messages between the United States and the Soviet Union.

(*d*) Each satellite communications circuit shall utilize an earth station in the territory of the United States, a communications satellite transponder, and an earth station in the territory of the Soviet Union. Each Party shall be responsible for linking the earth stations in its territory to its own terminals of the Direct Communications Link.

(*e*) For the circuits specified in paragraph I (*b*):—The Soviet side will provide and operate at least one earth station in its territory for the satellite communications circuit in the Intelsat system, and will also arrange for the use of suitable earth station facilities in its territory for the satellite communications circuit in the Molniya II system. The United States side, through a governmental agency or other United States legal entity, will make appropriate arrangements with Intelsat with regard to access for the Soviet Intelsat earth station to the Intelsat space segment, as well as for the use of the applicable portion of the Intelsat space segment. —The United States side will provide and operate at least one earth station in its territory for the satellite communications circuit in the Molniya II system, and will also arrange for the use of suitable earth station facilities in its territory for the satellite communications circuit in the Intelsat system.

(f) Each earth station shall conform to the performance specifications and operating procedures of the corresponding satellite communications system and the ratio of antenna gain to the equivalent noise temperature should be no less than 31 decibels. Any deviation from these specifications and procedures which may be required in any unusual situation shall be worked out and mutually agreed upon by the designated agencies of both Parties after consultation.

(g) The operational commissioning dates for the satellite communications circuits based on the Intelsat and Molniya II systems shall be as agreed upon by the designated agencies of the Parties through consultations.

(h) The United States side shall bear the costs of: (1) providing and operating the Molniya II earth station in its territory; (2) the use of the Intelsat earth station in its territory; and (3) the transmission of messages via the Intelsat system. The Soviet side shall bear the costs of: (1) providing and operating the Intelsat earth station in its territory; (2) the use of the Molniya II earth station in its territory; and (3) the transmission of messages via the Molniya II system. Payment of the costs of the satellite communications circuits shall be effected without any transfer of payments between the Parties.

(i) Each Party shall be responsible for providing to the other Party notification of any proposed modification or replacement of the communications satellite system containing the circuit provided by it that might require accommodation by earth stations using that system or otherwise affect the maintenance or operation of the Direct Communications Link. Such notification should be given sufficiently in advance to enable the designated agencies to consult and to make, before the modification or replacement is effected, such preparation as may be agreed upon for accommodation by the affected earth stations.

II. Terminals

(a) Each Party shall establish a system of terminals in its territory for the exchange of messages with the other Party, and shall determine the locations and number of terminals in such a system. Terminals of the Direct Communications Link shall be designated "USA" and "USSR".

(b) Each Party shall take necessary measures to provide for rapidly switching circuits among terminal points in such a manner that only one terminal location is connected to the circuits at any one time.

(c) Each Party shall use teleprinter equipment from its own sources to equip the additional terminals for the transmission and reception of messages from the United States to the Soviet Union in the English language and from the Soviet Union to the United States in the Russian language.

(d) The terminals of the Direct Communications Link shall be provided with encoding equipment. One-time tape encoding equipment shall be used for transmissions via the Direct Communications Link. A mutually agreed quantity of encoding equipment of a modern and reliable type selected by the United States side, with spares, test equipment, technical literature and operating supplies, shall be furnished by the United States side to the Soviet side against payment of the cost thereof by the Soviet side; additional spares for the encoding equipment supplied will be furnished as necessary.

(e) Keying tapes shall be supplied in accordance with the provisions set forth in paragraph 4 of the Annex to the Memorandum of Understanding, dated June 20, 1963. Each Party shall be responsible for reproducing and distributing additional keying tapes for its system of terminals and for implementing procedures which ensure that the required synchronization of encoding equipment can be effected from any one terminal at any time.

III. Other matters

Each Party shall designate the agencies responsible for arrangements regarding the establishment of the additional circuits and the systems of terminals provided for in this Agreement and Annex, for their operation and for their continuity and reliability. These agencies shall, on the basis of direct contacts:

(a) arrange for the exchange of required performance specifications and operating procedures for the earth stations of the communications systems using Intelsat and Molniya II satellites;

(b) arrange for testing, acceptance and commissioning of the satellite circuits and for operation of these circuits after commissioning; and,

(c) decide matters and develop instructions relating to the operation of the secondary teleprinter multiplex system used on the satellite circuits.

Source: *Treaties and Other International Acts, Series 7187* (US Department of State, Washington, D.C., 1971)

See also Amendment of 1975.

[1] International Telegraph and Telephone Consultative Committee.

AGREEMENT BETWEEN THE USA AND THE USSR ON MEASURES TO REDUCE THE RISK OF OUTBREAK OF NUCLEAR WAR

Signed at Washington, D.C. on
30 September 1971
Entered into force on 30 September 1971

The United States of America and the Union of Soviet Socialist Republics, hereinafter referred to as the Parties:

Taking into account the devastating consequences that nuclear war would have for all mankind, and recognizing the need to exert every effort to avert the risk of outbreak of such a war, including measures to guard against accidental or unauthorized use of nuclear weapons,

Believing that agreement on measures for reducing the risk of outbreak of nuclear war serves the interests of strengthening international peace and security, and is in no way contrary to the interests of any other country,

Bearing in mind that continued efforts are also needed in the future to seek ways of reducing the risk of outbreak of nuclear war,

Have agreed as follows:

Article 1

Each Party undertakes to maintain and to improve, as it deems necessary, its existing organizational and technical arrangements to guard against the accidental or unauthorized use of nuclear weapons under its control.

Article 2

The Parties undertake to notify each other immediately in the event of an accidental, unauthorized or any other unexplained incident involving a possible detonation of a nuclear weapon which could create a risk of outbreak of nuclear war. In the event of such an incident, the Party whose nuclear weapon is involved will immediately make every effort to take necessary measures to render harmless or destroy such weapon without its causing damage.

Article 3

The Parties undertake to notify each other immediately in the event of detection by missile warning systems of unidentified objects, or in the event of signs of interference with these systems or with related communications facilities, if such occurrences could create a risk of outbreak of nuclear war between the two countries.

Article 4

Each Party undertakes to notify the other Party in advance of any planned missile launches if such launches will extend beyond its national territory in the direction of the other Party.

Article 5

Each Party, in other situations involving unexplained nuclear incidents, undertakes to act in such a manner as to reduce the possibility of its actions being misinterpreted by the other Party. In any such situation, each Party may inform the other Party or request information when, in its view, this is warranted by the interests of averting the risk of outbreak of nuclear war.

Article 6

For transmission of urgent information, notifications and requests for information in situations requiring prompt clarification, the Parties shall make primary use of the Direct Communications Link between the Governments of the United States of America and the Union of Soviet Socialist Republics.[1]

For transmission of other information, notifications and requests for information, the Parties, at their own discretion, may use any communications facilities, including diplomatic channels, depending on the degree of urgency.

Article 7

The Parties undertake to hold consultations, as mutually agreed, to consider questions relating to implementation of the provisions of this Agreement, as well as to discuss possible amendments thereto aimed at further implementation of the purposes of this Agreement.

Article 8

This Agreement shall be of unlimited duration.

Article 9

This Agreement shall enter into force upon signature.

Source: *Treaty Series*, Vol. 807 (United Nations, New York)

CONVENTION ON THE PROHIBITION OF THE DEVELOPMENT, PRODUCTION AND STOCKPILING OF BACTERIOLOGICAL (BIOLOGICAL) AND TOXIN WEAPONS AND ON THEIR DESTRUCTION

Signed at London, Moscow and
Washington on 10 April 1972
Entered into force on 26 March 1975
Depositaries: UK, US and Soviet
governments

The States Parties to this Convention,
Determined to act with a view to achieving

effective progress towards general and complete disarmament, including the prohibition and elimination of all types of weapons of mass destruction, and convinced that the prohibition of the development, production and stockpiling of chemical and bacteriological (biological) weapons and their elimination, through effective measures, will facilitate the achievement of general and complete disarmament under strict and effective international control,

Recognizing the important significance of the Protocol for the Prohibition of the Use in War of Asphyxiating, Poisonous or Other Gases, and of Bacteriological Methods of Warfare, signed at Geneva on June 17, 1925, and conscious also of the contribution which the said Protocol has already made, and continues to make, to mitigating the horrors of war,

Reaffirming their adherence to the principles and objectives of that Protocol and calling upon all States to comply strictly with them,

Recalling that the General Assembly of the United Nations has repeatedly condemned all actions contrary to the principles and objectives of the Geneva Protocol of June 17, 1925,

Desiring to contribute to the strengthening of confidence between peoples and the general improvement of the international atmosphere,

Desiring also to contribute to the realization of the purposes and principles of the Charter of the United Nations,

Convinced of the importance and urgency of eliminating from the arsenals of States, through effective measures, such dangerous weapons of mass destruction as those using chemical or bacteriological (biological) agents,

Recognizing that an agreement on the prohibition of bacteriological (biological) and toxin weapons represents a first possible step towards the achievement of agreement on effective measures also for the prohibition of the development, production and stockpiling of chemical weapons, and determined to continue negotiations to that end,

Determined, for the sake of all mankind, to exclude completely the possibility of bacteriological (biological) agents and toxins being used as weapons,

Convinced that such use would be repugnant to the conscience of mankind and that no effort should be spared to minimize this risk,

Have agreed as follows:

Article I

Each State Party to this Convention undertakes never in any circumstances to develop, produce, stockpile or otherwise acquire or retain:

1. Microbial or other biological agents, or toxins whatever their origin or method of production, of types and in quantitites that have no justification for prophylactic, protective or other peaceful purposes;

2. Weapons, equipment or means of delivery designed to use such agents or toxins for hostile purposes or in armed conflict.

Article II

Each State Party to this Convention undertakes to destroy, or to divert to peaceful purposes, as soon as possible but not later than nine months after the entry into force of the Convention, all agents, toxins, weapons, equipment and means of delivery specified in article I of the Convention, which are in its possession or under its jurisdiction or control. In implementing the provisions of this article all necessary safety precautions shall be observed to protect populations and the environment.

Article III

Each State Party to this Convention undertakes not to transfer to any recipient whatsoever, directly or indirectly, and not in any way to assist, encourage, or induce any State, group of States or international organizations to manufacture or otherwise acquire any of the agents, toxins, weapons, equipment or means of delivery specified in article I of the Convention.

Article IV

Each State Party to this Convention shall, in accordance with its constitutional processes, take any necessary measures to prohibit and prevent the development, production, stockpiling, acquisition or retention of the agents, toxins, weapons, equipment and means of delivery specified in article I of the Convention, within the territory of such State, under its jurisdiction or under its control anywhere.

Article V

The States Parties to this Convention undertake to consult one another and to cooperate in solving any problems which may arise in relation to the objective of, or in the application of the provisions of, the Convention. Consultation and cooperation pursuant to this article may also be undertaken through appropriate international procedures within the framework of the United Nations and in accordance with its Charter.

Article VI

1. Any State Party to this Convention which finds that any other State Party is acting in breach of obligations deriving from the provisions of the Convention may lodge a complaint with the Security Council of the United Nations. Such a complaint should include all possible evidence confirming its validity, as well as a request for its consideration by the Security Council.

2. Each State Party to this Convention undertakes to cooperate in carrying out any investigation which the Security Council may initiate, in accordance with the provisions of the Charter of the United Nations, on the basis of the complaint received by the

Council. The Security Council shall inform the States Parties to the Convention of the results of the investigation.

Article VII

Each State Party to this Convention undertakes to provide or support assistance, in accordance with the United Nations Charter, to any Party to the Convention which so requests, if the Security Council decides that such Party has been exposed to danger as a result of violation of the Convention.

Article VIII

Nothing in this Convention shall be interpreted as in any way limiting or detracting from the obligations assumed by any State under the Protocol for the Prohibition of the Use in War of Asphyxiating, Poisonous or Other Gases, and of Bacteriological Methods of Warfare, signed at Geneva on June 17, 1925.

Article IX

Each State Party to this Convention affirms the recognized objective of effective prohibition of chemical weapons and, to this end, undertakes to continue negotiations in good faith with a view to reaching early agreement on effective measures for the prohibition of their development, production and stockpiling and for their destruction, and on appropriate measures concerning equipment and means of delivery specifically designed for the production or use of chemical agents for weapons purposes.

Article X

1. The States Parties to this Convention undertake to facilitate, and have the right to participate in, the fullest possible exchange of equipment, materials and scientific and technological information for the use of bacteriological (biological) agents and toxins for peaceful purposes. Parties to the Convention in a position to do so shall also cooperate in contributing individually or together with other States or international organizations to the further development and application of scientific discoveries in the field of bacteriology (biology) for prevention of disease, or for other peaceful purposes.

2. This Convention shall be implemented in a manner designed to avoid hampering the economic or technological development of States Parties to the Convention or international cooperation in the field of peaceful bacteriological (biological) activities, including the international exchange of bacteriological (biological) agents and toxins and equipment for the processing, use or production of bacteriological (biological) agents and toxins for peaceful purposes in accordance with the provisions of the Convention.

Article XI

Any State Party may propose amendments to this Convention. Amendments shall enter into force for each State Party accepting the amendments upon their acceptance by a majority of the States Parties to the Convention and thereafter for each remaining State Party on the date of acceptance by it.

Article XII

Five years after the entry into force of this Convention, or earlier if it is requested by a majority of Parties to the Convention by submitting a proposal to this effect to the Depositary Governments, a conference of States Parties to the Convention shall be held at Geneva, Switzerland, to review the operation of the Convention, with a view to assuring that the purposes of the preamble and the provisions of the Convention, including the provisions concerning negotiations on chemical weapons, are being realized. Such review shall take into account any new scientific and technological developments relevant to the Convention.

Article XIII

1. This Convention shall be of unlimited duration.

2. Each State Party to this Convention shall in exercising its national sovereignty have the right to withdraw from the Convention if it decides that extraordinary events, related to the subject matter of the Convention, have jeopardized the supreme interests of its country. It shall give notice of such withdrawal to all other States Parties to the Convention and to the United Nations Security Council three months in advance. Such notice shall include a statement of the extraordinary events it regards as having jeopardized its supreme interests.

Article XIV

1. This Convention shall be open to all States for signature. Any State which does not sign the Convention before its entry into force in accordance with paragraph (3) of this Article may accede to it at any time.

2. This Convention shall be subject to ratification by signatory States. Instruments of ratification and instruments of accession shall be deposited with the Governments of the United States of America, the United Kingdom of Great Britain and Northern Ireland and the Union of Soviet Socialist Republics, which are hereby designated the Depositary Governments.

3. This Convention shall enter into force after the deposit of instruments of ratification by twenty-two Governments, including the Governments designated as Depositaries of the Convention.

4. For States whose instruments of ratification or accession are deposited subsequent to the entry into force of this Convention, it shall enter into force on the date of the deposit of their instruments of ratification or accession.

5. The Depositary Governments shall promptly inform all signatory and acceding States of the date of each signature, the date

of deposit of each instrument of ratification or of accession and the date of the entry into force of this Convention, and of the receipt of other notices.

6. This Convention shall be registered by the Depositary Governments pursuant to Article 102 of the Charter of the United Nations.

Article XV

This Convention, the English, Russian, French, Spanish and Chinese texts of which are equally authentic, shall be deposited in the archives of the Depositary Governments. Duly certified copies of the Convention shall be transmitted by the Depositary Governments to the Governments of the signatory and acceding States.

Source: *Treaties and Other International Acts, Series 8062* (US Department of State, Washington, D.C., 1975)

For the list of states which have signed, ratified, acceded or succeded to the BW Convention, see Chapter 6.

AGREEMENT BETWEEN THE USA AND THE USSR ON THE PREVENTION OF INCIDENTS ON AND OVER THE HIGH SEAS

Signed at Moscow on 25 May 1972
Entered into force on 25 May 1972

The Government of the United States of America and the Government of the Union of Soviet Socialist Republics,

Desiring to assure the safety of navigation of the ships of their respective armed forces on the high seas and flight of their military aircraft over the high seas, and

Guided by the principles and rules of international law,

Have decided to conclude this Agreement and have agreed as follows:

Article I

For the purposes of this Agreement, the following definitions shall apply:

1. "Ship" means:

(*a*) A warship belonging to the naval forces of the Parties bearing the external marks distinguishing warships of its nationality, under the command of an officer duly commissioned by the government and whose name appears in the Navy list, and manned by a crew who are under regular naval discipline;

(*b*) Naval auxiliaries of the Parties, which include all naval ships authorized to fly the naval auxiliary flag where such a flag has been established by either Party.

2. "Aircraft" means all military manned heavier-than-air and lighter-than-air craft, excluding space craft.

3. "Formation" means an ordered arrangement of two or more ships proceeding together and normally maneuvered together.

Article II

The Parties shall take measures to instruct the commanding officers of their respective ships to observe strictly the letter and spirit of the International Regulations for Preventing Collisions at Sea, hereinafter referred to as the Rules of the Road. The Parties recognize that their freedom to conduct operations on the high seas is based on the principles established under recognized international law and codified in the 1958 Geneva Convention on the High Seas.

Article III

1. In all cases ships operating in proximity to each other, except when required to maintain course and speed under the Rules of the Road, shall remain well clear to avoid risk of collision.

2. Ships meeting or operating in the vicinity of a formation of the other Party shall, while conforming to the Rules of the Road, avoid maneuvering in a manner which would hinder the evolutions of the formation.

3. Formations shall not conduct maneuvers through areas of heavy traffic where internationally recognized traffic separation schemes are in effect.

4. Ships engaged in surveillance of other ships shall stay at a distance which avoids the risk of collision and also shall avoid executing maneuvers embarassing or endangering the ships under surveillance. Except when required to maintain course and speed under the Rules of the Road, a surveillant shall take positive early action so as, in the exercise of good seamanship, not to embarrass or endanger ships under surveillance.

5. When ships of both Parties maneuver in sight of one another, such signals (flag, sound, and light) as are prescribed by the Rules of the Road, the International Code of Signals, or other mutually agreed signals, shall be adhered to for signalling operations and intentions.

6. Ships of the Parties shall not simulate attacks by aiming guns, missile launchers, torpedo tubes, and other weapons in the direction of a passing ship of the other Party, not launch any object in the direction of passing ships of the other Party, and not use searchlights or other powerful illumination devices to illuminate the navigation bridges of passing ships of the other Party.

7. When conducting exercises with submerged submarines, exercising ships shall show the appropriate signals prescribed by the International Code of Signals to warn ships of the presence of submarines in the area.

8. Ships of one Party when approaching ships of the other Party conducting operations as set forth in Rule 4 (*c*) of the Rules of the Road, and particularly ships engaged in launching or landing aircraft as well as ships engaged in replenishment underway, shall take appropriate measures not to hinder maneuvers of such ships and shall remain well clear.

Article IV

Commanders of aircraft of the Parties shall use the greatest caution and prudence in approaching aircraft and ships of the other Party operating on and over the high seas, in particular, ships engaged in launching or landing aircraft, and in the interest of mutual safety shall not permit: simulated attacks by the simulated use of weapons against aircraft and ships, or performance of various aerobatics over ships, or dropping various objects near them in such a manner as to be hazardous to ships or to constitute a hazard to navigation.

Article V

1. Ships of the Parties operating in sight of one another shall raise proper signals concerning their intent to begin launching or landing aircraft.

2. Aircraft of the Parties flying over the high seas in darkness or under instrument conditions shall, whenever feasible, display navigation lights.

Article VI

Both Parties shall:

1. Provide through the established system of radio broadcasts of information and warning to mariners, not less than 3 to 5 days in advance as a rule, notification of actions on the high seas which represent a danger to navigation or to aircraft in flight.

2. Make increased use of the informative signals contained in the International Code of Signals to signify the intentions of their respective ships when maneuvering in proximity to one another. At night, or in conditions of reduced visibility, or under conditions of lighting and such distances when signal flags are not distinct, flashing light should be used to inform ships of maneuvers which may hinder the movements of others or involve a risk of collision.

3. Utilize on a trial basis signals additional to those in the International Code of Signals, submitting such signals to the Intergovernmental Maritime Consultative Organization for its consideration and for the information of other States.

Article VII

The Parties shall exchange appropriate information concerning instances of collision, incidents which result in damage, or other incidents at sea between ships and aircraft of the Parties. The United States Navy shall provide such information through the Soviet Naval Attache in Washington and the Soviet Navy shall provide such information through the United States Naval Attache in Moscow.

Article VIII

This Agreement shall enter into force on the date of its signature and shall remain in force for a period of three years. It will thereafter be renewed without further action by the Parties for successive periods of three years each.

This Agreement may be terminated by either Party upon six months written notice to the other Party.

Article IX

The Parties shall meet within one year after the date of the signing of this Agreement to review the implementation of its terms. Similar consultations shall be held thereafter annually, or more frequently as the Parties may decide.

Article X

The Parties shall designate members to form a Committee which will consider specific measures in conformity with this Agreement. The Committee will, as a particular part of its work, consider the practical workability of concrete fixed distances to be observed in encounters between ships, aircraft, and ships and aircraft. The Committee will meet within six months of the date of signature of this Agreement and submit its recommendations for decision by the Parties during the consultations prescribed in Article IX.

Source: *Treaties and Other International Acts, Series 7379* (US Department of State, Washington, D.C., 1972)

See also Protocol of 1973.

TREATY BETWEEN THE USA AND THE USSR ON THE LIMITATION OF ANTI-BALLISTIC MISSILE SYSTEMS (ABM TREATY)

Signed at Moscow on 26 May 1972
Entered into force on 3 October 1972

The United States of America and the Union of Soviet Socialist Republics, hereinafter referred to as the Parties,

Proceeding from the premise that nuclear war would have devasting consequences for all mankind,

Considering that effective measures to limit anti-ballistic missile systems would be a substantial factor in curbing the race in strategic offensive arms and would lead to a decrease in the risk of outbreak of war involving nuclear weapons,

Proceeding from the premise that the limitation of anti-ballistic missile systems, as well as certain agreed measures with respect to the limitation of strategic offensive arms, would contribute to the creation of more favorable conditions for further negotiations on limiting strategic arms,

Mindful of their obligations under Article VI of the Treaty on tne Non-Proliferation of Nuclear Weapons,

Declaring their intention to achieve at the earliest possible date the cessation of the nuclear arms race and to take effective measures toward reductions in strategic arms, nuclear disarmament, and general and complete disarmament,

Desiring to contribute to the relaxation of international tension and the strengthening of trust between States,

Have agreed as follows:

Article I

1. Each Party undertakes to limit anti-ballistic missile (ABM) systems and to adopt other measures in accordance with the provisions of this Treaty.

2. Each Party undertakes not to deploy ABM systems for a defense of the territory of its country and not to provide a base for such a defense, and not to deploy ABM systems for defense of an individual region except as provided for in Article III of this Treaty.

Article II

1. For the purposes of this Treaty an ABM system is a system to counter strategic ballistic missiles or their elements in flight trajectory, currently consisting of:

(a) ABM interceptor missiles, which are interceptor missiles constructed and deployed for an ABM role, or of a type tested in an ABM mode;

(b) ABM launchers, which are launchers constructed and deployed for launching ABM interceptor missiles; and

(c) ABM radars, which are radars constructed and deployed for an ABM role, or of a type tested in an ABM mode.

2. The ABM system components listed in paragraph 1 of this Article include those which are:

(a) operational;

(b) under construction;

(c) undergoing testing;

(d) undergoing overhaul, repair or conversion; or

(e) mothballed.

Article III

Each party undertakes not to deploy ABM systems or their components except that:

(a) within one ABM system deployment area having a radius of one hundred and fifty kilometers and centered on the Party's national capital, a Party may deploy: (1) no more than one hundred ABM launchers and no more than one hundred ABM interceptor missiles at launch sites, and (2) ABM radars within no more than six ABM radar complexes, the area of each complex being circular and having a diameter of no more than three kilometers; and

(b) within one ABM system deployment area having a radius of one hundred and fifty kilometers and containing ICBM silo launchers, a Party may deploy: (1) no more than one hundred ABM launchers and no more than one hundred ABM interceptor missiles at launch sites, (2) two large phased-array ABM radars comparable in potential to corresponding ABM radars operational or under construction on the date of signature of the Treaty in an ABM system deployment area containing ICBM silo launchers, and (3) no more than eighteen ABM radars each having a potential less than the potential of the smaller of the above-mentioned two large phased-array ABM radars.

Article IV

The limitations provided for in Article III shall not apply to ABM systems or their components used for development or testing, and located within current or additionally agreed test ranges. Each Party may have no more than a total of fifteen ABM launchers at test ranges.

Article V

1. Each Party undertakes not to develop, test, or deploy ABM systems or components which are sea-based, air-based, space-based, or mobile land-based.

2. Each Party undertakes not to develop, test, or deploy ABM launchers for launching more than one ABM interceptor missile at a time from each launcher, nor to modify deployed launchers to provide them with such a capability, nor to develop, test, or deploy automatic or semi-automatic or other similar systems for rapid reload of ABM launchers.

Article VI

To enhance assurance of the effectiveness of the limitations on ABM systems and their components provided by this Treaty, each Party undertakes:

(a) not to give missiles, launchers, or radars, other than ABM interceptor missiles, ABM launchers, or ABM radars, capabilities to counter strategic ballistic missiles or their elements in flight trajectory, and not to test them in an ABM mode; and

(b) not to deploy in the future radars for early warning of strategic ballistic missile attack except at locations along the periphery of its national territory and oriented outward.

Article VII

Subject to the provisions of this Treaty, modernization and replacement of ABM systems or their components may be carried out.

Article VIII

ABM systems or their components in excess of the numbers or outside the areas specified in this Treaty, as well as ABM systems or their components prohibited by this Treaty, shall be destroyed or dismantled under agreed procedures within the shortest possible agreed period of time.

Article IX

To assure the viability and effectiveness of this Treaty, each Party undertakes not to transfer to other States, and not to deploy outside its national territory, ABM systems or their components limited by this Treaty.

Article X

Each Party undertakes not to assume any international obligations which would conflict with this Treaty.

Article XI

The Parties undertake to continue active negotiations for limitations on strategic offensive arms.

Article XII

1. For the purpose of providing assurance of compliance with the provisions of this Treaty, each Party shall use national technical means of verification at its disposal in a manner consistent with generally recognized principles of international law.

2. Each party undertakes not to interfere with the national technical means of verification of the other Party operating in accordance with paragraph 1 of this Article.

3. Each party undertakes not to use deliberate concealment measures which impede verification by national technical means of compliance with the provisions of this Treaty. This obligation shall not require changes in current construction, assembly, conversion, or overhaul practices.

Article XIII

1. To promote the objectives and implementation of the provisions of this Treaty, the Parties shall establish promptly a Standing Consultative Commission, within the framework of which they will:

(a) consider questions concerning compliance with the obligations assumed and related situations which may be considered ambiguous;

(b) provide on a voluntary basis such information as either Party considers necessary to assure confidence in compliance with the obligations assumed;

(c) consider questions involving unintended interference with national technical means of verification;

(d) consider possible changes in the strategic situation which have a bearing on the provisions of this Treaty;

(e) agree upon procedures and dates for destruction or dismantling of ABM systems or their components in cases provided for by the provisions of this Treaty;

(f) consider, as appropriate, possible proposals for further increasing the viability of this Treaty, including proposals for amendments in accordance with the provisions of this Treaty;

(g) consider, as appropriate, proposals for further measures aimed at limiting strategic arms.

2. The Parties through consultation shall establish, and may amend as appropriate, Regulations for the Standing Consultative Commission governing procedures, composition and other relevant matters.

Article XIV

1. Each Party may propose amendments to this Treaty. Agreed amendments shall enter into force in accordance with the procedures governing the entry into force of this Treaty.

2. Five years after entry into force of this Treaty, and at five year intervals thereafter, the Parties shall together conduct a review of this Treaty.

Article XV

1. This Treaty shall be of unlimited duration.

2. Each Party shall, in exercising its national sovereignty, have the right to withdraw from this Treaty if it decides that extraordinary events related to the subject matter of this Treaty have jeopardized its supreme interests. It shall give notice of its decision to the other Party six months prior to withdrawal from the Treaty. Such notice shall include a statement of the extraordinary events the notifying Party regards as having jeopardized its supreme interests.

Article XVI

1. This Treaty shall be subject to ratification in accordance with the constitutional procedures of each Party. The Treaty shall enter into force on the day of the exchange of instruments of ratification.

2. This Treaty shall be registered pursuant to Article 102 of the Charter of the United Nations.

AGREED INTERPRETATIONS AND UNILATERAL STATEMENTS REGARDING THE ABM TREATY

1. Agreed interpretations

(a) *Initial Statements.* The document set forth below was agreed upon and initialed by the Heads of the Delegations on May 26, 1972:

[A]

The Parties understand that, in addition to the ABM radars which may be deployed in accordance with subparagraph (a) of Article III of the Treaty, those non-phased-array ABM radars operational on the date of signature of the Treaty within the ABM system deployment area for defense of the national capital may be retained.

[B]

The Parties understand that the potential (the product of mean emitted power in watts and antenna area in square meters) of the smaller of the two large phased-array ABM radars referred to in subparagraph (b) of Article III of the Treaty is considered for purposes of the Treaty to be three million.

[C]

The Parties understand that the center of the ABM system deployment area centered on the national capital and the center of the ABM system deployment area containing ICBM silo launchers for each Party shall be separated by no less than thirteen hundred kilometers.

[D]

In order to insure fulfillment of the obligation not to deploy ABM systems and their components except as provided in Article III of the Treaty, the Parties agree that in the event ABM systems based on other physical principles and including components capable of substituting for ABM interceptor missiles, ABM launchers, or ABM radars are created in the future, specific limitations on such systems and their components would be subject to discussion in accordance with Article XIII and agreement in accordance with Article XIV of the Treaty.

[E]

The Parties understand that Article V of the Treaty includes obligations not to develop, test or deploy ABM interceptor missiles for the delivery by each ABM interceptor missile of more than one independently guided warhead.

[F]

The Parties agree not to deploy phased-array radars having a potential (the product of mean emitted power in watts and antenna area in square meters) exceeding three million, except as provided for in Articles III, IV and VI of the Treaty, or except for the purposes of tracking objects in outer space or for use as national technical means of verification.

[G]

The Parties understand that Article IX of the Treaty includes the obligation of the US and the USSR not to provide to other States technical descriptions or blue prints specially worked out for the construction of ABM systems and their components limited by the Treaty.

(b) *Common Understandings.* Common understanding of the Parties on the following matters was reached during the negotiations:

A. Location of ICBM defenses

The U.S. Delegation made the following statement on May 26, 1972:

Article III of the ABM Treaty provides for each side one ABM system deployment area centered on its national capital and one ABM system deployment area containing ICBM silo launchers. The two sides have registered agreement on the following statement: "The Parties understand that the center of the ABM system deployment area centered on the national capital and the center of the ABM system deployment area containing ICBM silo launchers for each Party shall be separated by no less than thirteen hundred kilometers." In this connection, the U.S. side notes that its ABM system deployment area for defense of ICBM silo launchers, located west of the Mississippi River, will be centered in the Grand Forks ICBM silo launcher deployment area. (See Initialed Statement [C].)

B. ABM test ranges

The U.S. Delegation made the following statement on April 26, 1972:

Article IV of the ABM Treaty provides that "the limitations provided for in Article III shall not apply to ABM systems or their components used for development or testing, and located within current or additionally agreed test ranges." We believe it would be useful to assure that there is no misunderstanding as to current ABM test ranges. It is our understanding that ABM test ranges encompass the area within which ABM components are located for test purposes. The current U.S. ABM test ranges are at White Sands, New Mexico, and at Kwajalein Atoll, and the current Soviet ABM test range is near Sary Shagan in Kazakhstan. We consider that non-phased array radars of types used for range safety or instrumentation purposes may be located outside of ABM test ranges. We interpret the reference in Article IV to "additionally agreed test ranges" to mean that ABM components will not be located at any other test ranges without prior agreement between our Governments that there will be such additional ABM test ranges.

On May 5, 1972, the Soviet Delegation stated that there was a common understanding on what ABM test ranges were, that the use of the types of non-ABM radars for range safety or instrumentation was not limited under the Treaty, that the reference in Article IV to "additionally agreed" test ranges was sufficiently clear, and that national means permitted identifying current test ranges.

C. Mobile ABM systems

On January 28, 1972, the U.S. Delegation made the following statement:

Article V (1) of the Joint Draft Text of the ABM Treaty includes an undertaking not to develop, test, or deploy mobile land-based

ABM systems and their components. On May 5, 1971, the U.S. side indicated that, in its view, a prohibition on deployment of mobile ABM systems and components would rule out the deployment of ABM launchers and radars which were not permanent fixed types. At that time, we asked for the Soviet view of this interpretation. Does the Soviet side agree with the U.S. side's interpretation put forward on May 5, 1971?

On April 13, 1972, the Soviet Delegation said there is a general common understanding on this matter.

D. Standing Consultative Commission

Ambassador Smith made the following statement on May 22, 1972:

The United States proposes that the sides agree that, with regard to initial implementation of the ABM Treaty's Article XIII on the Standing Consultative Commission (SCC) and of the consultation Articles to the Interim Agreement on offensive arms and the Accidents Agreement, agreement establishing the SCC will be worked out early in the follow-on SALT negotiations; until that is completed, the following arrangements will prevail: when SALT is in session, any consultation desired by either side under these Articles be carried out by the two SALT Delegations; when SALT is not in session, *ad hoc* arrangements for any desired consultations under these Articles may be made through diplomatic channels.

Minister Semenov replied that, on an *ad referendum* basis, he could agree that the U.S. statement corresponded to the Soviet understanding.

E. Standstill

On May 6, 1972, Minister Semenov made the following statement:

In an effort to accommodate the wishes of the U.S. side, the Soviet Delegation is prepared to proceed on the basis that the two sides will in fact observe the obligations of both the Interim Agreement and the ABM Treaty beginning from the date of signature of these two documents.

In reply, the U.S. Delegation made the following statement on May 20, 1972:

The U.S. agrees in principle with the Soviet statement made on May 6 concerning observance of obligations beginning from date of signature but we would like to make clear our understanding that this means that, pending ratification and acceptance, neither side would take any action prohibited by the agreements after they had entered into force. This understanding would continue to apply in the absence of notification by either signatory of its intention not to proceed with ratification or approval.

The Soviet Delegation indicated agreement with the U.S. statement.

2. Unilateral statements

(*a*) The following noteworthy unilateral statements were made during the negotiations by the United States Delegation:

A. Withdrawal from the ABM Treaty

On May 9, 1972, Ambassador Smith made the following statement:

The U.S. Delegation has stressed the importance the U.S. Government attaches to achieving agreement on more complete limitations on strategic offensive arms, following agreement on an ABM Treaty and on an Interim Agreement on certain measures with respect to the limitation of strategic offensive arms. The U.S. Delegation believes that an objective of the follow-on negotiations should be to constrain and reduce on a long-term basis threats to the survivability of our respective strategic retaliatory forces. The USSR Delegation has also indicated that the objectives of SALT would remain unfulfilled without the achievement of an agreement providing for more complete limitations on strategic offensive arms. Both sides recognize that the initial agreements would be steps toward the achievement of more complete limitations on strategic arms. If an agreement providing for more complete strategic offensive arms limitations were not achieved within five years, U.S. supreme interests could be jeopardized. Should that occur, it would constitute a basis for withdrawal from the ABM Treaty. The U.S. does not wish to see such a situation occur, nor do we believe that the USSR does. It is because we wish to prevent such a situation that we emphasize the importance the U.S. Government attaches to achievement of more complete limitations on strategic offensive arms. The U.S. Executive will inform the Congress, in connection with Congressional consideration of the ABM Treaty and the Interim Agreement, of this statement of the U.S. position.

B. Tested in ABM mode

On April 7, 1972, the U.S. Delegation made the following statement:

Article II of the Joint Text Draft uses the term "tested in an ABM mode," in defining ABM components, and Article VI includes certain obligations concerning such testing. We believe that the sides should have a common understanding of this phrase. First, we would note that the testing provisions of the ABM Treaty are intended to apply to testing which occurs after the date of signature of the Treaty, and not to any testing which may have occurred in the past. Next, we would amplify the remarks we have made on this subject during the previous Helsinki phase by setting forth the objectives which govern the U.S. view on the subject, namely, while prohibiting testing of non-ABM components for ABM purposes: not to prevent testing of ABM components, and not to prevent testing of non-ABM components for non-ABM purposes. To clarify our interpretation of "tested in an ABM mode," we note that we would consider a launcher, missile or radar to be "tested in an ABM mode" if, for example, any of the following events occur: (1) a launcher is used to launch an ABM interceptor missile, (2) an interceptor missile is flight tested against a target vehicle which has a flight trajectory with characteristics of a strategic ballistic missile flight trajectory, or is flight tested in conjunction with the test of an ABM interceptor missile or an ABM radar at the same test range, or is flight tested to an altitude inconsistent with interception of targets against which air defenses are deployed, (3) a radar makes measurements on a cooperative target vehicle of the kind referred to in item (2) above during the reentry portion of its trajectory or makes measurements in conjunction with the test of an ABM interceptor missile or an ABM radar at the same test range. Radars used for purposes such as range safety or instrumentation would be exempt from application of these criteria.

C. No-transfer article of ABM Treaty

On April 18, 1972, the U.S. Delegation made the following statement:

In regard to this Article [IX], I have a brief and I believe self-explanatory statement to make. The U.S. side wishes to make clear that the provisions of this Article do not set a precedent for whatever provision may be considered for a Treaty on Limiting Strategic Offensive Arms. The question of transfer of strategic offensive arms is a far more complex issue, which may require a different solution.

D. No increase in defense of early warning radars

On July 28, 1970, the U.S. Delegation made the following statement:

Since Hen House radars [Soviet ballistic missile early warning radars] can detect and track ballistic missile warheads at great distances, they have a significant ABM potential. Accordingly, the U.S. would regard any increase in the defenses of such radars by surface-to-air missiles as inconsistent with an agreement.

Source: *Treaties and Other International Acts, Series 7503* (US Department of State, Washington, D.C., 1973)

See also Protocol of 1974.

INTERIM AGREEMENT BETWEEN THE USA AND THE USSR ON CERTAIN MEASURES WITH RESPECT TO THE LIMITATION OF STRATEGIC OFFENSIVE ARMS (SALT I AGREEMENT)

Signed at Moscow on 26 May 1972
Entered into force on 3 October 1972

The United States of America and the Union of Soviet Socialist Republics, hereinafter referred to as the Parties,

Convinced that the Treaty on the Limitation of Anti-Ballistic Missile Systems and this Interim Agreement on Certain Measures with Respect to the Limitation of Strategic Offensive Arms will contribute to the creation of more favorable conditions for active negotiations on limiting strategic arms as well as to the relaxation of international tension and the strengthening of trust between States,

Taking into account the relationship between strategic offensive and defensive arms,

Mindful of their obligations under Article VI of the Treaty on the Non-Proliferation of Nuclear Weapons,

Have agreed as follows:

Article I

The Parties undertake not to start construction of additional fixed land-based intercontinental ballistic missile (ICBM) launchers after July 1, 1972.

Article II

The Parties undertake not to convert land-based launchers for light ICBMs, or for ICBMs of older types deployed prior to 1964, into land-based launchers for heavy ICBMs of types deployed after that time.

Article III

The Parties undertake to limit submarine-launched ballistic missile (SLBM) launchers and modern ballistic missile submarines to the numbers operational and under construction on the date of signature of this Interim Agreement, and in addition to launchers and submarines constructed under procedures established by the Parties as replacements for an equal number of ICBM launchers of older types deployed prior to 1964 or for launchers on older submarines.

Article IV

Subject to the provisions of this Interim Agreement, modernization and replacement of strategic offensive ballistic missiles and launchers covered by this Interim Agreement may be undertaken.

Article V

1. For the purpose of providing assurance of compliance with the provisions of this Interim Agreement, each Party shall use

national technical means of verification at its disposal in a manner consistent with generally recognized principles of international law.

2. Each Party undertakes not to interfere with the national technical means of verification of the other Party operating in accordance with paragraph 1 of this Article.

3. Each Party undertakes not to use deliberate concealment measures which impede verification by national technical means of compliance with the provisions of this Interim Agreement. This obligation shall not require changes in current construction, assembly, conversion, or overhaul practices.

Article VI

To promote the objectives and implementation of the provisions of this Interim Agreement, the Parties shall use the Standing Consultative Commission established under Article XIII of the Treaty on the Limitation of Anti-Ballistic Missile Systems in accordance with the provisions of that Article.

Article VII

The Parties undertake to continue active negotiations for limitations on strategic offensive arms. The obligations provided for in this Interim Agreement shall not prejudice the scope or terms of the limitations on strategic offensive arms which may be worked out in the course of further negotiations.

Article VIII

1. This Interim Agreement shall enter into force upon exchange of written notices of acceptance by each Party, which exchange shall take place simultaneously with the exchange of instruments of ratification of the Treaty on the Limitation of Anti-Ballistic Missile Systems.

2. This Interim Agreement shall remain in force for a period of five years unless replaced earlier by an agreement on more complete measures limiting strategic offensive arms. It is the objective of the Parties to conduct active follow-on negotiations with the aim of concluding such an agreement as soon as possible.

3. Each Party shall, in exercising its national sovereignty, have the right to withdraw from this Interim Agreement if it decides that extraordinary events related to the subject matter of this Interim Agreement have jeopardized its supreme interests. It shall give notice of its decision to the other Party six months prior to withdrawal from this Interim Agreement. Such notice shall include a statement of the extraordinary events the notifying Party regards as having jeopardized its supreme interests.

PROTOCOL TO THE INTERIM AGREEMENT

The United States of America and the Union of Soviet Socialist Republics, hereinafter referred to as the Parties,

Having agreed on certain limitations relating to submarine-launched ballistic missile launchers and modern ballistic missile submarines, and to replacement procedures, in the Interim Agreement,

Have agreed as follows:

The Parties understand that, under Article III of the Interim Agreement, for the period during which that Agreement remains in force:

The US may have no more than 710 ballistic missile launchers on submarines (SLBMs) and no more than 44 modern ballistic missile submarines. The Soviet Union may have no more than 950 ballistic missile launchers on submarines and no more than 62 modern ballistic missile submarines.

Additional ballistic missile launchers on submarines up to the above-mentioned levels, in the U.S.—over 656 ballistic missile launchers on nuclear-powered submarines, and in the U.S.S.R.—over 740 ballistic missile launchers on nuclear-powered submarines, operational and under construction, may become operational as replacements for equal numbers of ballistic missile launchers of older types deployed prior to 1964 or of ballistic missile launchers on older submarines.

The deployment of modern SLBMs on any submarine, regardless of type, will be counted against the total level of SLBMs permitted for the U.S. and the U.S.S.R.

This Protocol shall be considered an integral part of the Interim Agreement.

AGREED INTERPRETATIONS AND UNILATERAL STATEMENTS REGARDING THE INTERIM AGREEMENT

1. Agreed interpretations

(a) *Initialed Statements.* The document set forth below was agreed upon and initialed by the Heads of the Delegations on May 26, 1972:

[A]

The Parties understand that land-based ICBM launchers referred to in the Interim Agreement are understood to be launchers for strategic ballistic missiles capable of ranges in excess of the shortest distance between the northeastern border of the continental U.S. and the northwestern border of the continental USSR.

[B]

The Parties understand that fixed land-based ICBM launchers under active construction as of the date of signature of the Interim Agreement may be completed.

[C]

The Parties understand that in the process of modernization and replacement the dimensions of land-based ICBM silo launchers will not be significantly increased.

[D]

The Parties understand that during the period of the Interim Agreement there shall be no significant increase in the number of ICBM or SLBM test and training launchers, or in the number of such launchers for modern land-based heavy ICBMs. The Parties further understand that construction or conversion of ICBM launchers at test ranges shall be undertaken only for purposes of testing and training.

[E]

The Parties understand that dismantling or destruction of ICBM launchers of older types deployed prior to 1964 and ballistic missile launchers on older submarines being replaced by new SLBM launchers on modern submarines will be initiated at the time of the beginning of sea trials of a replacement submarine, and will be completed in the shortest possible agreed period of time. Such dismantling or destruction, and timely notification thereof, will be accomplished under procedures to be agreed in the Standing Consultative Commission.

(b) *Common Understandings.* Common understanding of the Parties on the following matters was reached during the negotiations:

A. Increase in ICBM silo dimensions

Ambassador Smith made the following statement on May 26, 1972:

The Parties agreed that the term "significantly increased" means that an increase will not be greater than 10–15 percent of the present dimensions of land-based ICBM silo launchers.

Minister Semenov replied that this statement corresponded to the Soviet understanding.

B. Standing Consultative Commission

Ambassador Smith made the following statement on May 22, 1972:

The United States proposes that the sides agree that, with regard to initial implementation of the ABM Treaty's Article XIII on the Standing Consultative Commission (SCC) and of the consultation Articles to the Interim Agreement on offensive arms and the Accidents Agreement, agreement establishing the SCC will be worked out early in the follow-on SALT negotiations; until that is completed, the following arrangements will prevail: when SALT is in session, any consultation desired by either side under these Articles can be carried out by the two SALT Delegations; when SALT is not in session, *ad hoc* arrangements for any desired consultations under these Articles may be made through diplomatic channels.

Minister Semenov replied that, on an *ad referendum* basis, he could agree that the U.S. statement corresponded to the Soviet understanding.

C. Standstill

On May 6, 1972, Minister Semenov made the following statement:

In an effort to accommodate the wishes of the U.S. side, the Soviet Delegation is prepared to proceed on the basis that the two sides will in fact observe the obligations of both the Interim Agreement and the ABM Treaty beginning from the date of signature of these two documents.

In reply, the U.S. Delegation made the following statement on May 20, 1972:

The U.S. agrees in principle with the Soviet statement made on May 6 concerning observance of obligations beginning from date of signature but we would like to make clear our understanding that this means that, pending ratification and acceptance, neither side would take any action prohibited by the agreements after they had entered into force. This understanding would continue to apply in the absence of notification by either signatory of its intention not to proceed with ratification or approval.

The Soviet Delegation indicated agreement with the U.S. statement.

2. Unilateral statements

(a) The following noteworthy unilateral statements were made during the negotiations by the United States Delegation:

A. Withdrawal from the ABM Treaty

On May 9, 1972, Ambassador Smith made the following statement:

The U.S. Delegation has stressed the importance the U.S. Government attaches to achieving agreement on more complete limitations on strategic offensive arms, following agreement on an ABM Treaty and on an Interim Agreement on certain measures with respect to the limitation of strategic offensive arms. The U.S. Delegation believes that an objective of the follow-on negotiations should be to constrain and reduce on a long-term basis threats to the survivability of our respective strategic retaliatory forces. The USSR Delegation has also indicated that the objectives of SALT would remain unfulfilled without the achievement of an agreement providing for more complete limitations on strategic offensive arms. Both sides recognize that the initial agreements would be steps toward the achievement of more complete limitations on strategic arms. If an agreement providing for more complete strategic offensive arms limitations were not achieved within five years, U.S. supreme interests could be jeopardized. Should that occur, it would constitute a basis for withdrawal from the ABM Treaty. The U.S. does not wish to see such a situation occur, nor do we believe that the USSR does. It is because we wish to prevent such a situation that we emphasize the importance the U.S. Government attaches to achievement of more complete limitations on strategic offensive arms. The U.S. Executive will inform the Congress, in connection with Congressional consideration of the ABM Treaty and the Interim Agreement, of this statement of the U.S. position.

B. Land-mobile ICBM launchers

The U.S. Delegation made the following statement on May 20, 1972:

In connection with the important subject of land-mobile ICBM launchers, in the interest of concluding the Interim Agreement the U.S. Delegation now withdraws its proposal that Article I or an agreed statement explicitly prohibit the deployment of mobile land-based ICBM launchers. I have been instructed to inform you that, while agreeing to defer the question of limitation of operational land-mobile ICBM launchers to the subsequent negotiations on more complete limitations on strategic offensive arms, the U.S. would consider the deployment of operational land-mobile ICBM launchers during the period of the Interim Agreement as inconsistent with the objectives of that Agreement.

C. Covered facilities

The U.S. Delegation made the following statement on May 20, 1972:

I wish to emphasize the importance that the United States attaches to the provisions of Article V, including in particular their application to fitting out or berthing submarines.

D. "Heavy" ICBM's

The U.S. Delegation made the following statement on May 26, 1972:

The U.S. Delegation regrets that the Soviet Delegation has not been willing to agree on a common definition of a heavy missile. Under these circumstances, the U.S. Delegation believes it necessary to state the following: The United States would consider any ICBM having a volume significantly greater than that of the largest light ICBM now operational on either side to be a heavy ICBM. The U.S. proceeds on the premise that the Soviet side will give due account to this consideration.

(b) The following noteworthy unilateral statement was made by the Delegation of the U.S.S.R. and is shown here with the U.S. reply:

On May 17, 1972, Minister Semenov made the following unilateral "Statement of the Soviet Side":

Taking into account that modern ballistic missile submarines are presently in the possession of not only the U.S., but also of its NATO allies, the Soviet Union agrees that for the period of effectiveness of the Interim 'Freeze' Agreement the U.S. and its NATO allies have up to 50 such submarines with a total of up to 800 ballistic missile launchers thereon (including 41 U.S. submarines with 656 ballistic missile launchers). However, if during the period of effectiveness of the Agreement U.S. allies in NATO should increase the number of their modern submarines to exceed the numbers of submarines they would have operational or under construction on the date of signature of the Agreement, the Soviet Union will have the right to a corresponding increase in the number of its submarines. In the opinion of the Soviet side, the solution of the question of modern ballistic missile submarines provided for in the Interim Agreement only partially compensates for the strategic imbalance in the deployment of the nuclear-powered missile submarines of the USSR and the U.S. Therefore, the Soviet side believes that this whole question, and above all the question of liquidating the American missile submarine bases outside the U.S., will be appropriately resolved in the course of follow-on negotiations.

On May 24, Ambassador Smith made the following reply to Minister Semenov:

The United States side has studied the "statement made by the Soviet side" of May 17 concerning compensation for submarine basing and SLBM submarines belonging to third countries. The United States does not accept the validity of the considerations in that statement.

On May 26 Minister Semenov repeated the unilateral statement made on May 24. Ambassador Smith also repeated the U.S. rejection on May 26.

Source: *Treaties and Other International Acts, Series 7504* (US Department of State, Washington, D.C., 1972)

PROTOCOL TO THE AGREEMENT BETWEEN THE USA AND THE USSR ON THE PREVENTION OF INCIDENTS ON AND OVER THE HIGH SEAS

Signed at Washington, D.C. on 22 May 1973
Entered into force on 22 May 1973

The Government of the United States of America and the Government of the Union of Soviet Socialist Republics, herein referred to as the Parties;

Having agreed on measures directed to improve the safety of navigation of the ships of their respective armed forces on the high seas and flight of their military aircraft over the high seas,

Recognizing that the objectives of the Agreement may be furthered by additional understandings, in particular concerning actions of naval ships and military aircraft with respect to the non-military ships of each Party,

Further agree as follows:

Article I

The Parties shall take measures to notify the non-military ships of each Party on the provisions of the Agreement directed at securing mutual safety.

Article II

Ships and aircraft of the Parties shall not make simulated attacks by aiming guns, missile launchers, torpedo tubes and other weapons at non-military ships of the other Party, nor launch nor drop any objects near non-military ships of the other Party in such a manner as to be hazardous to these ships or to constitute a hazard to navigation.

Article III

This Protocol will enter into force on the day of its signing and will be considered as an integral part of the Agreement between the Government of the United States of America and the Government of the Union of Soviet Socialist Republics on the Prevention of Incidents On and Over the High Seas which was signed in Moscow on May 25, 1972.

Source: *Treaties and Other International Acts, Series 7624* (US Department of State, Washington, D.C., 1973)

AGREEMENT BETWEEN THE USA AND THE USSR ON BASIC PRINCIPLES OF NEGOTIATIONS ON THE FURTHER LIMITATION OF STRATEGIC OFFENSIVE ARMS

Signed at Washington, D.C. on 21 June 1973
Entered into force on 21 June 1973

The President of the United States of America, Richard Nixon, and the General Secretary of the Central Committee of the CPSU, L.I. Brezhnev,

Having thoroughly considered the question of the further limitation of strategic arms, and the progress already achieved in the current negotiations,

Reaffirming their conviction that the earliest adoption of further limitations of strategic arms would be a major contribution in reducing the danger of an outbreak of nuclear war and in strengthening international peace and security,

Have agreed as follows:

First. The two Sides will continue active negotiations in order to work out a permanent agreement on more complete measures on the limitation of strategic offensive arms, as well as their subsequent reduction, proceeding from the Basic Principles of Relations between the United States of America and the Union of Soviet Socialist Republics signed in Moscow on May 29, 1972, and from the Interim Agreement between the United States of America and the Union of Soviet Socialist Republics of May 26, 1972 on Certain Measures with Respect to the Limitation of Strategic Offensive Arms.

Over the course of the next year the two Sides will make serious efforts to work out the provisions of the permanent agreement on more complete measures on the limitation of strategic offensive arms with the objective of signing it in 1974.

Second. New agreements on the limitation of strategic offensive armaments will be based on the principles of the American-Soviet documents adopted in Moscow in May 1972 and the agreements reached in Washington in June 1973; and in particular, both Sides will be guided by the recognition of each other's equal security interests and by the recognition that efforts to obtain unilateral advantage, directly or indirectly, would be inconsistent with the strengthening of peaceful relations between the United States of America and the Union of Soviet Socialist Republics.

Third. The limitations placed on strategic offensive weapons can apply both to their quantitative aspects as well as to their qualitative improvement.

Fourth. Limitations on strategic offensive arms must be subject to adequate verification by national technical means.

Fifth. The modernization and replacement of strategic offensive arms would be permitted under conditions which will be formulated in the agreements to be concluded.

Sixth. Pending the completion of a permanent agreement on more complete measures of strategic offensive arms limitation, both Sides are prepared to reach agreements on separate measures to supplement the existing Interim Agreement of May 26, 1972.

Seventh. Each Side will continue to take necessary organizational and technical measures for preventing accidental or unauthorized use of nuclear weapons under its control in accordance with the Agreement of September 30, 1971 between the United States of America and the Union of Soviet Socialist Republics.

Source: *Treaties and Other International Acts, Series 7653* (US Department of State, Washington, D.C., 1973)

AGREEMENT BETWEEN THE USA AND THE USSR ON THE PREVENTION OF NUCLEAR WAR

Signed at Washington, D.C. on 22 June 1973
Entered into force on 22 June 1973

The United States of America and the Union of Soviet Socialist Republics, hereinafter referred to as the Parties,

Guided by the objectives of strengthening world peace and international security,

Conscious that nuclear war would have devastating consequences for mankind,

Proceeding from the desire to bring about conditions in which the danger of an outbreak of nuclear war anywhere in the world would be reduced and ultimately eliminated,

Proceeding from their obligations under the Charter of the United Nations regarding the maintenance of peace, refraining from the threat or use of force, and the avoidance of war, and in conformity with the agreements to which either Party has subscribed,

Proceeding from the Basic Principles of Relations between the United States of America and the Union of Soviet Socialist Republics signed in Moscow on May 29, 1972,

Reaffirming that the development of relations between the United States of America and the Union of Soviet Socialist Republics is not directed against other countries and their interests,

Have agreed as follows:

Article I

The United States and the Soviet Union agree that an objective of their policies is to remove the danger of nuclear war and of the use of nuclear weapons.

Accordingly, the Parties agree that they will act in such a manner as to prevent the development of situations capable of causing a dangerous exacerbation of their relations, as to avoid military confrontations, and as to exclude the outbreak of nuclear war between them and between either of the Parties and other countries.

Article II

The Parties agree, in accordance with Article I and to realize the objective stated in that Article, to proceed from the premise that each Party will refrain from the threat or use of force against the other Party, against the allies of the other Party and against other countries, in circumstances which may endanger international peace and security. The Parties agree that they will be guided by these considerations in the formulation of their foreign policies and in their actions in the field of international relations.

Article III

The Parties undertake to develop their relations with each other and with other countries in a way consistent with the purposes of this Agreement.

Article IV

If at any time relations between the Parties or between either Party and other countries appear to involve the risk of a nuclear conflict, or if relations between countries not parties to this Agreement appear to involve the risk of nuclear war between the United States of America and the Union of Soviet Socialist Republics or between either Party and other countries, the United States and the Soviet Union, acting in accordance with the provisions of this Agreement, shall immediately enter into urgent consultations with each other and make every effort to avert this risk.

Article V

Each Party shall be free to inform the Security Council of the United Nations, the Secretary General of the United Nations and the Governments of allied or other countries of the progress and outcome of consultations initiated in accordance with Article IV of this Agreement.

Article VI

Nothing in this Agreement shall effect or impair:

(*a*) the inherent right of individual or collective self-defense as envisaged by Article 51 of the Charter of the United Nations,

(*b*) the provisions of the Charter of the United Nations, including those relating to the maintenance or restoration of international peace and security, and

(*c*) the obligations undertaken by either Party towards its allies or other countries in treaties, agreements, and other appropriate documents.

Article VII

This Agreement shall be of unlimited duration.

Article VIII

This Agreement shall enter into force upon signature.

Source: *Treaties and Other International Acts, Series 7654* (US Department of State, Washington, D.C., 1973)

PROTOCOL TO THE TREATY BETWEEN THE USA AND THE USSR ON THE LIMITATION OF ANTI-BALLISTIC MISSILE SYSTEMS

Signed at Moscow on 3 July 1974
Entered into force on 24 May 1976

The United States of America and the Union of Soviet Socialist Republics, hereinafter referred to as the Parties,

Proceeding from the basic principles of relations between the United States of America and the Union of Soviet Socialist Republics signed on 29 May 1972,

Desiring to further the objectives of the Treaty between the United States of America and the Union of Soviet Socialist Republics on the Limitation of Anti-Ballistic Missile Systems signed on 26 May 1972, hereinafter referred to as the Treaty,

Reaffirming their conviction that the adoption of further measures for the limitation of strategic arms would contribute to strengthening international peace and security,

Proceeding from the premise that further limitation of anti-ballistic missile systems will create more favourable conditions for the completion of work on a permanent agreement on more complete measures for the limitation of strategic offensive arms,

Have agreed as follows:

Article I

1. Each Party shall be limited at any one time to a single area out of the two provided in article III of the Treaty for deployment of anti-ballistic missile (ABM) systems or their components and accordingly shall not exercise its right to deploy an ABM system or its components in the second of the two ABM system deployment areas permitted by article III of the Treaty, except as an exchange of one permitted area for the other in accordance with article II of this Protocol.

2. Accordingly, except as permitted by article II of this Protocol: The United States of America shall not deploy an ABM system or its components in the area centred on its capital, as permitted by article III (*a*) of the Treaty, and the Soviet Union shall not deploy an ABM system or its components in the deployment area of intercontinental ballistic missile (ICBM) silo launchers as permitted by article III (*b*) of the Treaty.

Article II

1. Each Party shall have the right to dismantle or destroy its ABM system and the components thereof in the area where they are presently deployed and to deploy an ABM system or its components in the alternative area permitted by article III of the Treaty, provided that prior to initiation of construction, notification is given in accord with the procedure agreed to in the Standing Consultative Commission during the year beginning 3 October 1977 and ending 2 October 1978, or during any year which commences at five-year intervals thereafter, those being the years for periodic review of the Treaty, as provided in article XIV of the Treaty. This right may be exercised only once.

2. Accordingly, in the event of such notice, the United States would have the right to dismantle or destroy the ABM system and its components in the deployment area of ICBM silo launchers and to deploy an ABM system or its components in an area centred on its capital, as permitted by article III (*a*) of the Treaty, and the Soviet Union would have the right to dismantle or destroy the ABM system and its components in the area centred on its capital and to deploy an ABM system or its components in an area containing ICBM silo launchers, as permitted by article III (*b*) of the Treaty.

3. Dismantling or destruction and deployment of ABM systems or their components and the notification thereof shall be carried out in accordance with article VIII of the ABM Treaty and procedures agreed to in the Standing Consultative Commission.

Article III

The rights and obligations established by the Treaty remain in force and shall be complied with by the Parties except to the extent modified by this Protocol. In particular, the deployment of an ABM system or its components within the area selected shall remain limited by the levels and other requirements established by the Treaty.

Article IV

This Protocol shall be subject to ratification in accordance with the constitutional procedures of each Party. It shall enter into force on the day of the exchange of instruments of ratification and shall thereafter be considered an integral part of the Treaty.

Source: UN document A/9698, Annex III, 9 August 1974

TREATY BETWEEN THE USA AND THE USSR ON THE LIMITATION OF UNDERGROUND NUCLEAR WEAPON TESTS (THRESHOLD TEST BAN TREATY)

Signed at Moscow on 3 July 1974
Not in force by 1 October 1981

The United States of America and the Union of Soviet Socialist Republics, hereinafter referred to as the Parties,

Declaring their intention to achieve at the earliest possible date the cessation of the nuclear arms race and to take effective measures towards reductions in strategic arms, nuclear disarmament, and general and complete disarmament under strict and effective international control,

Recalling the determination expressed by the Parties to the 1963 Treaty Banning Nuclear Weapon Tests in the Atmosphere, in Outer Space and Under Water in its preamble to seek to achieve the discontinuance of all test explosions of nuclear weapons for all time, and to continue negotiations to this end,

Noting that the adoption of measures for the further limitation of underground nuclear weapon tests would contribute to the achievement of these objectives and would meet the interests of strengthening peace and the further relaxation of international tension,

Reaffirming their adherence to the objectives and principles of the Treaty Banning Nuclear Weapon Tests in the Atmosphere, in Outer Space and Under Water and of the Treaty on the Non-Proliferation of Nuclear Weapons,

Have agreed as follows:

Article I

1. Each Party undertakes to prohibit, to prevent, and not to carry out any underground nuclear weapon test having a yield exceeding 150 kilotons at any place under its jurisdiction or control, beginning 31 March 1976.

2. Each Party shall limit the number of its underground nuclear weapon tests to a minimum.

3. The Parties shall continue their negotiations with a view towards achieving a solution to the problem of the cessation of all underground nuclear weapon tests.

Article II

1. For the purpose of providing assurance of compliance with the provisions of this Treaty, each Party shall use national technical means of verification at its disposal in a manner consistent with the generally recognized principles of international law.

2. Each Party undertakes not to interfere with the national technical means of verification of the other Party operating in accordance with paragraph 1 of this article.

3. To promote the objectives and implementation of the provisions of this Treaty the Parties shall, as necessary, consult with each other, make inquiries and furnish information in response to such inquiries.

Article III

The provisions of this Treaty do not extend to underground nuclear explosions carried out by the Parties for peaceful purposes. Underground nuclear explosions for peaceful purposes shall be governed by an agreement which is to be negotiated and concluded by the Parties at the earliest possible time.

Article IV

This Treaty shall be subject to ratification in accordance with the constitutional procedures of each Party. This Treaty shall enter into force on the day of the exchange of instruments of ratification.

Article V

1. This Treaty shall remain in force for a period of five years. Unless replaced earlier by an agreement in implementation of the objectives specified in paragraph 3 of article I of this Treaty, it shall be extended for successive five-year periods unless either Party notifies the other of its termination no later than six months prior to the expiration of the Treaty. Before the expiration of this period the Parties may, as necessary, hold consultations to consider the situation relevant to the substance of this Treaty and to introduce possible amendments to the text of the Treaty.

2. Each Party shall, in exercising its national sovereignty, have the right to withdraw from this Treaty if it decides that extraordinary events related to the subject matter of this Treaty have jeopardized its supreme interests. It shall give notice of its decision to the other Party six months prior to withdrawal from this Treaty. Such notice shall include a statement of the extraordinary events the notifying Party regards as having jeopardized its supreme interests.

3. This Treaty shall be registered pursuant to Article 102 of the Charter of the United Nations.

PROTOCOL TO THE THRESHOLD TEST BAN TREATY

The United States of America and the Union of Soviet Socialist Republics, hereinafter referred to as the Parties,

Having agreed to limit underground nuclear weapon tests,

Have agreed as follows:

1. For the purpose of ensuring verification of compliance with the obligations of the Parties under the Treaty by national technical means, the Parties shall, on the basis of reciprocity, exchange the following data:

(a) The geographic co-ordinates of the boundaries of each test site and of the boundaries of the geophysically distinct testing areas therein.

(b) Information on the geology of the testing areas of the sites (the rock characteristics of geological formations and the basic physical properties of the rock, i.e., density, seismic velocity, water saturation, porosity and depth of water table).

(c) The geographic co-ordinates of underground nuclear weapon tests, after they have been conducted.

(d) Yield, date, time, depth and co-ordinates for two nuclear weapon tests for calibration purposes from each geophysically distinct testing area where underground nuclear weapon tests have been and are to be conducted. In this connexion the yield of such explosions for calibration purposes should be as near as possible to the limit defined in article I of the Treaty and not less than one tenth of that limit. In the case of testing areas where data are not available on two tests for calibration purposes, the data pertaining to one such test shall be exchanged, if available, and the data pertaining to the second test shall be exchanged as soon as possible after a second test having a yield in the above-mentioned range. The provisions of this Protocol shall not require the Parties to conduct tests solely for calibration purposes.

2. The Parties agree that the exchange of data pursuant to subparagraphs (*a*), (*b*) and (*d*) of paragraph 1 shall be carried out simultaneously with the exchange of instruments of ratification of the Treaty, as provided in article IV of the Treaty, having in mind that the Parties shall, on the basis of reciprocity, afford each other the opportunity to familiarize themselves with these data before the exchange of instruments of ratification.

3. Should a Party specify a new test site or testing area after the entry into force of the Treaty, the data called for by subparagraphs (*a*) and (*b*) of paragraph 1 shall be transmitted to the other Party in advance of use of that site or area. The data called for by subparagraph (*d*) of paragraph 1 shall also be transmitted in advance of use of that site or area if they are available; if they are not available, they shall be transmitted as soon as possible after they have been obtained by the transmitting Party.

4. The Parties agree that the test sites of each Party shall be located at places under its jurisdiction or control and that all nuclear weapon tests shall be conducted solely within the testing areas specified in accordance with paragraph 1.

5. For the purposes of the Treaty, all underground nuclear explosions at the specified test sites shall be considered nuclear weapon tests and shall be subject to all the provisions of the Treaty relating to nuclear weapon tests. The provisions of article III of the Treaty apply to all underground nuclear explosions conducted outside of the specified test sites, and only to such explosions.

This Protocol shall be considered an integral part of the Treaty.

Source: UN document A/9698, Annex I and II, 9 August 1974

JOINT STATEMENT BY THE USA AND THE USSR ON STRATEGIC OFFENSIVE ARMS

Signed at Vladivostok, USSR, on 24 November 1974

During their working meeting in the area of Vladivostok on 23–24 November 1974, the President of the United States of America, Gerald R. Ford, and General Secretary of the Central Committee of the Communist Party of the Soviet Union, L. I. Brezhnev, discussed in detail the question of further limitations of strategic offensive arms.

They reaffirmed the great significance that both the United States and the USSR attach to the limitation of strategic offensive arms. They are convinced that a long-term agreement on this question would be a significant contribution to improving relations between the United States and the USSR, to reducing the danger of war and to enhancing world peace. Having noted the value of previous agreements on this question, including the Interim Agreement of 26 May 1972, they reaffirm the intention to conclude a new agreement on the limitation of strategic offensive arms, to last through 1985.

As a result of the exchange of views on the substance of such a new agreement, the President of the United States of America and the General Secretary of the Central Committee of the Communist Party of the Soviet Union concluded that favourable prospects exist for completing the work on this agreement in 1975.

Agreement was reached that further negotiations will be based on the following provisions:

1. The new agreement will incorporate the relevant provisions of the Interim Agreement of 26 May 1972, which will remain in force until October 1977.

2. The new agreement will cover the period from October 1977 through 31 December 1985.

3. Based on the principle of equality and equal security, the new agreement will include the following limitations:

(*a*) Both sides will be entitled to have a certain agreed aggregate number of strategic delivery vehicles;

(*b*) Both sides will be entitled to have a certain agreed aggregate number of ICBMs and SLBMs (intercontinental ballistic missiles; submarine-launched ballistic missiles) equipped with multiple independently targetable warheads (MIRVs).

4. The new agreement will include a provision for further negotiations beginning no later than 1980–1981 on the question of further limitations and possible reductions of strategic arms in the period after 1985.

5. Negotiations between the delegations of the United States and the USSR to work out the new agreement incorporating the foregoing points will resume in Geneva in January 1975.

Source: UN document A/C.1/1069, 25 November 1975

DECLARATION OF AYACUCHO

Signed at Lima, Peru, on 9 December 1974

EXCERPT:

Being assembled in the city of Lima at the

invitation of the President of Peru, Major-General Juan Velasco Alvarado, to commemorate the one hundred and fiftieth anniversary of the Battle of Ayacucho, we, the Heads of State and Government of Bolivia, Panama, Peru and Venezuela and the Representatives of the Heads of State of Argentina, Chile, Colombia and Ecuador, recognize the deep historical significance of that feat of arms, which was decisive in the saga of the emancipation of the American continent and which brought to its close a fundamental stage in the process of forging liberty for our peoples.

. . .

We reiterate our adherence to the principles of the legal equality of States, their territorial integrity, self-determination of peoples, ideological pluralism, respect for human rights, non-intervention and international co-operation, good faith in the fulfilment of obligations, the peaceful settlement of international disputes, and the prohibition of the threat or use of force and of armed aggression of economic or financial aggression in relations between States.

We condemn and repudiate the colonial situations which still exist in Latin America and which must be promptly eradicated because they are a potential threat to peace in the region. Our efforts are pledged to the attainment of that goal.

We undertake to promote and support the building of a lasting order of international peace and co-operation and to create the conditions which will make possible the effective limitation of armaments and an end to their acquisition for offensive purposes, so that all possible resources may be devoted to the economic and social development of every country in Latin America.

. . .

Source: UN document A/10044, Annex, 28 January 1975

AGREEMENT BETWEEN THE USA AND THE USSR AMENDING THE 1971 AGREEMENT ON MEASURES TO IMPROVE THE US–SOVIET DIRECT COMMUNICATIONS LINK

Effected by exchange of notes on 20 March and 29 April 1975
Entered into force on 29 April 1975

THE EMBASSY OF THE UNITED STATES OF AMERICA TO THE SOVIET MINISTRY OF FOREIGN AFFAIRS

The Embassy of the United States of America refers to the Ministry of Foreign Affairs of the Union of Soviet Socialist Republics to the Agreement between the United States of America and the Union of Soviet Socialist Republics on measures to improve the USA–USSR direct communications link, signed at Washington, September 30, 1971. With respect to the "Molniya II System(s)" and "Molniya II Earth Station" referred to in the Agreement, the Government of the United States of America proposes that the Agreement be modified to delete "II" in each case so that the references in the Annex would be to "Molniya System(s)" and "Molniya Earth Station."

If the foregoing is acceptable to the Government of the Union of Soviet Socialist Republics, the Government of the United States of America proposes that this Note and the reply thereto indicating acceptance and confirming that the technical information applicable to Molniya-2 is the same for Molniya-3, shall be considered as constituting an agreement between the two Governments concerning this matter, which shall come into force on the date of reply by the Government of the Union of Soviet Socialist Republics.

Moscow, March 20, 1975

THE SOVIET MINISTRY OF FOREIGN AFFAIRS TO THE EMBASSY OF THE UNITED STATES OF AMERICA

The Ministry of Foreign Affairs of the Union of Soviet Socialist Republics refers to the Note of the Embassy of the United States of America of March 20, 1975, which contains a suggestion for amending the Agreement between the Union of Soviet Socialist Republics and the United States of America on Measures to Improve the USSR–USA Direct Communications Link, as follows: to exclude from the nomenclature "Molniya II System" and "Molniya II Earth Station" the number "II" in each case, so that corresponding references in the Annex to the indicated Agreement, of which the Annex is an integral part, would thus refer to the "Molniya System" and "Molniya Earth Station."

The Soviet side agrees to these changes and confirms that the technical characteristics relating to the "Molniya System" fully correspond to those provided earlier to the American side.

Moscow, April 29, 1975

Source: *Treaties and Other International Acts, Series 8059* (US Department of State, Washington, D.C., 1975)

DOCUMENT ON CONFIDENCE-BUILDING MEASURES AND CERTAIN ASPECTS OF SECURITY AND DISARMAMENT, INCLUDED IN THE FINAL ACT OF THE CONFERENCE ON SECURITY AND CO-OPERATION IN EUROPE

Signed at Helsinki on 1 August 1975
The original of the Final Act was
  transmitted to the government of
  Finland, which retains it in its archives

The participating States,

Desirous of eliminating the causes of tension that may exist among them and thus of contributing to the strengthening of peace and security in the world;

Determined to strengthen confidence among them and thus to contribute to increasing stability and security in Europe;

Determined further to refrain in their mutual relations, as well as in their international relations in general, from the threat or use of force against the territorial integrity or political independence of any State, or in any other manner inconsistent with the purposes of the United Nations and with the Declaration on Principles Guiding Relations between Participating States as adopted in this Final Act;

Recognizing the need to contribute to reducing the dangers of armed conflict and of misunderstanding or miscalculation of military activities which could give rise to apprehension, particularly in a situation where the participating States lack clear and timely information about the nature of such activities;

Taking into account considerations relevant to efforts aimed at lessening tension and promoting disarmament;

Recognizing that the exchange of observers by invitation at military manœuvres will help to promote contacts and mutual understanding;

Having studied the question of prior notification of major military movements in the context of confidence-building;

Recognizing that there are other ways in which individual States can contribute further to their common objectives;

Convinced of the political importance of prior notification of major military manœuvres for the promotion of mutual understanding and the strengthening of confidence, stability and security;

Accepting the responsibility of each of them to promote these objectives and to implement this measure, in accordance with the accepted criteria and modalities, as essentials for the realization of these objectives;

Recognizing that this measure deriving from political decision rests upon a voluntary basis;

Have adopted the following:

I

PRIOR NOTIFICATION OF MAJOR MILITARY MANŒUVRES

They will notify their major military manœuvres to all other participating States through usual diplomatic channels in accordance with the following provisions:

Notification will be given of major military manœuvres exceeding a total of 25,000 troops, independently or combined with any possible air or naval components (in this context the word "troops" includes amphibious and airborne troops). In the case of independent manœuvres of amphibious or airborne troops, or of combined manœuvres involving them, these troops will be included in this total. Furthermore, in the case of combined manœuvres which do not reach the above total but which involve land forces together with significant numbers of either amphibious or airborne troops, or both, notification can also be given.

Notification will be given of major military manœuvres which take place on the territory, in Europe, of any participating State as well as, if applicable, in the adjoining sea area and air space.

In the case of a participating State whose territory extends beyond Europe, prior notification need be given only of manœuvres which take place in an area within 250 kilometres from its frontier facing or shared with any other European participating State, the participating State need not, however, give notification in cases in which that area is also contiguous to the participating State's frontier facing or shared with a non-European non-participating State.

Notification will be given 21 days or more in advance of the start of the manœuvre or in the case of a manœuvre arranged at shorter notice at the earliest possible opportunity prior to its starting date.

Notification will contain information of the designation, if any, the general purpose of and the States involved in the manœuvre, the type or types and numerical strength of the forces engaged, the area and estimated time-frame of its conduct. The participating States will also, if possible, provide additional relevant information, particularly that related to the components of the forces engaged and the period of involvement of these forces.

PRIOR NOTIFICATION OF OTHER MILITARY MANŒUVRES

The participating States recognize that they can contribute further to strengthening confidence and increasing security and stability, and to this end may also notify smaller-scale military manœuvres to other participating States, with special regard for those near the area of such manœuvres.

To the same end, the participating States also recognize that they may notify other military manœuvres conducted by them.

EXCHANGE OF OBSERVERS

The participating States will invite other participating States, voluntarily and on a bilateral basis, in a spirit of reciprocity and goodwill towards all participating States, to send observers to attend military manœuvres.

The inviting State will determine in each case the number of observers, the procedures and conditions of their participation, and give other information which it may consider useful. It will provide appropriate facilities and hospitality.

The invitation will be given as far ahead as is conveniently possible through usual diplomatic channels.

PRIOR NOTIFICATION OF MAJOR MILITARY MOVEMENTS

In accordance with the Final Recommendations of the Helsinki Consultations the participating States studied the question of prior notification of major military movements as a measure to strengthen confidence.

Accordingly, the participating States recognize that they may, at their own discretion and with a view to contributing to confidence-building, notify their major military movements.

In the same spirit, further consideration will be given by the States participating in the Conference on Security and Co-operation in Europe to the question of prior notification of major military movements, bearing in mind, in particular, the experience gained by the implementation of the measures which are set forth in this document.

OTHER CONFIDENCE-BUILDING MEASURES

The participating States recognize that there are other means by which their common objectives can be promoted.

In particular, they will, with due regard to reciprocity and with a view to better mutual understanding, promote exchanges by invitation among their military personnel, including visits by military delegations.

* * *

In order to make a fuller contribution to their common objective of confidence-building, the participating States, when conducting their military activities in the area covered by the provisions for the prior notification of major military manœuvres, will duly take into account and respect this objective.

They also recognize that the experience gained by the implementation of the provisions set forth above, together with further efforts, could lead to developing and enlarging measures aimed at strengthening confidence.

II

QUESTIONS RELATING TO DISARMAMENT

The participating States recognize the interest of all of them in efforts aimed at lessening military confrontation and promoting disarmament which are designed to complement political détente in Europe and to strengthen their security. They are convinced of the necessity to take effective measures in these fields which by their scope and by their nature constitute steps towards the ultimate achievement of general and complete disarmament under strict and effective international control, and which should result in strengthening peace and security throughout the world.

III

GENERAL CONSIDERATIONS

Having considered the views expressed on various subjects related to the strengthening of security in Europe through joint efforts aimed at promoting détente and disarmament, the participating States, when engaged in such efforts, will, in this context, proceed, in particular, from the following essential considerations:
— The complementary nature of the political and military aspects of security;
— The interrelation between the security of each participating State and security in Europe as a whole and the relationship which exists, in the broader context of world security, between security in Europe and security in the Mediterranean area;
— Respect for the security interests of all States participating in the Conference on Security and Co-operation in Europe inherent in their sovereign equality;
— The importance that participants in negotiating fora see to it that information about relevant developments, progress and results is provided on an appropriate basis to other States participating in the Conference on Security and Co-operation in Europe and, in return, the justified interest of any of those States in having their views considered.

Source: *The Conference on Security and Co-operation in Europe: Final Act* (Helsinki, 1975)

The Final Act was signed by Austria, Belgium, Bulgaria, Canada, Cyprus, Czechoslovakia, Denmark, Finland, France, German Democratic Republic, FR Germany, Greece, Holy See, Hungary, Iceland, Ireland, Italy, Liechtenstein, Luxembourg, Malta, Monaco, Netherlands, Norway, Poland, Portugal, Romania, San Marino, Spain, Sweden, Switzerland, Turkey, UK, USA, USSR, Yugoslavia

TREATY BETWEEN THE USA AND THE USSR ON UNDERGROUND NUCLEAR EXPLOSIONS FOR PEACEFUL PURPOSES

Signed at Moscow and Washington on 28 May 1976
Not in force by 1 October 1981

The United States of America and the Union of Soviet Socialist Republics, hereinafter referred to as the Parties,

Proceeding from a desire to implement Article III of the Treaty between the United States of America and the Union of Soviet Socialist Republics on the Limitation of Underground Nuclear Weapon Tests, which calls for the earliest possible conclusion of an agreement on underground nuclear explosions for peaceful purposes,

Reaffirming their adherence to the objectives and principles of the Treaty Banning Nuclear Weapon Tests in the Atmosphere, in Outer Space and Under Water, the Treaty on the Non-Proliferation of Nuclear Weapons, and the Treaty on the Limitation of Underground Nuclear Weapon Tests, and their determination to observe strictly the provisions of these international agreements,

Desiring to assure that underground nuclear explosions for peaceful purposes shall not be used for purposes related to nuclear weapons,

Desiring that utilization of nuclear energy be directed only toward peaceful purposes,

Desiring to develop appropriately co-operation in the field of underground nuclear explosions for peaceful purposes,

Have agreed as follows:

Article I

1. The Parties enter into this Treaty to satisfy the obligations in Article III of the Treaty on the Limitation of Underground Nuclear Weapon Tests, and assume additional obligations in accordance with the provisions of this Treaty.

2. This Treaty shall govern all underground nuclear explosions for peaceful purposes conducted by the Parties after 31 March 1976.

Article II

For the purposes of this Treaty:

(a) "explosion" means any individual or group underground nuclear explosion for peaceful purposes;

(b) "explosive" means any device, mechanism or system for producing an individual explosion;

(c) "group explosion" means two or more individual explosions for which the time interval between successive individual explosions does not exceed five seconds and for which the emplacement points of all explosives can be interconnected by straight line segments, each of which joins two emplacement points and each of which does not exceed 40 kilometres.

Article III

1. Each Party, subject to the obligations assumed under this Treaty and other international agreements, reserves the right to:

(a) carry out explosions at any place under its jurisdiction or control outside the geographical boundaries of test sites specified under the provisions of the Treaty on the Limitation of Underground Nuclear Weapon Tests; and

(b) carry out, participate or assist in carrying out explosions in the territory of another State at the request of such other State.

2. Each Party undertakes to prohibit, to prevent and not to carry out at any place under its jurisdiction or control, and further undertakes not to carry out, participate or assist in carrying out anywhere:

(a) any individual explosion having a yield exceeding 150 kilotons;

(b) any group explosion:

(1) having an aggregate yield exceeding 150 kilotons except in ways that will permit identification of each individual explosion and determination of the yield of each individual explosion in the group in accordance with the provisions of Article IV and the Protocol to this Treaty;

(2) having an aggregate yield exceeding one and one-half megatons;

(c) any explosion which does not carry out a peaceful application;

(d) any explosion except in compliance with the provisions of the Treaty Banning Nuclear Weapon Tests in the Atmosphere, in Outer Space and Under Water, the Treaty on Non-Proliferation of Nuclear Weapons, and other international agreements entered into by that Party.

3. The question of carrying out any individual explosion having a yield exceeding the yield specified in paragraph 2 (a) of this article will be considered by Parties at an appropriate time to be agreed.

Article IV

1. For the purpose of providing assurance of compliance with the provisions of this Treaty, each Party shall:

(a) use national technical means of verification at its disposal in a manner consistent with generally recognized principles of international law; and

(b) provide to the other Party information and access to sites of explosions and furnish assistance in accordance with the provisions set forth in the Protocol to this Treaty.

2. Each Party undertakes not to interfere with the national technical means of verification of the other Party operating in accordance with paragraph 1 (a) of this article, or with the implementation of the provisions of paragraph 1 (b) of this article.

Article V

1. To promote the objectives and implementation of the provisions of this Treaty, the Parties shall establish promptly a Joint

Consultative Commission within the framework of which they will:

(*a*) consult with each other, make inquiries and furnish information in response to such inquiries, to assure confidence in compliance with the obligations assumed;

(*b*) consider questions concerning compliance with the obligations assumed and related situations which may be considered ambiguous;

(*c*) consider questions involving unintended interference with the means for assuring compliance with the provisions of this Treaty;

(*d*) consider changes in technology or other new circumstances which have a bearing on the provisions of this Treaty; and

(*e*) consider possible amendments to provisions governing underground nuclear explosions for peaceful purposes.

2. The Parties through consultation shall establish, and may amend as appropriate, Regulations for the Joint Consultative Commission governing procedures, composition and other relevant matters.

Article VI

1. The Parties will develop co-operation on the basis of mutual benefit, equality, and reciprocity in various areas related to carrying out underground nuclear explosions for peaceful purposes.

2. The Joint Consultative Commission will facilitate this co-operation by considering specific areas and forms of co-operation which shall be determined by agreement between the Parties in accordance with their constitutional procedures.

3. The Parties will appropriately inform the International Atomic Energy Agency of results of their co-operation in the field of underground nuclear explosions for peaceful purposes.

Article VII

1. Each Party shall continue to promote the development of the international agreement or agreements and procedures provided for in Article V of the Treaty on the Non-Proliferation of Nuclear Weapons, and shall provide appropriate assistance to the International Atomic Energy Agency in this regard.

2. Each Party undertakes not to carry out, participate or assist in the carrying out of any explosion in the territory of another State unless that State agrees to the implementation in its territory of the international observation and procedures contemplated by Article V of the Treaty on the Non-Proliferation of Nuclear Weapons and the provisions of Article IV of and the Protocol to this Treaty, including the provision by that State of the assistance necessary for such implementation and of the privileges and immunities specified in the Protocol.

Article VIII

1. This Treaty shall remain in force for a period of five years, and it shall be extended for successive five-year periods unless either Party notifies the other of its termination no later than six months prior to its expiration. Before the expiration of this period the Parties may, as necessary, hold consultations to consider the situation relevant to the substance of this Treaty. However, under no circumstances shall either Party be entitled to terminate this Treaty while the Treaty on the Limitation of Underground Nuclear Weapon Tests remains in force.

2. Termination of the Treaty on the Limitation of Underground Nuclear Weapon Tests shall entitle either Party to withdraw from this Treaty at any time.

3. Each Party may propose amendments to this Treaty. Amendments shall enter into force on the day of the exchange of instruments of ratification of such amendments.

Article IX

1. This Treaty including the Protocol which forms an integral part hereof, shall be subject to ratification in accordance with the constitutional procedures of each Party. This Treaty shall enter into force on the day of the exchange of instruments of ratification which exchange shall take place simultaneously with the exchange of instruments of ratification of the Treaty on the Limitation of Underground Nuclear Weapon Tests.

2. This Treaty shall be registered pursuant to Article 102 of the Charter of the United Nations.

PROTOCOL TO THE TREATY ON UNDERGROUND NUCLEAR EXPLOSIONS FOR PEACEFUL PURPOSES

The United States of America and the Union of Soviet Socialist Republics, hereinafter referred to as the Parties,

Having agreed to the provisions in the Treaty on Underground Nuclear Explosions for Peaceful Purposes, hereinafter referred to as the Treaty,

Have agreed as follows:

Article I

1. No individual explosion shall take place at a distance, in metres, from the ground surface which is less than 30 times the 3.4 root of its planned yield in kilotons.

2. Any group explosion with a planned aggregate yield exceeding 500 kilotons shall not include more than five individual explosions, each of which has a planned yield not exceeding 50 kilotons.

Article II

1. For each explosion, the Party carrying out the explosion shall provide the other Party:

(*a*) not later than 90 days before the beginning of emplacement of the explosives when the planned aggregate yield of the explosion does not exceed 100 kilotons, or not later than 180 days before the beginning of emplacement of the explosives when the planned aggregate yield of the explosion exceeds 100 kilotons, with the following information to the extent and degree of precision available when it is conveyed:

(1) the purpose of the planned explosion;

(2) the location of the explosion expressed in geographical co-ordinates with a precision of four or less kilometres, planned date and aggregate yield of the explosion;

(3) the type or types of rock in which the explosion will be carried out, including the degree of liquid saturation of the rock at the point of emplacement of each explosive; and

(4) a description of specific technological features of the project, of which the explosion is a part, that could influence the determination of its yield and confirmation of purpose; and

(b) not later than 60 days before the beginning of emplacement of the explosives the information specified in subparagraph 1(a) of this article to the full extent and with the precision indicated in that subparagraph.

2. For each explosion with a planned aggregate yield exceeding 50 kilotons, the Party carrying out the explosion shall provide the other Party, not later than 60 days before the beginning of emplacement of the explosives, with the following information:

(a) the number of explosives, the planned yield of each explosive, the location of each explosive to be used in a group explosion relative to all other explosives in the group with a precision of 100 or less metres, the depth of emplacement of each explosive with a precision of one metre and the time intervals between individual explosions in any group explosion with a precision of one-tenth second; and

(b) a description of specific features of geological structure or other local conditions that could influence the determination of the yield.

3. For each explosion with a planned aggregate yield exceeding 75 kilotons, the Party carrying out the explosion shall provide the other Party, not later than 60 days before the beginning of emplacement of the explosives, with a description of the geological and geophysical characteristics of the site of each explosion which could influence determination of the yield, which shall include: the depth of the water table; a stratigraphic column above each emplacement point; the position of each emplacement point relative to nearby geological and other features which influenced the design of the project of which the explosion is a part; and the physical parameters of the rock, including density, seismic velocity, porosity, degree and liquid saturation, and rock strength, within the sphere centred on each emplacement point and having a radius, in metres, equal to 30 times the cube root of the planned yield in kilotons of the explosive emplaced at that point.

4. For each explosion with a planned aggregate yield exceeding 100 kilotons, the party carrying out the explosion shall provide the other Party, not later than 60 days before the beginning of emplacement of the explosives, with:

(a) information on locations and purposes of facilities and installations which are associated with the conduct of the explosion;

(b) information regarding the planned date of the beginning of emplacement of each explosive; and

(c) a topographic plan in local co-ordinates of the areas specified in paragraph 7 of Article IV, at a scale of 1:24,000 or 1:25,000 with a contour interval of 10 metres or less.

5. For application of an explosion to alleviate the consequences of an emergency situation involving an unforeseen combination of circumstances which calls for immediate action for which it would not be practicable to observe the timing requirements of paragraphs 1, 2 and 3 of this article, the following conditions shall be met:

(a) the Party deciding to carry out an explosion for such purposes shall inform the other Party of that decision immediately after it has been made and describe such circumstances;

(b) the planned aggregate yield of an explosion for such purpose shall not exceed 100 kilotons; and

(c) the Party carrying out an explosion for such purpose shall provide to the other Party the information specified in paragraph 1 of this article, and the information specified in paragraphs 2 and 3 of this article if applicable, after the decision to conduct the explosion is taken, but not later than 30 days before the beginning of emplacement of the explosives.

6. For each explosion, the Party carrying out the explosion shall inform the other Party, not later than two days before the explosion, of the planned time of detonation of each explosive with a precision of one second.

7. Prior to the explosion, the Party carrying out the explosion shall provide the other Party with timely notification of changes in the information provided in accordance with this article.

8. The explosion shall not be carried out earlier than 90 days after notification of any change in the information provided in accordance with this article which requires more extensive verification procedures than those required on the basis of the original information, unless an earlier time for carrying out the explosion is agreed between the Parties.

9. Not later than 90 days after each explosion the Party carrying out the explosion shall provide the other Party with the following information:

(a) the actual time of the explosion with a precision of one-tenth second and its aggregate yield;

(b) when the planned aggregate yield of a group explosion exceeds 50 kilotons, the actual time of the first individual explosion with a precision of one-tenth second, the time interval between individual explosions with a precision of one millisecond and the yield of each individual explosion; and

(c) confirmation of other information provided in accordance with paragraphs 1, 2, 3 and 4 of this article and explanation of any changes or corrections based on the results of the explosion.

10. At any time, but not later than one year after the explosion, the other Party may request the Party carrying out the explosion to clarify any item of the information provided in accordance with this article. Such clarification shall be provided as soon as practicable, but not later than 30 days after the request is made.

Article III

1. For the purposes of this Protocol:

(a) "designated personnel" means those nationals of the other Party identified to the Party carrying out an explosion as the persons who will exercise the rights and functions provided for in the Treaty and this Protocol; and

(b) "emplacement hole" means the entire interior of any drill-hole, shaft, adit or tunnel in which an explosive and associated cables and other equipment are to be installed.

2. For any explosion with a planned aggregate yield exceeding 100 kilotons but not exceeding 150 kilotons if the Parties, in consultation based on information provided in accordance with Article II and other information that may be introduced by either Party, deem it appropriate for the confirmation of the yield of the explosion, and for any explosion with a planned aggregate yield exceeding 150 kilotons, the Party carrying out the explosion shall allow designated personnel within the areas and at the locations described in Article V to exercise the following rights and functions:

(a) confirmation that the local circumstances, including facilities and installations associated with the project, are consistent with the stated peaceful purposes;

(b) confirmation of the validity of the geological and geophysical information provided in accordance with Article II through the following procedures:

(1) examination by designated personnel of research and measurement data of the Party carrying out the explosion and of rock core or rock fragments removed from each emplacement hole, and of any logs and drill core from existing exploratory holes which shall be provided to designated personnel upon their arrival at the site of the explosion;

(2) examination by designated personnel of rock core or rock fragments as they become available in accordance with the procedures specified in subparagraph 2(b)(3) of this article; and

(3) observation by designated person-

nel of implementation by the Party carrying out the explosion of one of the following four procedures, unless this right is waived by the other Party:

(i) construction of that portion of each emplacement hole starting from a point nearest the entrance of the emplacement hole which is at a distance, in metres, from the nearest emplacement point equal to 30 times the cube root of the planned yield in kilotons of the explosive to be emplaced at that point and continuing to the completion of the emplacement hole; or

(ii) construction of that portion of each emplacement hole starting from a point nearest the entrance of the emplacement hole which is at a distance, in metres, from the nearest emplacement point equal to six times the cube root of the planned yield in kilotons of the explosive to be emplaced at that point and continuing to the completion of the emplacement hole as well as the removal of rock core or rock fragments from the wall of an existing exploratory hole, which is substantially parallel with and at no point more than 100 metres from the emplacement hole, at locations specified by designated personnel which lie within a distance, in metres, from the same horizon as each emplacement point of 30 times the cube root of the planned yield in kilotons of the explosive to be emplaced at that point; or

(iii) removal of rock core or rock fragments from the wall of each emplacement hole at locations specified by designated personnel which lie within a distance, in metres, from each emplacement point of 30 times the cube root of the planned yield in kilotons of the explosive to be emplaced at each such point; or

(iv) construction of one or more new exploratory holes so that for each emplacement hole there will be a new exploratory hole to the same depth as that of the emplacement of the explosive, substantially parallel with and at no point more than 100 metres from each emplacement hole, from which rock cores would be removed at locations specified by designated personnel which lie within a distance, in metres, from the same horizon as each emplacement point of 30 times the cube root of the planned yield in kilotons of the explosive to be emplaced at each such point;

(c) observation of the emplacement of each explosive, confirmation of the depth of its emplacement and observation of the stemming of each emplacement hole;

(d) unobstructed visual observation of the area of the entrance to each emplacement hole at any time from the time of emplacement of each explosive until all personnel have been withdrawn from the site for the detonation of the explosion; and

(e) observation of each explosion.

3. Designated personnel, using equipment provided in accordance with paragraph 1 of Article IV, shall have the right, for any explosion with a planned aggregate yield exceeding 150 kilotons, to determine the yield of each individual explosion in a group explosion in accordance with the provisions of Article VI.

4. Designated personnel, when using their equipment in accordance with paragraph 1 of Article IV, shall have the right, for any explosion with a planned aggregate yield exceeding 500 kilotons, to emplace, install and operate under the observation and with the assistance of personnel of the Party carrying out the explosion, if such assistance is requested by designated personnel, a local seismic network in accordance with the provisions of paragraph 7 of Article IV. Radio links may be used for the transmission of data and control signals between the seismic stations and the control centre. Frequencies, maximum power output of radio transmitters, directivity of antennas and times of operation of the local seismic network radio transmitters before the explosion shall be agreed between the Parties in accordance with Article X and time of operation after the explosion shall conform to the time specified in paragraph 7 of Article IV.

5. Designated personnel shall have the right to:

(a) acquire photographs under the following conditions:

(1) the Party carrying out the explosion shall identify to the other Party those personnel of the Party carrying out the explosion who shall take photographs as requested by designation personnel;

(2) photographs shall be taken by personnel of the Party carrying out the explosion in the presence of designated personnel and at the time requested by designated personnel for taking such photographs. Designated personnel shall determine whether these photographs are in conformity with their requests and, if not, additional photographs shall be taken immediately;

(3) photographs shall be taken with cameras provided by the other Party having built-in, rapid developing capability and a copy of each photograph shall be provided at the completion of the development process to both Parties;

(4) cameras provided by designated personnel shall be kept in agreed secure storage when not in use; and

(5) the request for photographs can be made, at any time, of the following:

(i) exterior views of facilities and installations associated with the conduct of the explosion as described in subparagraph 4(a) of Article II;

(ii) geological samples used for confirmation of geological and geophysical information, as provided for in subparagraph 2(b) of this article and the equipment utilized in the acquisition of such samples;

(iii) emplacement and installation of equipment and associated cables used by designated personnel for yield determination;

(iv) emplacement and installation of the local seismic network used by designated personnel;

(v) emplacement of the explosives and the stemming of the emplacement hole; and

(vi) containers, facilities and installations for storage and operation of equipment used by designated personnel;

(b) photographs of visual displays and records produced by the equipment used by designated personnel and photographs within the control centres taken by cameras which are component parts of such equipment; and

(c) receive at the request of designated personnel and with the agreement of the Party carrying out the explosion supplementary photographs taken by the Party carrying out the explosion.

Article IV

1. Designated personnel in exercising their rights and functions may choose to use the following equipment of either Party, of which choice the Party carrying out the explosion shall be informed not later than 150 days before the beginning of emplacement of the explosives:

(a) electrical equipment for yield determination and equipment for a local seismic network as described in paragraphs 3, 4 and 7 of this article; and

(b) geologist's field tools and kits and equipment for recording of field notes.

2. Designated personnel shall have the right in exercising their rights and functions to utilize the following additional equipment which shall be provided by the Party carrying out the explosion, under procedures to be established in accordance with Article X to ensure that the equipment meets the specifications of the other Party: portable short-range communication equipment, field glasses, optical equipment for surveying and other items which may be specified by the other Party. A description of such equipment and operating instructions shall be provided to the other Party not later than 90 days before the beginning of emplacement of the explosives in connexion with which such equipment is to be used.

3. A complete set of electrical equipment for yield determination shall consist of:

(a) sensing elements and associated cables for transmission of electrical power, control signals and data;

(b) equipment of the control centre, electrical power supplies and cables for transmission of electrical power, control signals and data; and

(c) measuring and calibration instruments, maintenance equipment and spare parts necessary for ensuring the functioning of sensing elements, cables and equipment of the control centre.

4. A complete set of equipment for the local seismic network shall consist of:

(*a*) seismic stations each of which contains a seismic instrument, electrical power supply and associated cables and radio equipment for receiving and transmission of control signals and data or equipment for recording control signals and data;

(*b*) equipment of the control centre and electrical power supplies; and

(*c*) measuring and calibration instruments, maintenance equipment and spare parts necessary for ensuring the functioning of the complete network.

5. In case designated personnel, in accordance with paragraph 1 of this article, choose to use equipment of the Party carrying out the explosion for yield determination or for a local seismic network, a description of such equipment and installation and operating instructions shall be provided to the other Party not later than 90 days before the beginning of emplacement of the explosives in connexion with which such equipment is to be used. Personnel of the Party carrying out the explosion shall emplace, install and operate the equipment in the presence of designated personnel. After the explosion, designated personnel shall receive duplicate copies of the recorded data. Equipment for yield determination shall be emplaced in accordance with Article VI. Equipment for a local seismic network shall be emplaced in accordance with paragraph 7 of this article.

6. In case designated personnel, in accordance with paragraph 1 of this article, choose to use their own equipment for yield determination and their own equipment for a local seismic network, the following procedures shall apply:

(*a*) the Party carrying out the explosion shall be provided by the other Party with the equipment and information specified in subparagraphs (*a*) (1) and (*a*) (2) of this paragraph not later than 150 days prior to the beginning of emplacement of the explosives in connexion with which such equipment is to be used in order to permit the Party carrying out the explosion to familiarize itself with such equipment, if such equipment and information has not been previously provided, which equipment shall be returned to the other Party not later than 90 days before the beginning of emplacement of the explosives. The equipment and information to be provided are:

(1) one complete set of electrical equipment for yield determination as described in paragraph 3 of this article, electrical and mechanical design information, specifications and installation and operating instructions concerning this equipment; and

(2) one complete set of equipment for the local seismic network described in paragraph 4 of this article, including one seismic station, electrical and mechanical design information, specifications and installation and operating instructions concerning this equipment;

(*b*) not later than 35 days prior to the beginning of emplacement of the explosives in connexion with which the following equipment is to be used, two complete sets of electrical equipment for yield determination as described in paragraph 3 of this article and specific installation instructions for the emplacement of the sensing elements based on information provided in accordance with subparagraph 2 (*a*) of Article VI and two complete sets of equipment for the local seismic network as described in paragraph 4 of this article, which sets of equipment shall have the same components and technical characteristics as the corresponding equipment specified in subparagraph 6 (*a*) of this article, shall be delivered in sealed containers to the port of entry;

(*c*) the Party carrying out the explosion shall choose one of each of the two sets of equipment described above which shall be used by designated personnel in connexion with the explosion;

(*d*) the set or sets of equipment not chosen for use in connexion with the explosion shall be at the disposal of the Party carrying out the explosion for a period that may be as long as 30 days after the explosion at which time such equipment shall be returned to the other Party;

(*e*) the set or sets of equipment chosen for use shall be transported by the Party carrying out the explosion in the sealed containers in which this equipment arrived, after seals of the Party carrying out the explosion have been affixed to them, to the site of the explosion, so that this equipment is delivered to designated personnel for emplacement, installation and operation not later than 20 days before the beginning of emplacement of the explosives. This equipment shall remain in the custody of designated personnel in accordance with paragraph 7 of Article V or in agreed secure storage. Personnel of the Party carrying out the explosion shall have the right to observe the use of this equipment by designated personnel during the time the equipment is at the site of the explosion. Before the beginning of emplacement of the explosives, designated personnel shall demonstrate to personnel of the Party carrying out the explosion that this equipment is in working order;

(*f*) each set of equipment shall include two sets of components for recording data and associated calibration equipment. Both of these sets of components in the equipment chosen for use shall simultaneously record data. After the explosion, and after duplicate copies of all data have been obtained by designated personnel and the Party carrying out the explosion, one of each of the two sets of components for recording data and associated calibration equipment shall be selected, by an agreed process of chance, to be retained by designated personnel. Designated personnel shall pack and seal such components for recording data and associated calibration equipment which shall accompany them from the site of explosion to the port of exit; and

(*g*) all remaining equipment may be retained by the Party carrying out the explosion for a period that may be as long as 30 days, after which time this equipment shall be returned to the other Party.

7. For any explosion with a planned aggregate yield exceeding 500 kilotons, a local seismic network, the number of stations of which shall be determined by designated personnel but shall not exceed the number of explosives in the group plus five, shall be emplaced, installed and operated at agreed sites of emplacement within an area circumscribed by circles of 15 kilometres in radius centered on points on the surface of the earth above the points of emplacement of the explosives during a period beginning not later than 20 days before the beginning of emplacement of the explosives and continuing after the explosion not later than three days unless otherwise agreed between the Parties.

8. The Party carrying out the explosion shall have the right to examine in the presence of designated personnel all equipment, instruments and tools of designated personnel specified in subparagraph 1 (b) of this article.

9. The Joint Consultative Commission will consider proposals that either Party may put forward for the joint development of standardized equipment for verification purposes.

Article V

1. Except as limited by the provisions of paragraph 5 of this article, designated personnel in the exercise of their rights and functions shall have access along agreed routes:

(a) for an explosion with a planned aggregate yield exceeding 100 kilotons in accordance with paragraph 2 of Article III:

(1) to the locations of facilities and installations associated with the conduct of the explosion provided in accordance with subparagraph 4 (a) of Article II; and

(2) to the locations described in paragraph 2 of Article III; and

(b) for any explosion with a planned aggregate yield exceeding 150 kilotons, in addition to the access described in subparagraph 1 (a) of this article:

(1) to other locations within the area circumscribed by circles of 10 kilometres in radius centered on points on the surface of the earth above the points of emplacement of the explosives in order to confirm that the local circumstances are consistent with the stated peaceful purposes;

(2) to the locations of the components of the electrical equipment for yield determination to be used for recording data when, by agreement between the Parties, such equipment is located outside the area described in subparagraph 1 (b) (1) of this article; and

(3) to the sites of emplacement of the equipment of the local seismic network provided for in paragraph 7 of Article IV.

2. The Party carrying out the explosion shall notify the other Party of the procedure it has chosen from among those specified in subparagraph 2 (b) (3) of Article III not later than 30 days before beginning the implementation of such procedure. Designated personnel shall have the right to be present at the site of the explosion to exercise their rights and functions in the areas and at the locations described in paragraph 1 of this article for a period of time beginning two days before the beginning of the implementation of the procedure and continuing for a period of three days after the completion of this procedure.

3. Except as specified in paragraph 4 of this article, designated personnel shall have the right to be present in the areas and at the locations described in paragraph 1 of this article:

(a) for an explosion with a planned aggregate yield exceeding 100 kilotons but not exceeding 150 kilotons, in accordance with paragraph 2 of Article III, at any time beginning five days before the beginning of emplacement of the explosives and continuing after the explosion and after safe access to evacuated areas has been established according to standards determined by the Party carrying out the explosion for a period of two days; and

(b) for any explosion with a planned aggregate yield exceeding 150 kilotons, at any time beginning 20 days before the beginning of emplacement of the explosives and continuing after the explosion and after safe access to evacuated areas has been established according to standards determined by the Party carrying out the explosion for a period of:

(1) five days in the case of an explosion with a planned aggregate yield exceeding 150 kilotons but not exceeding 500 kilotons; or

(2) eight days in the case of an explosion with a planned aggregate yield exceeding 500 kilotons.

4. Designated personnel shall not have the right to be present in those areas from which all personnel have been evacuated in connexion with carrying out an explosion, but shall have the right to re-enter those areas at the same time as personnel of the Party carrying out the explosion.

5. Designated personnel shall not have or seek access by physical, visual, or technical means to the interior of the canister containing an explosive, to documentary or other information descriptive of the design of an explosive nor to equipment for control and firing of explosives. The Party carrying out the explosion shall not locate documentary or other information descriptive of the design of an explosive in such ways as to impede the designated personnel in the exercise of their rights and functions.

6. The number of designated personnel present at the site of an explosion shall not exceed:

(a) for the exercise of their rights and functions in connexion with the confirmation of the geographical and geophysical information in accordance with the provisions of subparagraph 2 (b) and applicable provisions of paragraph 5 of Article III—the number of emplacement holes plus three;

(b) for the exercise of their rights and functions in connexion with confirming that the local circumstances are consistent with the information provided and with the stated peaceful purposes in accordance with the provisions in sub-paragraphs 2 (a), 2 (c), 2 (d) and 2 (e) and applicable provisions of paragraph 5 of Article III—the number of explosives plus two;

(c) for the exercise of their rights and functions in connexion with confirming that the local circumstances are consistent with the information provided and with the stated peaceful purposes in accordance with the provisions in sub-paragraphs 2 (a), 2(c), 2(d) and 2(e) and applicable provisions of paragraph 5 of Article III and in connexion with the use of electrical equipment for determination of the yield in accordance with paragraph 3 of Article III—the number of explosives plus seven; and

(d) for the exercise of their rights and functions in connexion with confirming that the local circumstances are consistent with the information provided and with the stated peaceful purposes in accordance with the provisions in sub-paragraphs 2 (a), 2 (c), 2 (d) and 2 (e) and applicable provisions of paragraph 5 of Article III and in connexion with the use of electrical equipment for determination of the yield in accordance with paragraph 3 of Article III and with the use of the local seismic network in accordance with paragraph 4 of Article III—the number of explosives plus 10.

7. The Party carrying out the explosion shall have the right to assign its personnel to accompany designated personnel while the latter exercise their rights and functions.

8. The Party carrying out an explosion shall assure for designated personnel telecommunications with their authorities, transportation and other services appropriate to their presence and to the exercise of their rights and functions at the site of the explosion.

9. The expenses incurred for the transportation of designated personnel and their equipment to and from the site of the explosion, telecommunications provided for in paragraph 8 of this article, their living and working quarters, subsistence and all other personal expenses shall be the responsibility of the Party other than the Party carrying out the explosion.

10. Designated personnel shall consult with the Party carrying out the explosion in order to co-ordinate the planned programme and schedule of activities of designated personnel with the programme of the Party carrying out the explosion for the conduct of the project so as to ensure that designated personnel are able to conduct their activities in an orderly and timely way that is compatible with the implementation of the project. Procedures for such consultations shall be established in accordance with Article X.

Article VI

For any explosion with a planned aggregate yield exceeding 150 kilotons, determination of the yield of each explosive used shall be carried out in accordance with the following provisions:

1. Determination of the yield of each individual explosion in the group shall be based on measurements of the velocity of propagation, as a function of time, of the hydrodynamic shock wave generated by the explosion, taken by means of electrical equipment described in paragraph 3 of Article IV.

2. The Party carrying out the explosion shall provide the other Party with the following information:

(a) not later than 60 days before the beginning of emplacement of the explosives, the length of each canister in which the explosive will be contained in the corresponding emplacement hold, the dimensions of the tube or other device used to emplace the canister and the cross-sectional dimensions of the emplacement hole to a distance, in metres, from the emplacement point of 10 times the cube root of its yield in kilotons;

(b) not later than 60 days before the beginning of emplacement of the explosives, a description of materials, including their densities, to be used to stem each emplacement hole; and

(c) not later than 30 days before the beginning of emplacement of the explosives for each emplacement hole of a group explosion, the local co-ordinates of the point of emplacement of the explosive, the entrance of the emplacement hole, the point of the emplacement hole most distant from the entrance, the location of the emplacement hole at each 200 metres distance from the entrance and the configuration of any known void larger than one cubic metre located within the distance, in metres, of 10 times the cube root of the planned yield in kilotons measured from the bottom of the canister containing the explosive. The error in these co-ordinates shall not exceed 1 per cent of the distance between the emplacement hole and the nearest other emplacement hole or 1 per cent of the distance between the point of measurement and the entrance of the emplacement hole, whichever is smaller, but in no case shall the error be required to be less than one metre.

3. The Party carrying out the explosion shall emplace for each explosive that portion of the electrical equipment for yield determination described in sub-paragraph 3 (a) of Article IV, supplied in accordance with paragraph 1 of Article IV, in the same emplacement hole as the explosive in accordance with the installation instructions supplied under the provisions of paragraph 5 or 6 of Article IV. Such emplacement shall be carried out under the observation of designated personnel. Other equipment specified in sub-paragraph 3 (b) of Article IV shall be emplaced and installed:

(a) by designated personnel under the observation and with the assistance of personnel of the Party carrying out the explosion, if such assistance is requested by designated personnel; or

(b) in accordance with paragraph 5 of Article IV.

4. That portion of the electrical equipment for yield determination described in subparagraph 3 (a) of Article IV that is to be emplaced in each emplacement hole shall be located so that the end of the electrical equipment which is farthest from the entrance to the emplacement hole is at a distance, in metres, from the bottom of the canister containing the explosive equal to 3.5 times the cube root of the planned yield in kilotons of the explosive when the planned yield is less than 20 kilotons and three times the cube root of the planned yield in kilotons of the explosive when the planned yield is 20 kilotons or more. Canisters longer than 10 metres containing the explosive shall only be utilized if there is prior agreement between the Parties establishing provisions for their use. The Party carrying out the explosion shall provide the other Party with data on the distribution of density inside any other canister in the emplacement hole with a transverse cross-sectional area exceeding 10 square centimetres located within a distance, in metres, of 10 times the cube root of the planned yield in kilotons of the explosion from the bottom of the canister containing the explosive. The Party carrying out the explosion shall provide the other Party with access to confirm such data on density distribution within any such canister.

5. The Party carrying out an explosion shall fill each emplacement hole, including all pipes and tubes contained therein which have at any transverse section an aggregate cross-sectional area exceeding 10 square centimetres in the region containing the electrical equipment for yield determination and to a distance, in metres, of six times the cube root of the planned yield in kilotons of the explosive from the explosive emplacement point, with material having a densi_y not less than seven-tenths of the average density of the surrounding rock, and from that point to a distance of not less than 60 metres from the explosive emplacement point with material having a density greater than one gram per cubic centimetre.

6. Designated personnel shall have the right to:

(a) confirm information provided in accordance with sub-paragraph 2 (a) of this article;

(b) confirm information provided in accordance with sub-paragraph 2 (b) of this article and be provided, upon request, with a sample of each batch of stemming material as that material is put into the emplacement hole; and

(c) confirm the information provided in accordance with sub-paragraph 2 (c) of this article by having access to the data acquired and by observing, upon their request, the making of measurements.

7. For those explosives which are emplaced in separate emplacement holes, the emplacement shall be such that the distance D, in metres, between any explosive and any portion of the electrical equipment for determination of the yield of any other explosive in the group shall be not less than 10 times the cube root of the planned yield in kilotons of the larger explosive of such a pair of explosives. Individual explosions shall be separated by time intervals, in milliseconds, not greater than one-sixth the amount by which the distance D, in metres, exceeds 10 times the cube root of the planned yield in kilotons of the larger explosive of such a pair of explosives.

8. For those explosives in a group which are emplaced in a common emplacement hole, the distance, in metres, between each explosive and any other explosive in that emplacement hole shall be not less than 10 times the cube root of the planned yield in kilotons of the larger explosive of such a pair of explosives, and the explosives shall be detonated in sequential order, beginning with the explosive farthest from the entrance to the emplacement hole, with the individual detonations separated by time intervals, in milliseconds, of not less than one times the cube root of the planned yield in kilotons of the largest explosive in this emplacement hole.

Article VII

1. Designated personnel with their personal baggage and their equipment as provided in Article IV shall be permitted to enter the territory of the Party carrying out the explosion at an entry port to be agreed upon by the Parties, to remain in the territory of the Party carrying out the explosion for the purpose of fulfilling their rights and functions provided for in the Treaty and this Protocol, and to depart from an exit port to be agreed upon by the Parties.

2. At all times while designated personnel are in the territory of the Party carrying out the explosion, their persons, property, personal baggage, archives and documents as well as their temporary official and living quarters shall be accorded the same privileges and immunities as provided in Articles 22, 23, 24, 29, 30, 31, 34 and 36 of the Vienna Convention on Diplomatic Relations of 1961 to the persons, property, personal baggage, archives and documents of diplomatic agents as well as to the premises of diplomatic missions and private residences of diplomatic agents.

3. Without prejudice to their privileges and immunities it shall be the duty of designated personnel to respect the laws and regulations of the State in whose territory the explosion is to be carried out insofar as they do not impede in any way whatsoever the proper exercising of their rights and functions provided for by the Treaty and this Protocol.

Article VIII

The Party carrying out an explosion shall have sole and exclusive control over and full responsibility for the conduct of the explosion.

Article IX

1. Nothing in the Treaty and this Protocol shall affect proprietary rights in information made available under the Treaty and this Protocol and in information which may be disclosed in preparation for and carrying out of explosions; however, claims to such proprietary rights shall not impede implementation of the provisions of the Treaty and this Protocol.

2. Public release of the information provided in accordance with Article II or publication of material using such information, as well as public release of the results of observation and measurements obtained by designated personnel, may take place only by agreement with the Party carrying out an explosion; however, the other Party shall have the right to issue statements after the explosion that do not divulge information in which the Party carrying out the explosion has rights which are referred to in paragraph 1 of this article.

Article X

The joint Consultative Commission shall establish procedures through which the Parties will, as appropriate, consult with each other for the purpose of ensuring efficient implementation of this Protocol.

AGREED STATEMENT

The Parties to the Treaty Between the United States of America and the Union of Soviet Socialist Republics on Underground Nuclear Explosions for Peaceful Purposes, hereinafter referred to as the Treaty, agree that under sub-paragraph 2 (c) of Article III of the Treaty:

(a) Development testing of nuclear explosives does not constitute a "peaceful application" and any such development tests shall be carried out only within the boundaries of nuclear weapon test sites specified in accordance with the Treaty Between the United States of America and the Union of Soviet Socialist Republics on the Limitation of Underground Nuclear Weapon Tests;

(b) Associating test facilities, instrumentation or procedures related only to testing of nuclear weapons or their effects with any explosion carried out in accordance with the Treaty does not constitute a "peaceful application".

Source: Disarmament Conference documents CCD/496, 23 June 1976, and CCD/496/Corr. 1, 5 August 1976

AGREEMENT BETWEEN FRANCE AND THE USSR ON THE PREVENTION OF THE ACCIDENTAL OR UNAUTHORIZED USE OF NUCLEAR WEAPONS

Effected by exchange of letters on 16 July 1976 between the foreign ministers of France and the USSR
Entered into force on 16 July 1976

LETTER FROM THE MINISTER FOR FOREIGN AFFAIRS OF THE UNION OF SOVIET SOCIALIST REPUBLICS, MR ANDREI GROMYKO, ADDRESSED TO THE MINISTER FOR FOREIGN AFFAIRS OF FRANCE, MR JEAN SAUVAGNARGUES

As a result of our conversation of 28 April 1976, we considered it desirable to reaffirm the importance attached in the USSR and in France to the prevention of the accidental or unauthorized use of nuclear weapons. Such an initiative is in keeping with the special responsibilities incumbent on the Soviet Union and France as nuclear Powers.

Having regard to the views exchanged concerning measures to avoid any risk of such accidental or unauthorized use, it was agreed that the following provisions should be adopted:

1. Each Party undertakes to maintain and, possibly, improve, as it deems necessary, its existing organizational and technical arrangements to prevent the accidental or unauthorized use of nuclear weapons under its control.

2. The two Parties undertake to notify each other immediately of any accidental occurrence or any other unexplained incident that could lead to the explosion of one of their nuclear weapons and could be construed as likely to have harmful effects on the other Party.

3. In the event of an unexplained nuclear incident, each Party undertakes to act in such a manner as to avoid, as far as possible, the possibility of its actions being misinterpreted by the other Party. In any such situation, each Party may inform the other Party or request such information as it considers necessary.

4. For transmission of urgent information in situations requiring prompt clarification, the Parties shall make primary use of the Direct Communications Link between the Kremlin and the Elysée Palace.

5. The two Parties shall consider together the possibility of further improving, by mutual agreement, their means of direct communication.

If the above points meet with your approval, I have the honour to propose that this letter and your reply should constitute an agreement between the Soviet Union and France.

This agreement shall enter into force on today's date.

LETTER FROM THE MINISTER FOR FOREIGN AFFAIRS OF FRANCE, MR JEAN SAUVAGNARGUES, ADDRESSED TO THE MINISTER FOR FOREIGN AFFAIRS OF THE UNION OF SOVIET SOCIALIST REPUBLICS, MR ANDREI GROMYKO

As a result of our conversation of 28 April 1976, we considered it desirable to reaffirm the importance attached in France and the USSR to the prevention of the accidental or unauthorized use of nuclear weapons. Such an initiative is in keeping with the special responsibilities incumbent upon France and the Soviet Union as nuclear Powers.

Having regard to the views exchanged concerning measures to prevent any risk of such accidental or unauthorized use, it was agreed that the following provisions should be adopted:

1. Each Party shall undertake to maintain and, possibly, improve, as it deems necessary, its existing organizational and technical arrangements to prevent the accidental or unauthorized use of nuclear weapons under its control.

2. The two Parties undertake to notify each other immediately of any accidental occurrence or any other unexplained incident that could lead to the explosion of one of their nuclear weapons and could be construed as likely to have harmful effects on the other Party.

3. In the event of an unexplained nuclear incident, each Party undertakes to act in such a manner as to avoid, as far as possible, the possibility of its actions being misinterpreted by the other Party. In any such situation, each Party may inform the other Party or request such information as it considers necessary.

4. For transmission of urgent information in situations requiring prompt clarification, the Parties shall make primary use of the Direct Communications Link existing between the Elysée Palace and the Kremlin.

5. The two Parties shall consider together the possibility of further improving, by mutual agreement, their means of direct communication.

If the foregoing points meet with your approval, I have the honour to propose that this letter and your reply should constitute an agreement between France and the Soviet Union.

This agreement shall enter into force on to-day's date.

Source: UN document S/12161, Annex I and II, 4 August 1976

CONVENTION ON THE PROHIBITION OF MILITARY OR ANY OTHER HOSTILE USE OF ENVIRONMENTAL MODIFICATION TECHNIQUES

Signed at Geneva on 18 May 1977
Entered into force on 5 October 1978
Depositary: UN Secretary-General

The States Parties to this Convention,

Guided by the interest of consolidating peace, and wishing to contribute to the cause of halting the arms race, and of bringing about general and complete disarmament under strict and effective international control, and of saving mankind from the danger of using new means of warfare,

Determined to continue negotiations with a view to achieving effective progress towards further measures in the field of disarmament,

Recognizing that scientific and technical advances may open new possibilities with respect to modification of the environment,

Recalling the Declaration of the United Nations Conference on the Human Environment, adopted at Stockholm on 16 June 1972,

Realizing that the use of environmental modification techniques for peaceful purposes could improve the interrelationship of man and nature and contribute to the preservation and improvement of the environment for the benefit of present and future generations,

Recognizing, however, that military or any other hostile use of such techniques could have effects extremely harmful to human welfare,

Desiring to prohibit effectively military or any other hostile use of environmental modification techniques in order to eliminate the dangers to mankind from such use, and affirming their willingness to work towards the achievement of this objective,

Desiring also to contribute to the strengthening of trust among nations and to the further improvement of the international situation in accordance with the purposes and principles of the Charter of the United Nations,

Have agreed as follows:

Article I

1. Each State Party to this Convention undertakes not to engage in military or any other hostile use of environmental modification techniques having widespread, long-lasting or severe effects as the means of destruction, damage or injury to any other State Party.

2. Each State Party to this Convention undertakes not to assist, encourage or induce any State, group of States or international organization to engage in activities contrary to the provisions of paragraph 1 of this article.

Article II

As used in article I, the term "environmental modification techniques" refers to any technique for changing—through the deliberate manipulation of natural processes—the dynamics, composition or structure of the earth, including its biota, lithosphere, hydrosphere and atmosphere, or of outer space.

Article III

1. The provisions of this Convention shall not hinder the use of environmental modification techniques for peaceful purposes and shall be without prejudice to the generally recognized principles and applicable rules of international law concerning such use.

2. The States Parties to this Convention undertake to facilitate, and have the right to participate in, the fullest possible exchange of scientific and technological information on the use of environmental modification techniques for peaceful purposes. States Parties in a position to do so shall contribute, alone or together with other States or international organizations, to international economic and scientific co-operation in the preservation, improvement and peaceful utilization of the environment, with due consideration for the needs of the developing areas of the world.

Article IV

Each State Party to this Convention undertakes to take any measures it considers necessary in accordance with its constitutional processes to prohibit and prevent any activity in violation of the provisions of the Convention anywhere under its jurisdiction or control.

Article V

1. The States Parties to this Convention undertake to consult one another and to co-operate in solving any problems which may arise in relation to the objectives of, or in the application of the provisions of, the Convention. Consultation and co-operation pursuant to this article may also be undertaken through appropriate international procedures within the framework of the United Nations and in accordance with its Charter. These international procedures may include the services of appropriate international organizations, as well as of a Consultative Committee of Experts as provided for in paragraph 2 of this article.

2. For the purposes set forth in paragraph 1 of this article, the Depositary shall, within one month of the receipt of a request from any State Party to this Convention, convene a Consultative Committee of Experts. Any State Party may appoint an expert to the Committee whose functions and rules of procedure are set out in the annex, which constitutes an integral part of this Convention. The Committee shall transmit to the Depositary a summary of its findings of fact, incorporating all views and information presented to the Committee during its proceedings. The Depositary shall distribute the summary to all States Parties.

3. Any State Party to this Convention which has reason to believe that any other State Party is acting in breach of obligations deriving from the provisions of the Convention may lodge a complaint with the Security Council of the United Nations. Such a complaint should include all relevant information as well as all possible evidence supporting its validity.

4. Each State Party to this Convention undertakes to co-operate in carrying out any investigation which the Security Council may initiate, in accordance with the provisions of the Charter of the United Nations, on the basis of the complaint received by the Council. The Security Council shall inform the States Parties of the results of the investigation.

5. Each State Party to this Convention undertakes to provide or support assistance, in accordance with the provisions of the Charter of the United Nations, to any State Party which so requests, if the Security Council decides that such Party has been harmed or is likely to be harmed as a result of violation of the Convention.

Article VI

1. Any State Party to this Convention may propose amendments to the Convention. The text of any proposed amendment shall be submitted to the Depositary, who shall promptly circulate it to all States Parties.

2. An amendment shall enter into force for all States Parties to this Convention which have accepted it, upon the deposit with the Depositary of instruments of acceptance by a majority of States Parties. Thereafter it shall enter in force for any remaining State Party on the date of deposit of its instrument of acceptance.

Article VII

This Convention shall be of unlimited duration.

Article VIII

1. Five years after the entry into force of this Convention, a conference of the States Parties to the Convention shall be convened by the Depositary at Geneva, Switzerland. The conference shall review the operation of the Convention with a view to ensuring that its purposes and provisions are being realized, and shall in particular examine the effectiveness of the provisions of paragraph 1 of article I in eliminating the dangers of military or any other hostile use of environmental modification techniques.

2. At intervals of not less than five years thereafter, a majority of the States Parties to this Convention may obtain, by submitting a proposal to this effect to the Depositary, the convening of a conference with the same objectives.

3. If no conference has been convened pursuant to paragraph 2 of this article within

ten years following the conclusion of a previous conference, the Depositary shall solicit the views of all States Parties to this Convention, concerning the convening of such a conference. If one third or ten of the States Parties, whichever number is less, respond affirmatively, the Depositary shall take immediate steps to convene the conference.

Article IX

1. This Convention shall be open to all States for signature. Any State which does not sign the Convention before its entry into force in accordance with paragraph 3 of this article may accede to it at any time.

2. This Convention shall be subject to ratification by signatory States. Instruments of ratification or accession shall be deposited with the Secretary-General of the United Nations.

3. This Convention shall enter into force upon the deposit of instruments of ratification by twenty Governments in accordance with paragraph 2 of this article.

4. For those States whose instruments of ratification or accession are deposited after the entry into force of this Convention, it shall enter into force on the date of the deposit of their instruments of ratification or accession.

5. The Depositary shall promptly inform all signatory and acceding States of the date of each signature, the date of deposit of each instrument of ratification or accession and the date of the entry into force of this Convention and of any amendments thereto, as well as of the receipt of other notices.

6. This Convention shall be registered by the Depositary in accordance with Article 102 of the Charter of the United Nations.

Article X

This Convention, of which the English, Arabic, Chinese, French, Russian and Spanish texts are equally authentic, shall be deposited with the Secretary-General of the United Nations, who shall send duly certified copies thereof to the Governments of the signatory and acceding States.

In witness whereof, the undersigned, being duly authorized thereto by their respective Governments, have signed this Convention, opened for signature at Geneva on the eighteenth day of May, one thousand nine hundred and seventy-seven.

ANNEX

Consultative Committee of Experts

1. The Consultative Committee of Experts shall undertake to make appropriate findings of fact and provide expert views relevant to any problem raised pursuant to paragraph 1 of article V of this Convention by the State Party requesting the convening of the Committee.

2. The work of the Consultative Committee of Experts shall be organized in such a way as to permit it to perform the functions set forth in paragraph 1 of this annex. The Committee shall decide procedural questions relative to the organization of its work, where possible by consensus, but otherwise by a majority of those present and voting. There shall be no voting on matters of substance.

3. The Depositary or his representative shall serve as the Chairman of the Committee.

4. Each expert may be assisted at meetings by one or more advisers.

5. Each expert shall have the right, through the Chairman, to request from States, and from international organizations, such information and assistance as the expert considers desirable for the accomplishment of the Committee's work.

Source: *Convention on the Prohibition of Military or any other Hostile Use of Environmental Modification Techniques* (United Nations, New York, 1977)

For the list of states which have signed, ratified, acceded or succeeded to the Convention, see Chapter 6.

UNDERSTANDINGS RELATING TO THE CONVENTION ON THE PROHIBITION OF MILITARY OR ANY OTHER HOSTILE USE OF ENVIRONMENTAL MODIFICATION TECHNIQUES, WORKED OUT AT THE CONFERENCE OF THE COMMITTEE ON DISARMAMENT

Understanding relating to Article I

It is the understanding of the Committee that, for the purposes of this Convention, the terms "widespread", "long-lasting" and "severe" shall be interpreted as follows:

(*a*) "widespread": encompassing an area on the scale of several hundred square kilometers;

(*b*) "long-lasting': lasting for a period of months, or approximately a season;

(*c*) "severe": involving serious or significant disruption or harm to human life, natural and economic resources or other assets.

It is further understood that the interpretation set forth above is intended exclusively for this Convention and is not intended to prejudice the interpretation of the same or similar terms if used in connection with any other international agreement.

Understanding relating to Article II

It is the understanding of the Committee that the following examples are illustrative of phenomena that could be caused by the use of environmental modification techniques as defined in Article II of the Convention: earthquakes; tsunamis; an upset in the ecological balance of a region; changes in weather patterns (clouds, precipitation, cyclones of various types and tornadic storms); changes in climate patterns; changes in ocean currents; changes in the state of the ozone layer; and changes in the state of the ionosphere.

It is further understood that all the phenomena listed above, when produced by military or any other hostile use of environmental modification techniques, would result, or could reasonably be expected to result in widespread, long-lasting or severe destruction, damage or injury. Thus, military or any other hostile use of environmental modification techniques as defined in Article II, so as to cause those phenomena as a means of destruction, damage or injury to another State Party, would be prohibited.

It is recognized, moreover, that the list of examples set out above is not exhaustive. Other phenomena which could result from the use of environmental modification techniques as defined in Article II could also be appropriately included. The absence of such phenomena from the list does not in any way imply that the undertaking contained in Article I would not be applicable to those phenomena, provided the criteria set out in that Article were met.

Understanding relating to Article III

It is the understanding of the Committee that this Convention does not deal with the question whether or not a given use of environmental modification techniques for peaceful purposes is in accordance with generally recognized principles and applicable rules of international law.

Understanding relating to Article VIII

It is the understanding of the Committee that a proposal to amend the Convention may also be considered at any Conference of Parties held pursuant to Article VIII. It is further understood that any proposed amendment that is intended for such consideration should, if possible, be submitted to the Depositary no less than 90 days before the commencement of the Conference.

Source: Disarmament Conference document CCD/520, Annex A, 3 September 1976

Socialist Republics:

Conscious of the devastating results of any nuclear war, and of the special responsibilities incumbent upon the United Kingdom and the Soviet Union as nuclear powers to do everything possible to avoid the risk of outbreak of such a war:

Have agreed as follows:

Article I

Each Party undertakes to maintain and, whenever it believes it necessary, to improve its existing organisational and technical arrangements for guarding against the accidental or unauthorised use of nuclear weapons under its control.

Article II

The two Parties undertake to notify each other immediately of any accident or other unexplained or unauthorised incident which could result in the explosion of one of their nuclear weapons or could otherwise create the risk of outbreak of nuclear war. In the event of such an incident, the Party whose nuclear weapon is involved will immediately make every effort to take necessary measures to render harmless or destroy such weapon without its causing damage.

Article III

In the event of the occurrence of an incident of the type referred to in Article II of this Agreement each Party undertakes to act in such a manner as to reduce the possibilities of its action being misinterpreted by the other Party. In such circumstances each Party should provide to, or request from, the other such information as it considers necessary.

Article IV

The Parties shall use the direct communications link between their Governments for transmission of, or requests for, urgent information in situations requiring prompt clarification.

Article V

The Agreement shall enter into force on the date of signature.

Source: *Treaty Series No. 10 (1978)* (HMSO, London, 1978)

AGREEMENT BETWEEN THE UK AND THE USSR ON THE PREVENTION OF ACCIDENTAL NUCLEAR WAR

Signed at Moscow on 10 October 1977
Entered into force on 10 October 1977

The Government of the United Kingdom of Great Britain and Northern Ireland and the Government of the Union of Soviet

PROTOCOL (I) ADDITIONAL TO THE GENEVA CONVENTIONS OF 12 AUGUST 1949, AND RELATING TO THE PROTECTION OF VICTIMS OF INTERNATIONAL ARMED CONFLICTS

Signed at Bern on 12 December 1977
Entered into force on 7 December 1978
Depositary: Swiss Federal Council

PREAMBLE

The High Contracting Parties,

Proclaiming their earnest wish to see peace prevail among peoples,

Recalling that every State has the duty, in conformity with the Charter of the United Nations, to refrain in its international relations from the threat or use of force against the sovereignty, territorial integrity or political independence of any State, or in any other manner inconsistent with the purposes of the United Nations,

Believing it necessary nevertheless to re-affirm and develop the provisions protecting the victims of armed conflicts and to supplement measures intended to reinforce their application,

Expressing their conviction that nothing in this Protocol or in the Geneva Conventions of 12 August 1949 can be construed as legitimizing or authorizing any act of aggression or any other use of force inconsistent with the Charter of the United Nations,

Reaffirming further that the provisions of the Geneva Conventions of 12 August 1949 and of this Protocol must be fully applied in all circumstances to all persons who are protected by those instruments, without any adverse distinction based on the nature or origin of the armed conflict or on the causes espoused by or attributed to the Parties to the conflict,

Have agreed on the following:

PART I. GENERAL PROVISIONS

Article 1. *General principles and scope of application*

1. The High Contracting Parties undertake to respect and to ensure respect for this Protocol in all circumstances.

2. In cases not covered by this Protocol or by other international agreements, civilians and combatants remain under the protection and authority of the principles of international law derived from established custom, from the principles of humanity and from the dictates of public conscience.

3. This Protocol, which supplements the Geneva Conventions of 12 August 1949 for the protection of war victims, shall apply in the situations referred to in Article 2 common to those Conventions.

4. The situations referred to in the preceding paragraph include armed conflicts in which peoples are fighting against colonial domination and alien occupation and against racist régimes in the exercise of their right of self-determination, as enshrined in the Charter of the United Nations and the Declaration on Principles of International Law concerning Friendly Relations and Co-operation among States in accordance with the Charter of the United Nations.

Article 2. *Definitions*

For the purposes of this Protocol:

(*a*) "First Convention", "Second Convention", "Third Convention" and "Fourth Convention" mean, respectively, the Geneva Convention for the Amelioration of the Condition of the Wounded and Sick in Armed Forces in the Field of 12 August 1949; the Geneva Convention for the Amelioration of the Condition of Wounded, Sick and Shipwrecked Members of Armed Forces at Sea of 12 August 1949; the Geneva Convention relative to the Treatment of Prisoners of War of 12 August 1949; the Geneva Convention relative to the Protection of Civilian Persons in Time of War of 12 August 1949; "the Conventions" means the four Geneva Conventions of 12 August 1949 for the protection of war victims;

(*b*) "rules of international law applicable in armed conflict" means the rules applicable in armed conflict set forth in international agreements to which the Parties to the conflict are Parties and the generally recognized principles and rules of international law which are applicable to armed conflict;

(*c*) "Protecting Power" means a neutral or other State not a Party to the conflict which has been designated by a Party to the conflict and accepted by the adverse Party and has agreed to carry out the functions assigned to a Protecting Power under the Conventions and this Protocol;

(*d*) "substitute" means an organization acting in place of a Protecting Power in accordance with Article 5.

Article 3. *Beginning and end of application*

Without prejudice to the provisions which are applicable at all times:

(*a*) the Conventions and this Protocol shall apply from the beginning of any situation referred to in Article 1 of this Protocol;

(*b*) the application of the Conventions and of this Protocol shall cease, in the territory of Parties to the conflict, on the general close of military operations and, in the case of occupied territories, on the termination of the occupation, except, in either circumstance, for those persons whose final release, repatriation or re-establishment takes place thereafter. These persons shall continue to benefit from the relevant provisions of the Conventions and of this Protocol until their final release, repatriation or re-establishment.

Article 4. *Legal status of the Parties to the conflict*

The application of the Conventions and of this Protocol, as well as the conclusion of the agreements provided for therein, shall not affect the legal status of the Parties to the conflict. Neither the occupation of a territory nor the application of the Conventions and this Protocol shall affect the legal status of the territory in question.

. . .

PART III. METHODS AND MEANS OF WARFARE
COMBATANT AND PRISONER-OF-WAR STATUS

Section I. Methods and means of warfare

Article 35. *Basic rules*

1. In any armed conflict, the right of the Parties to the conflict to choose methods or means of warfare is not unlimited.

2. It is prohibited to employ weapons, projectiles and material and methods of warfare of a nature to cause superfluous injury or unnecessary suffering.

3. It is prohibited to employ methods or means of warfare which are intended, or may be expected, to cause widespread, long-term and severe damage to the natural environment.

Article 36. *New weapons*

In the study, development, acquisition or adoption of a new weapon, means or method of warfare, a High Contracting Party is under an obligation to determine whether its employment would, in some or all circumstances, be prohibited by this Protocol or by any other rule of international law applicable to the High Contracting Party.

Article 37. *Prohibition of perfidy*

1. It is prohibited to kill, injure or capture an adversary by resort to perfidy. Acts inviting the confidence of an adversary to lead him to believe that he is entitled to, or is obliged to accord, protection under the rules of international law applicable in armed conflict, with intent to betray that confidence, shall constitute perfidy. The following acts are examples of perfidy:

(a) the feigning of an intent to negotiate under a flag of truce or of a surrender;

(b) the feigning of an incapacitation by wounds or sickness;

(c) the feigning of civilian, non-combatant status; and

(d) the feigning of protected status by the use of signs, emblems or uniforms of the United Nations or of neutral or other States not Parties to the conflict.

2. Ruses of war are not prohibited. Such ruses are acts which are intended to mislead an adversary or to induce him to act recklessly but which infringe no rule of international law applicable in armed conflict and which are not perfidious because they do not invite the confidence of an adversary with respect to protection under that law. The following are examples of such ruses: the use of camouflage, decoys, mock operations and misinformation.

Article 38. *Recognized emblems*

1. It is prohibited to make improper use of the distinctive emblem of the red cross, red crescent or red lion and sun or of other emblems, signs or signals provided for by the Conventions or by this Protocol. It is also prohibited to misuse deliberately in an armed conflict other internationally recognized protective emblems, signs or signals, including the flag of truce, and the protective emblem of cultural property.

2. It is prohibited to make use of the distinctive emblem of the United Nations, except as authorized by that Organization.

Article 39. *Emblems of nationality*

1. It is prohibited to make use in an armed conflict of the flags or military emblems, insignia or uniforms of neutral or other States not Parties to the conflict.

2. It is prohibited to make use of the flags or military emblems, insignia or uniforms of adverse Parties while engaging in attacks or in order to shield, favour, protect or impede military operations.

3. Nothing in this Article or in Article 37, paragraph 1 (d), shall affect the existing generally recognized rules of international law applicable to espionage or to the use of flags in the conduct of armed conflict at sea.

Article 40. *Quarter*

It is prohibited to order that there shall be no survivors, to threaten an adversary therewith or to conduct hostilities on this basis.

Article 41. *Safeguard of an enemy hors de combat*

1. A person who is recognized or who, in the circumstances, should be recognized to be *hors de combat* shall not be made the object of attack.

2. A person is *hors de combat* if:

(a) he is in the power of an adverse Party;

(b) he clearly expresses an intention to surrender; or

(c) he has been rendered unconscious or is otherwise incapacitated by wounds or sickness, and therefore is incapable of defending himself;

provided that in any of these cases he abstains from any hostile act and does not attempt to escape.

3. When persons entitled to protection as prisoners of war have fallen into the power of an adverse Party under unusual conditions of combat which prevent their evacuation as provided for in Part III, Section I, of the Third Convention, they shall be released and all feasible precautions shall be taken to ensure their safety.

Article 42. *Occupants of aircraft*

1. No person parachuting from an aircraft in distress shall be made the object of attack during his descent.

2. Upon reaching the ground in territory controlled by an adverse Party, a person who has parachuted from an aircraft in distress shall be given an opportunity to surrender before being made the object of attack, unless it is apparent that he is engaging in a hostile act.

3. Airborne troops are not protected by this Article.

Section II. Combatant and prisoner-of-war status

Article 43. *Armed forces*

1. The armed forces of a Party to a conflict consist of all organized armed forces, groups and units which are under a command responsible to that Party for the conduct of its subordinates, even if that Party is represented by a government or an authority not recognized by an adverse Party. Such armed forces shall be subject to an internal disciplinary system which, *inter alia*, shall enforce compliance with the rules of international law applicable in armed conflict.

2. Members of the armed forces of a Party to a conflict (other than medical personnel and chaplains covered by Article 33 of the Third Convention) are combatants, that is to say, they have the right to participate directly in hostilities.

3. Whenever a Party to a conflict incorporates a paramilitary or armed law enforcement agency into its armed forces it shall so notify the other Parties to the conflict.

Article 44. *Combatants and prisoners of war*

1. Any combatant, as defined in Article 43, who falls into the power of an adverse Party shall be a prisoner of war.

2. While all combatants are obliged to comply with the rules of international law applicable in armed conflict, violations of these rules shall not deprive a combatant of his right to be a combatant or, if he falls into the power of an adverse Party, of his right to be a prisoner of war, except as provided in paragraphs 3 and 4.

3. In order to promote the protection of the civilian population from the effects of hostilities, combatants are obliged to distinguish themselves from the civilian population while they are engaged in an attack or in a military operation preparatory to an attack. Recognizing, however, that there are situations in armed conflicts where, owing to the nature of the hostilities an armed combatant cannot so distinguish himself, he shall retain his status as a combatant, provided that, in such situations, he carries his arms openly:

(*a*) during each military engagement, and

(*b*) during such time as he is visible to the adversary while he is engaged in a military deployment preceding the launching of an attack in which he is to participate.

Acts which comply with the requirements of this paragraph shall not be considered as perfidious within the meaning of Article 37, paragraph 1 (*c*).

4. A combatant who falls into the power of an adverse Party while failing to meet the requirements set forth in the second sentence of paragraph 3 shall forfeit his right to be a prisoner of war, but he shall, nevertheless, be given protections equivalent in all respects to those accorded to prisoners of war by the Third Convention and by this Protocol. This protection includes protections equivalent to those accorded to prisoners of war by the Third Convention in the case where such a person is tried and punished for any offences he has committed.

5. Any combatant who falls into the power of an adverse Party while not engaged in an attack or in a military operation preparatory to an attack shall not forfeit his rights to be a combatant and a prisoner of war by virtue of his prior activities.

6. This Article is without prejudice to the right of any person to be a prisoner of war pursuant to Article 4 of the Third Convention.

7. This Article is not intended to change the generally accepted practice of States with respect to the wearing of the uniform by combatants assigned to the regular, uniformed armed units of a Party to the conflict.

8. In addition to the categories of persons mentioned in Article 13 of the First and Second Conventions, all members of the armed forces of a Party to the conflict, as defined in Article 43 of this Protocol, shall be entitled to protection under those Conventions if they are wounded or sick or, in the case of the Second Convention, shipwrecked at sea or in other waters.

Article 45. *Protection of persons who have taken part in hostilities*

1. A person who takes part in hostilities and falls into the power of an adverse Party shall be presumed to be a prisoner of war, and therefore shall be protected by the Third Convention, if he claims the status of prisoner of war, or if he appears to be entitled to such status, or if the Party on which he depends claims such status on his behalf by notification to the detaining Power or to the Protecting Power. Should any doubt arise as to whether any such person is entitled to the status of prisoner of war, he shall continue to have such status and, therefore, to be protected by the Third Convention and this Protocol until such time as his status has been determined by a competent tribunal.

2. If a person who has fallen into the power of an adverse Party is not held as a prisoner of war and is to be tried by that Party for an offence arising out of the hostilities, he shall have the right to assert his entitlement to prisoner-of-war status before a judicial tribunal and to have that question adjudicated. Whenever possible under the applicable procedure, this adjudication shall occur before the trial for the offence. The representatives of the Protecting Power shall be entitled to attend the proceedings in which that question is adjudicated, unless, exceptionally, the proceedings are held *in camera* in the interest of State security. In such a case the detaining Power shall advise the Protecting Power accordingly.

3. Any person who has taken part in hostilities, who is not entitled to prisoner-of-war status and who does not benefit from more favourable treatment in accordance with the Fourth Convention shall have the right at all times to the protection of Article 75 of this Protocol. In occupied territory, any such person, unless he is held as a spy, shall also be

entitled, notwithstanding Article 5 of the Fourth Convention, to his rights of communication under that Convention.

Article 46. *Spies*

1. Notwithstanding any other provision of the Conventions or of this Protocol, any member of the armed forces of a Party to the conflict who falls into the power of an adverse Party while engaging in espionage shall not have the right to the status of prisoner of war and may be treated as a spy.

2. A member of the armed forces of a Party to the conflict who, on behalf of that Party and in territory controlled by an adverse Party, gathers or attempts to gather information shall not be considered as engaging in espionage if, while so acting, he is in the uniform of his armed forces.

3. A member of the armed forces of a Party to the conflict who is a resident of territory occupied by an adverse Party and who, on behalf of the Party on which he depends, gathers or attempts to gather information of military value within that territory shall not be considered as engaging in espionage unless he does so through an act of false pretences or deliberately in a clandestine manner. Moreover, such a resident shall not lose his right to the status of prisoner of war and may not be treated as a spy unless he is captured while engaging in espionage.

4. A member of the armed forces of a Party to the conflict who is not a resident of territory occupied by an adverse Party and who has engaged in espionage in that territory shall not lose his right to the status of prisoner of war and may not be treated as a spy unless he is captured before he has rejoined the armed forces to which he belongs.

Article 47. *Mercenaries*

1. A mercenary shall not have the right to be a combatant or a prisoner of war.

2. A mercenary is any person who:

(*a*) is specially recruited locally or abroad in order to fight in an armed conflict;

(*b*) does, in fact, take a direct part in the hostilities;

(*c*) is motivated to take part in the hostilities essentially by the desire for private gain and, in fact, is promised, by or on behalf of a Party to the conflict, material compensation substantially in excess of that promised or paid to combatants of similar ranks and functions in the armed forces of that Party;

(*d*) is neither a national of a Party to the conflict nor a resident of territory controlled by a Party to the conflict;

(*e*) is not a member of the armed forces of a Party to the conflict; and

(*f*) has not been sent by a State which is not a Party to the conflict on official duty as a member of its armed forces.

PART IV. CIVILIAN POPULATION

Section I. General protection against effects of hostilities

Chapter I. Basic rule and field of application

Article 48. *Basic rule*

In order to ensure respect for and protection of the civilian population and civilian objects, the Parties to the conflict shall at all times distinguish between the civilian population and combatants and between civilian objects and military objectives and accordingly shall direct their operations only against military objectives.

Article 49. *Definition of attacks and scope of application*

1. "Attacks" means acts of violence against the adversary, whether in offence or in defence.

2. The provisions of this Protocol with respect to attacks apply to all attacks in whatever territory conducted, including the national territory belonging to a Party to the conflict but under the control of an adverse Party.

3. The provisions of this Section apply to any land, air or sea warfare which may affect the civilian population, individual civilians or civilian objects on land. They further apply to all attacks from the sea or from the air against objectives on land but do not otherwise affect the rules of international law applicable in armed conflict at sea or in the air.

4. The provisions of this Section are additional to the rules concerning humanitarian protection contained in the Fourth Convention, particularly in Part II thereof, and in other international agreements binding upon the High Contracting Parties, as well as to other rules of international law relating to the protection of civilians and civilian objects on land, at sea or in the air against the effects of hostilities.

Chapter II. Civilians and civilian population

Article 50. *Definition of civilians and civilian population*

1. A civilian is any person who does not belong to one of the categories of persons referred to in Article 4 A (1), (2), (3) and (6) of the Third Convention and in Article 43 of this Protocol. In case of doubt whether a person is a civilian, that person shall be considered to be a civilian.

2. The civilian population comprises all persons who are civilians.

3. The presence within the civilian population of individuals who do not come within the definition of civilians does not deprive the population of its civilian character.

Article 51. *Protection of the civilian population*

1. The civilian population and individual civilians shall enjoy general protection against dangers arising from military operations. To give effect to this protection, the following rules, which are additional to other applicable rules of international law, shall be

observed in all circumstances.

2. The civilian population as such, as well as individual civilians, shall not be the object of attack. Acts or threats of violence the primary purpose of which is to spread terror among the civilian population are prohibited.

3. Civilians shall enjoy the protection afforded by this Section, unless and for such time as they take a direct part in hostilities.

4. Indiscriminate attacks are prohibited. Indiscriminate attacks are:

(a) those which are not directed at a specific military objective;

(b) those which employ a method or means of combat which cannot be directed at a specific military objective; or

(c) those which employ a method or means of combat the effects of which cannot be limited as required by this Protocol;

and consequently, in each such case, are of a nature to strike military objectives and civilians or civilian objects without distinction.

5. Among others, the following types of attacks are to be considered as indiscriminate:

(a) an attack by bombardment by any methods or means which treats as a single military objective a number of clearly separated and distinct military objectives located in a city, town, village or other area containing a similar concentration of civilians or civilian objects; and

(b) an attack which may be expected to cause incidental loss of civilian life, injury to civilians, damage to civilian objects, or a combination thereof, which would be excessive in relation to the concrete and direct military advantage anticipated.

6. Attacks against the civilian population or civilians by way of reprisals are prohibited.

7. The presence or movements of the civilian population or individual civilians shall not be used to render certain points or areas immune from military operations, in particular in attempts to shield military objectives from attacks or to shield, favour or impede military operations. The Parties to the conflict shall not direct the movement of the civilian population or individual civilians in order to attempt to shield military objectives from attacks or to shield military operations.

8. Any violation of these prohibitions shall not release the Parties to the conflict from their legal obligations with respect to the civilian population and civilians, including the obligation to take the precautionary measures provided for in Article 57.

Chapter III. Civilian objects

Article 52. *General protection of civilian objects*

1. Civilian objects shall not be the object of attack or of reprisals. Civilian objects are all objects which are not military objectives as defined in paragraph 2.

2. Attacks shall be limited strictly to military objectives. In so far as objects are concerned, military objectives are limited to those objects which by their nature, location, purpose or use make an effective contribution to military action and whose total or partial destruction, capture or neutralization, in the circumstances ruling at the time, offers a definite military advantage.

3. In case of doubt whether an object which is normally dedicated to civilian purposes, such as a place of worship, a house or other dwelling or a school, is being used to make an effective contribution to military action, it shall be presumed not to be so used.

Article 53. *Protection of cultural objects and of places of worship*

Without prejudice to the provisions of the Hague Convention for the Protection of Cultural Property in the Event of Armed Conflict of 14 May 1954, and of other relevant international instruments, it is prohibited:

(a) to commit any acts of hostility directed against the historic monuments, works of art or places of worship which constitute the cultural or spiritual heritage of peoples;

(b) to use such objects in support of the military effort;

(c) to make such objects the object of reprisals.

Article 54. *Protection of objects indispensable to the survival of the civilian population*

1. Starvation of civilians as a method of warfare is prohibited.

2. It is prohibited to attack, destroy, remove or render useless objects indispensable to the survival of the civilian population, such as foodstuffs, agricultural areas for the production of foodstuffs, crops, livestock, drinking water installations and supplies and irrigation works, for the specific purpose of denying them for their sustenance value to the civilian population or to the adverse Party, whatever the motive, whether in order to starve out civilians, to cause them to move away, or for any other motive.

3. The prohibitions in paragraph 2 shall not apply to such of the objects covered by it as are used by an adverse Party:

(a) as sustenance solely for the members of its armed forces; or

(b) if not as sustenance, then in direct support of military action, provided, however, that in no event shall actions against these objects be taken which may be expected to leave the civilian population with such inadequate food or water as to cause its starvation or force its movement.

4. These objects shall not be made the object of reprisals.

5. In recognition of the vital requirements of any Party to the conflict in the defence of its national territory against invasion, derogation from the prohibitions contained in paragraph 2 may be made by a Party to the conflict within such territory under its own control where required by imperative military necessity.

Article 55. *Protection of the natural environment*

1. Care shall be taken in warfare to protect the natural environment against widespread, long-term and severe damage. This protection includes a prohibition of the use of methods or means of warfare which are intended or may be expected to cause such damage to the natural environment and thereby to prejudice the health or survival of the population.

2. Attacks against the natural environment by way of reprisals are prohibited.

Article 56. *Protection of works and installations containing dangerous forces*

1. Works or installations containing dangerous forces, namely dams, dykes and nuclear electrical generating stations, shall not be made the object of attack, even where these objects are military objectives, if such attack may cause the release of dangerous forces and consequent severe losses among the civilian population. Other military objectives located at or in the vicinity of these works or installations shall not be made the object of attack if such attack may cause the release of dangerous forces from the works or installations and consequent severe losses among the civilian population.

2. The special protection against attack provided by paragraph 1 shall cease:

(*a*) for a dam or a dyke only if it is used for other than its normal function and in regular, significant and direct support of military operations and if such attack is the only feasible way to terminate such support;

(*b*) for a nuclear electrical generating station only if it provides electric power in regular, significant and direct support of military operations and if such attack is the only feasible way to terminate such support;

(*c*) for other military objectives located at or in the vicinity of these works or installations only if they are used in regular, significant and direct support of military operations and if such attack is the only feasible way to terminate such support.

3. In all cases, the civilian population and individual civilians shall remain entitled to all the protection accorded them by international law, including the protection of the precautionary measures provided for in Article 57. If the protection ceases and any of the works, installations or military objectives mentioned in paragraph 1 is attacked, all practical precautions shall be taken to avoid the release of the dangerous forces.

4. It is prohibited to make any of the works, installations or military objectives mentioned in paragraph 1 the object of reprisals.

5. The Parties to the conflict shall endeavour to avoid locating any military objectives in the vicinity of the works or installations mentioned in paragraph 1. Nevertheless, installations erected for the sole purpose of defending the protected works or installations from attack are permissible and shall not themselves be made the object of attack, provided that they are not used in hostilities except for defensive actions necessary to respond to attacks against the protected works or installations and that their armament is limited to weapons capable only of repelling hostile action against the protected works or installations.

6. The High Contracting Parties and the Parties to the conflict are urged to conclude further agreements among themselves to provide additional protection for objects containing dangerous forces.

7. In order to facilitate the identification of the objects protected by this article, the Parties to the conflict may mark them with a special sign consisting of a group of three bright orange circles placed on the same axis, as specified in Article 16 of Annex I to this Protocol. The absence of such marking in no way relieves any Party to the conflict of its obligations under this Article.

Chapter IV. Precautionary measures

Article 57. *Precautions in attack*

1. In the conduct of military operations, constant care shall be taken to spare the civilian population, civilians and civilian objects.

2. With respect to attacks, the following precautions shall be taken:

(*a*) those who plan or decide upon an attack shall:

(i) do everything feasible to verify that the objectives to be attacked are neither civilians nor civilian objects and are not subject to special protection but are military objectives within the meaning of paragraph 2 of Article 52 and that it is not prohibited by the provisions of this Protocol to attack them;

(ii) take all feasible precautions in the choice of means and methods of attack with a view to avoiding, and in any event to minimizing, incidental loss of civilian life, injury to civilians and damage to civilian objects;

(iii) refrain from deciding to launch any attack which may be expected to cause incidental loss of civilian life, injury to civilians, damage to civilian objects, or a combination thereof, which would be excessive in relation to the concrete and direct military advantage anticipated;

(*b*) an attack shall be cancelled or suspended if it becomes apparent that the objective is not a military one or is subject to special protection or that the attack may be expected to cause incidental loss of civilian life, injury to civilians, damage to civilian objects, or a combination thereof, which would be excessive in relation to the concrete and direct military advantage anticipated;

(*c*) effective advance warning shall be given of attacks which may affect the civilian population, unless circumstances do not permit.

3. When a choice is possible between several military objectives for obtaining a similar military advantage, the objective to be selected shall be that the attack on which may

be expected to cause the least danger to civilian lives and to civilian objects.

4. In the conduct of military operations at sea or in the air, each Party to the conflict shall, in conformity with its rights and duties under the rules of international law applicable in armed conflict, take all reasonable precautions to avoid losses of civilian lives and damage to civilian objects.

5. No provision of this article may be construed as authorizing any attacks against the civilian population, civilians or civilian objects.

Article 58. *Precautions against the effects of attacks*

The Parties to the conflict shall, to the maximum extent feasible:

(*a*) without prejudice to Article 49 of the Fourth Convention, endeavour to remove the civilian population, individual civilians and civilian objects under their control from the vicinity of military objectives;

(*b*) avoid locating military objectives within or near densely populated areas;

(*c*) take the other necessary precautions to protect the civilian population, individual civilians and civilian objects under their control against the dangers resulting from military operations.

Chapter V. Localities and zones under special protection

Article 59. *Non-defended localities*

1. It is prohibited for the Parties to the conflict to attack, by any means whatsoever, non-defended localities.

2. The appropriate authorities of a Party to the conflict may declare as a non-defended locality any inhabited place near or in a zone where armed forces are in contact which is open for occupation by an adverse Party. Such a locality shall fulfil the following conditions:

(*a*) all combatants, as well as mobile weapons and mobile military equipment must have been evacuated;

(*b*) no hostile use shall be made of fixed military installations or establishments;

(*c*) no acts of hostility shall be committed by the authorities or by the population; and

(*d*) no activities in support of military operations shall be undertaken.

3. The presence, in this locality, of persons specially protected under the Conventions and this Protocol, and of police forces retained for the sole purpose of maintaining law and order, is not contrary to the conditions laid down in paragraph 2.

4. The declaration made under paragraph 2 shall be addressed to the adverse Party and shall define and describe, as precisely as possible, the limits of the non-defended locality. The Party to the conflict to which the declaration is addressed shall acknowledge its receipt and shall treat locality as a non-defended locality unless the conditions laid down in paragraph 2 are not in fact fulfilled,

in which event it shall immediately so inform the Party making the declaration. Even if the conditions laid down in paragraph 2 are not fulfilled, the locality shall continue to enjoy the protection provided by the other provisions of this Protocol and the other rules of international law applicable in armed conflict.

5. The Parties to the conflict may agree on the establishment of non-defended localities even if such localities do not fulfil the conditions laid down in paragraph 2. The agreement should define and describe, as precisely as possible, the limits of the nondefended locality; if necessary, it may lay down the methods of supervision.

6. The Party which is in control of a locality governed by such an agreement shall mark it, so far as possible, by such signs as may be agreed upon with the other Party, which shall be displayed where they are clearly visible, especially on its perimeter and limits and on highways.

7. A locality loses its status as a non-defended locality when it ceases to fulfil the conditions laid down in paragraph 2 or in the agreement referred to in paragraph 5. In such an eventuality, the locality shall continue to enjoy the protection provided by the other provisions of this Protocol and the other rules of international law applicable in armed conflict.

Article 60. *Demilitarized zones*

1. It is prohibited for the Parties to the conflict to extend their military operations to zones on which they have conferred by agreement the status of demilitarized zone, if such extension is contrary to the terms of this agreement.

2. The agreement shall be an express agreement, may be concluded verbally or in writing, either directly or through a Protecting Power or any impartial humanitarian organization, and may consist of reciprocal and concordant declarations. The agreement may be concluded in peacetime, as well as after the outbreak of hostilities, and should define and describe, as precisely as possible, the limits of the demilitarized zone and, if necessary, lay down the methods of supervision.

3. The subject of such an agreement shall normally be any zone which fulfils the following conditions:

(*a*) all combatants, as well as mobile weapons and mobile military equipment, must have been evacuated;

(*b*) no hostile use shall be made of fixed military installations or establishments;

(*c*) no acts of hostility shall be committed by the authorities or by the population; and

(*d*) any activity linked to the military effort must have ceased.

The Parties to the conflict shall agree upon the interpretation to be given to the condition laid down in sub-paragraph (*d*) and upon persons to be admitted to the demilitarized zone other than those mentioned in paragraph 4.

4. The presence, in this zone, of persons specially protected under the Conventions and this Protocol, and of police forces retained for the sole purpose of maintaining law and order, is not contrary to the conditions laid down in paragraph 3.

5. The Party which is in control of such a zone shall mark it, so far as possible, by such signs as may be agreed upon with the other Party, which shall be displayed where they are clearly visible, especially on its perimeter and limits and on highways.

6. If the fighting draws near to a demilitarized zone, and if the Parties to the conflict have so agreed, none of them may use the zone for purposes related to the conduct of military operations or unilaterally revoke its status.

7. If one of the Parties to the conflict commits a material breach of the provisions of paragraphs 3 or 6, the other Party shall be released from its obligations under the agreement conferring upon the zone the status of demilitarized zone. In such an eventuality, the zone loses its status but shall continue to enjoy the protection provided by the other provisions of this Protocol and the other rules of international law applicable in armed conflict.

Chapter VI. Civil defence

Article 61. *Definitions and scope*

For the purposes of this Protocol:

(*a*) "civil defence" means the performance of some or all of the undermentioned humanitarian tasks intended to protect the civilian population against the dangers, and to help it to recover from the immediate effects, of hostilities or disasters and also to provide the conditions necessary for its survival. These tasks are:

(i) warning;
(ii) evacuation;
(iii) management of shelters;
(iv) management of blackout measures;
(v) rescue;
(vi) medical services, including first aid, and religious assistance;
(vii) fire-fighting;
(viii) detection and marking of danger areas;
(ix) decontamination and similar protective measures;
(x) provision of emergency accommodation and supplies;
(xi) emergency assistance in the restoration and maintenance of order in distressed areas;
(xii) emergency repair of indispensable public utilities;
(xiii) emergency disposal of the dead;
(xiv) assistance in the preservation of objects essential for survival;
(xv) complementary activities necessary to carry out any of the tasks mentioned above, including, but not limited to, planning and organization;

(*b*) "civil defence organizations" means those establishments and other units which are organized or authorized by the competent authorities of a Party to the conflict to perform any of the tasks mentioned under subparagraph (*a*), and which are assigned and devoted exclusively to such tasks;

(*c*) "personnel" of civil defence organizations means those persons assigned by a Party to the conflict exclusively to the performance of the tasks mentioned under subparagraph (*a*), including personnel assigned by the competent authority of that Party exclusively to the administration of these organizations;

(*d*) "*matériel*" of civil defence organizations means equipment, supplies and transports used by these organizations for the performance of the tasks mentioned under subparagraph (*a*).

Article 62. *General protection*

1. Civilian civil defence organizations and their personnel shall be respected and protected, subject to the provisions of this Protocol, particularly the provisions of this Section. They shall be entitled to perform their civil defence tasks except in case of imperative military necessity.

2. The provisions of paragraph 1 shall also apply to civilians who, although not members of civilian civil defence organizations, respond to an appeal from the competent authorities and perform civil defence tasks under their control.

3. Buildings and *matériel* used for civil defence purposes and shelters provided for the civilian population are covered by Article 52. Objects used for civil defence purposes may not be destroyed or diverted from their proper use except by the Party to which they belong.

Article 63. *Civil defence in occupied territories*

1. In occupied territories, civilian civil defence organizations shall receive from the authorities the facilities necessary for the performance of their tasks. In no circumstances shall their personnel be compelled to perform activities which would interfere with the proper performance of these tasks. The Occupying Power shall not change the structure or personnel of such organizations in any way which might jeopardize the efficient performance of their mission. These organizations shall not be required to give priority to the nationals or interests of that Power.

2. The Occupying Power shall not compel, coerce or induce civilian civil defence organizations to perform their tasks in any manner prejudicial to the interests of the civilian population.

3. The Occupying Power may disarm civil defence personnel for reasons of security.

4. The Occupying Power shall neither divert from their proper use nor requisition buildings or *matériel* belonging to or used by civil defence organizations if such diversion or requisition would be harmful to the

civilian population.

5. Provided that the general rule in paragraph 4 continues to be observed, the Occupying Power may requisition or divert these resources, subject to the following particular conditions:

(a) that the buildings or *matériel* are necessary for other needs of the civilian population; and

(b) that the requisition or diversion continues only while such necessity exists.

6. The Occupying Power shall neither divert nor requisition shelters provided for the use of the civilian population or needed by such population.

Article 64. *Civilian civil defence organizations of neutral or other States not Parties to the conflict and international co-ordinating organizations*

1. Articles 62, 63, 65 and 66 shall also apply to the personnel and *matériel* of civilian civil defence organizations of neutral or other States not Parties to the conflict which perform civil defence tasks mentioned in Article 61 in the territory of a Party to the conflict, with the consent and under the control of that Party. Notification of such assistance shall be given as soon as possible to any adverse Party concerned. In no circumstances shall this activity be deemed to be an interference in the conflict. This activity should, however, be performed with due regard to the security interests of the Parties to the conflict concerned.

2. The Parties to the conflict receiving the assistance referred to in paragraph 1 and the High Contracting Parties granting it should facilitate international co-ordination of such civil defence actions when appropriate. In such cases the relevant international organizations are covered by the provisions of this Chapter.

3. In occupied territories, the Occupying Power may only exclude or restrict the activities of civilian civil defence organizations of neutral or other States not Parties to the conflict and of international co-ordinating organizations if it can ensure the adequate performance of civil defence tasks from its own resources or those of the occupied territory.

Article 65. *Cessation of protection*

1. The protection to which civilian civil defence organizations, their personnel, buildings, shelters and *matériel* are entitled shall not cease unless they commit or are used to commit, outside their proper tasks, acts harmful to the enemy. Protection may, however, cease only after a warning has been given setting, whenever appropriate, a reasonable time limit, and after such warning has remained unheeded.

2. The following shall not be considered as acts harmful to the enemy:

(a) that civil defence tasks are carried out under the direction or control of military authorities;

(b) that civilian civil defence personnel co-operate with military personnel in the performance of civil defence tasks, or that some military personnel are attached to civilian civil defence organizations;

(c) that the performance of civil defence tasks may incidentally benefit military victims, particularly those who are *hors de combat*.

3. It shall also not be considered as an act harmful to the enemy that civilian civil defence personnel bear light individual weapons for the purpose of maintaining order or for self-defence. However, in areas where land fighting is taking place or is likely to take place, the Parties to the conflict shall undertake the appropriate measures to limit these weapons to handguns, such as pistols or revolvers, in order to assist in distinguishing between civil defence personnel and combatants. Although civil defence personnel bear other light individual weapons in such areas, they shall nevertheless be respected and protected as soon as they have been recognized as such.

4. The formation of civilian civil defence organizations along military lines, and compulsory service in them, shall also not deprive them of the protection conferred by this Chapter.

Article 66. *Identification*

1. Each Party to the conflict shall endeavour to ensure that its civil defence organizations, their personnel, buildings and *matériel*, are identifiable while they are exclusively devoted to the performance of civil defence tasks. Shelters provided for the civilian population should be similarly identifiable.

2. Each Party to the conflict shall also endeavour to adopt and implement methods and procedures which will make it possible to recognize civilian shelters as well as civil defence personnel, buildings and *matériel* on which the international distinctive sign of civil defence is displayed.

3. In occupied territories and in areas where fighting is taking place or is likely to take place, civilian civil defence personnel should be recognizable by the international distinctive sign of civil defence and by an identity card certifying their status.

4. The international distinctive sign of civil defence is an equilateral blue triangle on an orange ground when used for the protection of civil defence organizations, their personnel, buildings and *matériel* and for civilian shelters.

5. In addition to the distinctive sign, Parties to the conflict may agree upon the use of distinctive signals for civil defence identification purposes.

6. The application of the provisions of paragraphs 1 to 4 is governed by Chapter V of Annex I to this Protocol.

7. In time of peace, the sign described in paragraph 4 may, with the consent of the competent national authorities, be used for civil defence identification purposes.

8. The High Contracting Parties and the

Parties to the conflict shall take the measures necessary to supervise the display of the international distinctive sign of civil defence and to prevent and repress any misuse thereof.

9. The identification of civil defence medical and religious personnel, médical units and medical transports is also governed by Article 18.

Article 67. *Members of the armed forces and military units assigned to civil defence organizations*

1. Members of the armed forces and military units assigned to civil defence organizations shall be respected and protected, provided that:

(*a*) such personnel and such units are permanently assigned and exclusively devoted to the performance of any of the tasks mentioned in Article 61;

(*b*) if so assigned, such personnel do not perform any other military duties during the conflict;

(*c*) such personnel are clearly distinguishable from the other members of the armed forces by prominently displaying the international distinctive sign of civil defence, which shall be as large as appropriate, and such personnel are provided with the identity card referred to in Chapter V of Annex I to this Protocol certifying their status;

(*d*) such personnel and such units are equipped only with light individual weapons for the purpose of maintaining order or for self-defence. The provisions of Article 65, paragraph 3 shall also apply in this case;

(*e*) such personnel do not participate directly in hostilities, and do not commit, or are not used to commit, outside their civil defence tasks, acts harmful to the adverse Party;

(*f*) such personnel and such units perform their civil defence tasks only within the national territory of their Party.

The non-observance of the conditions stated in (*e*) above by any member of the armed forces who is bound by the conditions prescribed in (*a*) and (*b*) above is prohibited.

2. Military personnel serving within civil defence organizations shall, if they fall into the power of an adverse Party, be prisoners of war. In occupied territory they may, but only in the interest of the civilian population of that territory, be employed on civil defence tasks in so far as the need arises, provided however that, if such work is dangerous, they volunteer for such tasks.

3. The buildings and major items of equipment and transports of military units assigned to civil defence organizations shall be clearly marked with the international distinctive sign of civil defence. This distinctive sign shall be as large as appropriate.

4. The *matériel* and buildings of military units permanently assigned to civil defence organizations and exclusively devoted to the performance of civil defence tasks shall, if they fall into the hands of an adverse Party, remain subject to the laws of war. They may not be diverted from their civil defence purpose so long as they are required for the performance of civil defence tasks, except in case of imperative military necessity, unless previous arrangements have been made for adequate provision for the needs of the civilian population.

Section II. Relief in favour of the civilian population

Article 68. *Field of application*

The provisions of this Section apply to the civilian population as defined in this Protocol and are supplementary to Articles 23, 55, 59, 60, 61 and 62 and other relevant provisions of the Fourth Convention.

Article 69. *Basic needs in occupied territories*

1. In addition to the duties specified in Article 55 of the Fourth Convention concerning food and medical supplies, the Occupying Power shall, to the fullest extent of the means available to it and without any adverse distinction, also ensure the provision of clothing, bedding, means of shelter, other supplies essential to the survival of the civilian population of the occupied territory and objects necessary for religious worship.

2. Relief actions for the benefit of the civilian population of occupied territories are governed by Articles 59, 60, 61, 62, 108, 109, 110 and 111 of the Fourth Convention, and by Article 71 of this Protocol, and shall be implemented without delay.

Section III. Treatment of persons in the power of a party to the conflict

Chapter I. Field of application and protection of persons and objects
. . .

Article 75. *Fundamental guarantees*

1. In so far as they are affected by a situation referred to in Article 1 of this Protocol, persons who are in the power of a Party to the conflict and who do not benefit from more favourable treatment under the Conventions or under this Protocol shall be treated humanely in all circumstances and shall enjoy, as a minimum, the protection provided by this Article without any adverse distinction based upon race, colour, sex, language, religion or belief, political or other opinion, national or social origin, wealth, birth or other status, or on any other similar criteria. Each Party shall respect the person, honour, convictions and religious practices of all such persons.

2. The following acts are and shall remain prohibited at any time and in any place whatsoever, whether committed by civilian or by military agents:

(*a*) violence to the life, health, or physical or mental well-being of persons, in particular:
  (i) murder;
  (ii) torture of all kinds, whether physical or mental;
  (iii) corporal punishment; and

(iv) mutilation;

(*b*) outrages upon personal dignity, in particular humiliating and degrading treatment, enforced prostitution and any form of indecent assault;

(*c*) the taking of hostages;

(*d*) collective punishments; and

(*e*) threats to commit any of the foregoing acts.

3. Any person arrested, detained or interned for actions related to the armed conflict shall be informed promptly, in a language he understands, of the reasons why these measures have been taken. Except in cases of arrest or detention for penal offences, such persons shall be released with the minimum delay possible and in any event as soon as the circumstances justifying the arrest, detention or internment have ceased to exist.

4. No sentence may be passed and no penalty may be executed on a person found guilty of a penal offence related to the armed conflict except pursuant to a conviction pronounced by an impartial and regularly constituted court respecting the generally recognized principles of regular judicial procedure, which include the following:

(*a*) the procedure shall provide for an accused to be informed without delay of the particulars of the offence alleged against him and shall afford the accused before and during his trial all necessary rights and means of defence;

(*b*) no one shall be convicted of an offence except on the basis of individual penal responsibility;

(*c*) no one shall be accused or convicted of a criminal offence on account of any act or omission which did not constitute a criminal offence under the national or international law to which he was subject at the time when it was committed; nor shall a heavier penalty be imposed than that which was applicable at the time when the criminal offence was committed; if, after the commission of the offence, provision is made by law for the imposition of a lighter penalty, the offender shall benefit thereby;

(*d*) anyone charged with an offence is presumed innocent until proved guilty according to law;

(*e*) anyone charged with an offence shall have the right to be tried in his presence;

(*f*) no one shall be compelled to testify against himself or to confess guilt;

(*g*) anyone charged with an offence shall have the right to examine, or have examined, the witnesses against him and to obtain the attendance and examination of witnesses on his behalf under the same conditions as witnesses against him;

(*h*) no one shall be prosecuted or punished by the same Party for an offence in respect of which a final judgement acquitting or convicting that person has been previously pronounced under the same law and judicial procedure;

(*i*) anyone prosecuted for an offence shall have the right to have the judgement pronounced publicly; and

(*j*) a convicted person shall be advised on conviction of his judicial and other remedies and of the time limits within which they may be exercised.

. . .

Chapter III. Journalists

Article 79. *Measures of protection for journalists*

1. Journalists engaged in dangerous professional missions in areas of armed conflict shall be considered as civilians within the meaning of Article 50, paragraph 1.

. . .

PART V. EXECUTION OF THE CONVENTIONS AND OF THIS PROTOCOL

Section I. General provisions

Article 80. *Measures for execution*

1. The High Contracting Parties and the Parties to the conflict shall without delay take all necessary measures for the execution of their obligations under the Conventions and this Protocol.

2. The High Contracting Parties and the Parties to the conflict shall give orders and instructions to ensure observance of the Conventions and this Protocol, and shall supervise their execution.

. . .

Article 83. *Dissemination*

1. The High Contracting Parties undertake, in time of peace as in time of armed conflict, to disseminate the Conventions and this Protocol as widely as possible in their respective countries and, in particular, to include the study thereof in their programmes of military instruction and to encourage the study thereof by the civilian population, so that those instruments may become known to the armed forces and to the civilian population.

2. Any military or civilian authorities who, in time of armed conflict, assume responsibilities in respect of the application of the Conventions and this Protocol shall be fully acquainted with the text thereof.

Article 84. *Rules of application*

The High Contracting Parties shall communicate to one another, as soon as possible, through the depositary and, as appropriate, through the Protecting Powers, their official translations of this Protocol, as well as the laws and regulations which they may adopt to ensure its application.

Section II. Repression of breaches of the conventions, and of this Protocol

Article 85. *Repression of breaches of this Protocol*

1. The provisions of the Conventions relating to the repression of breaches and grave breaches, supplemented by this Section, shall apply to the repression of breaches and grave breaches of this Protocol.

2. Acts described as grave breaches in the Conventions are grave breaches of this Protocol if committed against persons in the power of an adverse Party protected by Articles 44, 45 and 73 of this Protocol, or against the wounded, sick and shipwrecked of the adverse Party who are protected by this Protocol, or against those medical or religious personnel, medical units or medical transports which are under the control of the adverse Party and are protected by this Protocol.

3. In addition to the grave breaches defined in Article 11, the following acts shall be regarded as grave breaches of this Protocol, when committed wilfully, in violation of the relevant provisions of this Protocol, and causing death or serious injury to body or health:

(a) making the civilian population or individual civilians the object of attack;

(b) launching an indiscriminate attack affecting the civilian population or civilian objects in the knowledge that such attack will cause excessive loss of life, injury to civilians or damage to civilian objects, as defined in Article 57, paragraph 2 (a) (iii);

(c) launching an attack against works or installations containing dangerous forces in the knowledge that such attack will cause excessive loss of life, injury to civilians or damage to civilian objects, as defined in Article 57, paragraph 2 (a) (iii);

(d) making non-defended localities and demilitarized zones the object of attack;

(e) making a person the object of attack in the knowledge that he is *hors de combat*;

(f) the perfidious use, in violation of Article 37, of the distinctive emblem of the red cross, red crescent or red lion and sun or of other protective signs recognized by the Conventions or this Protocol.

4. In addition to the grave breaches defined in the preceding paragraphs and in the Conventions, the following shall be regarded as grave breaches of this Protocol, when committed wilfully and in violation of the Conventions or the Protocol:

(a) the transfer by the occupying Power of parts of its own civilian population into the territory it occupies, or the deportation or transfer of all or parts of the population of the occupied territory within or outside this territory, in violation of Article 49 of the Fourth Convention;

(b) unjustifiable delay in the repatriation of prisoners of war or civilians;

(c) practices of *apartheid* and other inhuman and degrading practices involving outrages upon personal dignity, based on racial discrimination;

(d) making the clearly-recognized historic monuments, works of art or places of worship which constitute the cultural or spiritual heritage of peoples and to which special protection has been given by special arrangement, for example, within the framework of a competent international organization, the object of attack, causing as a result extensive destruction thereof, where there is no evidence of the violation by the adverse Party of Article 53, sub-paragraph (b), and when such historic monuments, works of art and places of worship are not located in the immediate proximity of military objectives;

(e) depriving a person protected by the Conventions or referred to in paragraph 2 of this Article of the rights of fair and regular trial.

5. Without prejudice to the application of the Conventions and of this Protocol, grave breaches of these instruments shall be regarded as war crimes.

Article 86. *Failure to act*

1. The High Contracting Parties and the Parties to the conflict shall repress grave breaches, and take measures necessary to suppress all other breaches, of the Conventions or of this Protocol which result from a failure to act when under a duty to do so.

2. The fact that a breach of the Conventions or of this Protocol was committed by a subordinate does not absolve his superiors from penal or disciplinary responsibility, as the case may be, if they knew, or had information which should have enabled them to conclude in the circumstances at the time, that he was committing or was going to commit such a breach and if they did not take all feasible measures within their power to prevent or repress the breach.

Article 87. *Duty of commanders*

1. The High Contracting Parties and the Parties to the conflict shall require military commanders, with respect to members of the armed forces under their command and other persons under their control, to prevent and, where necessary, to suppress and report to competent authorities breaches of the Conventions and of this Protocol.

2. In order to prevent and suppress breaches, High Contracting Parties and Parties to the conflict shall require that, commensurate with their level of responsibility, commanders ensure that members of the armed forces under their command are aware of their obligations under the Conventions and this Protocol.

3. The High Contracting Parties and Parties to the conflict shall require any commander who is aware that subordinates or other persons under his control are going to commit or have committed a breach of the Conventions or of this Protocol, to initiate such steps as are necessary to prevent such violations of the Conventions or this Protocol, and, where appropriate, to initiate disciplinary or penal action against violators thereof.

. . .

Article 90. *International Fact-Finding Commission*

1. (*a*) An International Fact-Finding Commission (hereinafter referred to as "the Commission") consisting of fifteen members of high moral standing and acknowledged impartiality shall be established.

(*b*) When not less than twenty High Contracting Parties have agreed to accept the competence of the Commission pursuant to paragraph 2, the depositary shall then, and at intervals of five years thereafter, convene a meeting of representatives of those High Contracting Parties for the purpose of electing the members of the Commission. At the meeting, the representatives shall elect the members of the Commission by secret ballot from a list of persons to which each of those High Contracting Parties may nominate one person.

(*c*) The members of the Commission shall serve in their personal capacity and shall hold office until the election of new members at the ensuing meeting.

(*d*) At the election, the High Contracting Parties shall ensure that the persons to be elected to the Commission individually possess the qualifications required and that, in the Commission as a whole, equitable geographical representation is assured.

(*e*) In the case of a casual vacancy, the Commission itself shall fill the vacancy, having due regard to the provisions of the preceding sub-paragraphs.

(*f*) The depositary shall make available to the Commission the necessary administrative facilities for the performance of its functions.

2. (*a*) The High Contracting Parties may at the time of signing, ratifying or acceding to the Protocol, or at any other subsequent time, declare that they recognize *ipso facto* and without special agreement, in relation to any other High Contracting Party accepting the same obligation, the competence of the Commission to enquire into allegations by such other Party, as authorized by this Article.

(*b*) The declarations referred to above shall be deposited with the depositary, which shall transmit copies thereof to the High Contracting Parties.

(*c*) The Commission shall be competent to:

(i) enquire into any facts alleged to be a grave breach as defined in the Conventions and this Protocol or other serious violation of the Conventions or of this Protocol;

(ii) facilitate, through its good offices, the restoration of an attitude of respect for the Conventions and this Protocol.

(*d*) In other situations, the Commission shall institute an enquiry at the request of a Party to the conflict only with the consent of the other Party or Parties concerned.

(*e*) Subject to the foregoing provisions of this paragraph, the provisions of Article 52 of the First Convention, Article 53 of the Second Convention, Article 132 of the Third Convention and Article 149 of the Fourth Convention shall continue to apply to any alleged violation of the Conventions and shall extend to any alleged violation of this Protocol.

3. (*a*) Unless otherwise agreed by the Parties concerned, all enquiries shall be undertaken by a Chamber consisting of seven members appointed as follows:

(i) five members of the Commission, not nationals of any Party to the conflict, appointed by the President of the Commission on the basis of equitable representation of the geographical areas, after consultation with the Parties to the conflict;

(ii) two *ad hoc* members, not nationals of any Party to the conflict, one to be appointed by each side.

(*b*) Upon receipt of the request for an enquiry, the President of the Commission shall specify an appropriate time limit for setting up a Chamber. If any *ad hoc* member has not been appointed within the time limit, the President shall immediately appoint such additional member or members of the Commission as may be necessary to complete the membership of the Chamber.

4. (*a*) The Chamber set up under paragraph 3 to undertake an enquiry shall invite the Parties to the conflict to assist it and to present evidence. The Chamber may also seek such other evidence as it deems appropriate and may carry out an investigation of the situation *in loco*.

(*b*) All evidence shall be fully disclosed to the Parties, which shall have the right to comment on it to the Commission.

(*c*) Each Party shall have the right to challenge such evidence.

5. (*a*) The Commission shall submit to the Parties a report on the findings of fact of the Chamber, with such recommendations as it may deem appropriate.

(*b*) If the Chamber is unable to secure sufficient evidence for factual and impartial findings, the Commission shall state the reasons for that inability.

(*c*) The Commission shall not report its findings publicly, unless all the Parties to the conflict have requested the Commission to do so.

6. The Commission shall establish its own rules, including rules for the presidency of the Commission and the presidency of the Chamber. Those rules shall ensure that the functions of the President of the Commission are exercised at all times and that, in the case of an enquiry, they are exercised by a person who is not a national of a Party to the conflict.

7. The administrative expenses of the Commission shall be met by contributions from the High Contracting Parties which made declarations under paragraph 2, and by voluntary contributions. The Party or Parties to the conflict requesting an enquiry shall advance the necessary funds for expenses incurred by a Chamber and shall be reimbursed by the Party or Parties against which the allegations are made to the extent of fifty percent

of the costs of the Chamber. Where there are counter-allegations before the Chamber each side shall advance fifty per cent of the necessary funds.

Article 91. *Responsibility*

A Party to the conflict which violates the provisions of the Conventions or of this Protocol shall, if the case demands, be liable to pay compensation. It shall be responsible for all acts committed by persons forming part of its armed forces.

PART VI. FINAL PROVISIONS

Article 92. *Signature*

This Protocol shall be open for signature by the Parties to the Conventions six months after the signing of the Final Act and will remain open for a period of twelve months.

Article 93. *Ratification*

This Protocol shall be ratified as soon as possible. The instruments of ratification shall be deposited with the Swiss Federal Council, depositary of the Conventions.

Article 94. *Accession*

This Protocol shall be open for accession by any Party to the Conventions which has not signed it. The instruments of accession shall be deposited with the depositary.

Article 95. *Entry into force*

1. This Protocol shall enter into force six months after two instruments of ratification or accession have been deposited.
2. For each Party to the Conventions thereafter ratifying or acceding to this Protocol, it shall enter into force six months after the deposit by such Party of its instrument of ratification or accession.

. . .

Article 99. *Denunciation*

1. In case a High Contracting Party should denounce this Protocol, the denunciation shall only take effect one year after receipt of the instrument of denunciation. If, however, on the expiry of that year the denouncing Party is engaged in one of the situations referred to in Article 1, the denunciation shall not take effect before the end of the armed conflict or occupation and not, in any case, before operations connected with the final release, repatriation or re-establishment of the persons protected by the Conventions or this Protocol have been terminated.
2. The denunciation shall be notified in writing to the depositary, which shall transmit it to all the High Contracting Parties.
3. The denunciation shall have effect only in respect of the denouncing Party.
4. Any denunciation under paragraph 1 shall not affect the obligations already incurred, by reason of the armed conflict, under this Protocol by such denouncing

Party in respect of any act committed before this denunciation becomes effective.

. . .

Protocol I was worked out at the Diplomatic Conference which held its sessions in 1974–77. At the same time the Conference adopted a Protocol additional to the Geneva Conventions of 12 August 1949 and relating to the protection of victims of non-international armed conflicts (Protocol II).

Source: *Protocols additional to the Geneva Conventions of 12 August 1949. Resolutions of the Diplomatic Conference. Extracts from the Final Act of the Diplomatic Conference (International Committee of the Red Cross, Geneva, 1977)*

Parties: Bangladesh, Bahamas, Botswana, Cyprus (only Protocol I), Ecuador, El Salvador, Finland, Gabon, Ghana, Jordan, Libya, Lao People's Democratic Republic, Mauritania, Niger, Sweden, Tunisia, Viet Nam (only Protocol I), Yugoslavia

---

STATEMENTS BY THE USSR, THE USA AND THE UK ON SECURITY ASSURANCES

STATEMENT BY THE FOREIGN MINISTER OF THE USSR, MADE AT NEW YORK ON 26 MAY 1978 (excerpt):

. . .

From the rostrum of the United Nations special session our country declares that the Soviet Union will never use nuclear weapons against those States which renounce the production and acquisition of such weapons and do not have them on their territories.

. . .

Source: UN document A/S–10/PV.5, 26 May 1978

STATEMENT BY THE US SECRETARY OF STATE, MADE AT WASHINGTON, D.C., ON 12 JUNE 1978 (excerpt):

. . .

The United States will not use nuclear weapons against any non-nuclear-weapon State party to the Treaty on the Non-Proliferation of Nuclear Weapons or any comparable internationally binding commitment not to acquire nuclear explosive devices, except in the case of an attack on the United States, its territories or armed forces, or its allies, by such a State allied to a nuclear-weapon State, or associated with a nuclear-weapon State in carrying out or sustaining the attack.

. . .

Source: UN document A/S–10/AC.1/30, 13 June 1978

211

STATEMENT BY THE UK
REPRESENTATIVE TO THE UN, MADE
AT NEW YORK ON 28 JUNE 1978
(excerpt):
. . .

I accordingly give the following assurance, on behalf of my Government, to non-nuclear-weapon States which are parties to the Non-Proliferation Treaty or to other internationally binding commitments not to manufacture or acquire nuclear explosive devices: Britain undertakes not to use nuclear weapons against such States except in the case of an attack on the United Kingdom, its dependent territories, its armed forces or its allies by such a State in association or alliance with a nuclear-weapon State.

Source: UN document A/S-10/PV.26, 28 June 1978

STATEMENT BY THE USSR ON THE BACKFIRE BOMBER

Signed at Vienna on 16 June 1979

On 16 June 1979, President Brezhnev handed President Carter the following written statement:

"The Soviet side informs the United States side that the Soviet 'Tu-22M' airplane, called 'Backfire' in the United States, is a medium-range bomber and that it does not intend to give this airplane the capability of operating at intercontinental distances. In this connexion, the Soviet side states that it will not increase the radius of action of this airplane in such a way as to enable it to strike targets on the territory of the United States. Nor does it intend to give it such a capability in any other manner, including by in-flight refuelling. At the same time, the Soviet side states that it will not increase the production rate of this airplane as compared to the present rate."

President Brezhnev confirmed that the Soviet Backfire production rate would not exceed 30 per year.

President Carter stated that the United States enters into the SALT II agreement on the basis of the commitments contained in the Soviet statement and that it considers the carrying out of these commitments to be essential to the obligations assumed under the Treaty.

Source: Committee on Disarmament document CD/29, 2 July 1979

TREATY BETWEEN THE USA AND THE USSR ON THE LIMITATION OF STRATEGIC OFFENSIVE ARMS (SALT II TREATY)*

PROTOCOL TO THE TREATY BETWEEN THE USA AND THE USSR ON THE LIMITATION OF STRATEGIC OFFENSIVE ARMS*

AGREED STATEMENTS AND COMMON UNDERSTANDINGS REGARDING THE TREATY BETWEEN THE USA AND THE USSR ON THE LIMITATION OF STRATEGIC OFFENSIVE ARMS

Signed at Vienna on 18 June 1979
Not in force by 1 October 1981

These documents were signed separately. However, for the convenience of the reader, the Treaty and the Protocol are reproduced jointly with the Agreed Statements and Common Understandings, as they pertain to particular Article paragraphs.

TREATY

The United States of America and the Union of Soviet Socialist Republics, hereinafter referred to as the Parties,

Conscious that nuclear war would have devastating consequences for all mankind,

Proceeding from the Basic Principles of Relations Between the United States of America and the Union of Soviet Socialist Republics of 29 May 1972,

Attaching particular significance to the limitation of strategic arms and determined to continue their efforts begun with the Treaty on the Limitation of Anti-Ballistic Missile Systems and the Interim Agreement on Certain Measures with Respect to the Limitation of Strategic Offensive Arms, of 26 May 1972,

Convinced that the additional measures limiting strategic offensive arms provided for in this Treaty will contribute to the improvement of relations between the Parties, help to reduce the risk of outbreak of nuclear war and strengthen international peace and security,

Mindful of their obligations under Article VI of the Treaty on the Non-Proliferation of Nuclear Weapons,

Guided by the principle of equality and equal security,

Recognizing that the strengthening of strategic stability meets the interests of the Parties and the interests of international security,

---

* Index to the SALT II Agreements can be found in Appendix B.

Reaffirming their desire to take measures for the further limitation and for the further reduction of strategic arms, having in mind the goal of achieving general and complete disarmament,

Declaring their intention to undertake in the near future negotiations further to limit and further to reduce strategic offensive arms,

Have agreed as follows:

Article I

Each Party undertakes, in accordance with the provisions of this Treaty, to limit strategic offensive arms quantitatively and qualitatively, to exercise restraint in the development of new types of strategic offensive arms, and to adopt other measures provided for in this Treaty.

Article II

For the purposes of this Treaty:

1. Intercontinental ballistic missile (ICBM) launchers are land-based launchers of ballistic missiles capable of a range in excess of the shortest distance between the northeastern border of the continental part of the territory of the United States of America and the northwestern border of the continental part of the territory of the Union of Soviet Socialist Republics, that is, a range in excess of 5,500 kilometres.

AGREED STATEMENTS AND COMMON UNDERSTANDINGS

To Paragraph 1 of Article II of the Treaty

First Agreed Statement. *The term "intercontinental ballistic missile launchers", as defined in paragraph 1 of Article II of the Treaty, includes all launchers which have been developed and tested for launching ICBMs. If a launcher has been developed and tested for launching an ICBM, all launchers of that type shall be considered to have been developed and tested for launching ICBMs.*

First Common Understanding. *If a launcher contains or launches an ICBM, that launcher shall be considered to have been developed and tested for launching ICBMs.*

Second Common Understanding. *If a launcher has been developed and tested for launching an ICBM, all launchers of that type, except for ICBM test and training launchers, shall be included in the aggregate numbers of strategic offensive arms provided for in Article III of the Treaty, pursuant to the provisions of Article VI of the Treaty.*

Third Common Understanding. *The 177 former Atlas and Titan I ICBM launchers of the United States of America, which are no longer operational and are partially dismantled, shall not be considered as subject to the limitations provided for in the Treaty.*

Second Agreed Statement. *After the date on which the Protocol ceases to be in force, mobile ICBM launchers shall be subject to the relevant limitations provided for in the Treaty which are applicable to ICBM launchers, unless the Parties agree that mobile ICBM launchers shall not be deployed after that date.*

2. Submarine-launched ballistic missile (SLBM) launchers are launchers of ballistic missiles installed on any nuclear-powered submarine or launchers of modern ballistic missiles installed on any submarine, regardless of its type.

To Paragraph 2 of Article II of the Treaty

Agreed Statement. *Modern submarine-launched ballistic missiles are: for the United States of America, missiles installed in all nuclear-powered submarines; for the Union of Soviet Socialist Republics, missiles of the type installed in nuclear-powered submarines made operational since 1965; and for both Parties, submarine-launched ballistic missiles first flight-tested since 1965 and installed in any submarine, regardless of its type.*

3. Heavy bombers are considered to be:

(a) currently, for the United States of America, bombers of the B-52 and B-1 types, and for the Union of Soviet Socialist Republics, bombers of the Tupolev-95 and Myasishchev types;

(b) in the future, types of bombers which can carry out the mission of a heavy bomber in a manner similar or superior to that of bombers listed in sub-paragraph (a) above;

(c) types of bombers equipped for cruise missiles capable of a range in excess of 600 kilometres; and

(d) types of bombers equipped for ASBMs.

To Paragraph 3 of Article II of the Treaty

First Agreed Statement. *The term "bombers", as used in paragraph 3 of Article II and other provisions of the Treaty, means airplanes of types initially constructed to be equipped for bombs or missiles.*

Second Agreed Statement. *The parties shall notify each other on a case-by-case basis in the Standing Consultative Commission of inclusion of types of bombers as heavy bombers pursuant to the provisions of paragraph 3 of Article II of the Treaty; in this connexion the Parties shall hold consultations, as appropriate, consistent with the provisions of paragraph 2 of Article XVII of the Treaty.*

Third Agreed Statement. *The criteria the Parties shall use to make case-by-case determinations of which types of bombers in the future can carry out the mission of a heavy bomber in a manner similar or superior to that of current heavy bombers, as referred to in subparagraph 3(b) of Article II of the*

Treaty, shall be agreed upon in the Standing Consultative Commission.

Fourth Agreed Statement. *Having agreed that every bomber of a type included in paragraph 3 of Atricle II of the Treaty is to be considered a heavy bomber, the Parties further agree that:*

(a) airplanes which otherwise would be bombers of a heavy bomber type shall not be considered to be bombers of a heavy bomber type if they have functionally related observable differences which indicate that they cannot perform the mission of a heavy bomber;

(b) airplanes which otherwise would be bombers of a type equipped for cruise missiles capable of a range in excess of 600 kilometres shall not be considered to be bombers of a type equipped for cruise missiles capable of a range in excess of 600 kilometres if they have functionally related observable differences which indicate that they cannot perform the mission of a bomber equipped for cruise missiles capable of a range in excess of 600 kilometres, except that heavy bombers of current types, as designated in subparagraph 3(a) of Article II of the Treaty, which otherwise would be of a type equipped for cruise missiles capable of a range in excess of 600 kilometres shall not be considered to be heavy bombers of a type equipped for cruise missiles capable of a range in excess of 600 kilometres if they are distinguishable on the basis of externally observable differences from heavy bombers of a type equipped for cruise missiles capable of a range in excess of 600 kilometres; and

(c) airplanes which otherwise would be bombers of a type equipped for ASBMs shall not be considered to be bombers of a type equipped for ASBMs if they have functionally related observable differences which indicate that they cannot perform the mission of a bomber equipped for ASBMs, except that heavy bombers of current types, as designated in subparagraph 3(a) of Article II of the Treaty, which otherwise would be of a type equipped for ASBMs shall not be considered to be heavy bombers of a type equipped for ASBMs if they are distinguishable on the basis of externally observable differences from heavy bombers of a type equipped for ASBMs.

First Common Understanding. *Functionally related observable differences are differences in the observable features of airplanes which indicate whether or not these airplanes can perform the mission of a heavy bomber, or whether or not they can perform the mission of a bomber equipped for cruise missiles capable of a range in excess of 600 kilometres or whether or not they can perform the mission of a bomber equipped for ASBMs. Functionally related observable differences shall be verifiable by national technical means. To this end, the Parties may take, as appropriate, co-operative measures contributing to the effectiveness of verification by national technical means.*

Fifth Agreed Statement. *Tupolev-142 air-* *planes in their current configuration, that is, in the configuration for anti-submarine warfare, are considered to be airplanes of a type different from types of heavy bombers referred to in subparagraph 3(a) of Article II of the Treaty and not subject to the Fourth Agreed Statement to paragraph 3 of Article II of the Treaty. This Agreed Statement does not preclude improvement of Tupolev-142 airplanes as an anti-submarine system, and does not prejudice or set a precedent for designation in the future of types of airplanes as heavy bombers pursuant to subparagraph 3(b) of Article II of the Treaty or for application of the Fourth Agreed Statement to paragraph 3 of Article II of the Treaty to such airplanes.*

Second Common Understanding. *Not later than six months after entry into force of the Treaty the Union of Soviet Socialist Republics will give its 31 Myasishchev airplanes used as tankers in existence as of the date of signature of the Treaty functionally related observable differences which indicate that they cannot perform the mission of a heavy bomber.*

Third Common Understanding. *The designations by the United States of America and by the Union of Soviet Socialist Republics for heavy bombers referred to in subparagraph 3(a) of Article II of the Treaty correspond in the following manner:*

Heavy bombers of the types designated by the United States of America as the B-52 and the B-1 are known to the Union of Soviet Socialist Republics by the same designations;

Heavy bombers of the type designated by the Union of Soviet Socialist Republics as the Tupolev-95 are known to the United States of America as heavy bombers of the Bear type; and

Heavy bombers of the type designated by the Union of Soviet Socialist Republics as the Myasishchev are known to the United States of America as heavy bombers of the Bison type.

---

4. Air-to-surface ballistic missiles (ASBMs) are any such missiles capable of a range in excess of 600 kilometres and installed in an aircraft or on its external mountings.

5. Launchers of ICBMs and SLBMs equipped with multiple independently targetable re-entry vehicles (MIRVs) are launchers of the types developed and tested for launching ICBMs or SLBMs equipped with MIRVs.

To Paragraph 5 of Article II of the Treaty

First Agreed Statement. *If a launcher has been developed and tested for launching an ICBM or an SLBM equipped with MIRVs, all launchers of that type shall be considered to have been developed and tested for launching*

214

ICBMs or SLBMs equipped with MIRVs.

First Common Understanding. *If a launcher contains or launches an ICBM or an SLBM equipped with MIRVs, that launcher shall be considered to have been developed and tested for launching ICBMs or SLBMs equipped with MIRVs.*

Second Common Understanding. *If a launcher has been developed and tested for launching an ICBM or an SLBM equipped with MIRVs, all launchers of that type, except for ICBM and SLBM test and training launchers, shall be included in the corresponding aggregate numbers provided for in Article V of the Treaty, pursuant to the provisions of Article VI of the Treaty.*

Second Agreed Statement. *ICBMs and SLBMs equipped with MIRVs are ICBMs and SLBMs of the types which have been flight-tested with two or more independently targetable re-entry vehicles, regardless of whether or not they have also been flight-tested with a single re-entry vehicle or with multiple re-entry vehicles which are not independently targetable. As of the date of signature of the Treaty, such ICBMs and SLBMs are: for the United States of America, Minuteman III ICBMs, Poseidon C-3 SLBMs, and Trident C-4 SLBMs; and for the Union of Soviet Socialist Republics, RS-16, RS-18, RS-20 ICBMs and RSM-50 SLBMs.*

Each Party will notify the other Party in the Standing Consultative Commission on a case-by-case basis of the designation of the one new type of light ICBM, if equipped with MIRVs, permitted pursuant to paragraph 9 of Article IV of the Treaty when first flight-tested; of designations of additional types of SLBMs equipped with MIRVs when first installed on a submarine; and of designations of types of ASBMs equipped with MIRVs when first flight-tested.

Third Common Understanding. *The designations by the United States of America and by the Union of Soviet Socialist Republics for ICBMs and SLBMs equipped with MIRVs correspond in the following manner:*

Missiles of the type designated by the United States of America as the Minuteman III and known to the Union of Soviet Socialist Republics by the same designation, a light ICBM that has been flight-tested with multiple independently targetable re-entry vehicles;

Missiles of the type designated by the United States of America as the Poseidon C-3 and known to the Union of Soviet Socialist Republics by the same designation, an SLBM that was first flight-tested in 1968 and that has been flight-tested with multiple independently targetable re-entry vehicles;

Missiles of the type designated by the United States of America as the Trident C-4 and known to the Union of Soviet Socialist Republics by the same designation, an SLBM that was first flight-

tested in 1977 and that has been flight-tested with multiple independently targetable re-entry vehicles;

Missiles of the type designated by the Union of Soviet Socialist Republics as the RS-16 and known to the United States of America as the SS-17, a light ICBM that has been flight-tested with a single re-entry vehicle and with multiple independently targetable re-entry vehicles;

Missiles of the type designated by the Union of Soviet Socialist Republics as the RS-18 and known to the United States of America as the SS-19, the heaviest in terms of launch-weight and throw-weight of light ICBMs, which has been flight-tested with a single re-entry vehicle and with multiple independently targetable re-entry vehicles;

Missiles of the type designated by the Union of Soviet Socialist Republics as the RS-20 and known to the United States of America as the SS-18, the heaviest in terms of launch-weight and throw-weight of heavy ICBMs, which has been flight-tested with a single re-entry vehicle and with multiple independently targetable re-entry vehicles;

Missiles of the type designated by the Union of Soviet Socialist Republics as the RSM-50 and known to the United States of America as the SS-N-18, an SLBM that has been flight-tested with a single re-entry vehicle and with multiple independently targetable re-entry vehicles.

Third Agreed Statement. *Re-entry vehicles are independently targetable:*

(a) if, after separation from the booster, manoeuvring and targeting of the re-entry vehicles to separate aim points along trajectories which are unrelated to each other are accomplished by means of devices which are installed in a self-contained dispensing mechanism or on the re-entry vehicles, and which are based on the use of electronic or other computers in combination with devices using jet engines, including rocket engines, or aerodynamic systems;

(b) if manoeuvring and targeting of the re-entry vehicles to separate aim points along trajectories which are unrelated to each other are accomplished by means of other devices which may be developed in the future.

Fourth Common Understanding. *For the purposes of this Treaty, all ICBM launchers in the Derazhnya and Pervomaysk areas in the Union of Soviet Socialist Republics are included in the aggregate numbers provided for in Article V of the Treaty.*

Fifth Common Understanding. *If ICBM or SLBM launchers are converted, constructed or undergo significant changes to their principal observable structural design features after entry into force of the Treaty, any such launchers which are launchers of missiles equipped with MIRVs shall be distinguishable from launchers of missiles not equipped with MIRVs, and any such laun-*

chers which are launchers of missiles not equipped with MIRVs shall be distinguishable from launchers of missiles equipped with MIRVs, on the basis of externally observable design features of the launchers. Submarines with launchers of SLBMs equipped with MIRVs shall be distinguishable from submarines with launchers of SLBMs not equipped with MIRVs on the basis of externally observable design features of the submarines.

This Common Understanding does not require changes to launcher conversion or construction programmes, or to programmes including significant changes to the principal observable structural design features of launchers, under way as of the date of signature of the Treaty.

---

6. ASBMs equipped with MIRVs are ASBMs of the types which have been flight-tested with MIRVs.

To Paragraph 6 of Article II of the Treaty

First Agreed Statement. *ASBMS of the types which have been flight-tested with MIRVs are all ASBMs of the types which have been flight-tested with two or more independently targetable re-entry vehicles, regardless of whether or not they have also been flight-tested with a single re-entry vehicle or with multiple re-entry vehicles which are not independently targetable.*

Second Agreed Statement. *Re-entry vehicles are independently targetable:*

(a) *if, after separation from the booster, manoeuvring and targeting of the re-entry vehicles to separate aim points along trajectories which are unrelated to each other are accomplished by means of devices which are installed in a self-contained dispensing mechanism or on the re-entry vehicles, and which are based on the use of electronic or other computers in combination with devices using jet engines, including rocket engines, or aerodynamic systems;*

(b) *if manoeuvring and targeting of the re-entry vehicles to separate aim points along trajectories which are unrelated to each other are accomplished by means of other devices which may be developed in the future.*

---

7. Heavy ICBMs are ICBMs which have a launch-weight greater or a throw-weight greater than that of the heaviest, in terms of either launch-weight or throw-weight, respectively, of the light ICBMs deployed by either Party as of the date of signature of this Treaty.

To Paragraph 7 of Article II of the Treaty

First Agreed Statement. *The launch-weight of an ICBM is the weight of the fully loaded missile itself at the time of launch.*

Second Agreed Statement. *The throw-weight of an ICBM is the sum of the weight of:*

(a) *its re-entry vehicle or re-entry vehicles;*

(b) *any self-contained dispensing mechanisms or other appropriate devices for targeting one re-entry vehicle, or for releasing or for dispensing and targeting two or more re-entry vehicles; and*

(c) *its penetration aids, including devices for their release.*

Common Understanding. *The term "other appropriate devices", as used in the definition of the throw-weight of an ICBM in the Second Agreed Statement to paragraph 7 of Article II of the Treaty, means any devices for dispensing and targeting two or more re-entry vehicles; and any devices for releasing two or more re-entry vehicles or for targeting one re-entry vehicle, which cannot provide their re-entry vehicles or re-entry vehicle with additional velocity of more than 1,000 metres per second.*

---

8. Cruise missiles are unmanned, self-propelled, guided, weapon-delivery vehicles which sustain flight through the use of aerodynamic lift over most of their flight path and which are flight-tested from or deployed on aircraft, that is, air-launched cruise missiles or such vehicles which are referred to as cruise missiles in subparagraph 1 (b) of Article IX.

To Paragraph 8 of Article II of the Treaty

First Agreed Statement. *If a cruise missile is capable of a range in excess of 600 kilometres, all cruise missiles of that type shall be considered to be cruise missiles capable of a range in excess of 600 kilometres.*

First Common Understanding. *If a cruise missile has been flight-tested to a range in excess of 600 kilometres, it shall be considered to be a cruise missile capable of a range in excess of 600 kilometres.*

Second Common Understanding. *Cruise missiles not capable of a range in excess of 600 kilometres shall not be considered to be of a type capable of a range in excess of 600 kilometres if they are distinguishable on the basis of externally observable design features from cruise missiles of types capable of a range in excess of 600 kilometres.*

Second Agreed Statement. *The range of which a cruise missile is capable is the maximum distance which can be covered by the missile in its standard design mode flying until fuel exhaustion, determined by projecting its flight path onto the Earth's sphere from the point of launch to the point of impact.*

Third Agreed Statement. *If an unmanned, self-propelled, guided vehicle which sustains flight through the use of aerodynamic lift over most if its flight path has been flight-tested or deployed for weapon delivery, all vehicles of that type shall be considered to be weapon-delivery vehicles.*

Third Common Understanding. *Unmanned, self-propelled, guided vehicles which sustain flight through the use of aerodynamic lift over most of their flight path and are not weapon-delivering vehicles, that is, unarmed, pilotless, guided vehicles, shall not be considered to be cruise missiles if such vehicles are distinguishable from cruise missiles on the basis of externally observable design features.*

Fourth Common Understanding. *Neither Party shall convert unarmed, pilotless, guided vehicles into cruise missiles capable of a range in excess of 600 kilometres, nor shall either Party convert cruise missiles capable of a range in excess of 600 kilometres into unarmed, pilotless, guided vehicles.*

Fifth Common Understanding. *Neither party has plans during the term of the Treaty to flight-test from or deploy on aircraft unarmed, pilotless, guided vehicles which are capable of a range in excess of 600 kilometres. In the future, should a Party have such plans, that Party will provide notification thereof to the other Party well in advance of such flight-testing or deployment. This Common Understanding does not apply to target drones.*

Article III

1. Upon entry into force of this Treaty, each Party undertakes to limit ICBM launchers, SLBM launchers, heavy bombers, and ASBMs to an aggregate number not to exceed 2,400.

2. Each Party undertakes to limit, from 1 January 1981, strategic offensive arms referred to in paragraph 1 of this Article to an aggregate number not to exceed 2,250, and to initiate reductions of those arms which as of that date would be in excess of this aggregate number.

3. Within the aggregate numbers provided for in paragraphs 1 and 2 of this Article and subject to the provisions of this Treaty, each Party has the right to determine the composition of these aggregates.

4. For each bomber of a type equipped for ASBMs, the aggregate numbers provided for in paragraphs 1 and 2 of this Article shall include the maximum number of such missiles for which a bomber of that type is equipped for one operational mission.

5. A heavy bomber equipped only for ASBMs shall not itself be included in the aggregate numbers provided for in paragraphs 1 and 2 of this Article.

6. Reductions of the numbers of strategic offensive arms required to comply with the provisions of paragraphs 1 and 2 of this Article shall be carried out as provided for in Article XI.

Article IV

1. Each Party undertakes not to start con-struction of additional fixed ICBM launchers.

2. Each Party undertakes not to relocate fixed ICBM launchers.

3. Each Party undertakes not to convert launchers of light ICBMs, or of ICBMs of older types deployed prior to 1964, into launchers of heavy ICBMs of types deployed after that time.

4. Each Party undertakes in the process of modernization and replacement of ICBM silo launchers not to increase the original internal volume of an ICBM silo launcher by more than thirty-two per cent. Within this limit each Party has the right to determine whether such an increase will be made through an increase in the original diameter or in the original depth of an ICBM silo launcher, or in both of these dimensions.

To Paragraph 4 of Article IV of the Treaty

Agreed Statement. *The word "original" in paragraph 4 of Article IV of the Treaty refers to the internal dimensions of an ICBM silo launcher, including its internal volume, as of 26 May 1972, or as of the date on which such launcher becomes operational, whichever is later.*

Common Understanding. *The obligations provided for in paragraph 4 of Article IV of the Treaty and in the Agreed Statement thereto mean that the original diameter or the original depth of an ICBM silo launcher may not be increased by an amount greater than that which would result in an increase in the original internal volume of the ICBM silo launcher by 32 per cent solely through an increase in one of these dimensions.*

5. Each Party undertakes:

(*a*) not to supply ICBM launcher deployment areas with intercontinental ballistic missiles in excess of a number consistent with normal deployment, maintenance, training, and replacement requirements;

(*b*) not to provide storage facilities for or to store ICBMs in excess of normal deployment requirements at launch sites of ICBM launchers;

(*c*) not to develop, test, or deploy systems for rapid reload of ICBM launchers.

To Paragraph 5 of Article IV of the Treaty

Agreed Statement. *The term "normal deployment requirements", as used in paragraph 5 of Article IV of the Treaty, means the deployment of one missile at each ICBM launcher.*

6. Subject to the provisions of this Treaty, each Party undertakes not to have under construction at any time strategic offensive arms referred to in paragraph 1 of Article III in excess of numbers consistent with a normal construction schedule.

To Paragraph 6 of Article IV of the Treaty

Common Understanding. *A normal construction schedule, in paragraph 6 of Article IV of the Treaty, is understood to be one consistent with the past or present construction practices of each Party.*

---

7. Each Party undertakes not to develop, test, or deploy ICBMs which have a launch-weight greater or a throw-weight greater than that of the heaviest, in terms of either launch-weight or throw-weight, respectively, of the heavy ICBMs deployed by either Party as of the date of signature of this Treaty.

To Paragraph 7 of Article IV of the Treaty

First Agreed Statement. *The launch-weight of an ICBM is the weight of the fully loaded missile itself at the time of launch.*

Second Agreed Statement. *The throw-weight of an ICBM is the sum of the weight of:*

(a) its re-entry vehicle or re-entry vehicles;

(b) any self-contained dispensing mechanisms or other appropriate devices for targeting one re-entry vehicle, or for releasing or for dispensing and targeting two or more re-entry vehicles; and

(c) its penetration aids, including devices for their release.

Common Understanding. *The term "other appropriate devices", as used in the definition of the throw-weight of an ICBM in the Second Agreed Statement to paragraph 7 of Article IV of the Treaty, means any devices for dispensing and targeting two or more re-entry vehicles; and any devices for releasing two or more re-entry vehicles or for targeting one re-entry vehicle, which cannot provide their re-entry vehicles or re-entry vehicle with additional velocity of more than 1,000 metres per second.*

---

8. Each Party undertakes not to convert land-based launchers of ballistic missiles which are not ICBMs into launchers for launching ICBMs, and not to test them for this purpose.

To Paragraph 8 of Article IV of the Treaty

Common Understanding. *During the term of the Treaty, the Union of Soviet Socialist Republics will not produce, test, or deploy ICBMs of the type designated by the Union of Soviet Socialist Republics as the RS-14 and known to the United States of America as the SS-16, a light ICBM first flight-tested after 1970 and flight-tested only with a single re-entry vehicle; this Common Understanding also means that the Union of Soviet Socialist Republics will not produce the third stage of that missile, the re-entry vehicle of that missile, or the appropriate device for targeting the re-entry vehicle of that missile.*

---

9. Each Party undertakes not to flight-test or deploy new types of ICBMs, that is, types of ICBMs not flight-tested as of 1 May 1979, except that each party may flight-test and deploy one new type of light ICBM.

To Paragraph 9 of Article IV of the Treaty

First Agreed Statement. *The term "new types of ICBMs", as used in paragraph 9 of Article IV of the Treaty, refers to any ICBM which is different from those ICBMs flight-tested as of 1 May 1979 in any one or more of the following respects:*

(a) the number of stages, the length, the largest diameter, the launch-weight, or the throw-weight, of the missile;

(b) the type of propellant (that is, liquid or solid) of any of its stages.

First Common Understanding. *As used in the First Agreed Statement to paragraph 9 of Article IV of the Treaty, the term "different", referring to the length, the diameter, the launch-weight, and the throw-weight, of the missile, means a difference in excess of 5 per cent.*

Second Agreed Statement. *Every ICBM of the one new type of light ICBM permitted to each Party pursuant to paragraph 9 of Article IV of the Treaty shall have the same number of stages and the same type of propellant (that is, liquid or solid) of each stage as the first ICBM of the one new type of light ICBM launched by that Party. In addition, after the twenty-fifth launch of an ICBM of that type, or after the last launch before deployment begins of ICBMs of that type, whichever occurs earlier, ICBMs of the one new type of light ICBM permitted to that Party shall not be different in any one or more of the following respects: the length, the largest diameter, the launch-weight, or the throw-weight, of the missile.*

A Party which launches ICBMs of the one new type of light ICBM permitted pursuant to paragraph 9 of Article IV of the Treaty shall promptly notify the other Party of the date of the first launch and of the date of either the twenty-fifth or the last launch before deployment begins of ICBMs of that type, whichever occurs earlier.

Second Common Understanding. *As used in the Second Agreed Statement to paragraph 9 of Article IV of the Treaty, the term "different", referring to the length, the diameter, the launch-weight, and the throw-weight, of the missile, means a difference in excess of 5 per cent from the value established for each of the above parameters as of the twenty-fifth launch or as of the last launch before deployment begins, whichever occurs earlier. The values demonstrated in each of the above parameters during the last 12 of the 25 launches or during the last 12 launches before deployment begins, whichever 12 launches occur earlier, shall not vary by more than 10 per cent from any other of the corresponding values demonstrated during those 12 launches.*

Third Common Understanding. *The limitations with respect to launch-weight and throw-weight, provided for in the First Agreed Statement and the First Common Understanding to paragraph 9 of Article IV of the Treaty, do not preclude the flight-testing or the deployment of ICBMs with fewer re-entry vehicles, or fewer penetration aids, or both, than the maximum number of re-entry vehicles and the maximum number of penetration aids with which ICBMs of that type have been flight-tested as of 1 May 1979, even if this results in a decrease in launch-weight or in throw-weight in excess of 5 per cent.*

In addition to the aforementioned cases, those limitations do not preclude a decrease in launch-weight or in throw-weight in excess of 5 per cent, in the case of the flight-testing or the deployment of ICBMs with a lesser quantity of propellant, including the propellant of a self-contained dispensing mechanism or other appropriate device, than the maximum quantity of propellant, including the propellant of a self-contained dispensing mechanism or other appropriate device, with which ICBMs of that type have been flight-tested as of 1 May 1979, provided that such an ICBM is at the same time flight-tested or deployed with fewer re-entry vehicles, or fewer penetration aids, or both, than the maximum number of re-entry vehicles and the maximum number of penetration aids with which ICBMs of that type have been flight-tested as of 1 May 1979, and the decrease in launch-weight and throw-weight in such cases results only from the reduction in the number of re-entry vehicles, or penetration aids, or both, and the reduction in the quantity of propellant.

Fourth Common Understanding. *The limitations with respect to launch-weight and throw-weight, provided for in the Second Agreed Statement and the Second Common Understanding to paragraph 9 of Article IV of the Treaty, do not preclude the flight-testing or the deployment of ICBMs of the one new type of light ICBM permitted to each Party pursuant to paragraph 9 of Article IV of the Treaty with fewer re-entry vehicles, or fewer penetration aids, or both, than the maximum number of re-entry vehicles and the maximum number of penetration aids with which ICBMs of that type have been flight-tested, even if this results in a decrease in launch-weight or in throw-weight in excess of 5 per cent.*

In addition to the aforementioned cases, those limitations do not preclude a decrease in launch-weight or in throw-weight in excess of 5 per cent, in the case of the flight-testing or the deployment of ICBMs of that type with a lesser quantity of propellant, including the propellant of a self-contained dispensing mechanism or other appropriate device, than the maximum quantity of propellant, including the propellant of a self-contained dispensing mechanism or other appropriate device, with which ICBMs of that type have been flight-tested, provided that such an ICBM is at the same time flight-tested or deployed with fewer re-entry vehicles, or fewer penetration aids, or both, than the maximum number of re-entry vehicles and the maximum number of penetration aids with which ICBMs of that type have been flight-tested, and the decrease in launch-weight and throw-weight in such cases results only from the reduction in the number of re-entry vehicles, or penetration aids, or both, and the reduction in the quantity of propellant.

10. Each Party undertakes not to flight-test or deploy ICBMs of a type flight-tested as of 1 May 1979, with a number of re-entry vehicles greater than the maximum number of re-entry vehicles with which an ICBM of that type has been flight-tested as of that date.

To Paragraph 10 of Article IV of the Treaty

First Agreed Statement. *The following types of ICBMs and SLBMs equipped with MIRVs have been flight-tested with the maximum number of re-entry vehicles set forth below:*

For the United States of America

ICBMs of the
Minuteman III type — 7 re-entry vehicles;
SLBMs of the
Poseidon C-3 type — 14 re-entry vehicles;
SLBMs of the
Trident C-4 type — 7 re-entry vehicles;

For the Union of Soviet Socialist Republics

ICBMs of the
RS-16 type — 4 re-entry vehicles;
ICBMs of the
RS-18 type — 6 re-entry vehicles;
ICBMs of the
RS-20 type — 10 re-entry vehicles;
SLBMs of the
RSM-50 type — 7 re-entry vehicles.

Common Understanding. *Minuteman III ICBMs of the United States of America have been deployed with no more than three re-entry vehicles. During the term of the Treaty, the United States of America has no plans to and will not flight-test or deploy missiles of this type with more than three re-entry vehicles.*

Second Agreed Statement. *During the flight-testing of any ICBM, SLBM, or ASBM after 1 May 1979 the number of procedures for releasing or for dispensing may not exceed the maximum number of re-entry vehicles established for missiles of corresponding types as provided for in paragraphs 10, 11, 12, and 13 of Article IV of the Treaty. In this Agreed Statement "procedures for releasing or for dispensing" are understood to mean manoeuvres of a missile associated with targeting and releasing or dispensing its re-entry vehicles to aim points, whether or not a re-entry vehicle is actually released or dis-*

pensed. *Procedures for releasing anti-missile defence penetration aids will not be considered to be procedures for releasing or for dispensing a re-entry vehicle so long as the procedures for releasing anti-missile defence penetration aids differ from those for releasing or for dispensing re-entry vehicles.*

Third Agreed Statement. *Each Party undertakes:*

(a) *not to flight-test or deploy ICBMs equipped with multiple re-entry vehicles, of a type flight-tested as of 1 May 1979, with re-entry vehicles the weight of any of which is less than the weight of the lightest of those re-entry vehicles with which an ICBM of that type has been flight-tested as of that date;*

(b) *not to flight-test or deploy ICBMs equipped with a single re-entry vehicle and without an appropriate device for targeting a re-entry vehicle, of a type flight-tested as of 1 May 1979, with a re-entry vehicle the weight of which is less than the weight of the lightest re-entry vehicle on an ICBM of a type equipped with MIRVs and flight-tested by that Party as of 1 May 1979; and*

(c) *not to flight-test or deploy ICBMs equipped with a single re-entry vehicle and with an appropriate device for targeting a re-entry vehicle, of a type flight-tested as of 1 May 1979, with a re-entry vehicle the weight of which is less than 50 per cent of the throw-weight of that ICBM.*

11. Each Party undertakes not to flight-test or deploy ICBMs of the one new type permitted pursuant to paragraph 9 of this Article with a number of re-entry vehicles greater than the maximum number of re-entry vehicles with which an ICBM of either Party has been flight-tested as of 1 May 1979, that is, ten.

To Paragraph 11 of Article IV of the Treaty

First Agreed Statement. *Each Party undertakes not to flight-test or deploy the one new type of light ICBM permitted to each Party pursuant to paragraph 9 of Article IV of the Treaty with a number of re-entry vehicles greater than the maximum number of re-entry vehicles with which an ICBM of that type has been flight-tested as of the twenty-fifth launch or the last launch before deployment begins of ICBMs of that type, whichever occurs earlier.*

Second Agreed Statement. *During the flight-testing of any ICBM, SLBM, or ASBM after 1 May 1979 the number of procedures for releasing or for dispensing may not exceed the maximum number of re-entry vehicles established for missiles of corresponding types as provided for in paragraphs 10, 11, 12 and 13 of Article IV of the Treaty. In this Agreed Statement "procedures for releasing or for dispensing" are understood to mean manoeuvres of a missile associated with targeting and releasing or dispensing its re-entry vehicles to aim points, whether or not a re-*entry vehicle is actually released or dispensed. *Procedures for releasing anti-missile defence penetration aids will not be considered to be procedures for releasing or for dispensing a re-entry vehicle so long as the procedures for releasing anti-missile defence penetration aids differ from those for releasing or for dispensing re-entry vehicles.*

12. Each Party undertakes not to flight-test or deploy SLBMs with a number of re-entry vehicles greater than the maximum number of re-entry vehicles with which an SLBM of either party has been flight-tested as of 1 May 1979, that is, 14.

To Paragraph 12 of Article IV of the Treaty

First Agreed Statement. *The following types of ICBMs and SLBMs equipped with MIRVs have been flight-tested with the maximum number of re-entry vehicles set forth below:*

For the United States of America

ICBMs of the
 Minuteman III type — 7 re-entry vehicles;
SLBMs of the
 Poseidon C-3 type —14 re-entry vehicles;
SLBMs of the
 Trident C-4 type — 7 re-entry vehicles.

For the Union of Soviet Socialist Republics

ICBMs of the
 RS-16 type — 4 re-entry vehicles;
ICBMs of the
 RS-18 type — 6 re-entry vehicles;
ICBMs of the
 RS-20 type —10 re-entry vehicles;
SLBMs of the
 RSM-50 type — 7 re-entry vehicles.

Second Agreed Statement. *During the flight-testing of any ICBM, SLBM, or ASBM after 1 May 1979 the number of procedures for releasing or for dispensing may not exceed the maximum number of re-entry vehicles established for missiles of corresponding types as provided for in paragraphs 10, 11, 12 and 13 of Article IV of the Treaty. In this Agreed Statement "procedures for releasing or for dispensing" are understood to mean manoeuvres of a missile associated with targeting and releasing or dispensing its re-entry vehicles to aim points, whether or not a re-entry vehicle is actually released or dispensed. Procedures for releasing anti-missile defence penetration aids will not be considered to be procedures for releasing or for dispensing a re-entry vehicle so long as the procedures for releasing anti-missile defence penetration aids differ from those for releasing or for dispensing re-entry vehicles.*

13. Each Party undertakes not to flight-test or deploy ASBMs with a number of re-entry vehicles greater than the maximum number of re-entry vehicles with which an

ICBM of either Party has been flight-tested as of 1 May 1979, that is, ten.

To Paragraph 13 of Article IV of the Treaty

Agreed Statement. *During the flight-testing of any ICBM, SLBM, or ASBM after 1 May 1979 the number of procedures for releasing or for dispensing may not exceed the maximum number of re-entry vehicles established for missiles of corresponding types as provided for in paragraphs 10, 11, 12 and 13 of Article IV of the Treaty. In this Agreed Statement "procedures for releasing or for dispensing" are understood to mean manoeuvres of a missile associated with targeting and releasing or dispensing its re-entry vehicles to aim points, whether or not a re-entry vehicle is actually released or dispensed. Procedures for releasing anti-missile defence penetration aids will not be considered to be procedures for releasing or for dispensing a re-entry vehicle so long as the procedures for releasing anti-missile defence penetration aids differ from those for releasing or for dispensing re-entry vehicles.*

---

14. Each Party undertakes not to deploy at any one time on heavy bombers equipped for cruise missiles capable of a range in excess of 600 kilometres a number of such cruise missiles which exceeds the product of 28 and the number of such heavy bombers.

To Paragraph 14 of Article IV of the Treaty

First Agreed Statement. *For the purposes of the limitation provided for in paragraph 14 of Article IV of the Treaty, there shall be considered to be deployed on each heavy bomber of a type equipped for cruise missiles capable of a range in excess of 600 kilometres the maximum number of such missiles for which any bomber of that type is equipped for one operational mission.*

Second Agreed Statement. *During the term of the Treaty no bomber of the B-52 or B-1 types of the United States of America and no bomber of the Tupolev-95 or Myasishchev types of the Union of Soviet Socialist Republics will be equipped for more than 20 cruise missiles capable of a range in excess of 600 kilometres.*

Article V

1. Within the aggregate numbers provided for in paragraphs 1 and 2 of Article III, each Party undertakes to limit launchers of ICBMs and SLBMs equipped with MIRVs, ASBMs equipped with MIRVs, and heavy bombers equipped for cruise missiles capable of a range in excess of 600 kilometres to an aggregate number not to exceed 1,320.

2. Within the aggregate number provided for in paragraph 1 of this Article, each Party undertakes to limit launchers of ICBMs and SLBMs equipped with MIRVs, and ASBMs equipped with MIRVs to an aggregate number not to exceed 1,200.

3. Within the aggregate number provided for in paragraph 2 of this Article, each Party undertakes to limit launchers of ICBMs equipped with MIRVs to an aggregate number not to exceed 820.

4. For each bomber of a type equipped for ASBMs equipped with MIRVs, the aggregate numbers provided for in paragraphs 1 and 2 of this Article shall include the maximum number of ASBMs for which a bomber of that type is equipped for one operational mission.

To Paragraph 4 of Article V of the Treaty

Agreed Statement. *If a bomber is equipped for ASBMs equipped with MIRVs, all bombers of that type shall be considered to be equipped for ASBMs equipped with MIRVs.*

---

5. Within the aggregate numbers provided for in paragraphs 1, 2, and 3 of this Article and subject to the provisions of this Treaty, each Party has the right to determine the composition of these aggregates.

Article VI

1. The limitations provided for in this Treaty shall apply to those arms which are:

   (*a*) operational;

   (*b*) in the final stage of construction;

   (*c*) in reserve, in storage, or mothballed;

   (*d*) undergoing overhaul, repair, modernization, or conversion.

2. Those arms in the final stage of construction are:

   (*a*) SLBM launchers on submarines which have begun sea trials;

   (*b*) ASBMs after a bomber of a type equipped for such missiles has been brought out of the shop, plant, or other facility where its final assembly or conversion for the purpose of equipping it for such missiles has been performed;

   (*c*) other strategic offensive arms which are finally assembled in a shop, plant, or other facility after they have been brought out of the shop, plant, or other facility where their final assembly has been performed.

3. ICBM and SLBM launchers of a type not subject to the limitation provided for in Article V, which undergo conversion into launchers of a type subject to that limitation, shall become subject to that limitation as follows:

   (*a*) fixed ICBM launchers when work on their conversion reaches the stage which first definitely indicates that they are being so converted;

   (*b*) SLBM launchers on a submarine when that submarine first goes to sea after their conversion has been performed.

To Paragraph 3 of Article VI of the Treaty

Agreed Statement. *The procedures referred to in paragraph 7 of Article VI of the Treaty shall include procedures determining the manner in which mobile ICBM launchers of a type not subject to the limitation provided for in Article V of the Treaty, which undergo conversion into launchers of a type subject to that limitation, shall become subject to that limitation, unless the Parties agree that mobile ICBM launchers shall not be deployed after the date on which the Protocol ceases to be in force.*

---

4. ASBMs on a bomber which undergoes conversion from a bomber of a type equipped for ASBMs which are not subject to the limitation provided for in Article V into a bomber of a type equipped for ASBMs which are subject to that limitation shall become subject to that limitation when the bomber is brought out of the shop, plant, or other facility where such conversion has been performed.

5. A heavy bomber of a type not subject to the limitation provided for in paragraph 1 of Article V shall become subject to that limitation when it is brought out of the shop, plant, or other facility where it has been converted into a heavy bomber of a type equipped for cruise missiles capable of a range in excess of 600 kilometres. A bomber of a type not subject to the limitation provided for in paragraph 1 or 2 of Article III shall become subject to that limitation and to the limitation provided for in paragraph 1 of Article V when it is brought out of the shop, plant, or other facility where it has been converted into a bomber of a type equipped for cruise missiles capable of a range in excess of 600 kilometres.

6. The arms subject to the limitations provided for in this Treaty shall continue to be subject to these limitations until they are dismantled, are destroyed, or otherwise cease to be subject to these limitations under procedures to be agreed upon.

To Paragraph 6 of Article VI of the Treaty

Agreed Statement. *The procedures for removal of strategic offensive arms from the aggregate numbers provided for in the Treaty, which are referred to in paragraph 6 of Article VI of the Treaty, and which are to be agreed upon in the Standing Consultative Commission, shall include:*

(a) procedures for removal from the aggregate numbers, provided for in Article V of the Treaty, of ICBM and SLBM launchers which are being converted from launchers of a type subject to the limitation provided for in Article V of the Treaty, into launchers of a type not subject to that limitation;

(b) procedures for removal from the aggregate numbers, provided for in Articles III and V of the Treaty, of bombers which are being converted from bombers of a type subject to the limitations provided for in Article III *of the Treaty or in Articles III and V of the Treaty into airplanes or bombers of a type not so subject.*

Common Understanding. *The procedures referred to in subparagraph (b) of the Agreed Statement to paragraph 6 of Article VI of the Treaty for removal of bombers from the aggregate numbers provided for in Articles III and V of the Treaty shall be based upon the existence of functionally related observable differences which indicate whether or not they can perform the mission of a heavy bomber, or whether or not they can perform the mission of a bomber equipped for cruise missiles capable of a range in excess of 600 kilometres.*

---

7. In accordance with the provisions of Article XVII, the Parties will agree in the Standing Consultative Commission upon procedures to implement the provisions of this Article.

Article VII

1. The limitations provided for in Article III shall not apply to ICBM and SLBM test and training launchers or to space vehicle launchers for exploration and use of outer space. ICBM and SLBM test and training launchers are ICBM and SLBM launchers used only for testing or training.

To Paragraph 1 of Article VII of the Treaty

Common Understanding. *The term "testing", as used in Article VII of the Treaty, includes research and development.*

---

2. The Parties agree that:

(a) there shall be no significant increase in the number of ICBM or SLBM test and training launchers or in the number of such launchers of heavy ICBMs;

(b) construction or conversion of ICBM launchers at test ranges shall be undertaken only for purposes of testing and training;

(c) there shall be no conversion of ICBM test and training launchers or of space vehicle launchers into ICBM launchers subject to the limitations provided for in Article III.

To Paragraph 2 of Article VII of the Treaty

First Agreed Statement. *The term "significant increase", as used in subparagraph 2(a) of Article VII of the Treaty, means an increase of 15 per cent or more. Any new ICBM test and training launchers which replace ICBM test and training launchers at test ranges will be located only at test ranges.*

Second Agreed Statement. *Current test ranges where ICBMs are tested are located: for the United States of America, near Santa Maria, California, and at Cape Canaveral, Florida; and for the Union of Soviet Socialist Republics, in the areas of Tyura-Tam and*

Plesetskaya. In the future, each Party shall provide notification in the Standing Consultative Commission of the location of any other test range used by that Party to test ICBMs.

First Common Understanding. *At test ranges where ICBMs are tested, other arms, including those not limited by the Treaty, may ·also be tested.*

Second Common Understanding. *Of the 18 launchers of fractional orbital missiles at the test range where ICBMs are tested in the area of Tyura-Tam, 12 launchers shall be dismantled or destroyed and six launchers may be converted to launchers for testing missiles undergoing modernization.*

Dismantling or destruction of the 12 launchers shall begin upon entry into force of the Treaty and shall be completed within eight months, under procedures for dismantling or destruction of these launchers to be agreed upon in the Standing Consultative Commission. These 12 launchers shall not be replaced.

Conversion of the six launchers may be carried out after entry into force of the Treaty. After entry into force of the Treaty, fractional orbital missiles shall be removed and shall be destroyed pursuant to the provisions of subparagraph 1(c) of Article IX and of Article XI of the Treaty and shall not be replaced by other missiles, except in the case of conversion of these six launchers for testing missiles undergoing modernization. After removal of the fractional orbital missiles, and prior to such conversion, any activities associated with these launchers shall be limited to normal maintenance requirements for launchers in which missiles are not deployed. These six launchers shall be subject to the provisions of Article VII of the Treaty and, if converted, to the provisions of the Fifth Common Understanding to paragraph 5 of Article II of the Treaty.

Article VIII

1. Each Party undertakes not to flight-test cruise missiles capable of a range in excess of 600 kilometres or ASBMs from aircraft other than bombers or to convert such aircraft into aircraft equipped for such missiles.

To Paragraph 1 of Article VIII of the Treaty

Agreed Statement. *For purposes of testing only, each Party has the right, through initial construction or, as an exception to the provisions of paragraph 1 of Article VIII of the Treaty, by conversion, to equip for cruise missiles, capable of a range in excess of 600 kilometres or for ASBMs no more than 16 airplanes, including airplanes which are prototypes of bombers equipped for such missiles. Each Party also has the right, as an exception to the provisions of paragraph 1 of Article VIII of the Treaty, to flight-test from such airplanes cruise missiles capable of a*

range in excess of 600 kilometres and, after ·the date on which the Protocol ceases to be in force, to flight-test ASBMs from such airplanes as well, unless the Parties agree that they will not flight-test ASBMs after that date. The limitations provided for in Article III of the Treaty shall not apply to such airplanes.

The aforementioned airplanes may include only:

(a) airplanes other than bombers which, as an exception to the provisions of paragraph 1 of Article VIII of the Treaty, have been converted into airplanes equipped for cruise missiles capable of a range in excess of 600 kilometres or for ASBMs;

(b) airplanes considered to be heavy bombers pursuant to subparagraphs 3(c) or (d) of Article II of the Treaty; and

(c) airplanes other than heavy bombers which, prior to 7 March 1979 were used for testing cruise missiles capable of a range in excess of 600 kilometres.

The airplanes referred to in subparagraphs (a) and (b) of this Agreed Statement shall be distinguishable on the basis of functionally related observable differences from airplanes which otherwise would be of the same type but cannot perform the mission of a bomber equipped for cruise missiles capable of a range in excess of 600 kilometres or for ASBMs.

The airplanes referred to in subparagraph (c) of this Agreed Statement shall not be used for testing cruise missiles capable of a range in excess of 600 kilometres after the expiration of a six-month period from the date of entry into force of the Treaty, unless by the expiration of that period they are distinguishable on the basis of functionally related observable differences from airplanes which otherwise would be of the same type but cannot perform the mission of a bomber equipped for cruise missiles capable of a range in excess of 600 kilometres.

First Common Understanding. *The term "testing", as used in the Agreed Statement to paragraph 1 of Article VIII of the Treaty, includes research and development.*

Second Common Understanding. *The Parties shall notify each other in the Standing Consultative Commission of the number of airplanes, according to type, used for testing pursuant to the Agreed Statement to paragraph 1 of Article VIII of the Treaty. Such notification shall be provided at the first regular session of the Standing Consultative Commission held after an airplane has been used for such testing.*

Third Common Understanding. *None of the 16 airplanes referred to in the Agreed Statement to paragraph 1 of Article VIII of the Treaty may be replaced, except in the event of the involuntary destruction of any such airplane or in the case of the dismantling or destruction of any such airplane. The procedures for such replacement and for removal of any such airplane from that number, in case of its conversion,· shall be agreed* upon in the Standing Consultative Commission.

---

2. Each Party undertakes not to convert aircraft other than bombers into aircraft which can carry out the mission of a heavy bomber as referred to in subparagraph 3 (b) of Article II.

Article IX

1. Each Party undertakes not to develop, test, or deploy:

(a) ballistic missiles capable of a range in excess of 600 kilometres for installation on waterborne vehicles other than submarines, or launchers of such missiles;

(b) fixed ballistic or cruise missile launchers for emplacement on the ocean floor, on the seabed, or on the beds of internal waters and inland waters, or in the subsoil thereof, or mobile launchers of such missiles, which move only in contact with the ocean floor, the seabed, or the beds of internal waters and inland waters, or missiles for such launchers;

(c) systems for placing into Earth orbit nuclear weapons or any other kind of weapons of mass destruction, including fractional orbital missiles;

(d) mobile launchers of heavy ICBMs;

(e) SLBMs which have a launch-weight or throw-weight greater than that of the heaviest, in terms of either launch-weight or throw-weight, respectively, of the light ICBMs deployed by either Party as of the date of signature of this Treaty, or launchers of such SLBMs; or

(f) ASBMs which have a launch-weight greater or a throw-weight greater than that of the heaviest, in terms of either launch-weight or throw-weight, respectively, of the light ICBMs deployed by either Party as of the date of signature of this Treaty.

To Paragraph 1 of Article IX of the Treaty

Common Understanding to subparagraph (a). *The obligations provided for in subparagraph 1(a) of Article IX of the Treaty do not affect current practices for transporting ballistic missiles.*

Agreed Statement to subparagraph (b). *The obligations provided for in subparagraph 1(b) of Article IX of the Treaty shall apply to all areas of the ocean floor and the seabed, including the seabed zone referred to in Article I and II of the 1971 Treaty on the Prohibition of the Emplacement of Nuclear Weapons and Other Weapons of Mass Destruction on the Seabed and the Ocean Floor and in the Subsoil Thereof.*

Common Understanding to subparagraph (c). *The provisions of subparagraph 1(c) of Article IX of the Treaty do not require the dismantling or destruction of any existing launchers of either Party.*

First Agreed Statement to subparagraphs (e) and (f). *The throw-weight of an SLBM or of an ASBM is the weight of the fully loaded missile itself at the time of launch.*

Second Agreed Statement to subparagraphs (e) and (f). 'The throw-weight of an SLBM or of an ASBM is the sum of the weight of:

(a) *its re-entry vehicle or re-entry vehicles;*

(b) *any self-contained dispensing mechanisms or other appropriate devices for targeting one re-entry vehicle, or for releasing or for dispensing and targeting two or more re-entry vehicles; and*

(c) *its penetration aids, including devices for their release.*

Common Understanding to subparagraphs (e) and (f). *The term "other appropriate devices", as used in the definition of the throw-weight of an SLBM or of an ASBM in the Second Agreed Statement to subparagraphs 1(e) and 1(f) of Article IX of the Treaty, means any devices for dispensing and targeting two or more re-entry vehicles; and any devices for releasing two or more re-entry vehicles or for targeting one re-entry vehicle, which cannot provide their re-entry vehicles or re-entry vehicle with additional velocity of more than 1,000 metres per second.*

---

2. Each Party undertakes not to flight-test from aircraft cruise missiles capable of a range in excess of 600 kilometres which are equipped with multiple independently targetable warheads and not to deploy such cruise missiles on aircraft.

To Paragraph 2 of Article IX of the Treaty

Agreed Statement. *Warheads of a cruise missile are independently targetable if manoeuvring or targeting of the warheads to separate aim points along ballistic trajectories or any other flight paths, which are unrelated to each other, is accomplished during a flight of a cruise missile.*

Article X

Subject to the provisions of this Treaty, modernization and replacement of strategic offensive arms may be carried out.

Article XI

1. Strategic offensive arms which would be in excess of the aggregate numbers provided for in this Treaty as well as strategic offensive arms prohibited by this Treaty shall be dismantled or destroyed under procedures to be agreed upon in the Standing Consultative Commission.

2. Dismantling or destruction of strategic offensive arms which would be in excess of the aggregate number provided for in paragraph 1 of Article III shall begin on the date of the entry into force of this Treaty and shall be completed within the following periods from that date: four months for ICBM launchers; six months for SLBM launchers; and three months for heavy bombers.

3. Dismantling or destruction of strategic offensive arms which would be in excess of the aggregate number provided for in paragraph 2 of Article III shall be initiated no later than 1 January 1981, shall be carried out throughout the ensuing twelve-month period, and shall be completed no later than 31 December 1981.

4. Dismantling or destruction of strategic offensive arms prohibited by this Treaty shall be completed within the shortest possible agreed period of time, but not later than six months after the entry into force of this Treaty.

Article XII

In order to ensure the viability and effectiveness of this Treaty, each Party undertakes not to circumvent the provisions of this Treaty, through any other state or states, or in any other manner.

Article XIII

Each Party undertakes not to assume any international obligations which would conflict with this Treaty.

Article XIV

The Parties undertake to begin, promptly after the entry into force of this Treaty, active negotiations with the objective of achieving, as soon as possible, agreement on further measures for the limitation and reduction of strategic arms. It is also the objective of the Parties to conclude well in advance of 1985 an agreement limiting strategic offensive arms to replace this Treaty upon its expiration.

Article XV

1. For the purpose of providing assurance of compliance with the provisions of this Treaty, each Party shall use national technical means of verification at its disposal in a manner consistent with generally recognized principles of international law.

2. Each Party undertakes not to interfere with the national technical means of verification of the other Party operating in accordance with paragraph 1 of this Article.

3. Each Party undertakes not to use deliberate concealment measures which impede verification by national technical means of compliance with the provisions of this Treaty. This obligation shall not require changes in current construction, assembly, conversion, or overhaul practices.

To Paragraph 3 of Article XV of the Treaty

First Agreed Statement. *Deliberate concealment measures, as referred to in paragraph 3 of Article XV of the Treaty, are measures carried out deliberately to hinder or deliberately to impede verification by national technical means of compliance with the provisions of the Treaty.*

Second Agreed Statement. *The obligation not to use deliberate concealment measures, provided for in paragraph 3 of Article XV of the Treaty, does not preclude the testing of anti-missile defence penetration aids.*

First Common Understanding. *The provisions of paragraph 3 of Article XV of the Treaty and the First Agreed Statement thereto apply to all provisions of the Treaty, including provisions associated with testing. In this connexion, the obligation not to use deliberate concealment measures includes the obligation not to use deliberate concealment measures associated with testing, including those measures aimed at concealing the association between ICBMs and launchers during testing.*

Second Common Understanding. *Each party is free to use various methods of transmitting telemetric information during testing, including its encryption, except that, in accordance with the provisions of paragraph 3 of Article XV of the Treaty, neither Party shall engage in deliberate denial of telemetric information, such as through the use of telemetry encryption, whenever such denial impedes verification of compliance with the provisions of the Treaty.*

Third Common Understanding. *In addition to the obligations provided for in paragraph 3 of Article XV of the Treaty, no shelters which impede verification by national technical means of compliance with the provisions of the Treaty shall be used over ICBM silo launchers.*

Article XVI

1. Each Party undertakes, before conducting each planned ICBM launch, to notify the other party well in advance on a case-by-case basis that such a launch will occur, except for single ICBM launches from test ranges or from ICBM launcher deployment areas, which are not planned to extend beyond its national territory.

To Paragraph 1 of Article XVI of the Treaty

First Common Understanding. *ICBM launches to which the obligations provided for in Article XVI of the Treaty apply, include, among others, those ICBM launches for which advance notification is required pursuant to the provisions of the Agreement on Measures to Reduce the Risk of Outbreak of Nuclear War Between the United States of America and the Union of Soviet Socialist Republics, signed 30 September 1971, and the Agreement Between the Government of the United States of America and the Government of the Union of Soviet Socialist Republics on the Prevention of Incidents On and Over the High Seas, signed 25 May 1972. Nothing in Article XVI of the Treaty is intended to inhibit advance notification, on a voluntary basis, of any ICBM launches not subject to its provisions, the advance notifi-*

cation of which would enhance confidence between the Parties.

Second Common Understanding. *A multiple ICBM launch conducted by a Party, as distinct from single ICBM launches referred to in Article XVI of the Treaty, is a launch which would result in two or more of its ICBMs being in flight at the same time.*

Third Common Understanding. *The test ranges referred to in Article XVI of the Treaty are those covered by the Second Agreed Statement to paragraph 2 of Article VII of the Treaty.*

2. The Parties shall agree in the Standing Consultative Commission upon procedures to implement the provisions of this Article.

Article XVII

1. To promote the objectives and implementation of the provisions of this Treaty, the Parties shall use the Standing Consultative Commission established by the Memorandum of Understanding Between the Government of the United States of America and the Government of the Union of Soviet Socialist Republics Regarding the Establishment of a Standing Consultative Commission of 21 December 1972.

2. Within the framework of the Standing Consultative Commission, with respect to this Treaty, the Parties will:

(a) consider questions concerning compliance with the obligations assumed and related situations which may be considered ambiguous;

(b) provide on a voluntary basis such information as either Party considers necessary to assure confidence in compliance with the obligation assumed;

(c) consider questions involving unintended interference with national technical means of verification, and questions involving unintended impeding of verification by national technical means of compliance with the provisions of this Treaty;

(d) consider possible changes in the strategic situation which have a bearing on the provisions of this Treaty;

(e) agree upon procedures for replacement, conversion, and dismantling or destruction, of strategic offensive arms in cases provided for in the provisions of this Treaty and upon procedures for removal of such arms from the aggregate numbers when they otherwise cease to be subject to the limitations provided for in this Treaty, and at regular sessions of the Standing Consultative Commission, notify each other in accordance with the aforementioned procedures, at least twice annually, of actions completed and those in process;

(f) consider, as appropriate, possible proposals for further increasing the viability of this Treaty, including proposals for amendments in accordance with the provisions of this Treaty;

(g) consider, as appropriate, proposals for further measures limiting strategic offensive arms.

3. In the Standing Consultative Commission the Parties shall maintain by category the agreed data base on the numbers of strategic offensive arms established by the Memorandum of Understanding Between the United States of America and the Union of Soviet Socialist Republics Regarding the Establishment of a Data Base on the Numbers of Strategic Offensive Arms of 18 June 1979.

To Paragraph 3 of Article XVII of the Treaty

Agreed Statement. *In order to maintain the agreed data base on the numbers of strategic offensive arms subject to the limitations provided for in the Treaty in accordance with paragraph 3 of Article XVII of the Treaty, at each regular session of the Standing Consultative Commission the Parties will notify each other of and consider changes in those numbers in the following categories: launchers of ICBMs; fixed launchers of ICBMs; launchers of ICBMs equipped with MIRVs; launchers of SLBMs; launchers of SLBMs equipped with MIRVs; heavy bombers; heavy bombers equipped for cruise missiles capable of a range in excess of 600 kilometres; heavy bombers equipped only for ASBMs; ASBMs; and ASBMs equipped with MIRVs.*

Article XVIII

Each Party may propose amendments to this Treaty. Agreed amendments shall enter into force in accordance with the procedures governing the entry into force of this Treaty.

Article XIX

1. This Treaty shall be subject to ratification in accordance with the constitutional procedures of each Party. This Treaty shall enter into force on the day of the exchange of instruments of ratification and shall remain in force through 31 December 1985, unless replaced earlier by an agreement further limiting strategic offensive arms.

2. This Treaty shall be registered pursuant to Article 102 of the Charter of the United Nations.

3. Each Party shall, in exercising its national sovereignty, have the right to withdraw from this Treaty if it decides that extraordinary events related to the subject matter of this Treaty have jeopardized its supreme interests. It shall give notice of its decision to the other party six months prior to withdrawal from the Treaty. Such notice shall include a statement of the extraordinary events the notifying Party regards as having jeopardized its supreme interests.

PROTOCOL

The United States of America and the Union of Soviet Socialist Republics, hereinafter referred to as the Parties,

Having agreed on limitations on strategic offensive arms in the Treaty,

Have agreed on additional limitations for the period during which this Protocol remains in force, as follows:

Article I

Each Party undertakes not to deploy mobile ICBM launchers or to flight-test ICBMs from such launchers.

Article II

1. Each Party undertakes not to deploy cruise missiles capable of a range in excess of 600 kilometers on sea-based launchers or on land-based launchers.

2. Each Party undertakes not to flight-test cruise missiles capable of a range in excess of 600 kilometers which are equipped with multiple independently targetable warheads from sea-based launchers or from land-based launchers.

To Paragraph 2 of Article II of the Protocol

Agreed Statement. *Warheads of a cruise missile are independently targetable if manoeuvring or targeting of the warheads to separate aim points along ballistic trajectories or any other flight paths, which are unrelated to each other, is accomplished during a flight of a cruise missile.*

---

3. For the purposes of this Protocol, cruise missiles are unmanned, self-propelled, guided, weapon-delivery vehicles which sustain flight through the use of aerodynamic lift over most of their flight path and which are flight-tested from or deployed on sea-based or land-based launchers, that is, sea-launched cruise missiles and ground-launched cruise missiles, repectively.

To Paragraph 3 of Article II of the Protocol

First Agreed Statement. *If a cruise missile is capable of a range in excess of 600 kilometres, all cruise missiles of that type shall be considered to be cruise missiles capable of a range in excess of 600 kilometres.*

First Common Understanding. *If a cruise missile has been flight-tested to a range in excess of 600 kilometres, it shall be considered to be a cruise missile capable of a range in excess of 600 kilometres.*

Second Common Understanding. *Cruise missiles not capable of a range in excess of 600 kilometres shall not be considered to be a type capable of a range in excess of 600 kilometres if they are distinguishable on the basis of externally observable design features from cruise missiles of types capable of a range in excess of 600 kilometres.*

Second Agreed Statement. *The range of which a cruise missile is capable is the maximum distance which can be covered by the missile in its standard design mode flying until fuel exhaustion, determined by projecting its flight path onto the Earth's sphere from the point of launch to the point of impact.*

Third Agreed Statement. *If an unmanned, self-propelled, guided vehicle which sustains flight through the use of aerodynamic lift over most of its flight path has been flight-tested or deployed for weapon delivery, all vehicles of that type shall be considered to be weapon-delivery vehicles.*

Third Common Understanding. *Unmanned, self-propelled, guided vehicles which sustain flight through the use of aerodynamic lift over most of their flight path and are not weapon-delivery vehicles, that is, unarmed, pilotless, guided vehicles, shall not be considered to be cruise missiles if such vehicles are distinguishable from cruise missiles on the basis of externally observable design features.*

Fourth Common Understanding. *Neither Party shall convert unarmed, pilotless, guided vehicles into cruise missiles capable of a range in excess of 600 kilometres, nor shall either Party convert cruise missiles capable of a range in excess of 600 kilometres into unarmed, pilotless, guided vehicles.*

Fifth Common Understanding. *Neither Party has plans during the term of the Protocol to flight-test from or deploy on sea-based or land-based launchers unarmed, pilotless, guided vehicles which are capable of a range in excess of 600 kilometres. In the future, should a Party have such plans, that Party will provide notification thereof to the other Party well in advance of such flight-testing or deployment. This Common Understanding does not apply to target drones.*

Article III

Each Party undertakes not to flight-test or deploy ASBMs.

Article IV

This Protocol shall be considered an integral part of the Treaty. It shall enter into force on the day of the entry into force of the Treaty and shall remain in force through 31 December 1981, unless replaced earlier by an agreement on further measures limiting strategic offensive arms.

Source: Committee on Disarmament documents CD/28, 27 June 1979 and CD/29, 2 July 1979

MEMORANDUM OF UNDERSTANDING BETWEEN THE USA AND THE USSR REGARDING THE ESTABLISHMENT OF A DATA BASE ON THE NUMBERS OF STRATEGIC OFFENSIVE ARMS

Signed at Vienna on 18 June 1979

For the purposes of the Treaty Between the United States of America and the Union of Soviet Socialist Republics on the Limitation of Strategic Offensive Arms, the Parties have considered data on numbers of strategic offensive arms and agree that as of 1 November 1978 there existed the following numbers of strategic offensive arms subject to the limitations provided for in the Treaty which is being signed today.

	United States	USSR
Launchers of ICBMs	1,054	1,398
Fixed launchers of ICBMs	1,054	1,398
Launchers of ICBMs equipped with MIRVs	550	576
Launchers of SLBMs	656	950
Launchers of SLBMs equipped with MIRVs	496	128
Heavy bombers	574	156
Heavy bombers equipped for cruise missiles capable of a range in excess of 600 kilometers	0	0
Heavy bombers equipped only for ASBMs	0	0
ASBMs	0	0
ASBMs equipped with MIRVs	0	0

At the time of entry into force of the Treaty the Parties will update the above agreed data in the categories listed in this Memorandum.

Source: Committee on Disarmament document CD/29, 2 July 1979

STATEMENT BY THE USA OF DATA ON THE NUMBERS OF STRATEGIC OFFENSIVE ARMS AS OF THE DATE OF SIGNATURE OF THE SALT II TREATY

Signed at Vienna on 18 June 1979

The United States of America declares that as of 18 June 1979, it possesses the following numbers of strategic offensive arms subject to the limitations provided for in the Treaty which is being signed today:

Launchers of ICBMs	1,054
Fixed launchers of ICBMs	1,054
Launchers of ICBMs equipped with MIRVs	550
Launchers of SLBMs	656
Launchers of SLBMs equipped with MIRVs	496
Heavy bombers	573
Heavy bombers equipped for cruise missiles capable of a range in excess of 600 kilometers	3
Heavy bombers equipped only for ASBMs	0
ASBMs	0
ASBMs equipped with MIRVs	0

Source: Committee on Disarmament document CD/29, 2 July 1979

STATEMENT BY THE USSR OF DATA ON THE NUMBERS OF STRATEGIC OFFENSIVE ARMS AS OF THE DATE OF SIGNATURE OF THE SALT II TREATY

Signed at Vienna on 18 June 1979

The Union of Soviet Socialist Republics declares that as of 18 June 1979 it possesses the following numbers of strategic offensive arms subject to the limitations provided for in the Treaty which is being signed today:

Launchers of ICBMs	1,398
Fixed launchers of ICBMs	1,398
Launchers of ICBMs equipped with MIRVs	608
Launchers of SLBMs	950
Launchers of SLBMs equipped with MIRVs	144
Heavy bombers	156
Heavy bombers equipped for cruise missiles capable of a range in excess of 600 kilometers	0
Heavy bombers equipped only for ASBMs	0
ASBMs	0
ASBMs equipped with MIRVs	0

Source: Committee on Disarmament document CD/29, 2 July 1979

JOINT STATEMENT BY THE USA AND THE USSR OF PRINCIPLES AND BASIC GUIDELINES FOR SUBSEQUENT NEGOTIATIONS ON THE LIMITATION OF STRATEGIC ARMS

Signed at Vienna on 18 June 1979

The United States of America and the

Union of Soviet Socialist Republics, hereinafter referred to as the Parties,

Having concluded the Treaty on the Limitation of Strategic Offensive Arms,

Reaffirming that the strengthening of strategic stability meets the interests of the Parties and the interests of international security,

Convinced that early agreement on the further limitation and further reduction of strategic arms would serve to strengthen international peace and security and to reduce the risk of outbreak of nuclear war,

Have agreed as follows:

First. The Parties will continue to pursue negotiations, in accordance with the principle of equality and equal security, on measures for the further limitation and reduction in the numbers of strategic arms, as well as for their further qualitative limitation.

In furtherance of existing agreements between the Parties on the limitation and reduction of strategic arms, the Parties will continue, for the purposes of reducing and averting the risk of outbreak of nuclear war, to seek measures to strengthen strategic stability by, among other things, limitations on strategic offensive arms most destabilizing to the strategic balance and by measures to reduce and to avert the risk of surprise attack.

Second. Further limitations and reductions of stategic arms must be subject to adequate verification by national technical means, using additionally, as appropriate, cooperative measures contributing to the effectiveness of verification by national technical means. The Parties will seek to strengthen verification and to perfect the operation of the Standing Consultative Commission in order to promote assurance of compliance with the obligations assumed by the Parties.

Third. The Parties shall pursue in the course of these negotiations, taking into consideration factors that determine the strategic situation, the following objectives:

1. significant and substantial reductions in the numbers of strategic offensive arms;

2. qualitative limitations on strategic offensive arms, including restrictions on the development, testing, and deployment of new types of strategic offensive arms and on the modernization of existing strategic offensive arms;

3. resolution of the issues included in the Protocol to the Treaty between the United States of America and the Union of Soviet Socialist Republics on the Limitation of Strategic Offensive Arms in the context of the negotiations relating to the implementation of the principles and objectives set out herein.

Fourth. The Parties will consider other steps to ensure and enhance strategic stability, to ensure the equality and equal security of the Parties, and to implement the above principles and objectives. Each Party will be free to raise any issue relative to the further limitation of strategic arms. The parties will also consider further joint measures, as appropriate, to strengthen international peace and security and to reduce the risk of outbreak of nuclear war.

Source: Committee on Disarmament document CD/28, 27 June 1979

JOINT US–SOVIET COMMUNIQUÉ IN CONNECTION WITH THE SIGNING OF THE SALT II TREATY

Issued at Vienna on 18 June 1979

EXCERPT:

. . .

I. General Aspects of US–Soviet Relations

There is agreement between the sides that the state of relations between the United States and the Soviet Union is of great importance for the fundamental interests of the peoples of both countries and that it significantly affects the development of the international situation as a whole. Recognizing the great responsibility connected with this, the sides have expressed their firm intent to continue working toward the establishment of a more stable and constructive foundation for US–Soviet relations. To this end, the two sides acknowledged the necessity of expanding areas of cooperation between them.

Such cooperation should be based on the principles of complete equality, equal security, respect for sovereignty and nonintervention in each other's internal affairs, and should facilitate the relaxation of international tension and the peaceful conduct of mutually beneficial relations between states, and thereby enhance international stability and world peace.

The sides reaffirmed their conviction that full implementation of each of the provisions of the "Basic Principles of Relations between the United States of America and the Union of Soviet Socialist **Republics**" as well as other treaties and agreements concluded between them would contribute to a more stable relationship between the two countries.

The two sides stressed the importance of peaceful resolution of disputes, respect for the sovereignty and territorial integrity of states, and of efforts so that conflicts or situations would not arise which could serve to increase international tensions. They recognize the right of the peoples of all states to determine their future without outside interference.

Recognizing that an armed world conflict can and must be avoided, the sides believe that at the present time there is no more important and urgent task for mankind than ending the arms race and preventing war. They expressed their intention to make every effort to attain that goal. To that end, they also recognized the value of consultation between themselves and with other governments, at the United Nations and elsewhere, in order to prevent and eliminate conflict in various regions of the world.

The sides note with satisfaction the growing practice of contacts between government officials of the USA and the USSR in the course of which key questions of US–Soviet relations and pressing international issues are discussed. The process of developing useful ties between the US Congress and the Supreme Soviet of the USSR and of exchanges between non-governmental organizations is continuing.

The talks again confirmed the specific significance of personal meetings between the leaders of the USA and the USSR in resolving the basic questions in the relations between the two states. In principle, it has been agreed that such meetings will be held in the future on a regular basis, with the understanding that the specific timing will be determined by mutual agreement.

Agreement has also been reached on broadening the practice of consultations and exchanges of opinion between representatives of the sides on other levels.

II. Limitations of Nuclear and Conventional Arms

The two sides reaffirmed their deep conviction that special importance should be attached to the problems of the prevention of nuclear war and to curbing the competition in strategic arms. Both sides recognized that nuclear war would be a disaster for all mankind. Each stated that it is not striving and will not strive for military superiority, since that can only result in dangerous instability, generating higher levels of armaments with no benefit to the security of either side.

Recognizing that the USA and the USSR have a special responsibility to reduce the risk of nuclear war and contribute to world peace, President Carter and President Brezhnev committed themselves to take major steps to limit nuclear weapons with the objective of ultimately eliminating them, and to complete successfully other arms limitation and disarmament negotiations.

SALT. In the course of the meeting, President Carter and President Brezhnev confirmed and signed the Treaty Between the USA and the USSR on the Limitation of Strategic Offensive Arms, the Protocol thereto, the Joint Statement of Principles and Basic Guidelines for Subsequent Negotiations on the Limitation of Strategic Arms and the document entitled Agreed Statements and Common Understandings Regarding the Treaty Between the USA and USSR on the Limitation of Strategic Offensive Arms.

At the same time, the sides again stressed the great significance of the Treaty on the Limitation of Anti-Ballistic Missile Systems and strict compliance with its provisions and of other agreements previously concluded between them in the field of strategic arms limitations and reducing the danger of nuclear war.

Both sides express their deep satisfaction with the process of the negotiations on strategic arms limitations and the fact that their persistent efforts for many years to conclude a new treaty have been crowned with success. This treaty sets equal ceilings on the nuclear delivery systems of both sides; to begin the process of reductions it requires the reduction of existing nuclear arms; to begin to limit the threat represented by the qualitative arms race it also places substantial constraints on the modernization of strategic offensive systems and the development of new ones.

The new Treaty on the Limitation of Strategic Offensive Arms and the Protocol thereto represent a mutually acceptable balance between the interests of the sides based on the principles of equality and equal security. These documents are a substantial contribution to the prevention of nuclear war and the deepening of detente, and thus serve the interests not only of the American and Soviet peoples, but the aspirations of mankind for peace.

The two sides reaffirmed their commitment strictly to observe every provision in the treaty.

President Carter and President Brezhnev discussed questions relating to the SALT III negotiations and in this connection expressed the firm intention of the sides to act in accordance with the Joint Statement of Principles and Basic Guidelines for Subsequent Negotiations on the Limitation of Strategic Arms.

Comprehensive Test Ban Treaty. It was noted that there has been definite progress at the negotiations, in which the UK is also participating, on an international treaty comprehensively banning test explosions of nuclear weapons in any environment and an associated protocol. They confirmed the intention of the USA and the USSR to work, together with the UK, to complete preparation of this treaty as soon as possible.

Non-proliferation. The two sides reaffirmed the importance they attach to nuclear non-proliferation. They consistently advocate the further strengthening of the regime of non-proliferation of nuclear weapons and confirm their resolve to continue to comply strictly with the obligations they have assumed under the Treaty on the Non-Proliferation of Nuclear Weapons. They stressed the importance of applying comprehensive international safeguards under the International Atomic Energy Agency and pledged to continue their efforts to strengthen these safeguards.

They noted the profound threat posed to

world security by the proliferation of nuclear weapons, and agreed that the states already possessing nuclear weapons bear a special responsibility to demonstrate restraint. To this end, they affirmed their joint conviction that further efforts are needed, including on a regional basis, and expressed the hope that the conclusion of the SALT II Treaty will make an important contribution toward non-proliferation objectives.

Both sides further committed themselves to close cooperation, along with other countries, to insure a successful conclusion to the Non-Proliferation Treaty Review Conference in 1980, and called upon all states which have not already done so to sign and ratify the Non-Proliferation Treaty.

Vienna Negotiations. President Carter and President Brezhnev emphasized the great importance the sides attached to the negotiations on the mutual reduction of forces and armaments and associated measures in Central Europe in which they are participating with other states. A reduction of the military forces of both sides and the implementation of associated measures in Central Europe would be a major contribution to stability and security.

ASAT. It was also agreed to continue actively searching for mutually acceptable agreement in the ongoing negotiations on anti-satellite systems.

Conventional Arms Transfers. The two sides agreed that their respective representatives will meet promptly to discuss questions related to the next round of negotiations on limiting conventional arms transfers.

Chemical Weapons. The two sides reaffirmed the importance of a general, complete and verifiable prohibition of chemical weapons and agreed to intensify their efforts to prepare an agreed joint proposal for presentation to the Committee on Disarmament.

Radiological Weapons. President Carter and President Brezhnev were pleased to be able to confirm that bilateral agreement on major elements of a treaty banning the development, production, stockpiling and use of radiological weapons has been reached. An agreed joint proposal will be presented to the Committee on Disarmament this year.

Indian Ocean. The two sides agreed that their respective representatives will meet promptly to discuss the resumption of the talks on questions concerning arms limitation measures in the Indian Ocean.

Other Questions of Arms Limitations and General Disarmament. In discussing other questions connected with solving the problems of limiting the arms race and of disarmament, the sides expressed their support for the Final Document adopted at the Special Session of the UN General Assembly on Disarmament. The sides noted their support for a second special session of the

UN General Assembly devoted to disarmament and for that session to be followed by the convocation of a World Disarmament Conference with universal participation, adequately prepared and at an appropriate time.

The USA and the USSR will continue to cooperate between themselves and with other member states of the Committee on Disarmament with its enlarged membership for the purpose of working out effective steps in the field of disarmament in that forum.

In summing up the exchange of views on the state of negotiations being conducted between the USA and the USSR, or with their participation, on a number of questions connected with arms limitation and disarmament, the sides agreed to give new impetus to the joint efforts to achieve practical results at these negotiations.

. . .

Source: United States Department of State, Bureau of Public Affairs, *Vienna Summit*, Department of State Publication 8985, General Foreign Policy Series 316 (Washington, D.C., 1979)

AGREEMENT GOVERNING THE ACTIVITIES OF STATES ON THE MOON AND OTHER CELESTIAL BODIES

Opened for signature at New York on 5 December 1979
Not in force by 1 October 1981
Depositary: UN Secretary-General

The States Parties to this Agreement,
Noting the achievements of States in the exploration and use of the moon and other celestial bodies,
Recognizing that the moon, as a natural satellite of the earth, has an important role to play in the exploration of outer space,
Determined to promote on the basis of equality the further development of co-operation among States in the exploration and use of the moon and other celestial bodies,
Desiring to prevent the moon from becoming an area of international conflict,
Bearing in mind the benefits which may be derived from the exploitation of the natural resources of the moon and other celestial bodies,
Recalling the Treaty on Principles Governing the Activities of States in the Exploration and Use of Outer Space, including the Moon and Other Celestial Bodies, the Agreement on

the Rescue of Astronauts, the Return of Astronauts and the Return of Objects Launched into Outer Space, the Convention on International Liability for Damage Caused by Space Objects and the Convention on Registration of Objects Launched into Outer Space,

Taking into account the need to define and develop the provisions of these international instruments in relation to the moon and other celestial bodies, having regard to further progress in the exploration and use of outer space,

Have agreed on the following:

Article 1

1. The provisions of this Agreement relating to the moon shall also apply to other celestial bodies within the solar system, other than the earth, except in so far as specific legal norms enter into force with respect to any of these celestial bodies.

2. For the purposes of this Agreement reference to the moon shall include orbits around or other trajectories to or around it.

3. This Agreement does not apply to extraterrestrial materials which reach the surface of the earth by natural means.

Article 2

All activites on the moon, including its exploration and use, shall be carried out in accordance with international law, in particular the Charter of the United Nations, and taking into account the Declaration on Principles of International Law concerning Friendly Relations and Co-operation among States in accordance with the Charter of the United Nations, adopted by the General Assembly on 24 October 1970, in the interests of maintaining international peace and security and promoting international co-operation and mutual understanding, and with due regard to the corresponding interests of all other States Parties.

Article 3

1. The moon shall be used by all States Parties exclusively for peaceful purposes.

2. Any threat or use of force or any other hostile act or threat of hostile act on the moon is prohibited. It is likewise prohibited to use the moon in order to commit any such act or to engage in any such threat in relation to the earth, the moon, spacecraft, the personnel of spacecraft or man-made space objects.

3. States Parties shall not place in orbit around or other trajectory to or around the moon objects carrying nuclear weapons or any other kinds of weapons of mass destruction or place or use such weapons on or in the moon.

4. The establishment of military bases, installations and fortifications, the testing of any type of weapons and the conduct of military manoeuvres on the moon shall be forbidden. The use of military personnel for scientific research or for any other peaceful

purposes shall not be prohibited. The use of any equipment or facility necessary for peaceful exploration and use of the moon shall also not be prohibited.

Article 4

1. The exploration and use of the moon shall be the province of all mankind and shall be carried out for the benefit and in the interests of all countries, irrespective of their degree of economic or scientific development. Due regard shall be paid to the interests of present and future generations as well as to the need to promote higher standards of living and conditions of economic and social progress and development in accordance with the Charter of the United Nations.

2. States Parties shall be guided by the principle of co-operation and mutual assistance in all their activities concerning the exploration and use of the moon. International co-operation in pursuance of this Agreement should be as wide as possible and may take place on a multilateral basis, on a bilateral basis or through international intergovernmental organizations.

Article 5

1. States Parties shall inform the Secretary-General of the United Nations as well as the public and the international scientific community, to the greatest extent feasible and practicable, of their activities concerned with the exploration and use of the moon. Information on the time, purposes, locations, orbital parameters and duration shall be given in respect of each mission to the moon as soon as possible after launching, while information on the results of each mission, including scientific results, shall be furnished upon completion of the mission. In the case of a mission lasting more than sixty days, information on conduct of the mission, including any scientific results, shall be given periodically at thirty day intervals. For missions lasting more than six months, only significant additions to such information need be reported thereafter.

2. If a State Party becomes aware that another State Party plans to operate simultaneously in the same area of or in the same orbit around or trajectory to or around the moon, it shall promptly inform the other State of the timing of and plans for its own operations.

3. In carrying out activities under this Agreement, States Parties shall promptly inform the Secretary-General, as well as the public and the international scientific community, of any phenomena they discover in outer space, including the moon, which could endanger human life or health, as well as of any indication of organic life.

Article 6

1. There shall be freedom of scientific investigation on the moon by all States Parties without discrimination of any kind, on

the basis of equality and in accordance with international law.

2. In carrying out scientific investigations and in furtherance of the provisions of this Agreement, the States Parties shall have the right to collect on and remove from the moon samples of its mineral and other substances. Such samples shall remain at the disposal of those States Parties which caused them to be collected and may be used by them for scientific purposes. States Parties shall have regard to the desirability of making a portion of such samples available to other interested States Parties and the international scientific community for scientific investigation. States Parties may in the course of scientific investigations also use mineral and other substances of the moon in quantities appropriate for the support of their missions.

3. States Parties agree on the desirability of exchanging scientific and other personnel on expeditions to or installations on the moon to the greatest extent feasible and practicable.

Article 7

1. In exploring and using the moon, States Parties shall take measures to prevent the disruption of the existing balance of its environment whether by introducing adverse changes in that environment, by its harmful contamination through the introduction of extra-environmental matter or otherwise. States Parties shall also take measures to avoid harmfully affecting the environment of the earth through the introduction of extra-terrestrial matter or otherwise.

2. States Parties shall inform the Secretary-General of the United Nations of the measures being adopted by them in accordance with paragraph 1 of this article and shall also, to the maximum extent feasible, notify him in advance of all placements by them of radio-active materials on the moon and of the purposes of such placements.

3. States Parties shall report to other States Parties and to the Secretary-General concerning areas of the moon having special scientific interest in order that, without prejudice to the rights of other States Parties, consideration may be given to the designation of such areas as international scientific preserves for which special protective arrangements are to be agreed upon in consultation with the competent bodies of the United Nations.

Article 8

1. States Parties may pursue their activities in the exploration and use of the moon anywhere on or below its surface, subject to the provisions of this Agreement.

2. For these purposes States Parties may, in particular:

(*a*) Land their space objects on the moon and launch them from the moon;

(*b*) Place their personnel, space vehicles, equipment, facilities, stations and instal-

lations anywhere on or below the surface of the moon.

Personnel, space vehicles, equipment, facilities, stations and installations may move or be moved freely over or below the surface of the moon.

3. Activities of States Parties in accordance with paragraphs 1 and 2 of this article shall not interfere with the activities of other States Parties on the moon. Where such interference may occur, the States Parties concerned shall undertake consultations in accordance with article 15, paragraphs 2 and 3 of this Agreement.

Article 9

1. States Parties may establish manned and unmanned stations on the moon. A State Party establishing a station shall use only that area which is required for the needs of the station and shall immediately inform the Secretary-General of the United Nations of the location and purposes of that station. Subsequently, at annual intervals that State shall likewise inform the Secretary-General whether the station continues in use and whether its purposes have changed.

2. Stations shall be installed in such a manner that they do not impede the free access to all areas of the moon by personnel, vehicles and equipment of other States Parties conducting activities on the moon in accordance with the provisions of this Agreement or of article I of the Treaty on Principles Governing the Activities of States in the Exploration and Use of Outer Space, including the Moon and Other Celestial Bodies.

Article 10

1. States Parties shall adopt all practicable measures to safeguard the life and health of persons on the moon. For this purpose they shall regard any person on the moon as an astronaut within the meaning of article V of the Treaty on Principles Governing the Activities of States in the Exploration and Use of Outer Space, including the Moon and Other Celestial Bodies and as part of the personnel of a spacecraft within the meaning of the Agreement of the Rescue of Astronauts, the Return of Astronauts and the Return of Objects Launched into Outer Space.

2. States Parties shall offer shelter in their stations, installations, vehicles and other facilities to persons in distress on the moon.

Article 11

1. The moon and its natural resources are the common heritage of mankind, which finds its expression in the provisions of this Agreement, in particular in paragraph 5 of this article.

2. The moon is not subject to national appropriation by any claim of sovereignty, by means of use or occupation, or by any other means.

3. Neither the surface nor the subsurface

of the moon, nor any part thereof or natural resources in place, shall become property of any State, international intergovernmental or non-governmental organization, national organization or non-governmental entity or of any natural person. The placement of personnel, space vehicles, equipment, facilities, stations and installations on or below the surface of the moon, including structures connected with its surface or sub-surface, shall not create a right of ownership over the surface or the subsurface of the moon or any areas thereof. The foregoing provisions are without prejudice to the international régime referred to in paragraph 5 of this article.

4. States Parties have the right to exploration and use of the moon without discrimination of any kind, on the basis of equality and in accordance with international law and the terms of this Agreement.

5. States Parties to this Ageement hereby undertake to establish an international régime, including appropriate procedures, to govern the exploitation of the natural resources of the moon as such exploitation is about to become feasible. This provision shall be implemented in accordance with article 18 of this Agreement.

6. In order to facilitate the establishment of the international régime referred to in paragraph 5 of this article, States Parties shall inform the Secretary-General of the United Nations as well as the public and the international scientific community, to the greatest extent feasible and practicable, of any natural resources they may discover on the moon.

7. The main purposes of the international régime to be established shall include:

(a) The orderly and safe development of the natural resources of the moon;

(b) The rational management of those resources;

(c) The expansion of opportunities in the use of those resources;

(d) An equitable sharing by all States Parties in the benefits derived from those resources, whereby the interests and needs of the developing countries, as well as the efforts of those countries which have contributed either directly or indirectly to the exploration of the moon, shall be given special consideration.

8. All the activities with respect to the natural resources of the moon shall be carried out in a manner compatible with the purposes specified in paragraph 7 of this article and the provisions of article 6, paragraph 2, of this Agreement.

Article 12

1. States Parties shall retain jurisdiction and control over their personnel, space vehicles, equipment, facilities, stations and installations on the moon. The ownership of space vehicles, equipment, facilities, stations and installations shall not be affected by their presence on the moon.

2. Vehicles, installations and equipment or their component parts found in places other than their intended location shall be dealt with in accordance with article 5 of the Agreement on Rescue of Astronauts, the Return of Astronauts and the Return of Objects Launched into Outer Space.

3. In the event of an emergency involving a threat to human life, States Parties may use the equipment, vehicles, installations, facilities or supplies of other States Parties on the moon. Prompt notification of such use shall be made to the Secretary-General of the United Nations or the State Party concerned.

Article 13

A State Party which learns of the crash landing, forced landing or other unintended landing on the moon of a space object, or its component parts, that were not launched by it, shall promptly inform the launching State party and the Secretary-General of the United Nations.

Article 14

1. States Parties to this Agreement shall bear international responsibility for national activities on the moon, whether such activities are carried out by governmental agencies or by non-governmental entities, and for assuring that national activities are carried out in conformity with the provisions set forth in this Agreement. States Parties shall ensure that non-governmental entities under their jurisdiction shall engage in activities on the moon only under the authority and continuing supervision of the appropriate State Party.

2. States Parties recognize that detailed arrangements concerning liability for damage caused on the moon, in addition to the provisions of the Treaty on Principles Governing the Activities of States in the Exploration and Use of Outer Space, including the Moon and Other Celestial Bodies and the Convention on International Liability for Damage Caused by Space Objects, may become necessary as a result of more extensive activities on the moon. Any such arrangements shall be elaborated in accordance with the procedure provided for in article 18 of this Agreement.

Article 15

1. Each State Party may assure itself that the activities of other States Parties in the exploration and use of the moon are compatible with the provisions of this Agreement. To this end, all space vehicles, equipment, facilities, stations and installations on the moon shall be open to other States Parties. Such States Parties shall give reasonable advance notice of a projected visit, in order that appropriate consultations may be held and that maximum precautions may be taken to assure safety and to avoid interference with normal operations in the facility to be visited. In pursuance of this article, any State Party may act on its own behalf or with the full or partial assistance of any other State

Party or through appropriate international procedures within the framework of the United Nations and in accordance with the Charter.

2. A State Party which has reason to believe that another State Party is not fulfilling the obligations incumbent upon it pursuant to this Agreement or that another State Party is interfering with the rights which the former State has under this Agreement may request consultations with that State Party. A State Party receiving such a request shall enter into such consultations without delay. Any other State Party which requests to do so shall be entitled to take part in the consultations. Each State Party participating in such consultations shall seek a mutually acceptable resolution of any controversy and shall bear in mind the rights and interests of all States Parties. The Secretary-General of the United Nations shall be informed of the results of the consultations and shall transmit the information received to all States Parties concerned.

3. If the consultations do not lead to a mutually acceptable settlement which has due regard for the rights and interests of all States parties, the parties concerned shall take all measures to settle the dispute by other peaceful means of their choice appropriate to the circumstances and the nature of the dispute. If difficulties arise in connexion with the opening of consultations or if consultations do not lead to a mutually acceptable settlement, any State Party may seek the assistance of the Secretary-General, without seeking the consent of any other State Party concerned, in order to resolve the controversy. A State Party which does not maintain diplomatic relations with another State party concerned shall participate in such consultations, at its choice, either itself or through another State Party or the Secretary-General as intermediary.

Article 16

With the exception of articles 17 to 21, references in this Agreement to States shall be deemed to apply to any international intergovernmental organization which conducts space activities if the organization declares its acceptance of the rights and obligations provided for in this Agreement and if a majority of the States members of the organization are States Parties to this Agreement and to the Treaty on Principles Governing the Activities of States in the Exploration and Use of Outer Space, including the Moon and Other Celestial Bodies. States members of any such organization which are States Parties to this Agreement shall take all appropriate steps to ensure that the organization makes a declaration in accordance with the foregoing.

Article 17

Any State Party to this Agreement may propose amendments to the Agreement. Amendments shall enter into force for each

State Party to the Agreement accepting the amendments upon their acceptance by a majority of the States Parties to the Agreement and thereafter for each remaining State Party to the Agreement on the date of acceptance by it.

Article 18

Ten years after the entry into force of this Agreement, the question of the review of the Agreement shall be included in the provisional agenda of the General Assembly of the United Nations in order to consider, in the light of past application of the Agreement, whether it requires revision. However, at any time after the Agreement has been in force for five years, the Secretary-General of the United Nations, as depository, shall, at the request of one third of the States Parties to the Agreement and with the concurrence of the majority of the States Parties, convene a conference of the States Parties to review this Agreement. A review conference shall also consider the question of the implementation of the provisions of article 11, paragraph 5, on the basis of the principle referred to in paragraph 1 of that article and taking into account in particular any relevant technological developments.

Article 19

1. This Agreement shall be open for signature by all States at United Nations Headquarters in New York.

2. This Agreement shall be subject to ratification by signatory States. Any State which does not sign this Agreement before its entry into force in accordance with paragraph 3 of this article may accede to it at any time. Instruments of ratification or accession shall be deposited with the Secretary-General of the United Nations.

3. This Agreement shall enter into force on the thirtieth day following the date of deposit of the fifth instrument of ratification.

4. For each State depositing its instrument of ratification or accession after the entry into force of this Agreement, it shall enter into force on the thirtieth day following the date of deposit of any such instrument.

5. The Secretary-General shall promptly inform all signatory and acceding States of the date of each signature, the date of deposit of each instrument of ratification or accession to this Agreement, the date of its entry into force and other notices.

Article 20

Any State Party to this Agreement may give notice of its withdrawal from the Agreement one year after its entry into force by written notification to the Secretary-General of the United Nations. Such withdrawal shall take effect one year from the date of receipt of this notification.

Article 21

The original of this Agreement, of which the Arabic, Chinese, English, French,

Russian and Spanish texts are equally authentic, shall be deposited with the Secretary-General of the United Nations, who shall send certified copies thereof to all signatory and acceding States.

Source: UN document, General Assembly Resolution 34/68, Annex

Ratified by: Philippines

CONVENTION ON THE PHYSICAL PROTECTION OF NUCLEAR MATERIAL

*Signed at Vienna and New York on
3 March 1980
Not in force by 1 October 1981
Depositary: IAEA Director General*

The states parties to this convention,
Recognizing the right of all States to develop and apply nuclear energy for peaceful purposes and their legitimate interests in the potential benefits to be derived from the peaceful application of nuclear energy,
Convinced of the need for facilitating international co-operation in the peaceful application of nuclear energy,
Desiring to avert the potential dangers posed by the unlawful taking and use of nuclear material,
Convinced that offences relating to nuclear material are a matter of grave concern and that there is an urgent need to adopt appropriate and effective measures to ensure the prevention, detection and punishment of such offences,
Aware of the need for international co-operation to establish, in conformity with the national law of each State Party and with this Convention, effective measures for the physical protection of nuclear material,
Convinced that this Convention should facilitate the safe transfer of nuclear material,
Stressing also the importance of the physical protection of nuclear material in domestic use, storage and transport,
Recognizing the importance of effective physical protection of nuclear material used for military purposes, and understanding that such material is and will continue to be accorded stringent physical protection,
Have agreed as follows:

Article 1

For the purposes of this Convention:
(*a*) "nuclear material" means plutonium except that with isotopic concentration exceeding 80% in plutonium-238; uranium-233; uranium enriched in the isotopes 235 or 233; uranium containing the mixture of isotopes as occurring in nature other than in the form of ore or ore-residue; any material containing one or more of the foregoing;
(*b*) "uranium enriched in the isotope 235 or 233" means uranium containing the isotopes 235 or 233 or both in an amount such that the abundance ratio of the sum of these isotopes to the isotope 238 is greater than the ratio of the isotope 235 to the isotope 238 occurring in nature;
(*c*) "international nuclear transport" means the carriage of a consignment of nuclear material by any means of transportation intended to go beyond the territory of the State where the shipment originates beginning with the departure from a facility of the shipper in that State and ending with the arrival at a facility of the receiver within the State of ultimate destination.

Article 2

1. This Convention shall apply to nuclear material used for peaceful purposes while in international nuclear transport.
2. With the exception of articles 3 and 4 and paragraph 3 of article 5, this Convention shall also apply to nuclear material used for peaceful purposes while in domestic use, storage and transport.
3. Apart from the commitments expressly undertaken by States Parties in the articles covered by paragraph 2 with respect to nuclear material used for peaceful purposes while in domestic use, storage and transport, nothing in this Convention shall be interpreted as affecting the sovereign rights of a State regarding the domestic use, storage and transport of such nuclear material.

Article 3

Each State Party shall take appropriate steps within the framework of its national law and consistent with international law to ensure as far as practicable that, during international nuclear transport, nuclear material within its territory, or on board a ship or aircraft under its jurisdiction insofar as such ship or aircraft is engaged in the transport to or from that State, is protected at the levels described in Annex I.

Article 4

1. Each State Party shall not export or authorize the export of nuclear material unless the State Party has received assurances that such material will be protected during the international nuclear transport at the levels described in Annex I.
2. Each State Party shall not import or authorize the import of nuclear material from a State not party to this Convention unless the State Party has received assurances that such material will during the international nuclear transport be protected at the levels described in Annex I.
3. A State Party shall not allow the transit through its territory by land or internal waterways or through its airports or seaports

of nuclear material between States that are not parties to this Convention unless the State Party has received assurances as far as practicable that this nuclear material will be protected during international nuclear transport at the levels described in Annex I.

4. Each State Party shall apply within the framework of its national law the levels of physical protection described in Annex I to nuclear material being transported from a part of that State to another part of the same State through international waters or airspace.

5. The State Party responsible for receiving assurances that the nuclear material will be protected at the levels described in Annex I according to paragraphs 1 to 3 shall identify and inform in advance States which the nuclear material is expected to transit by land or internal waterways, or whose airports or seaports it is expected to enter.

6. The responsibility for obtaining assurances referred to in paragraph 1 may be transferred, by mutual agreement, to the State Party involved in the transport as the importing State.

7. Nothing in this article shall be interpreted as in any way affecting the territorial sovereignty and jurisdiction of a State, including that over its airspace and territorial sea.

Article 5

1. States Parties shall identify and make known to each other directly or through the International Atomic Energy Agency their central authority and point of contact having responsibility for physical protection of nuclear material and for co-ordinating recovery and response operations in the event of any unauthorized removal, use or alteration of nuclear material or in the event of credible threat thereof.

2. In the case of theft, robbery or any other unlawful taking of nuclear material or of credible threat thereof, States Parties shall, in accordance with their national law, provide co-operation and assistance to the maximum feasible extent in the recovery and protection of such material to any State that so requests. In particular:

(a) a State Party shall take appropriate steps to inform as soon as possible other States, which appear to it to be concerned, of any theft, robbery or other unlawful taking of nuclear material or credible threat thereof and to inform, where appropriate, international organizations;

(b) as appropriate, the States Parties concerned shall exchange information with each other or international organizations with a view to protecting threatened nuclear material, verifying the integrity of the shipping container, or recovering unlawfully taken nuclear material and shall:

(i) co-ordinate their efforts through diplomatic and other agreed channels;
(ii) render assistance, if requested;
(iii) ensure the return of nuclear material stolen or missing as a conse-

quence of the above-mentioned events.
The means of implementation of this co-operation shall be determined by the States Parties concerned.

3. States Parties shall co-operate and consult as appropriate, with each other directly or through international organizations, with a view to obtaining guidance on the design, maintenance and improvement of systems of physical protection of nuclear material in international transport.

Article 6

1. States Parties shall take appropriate measures consistent with their national law to protect the confidentiality of any information which they receive in confidence by virtue of the provisions of this Convention from another State Party or through participation in an activity carried out for the implementation of this Convention. If States Parties provide information to international organizations in confidence, steps shall be taken to ensure that the confidentiality of such information is protected.

2. States Parties shall not be required by this Convention to provide any information which they are not permitted to communicate pursuant to national law or which would jeopardize the security of the State concerned or the physical protection of nuclear material.

Article 7

1. The intentional commission of:

(a) an act without lawful authority which constitutes the receipt, possession, use, transfer, alteration, disposal or dispersal of nuclear material and which causes or is likely to cause death or serious injury to any person or substantial damage to property;

(b) a theft or robbery of nuclear material;

(c) an embezzlement or fraudulent obtaining of nuclear material;

(d) an act constituting a demand for nuclear material by threat or use of force or by any other form of intimidation;

(e) a threat:

(i) to use nuclear material to cause death or serious injury to any person or substantial property damage, or

(ii) to commit an offence described in sub-paragraph (b) in order to compel a natural or legal person, international organization or State to do or to refrain from doing any act;

(f) an attempt to commit any offence described in paragraphs (a), (b) or (c); and

(g) an act which constitutes participation in any offence described in paragraphs (a) to (f) shall be made a punishable offence by each State Party under its national law.

2. Each State Party shall make the offences described in this article punishable by appropriate penalties which take into account their grave nature.

Article 8

1. Each State Party shall take such measures as may be necessary to establish its

jurisdiction over the offences set forth in article 7 in the following cases:

(a) when the offence is committed in the territory of that State or on board a ship or aircraft registered in that State;

(b) when the alleged offender is a national of that State.

2. Each State Party shall likewise take such measures as may be necessary to establish its jurisdiction over these offences in cases where the alleged offender is present in its territory and it does not extradite him pursuant to article 11 to any of the States mentioned in paragraph 1.

3. This Convention does not exclude any criminal jurisdiction exercised in accordance with national law.

4. In addition to the States Parties mentioned in paragraphs 1 and 2, each State Party may, consistent with international law, establish its jurisdiction over the offences set forth in article 7 when it is involved in international nuclear transport as the exporting or importing State.

Article 9

Upon being satisfied that the circumstances so warrant, the State Party in whose territory the alleged offender is present shall take appropriate measures, including detention, under its national law to ensure his presence for the purpose of prosecution or extradition. Measures taken according to this article shall be notified without delay to the States required to establish jurisdiction pursuant to article 8 and, where appropriate, all other States concerned.

Article 10

The State Party in whose territory the alleged offender is present shall, if it does not extradite him, submit, without exception whatsoever and without undue delay, the case to its competent authorities for the purpose of prosecution, through proceedings in accordance with the laws of that State.

Article 11

1. The offences in article 7 shall be deemed to be included as extraditable offences in any extradition treaty existing between States Parties. States Parties undertake to include those offences as extraditable offences in every future extradition treaty to be concluded between them.

2. If a State Party which makes extradition conditional on the existence of a treaty receives a request for extradition from another State Party with which it has no extradition treaty, it may at its option consider this Convention as the legal basis for extradition in respect of those offences. Extradition shall be subject to the other conditions provided by the law of the requested State.

3. States Parties which do not make extradition conditional on the existence of a treaty shall recognize those offences as extraditable offences between themselves subject to the conditions provided by the law of the re-

quested State.

4. Each of the offences shall be treated, for the purpose of extradition between State Parties, as if it had been committed not only in the place in which it occurred but also in the territories of the States Parties required to establish their jurisdiction in accordance with paragraph 1 of article 8.

Article 12

Any person regarding whom proceedings are being carried out in connection with any of the offences set forth in article 7 shall be guaranteed fair treatment at all stages of the proceedings.

Article 13

1. States Parties shall afford one another the greatest measure of assistance in connection with criminal proceedings brought in respect of the offences set forth in article 7, including the supply of evidence at their disposal necessary for the proceedings. The law of the State requested shall apply in all cases.

2. The provisions of paragraph 1 shall not affect obligations under any other treaty, bilateral or multilateral, which governs or will govern, in whole or in part, mutual assistance in criminal matters.

Article 14

1. Each State Party shall inform the depositary of its laws and regulations which give effect to this Convention. The depositary shall communicate such information periodically to all States Parties.

2. The State Party where an alleged offender is prosecuted shall, wherever practicable, first communicate the final outcome of the proceedings to the States directly concerned. The State Party shall also communicate the final outcome to the depositary who shall inform all States.

3. Where an offence involves nuclear material used for peaceful purposes in domestic use, storage or transport, and both the alleged offender and the nuclear material remain in the territory of the State Party in which the offence was committed, nothing in this Convention shall be interpreted as requiring that State Party to provide information concerning criminal proceedings arising out of such an offence.

Article 15

The Annexes constitute an integral part of this Convention.

Article 16

1. A conference of States Parties shall be convened by the depositary five years after the entry into force of this Convention to review the implementation of the Convention and its adequacy as concerns the preamble, the whole of the operative part and the annexes in the light of the then prevailing situation.

2. At intervals of not less than five years thereafter, the majority of States Parties may

obtain, by submitting a proposal to this effect to the depositary, the convening of further conferences with the same objective.

Article 17

1. In the event of a dispute between two or more States Parties concerning the interpretation or application of this Convention, such States Parties shall consult with a view to the settlement of the dispute by negotiation, or by any other peaceful means of settling disputes acceptable to all parties to the dispute.

2. Any dispute of this character which cannot be settled in the manner prescribed in paragraph 1 shall, at the request of any party to such dispute, be submitted to arbitration or referred to the International Court of Justice for decision. Where a dispute is submitted to arbitration, if, within six months from the date of the request, the parties to the dispute are unable to agree on the organization of the arbitration, a party may request the President of the International Court of Justice or the Secretary-General of the United Nations to appoint one or more arbitrators. In case of conflicting requests by the parties to the dispute, the request to the Secretary-General of the United Nations shall have priority.

3. Each State Party may at the time of signature, ratification, acceptance or approval of this Convention or accession thereto declare that it does not consider itself bound by either or both of the dispute settlement procedures provided for in paragraph 2. The other States Parties shall not be bound by a dispute settlement procedure provided for in paragraph 2, with respect to a State Party which has made a reservation to that procedure.

4. Any State Party which has made a reservation in accordance with paragraph 3 may at any time withdraw that reservation by notification to the depositary.

Article 18

1. This Convention shall be open for signature by all States at the Headquarters of the International Atomic Energy Agency in Vienna and at the Headquarters of the United Nations in New York from 3 March 1980 until its entry into force.

2. This Convention is subject to ratification, acceptance or approval by the signatory States.

3. After its entry into force, this Convention will be open for accession by all States.

4. (a) This Convention shall be open for signature or accession by international organizations and regional organizations of an integrated or other nature, provided that any such organization is constituted by sovereign States and has competence in respect of the negotiation, conclusion and application of international agreements in matters covered by this Convention.

(b) In matters within their competence, such organizations shall, on their own behalf, exercise the rights and fulfil the responsibilities which this Convention attributes to States Parties.

(c) When becoming party to this Convention such an organization shall communicate to the depositary a declaration indicating which States are members thereof and which articles of this Convention do not apply to it.

(d) Such an organization shall not hold any vote additional to those of its Member States.

5. Instruments of ratification, acceptance, approval or accession shall be deposited with the depositary.

Article 19

1. This Convention shall enter into force on the thirtieth day following the date of deposit of the twenty first instrument of ratification, acceptance or approval with the depositary.

2. For each State ratifying, accepting, approving or acceding to the Convention after the date of deposit of the twenty first instrument of ratification, acceptance or approval, the Convention shall enter into force on the thirtieth day after the deposit by such State of its instrument of ratification, acceptance, approval or accession.

Article 20

1. Without prejudice to article 16 a State Party may propose amendments to this Convention. The proposed amendment shall be submitted to the depositary who shall circulate it immediately to all States Parties. If a majority of States Parties request the depositary to convene a conference to consider the proposed amendments, the depositary shall invite all States Parties to attend such a conference to begin not sooner than thirty days after the invitations are issued. Any amendment adopted at the conference by a two-thirds majority of all States Parties shall be promptly circulated by the depositary to all States Parties.

2. The amendment shall enter into force for each State Party that deposits its instrument of ratification, acceptance or approval of the amendment on the thirtieth day after the date on which two thirds of the States Parties have deposited their instruments of ratification, acceptance or approval with the depositary. Thereafter, the amendment shall enter into force for any other State Party on the day on which that State Party deposits its instrument of ratification, acceptance or approval of the amendment.

Article 21

1. Any State Party may denounce this Convention by written notification to the depositary.

2. Denunciation shall take effect one hundred and eighty days following the date on which notification is received by the depositary.

Article 22

The depositary shall promptly notify all States of:

(a) each signature of this Convention;

(b) each deposit of an instrument of ratification, acceptance, approval or accession;

(c) any reservation or withdrawal in accordance with article 17;

(d) any communication made by an organization in accordance with paragraph 4(c) of article 18;

(e) the entry into force of this Convention;

(f) the entry into force of any amendment to this Convention; and

(g) any denunciation made under article 21.

Article 23

The original of this Convention, of which the Arabic, Chinese, English, French, Russian and Spanish texts are equally authentic, shall be deposited with the Director General of the International Atomic Energy Agency who shall send certified copies thereof to all States.

ANNEX I

Levels of physical protection to be applied in international transport of nuclear material as categorized in Annex II

1. Levels of physical protection for nuclear material during storage incidental to international nuclear transport include:

(a) For Category III materials, storage within an area to which access is controlled;

(b) For Category II materials, storage within an area under constant surveillance by guards or electronic devices, surrounded by a physical barrier with a limited number of points of entry under appropriate control or any area with an equivalent level of physical protection;

(c) For Category I material, storage within a protected area as defined for Category II above, to which, in addition, access is restricted to persons whose trustworthiness has been determined, and which is under surveillance by guards who are in close communication with appropriate response forces. Specific measures taken in this context should have as their object the detection and prevention of any assault, unauthorized access or unauthorized removal of material.

2. Levels of physical protection for nuclear material during international transport include:

(a) For Category II and III materials, transportation shall take place under special precautions including prior arrangements among sender, receiver, and carrier, and prior agreement between natural or legal persons subject to the jurisdiction and regulation of exporting and importing States, specifying time, place and procedures for transferring transport responsibility;

(b) For Category I materials, transportation shall take place under special precaution identified above for transportation of Category II and III materials, and in addition, under constant surveillance by escorts and under conditions which assure close communications with appropriate response forces;

(c) For natural uranium other than in the form of ore or ore-residue, transportation protection for quantities exceeding 500 kilograms U shall include advance notification of shipment specifying mode of transport, expected time of arrival and confirmation of receipt of shipment.

240

Table: Categorization of nuclear material

Material	Form	Category I	II	III[c]
1. Plutonium[a]	Unirradiated[b]	2 kg or more	Less than 2 kg but more than 500 g	500 g or less but more than 15 g
2. Uranium-235	Unirradiated[b] — uranium enriched to 20% ^{235}U or more	5 kg or more	Less than 5 kg but more than 1 kg	1 kg or less but more than 15 kg
	— uranium enriched to 10% ^{235}U but less than 20%		10 kg or more	Less than 10 kg but more than 1 kg
	— uranium enriched above natural, but less than 10% ^{235}U			10 kg or more
3. Uranium-233	Unirradiated[b]	2 kg or more	Less than 2 kg but more than 500 g	500 g or less but more than 15 g
4. Irradiated fuel			Depleted or natural uranium, thorium or low-enriched fuel (less than 10% fissile content)[d,e]	

[a] All plutonium except that with isotopic concentration exceeding 80% in plutonium-238.

[b] Material not irradiated in a reactor or material irradiated in a reactor but with a radiation level equal to or less than 100 rads/hour at one metre unshielded.

[c] Quantities not falling in Category III and natural uranium should be protected in accordance with prudent management practice.

[d] Although this level of protection is recommended, it would be open to States, upon evaluation of the specific circumstances, to assign a different category of physical protection.

[e] Other fuel which by virtue of its original fissile material content is classified as Category I or II before irradiation may be reduced one category level while the radiation level from the fuel exceeds 100 rads/hour at one metre unshielded.

Source: IAEA, Legal Division, Certified copy of the convention (Vienna, 1980)

Ratified by: German Democratic Republic, Philippines, Sweden

CONVENTION ON PROHIBITIONS OR RESTRICTIONS ON THE USE OF CERTAIN CONVENTIONAL WEAPONS WHICH MAY BE DEEMED TO BE EXCESSIVELY INJURIOUS OR TO HAVE INDISCRIMINATE EFFECTS

Signed at New York on 10 April 1981
Not in force by 1 October 1981
Depositary: UN Secretary-General

The High Contracting Parties,

Recalling that every State has the duty, in conformity with the Charter of the United Nations, to refrain in its international relations from the threat or use of force against the sovereignty, territorial integrity or political independence of any State, or in any other manner inconsistent with the purposes of the United Nations,

Further recalling the general principle of the protection of the civilian population against the effects of hostilities,

Basing themselves on the principle of international law that the right of the parties to an armed conflict to choose methods or means of warfare is not unlimited, and on the principle that prohibits the employment in armed conflicts of weapons, projectiles and material and methods of warfare of a nature to cause superfluous injury or unnecessary suffering,

Also recalling that it is prohibited to employ methods or means of warfare which are intended, or may be expected, to cause widespread, long-term and severe damage to the natural environment,

Confirming their determination that in cases not covered by this Convention and its annexed Protocols or by other international agreements, the civilian population and the combatants shall at all times remain under the protection and authority of the principles of international law derived from established custom, from the principles of humanity and from the dictates of public conscience,

Desiring to contribute to international détente, the ending of the arms race and the building of confidence among States, and hence to the realization of the aspiration of all peoples to live in peace,

Recognizing the importance of pursuing every effort which may contribute to progress towards general and complete disarmament under strict and effective international control,

Reaffirming the need to continue the codification and progressive development of the rules of international law applicable in armed conflict,

Wishing to prohibit or restrict further the use of certain conventional weapons and believing that the positive results achieved in this area may facilitate the main talks on disarmament with a view to putting an end to the production, stockpiling and proliferation of such weapons,

Emphasizing the desirability that all States become parties to this Convention and its annexed Protocols, especially the militarily significant States,

Bearing in mind that the General Assembly of the United Nations and the United Nations Disarmament Commission may decide to examine the question of a possible broadening of the scope of the prohibitions and restrictions contained in this Convention and its annexed Protocols,

Further bearing in mind that the Committee on Disarmament may decide to consider the question of adopting further measures to prohibit or restrict the use of certain conventional weapons,

Have agreed as follows:

Article 1. *Scope of application*

This Convention and its annexed Protocols shall apply in the situations referred to in Article 2 common to the Geneva Conventions of 12 August 1949 for the Protection of War Victims, including any situation described in paragraph 4 of Article 1 of Additional Protocol I to these Conventions.

Article 2. *Relations with other international agreements*

Nothing in this Convention or its annexed Protocols shall be interpreted as detracting from other obligations imposed upon the High Contracting Parties by international humanitarian law applicable in armed conflict.

Article 3. *Signature*

This Convention shall be open for signature by all States at United Nations Headquarters in New York for a period of twelve months from 10 April 1981.

Article 4. *Ratification, acceptance, approval or accession*

1. This Convention is subject to ratification, acceptance or approval by Signatories. Any State which has not signed this Convention may accede to it.

2. The instruments of ratification, acceptance, approval or accession shall be deposited with the Depositary.

3. Expressions of consent to be bound by any of the Protocols annexed to this Convention shall be optional for each State, provided that at the time of the deposit of its instrument of ratification, acceptance or approval of this Convention or of accession thereto, that State shall notify the Depositary of its consent to be bound by any two or more of these Protocols.

4. At any time after the deposit of its instrument of ratification, acceptance or

approval of this Convention or of accession thereto, a State may notify the Depositary of its consent to be bound by any annexed Protocol by which it is not already bound.

5. Any Protocol by which a High Contracting Party is bound shall for that Party form an integral part of this Convention.

Article 5. *Entry into force*

1. This Convention shall enter into force six months after the date of deposit of the twentieth instrument of ratification, acceptance, approval or accession.

2. For any State which deposits its instrument of ratification, acceptance, approval or accession after the date of the deposit of the twentieth instrument of ratification, acceptance, approval or accession, this Convention shall enter into force six months after the date on which that State has deposited its instrument of ratification, acceptance, approval or accession.

3. Each of the Protocols annexed to this Convention shall enter into force six months after the date by which twenty States have notified their consent to be bound by it in accordance with paragraph 3 or 4 of Article 4 of this Convention.

4. For any State which notifies its consent to be bound by a Protocol annexed to this Convention after the date by which twenty States have notified their consent to be bound by it, the Protocol shall enter into force six months after the date on which that State has notified its consent so to be bound.

Article 6. *Dissemination*

The High Contracting Parties undertake, in time of peace as in time of armed conflict, to disseminate this Convention and those of its annexed Protocols by which they are bound as widely as possible in their respective countries and, in particular, to include the study thereof in their programmes of military instruction, so that those instruments may become known to their armed forces.

Article 7. *Treaty relations upon entry into force of this Convention*

1. When one of the parties to a conflict is not bound by an annexed Protocol, the parties bound by this Convention and that annexed Protocol shall remain bound by them in their mutual relations.

2. Any High Contracting Party shall be bound by this Convention and any Protocol annexed thereto which is in force for it, in any situation contemplated by Article 1, in relation to any State which is not a party to this Convention or bound by the relevant annexed Protocol, if the latter accepts and applies this Convention or the relevant Protocol, and so notifies the Depositary.

3. The Depositary shall immediately inform the High Contracting Parties concerned of any notification received under paragraph 2 of this Article.

4. This Convention, and the annexed Protocols by which a High Contracting Party is bound, shall apply with respect to an armed conflict against that High Contracting Party of the type referred to in Article 1, paragraph 4, of Additional Protocol I to the Geneva Conventions of 12 August 1949 for the Protection of War Victims:

(a) where the High Contracting Party is also a party to Additional Protocol I and an authority referred to in Article 96, paragraph 3, of that Protocol has undertaken to apply the Geneva Conventions and Additional Protocol I in accordance with Article 96, paragraph 3, of the said Protocol, and undertakes to apply this Convention and the relevant annexed Protocols in relation to that conflict; or

(b) where the High Contracting Party is not a party to Additional Protocol I and an authority of the type referred to in subparagraph (a) above accepts and applies the obligations of the Geneva Conventions and of this Convention and the relevant annexed Protocols in relation to that conflict. Such an acceptance and application shall have in relation to that conflict the following effects:

(i) the Geneva Conventions and this Convention and its relevant annexed Protocols are brought into force for the parties to the conflict with immediate effect;

(ii) the said authority assumes the same rights and obligations as those which have been assumed by a High Contracting Party to the Geneva Conventions, this Convention and its relevant annexed Protocols; and

(iii) the Geneva Conventions, this Convention and its relevant annexed Protocols are equally binding upon all parties to the conflict.

The High Contracting Party and the authority may also agree to accept and apply the obligations of Additional Protocol I to the Geneva Conventions on a reciprocal basis.

Article 8. *Review and amendments*

1. (a) At any time after the entry into force of this Convention any High Contracting Party may propose amendments to this Convention or any annexed Protocol to which it is bound. Any proposal for an amendment shall be communicated to the Depositary, who shall notify it to all the High Contracting Parties, and shall seek their views on whether a conference should be convened to consider the proposal. If a majority, that shall not be less than eighteen of the High Contracting Parties so agree, he shall promptly convene a conference to which all High Contracting Parties shall be invited. States not parties to this Convention shall be invited to the conference as observers.

(b) Such a conference may agree upon amendments which shall be adopted and shall enter into force in the same manner as this Convention and the annexed Protocols, provided that amendments to this Convention may be adopted only by the High Contracting Parties and that amendments to a specific annexed Protocol may be adopted only by the High Contracting Parties which are bound by that Protocol.

2. (a) At any time after the entry into force of this Convention any High Contracting Party may propose additional protocols relating to other categories of conventional weapons not covered by the existing annexed protocols. Any such proposal for an additional protocol shall be communicated to the Depositary, who shall notify it to all the High Contracting Parties in accordance with subparagraph 1(a) of this Article. If a majority, that shall not be less than eighteen of the High Contracting Parties so agree, the Depositary shall promptly convene a conference to which all States shall be invited.

(b) Such a conference may agree, with the full participation of all States represented at the conference, upon additional protocols which shall be adopted in the same manner as this Convention, shall be annexed thereto and shall enter into force as provided in paragraphs 3 and 4 of Article 5 of this Convention.

3. (a) If, after a period of ten years following the entry into force of this Convention, no conference has been convened in accordance with subparagraph 1(a) or 2(a) of this Article, any High Contracting Party may request the Depositary to convene a conference to which all High Contracting Parties shall be invited to review the scope and operation of this Convention and the Protocols annexed thereto and to consider any proposal for amendments of this Convention or of the existing Protocols. States not parties to this Convention shall be invited as observers to the conference. The conference may agree upon amendments which shall be adopted and enter into force in accordance with subparagraph 1(b) above.

(b) At such conference consideration may also be given to any proposal for additional protocols relating to other categories of conventional weapons not covered by the existing annexed Protocols. All States represented at the conference may participate fully in such consideration. Any additional protocols shall be adopted in the same manner as this Convention, shall be annexed thereto and shall enter into force as provided in paragraphs 3 and 4 of Article 5 of this Convention.

(c) Such a conference may consider whether provision should be made for the convening of a further conference at the request of any High Contracting Party if, after a similar period to that referred to in subparagraph 3(a) of this Article, no conference has been convened in accordance with subparagraph 1(a) or 2(a) of this Article.

Article 9. *Denunciation*

1. Any High Contracting Party may denounce this Convention or any of its annexed Protocols by so notifying the Depositary.

2. Any such denunciation shall only take effect one year after receipt by the Depositary of the notification of denunciation. If, however, on the expiry of that year the denouncing High Contracting Party is engaged in one of the situations referred to in Article 1, the Party shall continue to be bound by the obligations of this Convention and of the relevant annexed Protocols until the end of the armed conflict or occupation and, in any case, until the termination of operations connected with the final release, repatriation or re-establishment of the persons protected by the rules of international law applicable in armed conflict, and in the case of any annexed Protocol containing provisions concerning situations in which peace-keeping, observation or similar functions are performed by United Nations forces or missions in the area concerned, until the termination of those functions.

3. Any denunciation of this Convention shall be considered as also applying to all annexed Protocols by which the denouncing High Contracting Party is bound.

4. Any denunciation shall have effect only in respect of the denouncing High Contracting Party.

5. Any denunciation shall not affect the obligations already incurred, by reason of an armed conflict, under this Convention and its annexed Protocols by such denouncing High Contracting Party in respect of any act committed before this denunciation becomes effective.

Article 10. *Depositary*

1. The Secretary-General of the United Nations shall be the Depositary of this Convention and of its annexed Protocols.

2. In addition to his usual functions, the Depositary shall inform all States of:

(a) signatures affixed to this Convention under Article 3;

(b) deposits of instruments of ratification, acceptance or approval of or accession to this Convention deposited under Article 4;

(c) notifications of consent to be bound by annexed Protocols under Article 4;

(d) the dates of entry into force of this Convention and of each of its annexed Protocols under Article 5; and

(e) notifications of denunciation received under Article 9 and their effective date.

Article 11. *Authentic texts*

The original of this Convention with the annexed Protocols, of which the Arabic, Chinese, English, Russian and Spanish texts are equally authentic, shall be deposited with the Depositary, who shall transmit certified true copies thereof to all States.

PROTOCOL (I) ON NON-DETECTABLE FRAGMENTS

It is prohibited to use any weapon the primary effect of which is to injure by fragments which in the human body escape detection by X-rays.

PROTOCOL (II) ON PROHIBITIONS OR RESTRICTIONS ON THE USE OF MINES, BOOBY-TRAPS AND OTHER DEVICES

Article 1. *Material scope of application*

This Protocol relates to the use on land of the mines, booby-traps and other devices defined herein, including mines laid to interdict beaches, waterway crossings or river crossings, but does not apply to the use of anti-ship mines at sea or in inland waterways.

Article 2. *Definitions*

For the purpose of this Protocol:
1. "Mine" means any munition placed under, on or near the ground or other surface area and designed to be detonated or exploded by the presence, proximity or contact of a person or vehicle, and "remotely delivered mine" means any mine so defined delivered by artillery, rocket, mortar or similar means or dropped from an aircraft.
2. "Booby-trap" means any device or material which is designed, constructed or adapted to kill or injure and which functions unexpectedly when a person disturbs or approaches an apparently harmless object or performs an apparently safe act.
3. "Other devices" means manually-emplaced munitions and devices designed to kill, injure or damage and which are actuated by remote control or automatically after a lapse of time.
4. "Military objective" means, so far as objects are concerned, any object which by its nature, location, purpose or use makes an effective contribution to military action and whose total or partial destruction, capture or neutralization, in the circumstances ruling at the time, offers a definite military advantage.
5. "Civilian objects" are all objects which are not military objectives as defined in paragraph 4.

6. "Recording" means a physical, administrative and technical operation designed to obtain, for the purpose of registration in the official records, all available information facilitating the location of minefields, mines and booby-traps.

Article 3. *General restrictions on the use of mines, booby-traps and other devices*

1. This Article applies to:
(*a*) mines;
(*b*) booby-traps; and
(*c*) other devices.
2. It is prohibited in all circumstances to direct weapons to which this Article applies, either in offence, defence or by way of reprisals, against the civilian population as such or against individual civilians.
3. The indiscriminate use of weapons to which this Article applies is prohibited. Indiscriminate use is any placement of such weapons:
(*a*) which is not on, or directed against, a military objective; or
(*b*) which employs a method or means of delivery which cannot be directed at a specific military objective; or
(*c*) which may be expected to cause incidental loss of civilian life, injury to civilians, damage to civilian objects, or a combination thereof, which would be excessive in relation to the concrete and direct military advantage anticipated.
4. All feasible precautions shall be taken to protect civilians from the effects of weapons to which this Article applies. Feasible precautions are those precautions which are practicable or practically possible taking into account all circumstances ruling at the time, including humanitarian and military considerations.

Article 4. *Restrictions on the use of mines other than remotely delivered mines, booby-traps and other devices in populated areas*

1. This Article applies to:
(*a*) mines other than remotely delivered mines;
(*b*) booby-traps; and
(*c*) other devices.
2. It is prohibited to use weapons to which this Article applies in any city, town, village or other area containing a similar concentration of civilians in which combat between ground forces is not taking place or does not appear to be imminent, unless either:
(*a*) they are placed on or in the close vicinity of a military objective belonging to or under the control of an adverse party; or
(*b*) measures are taken to protect civilians from their effects, for example, the posting of warning signs, the posting of sentries, the issue of warnings or the provision of fences.

Article 5. *Restrictions on the use of remotely delivered mines*

1. The use of remotely delivered mines is prohibited unless such mines are only used within an area which is itself a military objective or which contains military objectives, and unless:

(*a*) their location can be accurately recorded in accordance with Article 7(1)(*a*); or

(*b*) an effective neutralizing mechanism is used on each such mine, that is to say, a self-actuating mechanism which is designed to render a mine harmless or cause it to destroy itself when it is anticipated that the mine will no longer serve the military purpose for which it was placed in position, or a remotely-controlled mechanism which is designed to render harmless or destroy a mine when the mine no longer serves the military purpose for which it was placed in position.

2. Effective advance warning shall be given of any delivery or dropping of remotely delivered mines which may affect the civilian population, unless circumstances do not permit.

Article 6. *Prohibition on the use of certain booby-traps*

1. Without prejudice to the rules of international law applicable in armed conflict relating to treachery and perfidy, it is prohibited in all circumstances to use:

(*a*) any booby-trap in the form of an apparently harmless portable object which is specifically designed and constructed to contain explosive material and to detonate when it is disturbed or approached, or

(*b*) booby-traps which are in any way attached to or associated with:

(i) internationally recognized protective emblems, signs or signals;

(ii) sick, wounded or dead persons;

(iii) burial or cremation sites or graves;

(iv) medical facilities, medical equipment, medical supplies or medical transportation;

(v) children's toys or other portable objects or products specially designed for the feeding, health, hygiene, clothing or education of children;

(vi) food or drink;

(vii) kitchen utensils or appliances except in military establishments, military locations or military supply depots;

(viii) objects clearly of a religious nature;

(ix) historic monuments, works of art or places of worship which constitute the cultural or spiritual heritage of peoples;

(x) animals or their carcasses.

2. It is prohibited in all circumstances to use any booby-trap which is designed to cause superfluous injury or unnecessary suffering.

Article 7. *Recording and publication of the location of minefields, mines and booby-traps*

1. The parties to a conflict shall record the location of:

(*a*) all pre-planned minefields laid by them; and

(*b*) all areas in which they have made large-scale and pre-planned use of booby-traps.

2. The parties shall endeavour to ensure the recording of the location of all other minefields, mines and booby-traps which they have laid or placed in position.

3. All such records shall be retained by the parties who shall:

(*a*) immediately after the cessation of active hostilities:

(i) take all necessary and appropriate measures, including the use of such records, to protect civilians from the effects of minefields, mines and booby-traps; and either

(ii) in cases where the forces of neither party are in the territory of the adverse party, make available to each other and to the Secretary-General of the United Nations all information in their possession concerning the location of minefields, mines and booby-traps in the territory of the adverse party; or

(iii) once complete withdrawal of the forces of the parties from the territory of the adverse party has taken place, make available to the adverse party and to the Secretary-General of the United Nations all information in their possession concerning the location of minefields, mines and booby-traps in the territory of the adverse party;

(*b*) when a United Nations force or mission performs functions in any area, make available to the authority mentioned in Article 8 such information as is required by that Article;

(*c*) whenever possible, by mutual agreement, provide for the release of information concerning the location of minefields, mines and booby-traps, particularly in agreements governing the cessation of hostilities.

Article 8. *Protection of United Nations forces and missions from the effects of minefields, mines and booby-traps*

1. When a United Nations force or mission performs functions of peace-keeping, observation or similar functions in any area, each party to the conflict shall, if requested by the head of the United Nations force or mission in that area, as far as it is able:

(*a*) remove or render harmless all mines or booby-traps in that area;

(*b*) take such measures as may be necessary to protect the force or mission from the effects of minefields, mines and booby-traps while carrying out its duties, and

(c) make available to the head of the United Nations force or mission in that area, all information in the party's possession concerning the location of minefields, mines and booby-traps in that area.

2. When a United Nations fact-finding mission performs functions in any area, any party to the conflict concerned shall provide protection to that mission except where, because of the size of such mission, it cannot adequately provide such protection. In that case it shall make available to the head of the mission the information in its possession concerning the location of minefields, mines and booby-traps in that area.

Article 9. *International co-operation in the removal of minefields, mines and booby-traps*

After the cessation of active hostilities, the parties shall endeavour to reach agreement, both among themselves and, where appropriate, with other States and with international organizations, on the provision of information and technical and material assistance—including, in appropriate circumstances, joint operations—necessary to remove or otherwise render ineffective minefields, mines and booby-traps placed in position during the conflict.

TECHNICAL ANNEX TO THE PROTOCOL

Guidelines on recording

Whenever an obligation for the recording of the location of minefields, mines and booby-traps arises under the Protocol, the following guidelines shall be taken into account.

1. With regard to pre-planned minefields and large-scale and pre-planned use of booby-traps:

(a) maps, diagrams or other records should be made in such a way as to indicate the extent of the minefield or booby-trapped area; and

(b) the location of the minefield or booby-trapped area should be specified by relation to the co-ordinates of a single reference point and by the estimated dimensions of the area containing mines and booby-traps in relation to that single reference point.

2. With regard to other minefields, mines and booby-traps laid or placed in position:
In so far as possible, the relevant information specified in paragraph 1 above should be recorded so as to enable the areas containing minefields, mines and booby-traps to be identified.

PROTOCOL (III) ON PROHIBITIONS OR RESTRICTIONS ON THE USE OF INCENDIARY WEAPONS

Article 1. *Definitions*

For the purpose of this Protocol:

1. "Incendiary weapon" means any weapon or munition which is primarily designed to set fire to objects or to cause burn injury to persons through the action of flame, heat, or a combination thereof, produced by a chemical reaction of a substance delivered on the target.

(a) Incendiary weapons can take the form of, for example, flame throwers, fougasses, shells, rockets, grenades, mines, bombs and other containers of incendiary substances.

(b) Incendiary weapons do not include:

(i) Munitions which may have incendiary effects, such as illuminants, tracers, smoke or signalling systems;

(ii) Munitions designed to combine penetration, blast or fragmentation effects with an additional incendiary effect, such as armour-piercing projectiles, fragmentation shells, explosive bombs and similar combined-effects munitions in which the incendiary effect is not specifically designed to cause burn injury to persons, but to be used against military objectives, such as armoured vehicles, aircraft and installations or facilities.

2. "Concentration of civilians" means any concentration of civilians, be it permanent or temporary, such as in inhabited parts of cities, or inhabited towns or villages, or as in camps or columns of refugees or evacuees, or groups of nomads.

3. "Military objective" means, so far as objects are concerned, any object which by its nature, location, purpose or use makes an effective contribution to military action and whose total or partial destruction, capture or neutralization, in the circumstances ruling at the time, offers a definite military advantage.

4. "Civilian objects" are all objects which are not military objectives as defined in paragraph 3.

5. "Feasible precautions" are those precautions which are practicable or practically possible taking into account all circumstances ruling at the time, including humanitarian and military considerations.

Article 2. *Protection of civilians and civilian objects*

1. It is prohibited in all circumstances to make the civilian population as such, individual civilians or civilian objects the object of attack by incendiary weapons.

2. It is prohibited in all circumstances to make any military objective located within a

concentration of civilians the object of attack by air-delivered incendiary weapons.

3. It is further prohibited to make any military objective located within a concentration of civilians the object of attack by means of incendiary weapons other than air-delivered incendiary weapons, except when such military objective is clearly separated from the concentration of civilians and all feasible precautions are taken with a view to limiting the incendiary effects to the military objective and to avoiding, and in any event to minimizing, incidental loss of civilian life, injury to civilians and damage to civilian objects.

4. It is prohibited to make forests or other kinds of plant cover the object of attack by incendiary weapons except when such natural elements are used to cover, conceal or camouflage combatants or other military objectives, or are themselves military objectives.

Source: United Nations, Legal Counsel, Certified copy of the Convention (New York, 1981)

6. Status of the implementation of the major multilateral arms control agreements, as of 1 October 1981

Number of parties

Antarctic Treaty	24
Partial Test Ban Treaty	112
Outer Space Treaty	82
Treaty of Tlatelolco	22
Additional Protocol I	2[a]
Additional Protocol II	5
Non-Proliferation Treaty	116
NPT safeguards agreements (non-nuclear weapon states)	70
Sea-Bed Treaty	72
BW Convention (prohibiting biological weapons)	94
ENMOD Convention (prohibiting environmental modification)	33

Note

1. Key to abbreviations used in the table:
    S: signature
    R: deposit of instrument of ratification, accession or succession

Place of signature and/or deposit of the instrument of ratification, accession or succession:

L: London
M: Moscow
W: Washington

Under the Antarctic Treaty, the only depositary is the US government; under the Treaty of Tlatelolco, the Mexican government; and under the ENMOD Convention, the UN Secretary-General.

For the Treaty of Tlatelolco:
PI: Additional Protocol I
PII: Additional Protocol II

For the Treaty of Tlatelolco and the NPT:
SA: Safeguards agreement in force with the International Atomic Energy Agency (IAEA)

2. The footnotes are listed at the end of the table and are grouped separately under the heading for each agreement. The texts of the statements contained in the footnotes have been abridged, but the wording is close to the original version.

---

[a] The USA ratified on 23 November 1981, bringing the number of parties to Protocol I to 3 (out of a possible 4).

State	Antarctic Treaty	Partial Test Ban Treaty	Outer Space Treaty	Treaty of Tlatelolco

Afghanistan		S: 8 Aug 1963 LW
		    9 Aug 1963 M
		R: 12 Mar 1964 L
		   13 Mar 1964 W
		   23 Mar 1964 M
			S: 27 Jan 1967 W
			   30 Jan 1967 M	

Algeria		S: 14 Aug 1963 LW 19 Aug 1963 M		

Argentina	S: 1 Dec 1959
	R: 23 Jun 1961
		S: 8 Aug 1963 W
		   9 Aug 1963 LM
			S: 27 Jan 1967 W
			   18 Apr 1967 M
			R: 26 Mar 1969 MW
				S:[1] 27 Sep 1967

Australia	S: 1 Dec 1959 R: 23 Jun 1961	S: 8 Aug 1963 LMW R: 12 Nov 1963 LMW	S: 27 Jan 1967 W R: 10 Oct 1967 LMW	
Austria		S: 11 Sep 1963 MW 12 Sep 1963 L R: 17 Jul 1964 LMW	S: 20 Feb 1967 LMW R: 26 Feb 1968 LMW	

Bahamas		R:[1] 16 Jul 1976 LM
		   13 Aug 1976 W
			R:[1] 11 Aug 1976 L
			   13 Aug 1976 W
			   30 Aug 1976 M
				S: 29 Nov 1976
				R:[2] 26 Apr 1977

Bangladesh				
Barbados			R: 12 Sep 1968 W	S: 18 Oct 1968 R:[2] 25 Apr 1969

Belgium	S: 1 Dec 1959
	R: 26 Jul 1960
		S: 8 Aug 1963 LMW
		R: 1 Mar 1966 LMW
			S: 27 Jan 1967 LM
			   2 Feb 1967 W
			R: 30 Mar 1973 W
			   31 Mar 1973 LM	

Non-Proliferation Treaty	Sea-Bed Treaty	BW Convention	ENMOD Convention

S: 1 Jul   1968 LMW
R: 4 Feb 1970 W
  5 Feb 1970 M
  5 Mar 1970 L
SA: 20 Feb 1978
	S: 11 Feb 1971 LMW
	R: 22 Apr 1971 M
	 23 Apr 1971 L
	 21 May 1971 W
		S: 10 Apr 1972 LMW
		R: 26 Mar 1975 L	

	S:[1] 3 Sep 1971 LMW	S: 1 Aug 1972 M
		  3 Aug 1972 L
		  7 Aug 1972 W
		R: 27 Nov 1979 W
		  5 Dec 1979 L
		 27 Dec 1979 M	

S:[1] 27 Feb 1970 LMW R: 23 Jan 1973 LMW SA: 10 Jul 1974	S: 11 Feb 1971 LMW R: 23 Jan 1973 LMW	S: 10 Apr 1972 LMW R: 5 Oct 1977 LMW	S: 31 May 1978
S: 1 Jul 1968 LMW R: 27 Jun 1969 LMW SA: 23 Jul 1972	S: 11 Feb 1971 LMW R: 10 Aug 1972 LMW	S: 10 Apr 1972 LMW R:[1] 10 Aug 1973 LMW	
R:[2] 11 Aug 1976 L 13 Aug 1976 W 30 Aug 1976 M			
R: 31 Aug 1979 LM 27 Sep 1979 W			R: 3 Oct 1979
S: 1 Jul 1968 W R: 21 Feb 1980 W		S: 16 Feb 1973 W R: 16 Feb 1973 W	
S: 20 Aug 1968 LMW R: 2 May 1975 LW 4 May 1975 M SA: 21 Feb 1977	S: 11 Feb 1971 LMW R: 20 Nov 1972 LMW	S: 10 Apr 1972 LMW R: 15 Mar 1979 LMW	S: 18 May 1977

State	Antarctic Treaty	Partial Test Ban Treaty	Outer Space Treaty	Treaty of Tlatelolco

Benin		S:[2] 27 Aug 1963 W
		     3 Sep 1963 L
		     9 Oct 1963 M
		R: 15 Dec 1964 W
		    23 Dec 1964 M
		    22 Apr 1965 L		

Bhutan		R: 8 Jun 1978 W		

Bolivia		S: 8 Aug 1963 W
		   21 Aug 1963 L
		   20 Sep 1963 M
		R: 4 Aug 1965 MW
		   25 Jan 1966 L
			S: 27 Jan 1967 W	S: 14 Feb 1967
				R:[2] 18 Feb 1969

Botswana		R:[1] 5 Jan 1968 M
		   14 Feb 1968 L
		    4 Mar 1968 W
			S: 27 Jan 1967 W	

Brazil	R: 16 May 1975	S: 8 Aug 1963 LW
		    9 Aug 1963 M
		R: 15 Dec 1964 M
		   15 Jan 1965 W
		    4 Mar 1965 L
			S: 30 Jan 1967 M
			   2 Feb 1967 LW
			R:[2] 5 Mar 1969 LMW
				S:[3] 9 May 1967
				R:[3] 29 Jan 1968

Bulgaria		S: 8 Aug 1963 LMW
		R: 13 Nov 1963 W
		   21 Nov 1963 M
		    2 Dec 1963 L
			S: 27 Jan 1967 LMW
			R: 28 Mar 1967 M
			   11 Apr 1967 W
			   19 Apr 1967 L	

Burma		S: 14 Aug 1963 LMW R: 15 Nov 1963 LMW	S: 22 May 1967 LMW R: 18 Mar 1970 LMW	
Burundi		S: 4 Oct 1963 W	S: 27 Jan 1967 W	
Byelorussia		S: 8 Oct 1963 M R:[3] 16 Dec 1963 M	S: 10 Feb 1967 M R:[3] 31 Oct 1967 M	

Non-Proliferation Treaty	Sea-Bed Treaty	BW Convention	ENMOD Convention
S: 1 Jul 1968 W R: 31 Oct 1972 W	S: 18 Mar 1971 W	S: 10 Apr 1972 W R: 25 Apr 1975 W	S: 10 Jun 1977
		R: 8 Jun 1978 W	
S: 1 Jul 1968 W R: 26 May 1970 W	S: 11 Feb 1971 LMW	S: 10 Apr 1972 W R: 30 Oct 1975 W	S: 18 May 1977
S: 1 Jul 1968 W R: 28 Apr 1969 L	S: 11 Feb 1971 W R: 10 Nov 1972 W	S: 10 Apr 1972 W	
	S:[2] 3 Sep 1971 LMW	S: 10 Apr 1972 LMW R: 27 Feb 1973 LMW	S: 9 Nov 1977

S: 1 Jul 1968 LMW
R: 5 Sep 1969 W
    18 Sep 1969 M
    3 Nov 1969 L
SA: 29 Feb 1972
	S: 11 Feb 1971 LMW
	R: 16 Apr 1971 M
	    7 May 1971 W
	    26 May 1971 L
		S: 10 Apr 1972 LMW
		R: 2 Aug 1972 L
		    13 Sep 1972 W
		    19 Sep 1972 M
			S: 18 May 1977
			R: 31 May 1978

	S: 11 Feb 1971 LMW	S: 10 Apr 1972 LMW	
R: 19 Mar 1971 M	S: 11 Feb 1971 MW	S: 10 Apr 1972 MW	
	S: 3 Mar 1971 M R: 14 Sep 1971 M	S: 10 Apr 1972 M R: 26 Mar 1975 M	S: 18 May 1977 R: 7 Jun 1978 M

State	Antarctic Treaty	Partial Test Ban Treaty	Outer Space Treaty	Treaty of Tlatelolco
Cameroon		S:[2] 27 Aug 1963 W 6 Sep 1963 L	S: 27 Jan 1967 W	
Canada		S: 8 Aug 1963 LMW R: 28 Jan 1964 LMW	S: 27 Jan 1967 LMW R: 10 Oct 1967 LMW	
Cape Verde		R: 24 Oct 1979 M		

Central African Republic		R: 22 Dec 1964 W
		    24 Aug 1965 L
		    25 Sep 1965 M
			S: 27 Jan 1967 W	

Chad		S: 26 Aug 1963 W R: 1 Mar 1965 W		

Chile	S: 1 Dec 1959
	R: 23 Jun 1961
		S: 8 Aug 1963 W
		     9 Aug 1963 LM
		R: 6 Oct 1965 L
			S: 27 Jan 1967 W
			     3 Feb 1967 L
			    20 Feb 1967 M
				S: 14 Feb 1967
				R:[4] 9 Oct 1974

China				PII[5] S: 21 Aug 1973 R: 12 Jun 1974

Non-Proliferation Treaty	Sea-Bed Treaty	BW Convention	ENMOD Convention
S: 17 Jul 1968 W 18 Jul 1968 M R: 8 Jan 1969 W	S: 11 Nov 1971 M		
S: 23 Jul 1968 LW 29 Jul 1968 M R: 8 Jan 1969 LMW SA: 21 Feb 1972	S: 11 Feb 1971 LMW R:[3] 17 May 1972 LMW	S: 10 Apr 1972 LMW R: 18 Sep 1972 LMW	S: 18 May 1977 R: 11 Jun 1981
R: 24 Oct 1979 M	R: 24 Oct 1979 M	R: 20 Oct 1977 M	R: 3 Oct 1979
R: 25 Oct 1970 W	S: 11 Feb 1971 W R: 9 Jul 1981 W	S: 10 Apr 1972 W	
S: 1 Jul 1968 M R: 10 Mar 1971 W 11 Mar 1971 M 23 Mar 1971 L			
		S: 10 Apr 1972 LMW R: 22 Apr 1980 L	

State	Antarctic Treaty	Partial Test Ban Treaty	Outer Space Treaty	Treaty of Tlatelolco
Colombia		S: 16 Aug 1963 MW 20 Aug 1963 L	S: 27 Jan 1967 W	S: 14 Feb 1967 R:[2] 4 Aug 1972
Congo				
Costa Rica		S: 9 Aug 1963 L 13 Aug 1963 W 23 Aug 1963 M R: 10 Jul 1967 W		S: 14 Feb 1967 R:[2] 25 Aug 1969 SA:[16]
Cuba			R:[4] 3 Jun 1977 M	
Cyprus		S: 8 Aug 1963 LMW R: 15 Apr 1965 L 21 Apr 1965 M 7 May 1965 W	S: 27 Jan 1967 W 15 Feb 1967 M 16 Feb 1967 L R: 5 Jul 1972 LW 20 Sep 1972 M	
Czechoslovakia	R: 14 Jun 1962	S: 8 Aug 1963 LMW R: 14 Oct 1963 LM 17 Oct 1963 W	S: 27 Jan 1967 LMW R: 11 May 1967 L 18 May 1967 M 22 May 1967 W	
Denmark	R: 20 May 1965	S: 9 Aug 1963 LMW R: 15 Jan 1964 LMW	S: 27 Jan 1967 LMW R: 10 Oct 1967 LMW	
Dominican Republic		S: 16 Sep 1963 W 17 Sep 1963 L 19 Sep 1963 M R: 3 Jun 1964 M 18 Jun 1964 L 22 Jul 1964 W	S: 27 Jan 1967 W R: 21 Nov 1968 W	S: 28 Jul 1967 R:[2] 14 Jun 1968 SA:[16]
Ecuador		S: 27 Sep 1963 W 1 Oct 1963 LM R: 6 May 1964 W 8 May 1964 L 13 Nov 1964 M	S: 27 Jan 1967 W 16 May 1967 L 7 Jun 1967 M R: 7 Mar 1969 W	S: 14 Feb 1967 R:[2] 11 Feb 1969 SA:[16]

Non-Proliferation Treaty	Sea-Bed Treaty	BW Convention	ENMOD Convention
S: 1 Jul 1968 W	S: 11 Feb 1971 W	S: 10 Apr 1972 W	
R: 23 Oct 1978 W	R: 23 Oct 1978 W	R: 23 Oct 1978 W	
S: 1 Jul 1968 W R: 3 Mar 1970 W SA: 22 Nov 1979	S: 11 Feb 1971 W	S: 10 Apr 1972 W R: 17 Dec 1973 W	
	R:[4] 3 Jun 1977 M	S: 12 Apr 1972 M R: 21 Apr 1976 M	S: 23 Sep 1977 R: 10 Apr 1978
S: 1 Jul 1968 LMW R: 10 Feb 1970 M 16 Feb 1970 W 5 Mar 1970 L SA: 26 Jan 1973	S: 11 Feb 1971 LMW R: 17 Nov 1971 LM 30 Dec 1971 W	S: 10 Apr 1972 LW 14 Apr 1972 M R: 6 Nov 1973 L 13 Nov 1973 W 21 Nov 1973 M	S: 7 Oct 1977 R: 12 Apr 1978
S: 1 Jul 1968 LMW R: 22 Jul 1969 LMW SA: 3 Mar 1972	S: 11 Feb 1971 LMW R: 11 Jan 1972 LMW	S: 10 Apr 1972 LMW R: 30 Apr 1973 LMW	S: 18 May 1977 R: 12 May 1978
S: 1 Jul 1968 LMW R: 3 Jan 1969 LMW SA: 21 Feb 1977	S: 11 Feb 1971 LMW R: 15 Jun 1971 LMW	S: 10 Apr 1972 LMW R: 1 Mar 1973 LMW	S: 18 May 1977 R: 19 Apr 1978
S: 1 Jul 1968 W R: 24 Jul 1971 W SA: 11 Oct 1973	S: 11 Feb 1971 W R: 11 Feb 1972 W	S: 10·Apr 1972 W R: 23 Feb 1973 W	
S: 9 Jul 1968 W R: 7 Mar 1969 W SA: 10 Mar 1975		S: 14 Jun 1972 W R: 12 Mar 1975 W	

State	Antarctic Treaty	Partial Test Ban Treaty	Outer Space Treaty	Treaty of Tlatelolco
Egypt		S: 8 Aug 1963 LMW R: 10 Jan 1964 LMW	S: 27 Jan 1967 MW R: 10 Oct 1967 W 23 Jan 1968 M	
El Salvador		S: 21 Aug 1963 W 22 Aug 1963 L 23 Aug 1963 M R: 3 Dec 1964 W 7 Dec 1964 L 9 Feb 1965 M	S: 27 Jan 1967 W R: 15 Jan 1969 W	S: 14 Feb 1967 R:[2] 22 Apr 1968 SA:[16]
Equatorial Guinea				
Ethiopia		S: 9 Aug 1963 LW 19 Sep 1963 M	S: 27 Jan 1967 LW 10 Feb 1967 M	
Fiji		R:[1] 14 Jul 1972 M 18 Jul 1972 W 14 Aug 1972 L	R:[1] 18 Jul 1972 W 14 Aug 1972 L 29 Aug 1972 M	
Finland		S: 8 Aug 1963 LMW R: 9 Jan 1964 LMW	S: 27 Jan 1967 LMW R: 12 Jul 1967 LMW	
France	S: 1 Dec 1959 R: 16 Sep 1960		S: 25 Sep 1967 LMW R: 5 Aug 1970 LMW	PI[6] S: 2 Mar 1979 PII[7] S: 18 Jul 1973 R: 22 Mar 1974
Gabon		S: 10 Sep 1963 W R: 20 Feb 1964 W 4 Mar 1964 L 9 Mar 1964 M		
Gambia		R:[1] 27 Apr 1965 MW 6 May 1965 L	S: 2 Jun 1967 L	

Non-Proliferation Treaty	Sea-Bed Treaty	BW Convention	ENMOD Convention
S: 1 Jul 1968 LM R:[3] 26 Feb 1981 L		S: 10 Apr 1972 LM	
S: 1 Jul 1968 W R: 11 Jul 1972 W SA: 22 Apr 1975		S: 10 Apr 1972 W	
	S: 4 Jun 1971 W		

S: 5 Sep 1968 LMW
R: 5 Feb 1970 M
     5 Mar 1970 LW
SA: 2 Dec 1977
	S: 11 Feb 1971 LMW
	R: 12 Jul 1977 L
	    14 Jul 1977 MW
		S: 10 Apr 1972 LMW
		R: 26 May 1975 LM
		    26 Jun 1975 W
			S: 18 May 1977

R:[2] 21 Jul 1972 W
    14 Aug 1972 L
    29 Aug 1972 M
SA: 22 Mar 1973
		S: 22 Feb 1973 L
		R: 4 Sep 1973 W
		    1 Oct 1973 L
		    5 Oct 1973 M	

S: 1 Jul 1968 LMW R: 5 Feb 1969 LMW SA: 9 Feb 1972	S: 11 Feb 1971 LMW R: 8 Jun 1971 LMW	S: 10 Apr 1972 LMW R: 4 Feb 1974 LMW	S: 18 May 1977 R: 12 May 1978
SA:[4]			
R: 19 Feb 1974 W		S: 10 Apr 1972 L	

S:[3]   4 Sep 1968 L
    20 Sep 1968 W
    24 Sep 1968 M
R: 12 May 1975 W
SA: 8 Aug 1978
	S: 18 May 1971 L
	    21 May 1971 M
	    29 Oct 1971 W
		S: 2 Jun 1972 M
		    8 Aug 1972 L
		    9 Nov 1972 W	

State	Antarctic Treaty	Partial Test Ban Treaty	Outer Space Treaty	Treaty of Tlatelolco
German Democratic Republic	R:[1] 19 Nov 1974	S: 8 Aug 1963 M R: 30 Dec 1963 M	S: 27 Jan 1967 M R: 2 Feb 1967 M	
FR Germany	R:[2] 5 Feb 1979	S: 19 Aug 1963 LMW R:[4] 1 Dec 1964 LW	S: 27 Jan 1967 LMW R:[5] 10 Feb 1971 LW	
Ghana		S: 8 Aug 1963 M 9 Aug 1963 W 4 Sep 1963 L R: 27 Nov 1963 L 9 Jan 1964 W 31 May 1965 M	S: 27 Jan 1967 W 15 Feb 1967 M 3 Mar 1967 L	
Greece		S: 8 Aug 1963 W 9 Aug 1963 LM R: 18 Dec 1963 LMW	S: 27 Jan 1967 W R: 19 Jan 1971 L	
Grenada				S: 29 Apr 1975 R:[2] 20 Jun 1975
Guatemala		S: 23 Sep 1963 W R:[2] 6 Jan 1964 W		S: 14 Feb 1967 R:[2] 6 Feb 1970
Guinea				
Guinea-Bissau		R: 20 Aug 1976 M	R: 20 Aug 1976 M	
Guyana			S: 3 Feb 1967 W	
Haiti		S: 9 Oct 1963 W	S: 27 Jan 1967 W	S: 14 Feb 1967 R:[2] 23 May 1969
Holy See (Vatican City)			S: 5 Apr 1967 L	
Honduras		S: 8 Aug 1963 W 15 Aug 1963 L 16 Aug 1963 M R: 2 Oct 1964 W 2 Dec 1964 L	S: 27 Jan 1967 W	S: 14 Feb 1967 R:[2] 23 Sep 1968 SA:[16]

Non-Proliferation Treaty	Sea-Bed Treaty	BW Convention	ENMOD Convention
S: 1 Jul 1968 M R: 31 Oct 1969 M SA: 7 Mar 1972	S: 11 Feb 1971 M R: 27 Jul 1971 M	S: 10 Apr 1972 M R: 28 Nov 1972 M	S: 18 May 1977 R: 25 May 1978
S: 28 Nov 1969 LMW R:[5] 2 May 1975 LW SA: 21 Feb 1977	S: 8 Jun 1971 LMW R:[5] 18 Nov 1975 LW	S: 10 Apr 1972 LMW	S: 18 May 1977

S: 1 Jul 1968 MW
    24 Jul 1968 L
R: 4 May 1970 L
    5 May 1970 W
   11 May 1970 M
SA: 17 Feb 1975
	S: 11 Feb 1971 LMW
	R: 9 Aug 1972 W
		S: 10 Apr 1972 MW
		R: 6 Jun 1975 L
			S: 21 Mar 1978
			R: 22 Jun 1978

S: 1 Jul 1968 MW
R: 11 Mar 1970 W
SA: 1 Mar 1972
	S: 11 Feb 1971 M
	   12 Feb 1971 W
		S: 10 Apr 1972 L
		   12 Apr 1972 W
		   14 Apr 1972 M
		R: 10 Dec 1975 W	

R:[2] 2 Sep 1975 L 3 Dec 1975 W			
S: 26 Jul 1968 W R: 22 Sep 1970 W	S: 11 Feb 1971 W	S: 9 May 1972 W R: 19 Sep 1973 W	
	S: 11 Feb 1971 MW		
R: 20 Aug 1976 M	R: 20 Aug 1976 M	R: 20 Aug 1976 M	
		S: 3 Jan 1973 W	
S: 1 Jul 1968 W R: 2 Jun 1970 W		S: 10 Apr 1972 W	
R:[6] 25 Feb 1971 LMW SA: 1 Aug 1972			S: 27 May 1977
S: 1 Jul 1968 W R: 16 May 1973 W SA: 18 Apr 1975	S: 11 Feb 1971 W	S: 10 Apr 1972 W R: 14 Mar 1979 W	

State	Antarctic Treaty	Partial Test Ban Treaty	Outer Space Treaty	Treaty of Tlatelolco
Hungary		S: 8 Aug 1963 LMW R: 21 Oct 1963 L 22 Oct 1963 W 23 Oct 1963 M	S: 27 Jan 1967 LMW R: 26 Jun 1967 LMW	
Iceland		S: 12 Aug 1963 LMW R: 29 Apr 1964 LMW	S: 27 Jan 1967 LMW R: 5 Feb 1968 LMW	
India		S: 8 Aug 1963 LMW R: 10 Oct 1963 L 14 Oct 1963 M 18 Oct 1963 W	S: 3 Mar 1967 LMW	
Indonesia		S: 23 Aug 1963 LMW R: 20 Jan 1964 M 27 Jan 1964 W 8 May 1964 L	S: 27 Jan 1967 W 30 Jan 1967 M 14 Feb 1967 L	
Iran		S: 8 Aug 1963 LMW R: 5 May 1964 LMW	S: 27 Jan 1967 L	
Iraq		S: 13 Aug 1963 LMW R: 30 Nov 1964 L 1 Dec 1964 W 3 Dec 1964 M	S: 27 Feb 1967 LW 9 Mar 1967 M R: 4 Dec 1968 M 23 Sep 1969 L	
Ireland		S: 8 Aug 1963 LW 9 Aug 1963 M R: 18 Dec 1963 LW 20 Dec 1963 M	S: 27 Jan 1967 LW R: 17 Jul 1968 W 19 Jul 1968 L	
Israel		S: 8 Aug 1963 LMW R: 15 Jan 1964 LW 28 Jan 1964 M	S: 27 Jan 1967 LMW R: 18 Feb 1977 W 1 Mar 1977 L 4 Apr 1977 M	
Italy	R: 18 Mar 1981	S: 8 Aug 1963 LMW R: 10 Dec 1964 LMW	S: 27 Jan 1967 LMW R: 4 May 1972 LMW	

Non-Proliferation Treaty	Sea-Bed Treaty	BW Convention	ENMOD Convention
S: 1 Jul 1968 LMW R: 27 May 1969 LMW SA: 30 Mar 1972	S: 11 Feb 1971 LMW R: 13 Aug 1971 LMW	S: 10 Apr 1972 LMW R: 27 Dec 1972 LMW	S: 18 May 1977 R: 19 Apr 1978
S: 1 Jul 1968 LMW R: 18 Jul 1969 LMW SA: 16 Oct 1974	S: 11 Feb 1971 LMW R: 30 May 1972 LMW	S: 10 Apr 1972 LMW R: 15 Feb 1973 LMW	S: 18 May 1977
	R:[6] 20 Jul 1973 LMW	S:[2] 15 Jan 1973 LMW R:[2] 15 Jul 1974 LMW	S: 15 Dec 1977 R: 15 Dec 1978
S:[7] 2 Mar 1970 LMW R:[7] 12 Jul 1979 LMW SA: 14 Jul 1980		S: 20 Jun 1972 MW 21 Jun 1972 L	

S: 1 Jul 1968 LMW
R: 2 Feb 1970 W
    10 Feb 1970 M
     5 Mar 1970 L
SA: 15 May 1974
	S: 11 Feb 1971 LMW
	R: 26 Aug 1971 LW
	    6 Sep 1972 M
		S: 10 Apr 1972 MW
		    16 Nov 1972 L
		R: 22 Aug 1973 LW
		    27 Aug 1973 M
			S: 18 May 1977

S: 1 Jul 1968 M R: 29 Oct 1969 M SA: 29 Feb 1972	S: 22 Feb 1971 M R:[4] 13 Sep 1972 M	S: 11 May 1972 M	S: 15 Aug 1977

S: 1 Jul 1968 MW
    4 Jul 1968 L
R: 1 Jul 1968 W
    2 Jul 1968 M
    4 Jul 1968 L
SA: 21 Feb 1977
	S: 11 Feb 1971 LW
	R: 19 Aug 1971 LW
		S:[3] 10 Apr 1972 LW
		R: 27 Oct 1972 LW
			S: 18 May 1977

S: 28 Jan 1969 LMW R:[8] 2 May 1975 LW 4 May 1975 M SA: 21 Feb 1977	S:[7] 11 Feb 1971 LMW R:[7] 3 Sep 1974 LMW	S: 10 Apr 1972 LMW R: 30 May 1975 LMW	S: 18 May 1977

State	Antarctic Treaty	Partial Test Ban Treaty	Outer Space Treaty	Treaty of Tlatelolco
Ivory Coast		S: 5 Sep 1963 W R: 5 Feb 1965 W		
Jamaica		S: 13 Aug 1963 LMW	S: 29 Jun 1967 LMW R: 6 Aug 1970 W 10 Aug 1970 L 21 Aug 1970 M	S: 26 Oct 1967 R:[2] 26 Jun 1969 SA:[16]
Japan	S: 1 Dec 1959 R: 4 Aug 1960	S: 14 Aug 1963 LMW R: 15 Jun 1964 LMW	S: 27 Jan 1967 LMW R: 10 Oct 1967 LMW	
Jordan		S: 12 Aug 1963 LW 19 Aug 1963 M R: 29 May 1964 L 7 Jul 1964 M 10 Jul 1964 W	S: 2 Feb 1967 W	
Kampuchea				
Kenya		R: 10 Jun 1965 L 11 Jun 1965 W 30 Jun 1965 M		
Korea, Republic of (South)		S: 30 Aug 1963 LW R:[2] 24 Jul 1964 LW	S: 27 Jan 1967 W R:[4] 13 Oct 1967 W	
Kuwait		S: 20 Aug 1963 LMW R:[5] 20 May 1965 W 21 May 1965 L 17 Jun 1965 M	R:[6] 7 Jun 1972 W 20 Jun 1972 L 4 Jul 1972 M	
Lao People's Dem. Rep.		S: 12 Aug 1963 LMW R: 10 Feb 1965 L 12 Feb 1965 W 7 Apr 1965 M	S: 27 Jan 1967 W 30 Jan 1967 L 2 Feb 1967 M R: 27 Nov 1972 M 29 Nov 1972 W 15 Jan 1973 L	

264

Non-Proliferation Treaty	Sea-Bed Treaty	BW Convention	ENMOD Convention
S: 1 Jul 1968 W R: 6 Mar 1973 W	R: 14 Jan 1972 W	S: 23 May1972 W	
S: 14 Apr 1969 LMW R: 5 Mar 1970 LMW SA: 6 Nov 1978	S: 11 Oct 1971 LW 14 Oct 1971 M	R: 13 Aug 1975 L	
S: 3 Feb 1970 LMW R:[9] 8 Jun 1976 LMW SA: 2 Dec 1977	S: 11 Feb 1971 LMW R: 21 Jun 1971 LMW	S: 10 Apr 1972 LMW	
S: 10 Jul 1968 W R: 11 Feb 1970 W SA: 21 Feb 1978	S: 11 Feb 1971 LMW R: 17 Aug 1971 W 30 Aug 1971 M 1 Nov 1971 L	S: 10 Apr 1972 W 17 Apr 1972 L 24 Apr 1972 M R: 30 May1975 M 2 Jun 1975 W 27 Jun 1975 L	
R: 2 Jun 1972 W	S: 11 Feb 1971 W	S: 10 Apr 1972 W	
S: 1 Jul 1968 W R: 11 Jun 1970 M		R: 7 Jan 1976 L	
S:[10] 1 Jul 1968 W R:[11] 23 Apr 1975 W SA: 14 Nov 1975	S:[4] 11 Feb 1971 LW	S:[4] 10 Apr 1972 LW	
S: 15 Aug 1968 MW 22 Aug 1968 L		S: 14 Apr 1972 MW 27 Apr 1972 L R:[5] 18 Jul 1972 W 26 Jul 1972 L 1 Aug 1972 M	R:[1] 2 Jan 1980
S: 1 Jul 1968 LMW R: 20 Feb 1970 M 5 Mar 1970 LW	S: 11 Feb 1971 LW 15 Feb 1971 M R: 19 Oct 1971 L 22 Oct 1971 M 3 Nov 1971 W	S: 10 Apr 1972 LMW R: 20 Mar 1973 M 22 Mar 1973 W 25 Apr 1973 L	S: 13 Apr 1978 R: 5 Oct 1978

State	Antarctic Treaty	Partial Test Ban Treaty	Outer Space Treaty	Treaty of Tlatelolco
Lebanon		S: 12 Aug 1963 W 13 Aug 1963 LM R: 14 May 1965 W 20 May 1965 L 4 Jun 1965 M	S: 23 Feb 1967 LMW R: 31 Mar 1969 LM 30 Jun 1969 W	
Lesotho			S: 27 Jan 1967 W	
Liberia		S: 8 Aug 1963 W 16 Aug 1963 L 27 Aug 1963 M R: 19 May 1964 W 22 May 1964 L 16 Jun 1964 M		
Libya		S: 9 Aug 1963 L 16 Aug 1963 MW R: 15 Jul 1968 L	R: 3 Jul 1968 W	
Liechtenstein				
Luxembourg		S: 13 Aug 1963 L 3 Sep 1963 W 13 Sep 1963 M R: 10 Feb 1965 LMW	S: 27 Jan 1967 MW 31 Jan 1967 L	
Madagascar		S: 23 Sep 1963 W R: 15 Mar 1965 W	R:[7] 22 Aug 1968 W	
Malawi		R:[1] 26 Nov 1964 MW 7 Jan 1965 L		
Malaysia		S: 8 Aug 1963 W 12 Aug 1963 L 21 Aug 1963 M R: 15 Jul 1964 M 16 Jul 1964 LW	S: 20 Feb 1967 W 21 Feb 1967 L 3 May 1967 M	

Non-Proliferation Treaty	Sea-Bed Treaty	BW Convention	ENMOD Convention
S: 1 Jul 1968 LMW R: 15 Jul 1970 LM 20 Nov 1970 W SA: 5 Mar 1973	S: 11 Feb 1971 LMW	S: 10 Apr 1972 LW 21 Apr 1972 M R: 26 Mar 1975 L 2 Apr 1975 M 13 Jun 1975 W	S: 18 May 1977
S: 9 Jul 1968 W R: 20 May 1970 W SA: 12 Jun 1973	S: 8 Sep 1971 W R: 3 Apr 1973 W	S: 10 Apr 1972 W R: 6 Sep 1977 L	
S: 1 Jul 1968 W R: 5 Mar 1970 W	S: 11 Feb 1971 W	S: 10 Apr 1972 W 14 Apr 1972 L	S: 18 May 1977
S: 18 Jul 1968 L 19 Jul 1968 W 23 Jul 1968 M R: 26 May 1975 LMW SA: 8 Jul 1980			
R:[12] 20 Apr 1978 LMW SA: 4 Oct 1979			
S: 14 Aug 1968 LMW R: 2 May 1975 LW 4 May 1975 M SA: 21 Feb 1977	S: 11 Feb 1971 LMW	S: 10 Apr 1972 LM 12 Apr 1972 W R: 23 Mar 1976 LMW	S: 18 May 1977
S: 22 Aug 1968 W R: 8 Oct 1970 W SA: 14 Jun 1973	S: 14 Sep 1971 W	S: 13 Oct 1972 L	
		S: 10 Apr 1972 W	R: 5 Oct 1978
S: 1 Jul 1968 LMW R: 5 Mar 1970 LMW SA: 29 Feb 1972	S: 20 May 1971 LMW R: 21 Jun 1972 LMW	S: 10 Apr 1972 LMW	

State	Antarctic Treaty	Partial Test Ban Treaty	Outer Space Treaty	Treaty of Tlatelolco
Maldives				
Mali		S: 23 Aug 1963 LMW	R: 11 Jun 1968 M	
Malta		R:[1] 25 Nov 1964 MW 1 Dec 1964 L		
Mauritania		S: 13 Sep 1963 W 17 Sep 1963 L 8 Oct 1963 M R: 6 Apr 1964 W 15 Apr 1964 L 28 Apr 1964 M		
Mauritius		R:[1] 30 Apr 1969 MW 12 May 1969 L	R:[1] 16 Apr 1969 W 21 Apr 1969 L 13 May1969 M	
Mexico		S: 8 Aug 1963 LMW R: 27 Dec 1963 LMW	S: 27 Jan 1967 LMW R: 31 Jan 1968 LMW	S:[8] 14 Feb 1967 R:[2] 20 Sep 1967 SA: 6 Sep 1968
Mongolia		S: 8 Aug 1963 LM R: 1 Nov 1963 M 7 Nov 1963 L	S: 27 Jan 1967 M R: 10 Oct 1967 M	
Morocco		S: 27 Aug 1963 MW 30 Aug 1963 L R: 1 Feb 1966 L 18 Feb 1966 M 21 Feb 1966 W	R: 21 Dec 1967 LM 22 Dec 1967 W	
Nepal		S: 26 Aug 1963 LM 30 Aug 1963 W R: 7 Oct 1964 LMW	S: 3 Feb 1967 MW 6 Feb 1967 L R: 10 Oct 1967 L 16 Oct 1967 M 22 Nov 1967 W	

Non-Proliferation Treaty	Sea-Bed Treaty	BW Convention	ENMOD Convention
S: 11 Sep 1968 W R: 7 Apr 1970 W SA: 2 Oct 1977			

S: 14 Jul 1969 W
    15 Jul 1969 M
R: 10 Feb 1970 M
    5 Mar 1970 W
	S: 11 Feb 1971 W
	    15 Feb 1971 M
		S: 10 Apr 1972 W	

S: 17 Apr 1969 W R: 6 Feb 1970 W	S: 11 Feb 1971 LW R: 4 May 1971 W	S: 11 Sep 1972 L R: 7 Apr 1975 L	

S: 1 Jul 1968 W
R: 8 Apr 1969 W
    14 Apr 1969 L
    25 Apr 1969 M
SA: 31 Jan 1973
	S: 11 Feb 1971 W
	R: 23 Apr 1971 W
	    3 May 1971 L
	    18 May 1971 M
		S: 10 Apr 1972 W
		R: 7 Aug 1972 W
		    11 Jan 1973 L
		    15 Jan 1973 M	

S:[13] 26 Jul 1968 LMW R: 21 Jan 1969 LMW SA: 14 Sep 1973		S:[6] 10 Apr 1972 LMW R: 8 Apr 1974 LMW	

S: 1 Jul 1968 M
R: 14 May 1969 M
SA: 5 Sep 1972 '
	S: 11 Feb 1971 LM
	R: 8 Oct 1971 M
	    15 Nov 1971 L
		S: 10 Apr 1972 LMW
		R: 5 Sep 1972 W
		    14 Sep 1972 L
		    20 Oct 1972 M
			S: 18 May 1977
			R: 19 May 1978

S: 1 Jul 1968 LMW
R: 27 Nov 1970 M
    30 Nov 1970 L
    16 Dec 1970 W
SA: 18 Feb 1975
	S: 11 Feb 1971 MW
	    18 Feb 1971 L
	R: 26 Jul 1971 L
	    5 Aug 1971 W
	    18 Jan 1972 M
		S: 2 May 1972 L
		    3 May 1972 W
		    5 Jun 1972 M
			S: 18 May 1977

S: 1 Jul 1968 LMW
R: 5 Jan 1970 W
    9 Jan 1970 M
    3 Feb 1970 L
SA: 22 Jun 1972
	S: 11 Feb 1971 MW
	    24 Feb 1971 L
	R: 6 Jul 1971 L
	    29 Jul 1971 M
	    9 Aug 1971 W
		S: 10 Apr 1972 LMW	

State	Antarctic Treaty	Partial Test Ban Treaty	Outer Space Treaty	Treaty of Tlatelolco
Netherlands	R: 30 Mar 1967	S: 9 Aug 1963 LMW R: 14 Sep 1964 LMW	S: 10 Feb 1967 LMW R: 10 Oct 1969 LMW	PI[9] S: 15 Mar 1968 R: 26 Jul 1971
New Zealand	S: 1 Dec 1959 R: 1 Nov 1960	S: 8 Aug 1963 LMW R: 10 Oct 1963 LW 16 Oct 1963 M	S: 27 Jan 1967 LMW R: 31 May 1968 LMW	
Nicaragua		S: 13 Aug 1963 LW 16 Aug 1963 M R: 26 Jan 1965 L 26 Feb 1965 MW	S: 27 Jan 1967 W 13 Feb 1967 L	S: 15 Feb 1967 R:[2,10] 14 Oct 1968 SA:[16]
Niger		S: 24 Sep 1963 LW R: 3 Jul 1964 M 6 Jul 1964 L 9 Jul 1964 W	S: 1 Feb 1967 W R: 17 Apr 1967 L 3 May 1967 W	
Nigeria		S: 30 Aug 1963 M 2 Sep 1963 L 4 Sep 1963 W R: 17 Feb 1967 L 25 Feb 1967 M 28 Feb 1967 W	R: 14 Nov 1967 L	
Norway	S: 1 Dec 1959 R: 24 Aug 1960	S: 9 Aug 1963 LMW R: 21 Nov 1963 LMW	S: 3 Feb 1967 LMW R: 1 Jul 1969 LMW	
Pakistan		S: 14 Aug 1963 LMW	S: 12 Sep 1967 LMW R: 8 Apr 1968 LMW	
Panama		S: 20 Sep 1963 W R: 24 Feb 1966 W	S: 27 Jan 1967 W	S: 14 Feb 1967 R:[2] 11 Jun 1971
Papua New Guinea	R: 16 Mar 1981	R:[1] 27 Oct 1980 L 13 Nov 1980 M 16 Mar 1981 W	R:[1] 27 Oct 1980 L 13 Nov 1980 M 16 Mar 1981 W	
Paraguay		S: 15 Aug 1963 LW 21 Aug 1963 M		S: 26 Apr 1967 R:[2] 19 Mar 1969 SA:[16]

Non-Proliferation Treaty	Sea-Bed Treaty	BW Convention	ENMOD Convention
S: 20 Aug 1968 LMW R: 2 May 1975 LMW SA: 21 Feb 1977	S: 11 Feb 1971 LMW R: 14 Jan 1976 LMW	S: 10 Apr 1972 LMW R: 22 Jun 1981 LMW	S: 18 May 1977

S: 1 Jul 1968 LMW
R: 10 Sep 1969 LMW
SA: 29 Feb 1972
	S: 11 Feb 1971 LMW
	R: 24 Feb 1972 LMW
		S: 10 Apr 1972 LMW
		R: 13 Dec 1972 W
		       18 Dec 1972 L
		       10 Jan 1973 M	

S: 1 Jul 1968 LW R: 6 Mar 1973 W SA: 29 Dec 1976	S: 11 Feb 1971 W R: 7 Feb 1973 W	S: 10 Apr 1972 LW R: 7 Aug 1975 W	S: 11 Aug 1977
	S: 11 Feb 1971 W R: 9 Aug 1971 W	S: 21 Apr 1972 W R: 23 Jun 1972 W	

S: 1 Jul 1968 LMW
R: 27 Sep 1968 L
       7 Oct 1968 W
      14 Oct 1968 M
		S: 3 Jul 1972 M
		      10 Jul 1972 L
		       6 Dec 1972 W
		R: 3 Jul 1973 W
		       9 Jul 1973 L
		      20 Jul 1973 M	

S: 1 Jul 1968 LMW
R: 5 Feb 1969 LMW
SA: 1 Mar 1972
	S: 11 Feb 1971 LMW
	R: 28 Jun 1971 LM
	      29 Jun 1971 W
		S: 10 Apr 1972 LMW
		R: 1 Aug 1973 LW
		      23 Aug 1973 M
			S: 18 May 1977
			R: 15 Feb 1979

		S: 10 Apr 1972 LMW R: 25 Sep 1974 M 3 Oct 1974 LW	
S: 1 Jul 1968 W R: 13 Jan 1977 W	S: 11 Feb 1971 W R: 20 Mar 1974 W	S: 2 May 1972 W R: 20 Mar 1974 W	

		R: 27 Oct 1980 L
		      13 Nov 1980 M
		      16 Mar 1981 W
			R: 28 Oct 1980

S: 1 Jul 1968 W R: 4 Feb 1970 W 5 Mar 1970 L SA: 20 Mar 1979	S: 23 Feb 1971 W	R: 9 Jun 1976 W	

271

State	Antarctic Treaty	Partial Test Ban Treaty	Outer Space Treaty	Treaty of Tlatelolco

Peru	R: 10 Apr 1981	S: 23 Aug 1963 LMW
		R: 20 Jul 1964 W
		      4 Aug 1964 L
		      21 Aug 1964 M
			S: 30 Jun 1967 W
			R: 28 Feb 1979 M
			      1 Mar 1979 L
			      21 Mar 1979 W
				S: 14 Feb 1967
				R:[2] 4 Mar 1969

Philippines		S: 8 Aug 1963 LW
		      14 Aug 1963 M
		R:[2] 10 Nov 1965 L
		      15 Nov 1965 W
		      8 Feb 1966 M
			S: 27 Jan 1967 LW
			      29 Apr 1967 M	

Poland	R: 8 Jun 1961	S: 8 Aug 1963 LMW R: 14 Oct 1963 LMW	S: 27 Jan 1967 LMW R: 30 Jan 1968 LMW	
Portugal		S: 9 Oct 1963 LW		
Qatar				
Romania	R:[3] 15 Sep 1971	S: 8 Aug 1963 LMW R: 12 Dec 1963 LMW	S: 27 Jan 1967 LMW R: 9 Apr 1968 LMW	

Rwanda		S: 19 Sep 1963 W
		R: 22 Oct 1963 L
		      16 Dec 1963 M
		      27 Dec 1963 W
			S: 27 Jan 1967 W	

Saint Lucia				

Samoa		S: 5 Sep 1963 L
		      6 Sep 1963 MW
		R: 15 Jan 1965 W
		      19 Jan 1965 L
		      8 Feb 1965 M		

San Marino		S: 17 Sep 1963 W
		      20 Sep 1963 L
		      24 Sep 1963 M
		R: 3 Jul 1964 L
		      9 Jul 1964 W
		      27 Nov 1964 M
			S: 21 Apr 1967 W
			      24 Apr 1967 L
			      6 Jun 1967 M
			R: 29 Oct 1968 W
			      21 Nov 1968 M
			      3 Feb 1969 L	

Non-Proliferation Treaty	Sea-Bed Treaty	BW Convention	ENMOD Convention
S: 1 Jul 1968 W R: 3 Mar 1970 W SA: 1 Aug 1979		S: 10 Apr 1972 LMW	

S: 1 Jul 1968 W
    18 Jul 1968 M
R: 5 Oct 1972 W
    16 Oct 1972 L
    20 Oct 1972 M
SA: 16 Oct 1974
		S: 10 Apr 1972 LW
		    21 Jun 1972 M
		R: 21 May 1973 W	

S: 1 Jul 1968 LMW R: 12 Jun 1969 LMW SA: 11 Oct 1972	S: 11 Feb 1971 LMW R: 15 Nov 1971 LMW	S: 10 Apr 1972 LMW R: 25 Jan 1973 LMW	S: 18 May 1977 R: 8 Jun 1978
R: 15 Dec 1977 LMW SA: 14 Jun 1979	R: 24 Jun 1975 LMW	S: 29 Jun 1972 W R: 15 May 1975 LMW	S: 18 May 1977
	R: 12 Nov 1974 L	S: 14 Nov 1972 L R: 17 Apr 1975 L	

S: 1 Jul 1968 LMW
R: 4 Feb 1970 LMW
SA: 27 Oct 1972
	S: 11 Feb 1971 LMW
	R: 10 Jul 1972 LMW
		S: 10 Apr 1972 LMW
		R: 25 Jul 1979 W
		    26 Jul 1979 L
		    27 Jul 1979 M
			S: 18 May 1977

R: 20 May 1975 LMW	S: 11 Feb 1971 W R: 20 May 1975 LMW	S: 10 Apr 1972 MW R: 20 May 1975 LMW	
R:[2] 28 Dec 1979 L			

R: 17 Mar 1975 M
    18 Mar 1975 W
    26 Mar 1975 L
SA: 22 Jan 1979			

S:[10] 1 Jul 1968 W
    29 Jul 1968 L
    21 Nov 1968 M
R: 10 Aug 1970 L
    20 Aug 1970 M
    31 Aug 1970 W
		S: 12 Sep 1972 W
		    30 Jan 1973 M
		    21 Mar 1973 L
		R: 11 Mar 1975 L
		    17 Mar 1975 W
		    27 Mar 1975 M	

State	Antarctic Treaty	Partial Test Ban Treaty	Outer Space Treaty	Treaty of Tlatelolco
Sao Tome and Principe				
Saudi Arabia			R: 17 Dec 1976 W	
Senegal		S: 20 Sep 1963 W 23 Sep 1963 L 9 Oct 1963 M R: 6 May 1964 L 12 May 1964 M 2 Jun 1964 W		
Seychelles			R: 5 Jan 1978 L	
Sierra Leone		S: 4 Sep 1963 L 9 Sep 1963 M 11 Sep 1963 W R: 21 Feb 1964 L 4 Mar 1964 W 29 Apr 1964 M	S: 27 Jan 1967 LM 16 May 1967 W R: 13 Jul 1967 M 14 Jul 1967 W 25 Oct 1967 L	
Singapore		R:[1] 12 Jul 1968 MW 23 Jul 1968 L	R: 10 Sep 1976 LMW	
Solomon Islands				
Somalia		S: 19 Aug 1963 MW	S: 2 Feb 1967 W	
South Africa	S: 1 Dec 1959 R: 21 Jun 1960	R: 10 Oct 1963 LW 22 Nov 1963 M	S: 1 Mar 1967 W R: 30 Sep 1968 W 8 Oct 1968 L	
Spain		S: 13 Aug 1963 W 14 Aug 1963 L R: 17 Dec 1964 LW	R: 27 Nov 1968 L 7 Dec 1968 W	
Sri Lanka		S: 22 Aug 1963 LW 23 Aug 1963 M R: 5 Feb 1964 W 12 Feb 1964 M 13 Feb 1964 L	S: 10 Mar 1967 L	

Non-Proliferation Treaty	Sea-Bed Treaty	BW Convention	ENMOD Convention
	R: 24 Aug 1979 M	R: 24 Aug 1979 M	R: 5 Oct 1979
	S: 7 Jan 1972 W R: 23 Jun 1972 W	S: 12 Apr 1972 W R: 24 May 1972 W	
S: 1 Jul 1968 MW 26 Jul 1968 L R: 17 Dec 1970 M 22 Dec 1970 W 15 Jan 1971 L SA: 14 Jan 1980	S: 17 Mar 1971 W	S: 10 Apr 1972 W R: 26 Mar 1975 W	
	R: 29 Jun 1976 W	R: 11 Oct 1979 L 16 Oct 1979 W 24 Oct 1979 M	
R: 26 Feb 1975 LMW	S: 11 Feb 1971 L 12 Feb 1971 M 24 Feb 1971 W	S: 7 Nov 1972 W 24 Nov 1972 L R: 29 Jun 1976 LMW	S: 12 Apr 1978
S: 5 Feb 1970 LMW R: 10 Mar 1976 LMW SA: 18 Oct 1977	S: 5 May 1971 LMW R: 10 Sep 1976 LMW	S: 19 Jun 1972 LMW R: 2 Dec 1975 LMW	
R:[2] 17 Jun 1981 L	R: 17 Jun 1981 L	R:[10] 17 Jun 1981 L	R:[3] 19 Jun 1981
S: 1 Jul 1968 LMW R: 5 Mar 1970 L 12 Nov 1970 W		S: 3 Jul 1972 M	
	S: 11 Feb 1971 W R: 14 Nov 1973 W 26 Nov 1973 L	S: 10 Apr 1972 W R: 3 Nov 1975 W	
		S: 10 Apr 1972 LW R: 20 Jun 1979 LW	S: 18 May 1977 R: 19 Jul 1978
S: 1 Jul 1968 LMW R: 5 Mar 1979 LMW		S: 10 Apr 1972 LMW	S: 8 Jun 1977 R: 25 Apr 1978

State	Antarctic Treaty	Partial Test Ban Treaty	Outer Space Treaty	Treaty of Tlatelolco
Sudan		S: 9 Aug 1963 LMW R: 4 Mar 1966 LW 28 Mar 1966 M		
Suriname				S: 13 Feb 1976 R:[2] 10 Jun 1977 SA:[16]
Swaziland		R: 29 May 1969 LW 3 Jun 1969 M		
Sweden		S: 12 Aug 1963 LMW R: 9 Dec 1963 LMW	S: 27 Jan 1967 LMW R: 11 Oct 1967 LMW	
Switzerland		S: 26 Aug 1963 LMW R: 16 Jan 1964 LMW	S: 27 Jan 1967 LW 30 Jan 1967 M R: 18 Dec 1969 LMW	
Syria		S: 13 Aug 1963 LMW R: 1 Jun 1964 LMW	R:[8] 14 Nov 1968 M	
Taiwan		S: 23 Aug 1963 W R: 18 May 1964 W	S: 27 Jan 1967 W R: 24 Jul 1970 W	
Tanzania		S: 16 Sep 1963 L 18 Sep 1963 W 20 Sep 1963 M R: 6 Feb 1964 L		
Thailand		S: 8 Aug 1963 LMW R: 15 Nov 1963 L 21 Nov 1963 M 29 Nov 1963 W	S: 27 Jan 1967 LMW R: 5 Sep 1968 L 9 Sep 1968 M 10 Sep 1968 W	
Togo		S: 18 Sep 1963 W R: 7 Dec 1964 W	S: 27 Jan 1967 W	

Non-Proliferation Treaty	Sea-Bed Treaty	BW Convention	ENMOD Convention
S: 24 Dec 1968 M R: 31 Oct 1973 W 22 Nov 1973 M 10 Dec 1973 L SA: 7 Jan 1977	S: 11 Feb 1971 L 12 Feb 1971 M		
R:[2] 30 Jun 1976 W SA: 2 Feb 1979			
S: 24 Jun 1969 L R: 11 Dec 1969 L 16 Dec 1969 W 12 Jan 1970 M SA: 28 Jul 1975	S: 11 Feb 1971 W R: 9 Aug 1971 W		
S: 19 Aug 1968 LMW R: 9 Jan 1970 LMW SA: 14 Apr 1975	S: 11 Feb 1971 LMW R: 28 Apr 1972 LMW	S: 27 Feb 1975 LMW R: 5 Feb 1976 LMW	
S: 27 Nov 1969 LMW R:[12] 9 Mar 1977 LMW SA: 6 Sep 1978	S: 11 Feb 1971 LMW R: 4 May 1976 LMW	S: 10 Apr 1972 LMW R:[7] 4 May 1976 LMW	
S: 1 Jul 1968 M R:[10] 24 Sep 1969 M		S: 14 Apr 1972 M	S: 4 Aug 1977
S: 1 Jul 1968 W R: 27 Jan 1970 W	S: 11 Feb 1971 W R:[8] 22 Feb 1972 W	S: 10 Apr 1972 W R:[8] 9 Feb 1973 W	
	S: 11 Feb 1971 W	S: 16 Aug 1972 L	
R: 7 Dec 1972 L SA: 16 May 1974		S: 17 Jan 1973 W R: 28 May 1975 W	
S: 1 Jul 1968 W R: 26 Feb 1970 W	S: 2 Apr 1971 W R: 28 Jun 1971 W	S: 10 Apr 1972 W R: 10 Nov 1976 W	

State	Antarctic Treaty	Partial Test Ban Treaty	Outer Space Treaty	Treaty of Tlatelolco
Tonga		R:[1] 22 Jun 1971 M 7 Jul 1971 LW	R:[1] 22 Jun 1971 L 7 Jul 1971 W 24 Aug 1971 M	
Trinidad and Tobago		S: 12 Aug 1963 LW 13 Aug 1963 M R: 14 Jul 1964 W 16 Jul 1964 L 6 Aug 1964 M	S: 24 Jul 1967 L 17 Aug 1967 M 28 Sep 1967 W	S: 27 Jun 1967 R:[2] 3 Dec 1970
Tunisia		S: 8 Aug 1963 W 12 Aug 1963 L 13 Aug 1963 M R: 26 May 1965 LM 3 Jun 1965 W	S: 27 Jan 1967 LW 15 Feb 1967 M R: 28 Mar 1968 L 4 Apr 1968 M 17 Apr 1968 W	
Turkey		S: 9 Aug 1963 LMW R: 8 Jul 1965 LMW	S: 27 Jan 1967 LMW R: 27 Mar 1968 LMW	
Tuvalu				
Uganda		S: 29 Aug 1963 LW R: 24 Mar 1964 L 2 Apr 1964 W	R: 24 Apr 1968 W	
Ukraine		S: 8 Oct 1963 M R:[3] 30 Dec 1963 M	S: 10 Feb 1967 M R:[3] 31 Oct 1967 M	
Union of Soviet Socialist Republics	S: 1 Dec 1959 R: 2 Nov 1960	S: 5 Aug 1963 M R: 10 Oct 1963 LMW	S: 27 Jan 1967 LMW R: 10 Oct 1967 LMW	PII[11] S: 18 May 1978 R: 8 Jan 1979
United Arab Emirates				
United Kingdom	S: 1 Dec 1959 R: 31 May 1960	S: 5 Aug 1963 M R:[6] 10 Oct 1963 LMW	S: 27 Jan 1967 LMW R: 10 Oct 1967 LMW	PI[12] S: 20 Dec 1967 R: 11 Dec 1969 PII[12] S: 20 Dec 1967 R: 11 Dec 1969

Non-Proliferation Treaty	Sea-Bed Treaty	BW Convention	ENMOD Convention
R:[2] 7 Jul 1971 L 15 Jul 1971 W 24 Aug 1971 M		R: 28 Sep 1976 L	
S: 20 Aug 1968 W 22 Aug 1968 L			
S: 1 Jul 1968 LMW R: 26 Feb 1970 LMW	S: 11 Feb 1971 LMW R: 22 Oct 1971 M 28 Oct 1971 L 29 Oct 1971 W	S: 10 Apr 1972 LMW R: 18 May 1973 W 30 May 1973 M 6 Jun 1973 L	S: 11 May 1978 R: 11 May 1978
S: 28 Jan 1969 LMW R:[14] 17 Apr 1980 LMW SA: 1 Sep 1981	S: 25 Feb 1971 LMW R: 19 Oct 1972 W 25 Oct 1972 L 30 Oct 1972 M	S: 10 Apr 1972 LMW R: 25 Oct 1974 M 4 Nov 1974 L 5 Nov 1974 W	S:[2] 18 May 1977
R:[2] 19 Jan 1979 L			
			S: 18 May 1977
	S: 3 Mar 1971 M R: 3 Sep 1971 M	S: 10 Apr 1972 M R: 26 Mar 1975 M	S: 18 May 1977 R: 13 Jun 1978
S: 1 Jul 1968 LMW R: 5 Mar 1970 LMW	S: 11 Feb 1971 LMW R: 18 May 1972 LMW	S: 10 Apr 1972 LMW R: 26 Mar 1975 LMW	S: 18 May 1977 R: 30 May 1978
		S: 28 Sep 1972 L	
S: 1 Jul 1968 LMW R:[15] 27 Nov 1968 LW 29 Nov 1968 M SA:[16] 14 Aug 1978	S: 11 Feb 1971 LMW R:[9] 18 May 1972 LMW	S: 10 Apr 1972 LMW R:[9] 26 Mar 1975 LMW	S: 18 May 1977 R: 16 May 1978

279

State	Antarctic Treaty	Partial Test Ban Treaty	Outer Space Treaty	Treaty of Tlatelolco
United States	S: 1 Dec 1959 R: 18 Aug 1960	S: 5 Aug 1963 M R: 10 Oct 1963 LMW	S: 27 Jan 1967 LMW R: 10 Oct 1967 LMW	PI[13] S: 26 May 1977 R: 23 Nov 1981 PI![14] S: 1 Apr 1968 R: 12 May 1971
Upper Volta		S: 30 Aug 1963 W	S: 3 Mar 1967 W R: 18 Jun 1968 W	
Uruguay	R:[4] 11 Jan 1980	S: 12 Aug 1963 W 27 Sep 1963 LM R: 25 Feb 1969 L	S: 27 Jan 1967 W 30 Jan 1967 M R: 31 Aug 1970 W	S: 14 Feb 1967 R:[2] 20 Aug 1968 SA:[16]
Venezuela		S: 16 Aug 1963 MW 20 Aug 1963 L R: 22 Feb 1965 M 3 Mar 1965 L 29 Mar 1965 W	S: 27 Jan 1967 W R: 3 Mar 1970 W	S: 14 Feb 1967 R:[2,15] 23 Mar 1970
Viet Nam			R: 20 Jun 1980 M	
Yemen Arab Republic		S: 13 Aug 1963 M 6 Sep 1963 W		
Yemen, People's Dem. Rep. of		R: 1 Jun 1979 M	R: 1 Jun 1979 M	
Yugoslavia		S: 8 Aug 1963 LMW R: 15 Jan 1964 L 31 Jan 1964 M 3 Apr 1964 W	S: 27 Jan 1967 LMW	
Zaire		S: 9 Aug 1963 LW 12 Aug 1963 M R: 28 Oct 1965 W	S: 27 Jan 1967 W 29 Apr 1967 M 4 May 1967 L	
Zambia		R:[1] 11 Jan 1965 MW 8 Feb 1965 L	R: 20 Aug 1973 W 21 Aug 1973 M 28 Aug 1973 L	

Non-Proliferation Treaty	Sea-Bed Treaty	BW Convention	ENMOD Convention
S: 1 Jul 1968 LMW R: 5 Mar 1970 LMW SA:[17] 9 Dec 1980	S: 11 Feb 1971 LMW R: 18 May 1972 LMW	S: 10 Apr 1972 LMW R: 26 Mar 1975 LMW	S: 18 May 1977 R: 17 Jan 1980
S: 25 Nov 1968 W 11 Aug 1969 M R: 3 Mar 1970 W			
S: 1 Jul 1968 W R: 31 Aug 1970 W SA: 17 Sep 1976	S: 11 Feb 1971 W	R: 6 Apr 1981 W	

S: 1 Jul 1968 W
R: 25 Sep 1975 L
    26 Sep 1975 W
     3 Oct 1975 M
		S: 10 Apr 1972 W
		R: 18 Oct 1978 LMW	

	R:[10]20 Jun 1980 M	R: 20 Jun 1980 M	R: 26 Aug 1980

S: 23 Sep 1968 M	S: 23 Feb 1971 M	S: 10 Apr 1972 W
		    17 Apr 1972 M
		    10 May 1972 L
			S: 18 May 1977
			R: 20 Jul 1977

S: 14 Nov 1968 M R: 1 Jun 1979 M	S: 23 Feb 1971 M R: 1 Jun 1979 M	S: 26 Apr 1972 M R: 1 Jun 1979 M	R: 12 Jun 1979
S: 10 Jul 1968 LMW R:[18] 4 Mar 1970 W 5 Mar 1970 LM SA: 28 Dec 1973	S: 2 Mar 1971 LMW R:[11]25 Oct 1973 LMW	S: 10 Apr 1972 LMW R: 25 Oct 1973 LMW	

S: 22 Jul 1968 W
    26 Jul 1968 M
    17 Sep 1968 L
R: 4 Aug 1970 W
SA: 9 Nov 1972
		S: 10 Apr 1972 MW
		    16 Sep 1975 L
		R: 28 Jan 1977 W
			S: 28 Feb 1978

	R: 9 Oct 1972 L
	     1 Nov 1972 W
	     2 Nov 1972 M		

The Antarctic Treaty

[1] The German Democratic Republic stated that in its view Article XIII, paragraph 1 of the Treaty was inconsistent with the principle that all states whose policies are guided by the purposes and principles of the United Nations Charter have a right to become parties to treaties which affect the interests of all states.

[2] The Federal Republic of Germany stated that the Treaty applies also to Berlin (West).

[3] Romania stated that the provisions of Article XIII, paragraph 1 of the Treaty were not in accordance with the principle according to which multilateral treaties whose object and purposes concern the international community, as a whole, should be open for universal participation.

[4] In acceding to the Treaty, Uruguay proposed the establishment of a general and definitive statute on Antarctica in which the interests of all states involved and of the international community as a whole would be considered equitably. It also declared that it reserved its rights in Antarctica in accordance with international law.

The Partial Test Ban Treaty

[1] Notification of succession.

[2] With a statement that this does not imply the recognition of any territory or regime not recognized by this state.

[3] The United States considers that Byelorussia and Ukraine are already covered by the signature and ratification by the Soviet Union.

[4] The Federal Republic of Germany stated that the Treaty applies also to Berlin (West).

[5] Kuwait stated that its signature and ratification of the Treaty do not in any way imply its recognition of Israel nor oblige it to apply the provisions of the Treaty in respect of the said country.

[6] The United Kingdom stated its view that if a regime is not recognized as the government of a state, neither signature nor the deposit of any instrument by it, nor notification of any of those acts, will bring about recognition of that regime by any other state.

The Outer Space Treaty

[1] Notification of succession.

[2] The Brazilian government interprets Article X of the Treaty as a specific recognition that the granting of tracking facilities by the parties to the Treaty shall be subject to agreement between the states concerned.

[3] The United States considers that Byelorussia and Ukraine are already covered by the signature and ratification by the Soviet Union.

[4] With a statement that this does not imply the recognition of any territory or regime not recognized by this state.

[5] The Federal Republic of Germany stated that the Treaty applies also to Berlin (West).

[6] Kuwait acceded to the Treaty with the understanding that this does not in any way imply its recognition of Israel and does not oblige it to apply the provisions of the Treaty in respect of the said country.

[7] Madagascar acceded to the Treaty with the understanding that under Article X of the Treaty the state shall retain its freedom of decision with respect to the possible installation of foreign observation bases in its territory and shall continue to possess the right to fix, in each case, the conditions for such installation.

[8] Syria acceded to the Treaty with the understanding that this should not mean in any way the recognition of Israel, nor should it lead to any relationship with Israel that could arise from the Treaty.

The Treaty of Tlatelolco

[1] Argentina stated that it understands Article 18 as recognizing the right of parties to carry out, by their own means or in association with third parties, explosions of nuclear devices for peaceful purposes, including explosions which involve devices similar to those used in nuclear weapons.

[2] The Treaty is in force for this country due to a declaration, annexed to the instrument of ratification in accordance with Article 28, paragraph 2, which waived the requirements for the entry into force of the Treaty, specified in paragraph 1 of that Article: namely, that all states in the region deposit the instruments of ratification; that Protocol I and Protocol II be signed and ratified by those states to which they apply; and that agreements on safeguards be concluded with the IAEA. Colombia made this declaration subsequent to the deposit of ratification, namely, on 6 September 1972, as did Nicaragua, on 24 October 1968, and Trinidad and Tobago, on 27 June 1975.

[3] On signing the Treaty, Brazil stated that, according to its interpretation, Article 18 of the Treaty gives the signatories the right to carry out, by their own means or in association with third parties, nuclear explosions for peaceful purposes, including explosions which involve devices similar to those used in nuclear weapons. This statement was reiterated at the ratification. Brazil also stated that it did not waive the requirements for the entry into force of the Treaty laid down in Article 28. The Treaty is therefore not yet in force for Brazil.

[4] Chile has not waived the requirements for the entry into force of the Treaty laid down in Article 28. The Treaty is therefore not yet in force for Chile.

[5] On signing Protocol II, China stated, *inter alia*: China will never use or threaten to use nuclear weapons against non-nuclear Latin American countries and the Latin American nuclear weapon-free zone; nor will China test, manufacture, produce, stockpile, install or deploy nuclear weapons in these countries or in this zone, or send its means of transportation and delivery carrying nuclear weapons to cross the territory, territorial sea or airspace of Latin American countries. The signing of the Protocol does not imply any

change whatsoever in China's stand on the disarmament and nuclear weapons issue and, in particular, does not affect the Chinese government's stand against the Non-Proliferation Treaty and the Partial Test Ban Treaty.

The Chinese government holds that, in order that Latin America may truly become a nuclear weapon-free zone, all nuclear countries, and particularly the superpowers, must undertake not to use or threaten to use nuclear weapons against the Latin American countries and the Latin American nuclear weapon-free zone, and implement the following undertakings: (1) dismantle all foreign military bases in Latin America and refrain from establishing new bases there, and (2) prohibit the passage of any means of transportation and delivery carrying nuclear weapons through Latin American territory, territorial sea or airspace.

6 On signing Protocol I, France made the following reservations and interpretive statements: the Protocol, as well as the provisions of the Treaty to which it refers, will not affect the right of self-defence under Article 51 of the UN Charter; the application of the legislation referred to in Article 3 of the Treaty relates to legislation which is consistent with international law; the obligations under the Protocol shall not apply to transit across the territories of the French Republic situated in the zone of the Treaty, and destined to other territories of the French Republic; the Protocol shall not limit, in any way, the participation of the populations of the French territories in the activities mentioned in Article 1 of the Treaty, and in efforts connected with the national defence of France; the provisions of Articles 1 and 2 of the Protocol apply to the text of the Treaty as it stands at the time when the Protocol is signed by France, and consequently no amendment to the Treaty that might come into force under Article 29 thereof would be binding on the government of France without the latter's express consent.

7 On signing Protocol II, France stated that it interprets the undertaking contained in Article 3 of the Protocol to mean that it presents no obstacle to the full exercise of the right of self-defence enshrined in Article 51 of the United Nations Charter; it takes note of the interpretation of the Treaty given by the Preparatory Commission for the Denuclearization of Latin America and reproduced in the Final Act, according to which the Treaty does not apply to transit, the granting or denying of which lies within the exclusive competence of each state party in accordance with the pertinent principles and rules of international law; it considers that the application of the legislation referred to in Article 3 of the Treaty relates to legislation which is consistent with international law. The provisions of Articles 1 and 2 of the Protocol apply to the text of the Treaty as it stands at the time when the Protocol is signed by France. Consequently, no amendment to the Treaty that might come into force under the provision of Article 29 would be binding

on the government of France without the latter's express consent. If this declaration of interpretation is contested in part or in whole by one or more contracting parties to the Treaty or to Protocol II, these instruments would be null and void as far as relations between the French Republic and the contesting state or states are concerned. On depositing its instrument of ratification of Protocol II, France stated that it did so subject to the statement made on signing the Protocol. On 15 April 1974, France made a supplementary statement to the effect that it was prepared to consider its obligations under Protocol II as applying not only to the signatories of the Treaty, but also to the territories for which the statute of denuclearization was in force in conformity with Article 1 of Protocol I.

8 On signing the Treaty, Mexico said that if technological progress makes it possible to differentiate between nuclear weapons and nuclear devices for peaceful purposes, it will be necessary to amend the relevant provisions of the Treaty, according to the procedure established therein.

9 The Netherlands stated that Protocol I shall not be interpreted as prejudicing the position of the Netherlands as regards its recognition or non-recognition of the rights of or claims to sovereignty of the parties to the Treaty, or of the grounds on which such claims are made. With respect to nuclear explosions for peaceful purposes on the territory of Suriname and the Netherlands Antilles, no other rules apply than those operative for the parties to the Treaty. Upon Suriname's accession to independence on 25 November 1975, the obligations of the Netherlands under the Protocol apply only to the Netherlands Antilles.

10 Nicaragua stated that it reserved the right to use nuclear energy for peaceful purposes such as the removal of earth for the construction of canals, irrigation works, power plants, and so on, as well as to allow the transit of atomic material through its territory.

11 The Soviet Union signed and ratified Protocol II with the following statement:

The Soviet Union proceeds from the assumption that the effect of Article 1 of the Treaty extends, as specified in Article 5 of the Treaty, to any nuclear explosive device and that, accordingly, the carrying out by any party to the Treaty of explosions of nuclear devices for peaceful purposes would be a violation of its obligations under Article 1 and would be incompatible with its non-nuclear status. For states parties to the Treaty, a solution to the problem of peaceful nuclear explosions can be found in accordance with the provisions of Article V of the Non-Proliferation Treaty and within the framework of the international procedures of the IAEA. The signing of the Protocol by the Soviet Union does not in any way signify recognition of the possibility of the force of the Treaty being extended beyond the territories of the states parties to the Treaty, including airspace and territorial waters as defined in accordance with international law. With regard to the reference in Article 3 of the Treaty to "its own legislation" in connection with the territorial waters, airspace and any other space over which the states parties to the Treaty exercise sovereignty, the signing of the Protocol by the Soviet Union does not signify recognition of their claims to the exercise of sovereignty which are contrary to generally accepted standards of international law. The Soviet Union takes note of the interpretation of the Treaty given in the Final Act of the Preparatory Commission for the Denuclearization of Latin America to the effect that the transport of nuclear weapons by the parties to the Treaty is covered by the prohibitions in Article 1 of the Treaty. The Soviet Union re-affirms its position that authorizing the transit of nuclear weapons in any form would be contrary to the objectives of the Treaty, according to which, as specially mentioned in the preamble, Latin America must be completely free from nuclear weapons, and that it would be incompatible with the non-nuclear status of the states parties to the Treaty and with their obligations as laid down in Article 1 thereof.

Any actions undertaken by a state or states parties to the Treaty which are not compatible with their non-nuclear status, and also the commission by one or more states parties to the Treaty of an act of aggression with the support of a state which is in possession of nuclear weapons or together with such a state, will be regarded by the Soviet Union as incompatible with the obligations of those countries under the Treaty. In such cases the Soviet Union reserves the right to reconsider its obligations under Protocol II. It further reserves the right to reconsider its attitude to this Protocol in the event of any actions on the part of other states possessing nuclear weapons which are incompatible with their obligations under the said Protocol. The provisions of the articles of Protocol II are applicable to the text of the Treaty for the Prohibition of Nuclear Weapons in Latin America in the wording of the Treaty at the time of the signing of the Protocol by the Soviet Union, due account being taken of the position of the Soviet Union as set out in the present statement. Any amendment to the Treaty entering into force in accordance with the provisions of Articles 29 and 6 of the Treaty without the clearly expressed approval of the Soviet Union shall have no force as far as the Soviet Union is concerned.

In addition, the Soviet Union proceeds from the assumption that the obligations under Protocol II also apply to the territories for which the status of the denuclearized zone is in force in conformity with Protocol I of the Treaty.

[12] When signing and ratifying Protocol I and Protocol II, the United Kingdom made the following declarations of understanding:

In connection with Article 3 of the Treaty, defining the term "territory" as including the territorial sea, airspace and any other space over which the state exercises sovereignty in accordance with "its own legislation", the UK does not regard its signing or ratification of the Protocols as implying recognition of any legislation which does not, in its view, comply with the relevant rules of international law.

The Treaty does not permit the parties to carry out explosions of nuclear devices for peaceful purposes unless and until advances in technology have made possible the development of devices for such explosions which are not capable of being used for weapon purposes.

The signing and ratification by the UK could not be regarded as affecting in any way the legal status of any territory for the international relations of which the UK is responsible, lying within the limits of the geographical zone established by the Treaty.

Should a party to the Treaty carry out any act of aggression with the support of a nuclear weapon state, the UK would be free to reconsider the extent to which it could be regarded as committed by the provisions of Protocol II.

In addition, the UK declared that its undertaking under Article 3 of Protcol II not to use or threaten to use nuclear weapons against the parties to the Treaty extends also to territories in respect of which the undertaking under Article 1 of Protocol I becomes effective.

[13] The United States ratified Protocol I with the following understandings: The provisions of the Treaty made applicable by this Protocol do not affect the exclusive power and legal competence under international law of a state adhering to this Protocol to grant or deny transit and transport privileges to its own or any other vessels or aircraft irrespective of cargo or armaments; the provisions of the Treaty made applicable by this Protocol do not affect rights under international law of a state adhering to this Protocol regarding the exercise of the freedom of the seas, or regarding pasage through or over waters subject to the sovereignty of a state, and the declarations attached by the United States to its ratification of Protocol II apply also to its ratification of Protocol I.

[14] The United States signed and ratified Protocol II with the following declarations of understanding:

In connection with Article 3 of the Treaty, defining the term "territory" as including the territorial sea, airspace and any other space over which the state exercises sovereignty in accordance with "its own legislation", the US ratification of the Protocol could not be regarded as implying recognition of any legislation which did not, in its view, comply with the relevant rules of international law.

Each of the parties retains exclusive power and legal competence, unaffected by the terms of the Treaty, to grant or deny non-parties transit and transport privileges.

As regards the undertaking not to use or threaten to use nuclear weapons against the parties, the United States would consider that an armed attack by a party, in which it was assisted by a nuclear weapon state, would be incompatible with the party's obligations under Article 1 of the Treaty.

The definition contained in Article 5 of the Treaty is understood as encompassing all nuclear explosive devices; Articles 1 and 5 of the Treaty restrict accordingly the activities of the parties under paragraph 1 of Article 18.

Article 18, paragraph 4 permits, and US adherence to Protocol II will not prevent, collaboration by the USA with the parties to the Treaty for the purpose of carrying out explosions of nuclear devices for peaceful purposes in a manner consistent with a policy of not contributing to the proliferation of nuclear weapon capabilities.

The United States will act with respect to such territories of Protocol I adherents, as are within the geographical area defined in Article 4, paragraph 2 of the Treaty, in the same manner as Protocol II requires it to act with respect to the territories of the parties.

[15] Venezuela stated that in view of the existing controversy between Venezuela on the one hand and the United Kingdom and Guyana on the other, Article 25, paragraph 2 of the Treaty should apply to Guyana. This paragraph provides that no political entity should be admitted, part or all of whose territory is the subject of a dispute or claim between an extra-continental country and one or more Latin American states, so long as the dispute has not been settled by peaceful means.

[16] Safeguards under the Non-Proliferation Treaty cover the Treaty of Tlatelolco.

The Non-Proliferation Treaty

[1] On signing the Treaty, Australia stated, *inter alia*, that it regarded it as essential that the Treaty should not affect security commitments under existing treaties of mutual security.

[2] Notification of succession.

[3] On the occasion of the deposit of the instrument of ratification, Egypt stated that since it was embarking on the construction of nuclear power reactors, it expected assistance and support from industrialized nations with a developed nuclear industry. It called upon nuclear weapon states to promote research and development of peaceful applications of nuclear explosions in order to overcome all the difficulties presently involved therein. Egypt also appealed to these states to exert their efforts to conclude an agreement prohibiting the use or threat of use of nuclear weapons against any state, and expressed the view that the Middle East should remain completely free of nuclear weapons.

[4] France, not party to the Treaty, declared that it would behave like a state adhering to the Treaty and that it would follow a policy of strengthening appropriate safeguards relating to nuclear equipment, material and technology. On 12 September 1981 an agreement between France, the European Atomic Energy Community (Euratom) and the IAEA

for the application of safeguards in France entered into force. The agreement covers nuclear material and facilities notified to the IAEA by France, and is similar to the agreements concluded with the IAEA by the United Kingdom and the United States.

[5] On depositing the instrument of ratification, the Federal Republic of Germany reiterated the declaration made at the time of signing: it reaffirmed its expectation that the nuclear weapon states would intensify their efforts in accordance with the undertakings under Article VI of the Treaty, as well as its understanding that the security of FR Germany continued to be ensured by NATO; it stated that no provision of the Treaty may be interpreted in such a way as to hamper further development of European unification; that research, development and use of nuclear energy for peaceful purposes, as well as international and multinational cooperation in this field, must not be prejudiced by the Treaty; that the application of the Treaty, including the implementation of safeguards, must not lead to discrimination of the nuclear industry of FR Germany in international competition; and that it attached vital importance to the undertaking given by the United States and the United Kingdom concerning the application of safeguards to their peaceful nuclear facilities, hoping that other nuclear weapon states would assume similar obligations.

In a separate note, FR Germany declared that the Treaty will also apply to Berlin (West) without affecting Allied rights and responsibilities, including those relating to demilitarization. In notes of 24 July, 19 August, and 25 November 1975, respectively, addressed to the US Department of State, Czechoslovakia, the Soviet Union and the German Democratic Republic stated that this declaration by FR Germany had no legal effect.

[6] On acceding to the Treaty, the Holy See stated, *inter alia*, that the Treaty will attain in full the objectives of security and peace and justify the limitations to which the states party to the Treaty submit, only if it is fully executed in every clause and with all its implications. This concern's not only the obligations to be applied immediately but also those which envisage a process of ulterior commitments. Among the latter, the Holy See considers it suitable to point out the following:

(*a*) The adoption of appropriate measures to ensure, on a basis of equality, that all nonnuclear weapon states party to the Treaty will have available to them the benefits deriving from peaceful applications of nuclear technology.

(*b*) The pursuit of negotiations in good faith on effective measures relating to cessation of the nuclear arms race at an early date and to nuclear disarmament, and on a treaty on general and complete disarmament under strict and effective control.

[7] On signing the Treaty, Indonesia stated, *inter alia*, that the government of Indonesia

attaches great importance to the declarations of the United States, the United Kingdom and the Soviet Union affirming their intention to provide immediate assistance to any non-nuclear weapon state party to the Treaty that is a victim of an act of aggression in which nuclear weapons are used. Of utmost importance, however, is not the action *after* a nuclear attack has been committed but the guarantees to prevent such an attack. The Indonesian government trusts that the nuclear weapon states will study further this question of effective measures to ensure the security of the non-nuclear weapon states. On depositing the instrument of ratification, Indonesia expressed the hope that the nuclear countries would be prepared to co-operate with non-nuclear countries in the use of nuclear energy for peaceful purposes and implement the provisions of Article IV of the Treaty without discrimination. It also stated the view that the nuclear weapon states should observe the provisions of Article VI of the Treaty relating to the cessation of the nuclear arms race.

[8] Italy stated that in its belief nothing in the Treaty was an obstacle to the unification of the countries of Western Europe; it noted full compatibility of the Treaty with the existing security agreements; it noted further that when technological progress would allow the development of peaceful explosive devices different from nuclear weapons, the prohibition relating to their manufacture and use shall no longer apply; it interpreted the provisions of Article IX, paragraph 3 of the Treaty, concerning the definition of a military nuclear state, in the sense that it referred exclusively to the five countries which had manufactured and exploded a nuclear weapon or other nuclear explosive device prior to 1 January 1967, and stressed that under no circumstance would a claim of pertaining to such category be recognized by the Italian government to any other state.

[9] On depositing the instrument of ratification, Japan expressed the hope that France and China would accede to the Treaty; it urged a reduction of nuclear armaments and a comprehensive ban on nuclear testing; appealed to all states to refrain from the threat or use of force involving either nuclear or non-nuclear weapons; expressed the view that peaceful nuclear activities in non-nuclear weapon states party to the Treaty should not be hampered and that Japan should not be discriminated against in favour of other parties in any aspect of such activities. It also urged all nuclear weapon states to accept IAEA safeguards on their peaceful nuclear activities.

[10] A statement was made containing a disclaimer regarding the recognition of states party to the Treaty.

[11] On depositing the instrument of ratification, the Republic of Korea took note of the fact that the depositary governments of the three nuclear weapon states had made declarations in June 1968 to take immediate and effective measures to safeguard any non-nuclear weapon state which is a victim of an act or an object of a threat of aggression in which nuclear weapons are used. It recalled that the UN Security Council adopted a resolution to the same effect on 19 June 1968.

[12] On depositing the instruments of accession and ratification, Liechtenstein and Switzerland stated that activities not prohibited under Articles I and II of the Treaty include, in particular, the whole field of energy production and related operations, research and technology concerning future generations of nuclear reactors based on fission or fusion, as well as production of isotopes. Liechtenstein and Switzerland define the term "source or special fissionable material" in Article III of the Treaty as being in accordance with Article XX of the IAEA Statute, and a modification of this interpretation requires their formal consent; they will accept only such interpretations and definitions of the terms "equipment or material especially designed or prepared for the processing, use or production of special fissionable material", as mentioned in Article III of the Treaty, that they will expressly approve; and they understand that the application of the Treaty, especially of the control measures, will not lead to discrimination of their industry in international competition.

[13] On signing the Treaty, Mexico stated, *inter alia,* that none of the provisions of the Treaty shall be interpreted as affecting in any way whatsoever the rights and obligations of Mexico as a state party to the Treaty of Tlatelolco.

It is the understanding of Mexico that at the present time any nuclear explosive device is capable of being used as a nuclear weapon and that there is no indication that in the near future it will be possible to manufacture nuclear explosive devices that are not potentially nuclear weapons. However, if technological advances modify this situation, it will be necessary to amend the relevant provisions of the Treaty in accordance with the procedure established therein.

[14] The ratification was accompanied by a statement in which Turkey underlined the non-proliferation obligations of the nuclear weapon states, adding that measures must be taken to meet adequately the security requirements of non-nuclear weapon states. Turkey also stated that measures developed or to be developed at national and international levels to ensure the non-proliferation of nuclear weapons should in no case restrict the non-nuclear weapon states in their option for the application of nuclear energy for peaceful purposes.

[15] The United Kingdom recalled its view that if a regime is not recognized as the government of a state, neither signature nor the deposit of any instrument by it, nor notification of any of those acts, will bring about recognition of that regime by any other state.

[16] This agreement, signed between the United Kingdom, Euratom and the IAEA, provides for the submission of British non-military nuclear installations to safeguards under IAEA supervision.

[17] Together with the notification that the statutory and constitutional requirements for the entry into force of the agreement for the application of safeguards to US civilian nuclear installations had been met, the IAEA received a list of facilities in the United States eligible to be safeguarded.

[18] In connection with the ratification of the Treaty, Yugoslavia stated, *inter alia*, that it considered a ban on the development, manufacture and use of nuclear weapons and the destruction of all stockpiles of these weapons to be indispensable for the maintenance of a stable peace and international security; it held the view that the chief responsibility for progress in this direction rested with the nuclear weapon powers, and expected these powers to undertake not to use nuclear weapons against the countries which have renounced them as well as against non-nuclear weapon states in general, and to refrain from the threat to use them. It also emphasized the significance it attached to the universality of the efforts relating to the realization of the Non-Proliferation Treaty.

The Sea-Bed Treaty

[1] On signing the Treaty, Argentina stated that it interprets the references to the freedom of the high seas as in no way implying a pronouncement of judgement on the different positions relating to questions connected with international maritime law. It understands that the reference to the rights of exploration and exploitation by coastal states over their continental shelves was included solely because those could be the rights most frequently affected by verification procedures. Argentina precludes any possibility of strengthening, through this Treaty, certain positions concerning continental shelves to the detriment of others based on different criteria.

[2] On signing the Treaty, Brazil stated that nothing in the Treaty shall be interpreted as prejudicing in any way the sovereign rights of Brazil in the area of the sea, the sea-bed and the subsoil thereof adjacent to its coasts. It is the understanding of the Brazilian government that the word "observation", as it appears in paragraph 1 of Article III of the Treaty, refers only to observation that is incidental to the normal course of navigation in accordance with international law.

[3] In depositing the instrument of ratification Canada declared: Article I, paragraph 1, cannot be interpreted as indicating that any state has a right to implant or emplace any weapons not prohibited under Article I, paragraph 1, on the sea-bed and ocean floor, and in the subsoil thereof, beyond the limits of national jurisdiction, or as constituting any limitation on the principle that this area of the sea-bed and ocean floor and the subsoil thereof shall be reserved for exclusively peaceful purposes. Articles I, II and III cannot be interpreted as indicating that any state but the coastal state has any right to implant or emplace any weapon not prohibited under Article I, paragraph 1 on the con-

tinental shelf, or the subsoil thereof, appertaining to that coastal state, beyond the outer limit of the sea-bed zone referred to in Article I and defined in Article II. Article III cannot be interpreted as indicating any restrictions or limitation upon the rights of the coastal state, consistent with its exclusive sovereign rights with respect to the continental shelf, to verify, inspect or effect the removal of any weapon, structure, installation, facility or device implanted or emplaced on the continental shelf, or the subsoil thereof, appertaining to that coastal state, beyond the outer limit of the sea-bed zone referred to in Article I and defined in Article II. On 12 April 1976, the Federal Republic of Germany stated that the declaration by Canada is not of a nature to confer on the government of this country more far-reaching rights than those to which it is entitled under current international law, and that all rights existing under current international law which are not covered by the prohibitions are left intact by the Treaty.

[4] A statement was made containing a disclaimer regarding recognition of states party to the Treaty.

[5] On ratifying the Treaty, the Federal Republic of Germany declared that the Treaty will apply to Berlin (West).

[6] On the occasion of its accession to the Treaty, the government of India stated that as a coastal state, India has, and always has had, full and exclusive rights over the continental shelf adjoining its territory and beyond its territorial waters and the subsoil thereof. It is the considered view of India that other countries cannot use its continental shelf for military purposes. There cannot, therefore, be any restriction on, or limitation of, the sovereign right of India as a coastal state to verify, inspect, remove or destroy any weapon, device, structure, installation or facility, which might be implanted or emplaced on or beneath its continental shelf by any other country, or to take such other steps as may be considered necessary to safeguard its security. The accession by the government of India to the Treaty is based on this position. In response to the Indian statement, the US government expressed the view that, under existing international law, the rights of coastal states over their continental shelves are exclusive only for the purposes of exploration and exploitation of natural resources, and are otherwise limited by the 1958 Convention on the Continental Shelf and other principles of international law. On 12 April 1976, the Federal Republic of Germany stated that the declaration by India is not of a nature to confer on the government of this country more far-reaching rights than those to which it is entitled under current international law, and that all rights existing under current law which are not covered by the prohibitions are left intact by the Treaty.

[7] On signing the Treaty, Italy stated, *inter alia*, that in the case of agreements on further measures in the field of disarmament to prevent an arms race on the sea-bed and ocean

floor and in their subsoil, the question of the delimitation of the area within which these measures would find application shall have to be examined and solved in each instance in accordance with the nature of the measures to be adopted. The statement was repeated at the time of ratification.

8 Ratification of the Treaty by Taiwan is considered by Romania as null and void.

9 The United Kingdom recalled its view that if a regime is not recognized as the government of a state, neither signature nor the deposit of any instrument by it, nor notification of any of those acts, will bring about recognition of that regime by any other state.

10 Viet Nam stated that no provision of the Treaty should be interpreted in a way that would contradict the rights of the coastal states with regard to their continental shelf, including the right to take measures to ensure their security.

11 On 25 February 1974, the Ambassador of Yugoslavia transmitted to the US Secretary of State a note stating that in the view of the Yugoslav government, Article III, paragraph 1, of the Treaty should be interpreted in such a way that a state exercising its right under this Article shall be obliged to notify in advance the coastal state, in so far as its observations are to be carried out "within the stretch of the sea extending above the continental shelf of the said state". On 16 January 1975, the US Secretary of State presented the view of the United States concerning the Yugoslav note, as follows: In so far as the note is intended to be interpretative of the Treaty, the United States cannot accept it as a valid interpretation. In addition, the United States does not consider that it can have any effect on the existing law of the sea. In so far as the note was intended to be a reservation to the Treaty, the United States placed on record its formal objection to it on the grounds that it was incompatible with the object and purpose of the Treaty. The United States also drew attention to the fact that the note was submitted too late to be legally effective as a reservation. A similar exchange of notes took place between Yugoslavia and the United Kingdom. On 12 April 1976, the Federal Republic of Germany stated that the declaration by Yugoslavia is not of a nature to confer on the government of this country more far-reaching rights than those to which it is entitled under current international law, and that all rights existing under current international law which are not covered by the prohibitions are left intact by the Treaty.

The BW Convention

1 Considering the obligations resulting from its status as a permanently neutral state, Austria declares a reservation to the effect that its co-operation within the framework of this Convention cannot exceed the limits determined by the status of permanent neutrality and membership with the United Nations.

2 In a statement made on the occasion of the signature of the Convention, India reiterated its understanding that the objective of the Convention is to eliminate biological and toxin weapons, thereby excluding completely the possibility of their use, and that the exemption with regard to biological agents or toxins, which would be permitted for prophylactic, protective or other peaceful purposes, would not in any way create a loophole in regard to the production or retention of biological and toxin weapons. Also any assistance which might be furnished under the terms of the Convention would be of a medical or humanitarian nature and in conformity with the Charter of the United Nations. The statement was repeated at the time of the deposit of the instrument of ratification.

3 Ireland considers that the Convention could be undermined if the reservations made by the parties to the 1925 Geneva Protocol were allowed to stand, as the prohibition of possession is incompatible with the right to retaliate, and that there should be an absolute and universal prohibition of the use of the weapons in question. Ireland notified the depositary government for the Geneva Protocol of the withdrawal of its reservations to the Protocol, made at the time of accession in 1930. The withdrawal applies to chemical as well as to bacteriological (biological) and toxin agents of warfare.

4 The Republic of Korea stated that the signing of the Convention does not in any way mean or imply the recognition of any territory or regime which has not been recognized by the Republic of Korea as a state or government.

5 In the understanding of Kuwait, its ratification of the Convention does not in any way imply its recognition of Israel, nor does it oblige it to apply the provisions of the Convention in respect of the said country.

6 Mexico considers that the Convention is only a first step towards an agreement prohibiting also the development, production and stockpiling of all chemical weapons, and notes the fact that the Convention contains an express commitment to continue negotiations in good faith with the aim of arriving at such an agreement.

7 The ratification by Switzerland contains the following reservations:

1. Owing to the fact that the Convention also applies to weapons, equipment or means of delivery designed to use biological agents or toxins, the delimitation of its scope of application can cause difficulties since there are scarcely any weapons, equipment or means of delivery peculiar to such use; therefore, Switzerland reserves the right to decide for itself what auxiliary means fall within that definition.

2. By reason of the obligations resulting from its status as a perpetually neutral state, Switzerland is bound to make the general reservation that its collaboration within the framework of this Convention cannot go beyond the terms prescribed by that status. This reservation refers especially to Article VII of the Convention as well as to any

similar clause that could replace or supplement that provision of the Convention.

In a note of 18 August 1976, addressed to the Swiss Ambassador, the US Secretary of State stated the following view of the US government with regard to the first reservation: The prohibition would apply only to (a) weapons, equipment and means of delivery, the design of which indicated that they could have no other use than that specified, and (b) weapons, equipment and means of delivery, the design of which indicated that they were specifically intended to be capable of the use specified. The government of the United States shares the view of the government of Switzerland that there are few weapons, equipment or means of delivery peculiar to the uses referred to. It does not, however, believe that it would be appropriate, on this ground alone, for states to reserve unilaterally the right to decide which weapons, equipment or means of delivery fell within the definition. Therefore, while acknowledging the entry into force of the Convention between itself and the government of Switzerland, the US government enters its objection to this reservation.

[8] The deposit of the instrument of ratification by Taiwan is considered by the Soviet Union as an illegal act because the government of the People's Republic of China is regarded by the Soviet Union as the sole representative of China.

[9] The United Kingdom recalled its view that if a regime is not recognized as the government of a state, neither signature nor the deposit of any instrument by it nor notification of any of those acts will bring about recognition of that regime by any other state.

[10] Notification of succession.

The ENMOD Convention

[1] Kuwait made the following reservation and understanding: This Convention binds Kuwait only towards states parties thereto; its obligatory character shall *ipso facto* terminate with respect to any hostile state which does not abide by the prohibition contained therein. It is understood that accession to this Convention does not mean in any way recognition of Israel by Kuwait; furthermore, no treaty relation will arise between Kuwait and Israel.

On 23 June 1980, the UN Secretary-General, the depositary of the Convention, received from the government of Israel a communication stating that Israel would adopt towards Kuwait an attitude of complete reciprocity.

[2] On signing the Convention, Turkey declared that the terms "widespread", "long-lasting" and "severe effects" contained in the Convention need to be more clearly defined, and that so long as this clarification was not made, Turkey would be compelled to interpret for itself the terms in question and, consequently, reserved the right to do so as and when required. Turkey also stated its belief that the difference between "military or any other hostile purposes" and "peaceful purposes" should be more clearly defined so as to prevent subjective evaluations.

[3] Notification of succession.

7. The arms control machinery

Progress, or lack of progress, in the field of arms control is determined mainly by national interests. Policy decisions are a function of the interaction of various sectors of government; in the course of arms control negotiations, each side tries first to enlist the support of its own political and military establishments and sometimes also those of its allies. The outcome of the negotiations with other parties depends to a great extent on the general world political climate. Procedures for conducting negotiations are less important in this context, but adequate institutional mechanisms may further the pursued cause.

I. The deliberative bodies

UN General Assembly

Since the creation of the United Nations in 1945, the UN General Assembly—the most representative body of the international community—has been the principal forum for international policy debate. Arms control issues are debated primarily in the First (Political) Committee, or directly in the plenary sessions without recourse to subsidiary bodies.

The UN General Assembly provides opportunities for making official statements as well as for holding informal discussions. It thus serves as a sounding-board for ideas and proposals which are then usually incorporated in draft resolutions; a two-thirds majority of the members present and voting is required to adopt them. The General Assembly also attempts to influence negotiations by making specific recommendations. These recommendations have no binding force but may carry some political or moral weight, especially when made unanimously. Resolutions adopted 'without vote', 'without objection' or 'by consensus', rather than by a formal vote, are usually understood to denote broad agreement as regards the general lines of the text. In such cases, delegations sometimes make explanatory statements recording their positions, interpretations or reservations with respect to certain provisions of a resolution.

Several resolutions, such as the 1946 resolution calling for the use of atomic energy exclusively for peaceful purposes, the 1959 resolution on general and complete disarmament, the 1961 resolution on the non-proliferation of nuclear weapons, or the 1971 resolution condemning nuclear weapon tests, represent landmarks in the arms control deliberative process. However, most of the nearly 450 resolutions on arms control matters which have been adopted by the General Assembly since the founding of the United Nations (of which about 50 were voted upon at the 1981 session alone) have made little impact on the course of negotiations. Unless the proceedings are streamlined by reducing, through consolidation, the number of items on the agenda and consequently also the number of recommendations or declarations on overlapping subjects, the effectiveness of the Assembly will remain on the decline.

The 1978 General Assembly Special Session devoted to disarmament was convened to work out a disarmament strategy, to improve the machinery for discussing arms control and to stimulate public interest in disarmament. Indeed, at this largest international meeting ever held to deal exclusively with disarmament matters, the problems were discussed in greater depth than at regular UN Assemblies, and the Final Document adopted by the Session marked progress in several respects. Although a coherent strategy for disarmament could not be worked out, the negotiators were at least given an enlarged frame of reference. Moreover, the Special Session induced many governments to develop and articulate their disarmament policies. It also revitalized the negotiating machinery and enhanced the role of the non-aligned and other smaller states in dealing with world affairs. One of its accomplishments was to help the non-governmental organizations (NGOs) to mobilize public opinion for the cause of disarmament. For the first time in UN history, representatives from these organizations and research institutions could address the Assembly on issues of universal importance. The Session recognized the value of non-governmental scientific research in the field of armaments and disarmament, as well as the need for educational programmes for disarmament.

UN Disarmament Commission

The Special Session reactivated, as a subsidiary, deliberative, intersessional organ of the Assembly, the Disarmament Commission (DC), composed of all UN members. The DC was originally established in 1952, functioned intermittently until the summer of 1965, and had been inactive since then. Since 1978 the Commission's task has been to consider and make recommendations on various problems in the field of disarmament and to follow up the relevant decisions and recommendations of the Special Session—a wide and far-reaching but very imprecise mandate. So far, the Disarmament Commission, meeting for several weeks per year, has worked out "elements" of a comprehensive programme of disarmament as well as the text of the declaration of the 1980s as the Second Disarmament Decade.

With regard to the programme of disarmament, the Commission reiterated the principles that have been stated many times before in UN resolutions and summarized the relevant provisions of the Final Document of the Special Session. It thus produced no more than a catalogue of measures which are loosely related to each other and which already appear on the agendas of the existing bilateral, trilateral and multilateral (including regional) negotiating forums. As far as the Second Disarmament Decade is concerned, the drafting of a resolution proclaiming the Decade could have been entrusted directly to the First Committee of the General Assembly, which had worked out many equally important documents in the past, including the declaration of the First Disarmament Decade.

It is therefore doubtful whether routine meetings of the Disarmament Commission are necessary, especially since they take precious time from arms control negotiations. The Disarmament Commission could perhaps usefully perform *ad hoc* functions: those of examining and possibly amending texts agreed in the multilateral negotiating body before they are submitted to the General Assembly for commendation. Thereby the requirement expressed in the Final Document of the Special Session could be better met: that draft multilateral disarmament conventions should be subjected to the "normal procedures applicable in the law of treaties"—that is, that the draft conventions should not be presented to UN members for approval on a take-it-or-leave-it basis, as has often been the case.

UN studies

In 1978, a board of eminent persons was established to advise the Secretary-General on various aspects of studies to be made under the auspices of the United Nations in the field of disarmament. The purposes of these studies were defined by the Advisory Board as: to assist in ongoing negotiations, to assist in the identification of specific topics with a view to initiating new negotiations, to provide a general background to current deliberations and negotiations, and to assess and promote public awareness of the threat posed by nuclear weapons and the continuing arms race.

Since the 1978 Special Session, as many as 16 UN studies have been conducted on the technical, economic and political aspects of arms control. Those carried out by qualified experts contain useful information, thorough analyses of relevant problems and well-considered suggestions. Others are mere collections of official governmental views. To maintain and improve the quality of the studies, expert groups appointed by the Secretary-General would have to include a greater number of scholars than government officials and be given more time to prepare their reports. The recently established UN Institute for Disarmament Research may help to broaden the UN expertise in arms control matters. (For the list of UN arms control studies, including those carried out prior to 1978, see table 7.1.)

UN Security Council

The UN Security Council has as one of its statutory responsibilities the formulation of plans for the establishment of a system for the regulation of armaments. It is to be assisted in this work by the Military Staff Committee, consisting of the chiefs of staff of the permanent members of the Council or their representatives (Articles 26 and 47 of the UN Charter). In the early post-war period the Security Council was actively engaged in arms control

Table 7.1. UN arms control studies

Economic and social consequences of disarmament (1962).

Effects of the possible use of nuclear weapons and the security and economic implications for states of the acquisition and further development of these weapons (1967).

Chemical and bacteriological (biological) weapons and the effects of their possible use (1969).

Economic and social consequences of the arms race and of military expenditures (1971).

Napalm and other incendiary weapons and all aspects of their possible use (1972).

Disarmament and development: report of the group of experts on the economic and social consequences of disarmament (1972).

Declaration of the Indian Ocean as a zone of peace: factual statement pursuant to General Assembly resolution 3080 (1974).

Reduction of the military budgets of states permanent members of the Security Council by 10 per cent and utilization of part of the funds thus saved to provide assistance to developing countries (1974).

Comprehensive study of the question of nuclear-weapon-free zones in all its aspects: special report of the Conference of the Committee on Disarmament (1975).

Reduction of military budgets—measurement and international reporting of military expenditures (1976).

Reduction of military budgets (1977).

Economic and social consequences of the arms race and of military expenditures (1977).

Reports of the *ad hoc* group of scientific experts to consider international co-operative measures to detect and to identify seismic events (1978 and 1979).

Comprehensive study on nuclear weapons (1980).

Study on all the aspects of regional disarmament (1980).

Comprehensive report on South Africa's plan and capability in the nuclear field (1980).

Study on the question of a comprehensive nuclear test ban (1980).

Report of the *ad hoc* panel on military budgeting. Practical test of the proposed standard instrument for international reporting of military expenditures (1980).

Study on the relationship between disarmament and development (1981).

Study on the relationship between disarmament and international security (1981).

The technical, legal and financial implications of establishing an international satellite monitoring agency (1981).

Study on Israeli nuclear armament (1981).

Study on confidence-building measures (1981).

Study on the institutional arrangements relating to the process of disarmament (1981).

Study on the organization and financing of a world disarmament campaign (1981).

Study of the group of experts on the economic and social aspects of the arms race (1982).

Study on reduction of military budgets (1982).

Study of the group of experts to investigate reports of the alleged use of chemical weapons (1981–82).

discussions, but since the 1950s its role in this field has been reduced to nought. It has never requested assistance from the Military Staff Committee. Nevertheless, in the context of its responsibility for the maintenance of international peace and security, the UN Security Council has in several arms control agreements been assigned the role of dealing with complaints about breaches of obligations contracted under these agreements.

Other deliberative UN bodies

During the past 35 years a number of other deliberative UN bodies have been established to deal with arms control issues. Some of them ceased to function upon completion of their tasks, while others adjourned *sine die* or were simply dissolved. By the end of 1981, the following three UN bodies set up for specific arms control issues, in addition to those described above, were in existence.

The UN Scientific Committee on the Effects of Atomic Radiation (UNSCEAR), established in 1955, has been dealing with a question related to the cessation of nuclear weapon tests. The task of this Committee is to assemble, study and disseminate information on observed levels of ionizing radiation from all sources, and on the effects of such radiation on man and the environment.

The *Ad Hoc* Committee on the Indian Ocean considers questions related to the achievement of the objectives of the 1971 UN Declaration of the Indian Ocean as a zone of peace. The Committee consists of 46 member states and reports annually to the Assembly.

Another *ad hoc* committee, composed of 40 non-nuclear weapon states, examines the views and suggestions expressed by governments on the convening of a World Disarmament Conference. (States possessing nuclear weapons are invited to co-operate or maintain contact with the committee.) The purpose of this exercise, which has been going on for a number of years, is not clear. In view of the near-universality of the United Nations, a UN General Assembly devoted exclusively to disarmament is already, for all practical purposes, a world disarmament conference. It is hard to see what an international parley under a different label could achieve that a UN Assembly could not, unless the proposed conference is meant to negotiate rather than deliberate. However, drafting arms control treaties in a body of some 160 plenipotentiaries may well prove to be an impossible task. In any event, no treaty obligations can be imposed upon states by an international meeting, be it a UN Assembly or a world conference, bypassing national constitutional procedures.

UN Secretariat

The principal UN Secretariat unit dealing with arms control matters is the Centre for Disarmament (which in 1977 replaced the Disarmament Affairs Division), headed by an Assistant Secretary-General, but forming part of the Department for Political and Security Council Affairs. The role of the Centre consists of servicing conferences; assisting experts engaged in disarmament-related studies; following up General Assembly resolutions; administering a programme of fellowships on disarmament for government officials; maintaining liaison with non-governmental organizations; and disseminating relevant information, including publication of a disarmament yearbook and a disarmament periodical, as well as a variety of pamphlets on arms control. Moreover, under the 1977 Environmental Modification Convention, the UN Secretary-General, in his capacity of depositary, has the duty, upon request, to convene and chair a consultative committee of experts to examine problems which may arise in the application of the Convention and to distribute the committee's findings of fact to the parties. It is obvious that the Centre for Disarmament would be directly involved in carrying out these tasks.

To cope with the increasing workload, adjustments have continuously been made to the structure of the Centre. Proposals have also been put forward for the establishment of a separate department headed by an Under-Secretary-General or for the creation of a separate international organization. The latter proposal does not seem to enjoy wide support. Indeed, since arms control is intended to increase the security of nations, divorcing it from the United Nations, which bears primary responsibility for international security, would hardly be justified. However, considering the role that the United Nations is called upon to play in disarmament, the strengthening of the position of the Centre for Disarmament within the UN would certainly be in order. This could be achieved by giving the Centre a more autonomous status, which would ensure a more direct relationship to the UN Secretary-General, and the task of co-ordinating all UN arms control-related events.

Since the future of arms control may depend on the degree of openness among nations with regard to armament developments, the United Nations could be requested to collect and make available information about weapon production and deployment, arms transfers and military expenditures. But as long as governments cling to their conservative views on national security, they will be reluctant to provide such information to any inter-governmental body, and most states will have to rely on non-governmental data collection and analysis.

UN specialized agencies

Several UN specialized agencies are involved, in one way or another, in arms control activities.

The UN Educational, Scientific and Cultural Organization (UNESCO) conducts conferences and symposia and issues publications on the arms race and disarmament. In 1980 it held a World Congress on Disarmament Education.

The World Health Organization (WHO) conducts studies on specific arms control or military issues related to medical science and practice. Its report on the health aspects of chemical and biological weapons, issued in 1970, contributed significantly to the discussion of the ban on these weapons. In 1981 the World Health Assembly requested the WHO Director-General to collaborate with the UN Secretary-General in establishing an international committee of scientists and experts to study the threat of a nuclear war and its consequences for the life and health of people.

The World Meteorological Organization (WMO) exchanges information with the *Ad Hoc* group of experts which considers international co-operative measures to detect and identify seismic events. The WMO Global

Telecommunications System has been proposed to be used as part of the verification system for a comprehensive nuclear test ban treaty.

The International Labour Organization (ILO) envisages in its work programme the possibility of holding special consultations and seminars on ways and means of converting armaments production to peaceful production, as well as on socio-economic aspects of disarmament and the effective utilization of resources released by disarmament measures.

The United Nations Environment Programme (UNEP) gathers information on methods of dealing with environmental problems caused by the material remnants of war. It also renders assistance to governments in preparing their programmes for the elimination of mines in their territories and carries out studies on the environmental effects of the material remnants of war.

Finally, the International Atomic Energy Agency (IAEA) administers safeguards to ensure that special fissionable and other materials, services, equipment, facilities and information are not used in such a way as to further military purposes. In line with this mandate, the IAEA has been given specific control functions under the Non-Proliferation Treaty and the Treaty of Tlatelolco.

II. The negotiating bodies

For the sake of efficiency, negotiating bodies have a more restricted membership than deliberative bodies.

Committee on Disarmament

The central forum for multilateral arms control negotiations is the Geneva-based Committee on Disarmament (CD) which was established following the 1978 UN Special Session of the General Assembly to replace the Conference of the Committee on Disarmament (CCD). In 1981 the CD membership (subject to review) was as follows: Algeria, Argentina, Australia, Belgium, Brazil, Bulgaria, Burma, Canada, China, Cuba, Czechoslovakia, Egypt, Ethiopia, France, the German Democratic Republic, the Federal Republic of Germany, Hungary, India, Indonesia, Iran, Italy, Japan, Kenya, Mexico, Mongolia, Morocco, the Netherlands, Nigeria, Pakistan, Peru, Poland, Romania, Sri Lanka, Sweden, the Soviet Union, the United Kingdom, the United States, Venezuela, Yugoslavia and Zaire.

The CD membership thus includes states representing all geographical regions and political groupings. All the five nuclear weapon states and other militarily significant countries are members. Non-members may submit written proposals or working documents and may, upon invitation, participate in the discussions on substantive items figuring on the agenda of the Committee. Formal plenary CD meetings are open to the public.

In spite of a general recognition that the United Nations must play a central role in the sphere of disarmament, the CD was not set up as a UN body, mainly because of US and Soviet opposition to such a relationship. Nonetheless, close ties with the United Nations do exist. In adopting its agenda the CD takes into account the recommendations made by the UN General Assembly (the Secretary-General transmits to it the relevant resolutions) and regularly submits reports to the Assembly. The budget of the CD is included in the budget of the United Nations, and the Committee holds its meetings on UN premises and is serviced by UN personnel. Moreover, the secretary of the CD is appointed by the UN Secretary-General and acts as his personal representative.

The predecessor of the CD was initially established to negotiate general and complete disarmament. In the mid–1960s, however, its interest shifted to partial measures. Several multilateral arms control agreements were worked out there—the Non-Proliferation Treaty, the Sea-Bed Treaty, the Biological Weapons Convention and the Environmental Modification Convention—and the texts of these treaties were transmitted to the UN General Assembly with a request to have them recommended for signature and ratification by member states. The Partial Test Ban Treaty, which resulted from trilateral talks held in 1963 between the UK, the USA and the USSR, had been preceded by intensive negotiations in the multilateral negotiating body. The CD continues dealing with partial measures, but it has also taken up the task of elaborating a comprehensive programme of disarmament. The 'decalogue' of issues on the CD's agenda is as follows:

(1) Nuclear weapons in all aspects
(2) Chemical weapons
(3) Other weapons of mass destruction
(4) Conventional weapons
(5) Reduction of military budgets
(6) Reduction of armed forces
(7) Disarmament and development
(8) Disarmament and international security
(9) Collateral measures; confidence-building measures; effective verification methods in relation to appropriate disarmament measures, acceptable to all parties concerned
(10) Comprehensive programme of disarmament leading to general and complete disarmament under effective international control.

Since 1980, four *ad hoc* working groups of the CD (closed to the public and press) have been dealing with chemical weapons, radiological weapons (considered as 'other' weapons of mass destruction), security assurances to non-nuclear weapon states (as part of a system of international security) and a comprehensive programme of disarmament. Meetings of experts on these and other topics have been arranged to clarify technical problems. Nuclear disarmament and a comprehensive test ban have received considerable attention, but the debate has remained inconclusive. The subject of conventional disarmament has been almost totally ignored.

Due to structural modifications brought about as a result of the 1978 Special Session, the methods of work of the CD have improved. In particular, the abolition of the institution of US–Soviet co-chairmanship (and the consequential removal of an obstacle to the participation of China and France) has made the committee more suited to the prevailing political circumstances. However, this change has not affected the role the USA and the USSR are to play in bringing about disarmament by virtue of their political and military standing in the world. The most important arms control measures, those related to the limitation of nuclear weapons, are subject to bilateral talks, and the range of measures which the two powers 'allow' to be negotiated multilaterally is rather limited, the comprehensive agenda of the CD notwithstanding.

The USA and the USSR continue to exercise a decisive influence on the proceedings of the CD, taking advantage of the requirement of consensus embodied in the Committee's rules of procedure. It is generally recognized that, in international transactions, the consent and co-operation of states are essential to achieve meaningful results. Attempts at imposing the will of the majority on a dissenting minority by resorting to the traditional process of voting are usually fruitless and may even be counterproductive. This applies to substantive issues, when vital interests of states are involved, but it cannot apply to procedural matters, such as the establishment of subsidiary organs to discuss specific measures already on the agenda of the Committee. A clear understanding on this point appears imperative to prevent arbitrariness and abuse of the consensus rule.

To function effectively, a body which works out treaty texts should not be too large. In this respect the 40–member CD may have already reached the upper limit. The problem with such a limitation is that non-members are prevented from making contributions or having a say on matters which may involve their national interests. This shortcoming could be remedied if all states were informed, currently and in detail, about the talks and if they maintained the right to present their views or proposals both in writing and orally. To avoid diluting the singular character of the negotiating body, the rights of non-members must be clearly circumscribed.

Other multilateral negotiating bodies

The United Nations may organize conferences to elaborate agreements on specific arms control measures. A conference was convened in 1979 to deal with the so-called inhumane weapons, and a text of the convention containing prohibitions and restrictions on the use of a few of these weapons was adopted in 1980.

The Diplomatic Conference on the reaffirmation and development of international humanitarian law applicable in armed conflicts, which in 1977 worked out two protocols to the 1949 Geneva Conventions for the protection of war victims, was convened at the invitation of the Swiss government. Other multilateral disarmament forums outside the UN framework include a conference to negotiate the reduction of forces and armaments and "associated measures" in Central Europe, which has been meeting in Vienna since 1973. Eleven states, with indigenous or stationed forces in Central Europe, are full participants in this conference, while eight additional countries have special observer status. A second forum devoted to European matters, the Conference on Security and Co-operation in Europe (33 European states plus Canada and the USA), deals with confidence-building measures and questions related to disarmament, in accordance with the Final Act of the Conference, signed at Helsinki on 1 August 1975.

Trilateral and bilateral bodies

In 1977 the UK, the USA and the USSR engaged in trilateral talks to conclude a comprehensive test ban treaty. In 1980 these talks were suspended.

By 1981 certain bilateral US–Soviet talks were also in abeyance. These included negotiations on the prohibition of the development, production and stockpiling of chemical weapons and on controlling anti-satellite systems. In the 1970s the two powers discussed possible limitations on the international transfer of arms, as well as restrictions on military activities in the Indian Ocean, but the discussions broke off. Negotiations between the USA and the USSR on European nuclear weapons started in November 1981, while the Strategic Arms Limitation Talks (SALT) were scheduled to resume in 1982, after an interval of more than two and a half years.

The trilateral and especially bilateral bodies are less formal and have a more flexible procedure than multilateral bodies. However, the Standing Consultative Commission (SCC), set up following the SALT agreements, has operated strictly in accordance with the established regulations. The terms of reference of the SCC go beyond mere consultative duties: within its framework the USA and the USSR may examine proposals for further arms limitation measures and thereby use the Commission also for negotiating purposes.

Trilateral and bilateral negotiations are closed to the public and the press. Only under considerable pressure by other countries, mainly non-aligned, have the protagonists in these negotiations consented to submit reports to the Committee on Disarmament on the progress of their talks concerning a nuclear test ban and the prohibition of chemical weapons. US–Soviet negotiations on the limitation of nuclear weapons remain even more secret; the reiterated appeals of the UN General Assembly to the governments of the nuclear weapon powers to keep the world properly informed have so far gone unheeded.

8. Summary and conclusions

The idea of controlling the weapons of war has a strong appeal in today's world, troubled by insecurity, tension and, indeed, the threat of annihilation. In fact, while the use of weapons is already subject to limitation under the humanitarian laws of war, there is a growing body of opinion that the right of nations to possess arms should also be limited by law.

I. The functions and significance of arms control

Arms control measures clearly cannot remove the motives for acquiring arms, but they may help to minimize the risk of war started by accident or miscalculation, or even by design. They may also contribute to narrowing the disparity between heavily and lightly armed states, to mitigating the destruction and suffering in armed conflicts, to saving resources which could be used for economic and social development, and to diminishing the dangers to the environment.

Another important function of arms control agreements is to reduce suspicion and contribute to better understanding among nations. Thus, for example, the Non-Proliferation Treaty and the SALT I agreements formed the necessary prerequisites for creating the detente between the two major military blocs which culminated in the 1975 Helsinki Declaration on security and co-operation in Europe. Conversely, the failure to ratify the SALT II agreements marked a return to the cold war atmosphere, although one could also argue that it was international tension (mainly the events in Afghanistan) that rendered the ratification of the SALT II agreements impossible.

In this connection, a question has arisen as to whether arms control can or should be negotiated among states whose mutual relations are characterized by enmity. Obviously, arms control is not a matter for negotiation among friends; however, a modicum of sanguine expectation is indispensable. One can hardly imagine parties engaged in an armed conflict with each other discussing modalities for the destruction of weapons which they are using in the conflict. But apart from such extreme cases, and short of a complete breakdown of communication between states embarked on a collision course, there are few situations that could justify the abandonment of efforts to control armaments.

To the extent that arms control is to serve the security, economic and other interests of all parties, participating in negotiations for arms control agreements should not be treated as a favour done to another state or as a reward for 'good international behaviour'. Therefore, linking arms control talks with the global policies of the negotiators is bound to be futile: it impedes progress in arms control without promoting the solution of other international problems. If anything, it is a prescription for an uncontrolled arms race. At a time when the negotiating climate is not propitious for achieving early results, the mere fact of maintaining a continuous intergovernmental communication line to deal with the matters of armaments may be important for the preservation of peace.

International forums for negotiating arms control already exist or can be quickly created. What seems to be lacking is effective domestic mechanisms for harmonizing arms control strategies, as formulated by politicians, with national security requirements, as postulated by the military.

It is sometimes argued that unilateral cuts in, or restraints on the acquisition of, arms are preferable to formal international agreements. These arguments run as follows: unilateral decisions arouse less bureaucratic opposition within the countries concerned than do inter-state treaties; in the process of negotiations for international agreements each side often tries to improve its bargaining position by developing or deploying weapons it otherwise would not have had, thereby stimulating arms competition rather than abating it; and arms control agreements may provide a justification or an excuse for embarking on new weapon programmes not covered by the agreements.

Unilateral arms control measures would certainly be feasible in the rare cases in which states do not perceive a military threat and can therefore take unilateral action without requiring reciprocity. Unilateral cuts in arms could also be made by states with a substantial 'over-kill' capacity since this would pose no danger to their security: this would apply, in the first place, to the United States and the Soviet Union. However, significant unilateral arms reductions are unlikely for most nations: a country about to embark on such reductions would expect similar responses from other nations. Reciprocal restraints, assumed without formal treaty commitments—and there are many areas where this could be done without risk to the security of the nations concerned—may usefully supplement the present, conventional means of achieving arms control, but they could not replace them. Limitations resulting from parallel moves may in many instances need to be codified in treaties to become durable and enforceable: a treaty defines the range of prohibited activities and gives the prohibition the force of law. It also inhibits certain government decisions and neutralizes those forces within each state which would otherwise urge new arms acquisitions. Moreover, abrogation of a legally binding commitment is more complicated and politically hazardous than reversing a unilateral undertaking.

For all these reasons, arms control negotiations have become part and parcel of international diplomacy and a focus of world-wide attention.

Regrettably, the arms control agreements hitherto reached have not halted the arms race or reduced the military potential of states. In many cases, the weapons prohibited have had little, if any, military importance, and the outlawed activities have never been seriously contemplated as methods of war. Negotiations on measures which could make a significant impact on the arms situation in the world have stagnated for years. Thus, during the past decade, very little has been done in the field of nuclear arms control, even though the removal of the threat of nuclear war is generally considered to be the most urgent task of the international community.

II. Nuclear tests

In spite of more than 40 UN General Assembly resolutions calling for a cessation of nuclear weapon tests (including a condemnation of such tests), no comprehensive ban has been reached so far. The 1963 multilateral Partial Test Ban Treaty, the 1974 US–Soviet Threshold Test Ban Treaty and the 1976 US–Soviet Peaceful Nuclear Explosions Treaty, the three agreements which have been signed in this field, have only circumscribed the environment for nuclear testing and reduced the size of the explosions.

The latter two treaties have not yet entered into force; speeding up their ratification may seem to be an obvious step. However, the threshold for the yield of explosions which they have established is so high that, from the military point of view, the agreed limitations are nearly meaningless. On the other hand, there seem to be insurmountable obstacles to a complete renunciation of nuclear tests by *all* the nuclear weapon powers; moreover, it is highly unlikely, at least in the foreseeable future, that the three negotiating powers (the UK, the USA and the USSR) would agree to stop all tests *forever*. The treaty negotiated trilaterally was planned to have a duration of no more than three years. Resumption of tests upon the expiration of such a short-lived agreement would probably hurt the cause of arms control more than if the treaty had never been entered into. Some new partial, but more meaningful measures may be needed.

Thus, for instance, in continuing to abide by the 150-kt threshold limitation set by the unratified (but nevertheless observed) Threshold Test Ban Treaty, the parties could start negotiating the lowering, through successive agreements, of the yield ceiling and of the number of tests conducted annually—down to zero. It is common knowledge that detection and identification of explosions considerably smaller than those now permitted are possible with the existing means of verification. Also, the yearly quota of explosions could be considerably lower than the annual average of tests conducted in recent years, for the experience of the past three decades has shown that very few tests are needed to ensure the reliability of stockpiled weapons, this being the main reason (or excuse) put forward by the military to justify continued nuclear testing.

A reduced threshold test ban would, again, be only a half-measure, but it may constitute significant progress towards a comprehensive ban. Moreover, a gradual approach could be a way of involving China and France in the negotiations. Both countries have hitherto refused to negotiate, considering that a complete cessation of tests, brought about at this stage, would harm their security interests by helping to consolidate the US–Soviet superiority in the nuclear field.

III. Nuclear weapons

The 1979 SALT II agreements contain serious shortcomings, mainly because the strategic nuclear fire-power of both sides was allowed to increase in spite of the agreed limitations. Nevertheless, the failure to ratify these agreements is making the competition in nuclear arms even more dangerous and unpredictable. Readjustments, if not revisions, of the SALT II texts are probably unavoidable (most time-limits set by the Treaty, and especially by the Protocol, have already passed), but it should be possible to salvage the most important elements of the agreements. Otherwise, years of painstaking negotiations will have been in vain.

Short of formal ratification, the parties could, as in the case of the Threshold Test Ban, continue to observe the essential SALT II limitations until a new, mutually acceptable SALT III agreement has been reached. An early resumption of the talks, which were interrupted in 1979, is necessary to maintain the continuity of the SALT process, but real progress would require substantial reductions in the number of missiles and warheads, not just the disposal of excess, obsolete hardware. Furthermore, and this is equally important, severe constraints, if not a total prohibition, would have to be placed on the modernization of strategic nuclear forces. This would prevent quantitative cuts from being offset by qualitative improvements in the remaining weapons. The development of military technology must some-how be brought under control, because it tends to generate new military doctrines which impede arms limitations. Deployment of weapon systems having destabilizing effects and likely to provoke a new round of the strategic arms race, as well as systems that may defy adequate verification (such as mobile land-based ICBM launchers or long-range cruise missiles on sea-based launchers) should definitely be prohibited. Finally, to ensure that the strategic and other arms limitations verified from space by satellites are being complied with, a ban on anti-satellite weapon systems should figure high on the arms control agenda.

US–Soviet talks on the so-called European theatre nuclear weapons began in November 1981 without a clear understanding on what to negotiate. Therefore, no progress can be expected unless the parties at least agree on a common basis for discussion. It would seem that a quantitative freeze on warhead inventories at the levels which existed before the deployment of the controversial Soviet long-range SS-20 missiles might provide such a basis. Nevertheless, in view of the difficulty of differ-entiating between strategic and non-strategic missions of weapons, it may become necessary to consider the control of European nuclear forces in con-junction with US and Soviet intercontinental nuclear forces. (For example, long-range, land-based cruise missiles, the deployment of which is regulated in the Protocol to the SALT II Treaty, is to be on the agenda of the talks concerning European nuclear weapons.) In other words, there would be an advantage in merging the two sets of talks.

The success of these negotiations will, to a great extent, depend on whether the negotiating parties will give up aspirations for military superiority. For, in view of the present size of the forces on both sides, such aspirations have less to do with strategic deterrence than with the desire to acquire a nuclear first-strike capability.

IV. Denuclearized zones

Nuclear weapon free-zone arrangements could play a part in preventing further nuclearization of the world. It is, however, hard to see where in the present international situation such arrangements could be concluded. Even the Latin American denuclearized zone, established by the Treaty of Tlatelolco more than 15 years ago, has so far failed to include those countries in the area which have a nuclear weapon potential.

Many proposals for nuclear weapon-free zones concern regions where states have not yet joined the Non-Proliferation Treaty, which prohibits the acquisition of nuclear weapons by non-nuclear weapon states; it is precisely in these regions that nuclearization should be prevented in the first place. However, it would not be realistic to expect that the same states would renounce the nuclear weapon option under a zonal agreement, which is more exacting and also more comprehensive than the Non-Proliferation Treaty, because in addition to prohibiting the acquisition of nuclear weapons it would also proscribe the presence of foreign nuclear forces in a given geographical region. A promise of non-use of nuclear weapons, which the nuclear powers may give to the members of the zone, could not provide a sufficient incentive for most of the countries in question because the likelihood of nuclear weapons being used against them is very small.

One could, nevertheless, envisage a gradual process of establishing nuclear weapon-free zones. A logical sequence would be to require adherence to the NPT by all non-parties in the region, preferably simultaneously, as the first and most important step towards a denuclearized arrangement. Measures to prevent the introduction of foreign nuclear forces into the zone, though important, are less urgent. They could come later, in the second stage, complementing the non-proliferation obligations.

As regards nuclear weapons already deployed in foreign territories, the likelihood of their withdrawal is slight, especially from Europe, which is the area of confrontation between the two main military alliances, unless at the same time the levels of armed forces and conventional weapons accumulated there were very substantially reduced, and, wherever possible, equalized. For it is precisely the lack of balance in conventional armaments that served as justification (or alibi) for the introduction of nuclear weapons in the areas in question.

V. Nuclear weapon proliferation

The Non-Proliferation Treaty needs strengthening. Apart from the political motivations that may prompt states to choose a nuclear weapon option, it is the behaviour of the nuclear powers—their will, or lack of it, to reverse the nuclear arms race—that will determine the fate of the Treaty in the long run. But in the short run it is the pressure brought to bear upon non-parties, in particular on those refusing to accept full-scope safeguards, and the readiness of the parties to meet defiance of the Treaty or violation of the safeguards agreements with a rapid and adequate response, including sanctions, that may prevent or at least delay nuclear weapon proliferation. It is important to encourage a world-wide consensus that actions by non-nuclear weapon states to acquire weapon-grade nuclear material are contrary to the interests of international peace and security.

On the positive side, it would seem advisable to launch a world-wide investigation into all aspects of the possible internationalization of the most sensitive parts of the nuclear fuel cycle—uranium enrichment and plutonium reprocessing plants capable of producing fissile material directly usable for weapons. (The more restrictive study on "regional nuclear fuel cycle centres", carried out by the IAEA in 1977, has not been followed up.) Minimizing the danger of nuclear weapon proliferation through such internationalization would help to promote co-operation among states in the development of nuclear energy for peaceful purposes—the topic of a United Nations conference to be held in 1983.

VI. Chemical weapons

Another urgent matter is the prohibition of chemical weapons and the destruction of stockpiles. Here again, in view of the serious difficulties in reaching a comprehensive agreement, and especially in devising acceptable methods of verification, certain intermediate steps may help break the deadlock.

One such step could be a freeze on the production of chemical weapons. The freeze would affect, first of all, countries possessing or able to produce militarily significant supplies of these weapons, especially the most lethal chemical warfare agents, but a declaration of intent could be made by all states. This may suffice as a temporary, confidence-building measure paving the way towards a complete ban.

Furthermore, states may consider the advisability of setting up chemical weapon-free zones, the members of which would undertake not to develop, test, manufacture, acquire or allow the deployment or storage of chemical weapons. Such geographically restricted bans, established in different regions of the world, would prevent the proliferation of chemical weapons without affecting the balance of forces in these regions. They would be easier to monitor than a simultaneously introduced global ban, and the acuteness of the problem of so-called hidden stocks would be considerably attenuated, for the existing types of chemical weapons are not destined for long-distance or inter-continental use as are nuclear weapons. To be employed in combat, they would have to be stocked in areas of possible confrontation, and these are usually under close intelligence surveillance by the opposing sides. If not stocked in the areas in question, they would have to be shipped there before being used. The establishment of chemical weapon-free zones would make this impossible; thereby the very utility of chemical weapons could be brought to nought.

It is, of course, assumed that the members of a chemical weapon-free zone would, under all circumstances, observe their obligation not to allow chemical weapons in their territory. In any event, shipment of toxic munitions or bulk chemical warfare agents (especially nerve gas agents) is a complex and dangerous operation, which could not take place over long distances in absolute secrecy. The element of surprise, which is of paramount importance in chemical warfare, would disappear once preparations for a chemical attack were discovered.

Europe could be a suitable first candidate for a chemical weapon-free zone arrangement. It is in Europe that there is widespread concern that, in addition to the existing stocks of 'conventional' chemical weapons, new, so-called binary nerve gas munitions may soon be deployed.

VII. Conventional weapons

While weapons of mass destruction understandably deserve the highest priority, the problem of conventional armaments must not be ignored. In fact, considerably larger resources are spent on conventional arms than on nuclear and chemical arms combined. All the wars since 1945, even those in which the nuclear powers were directly or indirectly involved, have been fought with conventional means of warfare. It is now generally believed that an escalating conventional conflict is more likely to trigger a nuclear war than a deliberate surprise attack with nuclear weapons alone. And yet, proposals for constraints on conventional armaments on a global scale have so far aimed mainly at arms transfers. Hence the reluctance of the Third World countries, relying entirely or to a significant degree on imports of weapons, to discuss such restraints, as these would only widen the gap between the *haves* and *have-nots* in the field of conventional armaments.

One can hardly imagine workable or lasting arms transfer limitations without restrictions on arms manufacture, both in the recipient and the supplier states. A treaty prohibiting the proliferation of conventional weapons, analogous to the treaty prohibiting the proliferation of nuclear weapons, is unthinkable simply because conventional arms are easier to produce, or acquire by other means, than are nuclear arms. This applies both to major and small arms. Logically, however, a *production-cum-transfer* limitation process should start with the most advanced, as well as the most destructive categories of weapons. These could be the weapons which are particularly effective in offence, or particularly threatening to the civilian population, or particularly suited to provide an incentive for a conventional first strike. Surface-to-surface missile systems having a range beyond any defensive need, aircraft having a long-range strike role, heavy tanks or landing-ships are a few examples of such weapons.

One advantage of this approach is that there are still few producers and suppliers and, as yet, relatively few recipients of the most sophisticated military equipment. This makes an agreement on possible limitations, as well as verification of its compliance, easier to arrange than with more numerous partners. Those who import the equipment in question often lack the necessary trained personnel and management capabilities to operate a modern military establishment and are, therefore, dependent on outside support. To prevent indigenous production, limitations on arms exports would have to be accompanied by a ban on the transfer of relevant military technology. It is true that such a measure could give an impulse to the independent manufacture of arms in a few, more industrialized Third World countries, and thereby prove counter-productive; but an effective ban might at least delay the untoward development.

Arms restraints on the suppliers could not fully match those proposed for the recipients, the starting positions being different. However, the adoption by the former nations of numerical ceilings on specified types of advanced weapon systems, in combination with certain qualitative limitations, might constitute a *quid pro quo*. It is especially important that restrictions should be placed on the manufacture of weapons, because irrespective of the exporters' political and strategic considerations, large-scale manufacture stimulates, and even renders necessary, a search for foreign markets for purely economic reasons.

What matters most in this field is a clear demonstration that the arms exporters are prepared to balance possible arms importers' 'sacrifices' with their own restraints on arms acquisition and deployment and thereby to contribute jointly to the overall goal of the world armaments reduction. The participation of the militarily most significant states would be indispensable for such an undertaking to succeed.

VIII. Military expenditures

Proposals have been put forward for reducing military expenditures. Such a measure would certainly be beneficial to slowing the arms race if the difficulties of measurement, comparability and verification were overcome, and provided that reductions were substantial. A small single cut in overall military spending, without a follow-up, would probably amount only to better defence management without affecting the military power of states. However, arms control undertakings could be usefully accompanied by corresponding, proportionate cuts in military appropriations and foreign military assistance. This could be an additional check that agreed measures were actually carried out. It would also make it more difficult for the parties to compensate for armament restrictions in one area by an expansion elsewhere.

Greater openness in military matters may remove some of the fears and misconceptions that develop under conditions of secrecy. Publication of statistics on defence expenditures and on the international trade in arms, as has been repeatedly suggested, would be very useful, but would not suffice. To be of real value, the statistics would have to include data on arms production as well.

IX. An integrated approach

It may well be that the very tactic of discussing small, 'easy-to-achieve', unrelated steps, which are meant to produce incremental effects, is not adequate; negotiations have not kept pace with advancing military technology and the rising levels of armaments. A more integrated approach is perhaps needed.

One could conceive of balanced packages of measures, comprising quantitative across-the-board reductions and qualitative limitations on both conventional and non-conventional armaments, as well as restrictions on the production and transfer of weapons. The significance of such packages would be further enhanced if they provided for prohibitions of certain specific categories of arms, since the clandestine or speedy development of a conventional or nuclear weapon capability could hardly be made from a zero base, that is, after the destruction of stockpiles and the cessation of production. Also, no-first-use or even unconditional non-use undertakings might usefully be included since there is less incentive to develop or maintain weapons with an uncertain future. Verification would have to be adapted to the type of activity prohibited, and procedures would have to be devised guaranteeing equal rights for all parties to ensure that the obligations were being observed.

An integrated approach would allow for trade-offs necessitated by the wide variety of arms possessed by states, as well as the geographical and demographic differences among them. It might therefore improve the security of states in a more equitable way, and give better guarantees against unilateral advantages than piecemeal arms control. This implies that emphasis ought to be placed on multilateral negotiations. Thus, properly constituted packages of interrelated measures could be included in a multi-phased comprehensive programme, worked out and agreed multilaterally. To render their implementation realistic, the packages would have to be arranged in growing order of importance, and in such a way as to assure a steady lowering of the offensive potential of states. In this context, deployment modifications to reduce the risks of military provocations or fears of surprise attack would be particularly helpful.

Setting a time scale for the completion of the whole programme may be desirable, as target dates usually stimulate action, but it does not seem indispensable. It is the speedy realization of the first phase, however modest that phase might be, that would influence further developments, including the contents and duration of subsequent phases.

It should also be borne in mind that the relationship of the size and nature of a country's armed forces to the armed forces of other states within its own region is very often much more relevant to its security than the relationship between its forces and those of more distant nations; that neighbouring states generally tend to acquire similar and comparable military capabilities; and that in certain regions there already exist co-operative arrangements as well as regional institutions which could take action in the field of arms control. However, the initiative for a regional arrangement must come from the region concerned, and the arrangement should include all states whose participation is deemed important by the parties.

X. Prospects

Arms control, even when comprehensive in scope, presupposes the continued existence of national military establishments. It does not require radical changes in the present world order, because it makes no claim to abolish war. However, the ultimate goal of all peaceful endeavours is to abolish the use of force in inter-state relations by eliminating the instruments of war. Complete world-wide disarmament would call for international structures which would permit nations to relinquish the prerogative of providing for their own defence, and thereby render national forces superfluous. A more effective system of collective security than the one embodied in the UN Charter would have to be elaborated.

At the time of writing this book (spring 1982) the world political situation looks bleak. Armed interventions and occupation of foreign territories continue, human rights are violated in many parts of the world, inter-state conflicts have become even more acute, and the ideological propaganda war between the USA and the USSR is in full swing. Consequently, military expenditures are rising fast, and modern, ever more powerful weapons are spreading round the world unchecked. There is little official support for moves toward arms control.

One good omen is the growing public concern about the dangers of the arms race. The public is now better informed and makes its voice heard. Questions of arms control have ceased to be matters of interest to governments alone.

Appendix A

Glossary

ABM	Anti-ballistic missile	IRBM	Intermediate-range ballistic missile
AGM	Air-to-ground missile		
ALCM	Air-launched cruise missile	ISMA	International Satellite Monitoring Agency
ASAT	Anti-satellite		
ASBM	Air-to-surface ballistic missile	LRTNF	Long-range theatre nuclear forces
ASM	Air-to-surface missile	MAD	Mutual assured destruction
ASW	Anti-submarine warfare	MARV	Manoeuvrable re-entry vehicle
AWACS	Airborne warning and control system	M(B)FR	Mutual (balanced) force reduction
BMD	Ballistic missile defence		
BW	Biological weapon	MIRV	Multiple independently targetable re-entry vehicle
CBM	Confidence-building measure		
CBW	Chemical and biological warfare	MRV	Multiple re-entry vehicle
		MURFAAMCE	Mutual reduction of forces and armaments and associated measures in Central Europe
CCD	Conference of the Committee on Disarmament		
CD	Committee on Disarmament		
CEP	Circular error probability	NPT	Non-Proliferation Treaty
CSCE	Conference on Security and Co-operation in Europe	NWFZ	Nuclear weapon-free zone
		OPANAL	Agency for the Prohibition of Nuclear Weapons in Latin America
CTB	Comprehensive test ban		
CW	Chemical weapon		
ENDC	Eighteen-Nation Disarmament Committee	PNE(T)	Peaceful Nuclear Explosions (Treaty)
ENMOD	Environmental modification	PTB(T)	Partial Test Ban (Treaty)
ERW	Enhanced radiation weapon	RV	Re-entry vehicle
EURATOM	European Atomic Energy Community	RW	Radiological weapon
		SALT	Strategic Arms Limitation Talks
FOBS	Fractional orbital bombardment system	SAM	Surface-to-air missile
GLCM	Ground-launched cruise missile	SCC	Standing Consultative Commission (US–Soviet)
IAEA	International Atomic Energy Agency	SLBM	Submarine-launched ballistic missile
ICBM	Intercontinental ballistic missile	SLCM	Sea-launched cruise missile
		SSBN	Submarine, ballistic missile-equipped, nuclear-powered
INFCE	International Fuel Cycle Evaluation		
		TTBT	Threshold Test Ban Treaty
		WEU	Western European Union

310

Anti-ballistic missile (ABM) system	Weapon system for intercepting and destroying ballistic missiles.
Anti-satellite (ASAT) system	Weapon system for destroying, damaging or disturbing the normal function of, or changing the flight trajectory of, artificial Earth satellites.
Ballistic missile	Missile which follows a ballistic trajectory (part of which is outside the Earth's atmosphere) when thrust is terminated.
Battlefield nuclear weapons	*See:* Theatre nuclear weapons.
Binary chemical weapon	A shell or other device filled with two chemicals of relatively low toxicity which mix and react while the device is being delivered to the target, the reaction product being a supertoxic chemical warfare agent, such as nerve gas.
Biological weapons (BW)	Living organisms or infective material derived from them, which are intended for use in warfare to cause disease or death in man, animals or plants, and the means of their delivery.
Chemical weapons (CW)	Chemical substances—whether gaseous, liquid or solid—which might be employed as weapons in combat because of their direct toxic effects on man, animals or plants, and the means of their delivery.
Circular error probability (CEP)	A measure of missile accuracy: the radius of a circle, centred on the target, within which 50 per cent of the weapons aimed at the target are expected to fall.
Committee on Disarmament (CD)	Multilateral arms control negotiating body, based in Geneva, which is composed of 40 states (including all the nuclear weapon powers). The CD is the successor of the Eighteen-Nation Disarmament Committee, ENDC (1962–69), and the Conference of the Committee on Disarmament, CCD (1969–78).
Conventional weapons	Weapons not having mass destruction effects. *See also:* Weapons of mass destruction.
Counterforce attack	Attack directed against military targets.
Countervalue attack	Attack directed against civilian targets.
Cruise missile	Missile which can fly at very low altitudes (and can be programmed to follow the contours of the terrain) to minimize radar detection. It can be air-, ground- or sea-launched and carry a conventional or a nuclear warhead.
Enhanced radiation weapon (ERW)	*See:* Neutron weapon.
Enriched nuclear fuel	Nuclear fuel containing more than the natural contents of fissile isotopes.
Enrichment	*See:* Uranium enrichment.
Eurostrategic weapons	*See:* Theatre nuclear weapons.
Fall-out	Particles contaminated with radioactive material as well as radioactive nuclides, descending to the Earth's surface following a nuclear explosion.

311

First-strike capability	Capability to destroy within a very short period of time all or a very substantial portion of an adversary's strategic nuclear forces.
Fission	Process whereby the nucleus of a heavy atom splits into lighter nuclei with the release of substantial amounts of energy. At present the most important fissionable materials are uranium–235 and plutonium–239.
Flexible response capability	Capability to react to an attack with a full range of military options, including a limited use of nuclear weapons.
Fractional orbital bombardment system (FOBS)	System capable of launching nuclear weapons into orbit and bringing them back to Earth before a full orbit is completed.
Fuel cycle	*See:* Nuclear fuel cycle.
Fusion	Process whereby light atoms, especially those of the isotopes of hydrogen—deuterium and tritium—combine to form a heavy atom with the release of very substantial amounts of energy.
Genocide	Commission of acts intended to destroy, in whole or in part, a national, ethnical, racial or religious group.
Intercontinental ballistic missile (ICBM)	Ballistic missile with a range in excess of 5 500 km.
Intermediate-range nuclear weapons	US designation for long-range and possibly medium-range theatre nuclear weapons. *See also:* Theatre nuclear weapons.
International Nuclear Fuel Cycle Evaluation (INFCE)	International study conducted in 1978–80 on ways in which supplies of nuclear material, equipment and technology and fuel cycle services can be assured in accordance with non-proliferation considerations.
Kiloton (kt)	Measure of the explosive yield of a nuclear weapon equivalent to 1 000 metric tons of trinitrotoluene (TNT) high explosive. (The bomb detonated at Hiroshima in World War II had a yield of about 12–15 kilotons.)
Launcher	Equipment which launches a missile. ICBM launchers are land-based launchers which can be either fixed or mobile. SLBM launchers are missile tubes on submarines.
Manoeuvrable re-entry vehicle (MARV)	Re-entry vehicle whose flight can be adjusted so that it may evade ballistic missile defences and/or acquire increased accuracy.
Medium-range nuclear weapons	Soviet designation for long-range theatre nuclear weapons. *See also:* Theatre nuclear weapons.
Megaton (Mt)	Measure of the explosive yield of a nuclear weapon equivalent to one million metric tons of trinitrotoluene (TNT) high explosive.
Multiple independently targetable re-entry vehicles (MIRV)	Re-entry vehicles, carried by one missile, which can be directed to separate targets.
Mutual assured destruction (MAD)	Concept of reciprocal deterrence which rests on the ability of the nuclear weapon powers to inflict intolerable damage on one another after surviving a nuclear first strike.

Mutual reduction of forces and armaments and associated measures in Central Europe (MURFAAMCE)	Subject of negotiations between NATO and the Warsaw Treaty Organization, which began in Vienna in 1973. Often referred to as mutual (balanced) force reduction (M(B)FR).
Neutron weapon	Nuclear explosive device designed to maximize radiation effects and reduce blast and thermal effects.
Nuclear fuel cycle	Series of steps involved in preparation, use and disposal of fuel for nuclear power reactors. It includes uranium ore mining, ore refining (and possibly enrichment), fabrication of fuel elements and their use in a reactor, reprocessing of spent fuel, refabricating the recovered fissile material into new fuel elements and disposal of waste products.
Nuclear weapon	Device which is capable of releasing nuclear energy in an explosive manner and which has a group of characteristics that are appropriate for use for warlike purposes.
Nuclear weapon-free zone (NWFZ)	Zone which a group of states may establish by a treaty whereby the statute of total absence of nuclear weapons to which the zone shall be subject is defined, and a system of verification and control is set up to guarantee compliance.
Peaceful nuclear explosion (PNE)	Application of a nuclear explosion for such purposes as digging canals or harbours, creating underground cavities, etc.
Plutonium separation	Reprocessing of spent reactor fuel to separate plutonium.
Radiological weapon (RW)	Device, including any weapon or equipment, other than a nuclear explosive device, specifically designed to employ radioactive material by disseminating it to cause destruction, damage or injury by means of the radiation produced by the decay of such material, as well as radioactive material, other than that produced by a nuclear explosive device, specifically designed for such use.
Re-entry vehicle (RV)	Portion of a strategic ballistic missile designed to carry a nuclear warhead and to re-enter the Earth's atmosphere in the terminal phase of the trajectory.
Second-strike capability	Ability to survive a nuclear attack and launch a retaliatory blow large enough to inflict intolerable damage on the opponent. *See also:* Mutual assured destruction.
Standing Consultative Commission (SCC)	US–Soviet consultative body established in accordance with the SALT agreements.
Strategic Arms Limitation Talks (SALT)	Negotiations between the Soviet Union and the United States, initiated in 1969, which seek to limit the strategic nuclear forces, both offensive and defensive, of both sides.
Strategic nuclear forces	ICBMs, SLBMs, ASBMs and bomber aircraft of intercontinental range.
Tactical nuclear weapons	*See:* Theatre nuclear weapons.
Terminal guidance	Guidance provided in the final, near-target phase of the flight of a missile.

Theatre nuclear weapons	Nuclear weapons of a range less than 5 500 km. Often divided into long-range—over 1 000 km (for instance, so-called Eurostrategic weapons), medium-range, and short-range—up to 200 km (also referred to as tactical or battlefield nuclear weapons).
Thermonuclear weapon	Nuclear weapon (also referred to as hydrogen weapon) in which the main part of the explosive energy released results from thermonuclear fusion reactions. The high temperatures required for such reactions are obtained with a fission explosion.
Toxins	Poisonous substances which are products of organisms but are inanimate and incapable of reproducing themselves. Some toxins may also be produced by chemical synthesis.
Uranium enrichment	The process of increasing the content of uranium-235 above that found in natural uranium, for use in reactors or nuclear explosives.
Warhead	That part of a missile, torpedo, rocket or other munition which contains the explosive or other material intended to inflict damage.
Weapons of mass destruction	Nuclear weapons and any other weapons which may produce comparable effects, such as chemical and biological weapons.
Weapon-grade material	Material with a sufficiently high concentration either of uranium-233, uranium-235 or plutonium-239 to make it suitable for a nuclear weapon.
Yield	Released nuclear explosive energy expressed as the equivalent of the energy produced by a given number of metric tons of trinitrotoluene (TNT) high explosive. *See also:* Kiloton and Megaton.

Appendix B

Index to the SALT II Agreements

In this index, articles of the treaty and protocol are referred to by their Roman numerals; paragraphs of those articles are indicated by Arabic numerals. References to articles of the protocol contain that designation (e.g., "protocol II.2"). References to articles of the treaty contain no additional designation (e.g., "IV.14"). The following abbreviations are used:

MOU—Memorandum of Understanding Between the United States of America and the Union of Soviet Socialist Republics Regarding the Establishment of a Data Base on the Numbers of Strategic Offensive Arms
JSP—Joint Statement of Principles and Basic Guidelines for Subsequent Negotiations on the Limitation of Strategic Arms
SBS—Soviet Backfire Statement
AS—Agreed Statement
CU—Common Understanding

Aggregate limits
dismantling or destruction of arms in excess of, XI.1, XI.2, XI.3
exclusion for bombers equipped only for ASBMs, III.5
exclusion for test and training launchers, II.1(2d CU)
from 1 January 1981, III.2
procedures for removal of arms from, VI.6(AS)
right to determine force composition, III.3, V.5
sublimits, V.1, V.2, V.3
upon entry into force, III.1

Air-launched cruise missiles
included in definition of cruise missiles, II.8
limits on numbers deployed on heavy bombers, IV.14, IV.14(1st AS, 2nd AS)

Air-to-surface ballistic missiles (ASBMs)
application of limitations to converted bombers, VI.4
bombers carrying, counted as heavy bombers, II.3(d), II.3(4th AS)

conversion of non-MIRVed ASBMs into MIRVed ASBMs, VI.4
conversion of planes into ASBM carriers, VIII.1, VIII.1(AS)
counting rules for ASBMs, III.4, V.4, V.4(AS)
defined, II.4
equipped with MIRVs, II.5(2d AS), II.6, II.6(1st AS), V.1, V.2, V.3, V.4, V.4(AS)
flight-testing or deployment during protocol, protocol III
heavy bombers equipped only for ASBMs, III.5
limit on number of RVs, IV.13
limits on throw-weight and launch-weight, IX.1(f)
number of ASBMs on a bomber, III.4
procedures for releasing or dispensing RVs from, IV.10(2d AS), IV.11(2d AS), IV.12(2d AS), IV.13(AS)
testing, using 16 exempt airplanes, VIII.1(AS, 1st CU, 2nd CU, 3d CU)
when counted, VI.2

Antimissile defense penetration aids
procedures for releasing, IV.10(2d AS), IV.11(2d AS), IV.12(2d AS), IV.13 (AS)
testing not deliberate concealment, XV.3 (2d AS)

ASBMs (see Air-to-surface ballistic missiles)

B-1 airplanes
current heavy bombers, II.3(a)
designation, II.3(3d CU)
limits on cruise missiles carried, IV.14 (2d AS)

B-52 airplanes
current heavy bombers, II.3(a)
designation, II.3(3d CU)
limits on cruise missiles carried, IV.14 (2d AS)

Backfire bomber
constrained, SBS
in-flight refuelling, SBS
production rate, SBS
radius of action, SBS

316

deployed under water, IX.1(b)

flight-testing on aircraft other than bombers, VIII.1, VIII.1(AS)

flight-testing with independently targetable warheads on sea-based or land-based launchers, protocol II.2, II.2 (AS), II.3

number per heavy bomber, IV.14, IV. 4 (1st AS, 2d AS)

testing, using 16 exempt airplanes, VIII.1 (AS, 1st CU, 2d CU, 3d CU)

with multiple independently targetable warheads, IX.2, IX.2(AS), protocol II.2, II.2(AS)

Current types of heavy bombers
listed, II.3(a)

Data base
categories, XVII.3(AS), MOU
obligation to maintain, MOU
place to maintain, XVII.3
set out, MOU

Deliberate concealment measures
associated with testing, XV.3(1st CU)
defined, XV.3(1st AS)
encryption of telemetry, XV.3(2d CU)
impeding verification by NTM, XV.3, XV.3(1st AS, 2d AS)
of association between ICBMs and their launchers, XV.3(1st CU)
telemetry, XV.3(2d CU)

Dismantling and destruction of arms
date for beginning, XI.2
date for completion, XI.3, XI.4
end of application of limitations, VI.6
fractional orbital missile launchers at Tyura-Tam, VII.2(2d CU)
not required by IX.1(c) for existing launchers of certain systems, IX.1(c) (CU)
procedures to be agreed in SCC, XI.1
procedures to be considered in SCC, XVII.2(e)
reductions to comply with aggregate limits, III.6
test airplanes for cruise missiles, VIII.1 (3d CU)

Duration
of protocol, protocol IV
of treaty, XIX.1

Earth orbit
weapons of mass destruction prohibited, IX.1(c)

Encryption
of telemetry, XV.3(2d CU)

Entry into force
of amendments, XVIII
of protocol, protocol IV
of treaty, XIX.1

Externally observable design features (EODFs)
distinguishability rule for cruise missiles not capable of a range in excess of 600 kilometres, II.8(2d CU), protocol II.3(2d CU)
distinguishability rule for cruise missiles that are not weapon delivery vehicles, II.8(3d CU), protocol II.3(3d CU)
must be used to distinguish launchers of ICBMs and SLBMs equipped with MIRVs from launchers of such missiles not equipped with MIRVs, for newly constructed, converted, or significantly changed launchers, II.5 (5th CU)
must be used to distinguish submarines with launchers of MIRVed SLBMs from submarines that launch non-MIRVed SLBMs, II.5(5th CU)
programs under way as of signature, II.5(5th CU)

Externally observable differences (EODs)
heavy bombers of current types which otherwise would be of a type equipped for ASBMs, II.3(4th AS, 1st CU)
heavy bombers of current types which otherwise would be of a type equipped for cruise missiles, II.3(4th AS)

Fixed ICBM launchers
new launchers prohibited, IV.1
relocation prohibited, IV.2

Flight-testing
of ASBMs equipped with MIRVs, II.6, II.6(1st AS)
of ASBMs during protocol, protocol III
of cruise missiles for weapon delivery, II.8, II.8(3d AS)
of cruise missiles from aircraft other than bombers, VIII.1, VIII.1(AS)
of cruise missiles to a range in excess of 600 kilometres, II.8(1st CU)
of cruise missiles with independently targetable warheads from aircraft, IX.2, IX.2(CU), protocol II.2, II.2 (AS)
of ICBMs and SLBMs with two or more independently targetable re-entry vehicles, II.5(2d AS, 3d CU)
of ICBMs from mobile launchers, protocol I
of ICBMs of existing types with a greater number of RVs, IV.10

317

318

concealment of association with ICBMs, XV.3(1st CU)

construction of additional fixed ICBM silo launchers banned, IV.1

conversion of non-MIRVed ICBM launchers into MIRVed ICBM launchers, VI.3, VI.3(AS)

conversion into launchers of heavy ICBMs prohibited, IV.3

conversion of other land-based launchers into ICBM launchers prohibited, IV.8

defined, II.1, II.1(1st AS, 1st CU, 2d CU)

dismantling and destruction of excess, XI.2

distinguishability rule for new, converted, or changed launchers, II.5(5th CU)

for ICBMs equipped with MIRVs, II.5, II.5(1st AS, 1st CU, 2d CU, 5th CU)

limit on increases in volume of silo launchers, IV.4, IV.4(CU)

mobile ICBM launchers, II.1(2d AS)

modernization and replacement, IV.4 (AS, CU)

new fixed launchers prohibited, IV.1

relocation of fixed launchers prohibited IV.2

shelters over, XV.3(3d CU)

supply with ICBMs, IV.5, IV.5(AS)

Land-based launchers of cruise missiles
regulated, protocol II.1, II.2

Launch sites of ICBM launchers
storage of ICBMs in excess of normal deployment requirements prohibited, IV.5, IV.5(AS)

Launch-weight
of heavy ICBM, II.7, IV.7

of ICBM defined, II.7(1st AS), IV.7(1st AS)

of new type of ICBM, IV.9(1st AS, 1st CU, 2d AS, 2d CU, 3d CU, 4th CU)

of SLBM and ASBM defined, IX.1(e) and (f)(2d AS, CU)

of SS-18, II.5(3d CU)

of SS-19, II.5(3d CU)

Launcher deployment areas (ICBMs)
supply of excess ICBMs prohibited, IV.5

test launchers from, XVI.1

Launchers of ICBMs and SLBMs equipped with multiple independently targetable re-entry vehicles (MIRVs)
conversion of launchers of non-MIRVed missile into, VI.3, VI.3(AS)

defined, II.5, II.5(1st AS, 1st CU, 2d CU, 2d AS)

designations, II.5(3d CU)

independently targetable defined, II.5 (3d AS)

limited, V.1, V.2, V.3

which have been flight-tested as of the date of signature, II.5(2d AS)

Light ICBMs
conversion of launchers, IV.3

new type of ICBM must be, II.5(2d AS), IV.9

SS-16 banned, IV.8(CU)

SS-19 identified as heaviest, II.5(3d CU)

standard for defining heavy missiles, II.7, IX.1(e), IX.1(f)

Minuteman III missile
counted as MIRVed missile, II.5(2d AS)

designation in Soviet Union, II.5(3d CU)

limitation of three RVs, IV.10(CU)

maximum number of RVs tested, IV.10 (1st AS), IV.12(1st AS)

MIRV (see Launchers of ICBMs and SLBMs equipped with multiple independently targetable re-entry vehicles; see also ASBMs

Mobile ICBM launchers
conversion to mobile launchers of MIRVed ICBMs, VI.3(AS)

for heavy missiles prohibited, IX.1(d)

regulated for term of protocol, protocol I

subject to relevant limitations after the protocol expires, II.1(2d AS)

Modernization
application of limitations during modernization, VI.1

of ICBM silo launchers, IV.4, IV.4(CU)

permitted subject to provisions of treaty, X

Multiple ICBM launch
defined, XVI.1(2d CU)

Multiple re-entry vehicles
flight-testing ICBMs with RVs lighter than previously flight-tested, IV.10 (3d AS)

ICBMs and SLBMs, flight-tested with both MIRVs and, II.5(2d AS)

Myasishchev airplanes
current heavy bombers, II.3(a)

designation, II.3(3d CU)

limits on cruise missiles carried, IV.14 (2d AS)

used as tankers, II.3(2d CU)

323

Appendix C

Bibliography

SIPRI publications

Anti-Personnel Weapons (Taylor & Francis, London, 1978).

Armaments and Disarmament in the Nuclear Age, A Handbook (Almqvist & Wiksell, Stockholm, 1976).

Arms Control: A Survey and Appraisal of Multilateral Agreements (Taylor & Francis, London, 1978).

The Arms Trade with the Third World (Almqvist & Wiksell, Stockholm, 1971).

CB Disarmament Negotiations 1920–1970, Vol. 4 of *The Problem of Chemical and Biological Warfare* (Almqvist & Wiksell, Stockholm, 1979).

CB Weapons Today, Vol. 2 of *The Problem of Chemical and Biological Warfare* (Almqvist & Wiksell, Stockholm, 1973).

CBW and the Law of War, Vol. 3 of *The Problem of Chemical and Biological Warfare* (Almqvist & Wiksell, Stockholm, 1973).

Chemical Disarmament: New Weapons for Old (Almqvist & Wiksell, Stockholm, 1975).

Chemical Disarmament: Some Problems of Verification (Almqvist & Wiksell, Stockholm, 1973).

Chemical Weapons: Destruction and Conversion (Taylor & Francis, London, 1980).

Delayed Toxic Effects of Chemical Warfare Agents (Almqvist & Wiksell, Stockholm, 1975).

Force Reductions in Europe (Almqvist & Wiksell, Stockholm, 1974).

French Nuclear Tests in the Atmosphere: The Question of Legality (Almqvist & Wiksell, Stockholm, 1974).

Incendiary Weapons (Almqvist & Wiksell, Stockholm, 1975).

Internationalization to Prevent the Spread of Nuclear Weapons (Taylor & Francis, London, 1980).

The Law of War and Dubious Weapons (Almqvist & Wiksell, Stockholm, 1976).

The Near-Nuclear Countries and the NPT (Almqvist & Wiksell, Stockholm, 1972).

The NPT: The Main Political Barrier to Nuclear Weapon Proliferation (Taylor & Francis, London, 1980).

The Nuclear Age (Almqvist & Wiksell, Stockholm, 1975).

Nuclear Energy and Nuclear Weapon Proliferation (Taylor & Francis, London, 1979).

Nuclear Proliferation Problems (Almqvist & Wiksell, Stockholm, 1974).

Nuclear Radiation in Warfare (Taylor & Francis, London, 1981).

Oil and Security (Almqvist & Wiksell, Stockholm, 1974).

Outer Space—Battlefield of the Future? (Taylor & Francis, London, 1978).

Postures for Non-Proliferation, Arms Limitations and Security Policies to Minimize Nuclear Proliferation (Taylor & Francis, London, 1979).

The Prevention of CBW, Vol. 5 of *The Problem of Chemical and Biological Warfare* (Almqvist & Wiksell, Stockholm, 1971).

Resources Devoted to Military Research and Development, An International Comparison (Almqvist & Wiksell, Stockholm, 1972).

The Rise of CB Weapons, Vol. 1 of *The Problem of Chemical and Biological Warfare* (Almqvist & Wiksell, Stockholm, 1971).

Safeguards against Nuclear Proliferation (Almqvist & Wiksell, Stockholm, 1975).

Tactical and Strategic Antisubmarine Warfare (Almqvist & Wiksell, Stockholm, 1974).

Tactical Nuclear Weapons: European Perspectives (Taylor & Francis, London, 1978).

Towards a Better Use of the Ocean (Almqvist & Wiksell, Stockholm, 1969).

Weapons of Mass Destruction and the Environment (Taylor & Francis, London, 1977).

World Armaments and Disarmament, SIPRI Yearbooks 1968/69 . . . 1977. (Almqvist & Wiksell, Stockholm, 1969 . . . 1977).

World Armaments and Disarmament, SIPRI Yearbooks 1978 . . . 1982 (Taylor & Francis, London, 1978 . . . 1982).

World Armaments and Disarmament, SIPRI Yearbooks 1968–1979, Cumulative Index (Taylor & Francis, London, 1980).

UN publications

Basic Problems of Disarmament, Reports of the Secretary-General: Economic and Social Consequences of Disarmament; Effects of the Possible Use of Nuclear Weapons and the Security and Economic Implications for States of the Acquisition and Further Development of these Weapons; Chemical and Bacteriological (Biological) Weapons and the Effects of their Possible Use (United Nations, New York, 1970).

Comprehensive Nuclear Test Ban, Report of the Secretary-General (UN document A/35/257, 23 May 1980).

Comprehensive Study on Nuclear Weapons, Report of the Secretary-General (UN document A/35/392, 12 September 1980).

Economic and Social Consequences of the Arms Race and of Military Expenditures, Report of the Secretary-General (United Nations, New York, 1978, Department of Political and Security Council Affairs, United Nations Centre for Disarmament).

325

Health Aspects of Chemical and Biological Weapons, Report of a WHO Group of Consultants (World Health Organization, Geneva, 1970).

Study on the Relationship between Disarmament and Development, Report of the Secretary-General (UN document A/36/356, 5 October 1981).

The United Nations and Disarmament 1945-1970 (United Nations, New York, 1970).

The United Nations and Disarmament 1970-1975 (United Nations, New York, 1976).

The United Nations Disarmament Yearbooks, Vol. 1 (1976) ... 5 (1980) (United Nations, New York, 1977 ... 1981).

Other publications

Arms Control, Readings from Scientific American with introductions by H. F. York (W. H. Freeman Company, San Francisco, 1973).

Arms, Defense Policy, and Arms Control, ed. F. A. Long and G. W. Rathjens (Norton & Company, New York, 1976).

Aron, R., *Le Grand Débat, Initiation à la Stratégie Atomique* [The Great Debate: Introduction to Atomic Strategy] (Calmann-Lévy, Paris, 1963).

Beaton, L., *Must the Bomb Spread?* (Penguin, Harmondsworth, 1966).

Becker, A. S., *Military Expenditure Limitation for Arms Control: Problems and Prospects* (Ballinger Publishing Company, Cambridge, Mass., 1977).

Bogdanov, O. V., *Razoruzhenie Garantia Mira* [Disarmament—Guarantee of Peace] (Izdatelstvo Mezhdunarodnye Otnoshenia, Moscow, 1972).

Bull, H., *The Control of the Arms Race* (Praeger, New York, 1965).

Burns, E. L. M., *A Seat at the Table* (Clarke, Irwin & Company, Toronto, 1972).

Controlling the Conventional Arms Race (UNA-USA National Policy Panel on Conventional Arms Control, New York, 1976).

Dahlman, O. & Israelson, H., *Monitoring Underground Nuclear Explosions* (Elsevier Scientific Publishing Company, Amsterdam, 1977, National Defense Research Institute, Stockholm, Sweden).

Davidov, V. F., *Nerasprostranenie Yadernogo Oruzhiya i Politika S.Sh.A.* [Non-Proliferation of Nuclear Weapons and USA Policy] (Izdatelstvo Nauka, Moscow, 1980).

The Dynamics of the Arms Race, ed. D. Carlton and C. Shaerf (Croom Helm, London, 1975).

The Effects of Nuclear Weapons, ed. S. Glasstone and P. J. Dolan (US Department of Defense and US Department of Energy, Washington, D. C., 1977).

Elias, T. O., *The Modern Law of Treaties* (Oceana Publications–Dobbs Terry, New York, 1974).

Epstein, W., *The Last Chance, Nuclear Proliferation and Arms Control* (The Free Press, New York, 1976).

Etzioni, A., *The Hard Way to Peace, A New Strategy* (Collier, New York, 1962).

Existing Mechanisms of Arms Control, ed. W. Young (Pergamon Press, Oxford, 1966).

Fischer, G., *La Non-Prolifération des Armes Nucléaires* [The Non-Proliferation of Nuclear Weapons] (Pichon et Durant-Augias, Paris, 1969).

García Robles, A., *El Tratado de Tlatelolco, Génesis, Alcance y Propósitos de la Proscripción de las Armas Nucleares en la América Latina* [The Treaty of Tlatelolco: Origin, Scope and Purposes of the Ban on Nuclear Weapons in Latin America] (El Colegio de México, México, D. F., 1967).

Goldschmidt, B., *Le complexe atomique* [The Atomic Complex] (Fayard, Paris, 1980).

Hull, W. I., *The Two Hague Conferences and their Contributions to International Law* (Ginn & Company, Boston, Mass., 1908; and Kraus Reprint Co., New York, 1970).

International Arms Control, Issues and Agreements, ed. J. H. Barton and L. D. Weiler, Stanford Arms Control Group (Stanford University Press, Stanford, Calif., 1976).

Inspection for Disarmament, ed. S. Melman (Columbia University Press, New York, 1958).

Jacobson, H. and Stein, E., *Diplomats, Scientists and Politicians: The United States and the Nuclear Test Ban Negotiations* (University of Michigan Press, Ann Arbor, 1966).

Joyce, J. A., *The War Machine, The Case Against the Arms Race* (Quartet Books, London, 1980).

Kalyadin, A. N., *Problemy zapreshchenia ispytaniy i rasprostranenia yadernogo oruzhia* [Problems of the Prohibition of Tests and of the Proliferation of Nuclear Weapons] (Izdatelstvo Nauka, Moscow, 1976).

Kalshoven, F., *The Law of Warfare, A Summary of its Recent History and Trends in Development* (Sijthoff, Leiden, 1973, Henry Dunant Institute, Geneva).

Klein, J., *L'Entreprise du Désarmement depuis 1945* [The Affair of Disarmament since 1945] (Editions Cujas, Paris, 1964).

Lachs, M., *The Law of Outer Space, an Experience in Contemporary Law-making* (Sijthoff, Leiden, 1972).

McPhee, J., *The Curve of Binding Energy* (Farrar, Straus and Giroux, New York, 1974).

Moch, J., *Destin de la Paix* [The Future of Peace] (Mercure de France, 1969).

Myrdal, A., *The Game of Disarmament* (Pantheon, New York, 1976).

Nedrustning under Debatt 1978-1982 [Debate on Disarmament], ed U. Herz (Arbetsgruppen för Svensk Folkriksdag för Nedrustning, Stockholm, 1980).

Newhouse, J., *Cold Dawn. The Story of SALT* (Holt, Rinehart and Winston, New York, 1973).

Noel-Baker, P., *The Arms Race, A Programme for World Disarmament* (John Calder, London, 1958).

NPT: Paradoxes and Problems, ed. A. W. Marks (Arms Control Association, Carnegie Endowment for International Peace, Washington, D.C., 1975).

Nuclear Proliferation Factbook, Prepared for the Subcommittee on Energy, Nuclear Proliferation, and Federal Services of the Committee on Governmental Affairs, US Senate, and the Subcommittee on International Economic Policy and Trade of the Committee on Foreign Affairs, US House of Representatives, by the Environment and Natural Resources Policy Division, Congressional Research Service, Library of Congress (US Government Printing Office, Washington, D.C., 1980).

Opportunities for Disarmament, ed. J. M. D. Sharp (Carnegie Endowment for International Peace, New York, 1978).

Peace and Disarmament, ed. N. N. Inozemtsev (Progress Publishers, Moscow, 1980).

Rathjens, G., Chayes, A. and Ruina, J., *Nuclear Arms Control Agreements: Process and Input* (Carnegie Endowment for International Peace, Washington, D.C., 1974).

Roskill, S., *Naval Policy between the Wars* (Walker & Company, New York, 1968).

Scott, G., *The Rise and Fall of the League of Nations* (Hutchinson, London, 1973).

Security in Disarmament, ed. R. Barnet and R. Falk (Princeton, N. J., 1965).

Sims, N. A., *Approaches to Disarmament. An Introductory Analysis* (Friends Peace and International Relations Committee, London, 1974).

Towpik, A., *Bezpieczenstwo Miedzynarodowe a Rozbrojenie* [International Security and Disarmament] (Polski Instytut Spraw Miedzynarodowych, Warsaw, 1970).

US Activities in Antarctica, Hearing before the Committee on Energy and Natural Resources, US Senate (US Government Printing Office, Washington, D.C., 1979).

A Warless World, ed. A. Larson (McGraw-Hill, New York, 1962).

Willot, A., *Le désarmement général et complet, Une approche* [An Approach to General and Complete Disarmament] (Editions de l'institut de Sociologie, Université Libre de Bruxelles, 1964).

Willrich, M. and Taylor, T., *Nuclear Theft: Risks and Safeguards* (Cambridge, Mass., 1974).

Wright, M., *Disarm and Verify: An Explanation of the Central Difficulties and of National Policies* (Chatto and Windus, London, 1964).

York, H. F., *Race to Oblivion: A Participant's View of the Arms Race* (Simon and Schuster, New York, 1971).

About the Author

Jozef Goldblat, senior member of the Research Collegium of the Stockholm International Peace Research Institute (SIPRI), has university degrees in international relations, law, economics and linguistics. He has been studying the problems of arms control since the 1950s and has been involved in disarmament negotiations in Geneva and New York in different capacities, including service for the United Nations. He has also been active in international commissions supervising armistice agreements. He has written reports, articles and books on the arms race and arms control, which have appeared in several languages, and has lectured at US and European universities.